The Essential Guide to Western Civilization

The Essential Guide to Western Civilization offers a concise overview of European history developed to suit the undergraduate Western Civilization curriculum. Author Nicholas L. Waddy provides an accessible account of major developments in European history in a flexible format. The book will serve as a core text for instructors wishing to build a syllabus including primary sources, articles, and visual materials of their own choosing. Discussion questions and a list of key terms at the end of each chapter will help to guide conversation and assist students in navigating the Western Civilization survey.

Nicholas L. Waddy is Associate Professor of History at Alfred State College in Alfred, New York.

The Essential Guide to Western Civilization

Nicholas L. Waddy

NEW YORK AND LONDON

First published 2018
by Routledge
711 Third Avenue, New York, NY 10017

and by Routledge
2 Park Square, Milton Park, Abingdon, Oxon, OX14 4RN

Routledge is an imprint of the Taylor & Francis Group, an informa business

© 2018 Taylor & Francis

The right of Nicholas L. Waddy to be identified as author of this work has been asserted by him in accordance with sections 77 and 78 of the Copyright, Designs and Patents Act 1988.

All rights reserved. No part of this book may be reprinted or reproduced or utilised in any form or by any electronic, mechanical, or other means, now known or hereafter invented, including photocopying and recording, or in any information storage or retrieval system, without permission in writing from the publishers.

Trademark notice: Product or corporate names may be trademarks or registered trademarks, and are used only for identification and explanation without intent to infringe.

Library of Congress Cataloging-in-Publication Data
A catalog record for this book has been requested

ISBN: 978-1-138-71030-6 (hbk)
ISBN: 978-1-138-71031-3 (pbk)
ISBN: 978-1-315-16966-8 (ebk)

Typeset in Bembo
by Apex CoVantage, LLC

Ob ducem ob patriam

Contents

Prologue: The Value of European History   ix

1. Early Humans and the Dawn of Civilization   1
2. Ancient Greece: Politics and War   18
3. Ancient Greece: Society, Culture, and Daily Life   36
4. Ancient Rome: Politics and War   53
5. Ancient Rome: Society, Culture, and Daily Life   74
6. The Middle Ages: Politics and War, 500–1300   93
7. The Middle Ages: Society, Culture, and Daily Life   119
8. The Late Middle Ages and the Renaissance   140
9. The Age of Discovery, the Protestant Reformation, and the Wars of Religion, 1492–1648   160
10. Politics, Colonialism, and War, 1648–1789   180
11. European Society During the Scientific, Agricultural, and Industrial Revolutions, 1600–1800   205
12. The Enlightenment, the French Revolution, and the Age of Napoleon, 1700–1815   223

13	Challenging the Conservative Order: Liberalism, Nationalism, and Socioeconomic Change, 1815–50	247
14	Middle-Class Europe: The Triumph of Liberalism and Nationalism and the Rise of Socialism, 1850–1914	263
15	Industrialization, Imperialism, and Intellectual and Social Change, 1850–1914	281
16	World War I, 1914–18	299
17	Interwar Europe, 1919–39	318
18	World War II, 1939–45	341
19	The Cold War and the End of European Dominance, 1945–present	364
	Epilogue: Europe, the United States, and the World in the Twenty-First Century	389
	Index	393

Prologue
The Value of European History

To historians, it is obvious that the study of European history is worthwhile. To college students in the United States, however, it will perhaps seem equally obvious that it is not. I hope to convince you otherwise.

There are many reasons why learning about history in general is useful and illuminating. Studying history helps us to understand the challenges that human beings have faced over the centuries. It thus enhances our capacity for empathy and caring. Historical study also makes it possible to notice patterns in historical change that can make it easier to avoid the mistakes of the past. In addition, as you will find out by reading this book, the story of history is filled with drama. It is tragic and comic, glorious and repugnant, inspirational and depressing, all at the same time. It has, in short, much more "entertainment value" than many people seem to expect.

I would like to suggest one additional reason why you may wish to take the study of European history seriously. Please give my argument careful consideration.

The United States of America is 3,000 miles from Europe, and, to many of you, it doubtless seems that the unbridgeable expanse of the Atlantic Ocean makes whatever happens in Europe irrelevant to your own lives. The truth, though, is that America is much more than just a place on a map. It is, more significantly, a *community*. It is composed not only of mountains, rivers, and fertile fields, but also of individuals, families, and neighborhoods. Its geography is and always has been far less important than its people.

The American people, moreover, are unique in their outlook, their culture, their values, and their way of life. It is how we live and how we think that define us as Americans. It is also these things that define *you* as an American. So where, then, have our outlook, our culture, our values, and our way of life come from?

The fact is that our American identity is a blend of many influences. The societies of Africa, Asia, the Middle East, and of the native peoples of the Americas have all left indelible marks on modern American culture. Thus, the study of world history is a vital component of any effort to understand America itself.

Primarily, though, given the immense power and wealth possessed by Europe during the last five centuries, it is Western influences—in other words, European culture and history—that have molded us as Americans. The language that you speak, the food that you eat, the technology that you use, the place at which you may worship, even the basic ideas and categories that rattle around inside your brain—from your conception of yourself as an individual to your notion of the United States of America as a nation-state—all of this is part of the legacy that Europe, more than any other part of the world, has given us. In one sense, this should be obvious. Given the fact that our nation was founded mainly by European settlers, how could America be anything other than primarily Western in its cultural orientation? True, many immigrants have come to the United States from other parts of the world, but just stop to think how massively Africa, Asia, the Middle East, and Latin America were *themselves* affected by European imperialism and Westernization. Certainly, there are few corners of the globe that Europe has not profoundly influenced, for good or for ill. We are part of that phenomenon of Western expansion.

All of this helps to explain why we use the term Western Civilization. A civilization is a complex society that practices agriculture and includes urban centers. As we will see in Chapter 1, civilized life introduces many other enhancements, from writing to trade, from government to organized religion. The first civilized societies arose in the Middle East, but our own agricultural-urban society—the United States of America—is largely based on European influences and precedents. Thus, although the core of Western Civilization is in Europe, the United States is also part of Western Civilization.

Why, then, should we study European history? It is at least partly because when we learn about the history of Western Civilization (the history of Europe and the lands into which that culture extended its influence) we come to a better understanding of how much Europe is still a part of who we are today. At the same time, by studying European history we may also find that we have outgrown and discarded some aspects of our past. Whether we embrace or reject our European heritage, though, clearly we learn much about ourselves by studying it.

In a very real sense, therefore, European history is not just Europe's past—it is also *our* past. It is not dead and buried—it is alive in every one of us. That realization ought to provoke a sense of genuine curiosity as you explore the history of Western Civilization.

I hope it is in this spirit that you will read my book.

Dr. Nicholas L. Waddy
Geneseo, New York

1 Early Humans and the Dawn of Civilization

Introduction

Human beings lived as hunter-gatherers long before the first glimmers of civilization—including agriculture and cities—appeared in what is today the Middle East. There, starting about 5,000 years ago, three great cultures arose that had a particularly lasting impact on Western Civilization: ancient Mesopotamia, ancient Egypt, and ancient Israel. The elements of civilized life that we take for granted today—writing, law, long-distance trade, and many others—were pioneered in these societies. In the process, the mentality of civilized life also began to take shape.

Ironically, some of the first and greatest strides of humankind toward civilized living took place in regions of the Middle East that today Americans sometimes dismiss as "unstable" or "backward." The lesson we may learn from this is simple: the long and complex journey that we have taken in the formation of what we today call Western Civilization has required, and continues to require, the contributions of a startlingly diverse group of people. Western Civilization is rather like a recipe, into which every person who has lived in the Western world for the past 5,000 years—and quite a few who have lived elsewhere!—has added his or her own touch of flavoring. At certain times, and in certain places, though, cultural or technological innovations have been important enough that they have altered the whole trajectory of human history. Ancient Mesopotamia, ancient Egypt, and ancient Israel were such places, and thus it is worth remembering and appreciating their contributions to our Western way of life.

Early Humans and the Transition to Agriculture

The story of Western Civilization begins with the birth of humankind itself. Modern humans—*Homo sapiens sapiens*—first appeared roughly 200,000 years ago in Africa, and subsequently scattered themselves throughout Asia, Europe, and the Middle East. For about the next 190,000 years, during the Paleolithic (Old Stone) Age, humans lived exclusively as hunter-gatherers. Hunting wild animals was the primary responsibility of men and boys, while women and girls gathered edible fruits, vegetables, nuts, roots, and seeds. Tribes of about 1,000 people were the largest forms of social organization. There was no government, organized religion, or military forces.

Early humans left no written records, and only a few archaeological traces, so little is known about their daily lives, but we do know that the first humans developed two remarkable traits: language and culture. Although some other primates have demonstrated a capacity to understand and use symbolic communication, the full use of language is unique to modern humans. Likewise, culture—the practice of learning and passing on a way of life from generation to generation—has fully flowered only in humans, creating, among other things, the preconditions for spiritual thought.

Since early humans were engaged in a constant struggle to find enough food, water, and shelter, the first forms of religion centered on the forces of nature. Stone Age carvings and cave paintings usually depicted animals that were either frequently hunted or especially feared by early humans. Images connected to female fertility were also popular. Sacrifices were sometimes made to appease the spirits that were believed to inhabit the natural world. Early humans also mourned their dead. Initially, these religious practices do not seem to have been coordinated by any special class of priests, sorcerers, or witch doctors.

About 8000 BCE, at the beginning of the Neolithic (New Stone) Age, human societies in the Middle East underwent a remarkable transformation. They gradually gave up hunting and gathering and began to settle permanently in villages, to cultivate crops, and to domesticate animals. How and why humans made the transition from hunting and gathering to farming is enormously significant to the rise of Western Civilization.

The end of the last Ice Age, circa 8000 BCE, led to increasing human populations and to the profusion of wild grains in the Middle East. Initially, hunter-gatherers used sickles to harvest grain that grew naturally in scattered areas. Some of the first "farmers" were actually nomads who engaged only in limited cultivation of crops. In other words, at first, the Neolithic Revolution—the spread of agriculture—did not massively change the way of life of early humans.

In time, though, villages grew larger and more permanent, and small mud huts were replaced with sizable farmhouses. Crops were bred selectively, and they were cultivated more often. Early farmers engaged in limited trade. They began to brew beer and make wine. They also domesticated animals on an increasingly large scale. Dogs were among the first animals to be bred and tamed by man. Even before the Neolithic Revolution, humans were burying dogs along with people, suggesting close companionship between them. The domestication of goats, sheep, pigs, cows, camels, cats, horses, and donkeys eventually followed.

The Neolithic Revolution led to new technologies, including more sophisticated stone tools, the wheel, woven fabrics, pottery, musical instruments, and primitive sailing ships, all of which made early farmers (and fishermen) more productive. It is unclear whether agriculture spread because more and more hunter-gatherers were persuaded to adopt it, or because farmers displaced or killed hunter-gatherers. In any case, by the beginning of the Bronze Age (circa 3000 BCE–1200 BCE), when stone tools were gradually replaced by metal implements, settled agriculture had become the norm not just in the Middle East but in parts of Europe, Africa, Asia, Melanesia, and North and South America. Historians are not sure whether agriculture spread from a point of origin in the Middle East to other areas in Europe, Africa, and Asia, or developed independently in various places, but given their geographical isolation, Native Americans almost certainly developed agricultural techniques on their own.

Over time, agriculture allowed populations to grow and a modest surplus of food to be produced. Because not every person had to engage in farming, some could become skilled craftsmen or artists, and some could engage in trade, while others could simply live off the hard work of their neighbors. An ambitious minority began to use language, culture, and spirituality to dominate others. Religion was transformed into a highly formalized system arranged around the worship of specific deities, all under the supervision of an exclusive class of priests. The first temples were built. And, as Neolithic societies became more stratified, men asserted domination over women.

As the privileged few amassed increasing wealth, raiding parties sought to steal it. Hunter-gatherers had few possessions, but now a farming village's stored grain, livestock, tools, weapons, and religious icons were attractive prizes. The common people's need for protection further reinforced the power of the new leadership class.

By around 3300 BCE, hunter-gatherers had disappeared from much of the modern Middle East. Most of Europe, though, was several thousand years behind in agricultural and social development. In a very real sense, therefore, Western Civilization would be born not in Europe but in Egypt and in a region called Mesopotamia, located between the Tigris and Euphrates Rivers in present-day Iraq. In these two places, by 3300 BCE, farming was well established, and the first towns and long-distance trade routes had formed. The stage was set for cities, kingdoms, and empires to emerge.

How did the Neolithic Revolution affect how most people lived?

The Earliest Civilizations in the Middle East

No historical records exist that can tell us why the first cities in Mesopotamia and Egypt were created. It seems that, as agriculture grew more intensive and productive, cities developed naturally to facilitate trade. Mesopotamia's position in the midst of trade routes connecting the Mediterranean region with Central Asia may help to explain why civilization developed there first.

4 *Early Humans and the Dawn of Civilization*

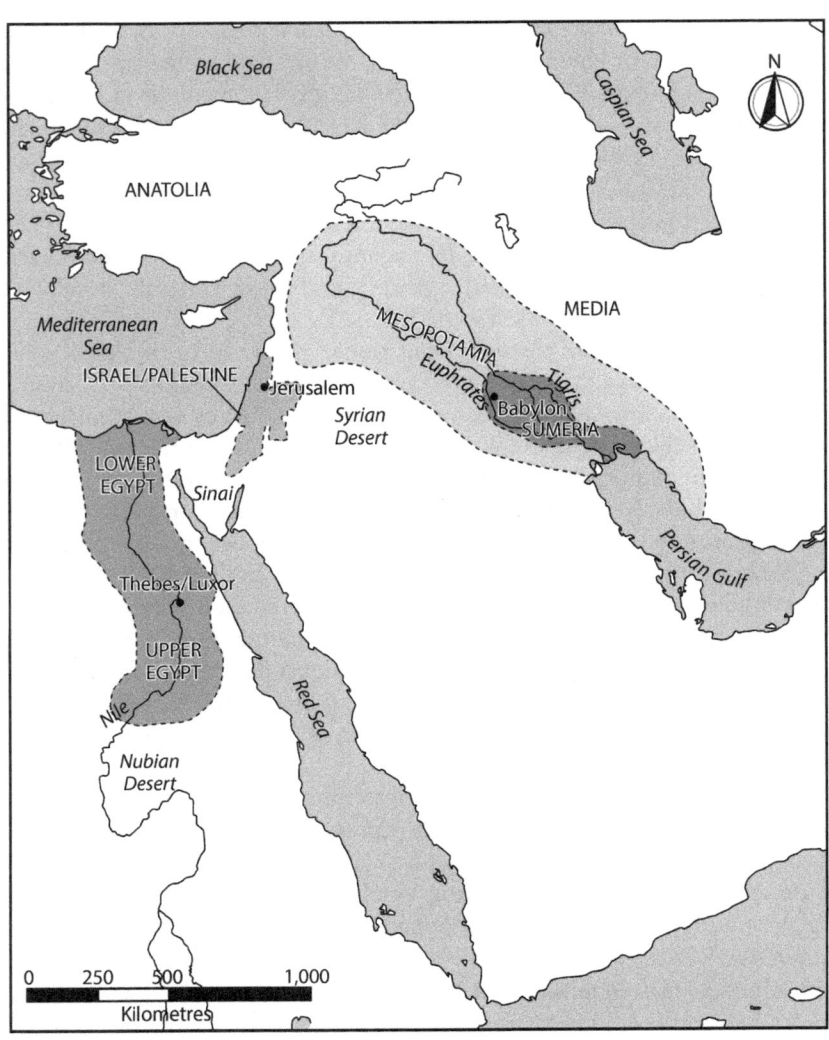

Map 1.1 Ancient Egypt, Israel, and Mesopotamia.

It would not be long before city-states arose that controlled one or more urban centers and their agricultural hinterlands. In time, warfare between city-states led to political consolidation that, in turn, created the first kingdoms and far-flung empires.

After 3000 BCE, civilization flourished in the southern part of Mesopotamia, between modern Baghdad and the Persian Gulf, in a region called Babylonia. Babylonia included the great city of Babylon in the north, and in the south an important sub-region called Sumeria. All this territory was united for the first time under King Sargon in 2300 BCE. Legend has it that Sargon was raised by a shepherd, and that he later became a cupbearer for the King of Kish, whom he eventually replaced on the throne. Sargon's realm was short-lived, but another empire eventually arose centered on glamorous Babylon, which reached its height under King Hammurabi from 1792 BCE to 1750 BCE.

Around 3100 BCE, Upper Egypt (the southern part of Egypt, closer to the source of the Nile River) and Lower Egypt (northern Egypt, where the Nile empties into the Mediterranean Sea) were united under a single, monarchical government. The reign of the pharaohs had begun.

Ancient Egyptian history is generally divided into three periods: the Old Kingdom, the Middle Kingdom, and the New Kingdom. Taken together, these three Kingdoms, and the short Intermediate Periods of relative instability between them, account for Egyptian history from 2700 BCE to 1075 BCE. For almost all of this time, Egypt was politically unified under the reign of the pharaohs, who exercised broad authority and even claimed to be gods themselves. In 1075 BCE, Egypt was conquered by the Assyrians, and later by the Persians, the Greeks, and the Romans.

The Hittites became the masters of most of modern Turkey from about 1400 BCE to 1200 BCE. Shortly after the decline of the Hittite empire, around 1100 BCE, historians mark the beginning of the Iron Age, when iron implements and weapons became more common than those made of bronze.

From about 1000 BCE to 600 BCE, a group called the Assyrians from what is today northern Iraq dominated much of the Middle East. They used military force, brutal atrocities, and, perhaps worst of all, an elaborate bureaucracy to subdue their enemies. Some of the Assyrians' victims were skinned alive or impaled. They also extracted considerable tax revenue, tribute, and forced labor from their subjects. Meanwhile, the Assyrian capital at Nineveh became one of the most splendid and luxurious cities in the ancient world. It had a population of over 100,000.

After the fall of the Assyrians, a Neo-Babylonian empire briefly prevailed and grew rich from international trade, but it was defeated by the Persians in 539 BCE. As discussed in Chapter 2, Persia's rapid rise would transform it into an ancient superpower that threatened to conquer the Greeks.

What follows is a consideration of the features that were shared by most ancient societies and by early civilization as a whole. Surprisingly, many of these Middle Eastern cities, kingdoms, and empires relied on institutions that people still take for granted today. Civilization, even though it began 5,000 years ago, has in some ways barely changed at all.

What were some of the first empires to form in ancient Mesopotamia and Egypt?

The Building Blocks of Civilization: Irrigation, Land Ownership, Trade, Social Hierarchy, Language, Writing, and Law

Ancient Mesopotamia and Egypt were both arid regions. The basis of the economy was agriculture, so careful engineering was required to store and channel precious water. Without irrigation, civilization would never have been possible. In addition, particularly in Mesopotamia, floods were a serious danger to farmland and cities alike. Dikes were therefore constructed to minimize flooding. In Egypt, by contrast, the annual flooding of the banks of the Nile River was seen in a much more positive light, since these floods deposited fertile soil that was the lifeblood of Egyptian agriculture.

Irrigation and flood control systems were often managed by royal officials. The farmland that was best situated for irrigation naturally became valuable, and great care was taken to establish who owned it. Deeds to the land were among the first written documents, and ancient law codes paid special attention to issues of land ownership.

In ancient Mesopotamia, kings, nobles, and high-ranking priests often owned large estates. Some of their land was worked by impoverished sharecroppers, while some was rented out to more prosperous farmers. Land was also bought and sold on an open market. In Egypt, by contrast, originally the pharaoh owned all the land. The country's agricultural system, granaries, and tax system were entirely coordinated by the central government. Later, leading nobles acquired control of some land in Egypt.

As agriculture became more efficient, more people could pursue occupations other than farming. Some became skilled craftsmen, such as bakers, weavers, or carpenters. Simultaneously, trade blossomed. Items exchanged included timber, metals, salt, textiles, wine, herds of animals, glassware, animal skins, ivory, precious gems, slaves, incense, perfume, and oils. Transport of these goods was facilitated by the construction of roads, canals, and ports. Pack animals and caravans became important to commerce. Nevertheless, a natural waterway like the Nile River was still the easiest way to transport goods.

The transition to agriculture, and the rise of trade, created societies that were decidedly hierarchical. The food surpluses and commercial wealth of ancient societies benefited primarily a small elite of kings, nobles, and priests. By contrast, at the very bottom of ancient Mesopotamian and Egyptian society were slaves. Slavery was not a major feature of every ancient culture, but it was extremely common. Ancient slavery was not based on race. Instead, most slaves were captured enemy soldiers (and their relatives), criminals, or debtors. Slaves could often earn or purchase their freedom. The law offered slaves some protections—they could, for example, marry as they pleased—but disobedient slaves could be whipped by their masters. In the end, slaves were an important source of cheap labor that ancient elites exploited mercilessly.

Semitic languages predominated in the ancient Middle East. (Arabic and Hebrew are modern Semitic languages.) The language of the Egyptians, however, was Afro-Asiatic, while that of the Sumerians was utterly distinct. The language of the Hittites, who had migrated from Europe to Turkey, was from the Indo-European language family. Ancient Greek, Latin, Persian, and Indian Sanskrit were also Indo-European languages. Virtually all modern European languages have Indo-European roots, reflecting the common linguistic and historical ties that modern Europeans (and Americans) share with ancient Greeks, Romans, Hittites, Persians, and Indians.

Initially, writing seems to have involved crude pictorial signs, but it gradually evolved into more abstract notations that were useful in administering cities, recording economic transactions, and proving ownership of land, livestock, or goods. Many historians date the beginning of civilization, and thus the dawn of history (as opposed to pre-history), to the invention of the first writing systems around 3300 BCE. The first form of writing was probably the cuneiform system used by the Sumerians that involved wedge-shaped characters made with reeds on clay tablets. Cuneiform became increasingly complex, and a specialized class of scribes became socially prominent and wealthy because of its valuable writing skills.

The Sumerians also developed one of the world's first sophisticated systems of numeracy. That is, they thought of and used numbers as abstract concepts, making complex mathematical calculations possible. This facilitated trade and finance, and it allowed advanced astronomical observations. The Sumerian number system was based on the number 60, which is why today we divide an hour into 60 minutes, a minute into 60 seconds, and a circle into 360 degrees.

The ancient Egyptians had a system of pictorial writing known (to the ancient Greeks, and thus to us) as hieroglyphics. This form of writing was only deciphered by Western scholars in the nineteenth century, after the unearthing of the Rosetta Stone in Egypt in 1799 by French soldiers fighting under Napoleon. The Egyptians used ink for writing, and they made a form of paper from the papyrus plant that grew along the banks of the Nile.

Initially, writing systems were used for specific, practical tasks, but over time the ancients wrote religious volumes, poems, plays, letters, songs, government dispatches, and, yes, even textbooks! The few documents that have survived give modern historians tantalizing glimpses into the way in which ancient peoples thought and lived.

Eventually, systems of writing allowed for the recording of elaborate law codes. The Babylonian King Hammurabi's renowned law code carefully regulated economic life, land ownership, and family relations. The code treated people differently based on social rank, and offenders could be punished with mutilation, beatings, enslavement, drowning, or impalement. Nevertheless, professional judges tried cases according to popularly accepted rules of justice and fair play, weighing documentary evidence and the testimony of witnesses. In some cases, mercy could also be shown by the king or by the victims of crime.

What sorts of people made up the elite in most ancient societies?

The Building Blocks of Civilization: Royal Government, Armies, Cities, and Organized Religion

Virtually every ancient society was a male-dominated hereditary monarchy. Some of the greatest strengths of hereditary monarchies are that they supply centralized and decisive leadership, especially in wartime, a clear line of succession, and, at least theoretically, political stability.

Ancient kings almost always led their armies into battle, and they inhabited grand palaces that symbolized their exalted status. When they were buried, their tombs were filled with gold and treasure, and sometimes even people—the Sumerian Queen Puabi, whose tomb was discovered by the English archaeologist Sir Leonard Woolley in the 1920s, was buried with five soldiers and 23 ladies-in-waiting, all of whom appear to have willingly joined their royal mistress in the afterlife.

Ancient monarchies did not all function in the same way. In ancient Egypt, the pharaoh was an absolute ruler who claimed divine status. To maintain the royal bloodline, the pharaoh often married his own sister or daughter. In Assyria, kings were both political leaders and high priests. In the Sumerian city-state of Uruk, kings derived their authority from having sexual relations with the goddess Inanna, although how they accomplished this feat remains a mystery. In Babylonia, by contrast, the offices of king and high priest were clearly distinct, and among the Hittites kings were advised by nobles, they did not claim divine sanction, and their succession had to be approved by the army.

Arguably the chief task of early royal governments was making war. Diplomacy and gift exchanges sometimes prevented war, but for most kings the temptation to seek territorial expansion, and perhaps even to conquer an empire, was hard to resist.

Ancient weapons included swords, daggers, spears, and bows and arrows. Catapults and battering rams were used against walled cities and forts. Defensive armor included shields and helmets made of bronze, iron, and sometimes gold and silver. Horse-drawn chariots were used by soldiers and military leaders during battles.

During Egypt's Middle and New Kingdoms, the pharaohs pursued territorial aggrandizement. Their armies temporarily conquered Syria and Israel/Palestine, and they pushed their way up the Nile River into modern-day Sudan. These campaigns netted Egypt both land and new economic resources, including slaves.

The Hittites were also successful warriors. The Hittite and Egyptian armies famously clashed in 1274 BCE at Qadesh, producing one of the largest battles in ancient history. As many as 80,000 soldiers may have been involved.

From about 1000 BCE to 600 BCE, the greatest empire in the ancient world was based in Assyria, in northern Mesopotamia. The Assyrians, like the Hittites, used iron weapons, and their vast armies were superbly organized. The Assyrians were especially famous for how they dealt with resistance to their authority. Terrible massacres persuaded many peoples that resisting Assyrian domination was futile. When the threat of violence was not enough, the Assyrians sometimes deported whole ethnic groups from one part of their empire to another. The Israelites were among the peoples who were scattered by the Assyrians.

Although the conquest of agricultural land and trade routes was important in the ancient world, the capture of cities was often the ultimate goal. Cities lay at the heart of ancient civilization. Although Jericho, in ancient Israel, is often considered to be the first town, the first sizable cities were established in Sumeria before 3000 BCE. In time, as much as 80 percent of the Sumerian population lived in cities, which could have populations as large as 80,000. As city-states were consolidated into kingdoms and empires, the capitals of these larger states grew in size and importance. They were generally enclosed by strong stone walls and included—in addition to the humble homes and workshops of the common people—palaces, forts, marketplaces, gardens, monuments, and temples, all of which demonstrated the wealth and power of the elite.

Ancient Mesopotamian cities such as Akkade, Nineveh, and Babylon were the focal points of great empires, and the Egyptian capital was also known for its splendor. During the Old Kingdom, the Egyptian capital was at Memphis, near modern Cairo, but it was later moved to Thebes, further up the Nile. Thebes was also known as Luxor, after which the opulent casino in Las Vegas is named.

Although many of the tangible achievements of ancient civilization have been lost to the ravages of time, some monumental building projects remain intact. Among the first such projects were the *ziggurat* temples built by the ancient Mesopotamians on the tops of man-made hills. Each temple, made of bricks of various colors, would sit high atop ascending layers of terraces, presumably so that the temple itself—presumed to be the home of one of the Mesopotamians' many gods—would be closer to heaven.

By far the most famous of the ancient building projects were the pyramids in Egypt. Of the original Seven Wonders of the Ancient World, only the pyramids remain. They were constructed during the Old Kingdom as massive mausoleums for the remains of the pharaoh. For approximately 4,000 years, the Great Pyramid at Giza (in sight of the ancient capital at Memphis, and now on the outskirts of Cairo) was the tallest man-made structure in the world. It rose to a height of 481 feet and was made of more than two million blocks of stone, each weighing about 2.5 tons. It took roughly 20 years to build, and, contrary to myth, was constructed not by slaves but by skilled workmen. The top of the pyramid was originally plated with gold.

10 Early Humans and the Dawn of Civilization

Figure 1.1 The Great Sphinx and the Pyramids at Giza, near Cairo, are among the most famous and most glorious remnants of ancient Egypt.

Pius Lee/Shutterstock.

The *ziggurats* and the pyramids, both of which required huge commitments of labor and resources to build, clearly demonstrate the high priority that many ancient leaders placed on organized religion. In Egypt, the pharaohs were considered gods, and indeed in almost every ancient society the official religion was closely linked to the royal government. Both civil and religious leaders also possessed enormous wealth in the form of agricultural estates, herds of livestock, multitudes of slaves, and control over trade.

In ancient Mesopotamia, religion was polytheistic—that is, the Mesopotamians worshiped many gods and goddesses. The gods were frequently linked to forces of nature. Certain gods were also associated with certain cities, and when a city increased its power and wealth, its resident god became more popular. Temples were not seen as houses of worship but as the homes of specific gods. Thus, within each temple, living quarters, food, servants, and entertainment were provided for the resident god to enjoy, while rituals and animal sacrifices were conducted to please him (or her). Predictably, most temples were run by men, although a Mesopotamian version of nuns, the *naditu*, were shown great respect. Ordinary Mesopotamians did not visit the grandest temples, nor did they worship the chief gods and goddesses; they prayed instead to lesser gods.

Divination—the reading of signs indicating the will of the gods or predicting the future—was an important part of Mesopotamian religion. The entrails of slaughtered animals, as well as astrological observations, were thought to give warning signs of dangerous developments in the future. Because the will of the gods seemed so fickle, the Mesopotamians developed a generally pessimistic attitude toward life and death, a viewpoint well illustrated in the classic poem, *The Epic of Gilgamesh*. They believed in the afterlife, but they generally expected it to be bleak and miserable.

Ancient Egyptian religion was also, in almost all cases, polytheistic. In addition to the pharaoh, Egyptians worshiped many gods and goddesses, most of whom had several names, were associated with forces of nature, and were portrayed either in human form or as hybrids of humans and animals or birds. Priests and priestesses conducted elaborate rituals in massive temples, but most Egyptians worshiped at smaller shrines or in their own homes. They often relied on magical spells or amulets to protect them from evil. Egyptians also participated in religious festivals and pilgrimages, some of which apparently involved drinking large amounts of wine or beer, since intoxication was thought to bring one closer to the gods.

Initially, it was believed that only the pharaoh enjoyed life after death. Eventually, though, ordinary Egyptians came to believe that they too could experience immortality if they were buried with sufficient offerings, and if they followed the rituals outlined in the *Book of the Dead*, including mummification. Egyptians looked forward to death, and they assumed that the next life would be characterized by pleasure, entertainment, and reunion with departed family members.

It is important to note that ancient religions in Mesopotamia and Egypt were extremely different from the dominant religious traditions in the modern Western world. Christianity, Judaism, and Islam are all monotheistic faiths—that is, they acknowledge the existence of only one God. They also assert that there is a clear link between spirituality and ethics, and they assume that God punishes the wicked and rewards the righteous. These ideas would have puzzled many ancient peoples in the Middle East.

As a rule, ancient societies were unabashedly male-dominated. Women contributed to many different commercial activities and were especially prominent as spinners and weavers, food retailers, nurses, merchants, and domestic servants. Their earnings were usually low, and once they married they were generally encouraged to focus their attention on their homes and families. Women's ability to own property was also restricted, and property was passed down from father to son. Marriages were often arranged, and a father could force his daughter to wed a man of his choice. As has been the case for the vast majority of human history, a woman's class standing had a huge impact on her marital prospects and her quality of life.

Predictably, family law was skewed toward male interests. Under the Babylonian Code of Hammurabi, a man could marry a second wife if his first wife proved unable to bear children. He could also freely engage in sexual relations with slave women, prostitutes, and concubines. A woman, by contrast, was required to be utterly faithful to her husband. If she committed adultery, the penalty outlined by Hammurabi was death by drowning.

Husbands were even permitted to sell their wives and children into slavery. A man could, in fact, sell his own mother.

Ancient women's status was seldom high, but they did benefit from some legal protections. Under the Code of Hammurabi and in ancient Egypt, women could divorce their husbands under certain conditions. Egyptian law also recognized women as full citizens, and it allowed unmarried girls a remarkable degree of sexual freedom.

Throughout the ancient world, the most influential women were always the wives and family members of kings, nobles, priests, and wealthy commoners. They were lavishly depicted in ancient art and literature. In addition, some women served as priestesses, and in very rare cases women ruled over city-states, kingdoms, and empires.

How did religion in the ancient Middle East differ from the forms of religion that dominate in the Western world today?

The Hebrews: Origins and History

The various building blocks of civilization discussed in the preceding sections worked together to propel ancient societies forward, even if they sometimes inflicted considerable suffering in the process. By 1200 BCE, when the ancient Hebrews settled in what is today Israel, most of the elements of civilization were firmly in place. The ancient Israelites would utilize and adapt all of these critical institutions as they constructed a novel society based on monotheism and religious ethics.

Historians disagree about the location of the original homeland of the ancient Hebrews, today called Jews, but many experts believe that they came from Mesopotamia, which they left around 2000 BCE. They then began to wander the Middle East as nomads, mingling with other Semitic peoples. They were led by chieftains called patriarchs, among them Abraham, Isaac, and Jacob.

According to the Bible, by the 1200s BCE the Hebrews were concentrated in Egypt, where they worked as slaves for the pharaoh. A man named Moses led them in a successful attempt to escape the clutches of the pharaoh. In the course of escaping, Moses famously held out his staff, and God parted the Red Sea. The Hebrews then wandered in the deserts of the Sinai Peninsula for 40 years. Atop Mount Sinai, Moses claimed that God, who the ancient Hebrews called Yahweh, gave him two stone tablets on which were engraved the Ten Commandments—the core ethical guidelines of the Jewish faith. The two tablets were to be stored in the Ark of the Covenant, a wooden chest covered in gold that few Hebrews, even priests, were ever permitted to set eyes upon.

Eventually, the Hebrews reached the land of Canaan. There they ceased to be nomads and concentrated on settled agriculture. The native Canaanites have largely been forgotten, but one of their most enduring accomplishments was the creation of a simplified alphabet that was transmitted to the Canaanites' most famous descendants, the Phoenicians. The Phoenicians were great seafarers, builders, craftsmen, and merchants whose colonies were scattered along the Mediterranean coasts of Africa, Asia, and Europe. Their alphabet passed to the Greeks, then to the Romans, and a variant of it is still in use by Americans and most Europeans today.

Predictably, the Hebrews fought bitterly with the Canaanites, enslaving some of them. When the Hebrews won out, the land of Canaan was given the new name of Israel. The 12 tribes of the ancient Hebrews, thereafter also known as Israelites, were finally united around 1000 BCE by Saul, the first King of Israel.

The greatest of the ancient Hebrew kings was David, who defeated the Philistines. Among David's other accomplishments was the conquest of Jerusalem, which became the new capital of the Kingdom of Israel and the center for Jewish culture. David was succeeded by his son Solomon.

King Solomon's reign, which lasted from roughly 965 BCE to 925 BCE, marked the high point of Hebrew unity, prosperity, and power. Solomon was rumored to have access to the abundant mineral wealth of a land called Ophir, where the legendary King Solomon's mines poured forth gold. No physical evidence of the mines has ever been discovered. It is more likely that the source of Solomon's wealth, and Israel's prosperity, was agriculture and trade.

Solomon built many roads, fortresses, and palaces, but he is best known for ordering the construction of a huge, ornate, and enormously costly temple in Jerusalem that would become the headquarters of the Jewish faith. The Temple would also house the Ark of the Covenant in a secure chamber, known as the Holy of Holies.

By this time, the Hebrew Scriptures, sometimes referred to by Christians as the Old Testament of the Bible, were being written down. Historians have verified the accuracy of some passages of the Hebrew Bible, but others appear to reflect Jewish mythology. Be that as it may, the Bible would go on to become the single most important document in the history of Western Civilization.

After Solomon's death, the 12 tribes split, and the Hebrews were conquered in stages by the Assyrians and the Neo-Babylonians. By about 586 BCE, the Jewish Temple in Jerusalem had been destroyed, the Ark of the Covenant had disappeared, and the Hebrews had forfeited their independence. They were sent into exile and were scattered throughout the Middle East in a period that became known as the Babylonian Captivity.

In 539 BCE, the Persians conquered Babylon. They permitted some Jews to return to Israel. The Israelites never recaptured their glory days under King Solomon, however. They were conquered in turn by Persians, Greeks, and Romans. In 70 CE, the Romans scattered the Hebrews once more and destroyed the rebuilt Temple in Jerusalem. A sizable Jewish community would not reemerge in the region until the twentieth century CE, when Jewish settlers founded the modern state of Israel.

Migration played an important role in the history of the Hebrew people. What were some of the migrations that the Hebrews undertook?

The Hebrews: God's "Chosen People"

The ancient Hebrews never conquered a historically significant empire—in fact, several times they came close to being wiped off the face of the earth. Their historical importance lies, therefore, not in their power, but in their faith. Although there were precedents for monotheism elsewhere, it is still fair to say that the Hebrews' monotheism set them apart from almost all the other peoples of the ancient world.

According to Hebrew tradition, there was only one God, Yahweh. His will was clearly manifested in the Hebrew scriptures, which continue to be important to modern Judaism, Christianity, and Islam. Yahweh was considered to be transcendent: in other words, he could not be pictured as a human being, nor did he have a beginning or an end. God had created nature, but he was also above it, and nature was not itself divine. Only God was worthy of worship. The ancient Hebrews were, in short, strict in their monotheism.

In general, the Hebrew religion stressed the importance of devotion and righteousness rather than the performance of rituals. According to the Bible, the Hebrews' founding father Abraham was once asked by God to sacrifice his son Isaac, but Isaac was spared at the last minute. God had only been testing Abraham's faith. This was evidence that Yahweh cared more about the character of his people than he did about extracting tribute or blood sacrifices from them.

According to Hebrew tradition, Abraham made a covenant, or a contract, with God that was later confirmed by Moses. According to the covenant, Yahweh selected the Hebrews as his "Chosen People," whom he would protect throughout history. "I will make of thee a great nation," God declared in the Book of Genesis. In return, the Hebrews agreed to worship only Yahweh and to obey the Ten Commandments as well as the lessons of the Hebrew scriptures. The Hebrews assumed that if they obeyed and worshiped God, then they would be rewarded in this life—they had little interest in the afterlife. If misfortune befell the Jews, on the other hand, they assumed that God was punishing them for sinfulness or disloyalty. The concept of the covenant gave the Hebrews a unique sense that they enjoyed a close relationship with God, although unfortunately this idea was also sometimes used to justify aggression and violence toward the enemies of Israel. Indeed, the Hebrew scriptures sanctioned violence against non-Jews repeatedly.

From the perspective of modern Western Civilization, though, perhaps the most critical element in the religion of the ancient Hebrews was its emphasis on character, which included compassion as well as respect for the dignity and worth of the individual. The Hebrew scriptures are full of calls to avoid lying, cheating, stealing, and violence against one's neighbors, while acts of charity are encouraged. Moreover, the Hebrew prophets (messengers of God) condemned Jews who merely observed the letter of God's laws and did not act humanely toward the weak and the vulnerable. This theme of compassion was largely absent from other ancient religions.

Admittedly, however, the Hebrews demonstrated considerably more compassion toward men than they did toward women. Hebrew traditions defined women as unclean and inferior beings who were not permitted to participate in some religious rituals or to enter many sacred areas. Marriages were arranged, and wives were subjected to the authority of their husbands. If a woman had sex outside of marriage, she could be stoned to death. In addition, women seldom inherited or controlled any property. Nevertheless, while women were subordinated to men, their moral dignity and their humanity were not questioned. The Hebrew scriptures made it clear that women were to be treated with respect, especially when they were faithful to God's laws and righteous in their conduct.

One final element of the ancient Hebrew faith would eventually play a decisive role in the emergence of Christianity. The Hebrew scriptures that were written in the difficult years after the Babylonian captivity, when many Jews had been scattered and foreigners ruled Israel, describe the need for a savior who would be sent by God to uplift his Chosen People. A Messiah, it was said, would end the oppression of the Jews and lead them to a new golden age. Christians believe that Jesus of Nazareth was that Messiah, and that the New Testament of the Bible reveals God's plan for humanity. Modern Jews, on the other hand, believe that the Messiah has not yet come.

How did the Hebrew religion differ from the religions of other ancient peoples?

Conclusions

The achievements of the ancient Mesopotamian and Egyptian civilizations are important to modern humans primarily because studying and refining them has taught us to live like civilized men and women. Indeed, there is far more continuity between their civilizations and ours than you might expect. Just because our contemporary institutions are more complex does not make them qualitatively different.

If the ancient Mesopotamians and Egyptians taught us how to live like civilized men and women, it was the ancient Hebrews who taught us invaluable lessons about the relationship between civilization and religion. It was the Hebrews who taught that religion is about more than prayers and ritual sacrifices. It is also about character, compassion, and human dignity. At the same time, the Hebrew scriptures remain central today to the monotheistic faiths of Judaism, Christianity, and Islam. That fact alone makes the ancient

Hebrews a necessary focus of any serious attempt to explain the history of Western Civilization.

It would, in short, be a mistake to imagine that, because ancient civilization unfolded thousands of years ago, it is therefore "dead" and has no relevance to modern life. On the contrary, even as you read this sentence, you are performing a task that only became possible because a few early farmers and city dwellers in what is today Iraq invented something that we now call "writing." As it turns out, they invented considerably more than that, and none of it should be taken for granted.

Key Terms for Chapter 1

Hunter-gatherers—people who obtain food from the natural environment without practicing agriculture.

Neolithic Revolution—circa 8000 BCE, this was the momentous step that human beings took away from hunting and gathering and toward agriculture.

Mesopotamia—an ancient term for the territory of present-day Iraq. Mesopotamia was one of the first areas to adopt civilization.

Pharaohs—the all-powerful monarchs of ancient Egypt, who were considered divine.

Cuneiform—perhaps the first form of writing, used by the Sumerians.

Pyramids—huge mausoleums built for the pharaohs, and which still stand today.

Hebrews—ancient name for the Jews. Once they conquered Canaan and renamed it Israel, the Hebrews were also known as Israelites.

Ten Commandments—the core directives of the Hebrew faith, communicated by God to Moses.

The Jewish Temple—a large religious complex built by King Solomon in Jerusalem, and later destroyed by the Neo-Babylonians, and then again by the Romans.

Messiah—"Anointed One." Christians believe that Jesus Christ was the fulfillment of the Hebrew scriptures' promise of a Messiah, while Jews believe that the Messiah has not yet come.

Review Questions for Chapter 1

1. What are the advantages and disadvantages of civilized living, especially compared to the lifestyle of hunter-gatherers?
2. Modern people seem much more fascinated by the ancient Egyptians than by the Mesopotamians, who were similarly instrumental in laying the foundation for Western Civilization. Describe at least three of the unique features of life in ancient Egypt that may explain this fascination.
3. Of the "Building Blocks of Civilization," choose two that you feel represent a positive change from a hunter-gatherer lifestyle, and two that you feel represent a negative change. Justify your selections.

4. The survival of the Jewish religion, despite the severe setbacks experienced by the ancient Hebrews, is remarkable. First, identify some of the challenges and misfortunes faced by the Hebrews. Next, discuss another historical example of a people who faced great adversity. Last, explain why, in your opinion, some groups prevail over difficult circumstances, whereas others are defeated by them.
5. Imagine you are a resident of ancient Mesopotamia or ancient Egypt. Recently, you visited Israel, where you were struck by the peculiar religious faith of the natives. Write a letter to a close relative in which you describe and critique ancient Judaism. Remember to do so from a polytheistic vantage point.

Further reading

Cottrell, Leonard. *The Quest for Sumer*. New York: Putnam. 1965.

Grabbe, Lester. *Ancient Israel: What Do We Know and How Do We Know It?* Revised Edition. New York: Bloomsbury T & T Clark. 2017.

Harris, David R. *Origins of Agriculture in West Central Asia: An Environmental-Archaeological Study*. Philadelphia, PA: University of Pennsylvania Press. 2011.

Hays, J. Daniel and Tremper Longman. *The Message of the Prophets: A Survey of the Prophetic and Apocalyptic Books of the Old Testament*. Grand Rapids, MI: Zondervan. 2010.

Inati, Shams C., ed. *Iraq: Its History, People, and Politics*. Amherst, NY: Humanity Books. 2003.

Kriwaczek, Paul. *Babylon: Mesopotamia and the Birth of Civilisation*. London: Atlantic Books. 2014.

Markoe, Glenn. *Peoples of the Past: Phoenicians*. London: British Museum Press. 2002.

Oakes, Lorna and Lucia Gahlin. *Ancient Egypt: An Illustrated Reference to the Myths, Religions, Pyramids and Temples of the Land of the Pharaohs*. London: Hermes House. 2010.

Redford, Donald B. *Egypt, Canaan, and Israel in Ancient Times*. Cairo: American University in Cairo Press. 1992.

Silverman, David P. *Ancient Egypt*. London: Duncan Baird. 2003.

Snell, Daniel C. *Life in the Ancient Near East, 3100–332 B.C.E.* New Haven, CT: Yale University Press. 1997.

Van De Mieroop, Marc. *A History of the Ancient Near East, ca.3000–323 B.C.* Oxford: Blackwell. 2007.

2 Ancient Greece
Politics and War

Introduction

When we think of ancient Greece, we often think of the practice of direct democracy in Athens, of beautiful classical art and architecture, of the great Greek philosophers, of the Olympic games, or of the birth of the scientific tradition. All of these accomplishments are indeed part of the heritage of ancient Greece and part of the legacy it has bestowed on modern Western Civilization.

The truth, though, is that all these achievements might never have played such a pivotal role in Western history were it not for another Greek specialty: war-making. Alexander the Great towers over ancient history as one of the greatest conquerors who ever lived, but in fact he was continuing a tradition of tactical and strategic brilliance, as well as courage and steadfastness on the battlefield, that Greeks—rich and poor, powerful and humble—had nurtured for centuries. This martial tradition made the Greeks masterful conquerors and able defenders of their liberty, when "barbarian" (i.e., foreign) enemies threatened their civilization, but it also made them quarrelsome, ferocious, and nearly impossible to unite under one banner.

The reality of ancient Greece, therefore, is that its magnificent cultural achievements were forged in the context of, and at the expense of, centuries of conflict and veritable rivers of blood. To know the Greeks, therefore, is first and foremost to know them as warriors, and so it is to the political and military history of ancient Greece that we now turn.

Bronze Age Greece, 2000 BCE–1100 BCE

The first civilized society that is known to have existed in Greece was that of the Minoans, a group of people named for their legendary King Minos. The Minoans lived mainly on the large Greek island of Crete. There they built elaborate stone palaces featuring indoor plumbing as well as lavish artwork, and they grew rich from trade with the city-states, kingdoms, and empires of the Middle East. The Minoans, however, were not Greek—that is, they were ethnically and linguistically distinct from the people who would later be called "Greek." They worshiped principally female goddesses, and they may have practiced human sacrifice.

The Minoan culture might have lasted longer, but the Minoans grew used to peaceful trade, or too reliant on their powerful navy, and so they failed to fortify their cities. By about 1400 BCE, Minoan society had been wiped out by invaders. The grand Minoan palace at Knossos, which had contained 1,300 rooms, many of them decorated with colorful frescoes, was left in ruins. The palace today has been partially reconstructed and can be visited by tourists.

The people who we know as the ancient Greeks, who spoke an Indo-European language, migrated into Greece around 2000 BCE. They were divided into hostile tribes, but they still had a strong sense of their common culture and language. Later, that sense of Greekness would find expression in the Olympic games, where political divisions were set aside.

The earliest Greeks displaced, and in some cases assimilated, the more primitive peoples already living in Greece. By about 1600 BCE, this blending of Greek and native peoples had produced a distinct culture known as Mycenaean, after one of its principal cities, Mycenae.

The Mycenaean world included mainland Greece, the Greek islands in the Aegean and Adriatic Seas, and Crete, which the Mycenaeans conquered around 1450 BCE. These areas were divided into several small kingdoms that frequently feuded, although peaceful trade was also common. Mycenaean traders reached as far as Egypt, Syria, Israel/Palestine, and southern Italy. Most Mycenaean Greeks were farmers or herders, but craftsmen, merchants, and noblemen also played major roles. The chief cities of the Mycenaeans, such as Athens, Thebes, and Mycenae, prospered, which we know today because their kings were commonly buried with heaps of treasure, especially gold.

Mycenaean government was monarchical, but kings shared power with nobles, most of whom were skilled warriors. Mycenaean politics revolved around war. The most famous event in Mycenaean history is recorded in Homer's epic poem, *The Iliad*, which centers on the Mycenaean siege, and eventual conquest, of a powerful and wealthy city, located in modern Turkey, called Troy.

According to Homer, the Greeks attacked Troy because Paris, a Trojan prince, had abducted Helen, the exceptionally beautiful wife of a Greek king. Hers was "the face that launched a thousand ships," each one of them filled with angry and well-armed Greeks. After a ten-year siege, a team of Greek warriors infiltrated Troy by hiding in a hollowed-out wooden statue of a horse. They then opened the gates to the city, Greek warriors rushed in, and Troy was destroyed. The ruins of Troy can be visited today in western Turkey.

For reasons that are not entirely clear to historians, the Mycenaean world collapsed around 1100 BCE. The ancient Greeks claimed that a less civilized people had invaded Greece from the north, leading to the disruption of

Mycenaean life. Instead, Mycenaean culture, which was always warlike, may have self-destructed. Whatever the cause, the end of the Mycenaean world led to serious consequences.

What factors led to the destruction of the Minoan and Mycenaean cultures?

The Greek "Dark Ages," 1100 BCE–800 BCE

The Dark Ages in Greece that followed the destruction of the Mycenaean culture were characterized by political instability, declining populations and trade, poverty, isolation, and cultural regression. Turmoil caused many Greeks to migrate to the islands in the Aegean Sea or to western Turkey. Since no written records from the Dark Ages exist, historians know relatively little about how Greek society functioned between 1100 BCE and 800 BCE. *The Iliad* and *The Odyssey*, two epic poems attributed to Homer, are among our best sources for reconstructing Greek life during the Dark Ages, although they include elements from the Mycenaean period as well.

In both the Mycenaean era and the Dark Ages, Greek society was extremely warlike. Monarchy was the predominant form of government, but kings depended on nobles for support and advice. Kings sometimes even consulted lowly soldiers.

The highest virtue acknowledged in the Homeric epics was *arete*, which means "excellence." The warrior society that existed during the Greek Dark Ages prized physical strength, bravery, loyalty, and glory. When Greek warrior-heroes were not engaging in one-on-one combat, they were satisfying their insatiable thirst for *arete* by competing in sports. The most famous Greek sporting competition was held at Olympia starting in 776 BCE. The modern Olympic games are based on this early Greek precedent.

In addition to engaging in battle and athletics, Greeks wishing to demonstrate *arete* could become public servants, they could give generously to various causes, or they could excel in wisdom. The ideal of *arete* applied mainly to the elite, especially to the warrior nobility, and seldom to women. Most Greeks were simple farmers, landless agricultural workers, or slaves whose lives and values were largely ignored by Homer.

The most important development of the Greek Dark Ages was the creation of a new form of political and social organization called the *polis* (plural: *poleis*). The idea of the *polis* has been so influential historically that even our modern English word politics is derived from *polis*. A *polis* was essentially an independent city-state. It was much more than just a municipality or a tiny nation, though. It was also a cultural and religious community. Members of a *polis* essentially thought of themselves as being part of a tribe. This was possible because most *poleis* had fewer than 5,000 male citizens—that is, full members of the state.

The *polis* inspired fierce loyalty in many Greeks, and the duties of citizenship were rigorously observed. Paradoxically, the *polis* was the strongest

Figure 2.1 This beautiful specimen of Athenian pottery, decorated with three runners, was presented as a prize to one of the victors in the Panathenaic Games. Athletic competition was central to ancient Greek culture and to the ideal of *arete*. Purchased from F.H.S Werry, 1856.

The British Museum/Wikimedia Commons.

institution in Greece, but it was also the biggest obstacle to Greek unification. The *poleis* often went to war with one another, and most attempts to consolidate multiple *poleis* into a federation or an empire ended in failure. At any given time, there were several hundred *poleis* in ancient Greece.

A *polis* was generally centered on a high, easily defensible plateau, called an *acropolis*. The most important temples and monuments were constructed on the *acropolis*. Nearby would be an *agora*, or marketplace. Here the political and commercial life of the *polis* would unfold. Outside of the town or city would be the *chora*, the farmland that sustained the community. Finally, every *polis* commonly had at least one *gymnasium*, where citizen-soldiers were expected to exercise.

Ancient Greeks experimented with a dizzying array of political philosophies, and democracy was by no means the most popular. Most *poleis* began as monarchies, but by the end of the Dark Ages few of the kings who still existed had significant power. Other common forms of government were aristocracy, in which a hereditary elite would rule; oligarchy, in which usually only a few rich citizens exercised real political power; and tyranny, in which a single man would rise to prominence, usually by appealing to populist sentiments. Democracies, which granted political authority to all male citizens (but not women, slaves, or persons born outside the *polis*), existed mainly in areas where the nobles or the wealthy had previously abused their powers. Many Greeks equated democracy with mob rule.

Each form of government had its strengths and weaknesses, and a given *polis* often lurched from one to another. Over time, though, Greek politics became more and more secular and pragmatic. The Greeks were often ready to embrace any form of government that promised them a better life.

What was the importance of the polis *in ancient Greece?*

Archaic Greece: The Rise of the Major Powers, 750 BCE–500 BCE

As the Dark Ages came to an end during the eighth century BCE, Greece became increasingly prosperous. Writing reemerged, trade flourished, and populations rose. In fact, overpopulation and food shortages developed, and many Greeks ventured across the Mediterranean Sea looking for land and opportunity. From about 750 BCE to 550 BCE, a wave of Greek colonization transformed the Mediterranean region. The site of each new colony and its first leader were chosen by its mother *polis*, which also provided ships and supplies. Once the colony was strong enough, however, it became self-governing. In this way, more than 1,000 new *poleis* were founded.

As Greek settlements proliferated throughout the Mediterranean region, the wealth of the Greeks increased, and their art and architecture grew more sophisticated—as did their approach to warfare. During the Dark Ages, Greek warfare had been dominated by noblemen on horseback. By the eighth century BCE, *poleis* expected all citizens to fight. The typical soldier was now a *hoplite*, a citizen-warrior armed with a long spear, a short sword, a bronze or iron helmet and armor, and a round shield. *Hoplites* fought in a formation known as a *phalanx*, a tightly packed square eight or more ranks deep on each side. The perimeter of the *phalanx* bristled with outstretched spears. So long as the *phalanx* stayed together, it was exceptionally difficult to attack. In battle, two opposing *phalanxes* would essentially ram into one another and engage in a pushing match. Generally, the most disciplined *phalanx* prevailed, and the losers fled.

The fact that most Greek warriors were citizen-soldiers had two important consequences. First, *hoplites* preferred short, decisive engagements close to home, preferably in the spring, before the harvesting of crops. Second, the traditional claim of the nobility to high status because of its monopoly on military expertise was undercut. Thus, hereditary aristocracies were shunted aside in many *poleis*, and forms of government with broader support, such as tyranny, democracy, and oligarchy, became more popular.

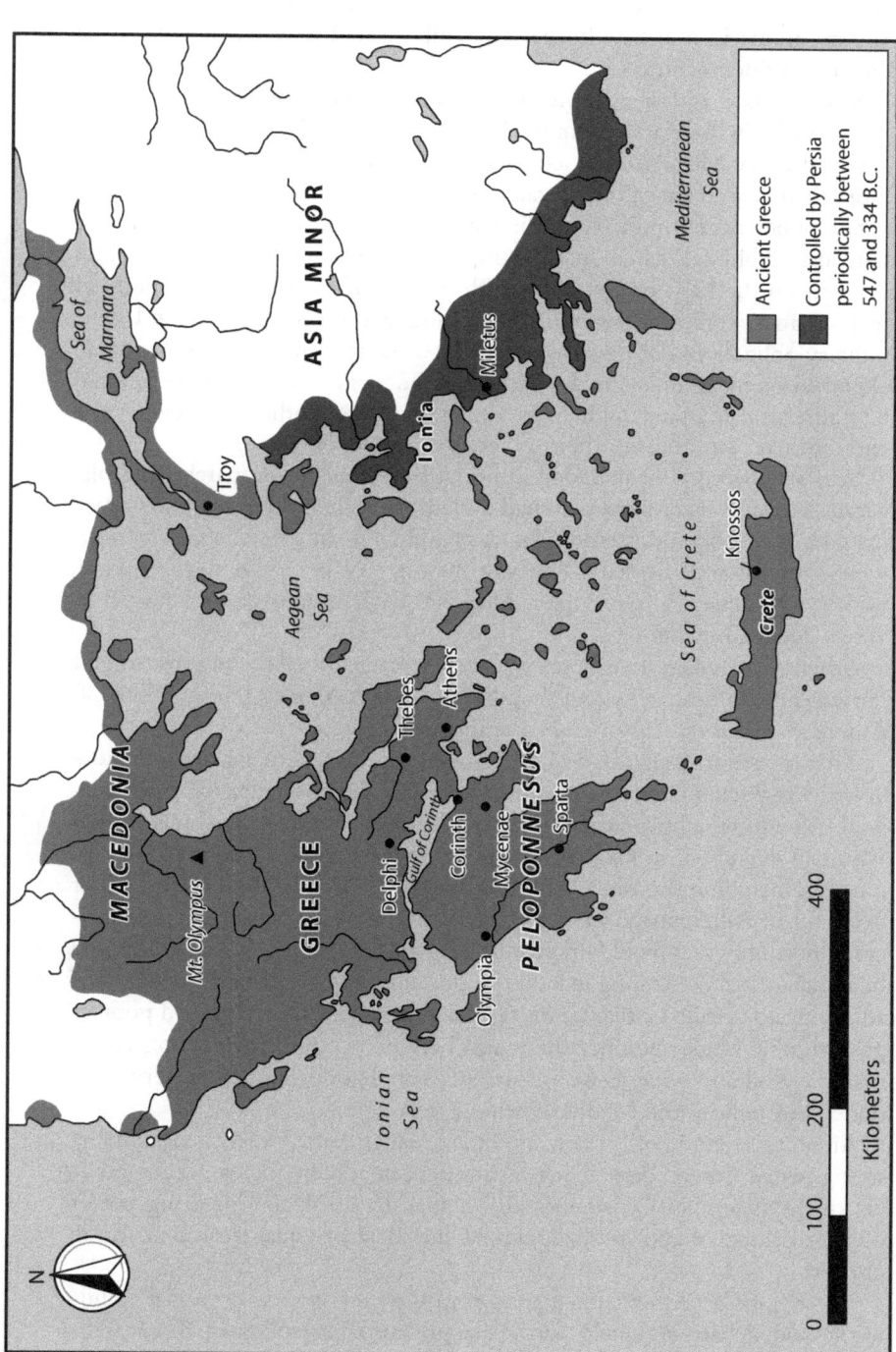

Map 2.1 Ancient Greece.

By far the most important *poleis* to emerge in Archaic Greece were Sparta and Athens, which followed remarkably different political paths. Sparta became militarized and authoritarian, while Athens moved gingerly in the direction of democracy.

Sparta was a sprawling state located on the Peloponnesian Peninsula. Around 715 BCE, Sparta conquered a neighboring *polis* called Messenia and enslaved every Messenian. Since slaves—called *helots* in Sparta—were now more than 90 percent of the overall population, free citizens had to maintain a state of permanent military readiness. Citizens of Sparta were held to high standards of physical fitness, patriotism, and self-sacrifice. Spartan authorities decided on the basis of physical health which infants would be permitted to live. Boys were sent for military training at the age of seven, and their military obligations did not end until age 60. Spartan men and women were expected to make do with the simplest food, drink, and clothing. Spartan discipline and military might were the envy of most other Greeks, but the extraordinary strictness of their society was often condemned.

Spartan government included important elements of monarchy and oligarchy, but all male citizens who had undergone military training also participated in a democratic assembly. That assembly, in turn, elected the five *ephors* who administered the state. The vast majority of people living in Sparta, however, had essentially no rights. After 500 BCE, moreover, the number of voters declined steadily.

Athens evolved in a completely different direction. Athens' government started out as a monarchy and then became an aristocracy, but by 500 BCE Athens was well on its way to becoming a democracy.

That transition began in 594 BCE, when the Athenian aristocracy chose Solon, a respected poet, to administer the *polis*. The poor, especially peasants, were close to rebellion. Many of them were deeply in debt, and an Athenian who had defaulted on his debts could be enslaved. Solon instituted massive reforms, including the cancellation of existing debts. He also began a major overhaul of Athenian government. Most importantly, he created a democratic Assembly that would empower the poor. The Assembly was composed of all male citizens. Among its other important duties, it helped elect Athens' administrators, called *archons*. This represented a critical shift toward popular government. Under Solon, Athens also became economically strong. Athenian olive oil and wine, as well as manufactured goods such as pottery, were traded throughout the Mediterranean region.

After an interlude of tyranny, a political leader named Cleisthenes further strengthened Athens' democratic institutions, mainly by increasing the powers of the Assembly. Cleisthenes also helped to break the lingering power of the aristocracy, and he championed the ideal of equal treatment for all citizens.

By 500 BCE, Athenian citizens, regardless of wealth or social standing, could debate and help formulate government policy in the Assembly. Women, as well as slaves and foreigners, were still excluded from the political process. Nevertheless, Athens was, in comparison to Sparta, a haven of democracy and freedom.

How did the governments of Sparta and Athens differ?

The Persian Menace

Starting in the sixth century BCE, the Greeks were threatened with invasion by a powerful eastern empire, Persia. From 546 BCE to 540 BCE, the Persians successfully conquered all of the Greek *poleis* in western Turkey, a region that the Greeks called Ionia. Who were the Persians, and why did they represent such a formidable threat to the Greeks?

The heartland of the Persian Empire lay in modern Iran. Before 559 BCE, the Persians had been a relatively unremarkable group of people. In that year, Cyrus the Great, founder of the Achaemenid dynasty, became the Persian king. He first absorbed a group called the Medes into Persia, and he then began a broader campaign of conquest. Cyrus the Great and his successors ultimately created the largest and greatest empire that the ancient Middle East had ever known.

One reason for Persia's success was its relatively gentle policies toward conquered peoples. Native customs, languages, and religions were generally left undisturbed (and sometimes they were even copied by the Persians themselves), so long as the Persians' subjects paid tribute and supplied military recruits. Among the subject peoples who were generally well treated by the Persians were the Hebrews, whom the Persians allowed to return to their homeland of Israel.

In theory, the Persian Empire was organized as an absolute monarchy. Its monarch, known as the *Shahanshah*, or King of Kings, owned all the land in the empire, and he could dispose of his subjects as he saw fit. In practice, because of the size and cultural diversity of the empire, Persia's kings had to delegate much of their power to bureaucrats and to regional governors known as *satraps*, who enjoyed considerable autonomy. The provinces, or *satrapies*, of the Persian Empire were, however, tied together by an advanced system of roads that facilitated trade and further conquest.

Religiously, the Persians were unique. Their faith, Zoroastrianism, named after the prophet Zoroaster, preached the existence of only one god, Ahura Mazda, who represented goodness, truth, and light. Ahura Mazda was opposed by his demonic enemy, Ahriman. According to Zoroaster, each person has the freedom to choose between good and evil. Ahura Mazda rewards the righteous and punishes the wicked. Some of these ideas may sound familiar, and indeed Judaism and Christianity may both have been influenced by Zoroastrianism.

The ancient Persian Empire experienced remarkable success in expanding to the west. From 540 BCE to 499 BCE, the Persians ruled every Greek *poleis* in Ionia, but they did so with considerable mildness. Beginning in

499 BCE, a scheming tyrant named Aristagoras, in the Ionian city of Miletus, led a rebellion against the Persians that the Athenians supported. The Persians prevailed, however, and they obliterated Miletus. More ominously, Persia's King Darius I made plans to invade the Greek mainland. In 490 BCE, Darius landed with as many as 50,000 men at the Plain of Marathon, north of Athens, hoping to make Greece his newest *satrapy*. About 10,000 Greeks opposed him at the Battle of Marathon, and they struggled to victory. Darius withdrew. According to legend, after the battle, a runner was sent from Marathon to Athens—a distance of roughly 25 miles—to announce the Greek triumph. After completing his mission, he promptly fell dead. This feat is the basis for our modern sporting event: the marathon.

Darius's successor, Xerxes, planned a much larger campaign in 481 BCE. He assembled a mighty army of 150,000 men to destroy Greek resistance. The Greeks responded, though, with an extraordinary show of unity against the Persian threat.

Xerxes's army took a circuitous route around the Aegean Sea, reaching the crucial mountain pass at Thermopylae in the summer of 480 BCE. There, a Greek force of less than 10,000 men tried to stem the Persian advance. After two days of bitter fighting, however, a Greek traitor showed the Persians how to outflank the Greek positions. Most of the Greek soldiers retreated, but a select force, including 300 Spartans, stayed to fight to the death. Die they did, and the Persians resumed their advance.

Luckily for the Greeks, the Athenians had invested in a naval buildup. At the Battle of Salamis in September 480 BCE, the Athenian fleet dealt a devastating defeat to the Persians despite the fact that the Athenian ships were outnumbered by more than two to one. Naval warfare at the time was conducted by triremes: long, narrow galley ships propelled by dozens of oarsmen. Triremes fought by ramming one another. Once a ship was rammed, it might sink, or it might be boarded by marines who fought hand-to-hand.

After the Battle of Salamis, King Xerxes returned home. The remnants of his army were convincingly defeated in 479 BCE at the Battle of Plataea, and Persian forces were swept from the entire Greek world. Thus, the Persian effort to conquer Greece, and to erase the liberties of the *poleis*, had been utterly crushed. Nonetheless, the Athenians proceeded to found a Delian League to continue the war against Persia. Although Sparta declined to support it, the Delian League brought unprecedented unity to the Greek *poleis*. It also, however, became a vehicle for Athenian imperialism. The allies of Athens, which at first joined willingly in the anti-Persian crusade, slowly became vassal states that owed tribute and obedience to Athens. Whenever they tried to reestablish their independence, Athens used force to restrain them. Before long, the ambition of the Athenians would make Athens and Sparta rivals, and Greece would be plunged into several generations of bitter fighting.

What were some of the most important battles fought between the Persians and the Greeks?

Classical Greece: Splendor and Strife, 478 BCE–338 BCE

As relations between Athens and Sparta unraveled, Athens used the wealth of the Delian League, much of it confiscated from Athens' client states, to fund monumental building projects and cultural events. It was in these years that the most famous buildings on the Acropolis in Athens were built. The majestic ruins of those buildings still stand today, and they even played an important role, albeit as scenery, in the 2004 Olympic games.

The flowering of Athenian architecture, art, drama, and philosophy during the fifth century BCE was impressive, but arguably the achievements of Athenian democracy were more significant. Starting in 461 BCE, the aristocratic politicians who traditionally had dominated the Athenian government, despite its democratic institutions, fell from favor, and a group of radical democrats took over. The most famous of these popular leaders was Pericles, a brilliant speaker and a visionary statesman. Thus, the period from about 460 BCE to 429 BCE, when democracy reached its height in Athens, and when Classical Greek art and culture flourished, is often referred to as the Age of Pericles.

During these years, Athenian political institutions were overhauled to give essentially unchecked power to the Assembly, in which all male citizens had the right to speak and vote. The Assembly met 40 times per year and voted directly on every issue—from budgets to criminal law to questions of war and peace. Predictably, skillful speakers often exercised disproportionate influence, and so the study of oratory and rhetoric became an Athenian obsession.

It was not only in the Assembly that ordinary citizens were represented. Property qualifications for those seeking political offices were eliminated. In fact, many public officials were chosen by lot, that is, at random, so all citizens were eligible. There was also frequent turnover in most government offices, and the people held public officials to account if they abused their powers. In addition, ordinary citizens served on the highest court in the *polis*, and jurors, who were paid for their service, judged many lesser cases. The Athenian justice system seems less progressive, however, when one considers that torture was regularly used on witnesses who were slaves.

Overall, Athenian democracy allowed, and it even relied upon, an extraordinarily high level of participation from ordinary citizens. At least in the Age of Pericles, Athenians seem to have attended to their public duties conscientiously. Remarkably, Athenian democracy also managed to minimize factionalism, no doubt partly because Athenians could vote to ostracize troublesome politicians, that is, expel them from the *polis* for a period of ten years! For the most part, the laws that were passed by the Assembly were also applied equally to everyone. In the ancient world, these were spectacular achievements.

As before, Athenian democracy had its limitations. Slaves, who represented perhaps 25 percent of the Athenian population, had no political input whatsoever. Strict rules also made it nearly impossible for immigrants from other *poleis* to become citizens. In addition, women were excluded from political life. As a matter of fact, during the Age of Pericles, Athenian women probably played a much smaller role in Greek politics than royal and aristocratic women had played before the advent of democracy. All in all, it is likely that less than ten percent of the Athenian population could vote.

It is also worth remembering that, while the Athenians were extending democracy in Athens itself, they were simultaneously imposing puppet regimes, with a democratic veneer, on the other Greek states that were enrolled in the Delian League. The Athenians were, in short, erasing the freedom of other Greeks at the very same time that they were maximizing it for themselves.

Modern democracy owes much to the example set by ancient Athens. Any American who studies the history of the American Revolution and the writing of the U.S. Constitution will soon learn that the Founding Fathers were intrigued and inspired by the history of democracy and personal freedom in ancient Athens. The truth, though, is that the Founders were equally aware of the failures of Athenian democracy, and they were determined to learn from those mistakes. And yet, despite the mixed record and the troubled history of democracy in ancient Greece, the fact remains that Athens and its Assembly have served for almost 2,500 years as one of the most shining examples of a government "of, by, and for the people."

Unfortunately for the Greeks, the democratic achievement in Athens would be largely overshadowed by warfare between Athens and Sparta. Friction between the two most powerful Greek *poleis* developed almost immediately after the end of the Persian Wars.

Sparta controlled a grand alliance of Greek states known as the Peloponnesian League, which was centered on the Greek mainland, and especially on the Peloponnesian Peninsula. The Athenians, of course, controlled the rival alliance, the Delian League, made up mostly of islands in the Aegean Sea and of various *poleis* spread along the Ionian coast. Predictably, the minor states in the Peloponnesian League and the Delian League often tested the limits of their respective alliances, resulting in political instability that drew Athens and Sparta into wider conflicts. From 460 BCE to 445 BCE, Athens and Sparta were at war. In this case, Sparta's mighty army, matched against Athens' unsurpassed navy, led to a stalemate.

As it turned out, this was merely a dress rehearsal for a much bigger conflict, the Peloponnesian War, which was fought between 431 BCE and 404 BCE. The pretext for the war was a dispute between two *poleis*, Corinth and Corcyra, but in reality the war was fought to determine once and for all which Greek superpower, Athens or Sparta, would predominate.

The war progressed according to the old pattern, with Sparta using its well-trained army to besiege Athens, while the Athenian navy harassed the coasts of Sparta and its allies. Athens' naval siege of the Spartan island of Sphacteria concluded with an unheard-of result: Spartan warriors, instead of fighting to the death, surrendered! Early in the war, Athens' respected leader, Pericles, died of plague. By 421 BCE, Athens and Sparta had fought, as before, to a stalemate, and a truce was declared. Still, however, ordinary Greeks suffered. In 416 BCE, the Athenians brutally invaded the island of Melos, which had stubbornly resisted Athenian domination. They killed the Melian men and enslaved the women and children.

In 413 BCE, Sparta renewed the war, and this time the Spartans won the assistance of a traditional Greek enemy, Persia, and they also benefited from the advice of an Athenian traitor, Alcibiades. The Persians built ships for a Spartan navy that convincingly defeated the Athenian fleet in 405 BCE. In 404, the Athenians, besieged on land and unable to receive supplies by sea, were forced to surrender. This outcome was a shock to many Greeks. Among the most important lessons of the war was the idea that, in the epic battle between democracy, represented by Athens, and authoritarian militarism, represented by Sparta, democracy had lost. Many Greeks wondered whether democratic ideals could survive such a humiliation.

Sparta now emerged as the dominant power throughout Greece. However, by imposing military occupation on many *poleis*, including Athens, and by installing pro-Spartan regimes, Sparta overplayed its hand. Persia eventually threw its support behind Sparta's enemies, and, during the first quarter of the fourth century BCE, both Athens and Thebes (a major *polis* in central Greece) managed to free themselves from Spartan domination. In 371 BCE, in fact, the Thebans defeated the Spartan army and proceeded to free the *helots* (Sparta's slaves). As a result, the power of Sparta was shattered.

The history of the Greek *poleis* from 371 BCE to 338 BCE reads like a soap opera, with alliances and empires forming and dissolving, with constant bickering and betrayals, and with the Persians playing the role of spoilers and exploiting the confusion to reestablish their control of Ionia. Throughout the fourth century BCE, in fact, the Greeks engaged in a vigorous debate over the nature, and even the survival, of the traditional *polis*. The squabbling between *poleis* that had defined so much of Greek history seemed to be reaching crisis proportions. Many Greeks yearned for order, and they feared that the Persians, who were still formidable, might try once more to impose a Middle Eastern despotism on the Greek world.

Amazingly, despite the instability of Greek politics, Greek art, architecture, drama, and philosophy reached incredible heights during the fourth century BCE. The two most famous Greek philosophers, Plato and Aristotle, both lived and worked in this era.

As it turned out, the Greeks need not have feared that the independence of their various *poleis* would be obliterated by Persia. Instead, the final and decisive blow to the institution of the *polis* would come not from the east, but from the north. There, the Macedonians, who were considered Greek only by courtesy, were slowly building an army and an empire that were destined to reshape the ancient world.

How was Athenian democracy similar to and different from modern democracy?

The Rise of Macedon and Alexander the Great

Macedon, or Macedonia as it is generally known today, lies in the very northern part of Greece. It is a mountainous but fertile region. Traditionally, the Greeks had seen it as a backward, impoverished land. By the standards of most Greeks, Macedonian culture was crude and semi-barbaric. The government of Macedon was in the hands of a hereditary king, supported by leading nobles, but the country was frequently threatened with internal strife and by hostile tribes to the north. Until the fourth century BCE, Macedon played only a minor role in Greek affairs.

All this changed when King Philip II took the throne in 359 BCE. Although other Greeks sometimes dismissed Philip as a country bumpkin, in reality he was intelligent, courageous, and ambitious. Philip had spent several years as an adolescent living as a hostage in Thebes. At the time, Thebes was the greatest military power in the Greek world, and Philip learned much by studying under the great Theban general, Epaminondas. Later, as king, Philip applied his knowledge to forge an imposing Macedonian army of 40,000 men.

Philip's soldiers were professionals, not amateur citizen-warriors, as most Greek *hoplites* had been for centuries. In addition, Philip hired military experts and mercenaries, he equipped his men with the finest weapons, and he deployed his aristocratic supporters as members of a superb force of cavalry. In short, Philip created an army that was by far the strongest in the Greek world. Interestingly, at the same time that Philip was working to improve his army, he also sought to refine Macedonian culture so that other Greeks would respect Macedon as a civilized land.

Gradually, the rest of Greece began to notice Philip and his army, and a debate began about how to meet the potential threat that the Macedonians posed. Some Greek politicians wanted to cooperate with Philip, while others, notably the great orator Demosthenes of Athens, wanted to oppose him. Demosthenes feared that Philip sought to impose Macedonian domination on the whole of Greece. In retrospect, Demosthenes was right about Philip's intentions, but he was wrong to suggest that the Greeks, given the weakness and indecision that characterized their political life at the time, could realistically have hoped to defeat Philip's army.

As it happened, the fate of Greece was decided in 338 BCE at the Battle of Chaeronea, where the Macedonians decisively defeated the Athenian and Theban armies. Philip's son, Alexander, played a leading role in Macedon's triumph. Philip proceeded to impose a League of Corinth, which he controlled, on virtually all the Greeks.

Although some of the local rights of the *poleis* were maintained, Macedonian rule effectively ended their independence. As a result, the Age of Classical Greece, which had been defined by the institution of the *polis*, came to a close in 338 BCE. A new era was dawning in which Greece would still be a beacon of high culture, but it would not be divided into innumerable small *poleis*, each jealously guarding its freedom, nor would it be a land in which democracy would flourish.

The Greeks, however, were not entirely displeased to be ruled by a Macedonian king. This was because Philip brought them unity, and he proposed a grand and seemingly noble purpose for his League of Corinth. He suggested that all the Greeks should combine their military forces and invade, occupy, and plunder the Persian Empire. The last few years of Philip's reign were dedicated to preparing for this great undertaking.

In 336 BCE, before the invasion of Persia could be launched, Philip of Macedon was assassinated. His successor was his 20-year-old son, Alexander, who became King Alexander III, usually known as Alexander the Great. Like his father, Alexander was a gifted political leader and military strategist—he had been tutored by none other than Aristotle—and he was determined to expand the empire controlled by Macedon.

In 334 BCE, Alexander led the Macedonian army and its Greek allies in the grand attack on Persia that had been planned by Philip. He brought with him Greek philosophers, poets, and scientists, plus a historian to record the mighty victories that he planned to win.

At the Battle of Granicus River in modern Turkey, Alexander boldly led the cavalry charge that broke the Persian lines. He narrowly escaped being killed. Then, at the Battle of Issus in Syria, Alexander faced the Persian King Darius III for the first time. Darius had brought with him much of his family and no less than 360 concubines. More importantly, Darius had huge numbers of troops at his disposal, including Greek mercenaries, and a much stronger navy than Alexander. Still, once again, Alexander personally led his men to victory. Darius fled, leaving his mother, wife, and two daughters behind to be captured, along with much treasure. Alexander even obtained, and happily made use of, Darius's ornamental bathtub! Macedonian and Greek troops proceeded to occupy Syria, Israel/Palestine, and Egypt. In the process, Alexander successfully captured all the ports used by the Persian navy, thus eliminating the threat it had posed. The high priests in Egypt then proclaimed Alexander Pharaoh. After visiting the Egyptian oracle at Siwa, Alexander even became convinced that he was the son of Zeus, and thus semi-divine.

Why were the Macedonians able to conquer the Greeks?

The Defeat of Persia and the Creation of the "Hellenistic World"

The climactic battle of the Macedonian invasion of the Persian Empire was fought on a dusty plain at Gaugamela, close to the modern Iraqi city of Mosul. Alexander's forces were, as usual, outnumbered, but Alexander managed nonetheless to outsmart the Persian generals and to defeat the Persian army. Darius fled again from the battlefield, but this time Alexander was able to occupy Mesopotamia and, in 330 BCE, he captured the magnificent Persian capital at Persepolis. In effect, the occupation of Persepolis spelled the end of the Persian Empire. Chased into the mountains, Darius was eventually killed by his own men. Alexander was now indisputably the greatest conqueror in the history of the ancient world.

Alexander was not a man to rest on his laurels. After occupying the heartland of the Persian Empire and dismissing his Greek troops, he led his Macedonian forces and some Greek mercenaries on a further campaign to pacify the eastern provinces of the Persian realm. Alexander's advance took him as far as India, where in 326 BCE he won the colorful Battle of the Hydaspes River. There he defeated masses of Indian soldiers, some of whom fought from the backs of elephants. Alexander's men, however, were exhausted. They mutinied, and Alexander was forced to retreat to the west, through the forbidding Gedrosian Desert.

Finally, Alexander and his surviving soldiers arrived in the ancient and luxurious city of Babylon, where Alexander, between wild drinking parties, began to plan the next phase of his reign. He may have toyed with the idea of conquering Arabia, or invading Italy, and he appears to have sent word to Greece that he expected to be worshiped as a god. Some historians even believe that around this time he went insane. Be that as it may, Alexander clearly wanted to found numerous new cities all over his empire, and to settle Greeks throughout the Middle East, who would lead, with Persian assistance, the native peoples of the region. He foresaw, in fact, a great new universal empire that would arise through the intermarriage and cooperation of a mainly Greek and Persian elite. Whether Alexander could have achieved this ambitious goal will never be known, because he died suddenly at Babylon in 323 BCE. He was only 32 years old. His death marks the beginning of a new period in ancient history: the Hellenistic Age, which would last from 323 BCE to 31 BCE.

After the death of Alexander the Great, although his rightful heir was his son, ambitious generals at Alexander's court decided to divide his gigantic empire among themselves. Alexander's 12-year-old son was therefore put to death.

The unity of Alexander's empire was thus shattered, but the domination of Macedonians and other Greeks throughout the Middle East lasted for several centuries. Politically, the Hellenistic world was divided between three royal families. The Antigonids ruled Macedonia and parts of Greece, at least until the Romans conquered the area in 168 BCE. One of Alexander's generals, Ptolemy, founded the Ptolemaic dynasty in Egypt. The Ptolemies would rule Egypt until 30 BCE, when the last member of the dynasty, Queen Cleopatra, died, and the Romans took over. The third large kingdom to emerge after Alexander's death was the Seleucid monarchy. The Seleucid dynasty ruled modern Iran, as well as Mesopotamia, Syria, and parts of Turkey and Central Asia. The Romans and the Parthians eventually conquered the Seleucid lands.

It is extremely important to note that the form of government that all the Hellenistic states had in common was monarchy. Even though Macedonians and other Greeks predominated, they made no attempt to carve the Hellenistic kingdoms into independent *poleis*. Indeed, the age of the *polis* was finished. Hellenistic kings (and, occasionally, queens) ruled not by consulting their citizens but by using force against any of their subjects who opposed them. In fact, many Hellenistic kings encouraged the idea that they were divine, or at least that the gods supported their absolute authority. In other words, religion had once again become the basis for political power, and democracy had once again become unthinkable. In truth, this was a trend that Alexander the Great himself had done much to encourage.

In some ways, then, the Hellenistic world was based on a betrayal of the ideals of Archaic and Classical Greece. In other ways, though, the Hellenistic Age spread traditional Greek ideals and culture, and many thousands of Greek settlers, throughout the Middle East. Hellenistic bureaucracies, cities, and armies were all primarily Greek, as was the economic elite. Thus, Greek art, architecture, drama, philosophy, commerce, and science all became enormously influential throughout the Hellenistic world, as Chapter 3 will make plain. At the same time, some Persian, Mesopotamian, Egyptian, and Hebrew traditions influenced Greece.

What characteristics did the Hellenistic kingdoms have in common?

Conclusions

It is worth remembering that all the cultural exchange that took place in the Hellenistic Age did not occur by accident. On the contrary, it was the simple fact of Alexander's conquest of the Middle East that made the Hellenistic world possible.

The greatest significance of ancient Greece for modern Western Civilization lies in the ideas that the Greeks contributed to the West—ideas such as democracy, individual freedom and dignity, classical beauty, and science. Nevertheless, it was not these ideas, but rather the often violent and unstable political and military history of ancient Greece, combined with its traditions of *arete* and selfless devotion to civic duty, that trained the Greeks to be great warriors. It was, moreover, Greek military superiority that allowed the Macedonians and the Greeks to conquer so much of the ancient world. Were it not for these conquests, it is entirely possible that the ancient Greeks, despite all of their political, cultural, artistic, and intellectual achievements, would have been far less influential in the history of the West.

We should thank Alexander the Great, therefore, just as much as we thank Plato, Pericles, or Sophocles, for the "Glory That Was Greece," and for the overwhelmingly positive legacy that ancient Greece has bestowed on modern Western Civilization.

Key Terms for Chapter 2

Minoans—the earliest civilized society in ancient Greece, based on the island of Crete.

Mycenaeans—an early Greek civilization dominated by kings and a warrior nobility. The Mycenaean attack on Troy was memorialized by the poet Homer in *The Iliad*.

Arete—"excellence," a Greek ideal framed by Homer.

Polis—a term for an ancient Greek city-state. Numerous forms of government were practiced in the various *poleis*, including democracy.

Greek colonization, 750 BCE–550 BCE—during the Archaic Period, a wave of Greek settlers washed over the Mediterranean region. They created many new *poleis*.

Hoplites—Greek citizen-warriors, who provided the backbone of most Greek armies. The military importance of ordinary citizens added to their political clout and helped to sideline the aristocracy.

Sparta—one of the most powerful of Greek *poleis*, notable for its high degree of militarization and its dependence on the labor of a vast population of slaves, known as *helots*.

Athens—one of the most powerful of Greek *poleis* and the source of many of the ancient Greek cultural and intellectual accomplishments that are most famous today. Athens evolved into an expansionist democracy.

Persian Empire—a large empire based in modern-day Iran, and ruling much of Central Asia, the Middle East, and North Africa. The Persians attempted to conquer the Greeks but were turned aside by a string of Greek victories facilitated by an unprecedented willingness among the Greeks to put aside their differences.

Peloponnesian War, 431 BCE–404 BCE—the most important war of the Classical Period, resulting in Athens' total defeat at the hands of Sparta.

Philip II—King of Macedonia from 359 BCE to 336 BCE. By forging a mighty army, he managed to unite all of Greece under his rule, but he was assassinated before he could commence an invasion of the Persian Empire.

Alexander III—King of Macedonia from 336 BCE to 323 BCE. Known as Alexander the Great, he realized his father's ambition of conquering the Persian Empire, but he died young, before his achievements could be consolidated.

Hellenistic world—a phrase describing the Greek-dominated eastern Mediterranean region from Alexander's death in 323 BCE until roughly 31 BCE, when Rome took over. The Hellenistic kingdoms were ruled by Macedonian/Greek monarchs, who encouraged the spread of Greek culture throughout much of the Middle East.

Review Questions for Chapter 2

1. The concept of *arete* exercised a profound influence on ancient Greek politics and society. Provide three examples of how the Greeks strove to embody *arete*.
2. The *polis* was arguably both a strength and a weakness for the ancient Greeks. First, explain at least one positive attribute of the *polis*. Then, explain at least one negative attribute.

3. Describe the major differences between the political system in ancient Sparta and the political system in ancient Athens. In your view, does Sparta's victory in the Peloponnesian War prove the superiority of Spartan ways? Why or why not?
4. You are a citizen of ancient Athens, and word has just reached the city of the untimely death of Alexander the Great. Write an obituary in which you recap some of the major achievements of his life, and in which you pass judgment on his reign. Consider, in particular, whether Alexander's career of conquest was good or bad for his fellow Greeks.
5. It is 481 BCE, and King Xerxes of Persia is preparing to launch a massive invasion of Greece. You are a Greek citizen of a minor *polis*. Write a letter in which you attempt to dissuade Xerxes from going through with his attack. Be creative in anticipating the arguments that Xerxes will find persuasive.

Further Reading

Brosius, Maria. *The Persians: An Introduction*. New York: Routledge. 2010.
Cartledge, Paul. *Alexander the Great: The Hunt for a New Past*. London: Pan Books. 2013.
Cartledge, Paul. *Spartans: The World of the Warrior-Heroes of Ancient Greece*. London: Pan Books. 2013.
Chamoux, François. *Hellenistic Civilization*. New York: John Wiley and Sons. 2008.
Everitt, Anthony. *The Rise of Athens: The Story of the World's Greatest Civilization*. New York: Random House. 2017.
Herman, Gabriel. *Morality and Behaviour in Democratic Athens*. Cambridge: Cambridge University Press. 2010.
Pomeroy, Sarah B., et al. *Ancient Greece: A Political, Social, and Cultural History*. Fourth Edition. New York: Oxford University Press. 2017.
Roberts, Jennifer. *The Plague of War: Athens, Sparta, and the Struggle for Ancient Greece*. New York: Oxford University Press. 2017.
Shipley, Graham. *The Greek World After Alexander, 323–30 B.C.* Hoboken, NJ: Taylor and Francis. 2014.
Spivey, Nigel. *The Ancient Olympics*. Oxford: Oxford University Press. 2012.
Taylour, Lord William. *The Mycenaeans*. London: Folio Society. 2004.
Van De Mieroop, Marc. *A History of the Ancient Near East, ca.3000–323 B.C.* Oxford: Blackwell. 2007.

3 Ancient Greece
Society, Culture, and Daily Life

Introduction

In the course of their efforts to achieve military glory, the Greeks founded one of the most brilliant and influential cultural traditions in all of human history. When modern people study the ancient Greeks, they are often deeply impressed by the Greeks' commitment to rationality and skepticism, their devotion to beauty and artistic excellence, their ethical moderation and humanity, their curiosity about the natural world, their boldness and integrity in the pursuit of wisdom and truth, and their willingness to experiment with a variety of political forms, including those that provided ordinary citizens with the opportunity to participate in decision making.

The ancient Greeks truly were different—sometimes radically so—from any people that had come before them. Because, as we have seen, their cultural and intellectual creativity was felicitously combined with military prowess, the Greeks were able to contribute to the long-term evolution of Western Civilization in a decisive way. Thus, the stamp of Greekness is still impressed on modern Western Civilization. The fact that the English language includes thousands of words with Greek roots is but one sign of this extraordinary influence.

Despite the greatness of their culture, most Greeks were neither artists nor philosophers. They were humble farmers, herders, fishermen, or traders. It is important for us to remember that "The Glory That Was Greece" was founded on the humdrum labors of a people who, at first glance, must have looked extremely ordinary, by ancient standards.

A Seafaring People, and a Survey of the Greek Economy

Homer's *The Odyssey*, the sequel to *The Iliad*, chronicled the remarkable ten-year voyage of Odysseus, a Greek king and warrior, from the defeated city of Troy to his home on the island of Ithaca. Much of the action takes place at sea, and Homer makes it clear that the sea was not just a natural phenomenon for the Greeks but also a cultural icon and even a spiritual force. In short, the Greek world was defined by the sea.

During the Archaic and Classical Periods—from about 750 BCE to 338 BCE—Greek colonization and sea-based trade flourished. At the height of Greek colonization in 750–550 BCE, Greek ships carried colonists to their new homes in Italy, Sicily, Spain, France, North Africa, and along the Black Sea coast. The resulting new *poleis* became vital trading partners for Greece itself. Mainland Greece, Ionia, and the Greek Isles exchanged wine, olive oil, pottery, jewelry, and weapons for grain, glassware, dyes, slaves, timber, metals, and precious and semi-precious stones. Meanwhile, Greek fishing vessels provided an important source of food. In time, oceangoing commerce would become a necessity for the ancient Greeks. The city of Athens, for example, relied upon Greek *poleis* along the Black Sea coast for much of its grain. When the Spartans built their own navy during the Peloponnesian War and cut off the Athenians' access to imported grain, therefore, Athens was forced to surrender.

The fate of Athens points out the extraordinary importance of naval combat to the history of ancient Greece. As we have seen already, perhaps the most important and decisive battle fought during ancient times was the Battle of Salamis, where the outnumbered Greek fleet defeated the mighty Persian navy. This Greek victory convinced the Persian "Great King," Xerxes, to abandon his invasion of Greece.

Although many Greeks were sailors, fishermen, or merchants (and a few were pirates), the majority were farmers or herders. In ancient Greece, as in every society before the Agricultural and Industrial Revolutions of the seventeenth, eighteenth, and nineteenth centuries CE, simply producing enough food to eat was a constant challenge.

In Minoan and Mycenaean times, farming was controlled by the central government, with surplus produce stored in royal palaces. By the Dark Ages, though, individual farmers decided for themselves what to grow and to whom they would sell their crops. Most Greek farmers seem to have owned only a small amount of land, and the entire family had to work very hard cultivating crops such as wheat, barley, olives, or grapes. Herders, meanwhile, raised pigs, goats, chickens, cows, oxen, and innumerable sheep.

Some rural Greeks owned no land, so they worked as sharecroppers or as agricultural laborers for the aristocracy. During hard times, Greeks often became indebted to noblemen. A farmer who could not pay his debts sometimes became the slave of his creditor. Not surprisingly, this caused tension between the different social classes.

In Archaic Greece, the power of the aristocracy steadily declined as tyrants, oligarchs, and democratic assemblies assumed political power. As we have seen, this was partly the result of the new *hoplite* style of warfare, which gave individual farmers greater clout in Greek politics. From time to time, governments even confiscated the land of noblemen and distributed it among the poor. Nevertheless, most aristocrats remained wealthy, and they continued to lead most *poleis*. Many prominent politicians in democratic Athens, for example, were nobles.

Tellingly, the aristocratic lifestyle, which revolved around the ideal of *arete*, or "excellence," endured long after most aristocratic governments had fallen. Nobles still fought bravely in wartime, they competed in athletic contests, they sponsored cultural events and building projects, and they enjoyed a form of entertainment called the *symposium*. A *symposium* was essentially a party at which noblemen would recline on couches and drink wine, play games, sing, engage in conversation, and enjoy the company of young women, often slaves, who would dance or play the flute. Aristocrats thus enjoyed a sophisticated, leisured lifestyle that they believed placed them above ordinary Greeks.

There was yet another important class in Archaic and Classical Greece: urban craftsmen, who produced some of the finest manufactured goods available in the ancient world. They made both ordinary and decorative pottery; they fashioned tools, utensils, jewelry, and weapons made of bronze, iron, silver, or gold; they practiced carpentry, woodcarving, tanning, and masonry; and they built graceful and sturdy ships. Skilled craftsmen were much respected in ancient Greece. In Athens, an artisan might refer to himself as a "lord of the hand." Some rose to high positions in the government.

As trade increased with Greek colonies and with the rich markets in Italy and the Middle East, Greek crafts became valuable exports. Athenian pottery, initially painted mainly with intricate geometrical patterns, and later with scenes of the gods, of animals, or of daily life, was especially popular. The wealth that Athens achieved through trade, in turn, made possible the great achievements in art, architecture, philosophy, and politics for which the city would later become famous.

Eventually, the standardization of weights and measures, as well as coinage, facilitated even greater levels of commerce and prosperity. The *agora*, or marketplace, in each *polis* hummed with activity. The Greeks were not just starry-eyed philosophers and poets, nor were they all bloodthirsty warriors. Most Greeks were practical farmers or small-scale entrepreneurs who worked hard to provide a decent life for their families.

What types of goods were important in Greek trade?

Greek Religion

In ancient Greece, as in Egypt and Mesopotamia, religion was polytheistic. In addition, the gods were almost always portrayed in human form. A god or goddess could be wounded; he or she could experience hunger, greed, or lust; and the powers of the gods were limited by nature or by fate. The boundary between humans and gods was also porous. Sometimes the gods had relationships with human beings that produced semi-divine children. Humans, by achieving superhuman feats, could also ascend to the status of partly godlike heroes. Hercules is the most famous of Greek heroes. The anthropomorphic qualities of Greek gods and goddesses sharply distinguish these deities from the transcendent God worshiped by Jews, Christians, and Muslims.

Twelve principal gods and goddesses were said to live on top of Mount Olympus, the highest mountain in Greece. The king of the gods was the sky-god Zeus, who had the power to hurl thunderbolts at those who displeased him. Zeus's brother Poseidon, god of the sea, was the cause of earthquakes and storms. Zeus had numerous divine children, including Athena, who was the goddess of wisdom, weaving, and crafts, as well as a capable warrior and the patron goddess of Athens; beautiful Aphrodite, the goddess of love; Apollo, god of the sun and of truth, as well as music, poetry, archery, and healing; and the god of war, Ares. The adventures and misadventures of these gods and goddesses were the prime subject matter of Greek mythology, which played a central role in Greek culture.

Greeks worshiped in a variety of ways. Temples were dedicated to the major gods and goddesses. The most important temples in a particular *polis* sat at the very center of the city, high atop its *acropolis*. Ordinary Greeks, however, seldom visited these temples, instead attending religious rituals nearby or at lesser shrines and altars in the countryside. In fact, the major deities and the great temples were the focus of Greek religion only when the *polis* came together as a whole. On a daily basis, average people prayed instead to lesser gods, or they invoked their ancestors. Some Greeks also became affiliated with mystery cults, explained in more detail in Chapter 5, which trained their followers in secret rituals.

Festivals were another major element of ancient Greek religion. An important festival in Athens was the elaborate annual Panathenaea that included a procession and competitions in athletics, music, and poetry. There was even a beauty contest for men. The Olympic games, held every four years in Olympia, took place on the grounds of a temple to Zeus and were effectively a festival held in his honor. Greek religious festivals often involved sacrificing large numbers of animals, some of which people then ate. Not surprisingly, such gatherings tended to be happy occasions. During important religious festivals, wars were usually suspended so that Greeks from various *poleis* could attend. Participation in religious rituals and festivals was even considered part of one's patriotic duty as a citizen of a particular *polis*. Women, who did not enjoy full citizenship rights, usually played a secondary role at festivals or were excluded altogether.

Another focus of Greek religion was divination, or the practice of predicting the future by reading signs attributed to the gods. The most important form of divination occurred at several special religious sites scattered throughout Greece called oracles. The famous oracle at Delphi was dedicated to the god Apollo. The priests and priestesses at Delphi conducted mysterious rituals that allowed them to answer questions posed by various Greeks. The oracles were also frequently the sites of festivals and games.

Ancient Greek religion had important limitations. First, it centered on rituals rather than morality. Greek religion suggested no clear interpretation of right and wrong. Second, although the Greeks believed in the afterlife, they did not focus on it, nor did they expect rewards and punishments for earthly conduct to be distributed in the hereafter. Last, although many ordinary Greeks were devoutly religious, over time religion became less influential. By the late Classical period, many Greeks had come to the conclusion that human beings could use their reason and their innate moral sense to solve practical problems without divine intervention.

The Greeks, more than any other ancient people, were rationalists: they believed that the human mind, when properly trained and disciplined, could find the answer to almost any problem. The Greeks also tended to be humanists, believing that the basic purpose of Greek culture, society, and government was not to fulfill the will of the gods, but to allow human beings to help themselves and to reach their fullest potential. Increasingly, therefore, many Greeks sought practical solutions to their problems, and religion became a secondary consideration in their lives.

Compare and contrast the practice of religion in ancient Greece with the practice of religion in most Western countries today.

Arts and Sciences

Greek poetry, literature, and drama were built on the foundation of Homer's epic poems, *The Iliad* and *The Odyssey*. During the Archaic and Classical Periods, however, there was a transition from epic poetry—poetry that tells long, inspiring stories—to lyric poetry, which captures the thoughts and feelings of daily life. Most lyric poets were aristocrats, and their poetry often celebrated the aristocratic lifestyle and the noble ideal of *arete*. Another theme was romance and eroticism. Sappho, a female aristocrat who lived on the island of Lesbos, wrote tender love poems about her relationships with both men and women.

Drama as we know it was invented by the ancient Greeks. Plays were performed in conjunction with religious festivals dedicated to the god Dionysus. A maximum of three actors, always men, performed in each play, but because actors wore masks a single actor could play many parts. Greek plays also included a chorus that would sing and dance at various points during the play.

The four most famous Athenian playwrights whose works have survived were Aeschylus, Sophocles, Euripides, and Aristophanes. Aeschylus, Sophocles, and Euripides all wrote tragedies. Sophocles's so-called Theban plays featuring Oedipus and Antigone are among the most famous. Aristophanes's plays, by contrast, were comedies that used coarse humor, including vivid sexual references, to amuse their audiences. Aristophanes sometimes poked fun at important generals, politicians, and thinkers. Despite the mixed reactions that many plays received, there is no evidence that they were censored.

Before the Classical Period, Greek sculpture portrayed the human body in stiff and formal postures. Over time, the humanist impulse caused the Greeks to portray the human form in increasingly realistic terms, although an ideal physical type was preferred. The Classical ideal of beauty stressed the importance of youthfulness, a well-proportioned, athletic physique, and the absence of any obvious defects. Classical Greek sculpture, which was usually executed in bronze, wood, limestone, or marble (and occasionally ivory), reached its height with Phidias, the ingenious sculptor who created the large statues of Zeus and Athena that stood in Olympia and Athens.

Ancient Greek architecture was best showcased in the precise workmanship and timeless elegance of the numerous temples that stood in most *poleis*. Pericles's determination to rebuild the temples and the ceremonial gateway on the Acropolis in Athens was as much a political decision as it was religious: the grandeur of the Athenian Acropolis served notice to the other Greek *poleis* that Athens had no equal.

The ruins that stand on the Acropolis today lead many visitors to assume that the exterior of all ancient Greek buildings was exposed white stone. On the contrary, ancient Greek temples and statues were originally painted in bright, even garish, colors. It is amusing to consider what neoclassical buildings, like the U.S. Capitol, would look like if the model of Greek architecture had been followed more faithfully!

Figure 3.1 A Romantic depiction of what the Acropolis may have looked like in its glory days during the Age of Pericles. Leo von Klenze, *The Acropolis at Athens*, 1846.
Neue Pinakothek/Wikimedia Commons.

The Greeks were among the first to analyze history rationally and objectively. The "father of history" was Herodotus, a chronicler of the Persian Wars. Herodotus included the gods in his accounts, but he also paid tribute to the decisions of political and military leaders, and to the superiority of the *polis* over (alleged) Persian tyranny.

The Greek study of history reached a climax with Thucydides, an Athenian who both fought in and wrote about the Peloponnesian War. Thucydides excluded the gods from his analysis, and he utilized the dramatic events of the Peloponnesian War to illustrate the strengths and weaknesses in human nature. He also weighed his evidence carefully. Thucydides preferred firsthand accounts, but he rejected claims made by historical actors who were obviously self-interested, misguided, or deceitful.

One of the preconditions for Greek progress in science was their discovery of the usefulness of mathematics to process and understand numerical data. The philosopher and mystic Pythagoras, who lived during the sixth century BCE, was among the first to realize the potential of mathematics. Pythagoras also gave us the Pythagorean Theorem. Later Greek thinkers attempted to explain systematically various mathematical laws and principles, as well as to relate mathematics to logic, a rational method of establishing the truth or falsehood of a particular claim.

Despite Greek scientists' sophistication, their work did not lead to large-scale technological innovation. For the Greeks, science was connected first and foremost to philosophy, and thus to pure thought. They generally did not see science as a method for solving real-world problems. Nevertheless, Greek scientists' consistent rejection of the idea that natural events were caused by the gods was in itself a major advance.

One area in which Greek science did produce significant practical achievements was in medicine. The Greek philosopher Hippocrates founded a school of medicine that boldly asserted that illnesses were not caused by the gods, demons, or magical spells. Hippocrates believed instead that diseases have natural causes, and the purpose of medicine is to treat diseases through knowledge of the natural processes that produce illness and recuperation. Hippocrates required each of his students to take the Hippocratic Oath, swearing to uphold scientific principles, respect patients' privacy, and give all patients—regardless of income or social standing—the full benefit of their medical knowledge. Doctors today still take a version of the Hippocratic Oath.

> *In which of the arts and sciences did the Greeks register their greatest accomplishments?*

Daily Life in Ancient Athens

Most of the written records that have survived from ancient Greece are Athenian, so we know far more about life there than in any other *polis*.

Daily life was, first and foremost, structured around the household to which one belonged. Most Athenian families—and their servants and slaves—lived in simple but comfortable homes that were arranged around a central courtyard. Houses were seldom decorated on the outside, and there were no windows. The most important rooms were a dining room for men and a sitting room where women and girls could spin thread and weave cloth. All rooms in the house were sparsely furnished. A well for drawing water and a religious altar were often found in the courtyard, along with chickens and goats that supplied the family with eggs, milk, and (rarely) meat. The Greek diet was dominated by bread and vegetables. Wine was the main beverage.

Ancient Greek clothing normally consisted of a loose-fitting tunic that was covered, especially in winter, with a cloak. Women's tunics as a rule concealed more of the body and were more colorful than men's, and women often wore jewelry, perfume, and makeup. Men carefully arranged their hair and beards. Men who were engaged in athletic competition or physical labor would sometimes discard their clothes altogether.

Games, such as dice and board games, were very popular in ancient Greece, along with amusements such as singing, dancing, storytelling, and the playing of music. By far the most popular form of recreation, though, was athletics. Men and boys loved to compete in sports such as running, discus and javelin tossing, and various forms of mock combat, including wrestling and boxing.

Most Greek *poleis* included at least one *gymnasium* or a smaller *palaistra* where men and boys would meet to exercise, practice their athletic skills, and compete in various games (they might also engage in conversation or amuse themselves with cat and dog fights). All this physical activity necessitated frequent baths. The ancient Greeks prized cleanliness. Public baths were popular, because sanitation in private homes was extremely primitive.

Although heterosexual relationships were the norm in ancient Greece, homosexual attractions were not always stigmatized. Among aristocrats, in particular, a romantic liaison between a young man and an adolescent boy was considered healthy. The young man was expected to serve as a mentor to his teenage counterpart, and there was often a sexual component as well. This sort of relationship is called pederasty, and one of its early sponsors was Solon, a political reformer in Athens.

Slaves made up a significant proportion of the Greek population. Greeks rarely enslaved members of their own *polis*, but foreigners from other *poleis* and barbarians who did not speak Greek were considered suitable for enslavement. Many slaves were soldiers who had become prisoners of war, civilians captured during wartime, or unfortunate Greeks who had been abducted by pirates.

Despite the fact that slaves could be beaten and were often subjected to sexual abuse and exploitation, they were not completely at the mercy of free citizens. Slaves who worked in the fields often toiled alongside their masters.

Many urban slaves were craftsmen, government employees, or domestic servants. Slaves were often paid the same wages as free men and women. The law protected slaves to some degree. Masters were not permitted to kill slaves, and it was fairly common for slaves either to buy their freedom or to be released from bondage. Additionally, there was never any clear racial component to slavery in ancient Greece, so free citizens did not necessarily see slaves as biologically inferior. Nevertheless, the omnipresence of slavery in ancient Greece will always complicate the modern image of the Greeks as a people dedicated to freedom and humane values.

How were slaves treated in ancient Greece?

The Status of Women

In ancient Greece, as in most of the ancient world, women were not greatly respected. Women were seldom considered to be participants in Greek rationalism, because they were thought to be incapable of reason. They were seldom included in Greek humanism, because their dignity, independence, and fulfillment were not high priorities in ancient Greek society. Most Greek women led circumscribed lives, had few legal protections, and were permanently under the control of men. Greek mythology reinforced the idea that women were dangerous, inferior beings, as did Greek science, drama, and philosophy. To Aristotle, a woman was simply a "mutilated male."

Most women in ancient Greece married very young, usually as teenagers. They often married significantly older men, and they seldom had any choice in the matter. Throughout a woman's life, legal responsibility for her was exercised first by her father and then by her husband. She controlled no property, she could not vote or hold public office, and she was, especially if she was from the aristocracy, rarely permitted to leave the women's quarters in her home without a chaperone. In fact, women were not even publicly referred to by name. They were described as possessions of their fathers or husbands.

As in most ancient societies, fidelity was expected of wives but not of husbands. Married men often visited prostitutes, they had sex with female slaves, or they kept mistresses. Women, by contrast, were encouraged to be chaste. Three of the six female goddesses in the Greek pantheon were virgins. Moreover, the ancient Greeks invented the legend of the Amazons: a tribe of women who rejected femininity, engaged in warfare, and reproduced by having promiscuous sex with random men. Needless to say, the Amazons were not admired.

Although ancient Greeks clearly lived in a male-dominated society, women were never as invisible and inconsequential as many men would have liked. In Homer's epic poems, for instance, women played major roles, and their virtues were often praised. We should not forget that, although the Greeks and Trojans fought over pride, they also fought over Helen, whose lovely face had "launched a thousand ships." Many other ancient Greek poems and plays had important female characters who used their wits and their beauty to influence men. The implication is clear: behind the scenes, Greek women often exercised considerable power. Pericles's beloved mistress, Aspasia, is an excellent example. Although she was vilified for her "meddling," and although she was accused of being a prostitute and a brothel owner, her opinions were respected by Pericles himself and by leading thinkers like Socrates. It is also important to note that a small number of ancient Greek women were able to take on a public role by becoming priestesses, who were widely revered.

Another example of the surprisingly vigorous role that some Greek women played in their communities comes from Sparta. Sparta was organized as a military state. Boys were taken from their mothers at age seven and given military training. (Athenian boys, by contrast, were given a liberal arts education stressing reading, writing, arithmetic, and music.) A Spartan man's term of military service did not end until he reached the age of 60. Because Spartan men spent so much time preparing for or at war, Spartan women had to be independent and resourceful enough to administer the homes and estates of their husbands. Some could read and write. Additionally, physical exercise—which was such an important part of the military training of men and boys—was also thought to be appropriate for Spartan women. Thus, Spartan women were famous throughout Greece for their physical and psychological toughness. They were also considered uncommonly beautiful.

We may never know how much the average wife and mother in ancient Greece led her life according to society's restrictive ideals, but it seems unlikely that she was totally marginalized. Poor women, for instance, did not have the luxury of remaining in the home, because their labor would have been needed to make ends meet. Women in wealthy families, moreover, would have had considerable power to direct the servants and slaves of the household, and to make purchases of food, furniture, clothing, and luxury goods. Thus, the ideal of a wife and mother who was largely invisible to men may have been impossible to achieve.

What is certain, however, is that the ancient Greeks never seriously contemplated granting women equal status and the same opportunities as men. It seldom occurred to the Greeks that their ideals of freedom, active citizenship, rational discourse, and the full cultivation of human potential were at odds with their scornful and patronizing attitudes toward women.

In what ways did Greek society treat women differently from men?

Ancient Greek Philosophy

Philosophy—literally, the love of wisdom—is the study and pursuit of truth. It involves questions about the origins, nature, and purpose of human life.

It should not surprise us that philosophy began in ancient Greece, since it revolves around the themes of rationalism and humanism, discussed above.

The very first philosophers concentrated their attention on the cosmos, and their activity was closely related to the rise of Greek science. Among the most important of the early Greek philosophers was Democritus, who theorized that the universe was made up of tiny, invisible particles called *atomoi*.

During the fifth century BCE, "the Golden Age of Classical Greece," a school of philosophers called the Sophists became influential. The Sophists concentrated their philosophical inquiries on practical problems of ethics, politics, religion, and social organization. They denied that any ethical principle could be absolute, since laws, moral codes, and even religion were human inventions. The skepticism of the Sophists was condemned by many Greeks. After all, if the laws of the *polis* were not backed by the authority of the gods, by traditional morality, or by absolute truth, then why should anyone bother to obey them?

One of the most celebrated of Greek philosophers was Socrates, who was often falsely accused of being a Sophist. Unlike the Sophists, however, Socrates believed in absolute truth. Socrates's method of seeking that truth was to question fellow Athenians who had strong convictions that they believed were rooted in reason. Socrates would use rational arguments to expose the weaknesses and inconsistencies in their views. His pointed questions, which lay at the heart of the Socratic method that is still popular today, were supposed to illuminate the path to wisdom. More often, though, they simply confused and humiliated his opponents.

In 399 BCE, in the wake of Athens' crushing defeat in the Peloponnesian War, Socrates was charged with corrupting the youth of Athens and undermining faith in the gods. At his trial, Socrates refused to apologize for his philosophizing. He claimed that he would never abandon the search for truth and goodness. He was therefore sentenced to death. His calm acceptance of his fate made him a hero to many Athenians.

Socrates's most devoted student was Plato. Like Socrates, Plato believed that reason, rather than tradition, was the most useful tool in the search for truth and virtue. Unlike Socrates, however, Plato did not merely expose the irrationality of others. He laid out clear, consistent answers to complex philosophical problems.

Plato believed that the knowledge that human beings regularly gain through their senses is imperfect. Perfect knowledge, on the other hand, consists of Ideas or Forms. For example, a man could never draw a perfect circle or a perfect square, but he can imagine what such a figure would look like. Thus, Plato asserted that ultimate reality exists in the realm of the mind rather than in matter. This concept, and other elements of Platonic thought, would later exercise a critical influence on early Christian theology.

Plato, like his mentor Socrates, believed that democracy is a deeply flawed form of government. It empowers the ignorant masses, claimed Plato, and it frequently leads to disorder and injustice.

Instead of democracy, Plato favored a form of aristocracy. Plato claimed that the ideal state is one that promotes reason and virtue, and who better to uphold reason and virtue than philosophers? Plato, therefore, in about 380 BCE, proposed in his masterwork, *The Republic*, that philosophers ought to have control over the government. He suggested that those who demonstrated exceptional gifts for rational discourse should become philosophers and, therefore, political leaders. Those who demonstrated exceptional courage should become soldiers. Everyone else should become a worker.

It is important to note that much of Socrates's and Plato's philosophizing took place during and after the Peloponnesian War, when many Greeks had lost faith in the *polis*, and when political confusion and violence were widespread. Many Greeks were therefore sympathetic to new philosophies, but also defensive when these philosophies challenged traditional beliefs. Socrates and Plato were brave to pursue their philosophical ideals when the risks were so great.

Plato's most famous student was Aristotle. Besides tutoring Alexander the Great, Aristotle wrote thoughtful essays on an amazing array of topics, including art and literature, ethics and society, physics and astronomy, and politics and rhetoric. He has been immensely influential throughout the last 2,400 years of Western Civilization, but never more so than during the medieval period, between 500 CE and 1500 CE.

Aristotle was, above all, a believer in reason and in evidence. Unlike Plato, who believed that abstract Forms or Ideas guided human reason, Aristotle believed that people needed to pay attention to the evidence provided by their sensory experiences. Thus, whenever Aristotle considered a complex problem, he sought to amass as much data as possible. He then tried to detect patterns in the data that could be rationally analyzed and described as universal laws. Aristotle's method of reasoning may sound familiar. It is closely related to the scientific method that has become one of the hallmarks of Western thought.

Aristotle analyzed Greek politics in this same objective spirit. Based on evidence he gathered related to the political systems in 158 Greek *poleis*, Aristotle advanced two seemingly sensible conclusions. First, he proposed that a *polis* with a moderate constitution that blended elements of various political philosophies was more likely to prosper and experience political stability than a *polis* that favored political extremes. Second, Aristotle concluded that a large middle class was a vital ingredient to good government. By contrast, a *polis* dominated by the arrogance of the wealthy, or by the envy of the poor, was likely to be overwhelmed by selfish passions.

Who were the most important ancient Greek philosophers?

The Hellenistic World

The Hellenistic Age, lasting from 323 BCE until the Roman conquest of the eastern Mediterranean region circa 31 BCE, may not have been as original and creative as the preceding Classical Period, but it was still crucially important to the long-term trajectory of Western Civilization. In the wake of Alexander the Great's conquests, Greek culture flourished and spread under the monarchies that ruled Greece as well as much of the Middle East.

Many Greeks and Middle Easterners lived in miserable poverty, but there were sizable upper and middle classes, concentrated in cities. High demand for luxury goods helped drive trade. The exports of the Hellenistic kingdoms reached as far as Spain in the west, India in the east, Russia in the north, and sub-Saharan Africa in the south. The construction of new cities, ports, and roads further expanded economic activity.

One of the main characteristics of the Hellenistic Age was cultural diffusion. The entire eastern Mediterranean region was at least superficially Hellenized. A version of the ancient Greek language, called *Koine*, became the common language. At the same time, elements of Egyptian, Mesopotamian, Persian, and Hebrew culture were introduced into Greece. Under Eastern influence, the traditionally conservative Greek attitude toward women became somewhat more flexible, and small numbers of women received a formal education. In addition, Middle Eastern religious cults and belief systems, including Judaism, became known to the Greeks. As a result, the Greeks became increasingly interested in the idea of an afterlife.

Hellenistic kings, like many rulers throughout history, used art and architecture to advertise their power. They hired skilled Greek artists, architects, and craftsmen for the purpose of giving an impressive Greek cultural veneer to their largely Eastern realms. The single most famous Hellenistic architectural achievement was the 384-foot tall Lighthouse of Alexandria, in Egypt, that stood for over a thousand years.

Although many Hellenistic artists and architects consciously copied Classical models, two innovations are noteworthy. First, much Hellenistic art and architecture represented a synthesis of Classical Greek and Middle Eastern influences. Second, Hellenistic art portrayed human figures in increasingly realistic and sentimentalized poses. More broadly, Greek culture now tended to focus on the individual and on his or her emotional needs.

Relatedly, Hellenistic philosophy diverged from Classical philosophy in several important respects. The Classical philosophy of Socrates, Plato, and Aristotle had assumed that rational individuals engaging in contemplation and discussion could find the truth, but Hellenistic kings did not wish their decisions to be rationally debated by the public. Therefore, Hellenistic philosophy turned away from politics and rational discourse. It emphasized instead the individual and the satisfaction of his or her craving for identity and fulfillment.

Some Hellenistic philosophers rejected the possibility that human beings could ever find the truth. The Skeptics advocated blind acceptance of conventional beliefs and values, whereas the Cynics endorsed the complete rejection of society's laws, norms, and values. The most famous Cynic, Diogenes, lived as a beggar. Neither Skepticism nor Cynicism was popular with ordinary Greeks.

Epicurus of Athens taught that fear of the gods and of death was irrational. Epicureanism instead suggested that the highest goal to which any person could aspire was serenity—a peace of mind that could only be achieved by rejecting the passions and living as independently as possible.

Stoicism was the most successful Hellenistic school of philosophy. The Stoics taught that the universe was governed by *logos*, a divine form of order and rationality. A spark of this universal order exists in every human being, and thus every person is equal. Virtue consists in accepting and understanding *logos*, fulfilling one's civic responsibilities, moderating one's passions, and living one's life honorably, justly, and bravely. The beliefs of the Stoics strongly influenced Roman philosophy, and elements of Stoicism were eventually incorporated into Christianity and into the modern idea of universal human rights.

Some of the greatest accomplishments of the Hellenistic Age were in the fields of science, mathematics, and medicine. Hellenistic science generally stressed pure theory, but some technological breakthroughs occurred, including the construction of steam engines and machines with gears. Science had its headquarters at the Library of Alexandria, generously supported by Egypt's Ptolemaic kings. The Library held the accumulated wisdom of the Greeks and other cultures, as well as a botanical garden, an observatory, and a staff of researchers.

Hellenistic astronomers debated whether the earth or the sun lay at the center of the universe. Aristarchus proposed a heliocentric, or sun-centered, model of the solar system, while the geocentric, or earth-centered, model became associated with Ptolemy (no relation to Egypt's dynasty of kings). The Ptolemaic theory was more popular, and it remained dominant until the work of Nicolaus Copernicus in the sixteenth century CE.

The most famous Hellenistic mathematician was Euclid, who wrote a textbook on geometry that is still read 2,300 years later. Eratosthenes used Hellenistic geometry to calculate the circumference of the earth, which he estimated at 24,675 miles. He was off by less than one percent. Archimedes, meanwhile, invented useful devices such as pulleys, levers, catapults, and the famous Archimedean Screw, used in irrigation. He also made major advances in physics. Modern physics students still repeat some of his basic experiments.

Hellenistic scientists and doctors performed dissections that greatly enhanced their knowledge of the human body. As a result, surgical techniques and drug treatments improved, although ordinary people continued to seek magical and religious cures for many illnesses.

What were the chief accomplishments of the Hellenistic Age?

Conclusions

Despite all of the independent achievements of the Hellenistic Age, its single greatest accomplishment was its success in spreading, popularizing, and recording for posterity the accumulated wisdom of the Classical Greeks.

The Greeks of the Classical Period contributed much to modern Western Civilization, including ideas about beauty, truth, and human dignity; methods of reasoning and of obtaining objective knowledge; ideals of freedom, civic engagement, ethical moderation, personal responsibility, and popular government; and, perhaps most importantly, an endless hunger for wisdom that did not recognize any artificial constraints or barriers.

The Greeks were bold adventurers in every sense of those words. They traveled widely, they fought bravely, and they conquered the mighty Persian Empire. Most of all, though, they *thought* about every conceivable problem and issue, and they were not afraid of where their thinking might take them. "We must follow wherever the argument will lead," said Socrates, and, given his fate, no one can question that he practiced what he preached.

From Archaic to Classical Greece, from the Hellenistic Age to the days of the Roman Empire, from the Middle Ages to the Renaissance, and finally on to modern Western Civilization, the transmission of ancient Greek ideas and ideals has continued to exercise a positive influence on humankind.

Key Terms for Chapter 3

Symposium—a drinking party for men in ancient Greece, usually featuring conversation and entertainment.

Oracles—religious sites at which ancient Greeks received advice and predictions about future events.

Rationalism—the idea that knowledge comes from pure thought, without recourse to emotion or prejudice.

Humanism—the idea that human beings, and the fulfillment of their potential, are what is important in life. Humanism led many Greeks to pursue achievements in the arts and sciences, or in practical domains such as athletics, politics, and warfare, rather than focusing on religion.

Greek drama—the Greeks largely invented plays, which for them involved a chorus and a maximum of three masked actors.

Science—the effort to understand nature through observation and reasoning.

Hippocrates—an ancient Greek doctor who attempted to ground medicine in scientific thinking and professional ethics.

Socrates—a famous ancient Greek philosopher who bravely questioned conventional wisdom and was executed for doing so.

Plato—Socrates's student, and a brilliant philosopher who suggested that ideas are more real than sensory perceptions and that philosophers should be given political power.

Aristotle—Plato's student, and one of the most influential philosophers in history. Aristotle, unlike Plato, believed that knowledge gained through the senses is valuable, and he asserted that moderation is crucial to political stability.

Koine—a version of ancient Greek that became the common language in the Hellenistic World.

Stoicism—a philosophy popular in ancient Greece and Rome. Stoics taught that the universe was governed by *logos*, a divine form of order and rationality that is accessible to all. *Logos* should be accepted calmly and dutifully.

Review Questions for Chapter 3

1. The religious context in which the ancient Greeks lived was very different from the religious context in which most people in the Western world live today. Explain at least three of the ways in which this is so.
2. The ancient Greeks are famous for their accomplishments in the arts and sciences. Describe at least three major Greek achievements in this realm, and indicate how each achievement has exercised an influence on modern Western Civilization.
3. Which one of the features of daily life in ancient Athens would you have found most agreeable? Which feature would you have found most disagreeable? By and large, would you prefer to live in ancient Athens or today?
4. From a modern perspective, it seems incongruous that the ancient Greeks were so enlightened in their thinking and yet they accorded women so little respect. First, list several of the ways in which women were marginalized in ancient Greece. Next, describe another society in the history of Western Civilization that simultaneously sought to maximize freedom for some, while ignoring the liberties and dignity of others. Finally, explain why, in your opinion, it is seemingly so easy for human beings to be selective in their thinking when it comes to issues of human rights.
5. Imagine that every trace of ancient Greek philosophy was lost during the Dark Ages, but that you, a famous archaeologist, recently unearthed evidence of the views of the philosophers and the schools of philosophy listed in this chapter. Write a brief argumentative essay in which you choose one philosopher or philosophical school to describe and to praise as particularly insightful. Then, conclude with a description and a critique of the philosopher or philosophical school that strikes you as the least sensible.

Further Reading

Brulé, Pierre. *Women of Ancient Greece*. Edinburgh: Edinburgh University Press. 2008.
Burkert, Walter and John Raffan. *Greek Religion: Archaic and Classical*. New York: John Wiley and Sons. 2013.
Chamoux, François. *Hellenistic Civilization*. New York: John Wiley and Sons. 2008.
DuBois, Page. *Slaves and Other Objects*. Chicago: University of Chicago Press. 2008.
Garland, Robert. *Ancient Greece: Everyday Life in the Birthplace of Western Civilization*. New York: Sterling. 2013.
Goodman, Martin, ed. *Jews in a Graeco-Roman World*. Oxford: Oxford University Press. 2006.

Herman, Gabriel. *Morality and Behaviour in Democratic Athens*. Cambridge: Cambridge University Press. 2010.

Patterson, Cynthia B. *The Family in Greek History*. Cambridge, MA: Harvard University Press. 2001.

Pomeroy, Sarah B. *Spartan Women*. New York: Oxford University Press. 2002.

Pomeroy, Sarah B., et al. *Ancient Greece: A Political, Social, and Cultural History*. Fourth Edition. New York: Oxford University Press. 2017.

Shipley, Graham. *The Greek World After Alexander, 323–30 B.C.* Hoboken, NJ: Taylor and Francis. 2014.

Spivey, Nigel. *The Ancient Olympics*. Oxford: Oxford University Press. 2012.

Zelnick-Abramovitz, Rachel. *Not Wholly Free: The Concept of Manumission and the Status of Manumitted Slaves in the Ancient Greek World*. Leiden, The Netherlands: Brill. 2005.

4 Ancient Rome

Politics and War

Introduction

Arguably the greatest empire in the history of Western Civilization (the British would almost certainly debate the point) was based in the ancient city of Rome. Rome progressed from being a sleepy peasant village, to a modest trading center, to a city-state, to the capital of an Italian confederation. It finally emerged as the glittering metropolis presiding over a vast Mediterranean empire. In the process, Rome extended its control over a wide array of lands and peoples, thus spreading Roman culture and institutions. At first, from 509 BCE to 27 BCE, Rome was a republic, governed by elected leaders, but, from 27 BCE until the Fall of Rome, circa 476 CE, Rome was governed instead by emperors.

When Roman power finally receded, the world had been remade in the image of Roman civilization. It was, in fact, only after the *Pax Romana* (the Roman peace) had broken down that Europeans were able to appreciate fully just what an accomplishment it had been—and how much their own societies continued to rely on the example set by Rome.

Humble Origins, and the Birth of the Roman Republic

According to Roman legend, the city was founded in 753 BCE by two abandoned boys, Romulus and Remus, who were nursed by a wolf and raised by a shepherd. Romulus eventually killed Remus and emerged as Rome's first king.

The truth is somewhat less dramatic. Migrating bands of shepherds and farmers, speaking Italic languages from the same Indo-European language group that included ancient Greek, were the first settlers in Rome. They chose the location due to its geographical advantages. Located in central Italy, Rome straddles the main north-south line of communications and trade in the Italian Peninsula. The city is located on seven hills, so it was easily defensible. Lastly, the River Tiber runs through Rome and was valuable both as a source of water and as a means of transport.

From Rome's foundation in the eighth century BCE until roughly 509 BCE, the city and the surrounding region, called Latium, were dominated by a group of foreigners known as Etruscans. Thanks to their military prowess, the Etruscans overawed the Romans and installed a succession of Etruscan kings to rule the city.

Under heavy Etruscan influence, Roman art, architecture, engineering, and religion blossomed. Rome progressed from being a simple peasant village to a significant trading and cultural center. Nevertheless, there were downsides to Etruscan rule. Romans later portrayed some of the city's Etruscan kings as oppressors, and they viewed Etruscan women as promiscuous and immodest.

Partly because the Etruscans were only loosely organized politically, Rome was able to chase away its last Etruscan king in 509 BCE. By the middle of the third century BCE, the Etruscans themselves were brought under Roman control.

Even after Rome was freed from Etruscan rule, only a small minority of Romans enjoyed real political influence. Roman society was divided into two basic classes: patricians and plebeians. The patricians were nobles from old and respected families. They wore gold rings and tunics adorned with a purple stripe to signify their status. Most patricians owned large amounts of land, and they dominated the economy, the government, the courts, and the official religion. Plebeians were commoners. While some were rich entrepreneurs or professionals, most were poor farmers, craftsmen, or unskilled urban workers. For a long time the plebeians, even though they represented the vast majority of Rome's population, had very little say in how their city was run.

The patricians chose to turn Rome into a republic—that is, a country without a king, over which the people rule. The government of the Roman Republic was led by two elected consuls who shared executive authority, or what the Romans called *imperium*—the power to command others and to punish disobedience. To prevent any consul from transforming himself into a king, however, not only were there two consuls, who could veto one another's actions, but consuls also served a term of only one year.

The two consuls shared governmental power with the Senate, which was an assembly of about 300 elder statesmen chosen by officials called censors. The Senate advised the consuls and directly administered Rome's public finances, its provinces, and its foreign policy. Senators, who generally served for life terms, tended to be from patrician families.

The last major pillar of the Republic was the Assembly: a legislature and court that represented all Roman male citizens, including both patricians and plebeians. It elected Rome's two consuls, it voted on most laws, it could declare war on Rome's enemies, and it served as the ultimate court of appeal in capital cases. In reality, though, the Senate used its superior status, as well as a great deal of manipulation and bribery, to prevail over the Assembly and, much of the time, to dominate the government. The notion that the Roman Republic was a democracy is therefore demonstrably false.

One reason for the Republic being ruled primarily by the patrician elite was that Roman elections were usually slanted in favor of the rich. The wealthy and highborn voted first, and their votes were weighted more heavily. Another reason was a Roman tradition known as clientage. A plebeian, if he needed a job, money, land, or legal advice, might turn to a wealthy patrician for help. The two might then enter into a formal relationship in which the patron would extend that help in return for loyalty and obedience. Finally, patricians dominated Rome partly because of their superior oratorical skills and because they could deliver games, feasts, and other seductive spectacles that the electorate craved.

Eventually, though, the plebeians did challenge the mastery of the patricians in the Struggle of the Orders that lasted from 494 BCE to 287 BCE. In the end, although patricians kept most of their privileges, plebeians won the right to marry patricians, to serve in high elective offices, including the consulship, to receive fair treatment in Roman courts, and to make laws in the Assembly that were binding on all Romans. They also insisted on the creation of a special form of public official: the tribune, whose job was to look out for plebeian interests.

As a result of the Struggle of the Orders, Roman law, which had previously been an oral tradition controlled by patricians, was published, circa 450 BCE, in a law code called the Twelve Tables. From this point on, Roman law became increasingly sophisticated, as judges, lawyers, and legal scholars analyzed and organized it. Roman law began with the *jus civile*, or the law for Roman citizens, but it eventually included the *jus gentium*, or the law of nations, which attempted to create a system of justice, based on fairness and the public good, that could be applied throughout Rome and its empire.

How did the government of the Roman Republic work?

The Roman Army and the Conquest of Italy, Carthage, and the Hellenistic Kingdoms

The early Roman Republic fought frequent skirmishes with its neighbors. Consequently, a tradition of bravery, tactical skill, and tenacity developed among Roman warriors. Importantly, Rome's government also provided reasonably effective commanders for the Roman army. Many leading Roman politicians actively sought military commands, since battlefield victories were the surest route to fame, fortune, and personal honor.

The Roman army was organized into large formations, each composed of about 5,000 men, called legions. There were also smaller units, of 100 men each, called centuries, led by a *centurion*. At first, the Romans believed that only citizens with a stake in the survival of the Republic should fight to preserve and expand it. Thus, only landowning citizens served in the army. Nevertheless, soldiers were paid while under arms, and they often received a share of the plunder from successful campaigns. As a result, Rome's army was well motivated.

In the Late Republic and in the days of the Roman Empire, recruitment policies would become much more flexible, and slaves, the urban and rural poor, provincials without citizenship, and even barbarians would be asked to fight for Rome. Their performance was inconsistent, at best. These problems had not yet appeared, though, when Rome was first beginning its program of territorial expansion.

Most Roman soldiers joined the light and heavy infantry, while a small number, usually recruited from rich families, served in the cavalry. The Roman army's principal weapons were similar to those employed by the ancient Greeks: swords, spears, and bows and arrows, along with some primitive forms of artillery, especially the catapult. Roman soldiers were well protected by helmets, wooden shields, and elaborate forms of armor. Most of all, Roman warriors were famous for their superb training and discipline. Rather than fight as heroic individuals, they fought as a coordinated team. Harsh punishments were inflicted on any soldier who did not properly execute his *sacramentum*, or military oath. He might be stoned to death, or, if his entire unit showed cowardice, it might be decimated. Decimation involved lining up a group of soldiers and killing every tenth man, to set an example to the others.

The first stage in Rome's rise to imperial greatness was the conquest of Italy. By 265 BCE, despite strong resistance from Gauls, Latins, Samnites, Etruscans, and Greeks, all of Italy south of the Po River was in Roman hands.

The Romans, though, did not conquer Italy by force of arms alone. Most of the time the Romans also used compromise and conciliation to achieve their ends. The Romans often signed treaties that gave defeated Italian cities special privileges and internal self-government in return for supplying recruits for the Roman army. Residents of some parts of Italy were granted Roman citizenship or the prospect of earning citizenship in the future. This proved to be an ingenious strategy for winning over the Italians and sharing the benefits of Roman expansion with the very people Rome was conquering. By contrast, it had never occurred to the Greeks to share citizenship with vanquished peoples.

It is also important to point out that the Roman army itself was much more than just a fighting force. Its engineers built Rome's outstanding network of roads, which boosted trade and created a broad network of Roman influence, while colonies of retired veterans spread Roman culture far and wide. Thus, for much of Rome's history, it was hard to portray the Roman army as a menacing or oppressive force.

While Rome was consolidating its hold on the Italian Peninsula, the Hellenistic kingdoms were jockeying for position in the eastern Mediterranean. The western Mediterranean, meanwhile, was dominated by a rich maritime empire based in the large North African port city of Carthage. Phoenicians had founded Carthage in the ninth century BCE. By the middle of the third century BCE, Carthage controlled an empire that included most of North Africa (except for Egypt), parts of Spain, the major Mediterranean islands of Corsica and Sardinia, and the western half of Sicily.

The Carthaginian government was based on a mixture of aristocracy and democracy, like the government of Rome. Carthage's polytheistic religion, however, involved child sacrifice, at least according to the scandalized Romans.

By 265 BCE, Rome had conquered all of southern Italy, and it began to see the Carthaginians in Sicily as a threat. This led to what the Romans called the First Punic War (the Romans referred to the Carthaginians as *Punici*, or Phoenicians), lasting from 264 BCE to 241 BCE. The war forced the Romans, who previously had relied on their outstanding army, to develop a sizable navy. They were astoundingly successful, winning control not only over Sicily but Corsica and Sardinia too. For the first time, Rome claimed an overseas empire.

The Carthaginian governor of Spain, Hamilcar Barca, decided that the best way to rebuild Carthaginian strength and prestige was to consolidate and enrich Carthage's Spanish domain. To undermine Hamilcar's success, Rome encouraged a rebellion in the Spanish city of Saguntum. Hamilcar's son, Hannibal, a brilliant military commander, put down the insurrection, which led the Romans to declare war. Thus began the Second Punic War, lasting from 218 BCE to 201 BCE.

The Romans were outfoxed by Hannibal, at least at first. They expected to go on the offensive and attack Carthage itself. Instead, Hannibal, who was based in Spain, marched his army, which included war elephants, through southern France, over the Alps, and into Italy. He won a number of crushing victories over the Roman legions, including one in 216 BCE at the Battle of Cannae, where as many as 70,000 Roman soldiers died along with scores of Roman senators and military commanders. The Carthaginians also systematically destroyed many Italian farms. A stalemate eventually developed in Italy. Critically, though, most of Rome's Italian allies refused to join forces with Hannibal. Rome's generous policies in Italy had forged a bond of loyalty and friendship between the Romans and their Italian neighbors.

It was a chivalrous young Roman commander known as Scipio Africanus who found a way to defeat Carthage. Leaving Hannibal to his own devices in Italy, Scipio launched attacks in Spain and North Africa. Worried, the Carthaginians considered suing for peace, but instead they recalled Hannibal to defend Carthage itself. The result was an epic clash at the Battle of Zama. Rome triumphed, and as a result Carthage was stripped of its navy and its empire. This was a stunning and decisive conclusion to the Second Punic War.

Roman mistrust of Carthage ran so deep, however, that in 149 BCE–146 BCE Rome fought the Third Punic War. This war ended with the complete obliteration of Carthage. Scipio Africanus's grandson, Scipio Aemilianus, gave the order to destroy the city and enslave all of the survivors. As it turned out, though, Rome's rise to power was only beginning.

With the destruction and absorption of the Carthaginian Empire, Rome found itself the unquestioned ruler of the western Mediterranean, but the

Romans proved surprisingly reluctant to undertake wars of expansion in the East. Many strong kingdoms, rich cities, and civilized peoples lived in the East, and the Romans knew that conquering these areas would be difficult. Nevertheless, slowly but surely, the Romans assumed control over the Hellenistic world.

The Roman conquest of the eastern Mediterranean began in the second century BCE, during the Punic Wars, with an invasion of Macedonia. The Romans at first claimed to be acting to secure Greek liberty from Macedonian tyranny. By 148 BCE, though, Macedonia had been declared a Roman province, and by 133 BCE all of Greece and western Turkey was in Roman hands.

Rome's triumph in the East was only partial, though. Egypt, under the Ptolemaic dynasty, remained independent for another century. Moreover, the Romans also failed, despite many attempts, to conquer the Parthians, who ruled much of the territory once held by ancient Persia. It is a myth, therefore, that the Roman legions were unstoppable.

Several troubling trends emerged as the Republic expanded its overseas possessions. First, the Romans took many military and civilian prisoners, millions of whom were sent to Italy to work as slaves. (Roman slavery is discussed in more detail in Chapter 5.) Few Romans were concerned about the moral implications of slavery, but the practical impact of this mass enslavement was largely negative. By the end of the Roman Republic, slaves made up perhaps a third of Italy's population, and slave revolts now represented a considerable threat to Rome's security. An enslaved gladiator named Spartacus launched a particularly large slave revolt in 73 BCE. His forces defeated several Roman armies. Only with great difficulty was the Spartacist revolt finally crushed. Several thousand of Spartacus's soldiers were then crucified on the road leading from southern Italy toward Rome so as to intimidate any slaves contemplating further resistance.

Increasingly, small farmers, who possessed few, if any, slaves, could not compete economically with the wealthy Romans whose *latifundia* (large estates) were worked by slave labor. Many ordinary Roman farmers, who had once formed the backbone of the Roman army, were pushed into poverty. Some became tenant farmers, but many ended up as part of the unemployed and sometimes violent rabble that milled about in the streets of Rome. These poor urban dwellers became a source of instability in Roman politics.

Another troubling development to emerge from the imperial expansion of the Roman Republic was misrule in the provinces. Generally speaking, ex-consuls and other experienced Roman politicians were designated to serve as governors in Rome's provinces. Because Rome's empire was acquired without any careful planning, though, few mechanisms existed to prevent these governors from using violence and trickery to milk their provinces for as much profit as possible. The Senate, which oversaw Roman provincial administration, generally preferred to let aristocratic governors do as they pleased. Many Romans therefore sadly concluded that the traditional

Roman virtues—simplicity, frugality, and dedication to the public good—were slipping away.

Luckily, as we have seen, there were also some positive aspects to Roman rule. Roman authorities often allowed their provincial subjects a certain measure of local autonomy, and they incorporated local elites in their system of rule. In addition, the enforcement of Roman order in the provinces brought an end, in most cases, to warfare. This created a secure environment that was favorable to economic progress and cultural exchange. Later, moreover, under Rome's first emperor, Augustus, the quality of Roman provincial administration would be dramatically improved.

Why was the Roman army so successful?

The Republic Unravels, 133 BCE–27 BCE

The growth in social inequality in the Late Republic, and the spread of corruption in the provinces, undercut the legitimacy of the Roman government. Increasingly, Roman patriotism ebbed, and selfishness, greed, ambition, and arrogance took over. Even as the Republic won amazing victories overseas, its internal stability and unity was disintegrating.

Two Roman brothers, both of whom served as tribunes, Tiberius Gracchus and Gaius Gracchus, realized that many of Rome's problems were caused by the impoverishment of small farmers who traditionally were the backbone of the Roman army and state. Many of these farmers had been forced to sell their land and now were destitute. To solve this problem, the two Gracchi proposed an ambitious program of land reform. State-owned land, much of which was then in use by wealthy owners of *latifundia*, would be redistributed to the poor. Predictably, rich landowners were outraged. When the Gracchi also began to suggest radical changes in the Roman constitution, the elite took action. Tiberius Gracchus was viciously murdered in 133 BCE, along with hundreds of his supporters, and a similar fate befell Gaius in 121 BCE. To the Roman elite, the Gracchi were dangerous demagogues who were stirring up trouble among the unruly masses. To the poor people of Rome, however, they were heroes and patriots whose deaths proved the ruthlessness of the patricians. Increasingly, class conflict was becoming a central theme in Republican politics.

The violence and acrimony between conservative and populist politicians might have been contained, and the Roman Republic might have endured, if the Roman army had preserved its professionalism and its neutrality in Roman elections. This, however, was not to be.

As the ranks of the small farmers were thinned by the rise of the *latifundia*, the old rule that only landowning citizens could serve in the army had to be relaxed. In 107 BCE, a Roman consul named Marius changed the recruitment policy. Marius managed to build a large and powerful army, filled mostly with poor, landless recruits, but it was a force that was loyal to Marius, not to Rome.

Eventually, Marius, the populist, came into conflict with Sulla, a patrician. For centuries, the city of Rome had been considered sacred ground, and soldiers had been required to keep their distance from it. Now, though, Rome found itself caught between Marius's and Sulla's opposing armies. After Marius's death, Sulla marched on Rome in 83 BCE and unleashed an extraordinary wave of bloodletting that targeted Marius's supporters. The murder of populist politicians was not only permitted—it was encouraged and richly rewarded. Sulla briefly ruled as a dictator, but he stepped down after reaffirming the powers of the aristocratic Senate. Sulla hoped that this would restore the traditional balance in the Republican constitution. Instead, by marching on Rome, Sulla had proven that the Republic was now at the mercy of its own armies.

In an attempt to bring order to the chaotic politics of the Late Republic, in 60 BCE three powerful men formed a Triumvirate (a three-man council) that would rule Rome while maintaining the illusion that the consuls, the Senate, and the Assembly were still in charge. Those three men were Pompey the Great, a successful general; Crassus, a military commander and a rich banker and businessman; and Julius Caesar, a patrician politician but also a populist who had almost been killed in Sulla's purges.

Of the three triumvirs, it is of course Julius Caesar who is the most memorable. In his early years, he was widely regarded as nothing more than an ambitious, vain, and clever young man with a knack for seducing other men's wives. As it turned out, though, Caesar outclassed both Pompey and Crassus in political savvy. It was not, however, until he demonstrated his genius as a military commander by conquering Gaul (modern France) in 58 BCE–51 BCE that the Romans fully appreciated his many gifts. His hard-won victories in Gaul were due mainly to his talents as a military strategist, but were also based on the exceptional maneuverability of his troops, his excellent military engineers, his fine handling of intelligence, and his decision to promote men based on skill and courage rather than parentage. Caesar also shared the adversities faced by his men, and he rewarded them generously with plunder. As a result of his campaign in Gaul, huge numbers of tribesmen were enslaved, and 1.2 million were killed, according to Caesar's own brilliant but propagandistic book, *The Gallic War*. More importantly, Gaul was conquered, and Caesar won fame, glory, and vast riches for himself.

Caesar's triumph in Gaul led some Romans to fear, justifiably, that he might use his growing popularity in Rome, and his loyal legions, to assume dictatorial power. Crassus, meanwhile, had died while leading an unsuccessful attack on the Parthians in the East. This left only Pompey and the Senate standing in Caesar's way.

In 49 BCE, Caesar defied the Senate and Roman tradition by marching his troops across the Rubicon River and into central Italy. A civil war then developed between Caesar and Pompey's armies. In 48 BCE, Pompey, after a terrible defeat at the Battle of Pharsalus, was treacherously murdered. Then, in 45 BCE, Caesar finally defeated the last of his opponents in the civil war.

Figure 4.1 Vercingetorix, a Gaulish king, attempted to unite the Gauls in a revolt against the Romans. He failed, becoming a prisoner of Julius Caesar. Caesar eventually had Vercingetorix strangled to death.

Lionel Royer, *Vercingetorix jette ses armes aux pieds de Jules César*, 1899. Musée CROZATIER du Puy-en-Velay/Wikimedia Commons.

In that year, the Senate, cowed into submission, named Julius Caesar dictator for life. Caesar began to wear a purple toga (purple was the color of royalty) and to sit on a golden throne. Also unprecedented was the fact that his face appeared on Roman coins. The Senate may even have authorized the worship of Caesar as a god. The Republic endured in name only.

Caesar's policies as dictator were bold and arguably farsighted. He pardoned many of his former enemies. He worked to improve the efficiency and integrity of Rome's administration of the provinces. He settled thousands of poor Romans in colonies throughout the Mediterranean world. He extended Roman citizenship to some provincials. He began the construction of beautiful new public buildings in Rome. Caesar also expanded the Senate, adding senators from Italy and Gaul. Whether these policies might have breathed new life into Rome, by reconciling the provinces to Roman rule and reducing class conflict, or whether they were only meant to create a monarchy with Caesar as Rome's first emperor, we will never know, because Julius Caesar was assassinated on March 15, 44 BCE, by a group of patrician senators who resented his arrogance and ambition. They stabbed him more than 20 times. Civil war now returned. This time, the Roman Republic would not survive the carnage.

Caesar had designated his adopted son Octavian as his heir. Octavian was only 18 years old upon Caesar's death, so initially he was forced to share power in a Second Triumvirate with two of Caesar's favorite generals: Mark Antony and Lepidus. The first task of the Triumvirate, besides deifying Caesar and naming the month of July in his honor, was to track down and kill Caesar's assassins as well as the political enemies of the triumvirs themselves. Once this had been accomplished, the triumvirs predictably turned on each other. Lepidus was sidelined, and a civil war between the forces of Octavian and Mark Antony ensued, unleashing yet more suffering on the Roman people. The struggle was finally decided at the naval battle of Actium off the western coast of Greece in 31 BCE.

Antony, who was in love with Cleopatra, the Queen of Egypt, had help at Actium from the Egyptian army and navy. Octavian, though, craftily used Antony's Eastern alliance and his love affair with an assertive Egyptian queen to brand him as a traitor to Rome. Thanks in part to this propaganda offensive, many of Antony's men deserted him. At Actium, therefore, Octavian triumphed. Not long thereafter, Antony and Cleopatra committed suicide, and Caesarion, a son that Julius Caesar had fathered with Cleopatra, was killed on Octavian's orders. At long last, therefore, one man, Octavian, at the age of 32, found himself in a position of undisputed mastery over Rome and all of its far-flung provinces. The Romans had a tantalizing opportunity to bring the age of interminable civil wars to a conclusive end. The question remained, however: what kind of ruler would Octavian prove to be?

On the surface, Octavian was a believer in the Republic, and he kept some of its key institutions in place. Though the Assembly was allowed to wither away, Octavian respected the Senate and restored some of its powers. In addition, Roman elections proceeded more or less as before, at least until 15 CE. Consuls continued to hold office, although the consulship became largely an honorary post. Octavian also refused to be called king or emperor. Instead, he designated himself as *princeps civitatis*, that is, First Citizen of the State.

In truth, however, the reign of Octavian brought an end to the Republic. Octavian held so many government positions, he controlled so much of Rome's tax revenue, and he maintained such absolute power over the Roman army that no one in Rome could think seriously about opposing him. In 27 BCE, Octavian shrewdly offered to give up all of his authority. The Senate, having been violently purged of Octavian's enemies, would not hear of it. Instead, the Senate bestowed on Octavian the semi-religious title of Augustus, that is, the revered one. (And, as of 8 BCE, the month of Sextilis would be renamed August.) From this point on, Octavian would be known as Augustus, and often as Caesar Augustus, a title that all future Roman leaders would claim. He was also referred to as *imperator*—a title that in the past had been applied to victorious generals but that now acquired monarchical overtones. For all practical purposes, Augustus had become the first Emperor of Rome.

What factors led to the destruction of the Roman Republic?

The Augustan Principate, 27 BCE–14 CE

Because Augustus called himself *princeps civitatis*, the period of his reign is often known as the Augustan Principate. This was, by most accounts, a glorious time for Rome. In addition to a flowering of Roman art, architecture, scholarship, and literature, the triumph of Augustus over his enemies meant that, at long last, there was order throughout Rome and its empire. Finally, therefore, the necessary conditions existed to permit economic expansion and bold political reform.

To begin with, Augustus put an end to the political confusion and corruption that had dominated Roman provincial administration during the Republic. He insisted that provincial governors and magistrates be experienced, honest men who were sincerely devoted to the welfare of Rome's citizens and subjects. Augustus also instituted new ways of supervising provincial officials, and those who abused their powers were harshly disciplined. In addition, Augustus gave many provincial cities increased powers of self-government, he shared Roman citizenship with more provincials, and he reformed and professionalized the system by which Rome collected taxes. Some Romans even began to talk about their empire as a world state. In other words, no longer did a few hundred Roman families rule the Mediterranean region as a personal fiefdom, exploiting it for selfish gain. Now, the Roman Empire was governed by a single magnanimous leader who valued the interests of all his people.

As Augustus was winning over the provinces, he also sought to reconcile the poor, unruly masses who lived in Rome itself to the new political order. Augustus, among his many titles, was granted *tribunicia potestas* by the Senate—in other words, he wielded personally the power of the tribunes. Historically, the tribunes had as their main responsibility the protection of the interests of the plebeian masses. Thus, Augustus, the populist emperor, initiated new policies that were designed to court the population of Rome. He constructed new buildings, roads, and aqueducts, thus employing many poor Romans. He created an organized police force and fire service. He ensured the delivery of grain at reasonable prices to the lower classes. To reduce Rome's problem of overcrowding, Augustus recruited many poor Romans into the army, and when their term of service was over he resettled them in Roman colonies scattered throughout the empire. Augustus also cleverly manipulated the poor people of Rome with spectacles such as gladiatorial contests and grand public ceremonies, and he used populist rhetoric to ensure the cooperation of the urban rabble at election time.

Another of Augustus's great accomplishments was his reorganization and professionalization of the Roman army. Under Augustus, promotions increasingly were based on performance. In addition, the standard tour of duty for Roman soldiers was fixed at 20 years, the army became an all-volunteer force, and Roman legionaries could expect regular pay, bonuses, competent commanders, a grant of Roman citizenship (if they did not already possess it), and generous retirement packages, sometimes including the gift of land

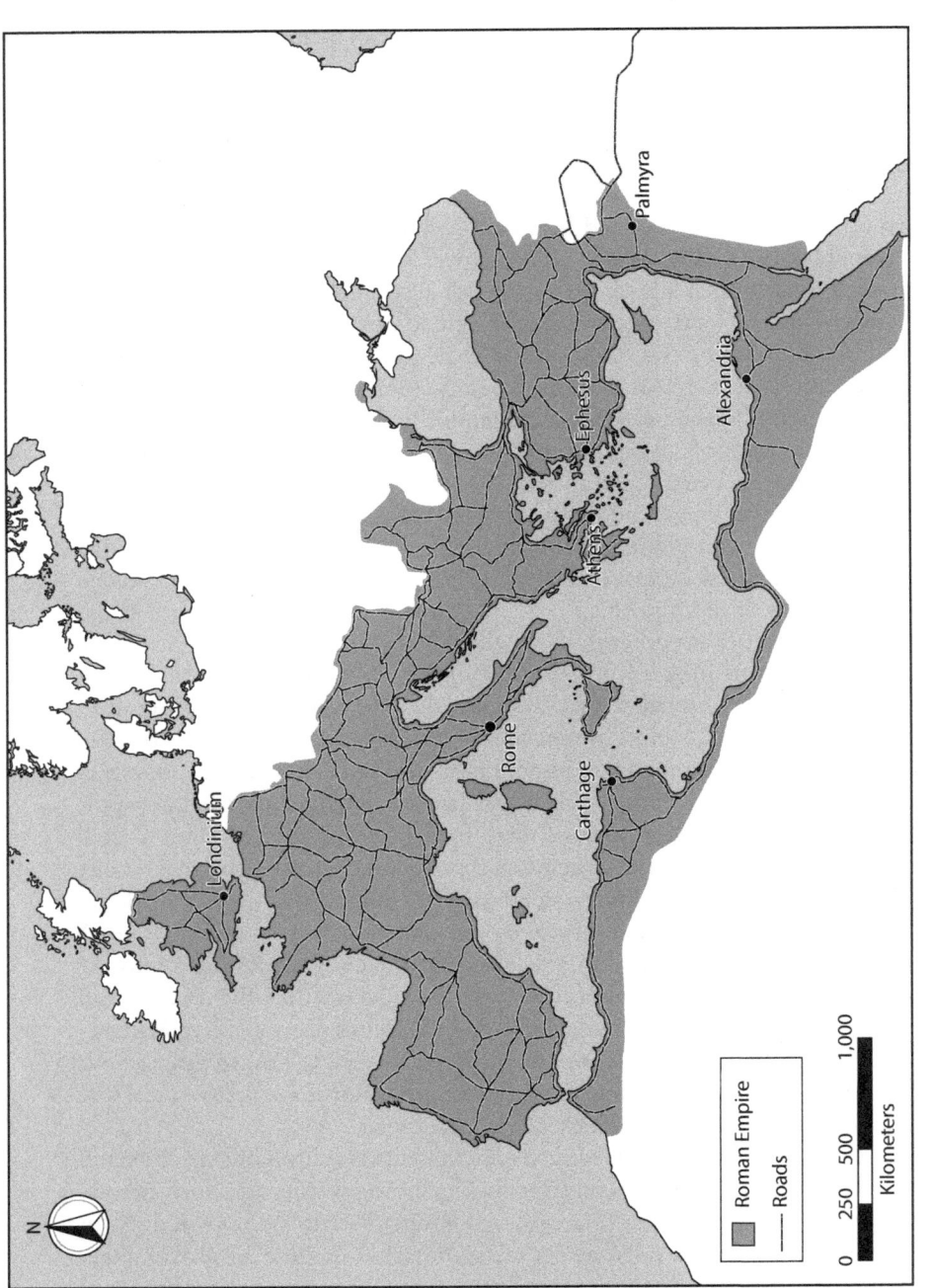

Map 4.1 The Roman Empire at its height, circa 125 CE.

in the provinces. These inducements motivated many provincials to become Roman soldiers. As a result, the percentage of Romans and Italians in the army declined.

The size of the Roman army as a whole was reduced under Augustus, but it continued to fight wars of expansion, at least initially. Augustus launched invasions of parts of Central and Eastern Europe. In Germany, however, a Roman army was destroyed in 9 CE. Despite the strength of its military forces, Rome never managed to win control over the Germanic tribes. Augustus eventually came to the conclusion, therefore, that Rome should be content with its existing borders.

Despite Augustus's successful military reforms, there was one ominous sign: the Roman army continued to be loyal to its commander-in-chief rather than to the government as a whole. This made it uncertain how the Roman army would behave after Augustus's death.

What were the main accomplishments of the Augustan Principate?

The *Pax Romana*

The era from the reign of Emperor Augustus to roughly 180 CE is known as the *Pax Romana*, that is, the Roman peace. That is because the Roman Empire for two centuries enjoyed relative political stability, good governance, economic prosperity, and cultural vitality. Nevertheless, Roman politics continued to be troubled by occasional incidents of assassination, rebellion, and civil war.

The four emperors who succeeded Augustus—Tiberius, Caligula, Claudius, and Nero—were all part of the Julio-Claudian dynasty, composed of various descendants of Augustus and his wife Livia. At first, the Julio-Claudians tried to cloak their imperial power in republican rhetoric, but it was not long before the Roman people grew accustomed to royalty, and so the pretense of republicanism was largely dropped.

Tiberius was an effective emperor who consolidated the numerous achievements of Augustus. Eventually, though, he became a reclusive figure who spent much of his reign on the sunny island of Capri. Whether he spent his time there brooding or engaging in wild debauchery is not entirely clear. It was under Tiberius's rule that Jesus Christ was crucified outside Jerusalem.

Caligula's short reign began in a celebratory mood, but he seems to have become both power-hungry and improvident with public funds. Many Roman emperors were officially deified after their deaths, but Caligula believed that he was a living god. He was eventually murdered by men serving in the elite Praetorian Guard, the very force that Augustus had created to protect the emperor.

Little was expected of Emperor Claudius, who suffered from a number of disabilities, but he turned out to be a capable and conscientious leader. Under his rule, Rome conquered Britain and many other provinces, judicial reforms were implemented, a rudimentary imperial bureaucracy took shape, and many roads, canals, aqueducts, and public buildings were constructed.

Claudius's successor, Nero, became emperor as a teenager. He had a lifelong love of acting and singing. He was also a populist ruler who fought corruption and the abuse of power. On the other hand, ancient historians allege that he was involved in the killings of his brother, his mother, his wife, and many political enemies. In 64 CE, a gigantic fire destroyed much of Rome, and Nero blamed the city's small community of Christians, many of whom were gruesomely put to death. In the aftermath of the fire, Nero spent public money wildly, particularly on a Golden Palace for himself that included an artificial lake and opulent rooms decorated with gold and precious stones. The dining area had a rotating ivory ceiling that dispensed perfume onto Nero's guests. Nero, however, had little chance to enjoy his new palace, because in 68 CE the Praetorian Guard forced him to commit suicide.

After Nero's death, Roman politics briefly veered once again into civil war. A general named Vespasian quickly restored order, though, and named himself emperor, despite his humble origins. This inaugurated the Flavian dynasty of emperors—made up of Vespasian and his two sons, Titus and Domitian—that lasted from 69 CE to 96 CE. Vespasian commissioned the construction of modern Rome's most famous ancient landmark, the *Colosseum*.

The assassination of Domitian in 96 CE, and the subsequent selection of a new emperor by the Senate, marked the beginning of a golden age for the Roman Empire that lasted until 180 CE. The Romans called this the era of the Five Good Emperors. These five emperors were: Nerva, Trajan, Hadrian, Antoninus Pius, and Marcus Aurelius. One reason for the excellence of Rome's imperial administration in this age was the happy coincidence that none of Rome's leaders, except Marcus Aurelius, had a biological son to succeed him. This forced the ruling emperor to name a talented general or public official as his successor.

Marcus Aurelius, the last of the Five Good Emperors, was an insightful philosopher as well as a great warrior. Ominously, however, Marcus Aurelius chose his son Commodus to succeed him. Commodus's unhappy reign, marred by his spectacular megalomania and cruelty, brought the age of the Five Good Emperors to a conclusive end. Commodus fancied himself a masterful gladiator and a reincarnation of the Greek hero Hercules. He was strangled to death in 192.

During the *Pax Romana* as a whole, Rome experienced few major rebellions. Although wealth was unevenly spread, the economy was generally strong. Most of the approximately 50 million citizens and subjects of the empire were content to enjoy the obvious benefits that the Roman peace provided, such as rising volumes of trade, law and order, and other, more tangible achievements, such as roads, aqueducts, public baths, theaters, temples, and irrigation systems. Many natives in the provinces became involved in local government, thus becoming junior members of the imperial elite.

Some groups, however, were unwilling to make the compromises that Roman rule required. Egyptians, residents of Gaul, and the scattered Germanic tribes were notoriously resistant to Roman authority. In addition, Queen Boudicca, a native leader, organized a particularly bloody revolt in Roman Britain. Most famously, the Jews rebelled on three separate occasions. After one of these revolts, in 70 CE, the Romans destroyed the Jewish Temple in Jerusalem. After the last major Jewish uprising, in 132 CE–135 CE, most Jews were either killed, enslaved, or exiled. In certain areas, therefore, the process of Romanization faced grave obstacles, and Roman rule could only be enforced through considerable bloodshed.

Why is the period from 27 BCE to 180 CE sometimes known as the Pax Romana?

The Rise of the Barbarians: The Decline and Fall of Rome or Late Antiquity?

Starting with the reign of Marcus Aurelius's son, Commodus, the quality of Roman leadership, and the reliability of the Roman army, began to decline. Rome also suffered from a variety of social and economic problems that, when combined with the increasing challenge of barbarian incursions on the Roman frontier, cast the very survival of the empire into doubt. A fierce debate rages among historians about how to characterize the outcome of this process.

Traditionally, the end of the Roman Empire has been seen, especially in the West, as a cataclysm that overturned most Roman achievements, and thus many historians talk about the Fall of Rome. Some modern historians, though, including the Princeton University scholar Peter Brown, have argued instead that the period from the third to the eighth centuries CE should be seen not as an epoch of collapse but as a time of gradual transition, cultural innovation, and in some cases positive change. They refer to this era not as the Fall of Rome, therefore, but as Late Antiquity. The truth is that both schools of thought are right to a certain extent, as we shall see.

After Commodus, Rome was ruled from 193 CE to 235 CE by the Severan dynasty, which accomplished the final extension of Roman citizenship to virtually all free men living in the empire. The Severi also began a military buildup and imposed higher taxes. After the Severi, Rome was governed from 235 CE to 284 CE by the barracks emperors, a series of military strongmen. In these years emperors were assassinated or killed in battle with such frequency that Roman politics frequently descended into utter chaos.

Amid this turmoil and violence, a number of disturbing trends began to emerge. Rome's economy withered. Rapid inflation and crumbling infrastructure hurt trade, while many Romans fled the cities, and sometimes their farms in the countryside, to escape rising taxes and predatory soldiers and public officials. Agricultural production declined, and food riots developed in the cities. Increasingly, owners of *latifundia* dominated agricultural production, and many ordinary Romans in the countryside were forced to become tenant farmers with few, if any, rights. Social inequality and crime rose, and the law now treated Romans differently depending on whether or not they came from the respectable classes. Another dangerous sign was that Romans and provincials no longer volunteered to serve in the imperial or local administration—now they had to be coerced. Under these circumstances, many Romans lost faith in the imperial system.

Despite all of this upheaval, Roman power proved remarkably resilient. Unfortunately for the empire, however, it faced yet another serious long-term threat: the migrating barbarian tribes. The barbarians, as the Romans called them, were a diverse set of peoples who generally lived in Northern, Central, and Eastern Europe, either in Rome's frontier provinces or beyond the borders of the empire. The most important tribes were the Goths, Allemani, Vandals, Franks, Lombards, Alans, Suebi, Angles, Saxons, Jutes, and Huns. Many barbarians spoke Germanic, Celtic, or Slavic languages, but others, like the Huns, were migrants from Asia. It is important to note that the barbarians had no sense of a common identity, and they did not coordinate their actions. Nevertheless, they shared certain characteristics. They had no written language, and no formal system of law; their political systems were usually based on chieftancies and tribal loyalties, and only occasionally on confederations or kingship; and they would often uproot themselves from the land and go marauding for loot. The Romans tended to concentrate on the violent and warlike nature of the barbarians. They often overlooked the fact that many barbarian tribes engaged in extensive farming and trade, built sizable towns, and excelled in metalworking and other crafts. Moreover, for centuries, Rome had lived more or less in equilibrium with the barbarians, many of whom had chosen to live within the borders of the empire. Some even became culturally Romanized.

For a long time, Rome's border defenses were sufficient to hold back the most recalcitrant of barbarians. During the third century, however, as Rome's generals increasingly turned on each other, the frontiers were left unguarded. This made it possible for some barbarian tribes to go on the offensive. In addition, as new barbarian groups were arriving from the East, other tribes were displaced and fled over the frontier. Some of these barbarian migrants had peaceful intentions, but others did not.

As dire as Rome's predicament in the third century was, the empire ultimately managed to defend itself from the barbarian hordes and to restore some semblance of order and prosperity. This process began with the Emperor Diocletian, who reigned from 284 to 305.

Diocletian was a commoner and a provincial who had risen to political prominence as a soldier. Once in power, he developed a simple and systematic way to bring the empire under control: he divided it into four zones. Each zone received a tetrarch as its leader. Senior tetrarchs were styled Augustus and junior tetrarchs were called Caesar. Diocletian simultaneously eliminated many of the powers of self-government that Rome's cities had traditionally enjoyed. The costs of defending Rome's borders forced Diocletian to raise taxes, to attempt to regulate prices and wages, and to coerce peasants into working for the state or for the rich owners of *latifundia*. He also instituted ancient Rome's most severe campaign of persecution against Christians. Increasingly, therefore, the empire was being run on clearly authoritarian lines.

In 305 CE, Diocletian retired: to what is now Split, Croatia. After a period of confusion, Constantine the Great, most recognizable as the first Christian emperor, emerged as the new leader. He abolished the tetrarchy, preferring to govern the empire as a single domain, but he inadvertently accelerated its disintegration by building a glamorous new capital at Constantinople, which today is Istanbul, Turkey. From this point on, the eastern empire and the western empire increasingly went their separate ways. A fair degree of urbanization, prosperity, and centralized control persisted in the East, offering historians ample evidence to support the concept of Late Antiquity, whereas poverty, crime, disorder, urban decline, and barbarian attacks plagued the West, indicating that here, at least, there really was a Fall of ancient Rome.

To further understand this process of imperial decline, it is necessary to appreciate just how radically the Roman army had changed from the days of the Early Republic to the Late Empire. When Rome was first expanding, its army was essentially a militia conscripted only from landowners. These citizen-warriors were devoted servants of the Republic. By the Late Empire, however, Roman soldiers might be either citizens or subjects; they might be Romans, provincials, or barbarians; they were often drawn from the ranks of the urban poor, the dispossessed peasantry, or from the wandering Germanic tribes; some were even slaves. They viewed military service as a means to achieve personal wealth, higher social status, and power. They also sought plunder from whatever source it could most easily be obtained—usually from fellow Romans!

Many historians would argue, therefore, that the eventual demise of the Roman Empire would occur not because barbarian military strength overwhelmed it. On the contrary, it would be more accurate to say that Rome fell because its own army decayed from within.

Clearly, the Roman Empire ruled by Constantine was one in peril. As discussed in Chapter 5, partly in order to breathe new life into his domain, Constantine took the bold step of adopting the new religion of Christianity. He also ended the persecution of Christians. The Emperor Theodosius, who reigned from 379 CE to 395 CE, went even further by making Christianity the official religion and outlawing paganism. It was too late, however, to save the empire by infusing it with a new sense of religious purpose.

The beginning of the end came in 376 CE, when the Goths, fleeing from the aggressive Huns, sought refuge in the empire. The Emperor Valens agreed to shelter the Goths, but fighting broke out between the Goths and the Roman legions. Valens himself was killed. The arrival of the Huns in Europe led numerous barbarian tribes to migrate into Roman territory.

These migrations often amounted to invasions. Symbolic of Rome's weakness was the sack of Rome itself by the Goths in 410 CE—the first foreign occupation of the city in roughly 800 years.

The borders of the empire, always porous, now fell apart. Hordes of barbarians traversed the Empire, from Germany, to Gaul, to Spain, to Italy, to North Africa. For the next several decades, a string of mediocre emperors tried vainly to stop the bleeding, but the empire, at least in the West, had ceased to function. Many Romans frankly preferred the protection offered by barbarian warlords to the rule of corrupt Roman officials and soldiers. In 476, the last Roman emperor, a teenage boy named Romulus Augustulus, was dethroned by a German general named Odoacer, who was declared King of Italy. By 500 CE, Germanic kings and nobles were in power throughout Western Europe.

As believers in Late Antiquity would hasten to point out, these dramatic events did not erase the glorious legacy of the Roman achievement. In many ways, the political, social, economic, and religious order that arose in Europe after 500 CE represented a blend of Greek, Roman, Christian, and barbarian influences. Nowhere was the Roman heritage simply forgotten.

In the West, for instance, many Germanic kings and nobles continued to speak Latin, which would remain the dominant literary language in Europe for another 1,000 years. (By some measures, even today the majority of words in English have Latin roots.) In addition, some barbarian warriors eventually settled in Roman villas and lived the lives of Roman country gentlemen. They often worshiped in basilicas of Roman design, and they admired the feats of Roman engineering, continuing for centuries to use Roman roads. Many Germanic peoples also embraced Christianity, which had itself been heavily Romanized.

Politically speaking, the new Germanic masters of Western Europe often consciously modeled their law codes on Roman legal traditions. The royal pretensions of some Germanic kings were also clearly inspired by the majesty and power of the Roman monarchy. As a matter of fact, virtually every Western monarchy that has existed during the last 1,500 years has based at least some of its institutions, ideology, or rituals on the example set by the Roman Empire. And the legacy of the Roman Republic was also strong: it provided inspiration for eighteenth-century revolutionaries in America and France.

Furthermore, in the East, lest we forget, not only did the Roman heritage remain influential, but the Roman Empire never fell at all! The cities, trade routes, infrastructure, ancient culture, Christian faith and Church organization, army, Roman law code, and imperial administration in the eastern half of the empire all survived the barbarian invasions. To easterners, therefore, it seemed that the Roman Empire was still in place.

Why, then, do we even talk of the Fall of Rome? We do so for two strong reasons. One, the triumph of the Germanic tribes in Western Europe did erase many important features of Roman civilization, not the least of which was the power and wealth of the city of Rome itself. Two, the persistence of the Roman Empire in the East is partly deceptive, because the East was still largely Hellenized, rather than Romanized—that is, the common language and culture in the East was Greek, a legacy of the Hellenistic Age. Historians usually describe this Hellenized eastern realm not as a continuation of Rome, but as something distinct: the Byzantine Empire (see Chapter 6). In short, much of the Roman heritage did survive after 476 CE, and yet the Fall of the Roman Empire truly was the end of an era. Rome would never again dominate Europe. Moreover, from this point on, *Romanitas*, or Romanness, would be just one of several key cultural influences on the shape of things to come in Western Civilization.

What role did the barbarians play in the Fall of Rome?

Conclusions

Many historians have agonized over the great question of why Rome fell. As you have seen, the potential answers are numerous. What we know for certain is the outcome of its fall.

By 500 CE, whatever order existed in Western Europe was provided by what is now known as the Catholic Church, an institution that was growing in power, and by the Germanic kings and nobles who were the new strongmen in Europe. Since most city dwellers had long since fled from marauding barbarians and exploitative Roman officials alike, the Europe over which the Germanic tribes and the Church now held sway was overwhelmingly rural. Wealth was in the form of land, and power was exercised by binding peasants, soldiers, and craftsmen to the service of a warrior nobility, settled on fortified agricultural estates, and ruling in cooperation with a clerical elite. The stage was thus set for feudalism, and for the Middle Ages.

For better or worse, after 500 CE, the Grandeur That Was Rome would no longer be the focus of Western Civilization.

Key Terms for Chapter 4

Etruscans—a group of people that dominated central Italy, including Rome, until the sixth century BCE.

Patricians—a hereditary class of elite Romans with extensive political, social, economic, and religious privileges that were somewhat diminished after the Struggle of the Orders.

Plebeians—the common people of Rome, who were traditionally ruled by the patricians.

Senate—a body of elder statesmen. It was at times the most powerful institution in the Roman Republic.

Legions—large formations of about 5,000 Roman soldiers.

Punic Wars—a series of conflicts between Rome and Carthage. Rome was victorious, leading to Roman hegemony in the western Mediterranean region.

The Gracchi—the brothers Tiberius and Gaius Gracchus attempted to improve conditions for, and enhance the political influence of, poor Roman farmers. They were assassinated at the behest of conservatives.

Julius Caesar—a brilliant Roman general, and, from 48 BCE to 44 BCE, dictator of Rome. He was assassinated by a group of senators who viewed him as a tyrant.

Augustus—originally known as Octavian, Augustus was Julius Caesar's heir and the founder of the Roman Empire.

Pax Romana—the Roman peace. It describes the period from roughly 27 BCE to 180 CE, during which Rome was generally led by competent emperors and enjoyed stable frontiers and general prosperity.

Barracks emperors—a series of third-century Roman military rulers who came and went with remarkable speed.

Barbarians—a diverse group of mostly Germanic, Celtic, and Slavic peoples who sometimes lived within the Roman Empire and sometimes lived beyond its frontiers. Barbarians, who were frequently on the move, would become a major military threat to Rome beginning in the third century.

Christianity—a new monotheistic religion that spread rapidly throughout the interconnected Roman world. Under Emperor Theodosius, it became Rome's official religion.

Review Questions for Chapter 4

1. Based on your understanding of the nature of the government of the Roman Republic, describe two ways in which it was similar, and two ways in which it was different, from the government of the United States today.
2. Class conflict was a major theme in Roman politics. Describe in detail two episodes in Rome's history in which class conflict played a significant role. Lastly, give your analysis as to whether, on balance, Rome dealt successfully or unsuccessfully with class tensions.
3. There were, for the peoples conquered by Rome, both costs and benefits to their inclusion in the Roman world. List at least two advantages, and two disadvantages, to being a provincial ruled by the Romans.
4. Julius Caesar and Augustus were two of the most compelling personalities in Roman history. Choose one, and write a thorough summary of his life and accomplishments.

5. The decline and fall of the Roman Empire is one of the most carefully researched phenomena in world history. First, describe in detail what you believe to be the two most important factors that contributed to the Roman Empire's demise. Next, consider whether either of these factors could, or will, produce the decline and fall of the United States of America.

Further Reading

Boatwright, Mary T., Daniel J. Gargola, and Richard J. A. Talbert. *The Romans: From Village to Empire*. Second Edition. New York: Oxford University Press. 2012.

Burns, Thomas S. *Rome and the Barbarians, 100 B.C.–A.D. 400*. Baltimore, MD: Johns Hopkins University Press. 2009.

Cunliffe, Barry. *The Ancient Celts*. London: Penguin Books. 1999.

Eckstein, Arthur M. *Mediterranean Anarchy, Interstate War, and the Rise of Rome*. Berkeley, CA: University of California Press. 2009.

Goffart, Walter. *Barbarian Tides: The Migration Age and the Later Roman Empire*. Philadelphia, PA: University of Pennsylvania Press. 2011.

Goldsworthy, Adrian. *Augustus: First Emperor of Rome*. New Haven, CT: Yale University Press. 2014.

Goldsworthy, Adrian. *Caesar: Life of a Colossus*. New Haven, CT: Yale University Press. 2008.

Goldsworthy, Adrian. *The Complete Roman Army*. London: Thames and Hudson. 2011.

Liebeschuetz, J.H.W.G. *Decline and Fall of the Roman City*. Oxford: Oxford University Press. 2007.

Mackay, Christopher. *Ancient Rome: A Military and Political History*. New York: Cambridge University Press. 2007.

MacMullen, Ramsay. *Romanization in the Time of Augustus*. New Haven, CT: Yale University Press. 2008.

Sumi, Geoffrey S. *Ceremony and Power: Performing Politics in Rome Between Republic and Empire*. Ann Arbor, MI: The University of Michigan Press. 2017.

Ward-Perkins, Bryan. *The Fall of Rome and the End of Civilization*. Oxford: Oxford University Press. 2006.

Wells, Peter S. *The Barbarians Speak: How the Conquered Peoples Shaped Roman Europe*. Princeton, NJ: Princeton University Press. 2001.

5 Ancient Rome
Society, Culture, and Daily Life

Introduction

The ancient Romans were among the most austere and self-disciplined people in all of world history, but they were also among the most decadent and debauched. They were alternately civic-minded and selfish, tolerant and brutal, law-abiding and corrupt, creative and anti-intellectual, urbane and primitive. Roman culture, in short, was based on a maze of contradictions that makes the understanding of *Romanitas*, or Romanness, frustratingly difficult. In a sense, though, this predicament should come as no surprise. The Roman Republic and the Roman Empire endured for about 1,000 years. Geographically, they embraced a huge portion of ancient Europe, Africa, and the Middle East; demographically, they comprised tens of millions of people of varying ethnic and religious backgrounds. How, then, could *Romanitas* be anything but a complicated idea?

Luckily, among the bewildering contradictions that characterize ancient Rome, there are recurring themes that make it possible to offer some accurate generalizations about the society, culture, and daily life of the ancient Romans. Certainly, theirs was a world that profoundly influenced the future course of Western Civilization. It has also captivated the historical imagination of Western peoples for the last 1,500 years. That is reason enough to ask the question: what did it mean to live as a Roman?

Agriculture, Commerce, and the Distribution of Wealth

When modern people imagine the ancient Romans, they think most often of city dwellers, especially the lucky residents of Rome itself. At least 80 percent of Romans, however, lived in the countryside, and agriculture was the mainstay of the economy. Most farmers produced grains, such as barley and wheat; some raised animals, especially sheep, pigs, and cattle; and there were vast profits to be made in the production of wine and olive oil, the latter used to heat and light Roman homes as well as for cooking and as a body oil.

In the early days of the Republic, as we have seen, small farmers formed the backbone of the Roman economy. As time went on, however, many ordinary farmers were reduced to poverty, and *latifundia* came to dominate Roman agriculture. By the end of the Roman Empire, the few small farmers who were left, in reaction to a multitude of threats, rushed to sign over their acres to the elite. In return, wealthy landowners promised their new clients jobs, food, shelter, and physical security. They expected loyalty and labor in return, not only from the client, but from the client's offspring as well.

Trade, finance, mining, quarrying, fishing, and the production of crafts were all important to the Roman economy. They were not, however, considered respectable professions: Roman senators, for example, were, at least theoretically, forbidden from engaging in commerce.

Roman trade reached as far as China and India. Across the Mediterranean region, the exchange of grains, wine, olive oil, fruits, nuts, vegetables, wool, animals, hides, furs, metals, salt, textiles, pottery, glassware, timber, slaves, precious stones, and assorted luxury goods was brisk, thanks to Rome's outstanding system of roads, its standardization of weights and measures, and its efficient harbors and merchant shipping companies.

During the Age of the Five Good Emperors, from 96 CE to 180 CE, the economy soared to new heights. Taxes were low, the currency was stable, pirates and brigands were controlled, government regulations were minimal, and strong population growth stimulated increased demand for consumer goods.

In the third century, however, the reign of the barracks emperors, followed by the autocratic rule of Emperors Diocletian and Constantine, produced economic decline. Generally speaking, the reaction of the Roman government to adversity was to tighten government control of the economy and expand military spending. Faced with excessive and unpredictable demands from the government, many Romans fled the cities, or they abandoned their small farms and sought the protection of agricultural magnates.

By the period of the Late Empire, trade had shrunk, pirates and criminals prowled transportation routes, cities were dwindling and in some cases abandoned, and villas in the countryside had become largely self-sufficient and self-contained, by necessity. Disease and violence had also produced a precipitous decline in the Roman population. The golden age of Roman prosperity was at an end.

The class system in ancient Rome underwent remarkable transformations. Under the Republic, the Struggle of the Orders (see Chapter 4) had reduced the traditional gap between the two hereditary classes: patricians and plebeians. Full-scale democracy and social equality had been avoided, but social mobility had increased.

In the Late Republic and in the empire, class divisions once again hardened and were enshrined in the law. Under the barracks emperors, soldiers began to treat civilians with contempt. Society was divided into *honestiores* (aristocrats, officials, and soldiers) and *humiliores* (ordinary Romans with inferior status). The imperial government also began to insist that merchants, craftsmen, and peasants be frozen into their economic and social roles, and that these professions be passed on to their children. By the era of the Late Empire, a rigid, hereditary class structure had taken shape, which would facilitate the rise of feudalism in the Middle Ages.

Why did the Roman economy decline starting in the third century?

Traditional Roman Religion

Ancient Rome's traditional religion was similar to religion in ancient Greece in several important respects. First, both faiths were polytheistic. Later, Christians would label Greek and Roman polytheists as pagans. Second, there was a distinction in both Greece and Rome between the state-endorsed religion and the religion of ordinary people. The state-sanctioned version of religion revolved around a pantheon of major gods and goddesses who were worshiped according to formal rituals. The religion of ordinary people, on the other hand, was usually based on the informal worship of ancestors and local deities.

The major gods and goddesses of the ancient Romans, who in many ways corresponded to the 12 principal gods and goddesses of the Greeks, were honored in and around grand temples by priests, priestesses, and *augurs* (seers who interpreted the will of the gods), who were often highborn patricians. Such worship customarily involved complex rituals that were designed to appease the gods and thus to ensure that they would show favor to Rome. The goddess Vesta, for instance, was worshiped by six Vestal Virgins who took a vow to remain chaste for 30 years. They enjoyed lives of privilege, but if they did not uphold their oath they were gruesomely put to death.

Like the Greeks, the Romans sponsored many festivals, games, and dramatic performances that they dedicated to the gods. *Saturnalia*, one of the most important festivals, occurred from December 17 to December 23 each year. It involved holidays and special privileges for slaves as well as the exchange of gifts, public ceremonies, feasting, casual attire, and general merriment. Some scholars have suggested that the date of Christmas, December 25, was chosen to coincide with the tradition of *Saturnalia* in order to make Christianity more appealing to pagans.

On the level of individuals and families, everyday religious practices revolved around honoring and placating spirits that lived in nature, along property lines or roadways, or within one's home. Consequently, small shrines at home or in the countryside were frequently the sites of religious observances, and religious processions were common. The most important spirits honored in such informal rituals were often those of one's own ancestors. Other outlets for Romans' religious impulses were the practice of sorcery, the interpretation of dreams, and astrology. Overall, the Romans were highly suspicious people, and they tended to believe that the gods controlled all natural phenomena. In almost all forms of popular religion, women played prominent roles.

One of the most remarkable aspects of official Roman policy toward religion was its flexibility. In most cases, the Romans gave wide latitude to provincials to practice their local religions as they saw fit. Only when Roman administrators sensed that a given religion might become a source of political unrest or social corruption did they act against it. Moreover, as the Romans conquered new areas, they spread the worship of their gods to new people. It was common under Augustus, for example, for temples dedicated to the minor goddess *Roma* to be built in far-flung provinces. The worship of *Roma*, combined with the veneration of Augustus himself, solidified the link between Rome and its empire. By the third century, the emperor cult had become a major feature of Roman religion. Interestingly, the Romans also sometimes embraced the gods of those whom they conquered. They appropriated large portions of Greek mythology, for instance.

Partly because of the highly formal nature of the state-endorsed version of Roman religion, few people felt a strong emotional connection to the major gods. Increasingly, Romans viewed participation in the state religion as a political duty rather than as an act of faith. Emperor Augustus, however, sought to reinvigorate Roman religion. He sponsored the construction of many new temples and funded the training of new priests. He also endorsed traditionalism both in the style of public worship and in questions of morality. Adultery, for example, was criminalized, and even Augustus's daughter, Julia, was punished severely for breaking her marriage vows.

Augustus's revival of Rome's pagan religion was not an unqualified success. By the first century CE, many Romans were looking for a new faith that addressed their most heartfelt spiritual needs, especially their fear of death.

In what ways were the ancient Greek and Roman religions similar?

Daily Life in Ancient Rome

Fortunately for us, some records revealing the character of daily life in ancient Rome survive. We also benefit from the work of archaeologists, which often allows us to view valuable evidence about how Romans lived. Some of the most intriguing evidence comes not from Rome itself but from the ruins of Pompeii, which was wiped off the map in a single day by the eruption of Mt. Vesuvius in 79 CE. Pompeii was essentially entombed and frozen in time for 2,000 years.

Dinner was the most important meal for Romans. Popular foods included bread, porridge, cheese, eggs, and vegetables, while wine was by far the most common beverage. *Garum* (a salty fish sauce), honey, and spices were widely used for flavoring. Most Romans rarely ate meat, fowl, or seafood, with the exception of the wealthy, who liked to dine extravagantly. For the rich, an especially noteworthy delicacy was a whole pig, stuffed with sausages.

Dinner parties would be served around a circular table, and guests would recline on couches.

Clothing in ancient Rome generally included a loose-fitting tunic, called a *stola* when worn by women, cinched around the waist. Over the tunic, men on important business would generally wrap a broad sash, usually white but sometimes dyed or decorated, called a *toga*, while women would wear a shawl. Shoes, boots, and sandals could be quite colorful and were an important sign of one's status. For women, jewelry, cosmetics, and perfumes were very popular.

Romans generally woke up early so as to make maximum use of the cool morning hours. When the day was at its hottest, Romans liked to take a nap. Bathing was an important custom, borrowed from the Greeks. In the cities, there were elaborate, even palatial, bathing establishments that provided the equivalent of saunas in addition to pools of hot, warm, and cold water. Shops, exercise rooms, libraries, gardens, food and drink vendors, and gathering spaces, not to mention prostitutes, were also frequently found in Roman baths.

Urban life in ancient Rome involved many downsides, such as high unemployment, crime, poor sanitation, epidemics, rickety and overcrowded apartment buildings, house fires, and expensive rents. Nevertheless, many Romans preferred city life because it provided numerous benefits. In the cities, an ordinary citizen might attach himself to a powerful and wealthy man and become his client, thereby gaining a protector and an avenue of advancement. In addition, in the cities, the government often distributed free or subsidized food and drink. In most cases, basic public services and transportation routes were well planned and well maintained. The vibrant urban economy centered on the Forum, a bustling meeting area and marketplace. Elsewhere, special areas were set aside for sports such as wrestling, boxing, ball games, and various elements of what today we would call track and field. All this was true not just in Rome but in other great imperial cities such as Ostia, Rome's thriving port; Athens, the impoverished but highly cultured center of Roman Greece; Ephesus, a glamorous and rich city in western Turkey; Palmyra, mistress of the caravan trade between Roman Syria and Mesopotamia; London, the prosperous capital of Roman Britain; and Alexandria, the greatest city in Roman Egypt, famous for its lighthouse and its library. In all these cities, politicians and rich businessmen sponsored spectacles, games, plays, or feasts for the urban population to enjoy.

Ancient Rome's most famous urban entertainments were chariot races and gladiatorial tournaments. The Circus Maximus, a gigantic arena for chariot racing on the outskirts of Rome, could accommodate upwards of 250,000 spectators. Betting was common, and victorious charioteers became folk heroes. Gladiatorial tournaments—which might involve death matches between wild animals, between animals and men, or between gladiators—were also very popular. Although some gladiators were volunteers, most were slaves who had no choice but to perform. Few Romans questioned the morality of such blood sports. In fact, over time these violent spectacles became even more extreme. Only after Christianity became the official religion were gladiatorial contests finally banned.

Roman education was an informal affair in the early days of the Republic, but, as Rome conquered more territory, and as Romans were exposed to the sophisticated culture of the Greeks, they began to reform their approach to education. Boys from well-to-do families were sent outside the home to learn about philosophy, rhetoric, history, law, literature, and mathematics. Their teachers were usually learned Greeks, often slaves, who taught in both Greek and Latin. For girls from elite families, a simplified version of this humanistic education was sometimes available, but girls were customarily tutored at home. Their education usually ended when they were married, often in their early teens to a significantly older man.

One of the least attractive features of Roman society was slavery, which reached such vast proportions that slave revolts became a serious threat to Rome's security. As with the ancient Greeks, although one's state of bondage could be inherited, the Romans acquired most slaves through warfare. Since these slaves were always of various racial and ethnic backgrounds, skin color meant little to the Romans. At all times, the physical and sexual abuse of slaves was commonplace, although only men were permitted sexual contact with slaves. In addition, slave marriages were not legally recognized. Nevertheless, some Roman emperors provided limited legal protection to slaves, and manumission, or the freeing of slaves, was a regular occurrence. The terms of manumission could be generous, and some former slaves even became wealthy slave owners themselves.

Most slaves worked as farmhands, craftsmen, domestic servants, or miners. They were a vital part of Roman society and economics. Only around the second century CE did slavery begin to decline.

What was life like in Roman cities?

The Status of Women, and the Question of Romanization

Women in ancient Rome enjoyed a superior social position and legal status compared with women in ancient Greece. Roman women could inherit and manage property; they could, in the days of the empire at least, refuse to marry a man of whom they disapproved; they often enjoyed marriages featuring close emotional attachments and mutual respect; they could travel as well as attend social functions; they could join women's associations; they possessed wide powers over the purchases and day-to-day management of their households; they had primary responsibility for raising their children, at least until the age of seven; they had access to birth control; they could divorce their husbands; they were often educated to a degree that was unheard of in Greece; and they were, in rare cases, taken seriously as writers and poets. Moreover, whereas in Greece it was considered scandalous for any woman to exercise political influence, in the Roman Empire it was expected that royal women would hold sway, to some degree, over the emperor. Many royal women were assassinated, precisely because they were so powerful in their own right.

There were, however, distinct limits to a Roman woman's freedom. Every woman, at least until the Late Empire, had to be under the legal guardianship of a man. She also commonly married at a very young age, so it was unlikely that her input into the choice of a husband would carry much weight. Many Romans also held traditional views about gender, so women were often chastised if they overstepped what were considered the proper bounds of feminine conduct. Most important of all, every Roman family was organized, at least in theory, as a sort of miniature despotism, with a *pater familias*, or father of the family, at its head. The *pater familias* could kill subordinate family members for disobedience; he could sell them into slavery; he could choose to abandon a newborn child; he could dispose of the entire family's property as he saw fit; and he could divorce his wife. Under these circumstances, whatever freedoms a woman might have enjoyed on paper were largely irrelevant if the dominant male figure in her life chose to command her absolute obedience.

In the period of the Roman Empire, the rights of Roman women were improved. Emperor Augustus, who wished to increase the birth rate, permitted women who bore numerous children to make legal decisions and to manage their property without the permission of a male guardian. Emperor Diocletian later did away entirely with the notion of male guardianship.

Christianity, when it began to spread in the Roman Empire starting in the first century CE, benefited enormously from the contributions of its active female devotees. By contrast, in ancient Mesopotamia, Egypt, Israel, or Greece, it would have been highly unlikely that women would have played such a decisive role in the popularization of a new faith. In ancient Rome, there were fewer limits on what women could accomplish.

One of the most interesting and controversial questions about ancient Rome revolves around the degree to which people in the provinces were exposed to, and chose to adopt, Roman culture, including its relatively liberal attitudes toward women. Some historians claim that only a superficial veneer of Romanization was achieved in the provinces, and that barbarian influences in Rome may ultimately have been stronger. Other historians claim that the Romans, through coercion, persuasion, and commerce, massively altered the way of life of all or most of their subject peoples.

The Romans undoubtedly enjoyed their greatest successes in assimilating provincials in the cities. Residents of provincial cities often adopted elements of Roman religion; learned Latin; turned to Roman courts; enjoyed the use of Roman-style baths, libraries, basilicas, arenas, and amphitheaters; purchased Roman luxury goods; and valued the opportunity to become Roman citizens. The Roman government frequently gave important local administrative responsibilities to members of the native aristocracy and the urban elite. These provincial opinion leaders were among the most likely to become Romanized. People who lived around Roman roads or military encampments, who served in the Roman army, or who traded with the Romans, were also subjected to strong Roman influences.

Of course, the vast majority of provincials were peasants who seldom, if ever, visited cities and had no hope of becoming part of the imperial elite. Although they may have learned a small amount of Latin, their daily lives, their grinding poverty, and their fundamental political, social, cultural, and religious outlook probably did not change at all when the Romans first arrived. As the years passed, however, even peasants were modestly Romanized. After all, some provinces lived under Roman rule for 500 years or more.

It is also important to recognize that Romans who moved to the provinces—as soldiers, administrators, or businessmen, for instance—often felt pressure to adopt some elements of the regional culture, including the worship of local gods. The Romans seldom hesitated to do so, if there was a clear advantage in going native.

In the end, the question of to what degree the provinces were Romanized is not entirely apt. In what is today France, for example, the long-term effect of Roman rule was not Romanization, nor the stubborn persistence of barbarian, Gaulish culture. It was instead the evolution of something new and different: *France*, which, although it uses a Romance language, is neither Roman nor barbarian. It is an original creation.

What advantages did Roman women enjoy over Greek women?

The Greek Inheritance, and the Arts and Sciences in Ancient Rome

One of the most critical questions in Roman culture was to what degree Romans ought to emulate the Greeks. Some Romans, such as Scipio Aemilianus, the conqueror of Carthage, cherished the sophistication and learning of the Greeks. Scipio, like many Romans, studied under Greek scholars, befriended Greek intellectuals, and sought to include elements of Greek literature, poetry, rhetoric, and art in Roman culture. Scipio believed that Rome's traditional culture, which revolved around agriculture and warfare, was far too simplistic to sustain Rome's new role as mistress of the Mediterranean region. Hellenistic culture, by contrast, had held the eastern Mediterranean in thrall for several centuries, so why should the Romans not learn from the Greek example?

Other Romans, however, held the Greeks in contempt. Cato the Elder, a traditionalist writer and politician who lived from 234 BCE to 149 BCE, condemned the Greeks as effeminate, cowardly, sexually perverted, quarrelsome, untrustworthy, greedy, impractical, pretentious, and weak. And, he argued, was not Rome's conquest of Greece the ultimate proof of the decadence of Greek culture?

Despite Cato's doubts, Greek cultural influences steadily infiltrated ancient Rome. Many Roman artists, writers, and architects shamelessly copied Greek models. In addition, most elite Romans were taught by Greek tutors and scholars, rendering them bilingual in Greek and Latin. Some of them traveled to Greece itself to learn from the Mediterranean world's most celebrated thinkers. The end result of this process of Hellenization was a cultural amalgam that is sometimes known as Greco-Roman.

The vast majority of Roman literature did not survive the collapse of the Roman Empire, but the literature that we do possess makes it clear that the Greek influence on Roman authors was very strong. Much of the Roman literature that is still accessible is historical in nature. By modern standards, many Roman historians were essentially propagandists who were extremely careless in screening their evidence.

Many of the historians in the imperial period were members of the senatorial elite. They were jealous of the power of the emperors, and thus their historical accounts tended to highlight the personal and political faults of Rome's leaders. Tacitus, a senator, wrote brilliant but critical histories of the reigns of numerous emperors as well as a fascinating treatise on the Germanic tribes.

By contrast, some literary figures were paid directly by the emperor. Livy, for example, was one of the most prolific and accomplished historians during the reign of Emperor Augustus. He wrote with a strongly pro-establishment bias. Also notable is the work of the historian and essayist Plutarch, who wrote intriguing biographical portraits of prominent Greek and Roman statesmen.

Besides history, the Romans showed a fondness for romantic and comic literature—some of it inspiring, some of it downright obscene. In almost all cases, the focus of Roman literature was on the problems of human beings, not on issues of religion.

One of the few Roman writers whose work has been largely preserved is Cicero. He lived in the first century BCE, in the dying days of the Republic. His speeches, tracts, and private letters would be read especially avidly during the Middle Ages and the Renaissance, but even today they are admired for their humanity and literary flair. Cicero was a conservative statesman and philosopher who struggled to deal with the political violence and instability that surrounded him. He was a successful politician too—he once served as consul, and he promoted cooperation across class and political divides. He was, however, eventually killed in a political purge.

Roman poetry, which peaked in the era of the Late Republic and early empire, owed much to Greek influences. Horace, one of the greatest poets of the Age of Augustus, studied in Athens and adapted the forms of Greek lyric poetry for use in Latin. Rome's preeminent poet was Virgil. His masterwork, the epic poem *The Aeneid*, retold the history of Rome by interweaving it with the story of the Mycenaeans' attack on Troy. Thus, Virgil drew on Homer's *The Iliad* and *The Odyssey*. Another great Roman poet was Catullus, who wrote stirringly of the highs and lows of romantic love. Ovid was a more earthy poet who tackled overtly sexual themes. He also drew heavily on Greek mythology, and he praised the simple life of Roman farmers.

Roman drama drew heavily on Greek influences, though it was never as popular or as refined as Greek drama. Romans preferred raucous comedies, often with satirical overtones.

The Romans, unlike the Greeks, did not value abstract thought for its own sake. Nevertheless, some Roman philosophers made significant contributions to the history of Western thought.

Lucretius was Rome's leading advocate of Epicureanism, a philosophy that had its roots in ancient Greece, and which encouraged its adherents to strive for a life that is serene and independent. The great orator Cicero was a member of the most popular philosophical school in ancient Rome: the Stoics (see also Chapter 3). Other important Stoic thinkers included Seneca, Epictetus, and the Emperor Marcus Aurelius. Stoicism taught that all men and women share the faculty of reason and are bound by natural law. Stoics also stressed the importance of duty, self-control, and virtue. At first, Stoics saw God mainly as an impersonal force that embodied abstract reason. Later, though, they began to conceive of God as a caring being who offered help to people trying to live virtuously. The Stoic perspective on God influenced early Christianity. By the Late Empire, a new philosophical school had emerged called Neo-Platonism that was more mystical than rational. By emphasizing the importance of a transcendent God, Neo-Platonism also helped to prepare the way for Christianity.

Predictably, Roman sculpture was based on Greek precedents. The classical beauty and ideal proportions that characterized much of Greek sculpture were duplicated by the Romans, as were the more realistic features of Hellenistic sculpture. Roman portraiture, however, in the form of wall paintings, mosaics, and busts, was more original. In addition to portraits, Romans enjoyed depictions of landscapes, military triumphs, real and mythical animals, geometric designs, mythological scenes, architecture images, and snapshots of daily life.

Roman architecture was famous for its grandeur. This was due in part to the fact that the Romans were superb engineers. True, the style of many Roman temples, libraries, palaces, monuments, theaters, and baths was influenced by Greek designs, but Roman architects were also innovators. In particular, the Romans used vaults, arches, domes, concrete and brick construction, and marble to produce impressive interiors—something that had eluded the Greeks. Perhaps most importantly, the Romans did not just build magnificent buildings in the city of Rome itself. They succeeded in exporting their architectural creations to cities across the Mediterranean world.

Even in the Late Empire, the Roman passion for building did not ebb. Increasingly, basilicas, which had traditionally been used as secular gathering spaces, were used instead as churches. Another sign of the vitality of Roman architecture in the Late Empire was the ongoing construction of villas. For centuries, Romans had lived in houses arranged, as in Greece, around a central courtyard. Villas were based on this same pattern, but they were large residential complexes at the center of vast agricultural estates. They included spacious living quarters for the wealthy owners as well as housing for servants, bathing facilities, ornamental and vegetable gardens, barns, storage areas, workshops, kitchens, and a church or a temple. What is most extraordinary about Roman villas, though, is that they were to be found in almost every corner of the empire. The Romans thus exported not just their architectural preferences and their building techniques but their very notions of space and of rural social organization throughout Europe, the Middle East, and North Africa.

With only a few exceptions, the Romans were not technological trailblazers. Some historians argue that the principal reason for this technological stagnation was slavery. Cheap and pliable slave labor made it possible to manufacture goods without mechanization or technological enhancements.

Where the Romans truly excelled was in engineering. It was the Etruscans who first taught the Romans about water management, but the Romans developed this technology to become masters of water delivery, water mills, irrigation, drainage, and sewage removal.

Many people today are familiar with the massive, yet graceful, aboveground components of Roman aqueducts, which take the form of a series of arches made of stone. Over the top of these arches, water traveled (and in some cases still travels) down a very slight gradient to its planned destination. In reality, though, the Roman system for water management was mostly underground, and it was far more complex and efficient than anything that had ever been built before. Because gravity was the means by which water was moved from place to place, Roman aqueducts had to be planned and constructed with incredible precision, and they had to be very durable. Rome itself was served by no less than 11 aqueducts, which together delivered at least 200,000,000 gallons of water to the city each day. As a result, some Roman homes enjoyed running water, and sewage was efficiently removed. In rare cases, Roman homes even enjoyed a system of under-floor heating called a *hypocaust*.

Roman roads were among the most outstanding feats of Roman engineering. Some of them are still in use today. In total, Roman soldiers and military engineers built over 50,000 miles of roads. They tended to make roads as straight as possible and to use similar layered construction methods wherever they went. Rest areas were constructed at specified intervals, and milestones were laid. For most of Rome's history, the roads were well maintained and well guarded. Many historians believe that the creation and administration of the vast empire of the Romans would not have been possible without the help of the Roman roads.

Sadly, in the Late Empire, Roman infrastructure fell into disrepair. Roads and water systems of such high quality would not be built again in Europe for more than 1,000 years.

The greatest scientist and mathematician of the Roman era was Ptolemy, a Greek who lived in Alexandria, Egypt (see Chapter 3). Ptolemy formulated the geocentric (i.e., earth-centered) theory of the solar system that remained dominant until the sixteenth and seventeenth centuries CE. Galen, another Greek, was a doctor and a scientist who studied the anatomy of human beings and animals. He greatly expanded medical knowledge by performing animal dissections.

Although the achievements of Ptolemy and Galen were impressive, it is instructive that both men were Greek, not Roman. The Romans did not value intellectual inquiry for its own sake, and in ancient times few people understood the practical uses of science. Scientific work, therefore, did not progress very far under the Romans.

In which of the arts and sciences did the Romans excel?

The Rise of Christianity

Mystery cults had begun to spread from the Middle East into Greece as early as the Hellenistic Age. Eventually, they made their way to Rome as well. These cults were diverse, but they possessed common elements, including secrecy, initiation rites, baptism, rituals involving eating or drinking, public professions of faith, an emphasis on emotion rather than reason, and, most importantly, a promise of security and happiness in the afterlife. The success of the mystery cults reflected Romans' dissatisfaction with traditional pagan religious traditions.

Into this climate of spiritual upheaval stepped Jesus Christ, also known as Jesus of Nazareth, who lived from about 4 BCE to 30 CE. Jesus was born a Jew in a time of special anxiety for Judaism. Israel had been conquered by the Romans, who ruled in conjunction with a Jewish elite of priests and landowners. Roman rule, and especially Roman taxation, was deeply unpopular. In addition, the ravages of warfare and problems such as plague and famine made life for the Jews even more miserable. In response to these challenges, two religious movements arose in Israel. One suggested that a Messiah would soon come who would defeat the Jews' enemies and usher in an age of peace, prosperity, and national independence. The other movement suggested that the Jews' misfortunes were a sign of the coming apocalypse, and that every man, woman, and child ought to repent and prepare for the destruction of the world.

According to the Gospels, which were written down decades later, Jesus preached that he was the Messiah and the Son of God. He claimed, furthermore, that he had come to deliver the Jews from their oppressors, but that he would do so in heaven and not on earth. In fact, he promised anyone who believed in him eternal life—a concept that had never been prominent in Judaism. Jesus also endorsed the notion that an earthly apocalypse was on the horizon, so Jews should ready themselves for the Day of Judgment. Jesus asserted, contrary to the high priests of the Jewish Temple, that observing rituals and obeying the Jewish Law did not in itself make one worthy. It was only by living according to the loving, selfless, and generous spirit of the Prophets—as well as by believing in Jesus himself—that one earned salvation.

Because Jesus had challenged the power and doctrines of the Jewish elite, and because he was amassing a large following, the Roman and Jewish authorities in Jerusalem decided to put him to death. He was beaten and then crucified on a hilltop outside the city. Jesus's spiritual movement did not disappear, however. Three days after his death, rumors spread that his body was missing, and that he had risen from the dead.

Modern historians cannot prove or disprove the vast majority of the assertions in the Gospels. What is clear, however, is that Jesus's message was an eclectic mixture of themes that were already present in Jewish thought.

The person most instrumental in taking Jesus's message to the wider Roman world was Saul of Tarsus. He started out as a devout Jew who helped persecute Christians. According to Saul, however, he was miraculously converted to Christianity on the road to Damascus and renamed Paul. As a Roman citizen who was friendly with Jews, Greeks, and Romans, Paul was the ideal man to take the Christian movement beyond Israel. Importantly, Paul chose to turn Christianity into a universal religion. In other words, not only Jews, but also Gentiles (the Jewish term for non-Jews) would be welcomed into the Church.

Paul's attempt to export Christianity to Gentile communities throughout the Mediterranean world was a dramatic success. Women, the poor, and slaves joined Christian churches in large numbers, as did members of the Romanized and Hellenized middle class. For many, Christianity's utilization of some of the characteristics of the Eastern mystery cults—such as baptism; the promotion of a close, emotional relationship between God and his worshipers; and the offer of eternal salvation—made the decision to convert to Christianity much easier.

Jews, however, often refused to join the Christian movement. Many of them did not approve of Christianity's universalism. Many also objected to Paul's willingness to downplay Hebrew traditions, such as circumcision. As a result, Christianity and Judaism increasingly followed separate paths. Some Christians even demonized the Jews.

During the second and third centuries, Christianity spread widely throughout the Roman Empire. Christians were still in the minority, however.

The Roman authorities viewed Christianity with suspicion. They were alarmed by Christianity's denial of the existence of the official pagan gods (Jewish monotheism was considered less threatening). Also worrisome was the Christians' refusal to participate in emperor-worship; their active

Figure 5.1 A Renaissance depiction of St. Peter and St. Paul. Peter holds the keys to the Kingdom of Heaven, symbolizing the powerful role of the Church in guiding Christians toward salvation. Painting by Fray Juan Sanchez Cotan.

Courtesy of Renata Sedmakova / Shutterstock.com

attempts to spread their faith; their secretive rituals; their eccentric fondness for celibacy; their occasional condemnation of material wealth, violence, and slavery; and their belief that an apocalypse would soon destroy the Roman Empire. When disasters did befall the empire, some Romans put the blame on the Christians and their refusal to honor the pagan gods.

The persecution of Christians was rare in the history of ancient Rome, but it is true that some Christian martyrs were torn limb-from-limb by wild animals in the arena. Paul himself was executed. In all likelihood, though, the government's sporadic attempts at repression, coupled with the bravery of beleaguered Christians, only increased the religion's appeal.

During the second and third centuries, Christianity became somewhat less idealistic and more worldly. Christian communities were so widespread that they required coordination, and thus bishops, elected by the various congregations under their charge, became a fixture in the Church. Only bishops had the authority to confirm new members of the faith and to ordain priests.

Why were Christians sometimes persecuted in ancient Rome?

The Triumph of Christianity

Ultimately, it would be the Emperor Constantine the Great who would be most responsible for the Christianization of the Roman Empire. Inspired partly by the Christian faith of his mother, St. Helena, Constantine became a Christian himself. In 313, he issued the Edict of Milan, which ended the persecution of Christians. Just as importantly, he appointed Christians to senior administrative jobs, made Sunday a day of rest, exempted the Christian clergy from taxation, helped to settle doctrinal disputes, and funded the construction of churches and the training of new priests. Not surprisingly, under these circumstances, the popularity of Christianity surged throughout the fourth century.

Finally, during the reign of Emperor Theodosius, in 379–395, Christianity became Rome's official religion. It was now the pagans' turn to be persecuted. Moreover, at least in the spiritual realm, Theodosius declared that the Church would be supreme over the emperor himself. Clearly, Christians had come a long way from the dark days of martyrdom!

Several trends benefited the Church in the Late Empire. As the infrastructure and bureaucracy of the imperial government disintegrated, Church officials were often the only ones left to provide needed services. This greatly improved the prestige of the Church. In addition, the Church frequently benefited from outstanding leadership, because members of the Roman elite increasingly sought high positions in the Church instead of in the government. Also, by the end of the fourth century, the Bible as we know it, including the Old and New Testaments, had taken shape after the intervention of several Church councils. It was St. Jerome who issued the definitive Latin translation of the Bible, the standardization of which greatly aided in the popularization of the Church.

In the fourth century, as Roman emperors began to spend less time in Rome itself, the bishop of Rome became the most powerful figure in the city. Given Rome's great renown, he claimed to be the most important bishop of all. In the Bible, Jesus appeared to delegate authority over the Church to one of his disciples, Peter, who was eventually executed in Rome. Later, the bishops of Rome claimed to have inherited Peter's authority. By the fifth century, the bishop of Rome was the first among equals, at least in Western Europe. He was also now known as the pope.

As Christianity spread, the first serious cracks began to appear in the movement. One of the most popular forms of heresy (i.e., a belief, or set of beliefs, that goes against the official position of the Church) was Arianism. Arius of Alexandria proposed that Jesus Christ was created by, and was subordinate to, God the Father. Arius was thus opposing the doctrine of the Trinity, which states that God the Father, Jesus Christ, and the Holy Spirit are all equal, divine, and eternal components of God as a whole. Arianism was condemned at the Council of Nicaea in 325, which had been convened by the Emperor Constantine. Arianism, however, survived for centuries.

Despite such doctrinal battles, a body of Christian literature and theology emerged that brought unity to the Church. By far the most significant early Christian writer and thinker was St. Augustine, who began as a wayward and womanizing student of classical learning, but who ended up serving as the bishop of the North African city of Hippo Regius. Augustine wrote an autobiography called *The Confessions* that brilliantly explained his own past struggles with sin and his journey toward faith. Augustine believed that all human beings are born innately sinful. To overcome our corrupted natures, we require the grace of God, transmitted through the sacraments of the Church, such as baptism and the Eucharist. Augustine identified sexual desire as one of the most sinful appetites of all. Although Augustine believed that faith should dominate over reason, he also argued that classical learning and rational inquiry can help us to unlock God's plan for our lives.

One of the most important features of early Christian thought was that it was predominantly otherworldly rather than humanistic. Classical humanism had stressed the importance of developing the full capacities of human beings, including reason, to make life better in the here and now. Christianity, on the other hand, viewed life on earth as burdensome and fleeting. Christians therefore were urged to concentrate on their faith and on the promise of eternal life.

There is no greater sign of the otherworldly nature of Christianity than the phenomenon of monasticism. Christian monks had their origins in various hermits who retreated in the third and fourth centuries from the turbulent Roman world to live in the desert or in remote mountain areas. These zealots embraced solitude and deprivation in order to escape the sins of this world and prepare themselves for the next.

In the fourth, fifth, and sixth centuries, the high esteem in which such hermits were held led to the creation of communities of dedicated Christians who took vows of chastity, poverty, and obedience. Most such communities were only for men, but some convents also appeared for women. One of the most important of the early monastic communities was the Order of Saint Benedict, created in Italy in 529. Its founding document, the Benedictine Rule, was enormously influential in the development of Christian monasticism.

Monastic life had several defining features. Monks commonly followed a schedule of daily tasks and worship services; they wore simple clothing; they did manual labor; they performed acts of charity; they sometimes worked as scholars or teachers (and during the Middle Ages acquired a virtual monopoly on advanced learning); and they served as missionaries. The monastic lifestyle represented a complete rejection of earthly pleasures, family life, self-indulgence, rational inquiry, political and civic involvement, and the accumulation of wealth. Monasteries held their property in common, and they prided themselves on rising above the standards of ordinary people, from whom they sought to be isolated.

Monks were instrumental in facilitating the spread of Christianity, which continued unabated long after the Roman Empire had ceased to exist. As a result, a chain reaction of Christianization occurred in Europe that lasted for about 1,000 years. By the time of the Crusades, in the eleventh through the thirteenth centuries, virtually all of Europe had become Christian, and paganism had largely been extinguished.

What factors explain the extraordinary spread of Christianity?

Conclusions

Although most Romans and provincials had always lived in the countryside, at the heart of Roman society and civilization had been cities. The decline of urban areas in the period of the Late Empire and after the Fall of Rome therefore signaled the end of the Roman world. Although some Roman aristocrats made an easy transition to serving as bishops and other high clergy in the Catholic Church, in most of Western and Central Europe a new elite, a new form of government, a new social system, and a new economy was soon in place. For better or worse, Germanic nobles and warlords, who were proprietors of self-sufficient agricultural estates, were Europe's new masters.

As we saw in Chapter 4, the legacy of the Roman world lived on in the form of language, culture, technology, and political ideas and institutions. Nevertheless, by 500 CE, a new era was dawning: the Middle Ages.

Key Terms for Chapter 5

Latifundia—large estates, which increasingly swallowed up the holdings of ordinary Roman farmers.

Forum—the main marketplace at the center of Roman cities.

Pater familias—father of the family. The patriarch of each Roman household theoretically enjoyed virtually unlimited authority over those living under his roof, including his wife and children.

Romanization—the uneven process by which provincials adopted elements of Roman culture.

Cicero—a Roman statesman and author, many of whose works have survived to be admired by modern readers.

Virgil—the greatest Roman poet, whose epic poem *The Aeneid* cast the Romans as Homeric heroes.

Roman roads—Roman soldiers and engineers built over 50,000 miles of well-maintained thoroughfares that helped to bind the Roman world together.

Jesus of Nazareth—according to Christians, he was the fulfillment of the Jewish faith's promise of a Messiah. Despite his execution at the hands of Roman and Jewish authorities, Jesus's message spread quickly throughout the Roman world.

Bible—the books of the Bible, as Christians know them today, coalesced under the influence of Church authorities in the fourth century.

Monk—a devout religious person who separates himself from society in order to concentrate on the cultivation of his faith. The female equivalent is called a nun.

Review Questions for Chapter 5

1. The state-endorsed version of traditional Roman religion appears to have left many Romans dissatisfied. Imagine yourself as a recent convert to Christianity, and write a letter to a pagan friend in which you provide at least three arguments for the superiority of your faith.
2. One reason that people today demonstrate so much interest in the Roman world is because the behavior and attitudes of the Romans appear surprisingly modern, at least in certain ways. Describe two ways in which daily life and/or the Roman approach to gender relations was arguably modern. Then describe two ways in which the Romans were decidedly different from us in their behavior or their thinking.
3. Although the Romans are known primarily as great empire-builders, their accomplishments in the arts and sciences were notable. Describe in detail three of the Romans' non-political achievements.
4. Roman roads were particularly important in joining together the Roman world. Imagine yourself as a traveler on one of these roads. Write a letter to a close relative in which you describe at least three experiences during your journey that symbolized for you *Romanitas*, or Romanness.
5. Christianity brought many cultural changes to the Roman world. Monasticism, in particular, represented a rejection of many of the values and practices that had helped to define Roman culture. Describe at least three ways in which a Christian monk lived or thought differently from a respectable Roman citizen before the advent of Christianity.

Further Reading

Aldrete, Gregory S. *Daily Life in the Roman City: Rome, Pompeii, and Ostia*. Norman, OK: University of Oklahoma Press. 2008.

Alföldy, Géza. *The Social History of Rome*. New York: Routledge. 2015.

Beard, Mary. *The Fires of Vesuvius: Pompeii Lost and Found*. Cambridge, MA: Belknap Press. 2010.

Brown, Peter. *The Rise of Western Christendom: Triumph and Diversity, A.D. 200–1000*. Malden, MA: Wiley-Blackwell. 2013.

D'Ambra, Eve. *Roman Women*. Cambridge: Cambridge University Press. 2007.

Ferguson, Everett. *Backgrounds of Early Christianity*. Grand Rapids, MI: Eerdmans. 2009.

Gonzalez, Justo L. *The Story of Christianity: Volume I: The Early Church to the Reformation*. New York: HarperOne. 2010.

Johnson, Luke Timothy. *Among the Gentiles: Greco-Roman Religion and Christianity*. New Haven, CT: Yale University Press. 2010.

Rodgers, Nigel. *Life in Ancient Rome: People and Places*. London: Hermes House. 2014.

Rüpke, Jörg. *Religion of the Romans*. Cambridge: Polity Press. 2009.

Skinner, Marilyn B. *Sexuality in Greek and Roman Culture*. Malden, MA: Wiley-Blackwell. 2014.

Turcan, Robert. *The Gods of Ancient Rome: Religion in Everyday Life From Archaic to Imperial Times*. New York: Routledge. 2013.

Ward-Perkins, Bryan. *The Fall of Rome and the End of Civilization*. Oxford: Oxford University Press. 2006.

6 The Middle Ages
Politics and War, 500–1300

Introduction

It is a common misconception that the thousand-year period of the Middle Ages (roughly 500 CE to 1500 CE) is synonymous with the Dark Ages, and that, with few exceptions, it was an era characterized by disorder, warfare, plague, poverty, ignorance, and superstition. Only the first half of the medieval period, however, could plausibly be labeled the Dark Ages, and in fact many historians have chosen to discard the term altogether, and for good reasons. While it is true that, during the Middle Ages as a whole, the levels of political order, trade, material comfort, learning, and humane and rational thought never matched the high points of ancient Greece and Rome, it is also indisputable that considerable progress was made by medieval men and women. Some of their accomplishments still impress us today. The towering Gothic cathedrals that are found across Europe are perhaps the most familiar manifestation of medieval brilliance. More important, as we shall see, are the other, less tangible achievements of the Middle Ages. It is no exaggeration to say that medieval institutions and ideas helped to set the stage for modern Western Civilization. Indeed, the West as we know it is built on a medieval foundation.

Another misconception that many people have about the Middle Ages is the idea that medieval society was cut off from the rest of the world. This is far from the case. Several external influences on the core areas of the West are especially noteworthy. One such influence was the Byzantine Empire, also called Byzantium, which lasted roughly 1,000 years in Turkey, the Middle East, and southeastern Europe. Because of its distinct Greco-Roman culture, it served as a repository for various elements of classical scholarship and literature that Western Europeans later rediscovered. Byzantium was also a hub for East-West trade as well as the headquarters for Orthodox Christianity, a strain of Christian worship that vied with Catholicism. Another external influence on medieval Europe was Islam, a religion founded in Arabia in the seventh century CE, and which quickly expanded its reach into parts of Europe, producing a defensive reaction. The Crusades, which aimed to wrest control of the Holy Land from the Muslims, were largely unsuccessful.

Despite the hostility between Christians and Muslims, in many instances the two groups found ways to coexist peacefully and profitably.

We have remarked before on the fact that Western Civilization today is the result of the blending of a remarkable and diverse array of ingredients. This is true of Western culture in the Middle Ages too, despite the era's reputation for insularity and ignorance.

The Barbarian Legacy

One of the strongest elements in the new civilization that we label as medieval was the culture of the so-called barbarians who had conquered ancient Rome. One thing about barbarian culture must be made very clear: the tribes, which historians often describe as representing the highest level of social organization achieved by the barbarians, were unstable, flexible entities. Germanic tribes, such as the Franks, Burgundians, Vandals, Visigoths, and Ostrogoths, tended to be ruled by a royal family that claimed divine descent but whose power was in fact based on a reputation for military glory. Thus, when military disaster befell the tribe, its leading family would often fall from grace, and sometimes the members of the tribe would disperse. Assassinations and infighting also plagued many tribes. Moreover, barbarian kings had uncertain powers, not unlike medieval kings. All these factors made tribal unity difficult to achieve and almost impossible to maintain. Non-Germanic tribes—such as the Huns and various Celtic and Slavic groups—also tended to form identities that were opportunistic and fleeting. Thus, any notion that the barbarians were formed into modern nations or states is simply wrong.

The Germanic tribes were warlike, but they also practiced agriculture, metalworking, and crafts. Their religion was polytheistic, as in pagan Greece and Rome, and it centered on outdoor worship and the veneration of spirits in nature. Priests and storytellers were held in high esteem. Women were valued for their spiritual insight and for their ability to predict the future. Germanic law was customary rather than written, although often a form of Roman law was selectively applied.

Germanic social organization was distinctive. Barbarian society was unabashedly male-dominated, and some men even had several wives, but women were still prized as workers and for their role in family life. Women even cheered on their menfolk in battle. An important social institution for men was the *comitatus*, or war band, that fought alongside the king or chieftain. Not surprisingly, a man's social status was usually based on his military skill, and battlefield victories were also the best route to obtaining greater wealth in the form of land, cattle, and slaves. A common custom that solidified alliances and friendships was gift-giving.

The forging of a medieval worldview among the barbarians was facilitated by the spread of Christianity. Often Christianity first arrived in barbarian lands in the form of bold missionaries who strove to convert kings or tribal chieftains. Alternatively, the conversion of royal or elite Germanic women was frequently a path to winning over an entire tribe. The power of the Christian God to bring victory on the battlefield, the usefulness of Christian learning and bureaucratic skills, and the support that Christian theology gave to kingly authority, were vital factors that persuaded barbarian leaders to adopt the new faith. St. Patrick, who converted much of Ireland to Catholic Christianity in the fifth century, first targeted tribal kings who then required their subjects to undergo baptism.

The formalities of Christian conversion were customarily followed up by a drawn-out process of indoctrination that familiarized former pagans with Christian theology, the Bible, the sacraments, and the need for confession of sins. Usually, stern consequences were applied to elements of the population that rejected all or part of the Christian message. At the same time, however, compromises were made with paganism. Pagan holidays became Christian holy days. Pagan gods were sometimes recast as Christian saints, both male and female. Pagan temples were re-sanctified as Christian churches. All in all, Christian missionaries pursued new converts with incredible courage and tenacity but also with remarkable savvy and versatility. The result was the creation of thousands of distinct local interpretations of the faith that nevertheless were similar enough to merit the collective term Catholic Christianity.

By the eleventh and twelfth centuries, the Catholic Church had spread as far north as Scandinavia, and in the tenth through thirteenth centuries German conquerors, settlers, and missionaries spread the faith in Poland, Hungary, the Baltic states, and other parts of Eastern Europe. The Church had thus become very nearly "catholic," or universal, in scope. Virtually all of Western, Central, and Southern Europe—and large parts of Eastern Europe—were under its sway. In the process, many barbarians were convinced to moderate their allegedly primitive, warlike ways, and to partake in Christendom, which provided medieval Europe with the closest thing to a common identity that it would ever possess.

What were some of the features of barbarian life?

The Catholic Church: The Great Unifier of Medieval Europe

The Catholic Church, based in Rome, was by far the most powerful institution during the Middle Ages. The papacy provided a strong, centralized government for the Church. The pope presided over a bureaucracy; a large number of monasteries and convents; hundreds of bishops and cardinals; hundreds of thousands of priests, monks, and nuns; a tax collection system; and a series of courts. The medieval Church also claimed a monopoly on higher education and scholarship as well as control over most charitable organizations. At times, the pope even interfered directly in the political administration of Catholic areas. Meanwhile, attendance at Mass, confession, pilgrimage, veneration of the saints, and prayer were common features of everyday life.

The secret to the success of the Catholic Church lay in a curious combination of centralization and standardization, on one hand, and flexibility and adaptability, on the other. For example, the Catholic Church did a superb job of enforcing a reasonable degree of theological and liturgical uniformity across Europe. Simultaneously, in its relationship with the political, civil, and military power structure, the Church proved surprisingly flexible. At times, the Church succeeded in imposing its will on political leaders. At other times, though, Church leaders such as bishops and cardinals were appointed by kings or leading nobles, and the Church was thus subordinated to the secular government.

A number of medieval popes played particularly influential roles in the history of the Church. Among these, Gregory VII, who ruled as pope from 1073 to 1085, and who was later raised to sainthood, stands out as one of the most effective champions of the papacy and of Church reform.

In the tenth century, a movement for ecclesiastical reform had begun at a monastery in Cluny, France. Its goals were ambitious: to reduce Church corruption; to encourage higher moral standards among the clergy, and in particular to insist on clerical celibacy; to discourage warfare; and to make the Church less susceptible to monarchical and noble influences. This last point was critical. In the tenth century, many bishops and abbots (the leaders of monasteries) were appointed not by the pope but by kings and powerful lords. Even the pope was effectively chosen by Italian aristocrats, at least until the College of Cardinals gained the right to elect the pope in 1059. Cluniacs believed that all of this secular influence was extremely harmful. They proposed that, in the future, all ecclesiastical appointments be made by Church officials, not by laymen.

Pope Gregory VII, a devout, austere, and somewhat stubborn man, was a firm believer in papal power and in the broad authority of the Church. He therefore took a brave stand on behalf of the Cluniacs' ideals. He strongly condemned priests and bishops who married. More importantly, he fought for years with the German Emperor Henry IV over the practice of lay investiture.

What was lay investiture? Traditionally, in Germany and elsewhere, the monarch had invested new bishops with the symbols of their authority, making it clear that bishops were beholden to the secular government. Gregory believed that only the pope and his designated representatives should have the power to confirm new bishops in their offices. In 1076, as a result of this disagreement, Emperor Henry IV arranged for some of his most loyal bishops to repudiate Gregory's authority, and Gregory excommunicated Henry in response. He also removed Henry from Germany's throne. A civil war began to brew in Germany, and Henry came close to being overthrown. Desperate, Henry traveled to Canossa, Italy, where the pope was staying. By groveling barefoot in the snow for three days, by fasting, and by beseeching the pope for forgiveness, Henry succeeded in convincing a dubious Gregory to lift his sentence of excommunication.

The story does not end there, however. Henry's abasement was a symbolic victory for the pope, but it involved no real resolution of the problem of lay investiture. Gregory later tried to resume the battle over lay investiture, but this time Henry simply marched on Rome, drove Gregory into exile, and helped to choose a new pope.

It may seem, therefore, that Gregory VII's career as Pontiff was a failure, but his determined stand against lay investiture ultimately bore fruit. In 1122, Pope Calixtus II and Emperor Henry V (Henry IV's successor) announced a compromise, called the Concordat of Worms. Bishops in Germany would still be subordinate to the emperor, but they would be chosen by the Church and would receive the symbols of their spiritual authority from representatives of the pope. This was an important result for two reasons.

One, the independence of the Church from secular meddling was greatly enhanced. In fact, under future popes, such as Innocent III, who ruled from 1198 to 1216, the powers, wealth, and independence of the papacy and the Church would reach unprecedented heights.

The other reason why the Concordat was so significant, however, was almost certainly a surprise to the Church itself. The weakening of the emperor's control over the Church in Germany had the effect of reducing the overall power of the emperor and increasing the power of various regional and local lords. The net result of the Concordat, therefore, was to weaken German unity. The battle over lay investiture did not produce, therefore, the clear victory that the Church had been seeking. In some ways, in fact, the nobles emerged as the real winners.

> *In the Middle Ages, what was the relationship between the Catholic Church and secular political authorities?*

Orthodox Christianity, the Byzantine Empire, and Other Limitations on the Power and Scope of the Catholic Church

For most of the Middle Ages, the relative independence of the Catholic Church from secular control contrasted remarkably with the strong role that the Byzantine emperor played in the Orthodox Church, a separate form of Christianity popular in parts of Eastern Europe and in the eastern Mediterranean. The belief of the Byzantine emperors that they should play a leading role in the Orthodox Church is sometimes controversially referred to as Caesaropapism. In effect, the Byzantine Empire was a theocratic state, although there was also a figure known as the Patriarch of Constantinople, who played a role somewhat analogous to that of the pope in the West.

In the long run, disagreements between the Catholic Church and the Orthodox Church over a variety of doctrinal and liturgical issues made reconciliation impossible. In 1054, the Catholic Church formally excommunicated the Patriarch of Constantinople, who returned the favor by excommunicating the pope's legate, and from that point on the estrangement between the two churches became more or less permanent. The western border of the Byzantine Empire became, in effect, the eastern frontier of Catholic Christianity. Church leaders made some efforts at bridging the gap, but these were seriously undermined in 1204, when Catholics sacked the city of Constantinople and imposed a Latin Empire on its inhabitants. Even today, Catholics and Orthodox Christians do not see eye to eye.

Undeterred by the formal split between Catholicism and Orthodoxy in 1054, Byzantine missionaries continued to expand the Orthodox faith by sharing it with many Slavic peoples, such as the Russians, Ukrainians, Serbs, and Bulgarians. As a result, these peoples adopted Orthodoxy, and they began to use the Cyrillic alphabet, which had been devised for them by two Byzantine holy men. Even today, these Slavic peoples remain primarily Orthodox, and they continue to write in Cyrillic script.

In some ways, the Byzantine Empire had been born as early as 324 CE, when the Roman Emperor Constantine decided to build a new capital city, called Constantinople, for the richer, more populated eastern half of the empire. Constantinople, a cosmopolitan port city located on the Bosphorus Strait that connects the Mediterranean to the Black Sea, would serve for 1,000 years as the center point of the Byzantine Empire, as well as the headquarters of the Orthodox religion. At its height in the sixth century, Byzantium ruled modern Turkey, as well as Greece, Italy, Syria, Israel/Palestine, and parts of North Africa, Spain, and the Balkans.

The Byzantine emperors called themselves Roman, and they struggled to uphold Roman traditions, but it is probably more accurate to think of Byzantium as essentially Greek. Greek was the common language spoken by the elite. Byzantine scholars also took care to preserve the intellectual heritage of ancient Greece. In addition, the Byzantines constructed a political system that granted the vast majority of political power to the emperor. This form of government was heavily influenced by the history of religiously backed monarchies during the (Greek-dominated) Hellenistic Age. While the Byzantines called their country The Empire of the Romans, therefore, Western Europeans, perhaps more perceptively, called it The Empire of the Greeks.

Although Byzantium was wealthy and powerful, it faced several threats. Religious divisions within Orthodoxy threatened to tear Byzantine society apart. Epidemic diseases periodically ravaged the empire's crowded cities. Just as importantly, long-running military campaigns waged against Germanic kings and Vikings; against Huns, Avars, and Slavs in the Balkans; and against Persians, Arabs, and Turks in the Middle East, drained the resources of the Byzantine state. Much territory was lost. Luckily, though, the capital at Constantinople was heavily fortified and thus managed to repulse almost all attacks. As a matter of fact, according to some historians, Byzantium's military successes, spread over more than 1,000 years, were a critical factor in the history of Western Civilization, since the Byzantines provided a sort of defensive perimeter that protected Western Europe from Persian, Arab, and Turkish assaults. Simultaneously, the Byzantines provided, in Constantinople, a convenient venue for trade and cultural exchange with the East.

One of the most noteworthy of Byzantine emperors was Justinian, who ruled from 527 to 565. Justinian was a great conqueror and builder, a zealous defender of Orthodox Christianity, and a devoted husband to his strong-willed and intelligent wife Theodora, who ruled as a virtual co-emperor. But Justinian is best remembered today for the Justinian Code, also known as the *Corpus Juris Civilis*, or Body of Civil Law. The Code was a massive and systematic compilation of Roman laws and legal commentary assembled at the emperor's request. For the next 1,500 years, and counting, it would serve as one of the most important influences on the development of the European legal tradition.

In 1453, Byzantium's luck finally ran out. The Ottoman Turks, described in Chapter 8, succeeded in occupying Constantinople and destroying the Byzantine state. The Byzantine era therefore came to an ignominious end.

Besides Orthodox Christianity, headquartered in Byzantium, another limitation on the power and scope of the Catholic Church in the Middle Ages was the occasional appearance of heretical reform movements, some of which enjoyed considerable popularity. The Waldensians were a group of Catholics, spread out across Europe, who rejected material wealth, preferring to give their money to the poor. Laymen who believed in the Waldensian message also took it upon themselves to preach the Gospel, even though this was an activity normally reserved for priests and monks. Not surprisingly, the Waldensians were harshly persecuted.

A much more radical and dangerous heretical movement emerged in twelfth- and thirteenth-century France, called Albigensianism, or Catharism. The Cathars rejected some of the principal tenets of Catholic theology. They associated the Hebrew God of the Old Testament with evil and the desires of the flesh. They also denied that Jesus Christ had ever taken human form. Perhaps most distressing from the perspective of Catholic leaders was the Cathars' belief that the Church itself was wicked and corrupt. Pope Innocent III initiated a sustained and bloody crusade against the Cathars in the early thirteenth century. Their movement was eventually eradicated, but only after a wave of persecution had washed over southern France for more than a century.

The desire to stamp out Catharism caused the Church to found a new institution: the Inquisition, which primarily took the form of special courts that targeted heresy. Persons accused of heresy had few legal protections. They were sometimes tortured, within prescribed limits. Executions were rare, but common penalties included public humiliation and the forfeiture of property. The goal was not to inflict punishment, however, but to save the soul of the accused.

Although heresy represented a considerable danger to the Church, the Catholic hierarchy was generally successful in combating it. Until the Protestant Reformation in the sixteenth century, the doctrines and the liturgy of the Catholic Church were seldom openly questioned, at least in Catholic areas—and those who did repudiate Catholic beliefs or practices faced dire consequences.

Besides Orthodox Christians, the only large group of Europeans who steadfastly rejected Catholic Christianity throughout the Middle Ages was the Jews. Before the Crusades, the Jews were generally tolerated, but starting with the First Crusade in the eleventh century, Christians' hostility toward nonbelievers increased, and this poisoned Christian-Jewish relations.

Why were Jews so often hated? Since Jews were barred from many professions and from owning land, they often became merchants or moneylenders, and their financial success led to fierce resentment. In addition, because Jesus had been executed partly at the instigation of the Jewish hierarchy in Jerusalem, medieval Christians commonly condemned the Jews as Christ-killers. Wild rumors also circulated in the Middle Ages that the Jews practiced bizarre rituals that involved sacrificing Christian children, among other outrages. Responsible Church authorities condemned such fabrications, but many ordinary Catholics believed that Jews were in league with the Devil. As a result, Jews were often segregated, denied access to many professions and offices, required to pay special taxes, permitted only minimal social contact with Christians, and otherwise persecuted. In extreme cases, Jewish communities were simply slaughtered, and Jews were also periodically expelled from countries such as England and France.

Catholic Christianity was consistent in one respect: it prized conformity over tolerance. The Jews were not the only victims of Catholic persecution, but they were among the most frequent targets. It is nothing less than astounding, therefore, that European Jews were able to sustain a vibrant Jewish culture in the midst of such harsh repression.

How did the Catholic Church respond to heresy?

Feudalism and Medieval Warfare

Feudalism, a word unknown in the Middle Ages, refers to a hierarchical social system common, although not universal, in the medieval period that traded personal loyalty and military service in return for grants of land or financial support. The dominant member of a feudal relationship was known as a lord, and his subordinate was known as a vassal. (Thus, feudalism can also be referred to as vassalage.) The vassal would take an oath of fealty, that is, loyalty and obedience, to his lord, and in return he would receive a fief, usually an allotment of land, including control over the peasants who worked that land. The income from this fief would allow the vassal to support himself and to purchase military equipment and horses with which he would discharge his military obligations to his lord.

Although feudalism seems to have been inspired partly by the tradition of the Germanic war band, arguably the first vassals were counts, who were regional governors appointed by Germanic kings. These counts received control over vast estates in return for faithful service to the king, including fighting in the king's army. Over time, the position of these counts tended to become hereditary. Eventually, there arose not only counts, but dukes, earls, and barons. In addition, high Church officials, such as bishops, archbishops, abbots, and cardinals, sometimes served as either lords or vassals.

To make matters even more complicated, sometimes vassals would choose to subdivide their fiefs and take on vassals of their own. These lower-ranking vassals were often known as knights, and they did much of the fighting in medieval wars. In the Early Middle Ages knights were relatively humble soldiers, but by the Late Middle Ages they were usually landowners and were thought of as junior members of the nobility.

What made this feudal system even more confusing was the fact that sometimes a vassal, seeking to expand his fiefs, would acquire more than one lord. In this case, he might find it necessary to identify a liege lord to whom he owed primary obedience. Elaborate codes of honor were created, and sanctified by the Church, in order to try to prevent lords and vassals from taking advantage of their feudal roles. Nonetheless, conflicts were commonplace. Vassals' positions were surprisingly strong because, once a vassal occupied a fief, especially one that centered on a fortified castle, it could take a considerable amount of military force to dislodge him.

The feudal system provided basic order to large parts of medieval Europe. In many areas feudal lords, not kings, were the main providers of legal protection, physical security, and employment to ordinary Europeans. Nevertheless, feudalism was an *ad hoc* system, in which, for all practical purposes, each lord and each vassal possessed as much power and wealth as he could take from others. This produced massive instability and uncertainty.

Predictably, many kings argued that the centralization of power in their hands was the surest way to overcome the chaos of feudalism. And it is true that the rise of effective royal governments eventually spelled the end of feudalism, although it took many centuries for this process to unfold.

Undeniably, warfare was a way of life in the Middle Ages. Most nobles and knights had inherited from their Germanic ancestors a love of combat. Military valor was seen as one of the highest virtues, and success on the battlefield was an indispensable source of glory, power, and riches. Chivalry, the set of ideals to which nobles and knights subscribed, discussed in Chapter 7, was essentially a warrior's code.

Even when medieval nobles and knights were not fighting, they spent much of their time hunting or participating in colorful and dangerous tournaments. They might also play strategy games, such as chess. Thus, even their leisure activities revolved around martial themes.

Although nobles and knights were in almost universal agreement that warfare was honorable and desirable, many other members of medieval society disagreed. Peasants, townspeople, and clergymen were all frequently victimized by senseless violence. Church authorities repeatedly tried to reduce the amount of fighting done by nobles and knights. The Church sometimes formed protection societies, and it published decrees and organized

Figure 6.1 The mounted knight was the mainstay of medieval warfare.
Slawomir Fajer/Shutterstock.

agreements to try to limit when fighting could occur and who could be legitimately targeted. The most ambitious attempts to regulate medieval warfare were the Catholic Church's Peace of God and Truce of God movements, which achieved limited success.

Although infantrymen and archers played important roles on medieval battlefields, by far the most prestigious warriors were the mounted knights, armed usually with a sword and a spear or lance. The role of the cavalry had already increased in the days of the Late Roman Empire. Beginning in the eighth century, the introduction of the stirrup made cavalry tactics even more effective. The only downside to mounted warfare, from the knight's perspective, was the expense of the armor, weapons, training, and horses that it required. Thus, in order to make the aggressive, violent lifestyle of the medieval aristocracy feasible, a huge fraction of the meager economic resources of medieval society had to be diverted to fund military needs. Thus, warfare was a source of great profit in the Middle Ages, but it was also the leading cause of the miserable poverty that afflicted most Europeans.

What is the relationship between feudalism and medieval warfare?

The Kingdom of the Franks, and the Reign of Charlemagne

After the collapse of the Roman Empire, a number of barbarian kingdoms were formed. Most were short-lived, but not the Kingdom of the Franks, after which modern France is named.

Around 500, the first true Frankish king, named Clovis, guided by his wife Clotild, decided to convert to Catholicism. The Kingdom of the Franks quickly forged a close relationship with the Catholic Church and the papacy. Based on its alliance with the Church and on its military strength, the Kingdom of the Franks eventually expanded to include all of modern France, Belgium, the Netherlands, and Luxembourg, plus parts of Germany, Switzerland, and northern Italy.

From the reign of Clovis until 751, the Frankish kingdom was led by the Merovingian dynasty. The Merovingian kings constructed an effective system of regional government, led by counts and dukes. Counts presided over tax collection, law enforcement, the courts, and the recruitment of soldiers, while dukes held major military commands. Latin was the language of politics, justice, and administration.

The accomplishments of the Merovingians were impressive, but their kingdom suffered from two critical weaknesses. First, Frankish inheritance law required the king's domain to be divided at his death among all his sons, which caused considerable confusion, rivalry, and violence. Second, the Merovingian kings gradually became dependent on the support of their highest-ranking subordinate, known as the Mayor of the Palace. Starting in the seventh century, this position was monopolized by members of the Carolingian family: Pepin I, Pepin II, Charles Martel, and finally Pepin III.

In 751, Pepin III cunningly made a pact with the pope to overthrow the Merovingian king. Thus, the Carolingian dynasty was born. In 754, Pope Stephen II personally anointed Pepin as *rex et sacerdos* (king and priest).

The Carolingians made alliances not just with the Church, but also with the landed aristocracy. The Carolingians were among the first to grant fiefs, and they stressed the importance of a well-trained, well-equipped cavalry in the Frankish army. Thus, the Carolingians laid the foundations for some of the central elements of feudalism and medieval warfare.

The most powerful Carolingian ruler by far was Charlemagne (Charles the Great), who reigned from 768 to 814. Charlemagne was unusually tall at six feet four. He was also outgoing and intelligent. Above all, though, he was an enormously successful conqueror. He brought most of Western and Central Europe under Frankish control, including new territories in northern Spain, Germany, and Italy.

Like his predecessors, Charlemagne used counts and other royal officials to administer his domain, but their reliability was always doubtful. Charlemagne tried to keep a close eye on his counts by sending deputations of trusted officials to check up on them. Charlemagne's empire was, however, ultimately more a set of personal relationships and alliances than a state.

On Christmas Day in the year 800, Charlemagne, who was visiting Rome, was crowned Roman Emperor by Pope Leo III. It was an important turning point for the Carolingian Empire and for Catholic Christianity. For Charlemagne, the title of Roman Emperor was a clear source of legitimation for his rule. Perhaps even more significant, though, was the pope's leading role in Charlemagne's coronation. This emphasized the sacred character of Frankish kingship, and to some churchmen it also implied that the pope was superior to the emperor. After all, if the pope could grant the imperial crown, then presumably he could also take it away. Be that as it may, Charlemagne, as a staunchly Catholic monarch, sought the conversion of all of his subjects to Catholicism, and he utilized many bishops, abbots, priests, and monks in his royal administration.

One of the most impressive achievements of Charlemagne's reign was the Carolingian Renaissance, which involved Charlemagne's patronage of artists, writers, architects, and scholars. Primarily, Charlemagne was interested in creating schools that could train and civilize the next generation of clerics, bureaucrats, and military officers. Charlemagne was also keen to improve his subjects' knowledge of and appreciation for scripture and Christian traditions. The head of this civilizing effort was Alcuin, an English scholar and educator.

Thanks to the Carolingian Renaissance, greater effort was put into copying and preserving ancient texts. Many Greek and Roman manuscripts would not have survived to this day were it not for the work of Carolingian scholars. In addition, it was during the Carolingian Renaissance that some of our modern writing conventions, such as capitalization and spacing between words, became widespread. These innovations lastingly improved the legibility and accessibility of the written word.

It was in Charlemagne's realm that the essential features of medieval civilization flowed together for the first time: Catholic Christianity, Germanic traditions, the Greek and Roman heritage, and feudalism. The political order that Charlemagne had forged, though, did not long outlast him. By the middle of the ninth century, Charlemagne's three grandsons had divided the empire between them. It was not long before internal conflict, combined with external pressures, produced the complete collapse of the Carolingian regime.

The external threats facing the Carolingians were formidable. Repeated invasions and raids by Muslims to the south, Vikings (or Northmen) to the north, and Magyars (Hungarians) to the east brought the Carolingian Empire to its knees. The Vikings were especially fierce. Their opportunistic plundering of Carolingian villages, towns, and especially monasteries and convents, was a complex military challenge that overwhelmed the Carolingian monarchy. Needing protection from these marauding outsiders, Europeans turned increasingly to their local lords. Feudalism, rather than strong, centralized monarchical government, was confirmed as the dominant political system of the Middle Ages.

Which parts of Europe did Emperor Charlemagne control?

The Rise of Islam

In the seventh century, a powerful new faith developed in what is today Saudi Arabia. Its leader was a man named Muhammad, a caravan trader in the city of Mecca. Around the age of 40, Muhammad asserted that he was visited by the angel Gabriel, who revealed to him that he had been chosen as God's last and definitive prophet. Muhammad soon began to preach to his neighbors about the new religion of Islam, or submission to God. At the time, most Arabs were pagans who believed in many gods. In 622, therefore, Muhammad and his followers were expelled from Mecca because their monotheistic religion offended traditionalists. Nevertheless, Islam continued to grow in popularity, and in 630 Muhammad was able to conquer Mecca with a large army. By his death in 632, Muhammad had triumphed over all of the Arab tribes living around Mecca, bringing them under his authority and converting them to Islam.

Muhammad preached that there was only one God, called Allah, and that many past prophets had provided insight into his nature. In fact, even the Jewish prophets and Jesus Christ are considered by Muslims to have been messengers of God. Muslims also believe, however, that Muhammad's teachings supersede all that came before.

In the 650s, Islam's holy book, the *Quran*, was written down. Within it, and also in the *hadith*, which were collections of Muhammad's spiritual wisdom and practical advice, a complete plan was provided for how a Muslim was to live, and how a Muslim society was to be run. This plan

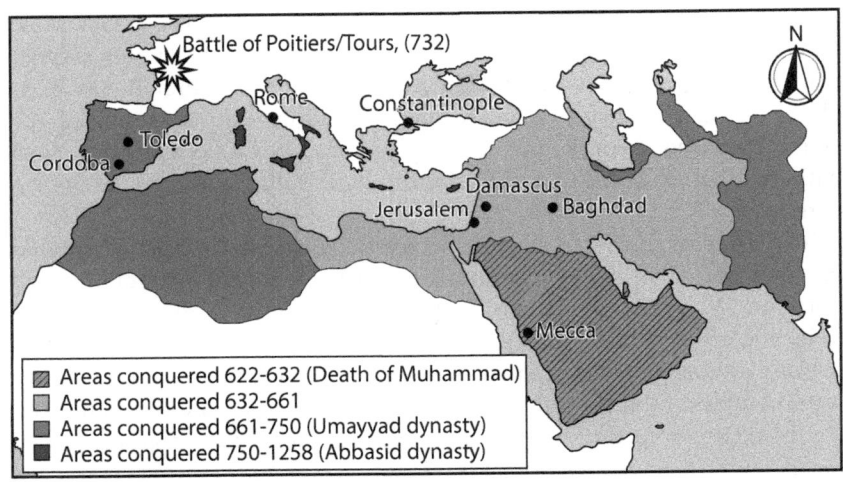

Map 6.1 The expansion of Islam.

included explicit instructions for how Muslims were to fast, pray, give alms to the poor, avoid pork and alcohol, visit Mecca as pilgrims, and perform other religious duties. It also described how women were to submit to men, sometimes in polygynous marriages, although women's ability to own property was protected.

Importantly, the *Quran* contains the outline of Sharia law, a legal system based on God's will as expressed by Muhammad. Muslims believe, like Jews and Christians, in the importance of honesty, piety, charity, self-control, and moral purity, but they also tend to believe in a close alliance between religious and political authority. For many years, in fact, Muslims were led by caliphs, who wielded both religious and secular power, since they claimed to be Muhammad's successors. Eventually, though, the political power of the caliphs waned. Alternatively, some monarchs simply appropriated the title of caliph for themselves. A portion of modern Muslims would like to reintroduce a form of caliphate, based on Sharia law, because they feel that today's secular rulers of Muslim states are not sufficiently devoted to traditional Islam.

Muslims believe that those who follow Islamic precepts, honor Allah, and engage in *jihad*—that is, struggle, in the broadest possible sense, including the struggle to live righteously—will experience, after their deaths, physical and spiritual pleasures in paradise. Those who do not follow the straight path of Islam, on the other hand, will be consigned to hell. Nevertheless, Islam does not necessarily persecute nonbelievers, much less seek their annihilation. Historically, Arab Muslims, and later on the Ottoman Turks, respected Christians and Jews. Members of these faith communities who lived in Muslim lands were encouraged to convert and were in some respects treated as second-class citizens, but they were not massacred or expelled, as sometimes happened to Jews and Muslims in the West. Primarily, the attitude of early Muslims to non-Muslims was a fervent desire to conquer them, and thus early Islam fostered expansionism and nearly continuous war.

In the seventh and eighth centuries, Arab Muslims, under a succession of powerful caliphs, proved enormously successful in expanding the domain under their control, establishing, in effect, one of the greatest and most far-flung empires in world history. They conquered Egypt and the rest of North Africa, Spain, Sicily, Syria, Israel/Palestine, modern Iraq, Persia, Afghanistan, Pakistan, western India, and parts of Turkey. Their capital moved from Mecca, to Damascus, to Baghdad, and the Arabs' language and culture were popularized as never before. The Byzantines were only able to hang on to Constantinople with great difficulty. Moreover, in 732, Frankish warriors under Charles Martel barely managed to defeat an Arab thrust into Western Europe. They did so at the Battle of Poitiers, also known as the Battle of Tours, an event that some historians see as a critical turning point in the history of Western Civilization. Historical experts are divided, though, on whether the Arab force at Poitiers represented an advance guard for a Muslim invasion of Europe or was merely a raiding party with far more limited objectives. Be that as it may, many Christians were shaken to the core by the looming threat that Islam seemed to pose.

In 750, the Abbasid dynasty of caliphs succeeded the Umayyad dynasty. Under the Abbasids, the Arab empire reached its greatest territorial extent. The Abbasids brilliantly blended the cultures of the great societies under their rule, showing tremendous respect, in particular, for the civilizations of Persia and ancient Greece. When medieval Europe intensified its interest in Aristotle in the twelfth century, this was partly because it had recently received some of the great Greek philosopher's works from the Arabs, who had preserved and expanded on them. In short, much of the best artistic, philosophical, literary, scientific, medical, and mathematical work of the Middle Ages was done by Muslim Arabs.

What are some of the similarities and differences between Islam and Christianity?

The Crusades

When the Arabs first advanced into Europe in the eighth and ninth centuries, moving through Spain, briefly into France, and obtaining control of Sicily and other Mediterranean islands, Europeans failed to come together to resist them. Most Europeans were too caught up in interminable feudal bloodletting to contemplate a united front against Islam.

By the eleventh and twelfth centuries, as we shall see, Europe was a very different place. Cities and trade had expanded, literacy and learning were beginning to flourish, and royal governments were asserting their authority over nobles and knights. Flush with self-confidence, the Europeans were in a position to expand the area under their control. They were also in a position to take on the Muslims, whose heathen faith the Church had always condemned.

By the end of the twelfth century, Corsica, Sardinia, and Sicily, along with large parts of Spain, had been wrested from Muslim control. The *Reconquista* (Reconquest) in Spain provided a particularly compelling model of how a holy war could be fought.

Especially galling to Christians in this era was the fact that Muslims—in this case the Seljuk Turks—were still in control of Jerusalem and the Holy Land. On rare occasions, the Turks had even sponsored discrimination and violence against Christian pilgrims visiting Israel/Palestine.

In 1095, Pope Urban II addressed the Council of Clermont, encouraging his listeners to join a righteous effort to expel the Turks from Byzantine lands and, most importantly, from Jerusalem. He cited lurid stories about torture, rape, desecration and destruction of churches, and massacres of Christians. Furthermore, he promised any noble or knight who volunteered to go on crusade virtually automatic entrance into heaven.

Many European warriors, and some ordinary peasants and townsmen, responded positively to Urban's appeal. Undoubtedly, numerous crusaders believed the exaggerated stories about the misrule of the Seljuk Turks. In addition, however, it is clear that many Europeans saw the Crusades as a great opportunity for glory, adventure, and self-enrichment. At the same time, European monarchs were quite happy to send wave after wave of troublesome nobles and knights to Israel/Palestine to be killed in battle. The papacy, meanwhile, viewed the whole phenomenon of the Crusades as a boon to its prestige and authority, as a means to channel Europeans' violent impulses in a godly direction, and as a way to promote reconciliation, on Catholic terms, with Orthodox Christians. In the final analysis, therefore, many in Europe saw ways to gain advantage from the Crusades, spiritually and otherwise. It was not long before thousands had eagerly joined the effort.

The First Crusade, from 1095 to 1099, was by far the most successful. By amassing a Christian army of up to 100,000 men, it defeated the Seljuk Turks and seized control of Jerusalem and the Holy Land. Four Christian kingdoms were carved out of the areas conquered by the crusaders. The Second Crusade, from 1147 to 1149, was an abject failure. The Third Crusade, from 1189 to 1192, aimed to take control of Jerusalem from Saladin, a masterful and chivalrous Muslim commander who had recently conquered the city. Although the crusaders won some impressive victories, Jerusalem remained in Muslim hands. The Fourth Crusade, from 1202 to 1204, was a shameful farce. Far from advancing the interests of Christendom, the crusaders simply sacked several Christian cities, including Constantinople. After this debacle, Europeans' crusading zeal understandably ebbed.

In hindsight, it may appear that the Crusades were a failure, and in simple terms they were: Jerusalem and the Holy Land were only liberated from their Islamic occupiers temporarily, and this liberation involved massacring most of the Muslim and Jewish population. Moreover, the Crusades also unleashed great waves of intolerance in Europe itself. Many heretics and Jews suffered terribly as a result.

Nevertheless, the Crusades were a vivid demonstration of the self-confidence, the wealth, and the military power that Europe had amassed. As such, they were celebrated and romanticized in medieval poetry and literature. The Crusades were also a sign that the balance of power between Christian areas and Muslim areas had shifted decisively. By the eleventh and twelfth centuries, Europe was on the march.

Not surprisingly, Christian-Muslim relations were damaged by the Crusades. Some historians also believe that the Crusades may have contributed to a tendency within Islam to spurn contact with outsiders. This point is debatable, however, because Christian efforts to reconquer the Holy Land brought many Europeans into contact with the peoples of the Middle East, and some of the most fruitful of these contacts endured long after the Crusades themselves had ended. As we shall see in Chapter 7, a great deal of trade and cultural exchange occurred as a result, and often both Christians and Muslims benefited.

What was the main goal of the Crusades, and to what extent was it achieved?

Monarchy Falters in Germany and Rises in France

After the collapse of the Carolingian Empire, a long period of chaos ensued in France and Germany. In the middle of the tenth century, though, a powerful German king named Otto emerged. He won primacy over the other princes, dukes, bishops, and archbishops in Germany partly by defeating the Hungarians. In 962, Pope John XII recognized Otto's preeminence by naming him emperor, a title that under Otto's successors would evolve into Holy Roman Emperor. Once again, in the tradition of Charlemagne, it appeared that a strong-willed monarch was ready to impose order on Europe.

The problem with Otto's empire, however, was that it was difficult to sustain the support of the Church and the nobility for centralized imperial government. Otto's successors, Otto II and Otto III, also wasted much time, money, and energy trying to establish the dominance of the Holy Roman Emperor in Italy.

In the eleventh century, as we have seen, Emperor Henry IV became embroiled in a long struggle with Pope Gregory VII over which of them should have the power to make ecclesiastical appointments. In the end, the authority of the emperor was curtailed. This reduced the unity of the Holy Roman Empire. The main beneficiaries were the princes, dukes, archbishops, and bishops who ruled over the small feudal states in Germany. Thanks to their stubborn independence, Germany would not be effectively united under one government until the nineteenth century.

In the twelfth century, another attempt was made to bring cohesion to the Holy Roman Empire by a new royal family, the Hohenstaufens.

Frederick Barbarossa, who ruled from 1152 to 1190, sought to enforce Roman law in his domain, and for a while he brought the leading nobles to heel. He also repeatedly tried to subdue the papacy and the largely autonomous city-states of northern Italy, but on these two fronts he ultimately failed. At the Battle of Legnano in 1176, Italian cavalry and foot soldiers defeated Frederick's knights, marking a symbolic victory for the papacy and a decisive blow to the drive for unity in the Holy Roman Empire. Frederick Barbarossa's eventual successor, Emperor Frederick II, made many of the same mistakes, and as a result the authority of the imperial government in Germany sank even lower. By the middle of the thirteenth century, the Holy Roman Empire had effectively become a mere confederation of independent states.

From the death of Charlemagne in 814 until the foundation of the Capetian dynasty of French kings in 987, the history of France was a sad tale of civil war, assassination, economic collapse, and foreign invasion. In 987, the leading nobles in France, hoping for stability and unity, elected Hugh Capet as their new king (he was still called King of the Franks, not King of France). Despite Hugh Capet's coronation, though, the feudal princes still controlled most land and soldiers in France, so at first the monarchy's power was confined mainly to the area around Paris, known as the *Île-de-France*.

Gradually, the Capetians convinced France's feudal lords to recognize their hereditary right to the throne, and they slowly expanded the territory under royal control. Their job was made easier by the fact that the English held a large fraction of French lands. This increased the willingness of the French nobility to accept unified leadership in order to defeat a foreign threat.

By most accounts, the Capetian king who did the most to strengthen the monarchy in France was Philip II, known as Philip Augustus, who reigned from 1180 to 1223. Philip Augustus retook most of the English territories in France and added them to the lands controlled directly by the French king, which tripled in size as a result. The King of England and the Holy Roman Emperor then tried to reverse these French gains at the Battle of Bouvines, in which perhaps 80,000 soldiers participated, but Philip Augustus's forces triumphed. The prestige and power of the French monarchy soared.

Philip Augustus's grandson, King Louis IX, who reigned from 1226 to 1270, was an even more popular monarch. Louis was so devoted to the Church, and so upright in his conduct, that he was canonized as a saint after his death (the city of St. Louis, Missouri, is named after him). Not surprisingly, St. Louis was a strong supporter of the Crusades, and he patronized the construction of numerous Gothic cathedrals and churches.

In addition to being a zealous Christian, Louis was also an outstanding and pragmatic political leader. He worked to ensure that the king's agents were honest and loyal, and he made it clear that royal edicts applied everywhere in France. In addition, he enhanced the legal standing of peasants and increased the power of the royal courts, the judgments of which were based on Roman law.

By the end of St. Louis's reign, although the English still had not been evicted from French soil, France was as strong a kingdom as any in Europe. Its feudal lords retained great wealth, power, and privilege, but most of the time the King of France could count on their obedience and support.

Unlike in England, where the Parliament evolved into a branch of government that shared power with the king, in France the king's power was limited only by practical considerations and by local and feudal traditions. Occasionally, starting in the fourteenth century, the king consulted with nobles and commoners, who met in an emergency assembly called the Estates-General, but this body never acquired a permanent presence in, or a sizable influence over, the French government.

Why did the Holy Roman Emperors fail in their efforts to bring a strong, centralized government to Germany?

Monarchy in England

In Roman times, the native population of England was mostly Celtic. After the collapse of Roman Britain, however, various Germanic invaders and migrants arrived, including the Angles and the Saxons, and by the seventh and eighth centuries they had established powerful kingdoms that covered most of the country. Finally, in the ninth century, the Anglo-Saxons and the Celtic Britons were united under the leadership of King Alfred.

As it happened, the destinies of England and France would be closely intertwined. In the early 900s, the King of France gave a large tract of land to a group of Vikings, or Northmen. This sprawling fiefdom became known as the Duchy of Normandy, and the Vikings who ruled it became known as Normans. The Normans settled on the land, became Christians, and learned to speak French, but they never forgot how to fight like Vikings. In 1066, William, the Duke of Normandy, invaded England, enforcing a claim that he had on the English throne. Norman forces won a crushing victory at the Battle of Hastings, and William the Conqueror became King of England. He reigned from 1066 to 1087.

Thus began a rather uncomfortable international relationship, because William, as Duke of Normandy, was a vassal of the King of France, but as King of England he was also the equal of the King of France. To make matters even more complicated, for many years the kings of England actually controlled more land in France than did the French kings. To say, therefore, that medieval England and France were closely but problematically related would be a considerable understatement.

As King of England, William established one of the strongest monarchies in the Middle Ages. He ordered an exhaustive census taken of all persons, animals, and farm implements. This information was then collected in the Domesday Book, which was used to enforce an effective system of tax collection. William also required all landowners to swear fealty to him, and he redistributed large tracts of land to his Norman vassals. Lastly, William continued the Anglo-Saxon practice of dividing England into administrative units known as shires, led by sheriffs, who were chosen by and accountable to the king.

Under William's successors, Henry I and Henry II, Norman and Anglo-Saxon ideas and practices were gradually reconciled. An English identity started to take shape.

In 1154, Henry II founded the new Plantagenet dynasty that ruled England until 1485. Partly by marrying the forceful, intelligent, and beautiful Eleanor of Aquitaine, Henry greatly expanded England's territories in France, and he dominated Scotland and parts of Ireland as well. Henry II also tried to establish firm royal control over the Church. In 1170, several of Henry's knights brutally murdered the head of the English Church, the Archbishop of Canterbury, Thomas Becket, who had challenged the king. Becket became a martyr, and Henry had to back down.

In these years, the court system in England was increasingly placed under royal control. At the same time, a body of law known as the common law developed, based on the idea that lawyers, legal scholars, and judges should appeal to precedents established elsewhere, instead of relying mainly on local customs, and to broad notions about justice to which a nation's people subscribe. Today, the legal systems in Britain and the United States are still based on this common law foundation, which contrasts with the system based on Roman law that is found elsewhere in the world, especially in continental Europe. Roman law is based more on abstract reasoning and less on the analysis of precedents and legal and cultural traditions.

The most important legal and constitutional innovation in medieval England was yet to come. In 1215, King John, in a weakened position politically, was compelled to sign a historic document called *Magna Carta*, or Great Charter. It stated explicitly that even the king was bound to obey English laws. Moreover, it said that no Englishman should be imprisoned or punished unless he was found guilty by a jury of his peers, according to established procedures of justice. *Magna Carta* also stated that new taxes should not be imposed on the English unless they were consulted in the matter first.

These progressive ideas came with strings attached. It was England's feudal lords who had imposed *Magna Carta* on King John, and they did not necessarily intend that the rights outlined therein should apply to commoners. Moreover, John himself did not necessarily intend to keep his word. Even the pope declared *Magna Carta* null and void. Nevertheless, few documents in the history of Western politics have been as influential in the long run. *Magna Carta* established the ideal of a government that is respectful of the rights, interests, and views of its people.

As important as the appearance of *Magna Carta* was, every bit as significant was the continuation under William the Conqueror and his successors of the Anglo-Saxon tradition of consulting England's feudal lords in major royal decisions. By the thirteenth century, a Great Council of nobles and bishops existed to advise the king. By the fourteenth century, the nucleus of the English Parliament was in place, with a House of Lords for the nobles and bishops, and a House of Commons to represent propertied citizens in the countryside and in the towns. Parliament also gradually acquired both lawmaking powers and the ability to grant or refuse permission to raise taxes.

By the Late Middle Ages, therefore, England was well on its way to developing a strong, unified royal administration. It was, moreover, an administration supported by the active participation of nobles and some commoners in governmental affairs.

In what ways are modern American law and government based on precedents from medieval England?

Other Strong European Monarchies

Although historically the establishment of powerful royal governments in England and France was especially important, strong states also appeared in other parts of Europe.

Most people today think of the Vikings as bloodthirsty marauders, but they were also the founders of numerous states. Not only did they control Scandinavia, but they became the masters of Normandy, England, and Sicily. They also raided, traded, and settled extensively in what is today Russia and Ukraine. Kievan Rus, a medieval state that was the starting point for Russia, was founded and ruled by Vikings. It lasted from 878 until the middle of the thirteenth century.

In 988, Grand Prince Vladimir, ruler of Kievan Rus, embraced Orthodox Christianity, under the influence of officials from Byzantium. Ever since, most Russians, Ukrainians, and Belorussians have been Orthodox Christians. In 1453, when the Byzantine capital of Constantinople fell to the invading Ottoman Turks, the political and religious elite in Moscow (rather than Kiev) declared their city to be the Third Rome, and thus the new headquarters of Orthodox Christianity. The relationship between the Russian people, the Russian state, and the Orthodox Church would remain extremely close up until the beginning of the twentieth century, when the Bolshevik Revolution brought atheistic communists to power.

In the thirteenth century, Russia, along with large parts of the Muslim world, was subjected to brutal Mongol attacks, emanating from what is today Mongolia, Siberia, Central Asia, and northern China. From 1243 to 1480, Russia was effectively ruled by a Mongol state known as the Golden Horde, founded by a grandson of the great conqueror Genghis Khan. Many Russians complained bitterly about the "Mongol Yoke," especially in the city of Moscow, which became a focal point of resistance against the Mongols, also known as Tatars. Over the years, the hated Mongols destroyed many Russian cities, and they killed vast numbers of nobles and ordinary citizens—perhaps as much as half of the population. While the Mongols encouraged trade, Russian culture withered under their rule.

Mongol domination was finally ended in Russia in 1480 by Moscow's Grand Prince Ivan III, known as Ivan the Great. In addition to evicting the Mongols, Ivan greatly expanded Moscow's territory, tripling it in size; he curtailed the power of the nobility; and, to seal Russia's status as the new headquarters of the Orthodox faith, he married the niece of the last reigning Byzantine emperor.

The end of Mongol rule did not necessarily mean liberty for the Russian people. In the sixteenth century, Ivan III's grandson became Ivan IV, better known as Ivan the Terrible. Ivan IV declared himself Tsar, the Russian term for Emperor, derived from Caesar. Ivan added further to the lands ruled by Moscow, so much so that many historians believe that the country of Russia was born at this time. He also reformed Russia's law code and administration. Tragically, though, Ivan instituted a reign of terror, essentially confiscating all land and property in the country and meddling in the affairs of all his subjects. Ivan suffered from paranoid delusions about conspiracies against him, and thus he employed a small army of black-clad executioners to terrorize his people. Members of these medieval death squads dressed like monks, and they carried severed dogs' heads and brooms to symbolize their mission of sniffing out and sweeping away enemies of the Tsar. They killed many leading nobles who Ivan distrusted, along with their family members, friends, and even the peasants who toiled on their lands. To top it all off, Ivan the Terrible murdered his own son.

Ivan died in 1584. Although many Russians were relieved, decades of internal conflict ensued before a member of the Romanov family claimed the throne in 1613. The Romanov dynasty would rule Russia until 1917. In the intervening three hundred years Russia would ascend steadily to the status of a great power.

As we shall see in later chapters, Russia rose to greatness while making concerted efforts to portray itself as a Western country. In fact, though, one of Russia's most important historical strengths has been its ability to synthesize Western, Byzantine/Greek, and Asian influences. Russia is, and always has been, a cultural crossroads.

Strong medieval states also appeared in Poland and Bulgaria. Poland evolved into one of the largest states in Europe. Meanwhile, Bulgaria grew strong enough to launch formidable attacks on the Byzantine Empire in the tenth century.

The Russians, the Poles, and the Bulgarians are all Slavs—the ethnic and language group that predominates in Eastern Europe—but the Poles embraced Catholicism, while the Russians and Bulgarians, influenced by missionaries from the Byzantine Empire, became Orthodox Christians. Other Slavic groups also had to choose between Catholic Christianity and Orthodoxy, and for the most part their choices in the Middle Ages still determine their modern religious views. Today, Poles, Czechs, Slovaks, Slovenes, and Croats are all Slavic and Catholic, while Serbs, Bulgarians, Ukrainians, and Russians are Slavic and Orthodox. The Magyars, or Hungarians, are not Slavs and speak a language with roots in Asia. In the ninth century, they were fierce horsemen who launched raids across Europe. In the tenth century, though, they settled in Central Europe and embraced Catholicism. The Romanians, for their part, are not Slavs, practice Orthodoxy, and speak a language based on Latin. Ethnically, religiously, and linguistically, therefore, Eastern Europe is a complicated place!

Some of the greatest strides toward the formation of strong royal governments were made in Spain and Portugal, where indigenous peoples struggled throughout the Middle Ages to overthrow the Muslim rulers who had conquered most of the Iberian Peninsula in the seventh and eighth centuries. As we have seen, the attempt to drive out the Muslims was known as the *Reconquista*, and many Christians considered it a religious duty. The kings of Castile, Aragon, and Portugal were especially successful at marshaling the military resources of their peoples to win victories over the Muslims. By 1248, the vast majority of the Iberian Peninsula had been liberated from Muslim control. Many European immigrants flocked to Spain and Portugal to live in these newly Christianized areas.

In the Spanish kingdoms of Castile and Aragon, as in England and France, assemblies were created that gave some representation to the people. Specifically, there were bodies called *Cortés* that enabled nobles, clergymen, and town dwellers to have a say in royal policy. Iberian kings had the last word, though, partly because there was a pressing need for unity and decisive leadership in the ongoing wars against the Muslims in southern Spain, who were not fully defeated until 1492.

The last corner of Europe where strong royal authority prevailed was in Sicily, which, as previously mentioned, was conquered by the Vikings, or, more accurately, by the Normans. Between 1061 and 1091, Roger de Hauteville subdued the island and created a well-managed government and a tolerant society that respected the cultural traditions of all who lived there: the Sicilian natives, Muslims, Greeks, Jews, and Normans. Count Roger, and his son and heir, Roger II, utilized the services of Muslim bureaucrats who presided over one of the most efficient tax collection systems in Europe. By the end of his reign, Roger II had expanded his realm to include much of southern Italy. His domain, which became a center for medieval scholarship, eventually became known as the Kingdom of Sicily, or the Kingdom of the Two Sicilies, and the pope promoted Roger himself from count, to duke, to king.

The centralized royal government in Sicily was strengthened even further by Frederick I, who reigned from 1212 to 1250. (He also served as Holy Roman Emperor, but in that capacity he was known as Frederick II.) Frederick banned private warfare, popularized Roman law, continued the policy of toleration toward non-Christians, and patronized art, poetry, and scholarship. He was widely regarded as one of the most enlightened of medieval

116   *Politics and War, 500–1300*

rulers. Unfortunately, after his death, the strong administration that he had helped to build in Sicily collapsed.

Which Slavic peoples built strong states in the Middle Ages?

Conclusions

The history of politics and warfare in medieval Europe from 500 to 1300 is arguably a history of failure. Although Europeans managed to match the military strength of the Muslims to their south, they ultimately failed to liberate the Holy Land, which was the chief goal of the Crusades. Moreover, in most of Europe, the effort to bring feudal lords to heel, to create strong royal administrations, and to uphold the rule of law, repeatedly fell short. Luckily, in a few places, such as England and France, the drive to reestablish order, and to reinforce royal authority, succeeded. As a result, by the end of the Middle Ages, England and France were among the most powerful and prosperous states in Europe.

It is important to point out, though, that the seeds of royal centralization were not the only contribution that the Middle Ages made to the long-term political development of Western Civilization. Feudalism gave many Europeans an acute awareness of their rights and privileges, while medieval Christianity convinced many Europeans that resistance to oppression can sometimes be justified by appealing to a higher power. Feudalism and medieval religion thus provided sources of inspiration to later proponents of individual rights. At the same time, medieval laws, charters, and assemblies provided an opening, however narrow, for popular participation in government. They therefore laid the groundwork for representative government. Lastly, the Western legal tradition coalesced in the Middle Ages. Indeed, our modern rule of law relies on a great many medieval precedents.

In short, the political ideas and institutions of the medieval period, which may seem alien and distant, were in many ways precursors of modern political values and practices. As we shall see, the economic, social, religious, artistic, and intellectual accomplishments of medieval men and women were, arguably, even more influential.

Key Terms for Chapter 6

Gregory VII—pope from 1073 to 1085. He battled against Germany's Emperor Henry IV in an attempt to secure the papacy's authority over ecclesiastical appointments.

Cluniacs—members of a reform movement in the medieval Catholic Church. Cluniacs sought a more morally upright clergy, and one less susceptible to corrupting external influences.

Orthodox Church—the most popular strain of Christianity in the Byzantine Empire and in much of Eastern Europe. Orthodox Christians rejected the authority of the pope.

Inquisition—an institution in the Catholic Church dedicated to rooting out and punishing heretics.

Feudalism—the dominant social system during the Middle Ages, in which lords (who could be monarchs, nobles, or churchmen) granted their vassals (subordinates) fiefs (usually land) in return for loyalty and military service.

Charlemagne—the most powerful monarch of the Middle Ages. He was crowned Roman Emperor by the pope, and ruled most of Western and Central Europe. His empire fell apart soon after his death.

Carolingian Renaissance—a term describing the blossoming of art, literature, and scholarship under Charlemagne, who was a member of the Carolingian dynasty.

Vikings—one of several groups of invaders who terrorized Europe in the ninth and tenth centuries. The Vikings eventually settled in and ruled over many parts of Europe.

Muhammad—seventh-century founder of Islam, a dynamic new monotheistic religion. Muslims believe that Muhammad was God's definitive prophet.

Quran—the holy book of the Islamic faith, in which the spiritual wisdom of Muhammad is collected.

Crusades—a series of invasions of the Holy Land in Israel/Palestine, organized by the Catholic Church. Ultimately, the Church was unsuccessful in its attempts to free the Holy Land from Muslim occupation.

Frederick Barbarossa—King of Germany and Holy Roman Emperor from 1152 to 1190. Although he was one of the most forceful, charismatic, and successful of medieval monarchs, he failed to bring lasting unity to the Holy Roman Empire, and could not subdue resistance in his Italian domain.

William the Conqueror—nickname for King William I of England, who ruled from 1066 to 1087. William, who started out as the Duke of Normandy, obtained the English crown by invading the country and defeating its sitting king.

Magna Carta—Great Charter. This was an agreement between King John and leading English nobles that the king would thereafter obey English laws and respect the rights and views of his subjects.

Slavs—a broad ethnic category embracing most of the peoples of Eastern Europe.

Review Questions for Chapter 6

1. There is no debating the fact that the Catholic Church was a very different institution during the Middle Ages than it is today. Describe three ways in which this is so.
2. While feudalism may seem like a way to organize a society that is completely alien to our own beliefs and methods, in fact some elements or traces of feudalism survive in modern life. Provide three examples of aspects of modern Western Civilization that are either based on feudal precedents or that remind you of feudalism.

3. Compare and contrast Christianity and Islam by describing in detail two similarities and two differences between the faiths.
4. Many historians believe that the appearance of *Magna Carta* in medieval England, along with the rise of Parliament, paved the way for the eventual triumph of representative democracy in Western Civilization. Provide at least one detailed argument for why this may be so, and provide at least one detailed argument for why it may be an exaggeration.
5. War was a defining feature of medieval society. Imagine that you are a knight who has fought in one of the wars or campaigns mentioned in Chapter 6. Write a letter to your family in which you describe what your military experiences were like, and in which you make a case, based on your medieval worldview, for why your actions were justified.

Further Reading

Barbero, Alessandro. *Charlemagne: Father of a Continent*. London: Folio Society. 2006.

Barford, P. M. *The Early Slavs: Culture and Society in Early Medieval Eastern Europe*. London: British Museum Press. 2001.

Brown, Peter. *The Rise of Western Christendom: Triumph and Diversity, A.D. 200–1000*. Malden, MA: Wiley-Blackwell. 2013.

Donner, Fred McGraw. *Muhammad and the Believers: At the Origins of Islam*. Cambridge, MA: Belknap Press. 2012.

Esposito, John L. *Islam: The Straight Path*. Fifth Edition. New York: Oxford University Press. 2016.

Finkel, Caroline. *Osman's Dream: The Story of the Ottoman Empire, 1300–1923*. New York: Basic Books. 2007.

Hallam, Elizabeth. *Capetian France, 987–1328*. Abingdon, UK: Taylor and Francis. 2015.

Herrin, Judith. *Byzantium: The Surprising Life of a Medieval Empire*. Princeton, NJ: Princeton University Press. 2009.

Housley, Norman. *Fighting for the Cross: Crusading to the Holy Land*. New Haven, CT: Yale University Press. 2008.

Lynch, Joseph. *The Medieval Church: A Brief History*. Second Edition. New York: Routledge. 2014.

Martin, Janet. *Medieval Russia, 980–1584*. Cambridge: Cambridge University Press. 2011.

Norman, Vesey. *The Medieval Soldier*. Barnsley, UK: Pen and Sword Military. 2010.

Reynolds, Susan. *Fiefs and Vassals: The Medieval Evidence Reinterpreted*. Oxford: Clarendon Press. 2001.

Starkey, David. *Crown and Country: A History of England Through the Monarchy*. London: HarperPress. 2011.

Wells, Colin. *Sailing From Byzantium: How a Lost Empire Shaped the World*. New York: Bantam Dell. 2007.

7 The Middle Ages
Society, Culture, and Daily Life

Introduction

Many of the greatest cultural achievements of the medieval period occurred between 1050 and 1300, in what is known as the High Middle Ages. Feudal society at this time was strictly hierarchical, and it was organized around three major groups: nobles, peasants, and clergy. Each group, or order, had distinct privileges and responsibilities, and each individual member of these groups was encouraged to view his or her role as part of God's plan for humanity. Generally speaking, clergymen existed to pray, nobles lived to fight, and peasants grew food. Each group was seen as thoroughly indispensable to medieval society.

The medieval social construct was, from the start, somewhat mythical. Within each of the three groups that made up medieval society, there were major differences and conflicts, based on wealth, power, privileges, education, gender, geography, family connections, and other factors. In addition, there were some people, such as townsmen and merchants, who did not fit neatly into any of the three orders. Thus, the categorization of people in the Middle Ages as belonging either to the clergy, nobility, or peasantry, although undeniably useful, was simplistic to begin with, and it became less and less accurate over time.

The Nobility

The medieval nobility usually made up less than five percent of the total population, but to a large degree it dominated medieval society. The nobility had its origins in the war bands that had surrounded Germanic kings and chieftains, and in the regional administrators who had been appointed by Merovingian and Carolingian kings. By the High Middle Ages, in the wake of the chaos of the ninth and tenth centuries, nobles had acquired hereditary control over the lands that had been granted to them, or to their forebears, as fiefs. Some important nobles, such as dukes, counts, and earls, owned vast estates that were occasionally greater in size than the territories ruled by kings. Other nobles, such as knights, were of much lower rank, and their lands sometimes included only one small village and the farmland surrounding it.

On the nobleman's land lived peasants, who toiled under the supervision of their lord to produce food and other basic necessities. They thus provided their local nobleman with his principal source of income. Nobles used this income, supplemented by plunder, to sustain a lavish lifestyle, by medieval standards, that featured rich foods, the finest clothing, and various luxury goods imported from the East. They also built large manor houses or castles that provided comfortable accommodations—and, if needed, refuge from attackers. Income from his fief allowed a nobleman to perform his chief function in life: he provided protection to those who lived on his land, and he rendered military service to the king, or to whomever was his lord.

The military orientation of the nobility is demonstrated by the ideal set of values for nobles and knights that came to be known as chivalry. According to the code of chivalry, a nobleman was supposed to be an accomplished and courageous warrior. He was also expected to be obedient and respectful toward his king or lord, courteous toward women, temperate in his conduct, conscientious in following Christian precepts, merciful to clergymen and other non-combatants, fair and generous in his treatment of vassals and underlings, and capable of appreciating literature, poetry, and the arts. Unlike his barbarian forebears, therefore, a nobleman or knight in the High Middle Ages was expected to be self-controlled, pious, compassionate, and genteel. Naturally, some nobles and knights preferred a more rough-and-ready Germanic lifestyle, but nonetheless chivalric ideals had a wide impact.

Ordinarily, noble status was inherited from one's parents, but a man became a knight rather differently. First, as a boy, he would undergo a sort of apprenticeship, and he would serve as a retainer to his knightly tutor, both on and off the battlefield. Around age 21, he would be formally welcomed into knighthood through a ceremonial process of knighting, or "dubbing." He would bathe, participate in religious rituals, present himself and his weapons to be blessed by a priest, and would then be tapped on the shoulder (dubbed) with the sword of his king or lord, signifying that he was now a member of the knightly class. This ceremony might be followed by an oath, by the joining of hands, by a kiss, or by the signing of a specially prepared document.

Young men from noble families were dubbed as a matter of course, but wealthy merchants, farmers, and townsmen could sometimes gain entrance to the knighthood by persuading (or bribing) a king or a nobleman to accept them as vassals. For the most part, knighthood and ennoblement were coveted honors. Toward the end of the Middle Ages, however, kings made increasing demands on the knights in their service, and some young men actually sought to evade the burdens of knighthood.

What were the advantages and disadvantages of being a noble in the Middle Ages?

Peasants, Serfs, and Slaves

The vast majority of people who lived in Europe during the Middle Ages were peasants—that is, poor farmers. Among the peasantry, however, there was an important distinction between free peasants and unfree peasants, also called serfs. A free peasant is a farmer who may or may not own his own land, but generally decides for himself what to grow, to whom to sell his crops, whom to marry, and whether or not he should migrate beyond his village. He is, in other words, legally free to make most of his own decisions.

An unfree peasant, or serf, by contrast, is a farmer or an agricultural worker who owns little or no land, and who generally must take orders from his local lord. His choices about what to cultivate, how and where to market his crops, whom to marry, and whether he would ever leave his village, are all made with substantial input from his lord. He also frequently owes his lord money in the form of fines, fees, or payments in kind. He may also owe him labor in the form of participation in work gangs, work as a craftsman, or through domestic service in the lord's home. The severity of these obligations varied, but in almost all cases they were passed down from generation to generation.

Throughout the Middle Ages, besides free peasants and serfs, there were also small numbers of slaves in Europe who could be bought and sold. Before the fifteenth century, many slaves were pagan Slavs imported to the West from Eastern Europe. Indeed, the modern word slave is derived from Slav.

In the High Middle Ages, it was serfs who were clearly in the majority, both in the peasant population and in the population as a whole. What, then, was life like for most serfs? Serfs lived on manors, that is, estates, centered on the lord's manor house or castle, and usually including one or more villages and the surrounding farmland. Serfs lived and worked under the supervision of their lord, or his representative, who ran the manorial economy and administered justice according to traditional practices. The lord might be a nobleman; he might be an abbot, bishop, or other Church official; or he might be a king.

Why would serfs, who were so vital to the medieval economy, have accepted a system that granted them so few rights? The answer is that most of the time the security from invaders and criminals, and the humanitarian assistance, that lords promised to their serfs were extremely valuable. By contrast, a village of free peasants that did not enjoy the protection of a powerful, well-armed, and well-fortified nobleman could be pillaged or overrun, and in the event of famine it would face starvation. Historically, therefore, peasants have often been willing to trade away their freedom in exchange for security and humanitarian relief.

Medieval manors tended to follow a set pattern. They included a church and a priest. There was also a blacksmith, a carpenter, a stonemason, and a few other specialized workers. Few goods were imported from outside the manor. Generally speaking, serfs would devote about half of their labor to their lord, and the other half to growing crops on their own land and running their own households. Villagers from different families often cooperated on projects that were for the benefit of the whole community. In some cases, they may even have elected their own leaders.

In the High Middle Ages, the position of serfs gradually improved in Western Europe. This was because the worst violence of the ninth and tenth centuries was long over, and royal governments and Church authorities were succeeding in imposing order on some regions. Serfs thus had less need for the protection provided by their local lord, so if serfs did not like the way they were treated they could simply vote with their feet and leave the manor, moving in some cases to the towns, which were increasingly prosperous. Meanwhile, some serfs acquired the means to purchase their freedom. At the same time, casualties from peasant rebellions and population losses due to disease could make laborers scarce, and thus more valuable, putting pressure on nobles and royal administrations to alleviate serfdom, or abolish it altogether. In short, during the High Middle Ages many Western European serfs were transforming themselves into free peasants. In Central and Eastern Europe, by contrast, conditions of serfdom continued to worsen well into the eighteenth century. The main reason was apparently the lack of agricultural laborers in these regions. The response of Central and Eastern European nobles to this challenge was not to improve the treatment of their labor force but to use coercion and naked force, if need be, to keep serfs on the land.

Even though some improvements occurred in the lives of Western European peasants and serfs in the High Middle Ages, it would be irresponsible to romanticize their lifestyle. Peasants and serfs usually lived alongside chickens and other livestock in small, thatched, one-room cottages with dirt floors. There was little heat in winter, little protection from disease, and little help when crops failed and food supplies dwindled. Lords, clergy, and townsmen alike looked down on peasants and serfs, often viewing them as indistinguishable from filthy barnyard animals. Drunkenness appears to have been a common peasant vice. The ability to read and write was almost unheard of. There was only a small chance that a peasant or a serf, through hard work, could improve his or her lot. Ballgames, dancing, music, feasting, and gambling may have provided some diversions for medieval peasants and serfs, but generally their lives were bleak. It is no wonder, therefore, that they looked principally to religion, and to the afterlife, to give them hope.

What was life like for medieval peasants?

Clergy

The three principal groups in medieval society—clergymen, nobles, and peasants—were sometimes referred to as the three estates, and the clergy, because of its exalted spiritual functions, was known as the First Estate. Nobles were the Second Estate, and commoners were the Third.

At its height, the clergy comprised between one and two percent of the medieval European population, but the power, wealth, status, and independence of the Church made the clergy far more important than its small numbers might suggest. Vast tracts of land were controlled by the Church, and it completely dominated European art, high culture, and intellectual life. Meanwhile, almost all Europeans were dependent on the Church, which they believed controlled access to God's grace.

Based on their special functions, clergymen enjoyed immunity from many laws and taxes that applied to noblemen, townspeople, and peasants. In addition, clergymen were judged not in secular courts but by their peers in ecclesiastical courts.

Not surprisingly, in some cases, the wealth and privileges of the Church spawned corruption and the abuse of power. To some degree, these problems were addressed by Church reforms, but popular resentment of the clergy was nevertheless widespread.

The clergy included high officials in the Church, such as cardinals, bishops, archbishops, and Church bureaucrats, all of whom were increasingly likely to hold university degrees. It also included monks, nuns, and ordinary parish priests (nuns, because they were female, were technically not part of the clergy, but they were widely acknowledged to have clerical status regardless). The high clergy, monks, and nuns were often drawn from the nobility. Ordinary priests in the countryside were usually drawn from the ranks of the serfs. Many of them were uneducated, and most were desperately poor, much like their parishioners.

Monasteries and convents, discussed also in Chapter 5, varied enormously in how strictly they enforced the rules regulating the behavior of monks and nuns, and also in how luxurious the accommodations were that they provided. Some monasteries grew so rich from generations of bequests and contributions, and from the wise administration of monastic manors and business interests, that their monks could live in opulence and splendor. This was especially true of monasteries run according to the Benedictine Rule. Other medieval monastic orders, however, such as the Cistercians and the Carthusians, stressed the importance of poverty, isolation, and self-discipline. Cistercian monks were required to avoid any contact with women, while Carthusian monks practiced self-flagellation, that is, whipping of one's flesh, to atone for their sins. Some monks were also great scholars, physicians, musicians, writers, teachers, and artists. Primarily, though, they spent an extraordinary amount of time in prayer, because monastic prayer was thought to be highly effective in protecting society from divine retribution.

In many parts of medieval Europe, convents were the only organizations that provided education, a degree of independence, and a form of upward mobility for women. Some nuns became noted scholars, artists, theologians, and literary figures, while abbesses, the female administrators of convents, were among the most revered members of medieval society. Hildegard of Bingen, who lived in the twelfth century, was a celebrated abbess, artist, poet, playwright, author, scientist, composer, and moral and theological expert. Popes and emperors respected her views.

Many thousands of women who were not eligible to become nuns joined Beguine houses, communities of unmarried women who lived and prayed together. Eventually, Beguine women became associated with mysticism and heresy, and their organizations were suppressed.

Lastly, the medieval clergy included a group that emerged only in the thirteenth century—the friars—who were preachers of the Gospel who often moved from place to place, tending to the needs of the sick and the poor, and carrying out whatever tasks the Church required of them. Frequently, friars concentrated on ministering to city dwellers, whose spiritual needs were neglected by most priests and monks, who lived in the countryside. Unlike monks, friars did not live segregated from mainstream society. They felt that by living and praying among the laity they were imitating Christ himself. Over time, many friars ended up serving as professors, teachers, or missionaries.

St. Francis of Assisi, the son of an Italian cloth merchant, yearned to be a poet as a young man. Instead he served as a soldier, but he was haunted by visions that called him to devote his life to Christ. Eventually, Francis decided to give up all of his worldly possessions. He began to wander, preaching as he went. He soon attracted a small group of followers. Since he preached not only to people but also to birds and animals, he was later recognized as the patron saint of the environment.

Francis founded the Franciscan Order of friars in 1210. The Franciscans at first moved from town to town, carefully observing a vow of poverty and dedicating all their time and energy to preaching and to helping the needy. Eventually, however, the Church asserted control over the Franciscans, and the Order was required to accept donations of money and property that would be held in trust by Church authorities. The Franciscans were often tasked with running schools and universities.

In 1216, the Dominican Order of friars, also called the Order of Preachers, was created. The Dominicans were especially active in combating heresy, often serving in the Inquisition. A Dominican friar, St. Thomas Aquinas, discussed later in the text, became the leading theologian and philosopher of the medieval Church.

What social roles did the clergy take on during the Middle Ages?

Townspeople

The last category within medieval society—although it was not recognized as one of the three major orders—was the townspeople. Only about five percent of the population lived in towns.

Urban life had more or less evaporated in most of Europe with the collapse of the Roman Empire. Some towns recovered under Charlemagne, but later, in the ninth and tenth centuries, wide-ranging violence caused many towns to disappear altogether. Only in the Byzantine realm did cities continue to flourish. There, Constantinople had a population of perhaps half a million—comparable to the population of ancient Rome.

In the eleventh century, town life began to regenerate in the West. Trade increased, monarchs succeeded in establishing some semblance of order, the food supply improved, and a rising number of serfs migrated to urban areas. By this time, the largest cities were in Italy. Tens of thousands of people lived in places like Florence, Genoa, Milan, Naples, Palermo, Rome, and Venice. By 1300, Paris was Europe's largest city, with a population of about 200,000. Most towns were far smaller, with less than 1,000 inhabitants.

Townspeople were often known as burghers. In France, a burgher was known as a *bourgeois*, and, collectively, urban professionals, merchants, and business owners were called the *bourgeoisie*. Although it would take hundreds of years, eventually the *bourgeoisie* would evolve into what we today call the middle class.

Most medieval towns started out as walled enclaves centered around a marketplace. They were generally established on the land of rich nobles or powerful bishops. These lords and Churchmen embraced the trend toward urbanization because townspeople were a valuable source of income. Townsmen, however, were uncomfortable living like vassals of the local lord. Luckily, nobles and bishops were often willing to grant charters to towns that stood within their fiefs—charters that granted urban citizens extensive privileges and considerable independence if townspeople paid the local lord handsomely in return. Thus, most towns were eventually able to buy their way out of feudal and manorial obligations.

The principal function of medieval towns was to facilitate trade. Thus, the most successful towns were usually located near major ports or at crossroads. They teemed with life and were among the most economically dynamic places in medieval Europe. True, medieval towns suffered from overcrowding, house fires, poor sanitation, crime, and disease, but, despite such challenges, during the High Middle Ages the migration of people from the countryside to the towns continued unabated.

Around this time, the urban social structure solidified in a way that protected the interests of a small urban elite. Old and respected families, some of them boasting noble origins, dominated most towns, intermarrying with the families of the wealthiest merchants and entrepreneurs. In addition, small business owners and craftsmen demanded, and usually received, a modest amount of representation on town councils. Women and the urban poor—apprentice craftsmen and domestic servants, for example—were wholly excluded from political representation, as were Jews, who often lived in cities, too, but separately from the Christian majority.

Small business owners and craftsmen were the towns' economic backbone. Their interests were safeguarded through the formation of guilds, which were associations of master and junior craftsmen who were given a monopoly over a certain trade in a defined geographical area. All the cobblers in Paris, for instance, might form an exclusive guild, and the town's laws would prevent anyone who was not a member of the guild from producing or selling shoes in Paris. Furthermore, the members of the guild agreed to abide by common rules. A guild of cobblers would develop strict standards for how much an apprentice cobbler should be paid, what materials he should use, and how much a finished pair of shoes should cost. In effect, therefore, guilds were associations of small businesses, run by master craftsmen, who all agreed to play by the same rules, thus eliminating competition between them and securing exclusive control over a sector of the local economy. To increase their sense of solidarity even further, those belonging to a guild would often socialize with one another, wear distinctive outfits, and provide charitable support to guild members who had fallen on hard times.

Medieval guilds may have done their job too well. Guilds promoted stability in many economic sectors and trades, but, by reducing competition, they also undercut innovation in business practices and technology. As a result, medieval businesses seldom improved efficiency, and living standards remained low. It would take roughly another 500 years before Europeans were ready for a free enterprise, capitalist economy.

By the thirteenth century, a critical alliance founded on mutual self-interest had emerged between the *bourgeoisie*, that is, successful townspeople, and monarchs. Townspeople generally supported the centralization of political power in the hands of kings, because they viewed the private warfare and economic meddling of feudal lords as injurious to trade. Kings seemed to be the only force in society that could bring the nobility to heel. In addition, kings tended to create uniform systems of taxation, reasonably fair trade regulations, and improvements in communications and transportation infrastructure.

For their part, kings were only too happy to ally themselves with townspeople, because the towns were often extremely wealthy. Towns were also repositories of skilled professionals, such as lawyers, bureaucrats, and professors.

In the Middle Ages, the vision of a Europe ruled by kings and the *bourgeoisie* was unrealistic, given the fact that so few people lived in towns to begin with, and in the countryside the nobility still reigned supreme. By the eighteenth century, though, during the early stages of the Industrial Revolution, monarchs and the urban middle class started to elbow aside the nobility. In time, the *bourgeoisie* itself would come to dominate Europe.

What was the hierarchical social structure like in a typical medieval town?

Popular Religion, Economics, and Agriculture

It is difficult to overstate the influence of religion on the daily lives of medieval Europeans. The Catholic faith was, quite simply, the focal point of the Middle Ages.

For most nobles, attendance at Mass was a regular event. A significant proportion of nobles also ended up as monks and nuns, or as members of the high clergy.

Peasants and serfs were religious, too, but theirs was a simpler form of faith. Masses were sung in Latin throughout the Church, which few if any serfs understood. They would struggle to memorize the Latin version of the Lord's Prayer, and they would certainly participate in the sacraments, such as baptism, the Eucharist, marriage, and the last rites, but otherwise they had only a vague understanding of Catholic liturgy. What little they knew of the Bible often came from staring at religious paintings, from attending religious plays, or from listening to sermons.

Popular religion included elements that Protestants would later condemn as a perversion of the Christian message (see Chapter 9). Many medieval Europeans prayed not to God, but to the saints, especially the Virgin Mary. Europeans also grew closer to the saints by purchasing charms, participating in processions, celebrating Church holy days, admiring religious art, and going on pilgrimages to shrines and reliquaries, where relics such as the bones or tattered clothing of a saint might be kept.

The Church's influence on daily life did not end there. As noted already, the Church claimed a dominant role in education, the arts, and intellectual life. It also provided most social services. In the Middle Ages, the needy would invariably rely on the Church for assistance, especially on monasteries, which in many places were effectively the only hotels, hospitals, libraries, and schools available.

Turning now to the medieval economy, we find that it was strongly affected by politics. When warfare, chaos, and corruption were widespread, as in the ninth and tenth centuries, towns shrank, trade declined, and manors were forced to provide for their own needs. In the High Middle Ages, politics became more orderly, which, combined with population growth, provided a more propitious environment for economic expansion. Historians talk, therefore, of a commercial revolution that occurred from roughly 1050 to 1300.

The revival of medieval trade was closely connected to the resurgence of many urban communities. At the very heart of the medieval commercial revolution was the fair: a periodic gathering of traders at the site of a bustling marketplace lined with stalls, usually outdoors, where goods were exchanged from all over Europe, and sometimes from as far afield as the Middle East, Africa, China, and India. Marco Polo's famous voyage to China along the Silk Road was a testament to the wide reach of European commercial interests during the Middle Ages.

Merchants grew more sophisticated in the twelfth, thirteenth, and fourteenth centuries. They formed partnerships, opened new trade routes, purchased insurance, improved their accounting practices, signed binding contracts, and established inventive ways to deal in multiple currencies. Merchants also lent and borrowed money, despite the Church's prohibition of usury, that is, collecting interest on loans, that was only gradually relaxed. In addition, merchants negotiated with nobles and kings to enhance security along major thoroughfares, to improve transportation infrastructure, and to reform laws affecting commerce. Merchants sometimes even grew powerful enough to establish broad trading alliances that enrolled whole cities and regions.

In the Middle Ages, long-distance trade occurred all over Europe, but it was concentrated, as in Roman times, around the Mediterranean Sea, and it was thus cities in Italy that grew especially wealthy from commerce and finance. Most trade was in agricultural commodities, but textiles, luxury goods, tools, weapons, household items, timber, slaves, salt, and metals were bought and sold as well. Merchants were usually commoners, but quite a few nobles and Churchmen partook in trade as well.

All this economic activity may have created an early version of the capitalist spirit, according to which the individual accumulation of wealth was desirable. For most medieval Europeans, however, profits made through the exchange of goods were still considered suspect. Praying, fighting, and tilling the soil, by contrast, were considered honorable livelihoods.

Agriculture was by far the dominant sector of the economy. All the hard work on medieval farms, of course, was done by free peasants and serfs. In addition to raising crops, a peasant or a serf would spend much time gathering wood and manure; building and maintaining roads, fences, and other infrastructure; and sewing and weaving. Peasants and serfs most often grew grain and raised farm animals. The main foods in their diet were bread, porridge, vegetables, milk, eggs, and modest quantities of meat. Spices were imported and extremely expensive. Various forms of beer and ale were by far the most common beverages, except in southern Europe, where wine was preferred.

Agricultural methods improved greatly in the Middle Ages, leading to higher crop yields, better diets, and population growth. The use of heavier plows allowed for a wider variety of soil types to be brought under cultivation. In addition, a new type of collar was invented for horses, along with horseshoes, which allowed them to be used more effectively on farms. The widespread use of water mills and windmills to grind grain and to perform other vital tasks was another crucial innovation. Perhaps most significant was the gradual introduction of the three-field system of crop rotation. Previously, under the two-field system, 50 percent of farm fields were allowed to lie fallow at any given time. Under the three-field system, only 33 percent lay fallow, while the remaining fields were planted with a strategic mixture of grains and vegetables. Overall, during the High Middle Ages, average agricultural yields may have doubled, although famine still threatened periodically.

In what ways did the medieval economy grow more sophisticated over time?

Trade and Cultural Exchange between East and West

As we saw in Chapter 6, the relationships between Western Europe and Byzantium, and between Western Europe and Islam, were frequently bedeviled by misconceptions and animosity, leading all too often to violence and cruelty. Nonetheless, as has also been made clear, Europeans often managed to find common ground with Byzantines and Muslims. Moreover, some of the greatest achievements of Western, Byzantine, and Islamic societies occurred at times when, and in places where, these three traditions blended together.

The chief accomplishment of the Byzantines—the feat of preserving much of the heritage of classical civilization, and then passing along this cultural legacy to Western Europeans, Muslims, and Slavs—has been noted already. Likewise, the achievements of the Arabs, especially at their peak in the eighth and ninth centuries, are extraordinary. Arab scholars in wealthy and cosmopolitan cities such as Baghdad and Córdoba not only recorded the wisdom of the ancients but also commented on, applied, and expanded this knowledge. In addition, Arab scientific, medical, and mathematical expertise, agricultural know-how, technology (such as paper-making), and literary and poetic styles were all extremely influential in medieval Europe. Even today we use Arabic numerals, that is, 0, 1, 2, 3, 4, 5, 6, 7, 8, and 9, as opposed to Roman numerals, which previously had dominated. The Arabic numbering system has its origins in India, but it was the Arabs who transmitted it to the West. And Arabs would not be the only Muslims to contribute to Western cultural and intellectual progress in the Middle Ages. Western thinkers owed a huge debt to Avicenna, an eleventh-century Persian philosopher and scientist who was particularly admired for his masterful work *The Canon of Medicine*.

Nowhere was the potential for positive interaction between Christians and Muslims (and Jews as well) made more manifest than in Arab-ruled Spain, and in the prosperous and relatively harmonious society that was built there from the eighth to the twelfth centuries. In Spanish, this era is sometimes called *La Convivencia* (The Coexistence).

The Muslim Arab rulers of Spain showed surprising tolerance for Christians and Jews. A distinct term, Mozarabs, is used to describe Spanish Christians who assimilated some aspects of Arab culture and who occasionally even served in high positions in the government. Some free-thinking Christians and Jews actually fled from Catholic territories into Arab-ruled areas and later into Ottoman lands to escape persecution. Nevertheless, Christians in Muslim Spain had to pay a special tax, and they endured some forms of discrimination.

Besides fostering a degree of religious toleration, Arab Spain registered a number of other accomplishments. Cities there were thriving, orderly metropolises, Spanish agriculture was multifaceted and productive, and education and literacy were far more advanced than anything seen in the West. The vast libraries at Córdoba and Toledo were emporiums of knowledge, especially when compared to the tiny collections of books that Catholic monasteries could muster. At the same time, inventors, scientists, mathematicians, and doctors in Muslim Spain made critical advances. In particular, the towering intellect of Ibn Rushd, known in the West as Averroes, exerted a strong influence in fields as diverse as astronomy, law, philosophy, and medicine.

Unfortunately, by the twelfth century, Arab Spain's golden age had passed, and a less tolerant and more religiously, culturally, and politically divided Spain would thereafter succumb, albeit gradually, to Christian invaders. By 1492, the Christian *Reconquista* was complete.

The Crusades seem, on the face of it, to be the ultimate example of bitter conflict between East and West, but they also functioned to bridge the gap between Christians and Muslims in some important ways. Christians traveling to the Holy Land, either as would-be conquerors, as merchants, or as pilgrims, acquired an interest in Middle Eastern culture and geography. In addition, some Europeans, especially Italian merchants and shippers, profited enormously from provisioning the crusaders. Moreover, once the crusaders had founded a number of small Christian states in the Holy Land, these outposts of Catholic Christianity became hubs for East-West trade. Many crusaders went home having acquired a taste for Arab and Turkish food, art, clothing, architecture, and luxury goods. This led merchants to redouble their efforts to cater to these exotic appetites.

Because of the boom in trade between East and West, Venice and Genoa, in particular, rose from being modest towns to vibrant cities adorned with extravagant buildings that showcased the wealth of merchants and financiers. Venice dominated the European trade in spices with the East, so much so that the Venetians amassed the resources to build one of the Mediterranean's strongest navies. They also established colonial dominion over Crete, Cyprus, and much of the Adriatic coast. By the close of the Middle Ages, Venice had a population of 120,000 and was one of Europe's largest, most cosmopolitan, and most prosperous cities. Genoa, for its part, excelled in finance, shipping, and the slave trade. Both cities built up a reservoir of commercial and maritime skill that was drawn on by both the Portuguese and the Spanish when they began their voyages of discovery in the fifteenth century—voyages that aimed, ironically, to break the Italian stranglehold on East-West trade.

Of course, despite the fact that trade flourished between Muslims and Europeans, most Christians and Muslims continued to despise one another. Nevertheless, by the close of the medieval period, Christian Europeans and Muslim Arabs and Turks understood one another better than ever before. They had also proven that, when the circumstances were right, Christians and Muslims could live together in prosperity and peace.

What was La Convivencia?

Women and Family Life

Medieval society was thoroughly male-dominated and even hostile to women in many respects, but women nevertheless played prominent roles in all four major social groups.

As we have seen, a significant minority of aristocratic women became nuns. Although there were many benefits to life in the cloister, few women became nuns by choice. They became oblates, or trainees, in a convent at a young age, often because their parents decided that the marriage market was unfavorable to them.

Most noblewomen did marry. Customarily, a girl's father would choose her husband for her, often when she was in her teens. Since her dowry usually included land, a valuable resource, it was in the interests of her family to choose her husband carefully.

The Church taught wives that they should submit to the authority of their husbands, but in fact many noblewomen had substantial power in their households. They purchased food and luxury goods; they supervised the upbringing of the couple's children, especially girls; they administered servants; and they managed the manor when the husband was away. Noblewomen also frequently became widows. A widow inherited many of her husband's privileges and obligations. She became, in effect, a vassal to her husband's lord, controlling his fief. The fact that medieval women could own and administer property is a sign that the patriarchal structure of medieval society was not as strict as many people suppose.

Among townspeople and peasants, women were, if anything, even more prominent than among the clergy and nobility. In addition to cooking, cleaning, and fulfilling other household responsibilities, they were primarily responsible for raising children. They were also just as economically active as men.

In the towns, women and girls often worked as domestic servants or in the retail sector. Women also managed inns, engaged in prostitution, and worked in certain crafts. Some women joined guilds and became business owners. In most cases, though, women held subordinate jobs, they were poorly paid, or they simply worked alongside their husbands as unpaid auxiliary employees.

Peasant women toiled in the fields along with everyone else in the village. Peasant women also had distinctive responsibilities of their own, such as brewing beer, sewing and weaving, cooking, and tending to vegetable gardens and livestock.

Despite the important roles played by women in all classes of medieval society, the Church taught that women were inferior to men. Many theologians held that women were wild temptresses who required constant male supervision. Even nuns were viewed with suspicion. Meanwhile, spousal abuse was widely tolerated, and even recommended by some authorities.

Why was medieval society so misogynistic? Elite opinion regarding women's roles was largely formulated by the clergy, which was, at least in theory, celibate. The Church believed that anyone who engaged in sexual relations, even within marriage, was tainted by the sins of the flesh. Women were therefore blamed for causing sexual desire in men, and for drawing them away from God. Importantly, though, the Christian faith also taught that both men and women were children of God. Both could receive salvation, and both merited respect. Moreover, the veneration of female saints, especially the Virgin Mary, played a central role in Catholic practices.

Family life was extremely important in the Middle Ages. When political and social order disintegrated, or when famine or epidemics struck, family ties were one of the few bonds on which people could rely.

Although the households of the wealthy might contain a vast array of servants, clients, and distant relations, most medieval homes contained nuclear families, even though one's extended family often lived nearby. Family life was close and usually supportive and caring, but tensions could arise. Noble sons, for example, sometimes waited impatiently for their share of their father's estate. Married life could also be problematic, especially since marriages were generally arranged and the Church did not recognize divorce.

Approximately 50 percent of medieval children did not live to be five years old, but this did not prevent parents from forming close emotional bonds with them. Nonetheless, children were put to work as soon as they were old enough to handle simple physical tasks, usually well before the age of ten. As a last resort, if a family felt it did not have the resources to care for a child, he or she might be abandoned, sold, or handed over to a monastery or a convent.

Although it may come as a surprise to us today, medieval sexual morality was quite liberal. In theory, Christians were supposed to avoid premarital and extramarital sex, as well as sex on Sundays; on other holy days (including all 40 days of Lent); when women were menstruating, pregnant, or nursing; and when pleasure rather than procreation was the goal. There is little evidence, however, that these guidelines were observed. There was even a certain bawdy tone in much of medieval culture that suggests that sex was widely enjoyed.

What restrictions did medieval society impose on women?

The Arts and Sciences

At the beginning of the High Middle Ages, formal education was extremely rudimentary, and less than one percent of the European population could read and write. In most cases, monasteries and convents were the only places where advanced learning thrived. This situation began to change in the eleventh century.

First, a number of classical texts reached Europe via the Byzantines and the Arabs, who had carefully preserved them. The works of Aristotle, in particular, encouraged renewed interest in many scholarly disciplines. Second, enhanced levels of public order and prosperity meant that there was greater opportunity for inquisitive people to pursue formal learning. Lastly, the rise of European cities provided convenient locations at which major new educational facilities could be established as well as an increased demand for their services.

The rise in formal education and scholarship was demonstrated by the creation of a new institution: the medieval university. A university would often develop from a school associated with a cathedral or a monastery. Alternatively, conglomerations of inquisitive young men in urban centers would form guilds of students who hired lecturers to teach them. Most university students were the sons of noblemen or urban merchants and professionals. Instruction was based overwhelmingly on students listening to, taking notes on, and sometimes memorizing, what the master had to say about an old and respected text. Although a high proportion of university students aimed to become priests, monks, or Church functionaries, by the twelfth and thirteenth centuries many students intended instead to pursue careers in law or business.

Another development that gave impetus to medieval scholarship was the creation of a systematic way of viewing the world that has become known as scholasticism, the practitioners of which were called scholastics. According to scholasticism, the chief task of scholarship is to bring classical learning, usually equated with reason, into harmony with Christian beliefs, usually equated with faith. Thus, scholastics used the Latin language, drew upon classical and ecclesiastical traditions, and utilized logic and debate in order to eliminate any seeming contradictions between the wisdom of the ancients and the teachings of the Church.

Figure 7.1 Modern institutions of higher education are based on the precedent of the medieval university. *Laurentius de Voltolina, Liber ethicorum des Henricus de Alemannia.*
Museum of Prints and Drawings Berlin/Wikimedia Commons.

The great advantage of the scholastic approach was that it introduced a uniform body of assumptions and texts that every medieval scholar and student was supposed to use. The downside to scholasticism, however, was that it generally took for granted that all the wisdom that the world would ever need was contained in the writings of classical philosophers, especially Aristotle, in the Bible, and in the traditions of the Church. These preconceptions sometimes prevented medieval scholars and students from thinking for themselves.

Theology was the most important discipline in many medieval universities. The most revered medieval theologian was St. Thomas Aquinas, a Dominican friar. Aquinas asserted that reason, properly employed, can never contradict faith, because both originate with God. Aquinas admitted the primacy of faith, but he asserted that when we use reason, our senses, and experimentation in order to improve our knowledge of nature, we can also come to a better understanding of God, who created nature in the first place. From a scholastic perspective, the great strength of Aquinas's worldview, which was laid out in his masterwork, *Summa Theologica*, was that it affirmed fully the dignity of both reason and faith.

In terms of architecture, the medieval period is known as an age of high achievement. Byzantine architecture culminated in the construction of the domed and richly decorated Church of Hagia Sophia in Constantinople, later transformed into a mosque. It was the largest church in the world for almost 1,000 years.

In the High Middle Ages, architecture was the dominant art form. From the tenth to the twelfth centuries, Western Europeans built churches, monasteries, and other buildings in the Romanesque style. As the name implies, Romanesque churches bore a resemblance to Roman public buildings such as basilicas, with their heavy rounded ceilings supported by thick stone walls. Windows were scarce, and little sunlight penetrated the cavernous interiors, which were therefore decorated with brightly colored paintings, tapestries, and gleaming gold and silver objects.

In the twelfth century, a new architectural style emerged: the Gothic style. Gothic architecture radiated outward from France and dominated parts of Europe as late as the 1500s. In fact, versions of neo-Gothic architecture were popular in Europe and the Americas well into the twentieth century.

The ceilings in Gothic churches and cathedrals were much less heavy than in Romanesque structures. Partly because of this, Gothic churches and cathedrals could be built much taller: the highest ceiling in Beauvais Cathedral, begun in the thirteenth century, was over 150 feet high, while the top of some Gothic spires rose to over 500 feet. In addition, because of their ingenious construction and relatively thin walls, Gothic churches could accommodate many more windows than their Romanesque counterparts. In many cases, these windows were filled with beautiful stained-glass depictions of scenes from the Bible, portraits of saints, images of the elite, and sketches of everyday life. The effect on visitors was profound: Gothic churches seemed to reach heavenward, and they drenched medieval congregations in ethereal, multicolored light.

The construction of Gothic churches could take decades, or even centuries, to complete. Many Europeans were eager to demonstrate their piety, their worldly success, and their civic pride by contributing to the construction and decoration of Gothic churches, but in addition these structures served some very practical functions. Especially if they contained saintly relics, churches could attract droves of pilgrims, who were a valuable source of revenue. As well as hosting religious ceremonies, churches were the scene of town meetings, plays, business deals, and feasts. Today, Gothic churches are among Europe's most popular tourist attractions.

Other forms of medieval art also had a direct connection to religion. Murals, illuminated (i.e., decorated) manuscripts, and medieval statuary and reliefs frequently centered on religious themes, as did medieval tapestries, although as time went on images of battles, landscapes, hunting expeditions, and life at court also became popular. For their part, Byzantine artists produced beautiful frescoes, mosaics, illuminated manuscripts, and carvings.

As we have seen, medieval literature first flourished in the midst of the Carolingian Renaissance. During the High Middle Ages, medieval literature again made enormous strides. By this time, although Latin still predominated, a growing proportion of literature was written in early versions of English, French, German, Italian, and other vernacular (i.e., native, or commonly spoken) languages.

Even before the Carolingian Renaissance, an Anglo-Saxon monk had set down in writing the great Germanic epic poem, *Beowulf*. In the High Middle Ages, French epic poems, called *chansons de geste*, or songs of great deeds, became extremely popular among the nobility. Such poems exalted aristocratic virtues such as bravery, piety, and loyalty, and they frequently revolved around pursuits such as war and hunting.

Medieval romances were a form of epic poem that combined the chivalric and Christian emphases of the *chansons de geste* with fantastic elements taken from popular (often Germanic) legends. Chrétien de Troye's versions of the legends of King Arthur are perhaps the best examples of medieval romances.

Other noteworthy medieval poets include Dante Alighieri and Geoffrey Chaucer. Dante's *The Divine Comedy* explored the nature of heaven and hell, while Chaucer's *Canterbury Tales* chronicled the often amusing adventures of 29 pilgrims on their way to Canterbury Cathedral. Both men wrote in vernacular languages—Italian and English, respectively.

Perhaps the most distinctive form of medieval poetry was troubadour poetry, which originated in southern France. Troubadours sang their poems at royal and noble courts. Their theme was courtly love, or the selfless and devoted love that a nobleman felt, usually from afar, for a noblewoman. Courtly love was supposed to be spiritually uplifting, but it was nonetheless rife with sexual tension.

Medieval science, compared to Greek or Arab science, achieved little. One of the few medieval thinkers who attempted to separate rational, scientific learning from religion was William of Ockham, a Franciscan friar. Another Franciscan, the English scholar Roger Bacon, suggested that experimentation and mathematical calculations could be the keys to unlocking the mysteries of nature.

European science received a boost during the High Middle Ages from the acquisition of a treasure trove of Byzantine and Arab scientific and medical texts, some of them original, and some of them preserved from ancient times. As a result of this infusion of knowledge, medieval science blossomed, relatively speaking, in the thirteenth and fourteenth centuries. In fact, some historians go so far as to argue that the scholastics laid the groundwork for the Scientific Revolution of the sixteenth to eighteenth centuries. Be that as it may, medieval thinkers were always far more devoted to theology than to science.

Astronomy was the most popular branch of medieval science. Predictably, it was based on a curious mixture of ideas from classical scholarship and Christian doctrine. Most medieval thinkers believed that the universe was geocentric. In other words, they had inherited from Aristotle and Ptolemy the idea that the earth is at the center of the universe.

Medieval men and women registered some significant technological achievements, besides the major improvements in agricultural productivity mentioned already. The Byzantines developed a powerful new weapon, Greek fire, an incendiary liquid that was deployed via a primitive flamethrower. Greek fire was used effectively against the Arabs, among others. In the Late Middle Ages, mechanical clocks began to be built in the center of many European towns. On the battlefield, the innovative use of gunpowder, starting in the fourteenth century, would have earth-shattering ramifications, leading to the widespread use of firearms and cannons. Important navigational devices, such as the astrolabe and the compass, laid the groundwork for the "voyages of discovery," starting in the fifteenth century. In truth, though, few of these inventions were original creations. In most cases, they were instead ingenious adaptations of either ancient or non-European technology.

Medieval medicine is often seen as unsophisticated, but in fact as early as the ninth century a medical school had been established at Salerno, south of Rome. In the High Middle Ages, the study of medicine became one of the most respected disciplines at medieval universities, although its emphasis was more theoretical than clinical, and it still relied heavily on ancient medical knowledge. For instance, it was widely believed that a person's health depended on the balance of four humors, or fluids, in the body: blood, phlegm, and black and yellow bile. This was a view inherited from the ancient Greeks. According to this approach, an accurate diagnosis of a patient's ailment often depended on the observation of his or her fluids, especially urine. Frequently, doctors would prescribe a cure involving an herbal remedy or bleeding.

In the Middle Ages, only the very rich would have been treated by university-trained doctors. Among the masses, medical services and advice were dispensed by barber-surgeons, traditional healers, midwives, dentists, apothecaries, herbalists, astrologers, mystics, and family and friends. Only in

Byzantium would one have found anything resembling a modern hospital. Contraceptives and abortion, although forbidden by the Catholic Church, were often available to women.

Whether most forms of medieval medical care did much good is an open question, but we do know that if a person survived childhood diseases and had adequate food and shelter, it was not uncommon to survive to age 50 and beyond.

In which of the arts and sciences did medieval society excel?

Conclusions

We saw in Chapter 6 that many modern political institutions and ideas have their origins partly in the Middle Ages. Medieval culture has also had an enduring influence.

First, the medieval division of society into three groups, nobles, peasants, and clergy, supplemented by a fourth group, the townspeople, remained the foundation of the social structure in Europe at least until the second half of the nineteenth century.

In terms of religion, modern Catholics still venerate the saints and respect the authority of the clergy and the pope, Christians of all denominations continue to debate the relationship between reason and faith, and many elements of medieval theology and popular religion remain influential to this day.

In the realm of economics and society, modern businessmen still form partnerships and hold fairs, while also utilizing banking and financial practices developed in the Middle Ages; craftsmen still undergo apprenticeships; Western merchants still buy and sell goods worldwide; and modern unions, corporations, and chambers of commerce are based partly on medieval guilds.

In the area of intellectual growth and education, meanwhile, modern universities still garb their professors and students in medieval costumes, and they still grant degrees with medieval roots. Often, they concentrate on a liberal arts core that is based on the medieval curriculum.

In the cultural domain, modern lovers still make reference to the medieval ideals of chivalry and courtly love, while medieval romances and poetry, along with medieval art and Gothic architecture, still evoke awe and admiration.

Finally, medieval accomplishments in science, technology, and medicine, while modest, set the stage for the unprecedented wave of experimentation and discovery that Western peoples have sustained over the last 500 years.

And yet, despite the great accomplishments of medieval society, by the close of the High Middle Ages the progress of medieval civilization had stalled. To make matters worse, after 1300, a series of crises beset Europe, leading members of the ecclesiastical and noble elite, and many ordinary townsmen and peasants, to question whether the values, institutions, and practices of the Middle Ages were sustainable. Some began to argue that there were better ways forward. It was only a matter of time before the medieval world would come to an end.

Key Terms for Chapter 7

Chivalry—a code of behavior to which nobles and knights were supposed to adhere, involving virtues such as bravery, compassion, and self-control.

Serfs—peasants who are tied to the land and live under the control of the local nobleman.

Manor—a medieval agricultural estate, including the house or castle of the proprietor, usually a nobleman or knight, and the surrounding farmland. Local peasants and serfs were subject to the supervision of the lord of the manor. The medieval economic system is sometimes referred to as manorialism.

Hildegard of Bingen—a prominent and highly respected medieval abbess who was accomplished in a variety of artistic, literary, and scientific fields.

Friars—starting in the thirteenth century, a new category of clergymen. Friars were preachers unconnected with a specific parish who often served the Church as missionaries or educators.

Bourgeoisie—a French term referring to urban professionals, merchants, and business owners, later collectively labeled as the middle class.

Guild system—a method of producing goods popular during the Middle Ages, involving associations of local craftsmen who all agree to use similar business practices.

La Convivencia—the Coexistence. This is a Spanish phrase describing the period from the eighth to twelfth centuries when Spain was ruled by Arab Muslims, but Muslims, Christians, and Jews lived relatively happily side by side.

Universities—a medieval innovation in higher education involving guilds of students who were instructed by masters in disciplines such as theology, law, and medicine.

Scholasticism—a medieval intellectual tradition that sought to harmonize reason and faith.

St. Thomas Aquinas—the most important medieval theologian, and an advocate of scholasticism.

Gothic architecture—a building style that flourished in the High and Late Middle Ages. Gothic churches were tall, spacious, richly decorated, and, because they had many windows, brightly illuminated.

Review Questions for Chapter 7

1. Many people seem to believe that chivalry is dead in modern Western Civilization. Provide one compelling argument for why this may be so, and one compelling argument for why it may not be.

2. Imagine that you are either a noble, a free peasant or serf, a member of the clergy, or a town-dweller in the Middle Ages. Write a short essay describing why you are either pleased or displeased to be a member of your particular class. Then, give your opinion on whether it would be a good idea or a bad idea to allow people to change their class status.
3. Gender relations and family life were very different in the Middle Ages than they are today. List at least five ways in which this was so.
4. Describe one major similarity and one major difference between medieval and modern universities.
5. The legacy of medieval achievements in the arts and sciences is profound, even if it is seldom recognized. Which medieval accomplishment in the arts and sciences do you feel was the most important in shaping the long-term development of Western Civilization? Justify your choice.

Further Reading

Bitel, Lisa M. *Women in Early Medieval Europe, 400–1100*. Cambridge: Cambridge University Press. 2006.

Blamires, Alcuin. *The Case for Women in Medieval Culture*. Oxford: Clarendon Press. 2005.

Colish, Marcia L. *Medieval Foundations of the Western Intellectual Tradition: 400–1400*. New Haven, CT: Yale University Press. 2009.

French, Roger. *Medicine Before Science: The Business of Medicine From the Middle Ages to the Enlightenment*. New York: Cambridge University Press. 2009.

Gies, Frances and Joseph Gies. *Life in a Medieval City*. New York: Harper Perennial. 2016.

Grant, Edward. *God and Reason in the Middle Ages*. Cambridge: Cambridge University Press. 2009.

Herlihy, David. *The Black Death and the Transformation of the West*. Cambridge, MA: Harvard University Press. 2001.

Karras, Ruth Mazo. *Sexuality in Medieval Europe: Doing Unto Others*. New York: Routledge. 2017.

Lowney, Chris. *A Vanished World: Medieval Spain's Golden Age of Enlightenment*. Oxford: Oxford University Press. 2006.

Magnusson, Roberta J. *Water Technology in the Middle Ages: Cities, Monasteries, and Waterworks After the Roman Empire*. Baltimore, MD: Johns Hopkins University Press. 2003.

Newman, Paul B. *Travel and Trade in the Middle Ages*. Jefferson, NC: McFarland. 2011.

Pounds, Norman. *The Medieval City*. Westport, CT: Greenwood Press. 2005.

Rubenstein, Richard E. *Aristotle's Children: How Christians, Muslims, and Jews Rediscovered Ancient Wisdom and Illuminated the Middle Ages*. Orlando, FL: Harcourt. 2004.

Rudolph, Conrad, ed. *A Companion to Medieval Art: Romanesque and Gothic in Northern Europe*. Malden, MA: Blackwell. 2006.

Swanson, R. N. *Religion and Devotion in Europe, c.1215–c.1515*. New York: Cambridge University Press. 1995.

8 The Late Middle Ages and the Renaissance

Introduction

In the fourteenth and fifteenth centuries, a number of factors began to undermine medieval society. The political, economic, religious, intellectual, and artistic progress of the High Middle Ages, from 1050 to 1300, seemed to have stalled. Then, a colder climate suddenly befell Europe in the fourteenth century. This, combined with warfare and the ravages of the Black Death, caused massive turmoil and death on a vast scale. At the same time, the old patchwork system of feudalism and manorialism started to fray, while the Catholic Church entered a period of profound confusion. The prestige and independence of the papacy reached new lows. Meanwhile, a new Islamic empire, led by the Ottoman Turks, loomed as a potential threat to Christian Europe. Under these circumstances, Europeans began to question many of their medieval preconceptions.

By the end of the fifteenth century, the medieval outlook was gradually fading, while something recognizably more modern was taking its place. Many Europeans thought they had found—in national unity, bureaucratic centralization, royal absolutism, capitalism, religious reform, and most of all in the secular, rational, individualistic, humanistic, and optimistic values of the Renaissance (i.e., Rebirth)—a new and better way to organize their states, economies, and cultures. Thanks to the invention of the printing press, these new values, ideas, and institutions spread rapidly throughout Europe, ushering in an era of rapid change and political, social, economic, and cultural development. In some ways, that era of change and development has lasted all the way to the present.

Late Medieval Crises: The Black Death and the Hundred Years' War

Prior to the onset of the Black Death in the mid-fourteenth century, there was already an agricultural and health crisis in medieval Europe. Agricultural productivity had increased in the High Middle Ages, but Europe's population had doubled. Peasants were straining to produce enough food for everyone to eat. At the same time, topsoils had been depleted in some areas, and a notable cooling trend shortened the growing season. Some climatologists believe, in fact, that there was a Little Ice Age in the fourteenth and early fifteenth centuries (and perhaps extending to the nineteenth century) that, because of its agricultural impact, explains much of the turmoil that took place in the Late Middle Ages. Due to these multiple challenges, from 1315 to 1317 Europe faced the worst series of famines that it had endured in centuries.

Europe's problem with food scarcity was compounded by the arrival of the Black Death from 1347 to 1351. The Black Death, also called bubonic plague, resulted from a bacterial infection. It originated in Asia and first affected Europe in the Black Sea region, from which it migrated to Mediterranean ports in Sicily and Italy. Trade routes then carried the plague to most corners of Europe, sparing only the most isolated areas. Mortality rates were highest in cities, where large numbers of people lived close together, usually in squalid conditions. Rats carried the bacteria of the bubonic plague and passed it to the fleas that bit them. Those fleas would then bite human beings, leading to infection. After one person became infected, others who came into direct contact with his or her contaminated body fluids would be at severe risk of contracting the disease.

First, a plague victim would be struck by the appearance of a painful bubo, or a swelling of the lymph nodes, in the armpit, neck, or groin. Buboes would normally ooze blood and pus. The victim's body might become discolored by internal bleeding. Carriers of the plague would also become tired, nauseated, and feverish. Sometimes the patient would cough up blood. European doctors, pharmacists, astrologers, and traditional healers were utterly unable to cope with the epidemic. Most who contracted the disease were dead within a week.

Many Europeans interpreted the plague as a punishment inflicted by God. Thus, interest in the darker, more morbid aspects of the Christian faith—especially in the Book of Revelation—exploded. Art and literature related to death became immensely popular. Crime also rose. Some Europeans beat themselves with whips and sticks, hoping to appease God. Others became desperate to experience as much physical pleasure as possible. Still others attacked the Jews as convenient scapegoats.

In the end, the Black Death appears to have killed roughly half of Europe's population. All social classes were hit, but priests and monks died in especially high numbers, because they were the ones who cared for the sick. The first outbreak of the plague was followed by subsequent outbreaks, of diminished severity, that only fully receded in the eighteenth century. Europe's population would not recover to pre-plague levels until around 1500. Not surprisingly, the political, social, and economic effects of the Black Death were sweeping.

First and foremost, the Black Death enfeebled the feudal nobility, because it killed off a large portion of the serfs upon whom landed nobles depended

Figure 8.1 Medieval depiction of patients suffering from bubonic plague, covered with the disease's characteristic buboes (swollen lymph nodes).
Everett Historical/Shutterstock.

for their livelihood. As a consequence, food production declined. Nobles tried to reassert themselves politically and economically, with some success, but in the final analysis many nobles lost a significant fraction of their power and wealth. In fact, some knights were so hard-pressed that they formed criminal gangs that engaged in robbery, kidnapping, and extortion.

Inevitably, the Black Death caused enormous friction between various classes and interest groups. In the cities, craftsmen and members of the rising *bourgeoisie* grew angry with urban elites, and sometimes with each other, leading to riots and rebellions. More significantly, when kings and nobles tried to minimize their economic losses in the countryside by imposing new obligations on free peasants and serfs, the result was some of the largest peasant uprisings that Europe had ever seen. The *Jacquerie* in France in 1358, and the Peasants' Revolt in England in 1381, led to indiscriminate violence and many deaths. In almost every case, peasant rebellions were crushed by force, but kings and nobles could not entirely prevent free peasants, serfs, and urban craftsmen from capitalizing on their newfound economic leverage. Simply put, the fact that there were now fewer workers meant that those workers were more valuable, so employers generally had to treat them better.

Economically and socially, therefore, one of the principal effects of the Black Death was to hasten the decline of serfdom. As we saw in Chapter 7, many serfs were freed in the Late Middle Ages. True, they remained subordinate to nobles and large landowners, and their wages, diets, and standard of living were appallingly bad by modern standards, but their legal situation had decisively changed for the better. By 1550, serfdom had ceased to exist in England and was on its way out elsewhere in Western Europe (in Eastern Europe, by contrast, serfdom was widespread even as late as the nineteenth century). In many cases, free peasants and serfs also saw the rents and fees that they paid to local noblemen reduced. At the same time, the rising cost of labor forced Europeans to experiment with ways to make the production of goods more efficient. The first glimmerings of mechanization could be espied across Europe that would lead eventually to the Industrial Revolution.

As if the suffering and instability caused by the Black Death were not enough, a series of military conflicts between England and France developed in the fourteenth and fifteenth centuries that caused enormous devastation. Collectively, these conflicts are known as the Hundred Years' War, which lasted from 1337 to 1453. The chief cause of this war was the desire of the English to rule France. This was, in feudal terms, not an unreasonable goal, since the degree of intermarriage between the English and French royal houses meant that the King of England, Edward III, who reigned from 1327 to 1377, had a plausible claim to be the rightful King of France. The French nobility, however, preferred to support the claim of Philip VI, a Frenchman who was crowned in 1328 as the first king from the House of Valois.

In the course of the many battles that followed, England managed to divide the French and find allies among those who were dissatisfied with the new Valois monarchy. As a result, by 1429, England had conquered most of France, including Paris. English victories, such as their triumph at the Battle of Agincourt in 1415, memorialized by Shakespeare in his brilliant play *Henry V*, were due in large part to superior military organization and equipment. Toward the end of the war, however, the two sides became more evenly matched, and, ominously, both were starting to employ gunpowder and artillery.

Although most of the early victories went to the English, the tide of battle turned starting in 1429, when a 17-year-old French peasant girl, nowadays referred to as Joan of Arc, visited the court of the King of France, Charles VII. Joan claimed that God had appointed her as France's savior, and that she would lead the French to victory. By successfully lifting the English siege of Orléans, she did exactly that.

After Orléans, more victories ensued, and slowly the French, with Joan's help, began to evict the English from their soil. Charles VII, though, had lost his enthusiasm for Joan. She was captured by the French allies of the English, tried for heresy, and burned at the stake in 1431. In 1456, an ecclesiastical tribunal posthumously overturned Joan's conviction. She was declared a saint in 1920 and remains a heroine of French nationalism today.

The Hundred Years' War had wide-ranging consequences. First, England's drive to conquer France and merge the two realms was narrowly beaten back. As a result, French pride rose to new heights.

Second, the English and French monarchs, along with England's Parliament, were able to expand their authority as a result of the fighting. They raised taxes and fielded massive armies. Increasingly, those armies were manned by professional soldiers and mercenaries rather than by knights, and pay and plunder rather than chivalry motivated most of those who fought.

Finally, the combat itself, and the heavy burdens of taxation that the Hundred Years' War caused, created enormous suffering, especially for the peasantry. As previously mentioned, the *Jacquerie* in France and the Peasants' Revolt in England were both partly the result of the ravages of the Black Death. They were also abetted, though, by the hardships that the common people had shouldered in the course of the Hundred Years' War.

What were the long-term consequences of the Black Death?

Late Medieval Crises: The Church Falters

Given the horrors of the Black Death and the Hundred Years' War, Europe needed the reassurance provided by Catholic Christianity more than ever. The Church, however, spent most of the Late Middle Ages in a weakened and chaotic state.

First, the extravagant claims to secular power made by various popes in the High Middle Ages were severely tested during the pontificate of Boniface VIII, lasting from 1294 to 1303. Boniface attempted to prevent the French King Philip IV (called Philip the Fair) from imposing taxes on the French clergy, using the threat of excommunication as a powerful motivator. The disagreement climaxed when an enraged Philip accused Boniface of a multitude of sins, including sodomy and heresy, and ordered a raid on the pope's summer palace, during which Boniface was severely beaten. The sickly pope died one month later. Philip's contemptuous treatment of Boniface made the papacy seem weak, and its pretensions to absolute power collapsed.

In 1309–77, the respect that many Europeans felt for the papacy reached new lows during a period known as the Babylonian Captivity (named after the period chronicled in the Hebrew scriptures, when the Jews were forced to move from Israel/Palestine to Babylon). In 1309, to conciliate Philip IV, Pope Clement V moved his residence from Rome to Avignon, a town under Church control in what is today southeastern France. For the next 70 years, every single pope lived in Avignon and was a Frenchman who was closely allied with the French monarchy. Thus, many Europeans began to view the papacy as servile and browbeaten.

The end of the Babylonian Captivity, and the return of the pope to Rome in 1377, did not restore the fortunes of the papacy. In 1378, a dispute developed over who the real pope was: Urban VI or Clement VII. Finally, after decades of acrimony, the Council of Constance, which met from 1414 to 1418, succeeded in clearing the way for a new pope to take over.

All this confusion caused some Christians to suggest that a new form of Church governance was needed. A Conciliar Movement developed that proposed that meetings of Church officials and dignitaries, like the Council of Constance, should be empowered to override the dictates of the pope. The papacy, however, managed to beat back this challenge to its authority. The Conciliar Movement was declared heretical in 1460.

Yet another sign of crisis in the Church was the rise of new heretical reform movements, such as those of John Wycliffe in England and Jan Hus in what is today the Czech Republic. Wycliffe and Hus had similar ideas. They both rejected the wealth, power, and privileges of the clergy. They also asserted that the supposedly supernatural sacraments performed by clergymen should be de-emphasized, as should the veneration of saintly images and relics. Instead, Christians should read the Bible, translated into their own languages, in order to come to an understanding of their faith. Both Wycliffe and Hus were also patriots who favored the autonomy of their own regional and national churches rather than blind submission to the ecclesiastical authorities in Rome.

To some extent, the beliefs and goals of Wycliffe's and Hus's supporters, known as Lollards and Hussites, respectively, presaged those of the Protestant reformers of the sixteenth century. In the Late Middle Ages, in any case, the Church was in no mood to listen to the radical pronouncements of heretics. Both Wycliffe's and Hus's movements were suppressed by force. John Wycliffe was posthumously burned, while Jan Hus was burned alive. And yet the Hussites, after a series of armed uprisings, ultimately succeeded in transforming some aspects of the Church in Czech areas.

Heresy was not the only outlet available to Christians who were dissatisfied with the late medieval Church. Some believers, especially women, were instead attracted by mysticism, which offered a way to commune with God without the assistance of the clergy. Mystics might have visions or vivid dreams; they might experience seizures or trances; they might communicate with God, the Virgin Mary, angels, or saints; and they sometimes exhibited wounds similar to those received by Jesus Christ at his crucifixion. As an alternative to mysticism, some Europeans joined lay movements that stressed self-improvement and simple piety. In short, an increasing number of Europeans were finding sources of spiritual fulfillment outside the walls of their churches.

Another dangerous sign for the Church was a faltering of scholasticism. The scholastics had taught that faith and reason were complementary. In the Late Middle Ages, though, thinkers such as William of Ockham suggested that the two were distinct. Another skeptic, Marsiglio of Padua, proposed that, if faith and reason were fundamentally different, then theology and politics should also be considered separately. This meant that the Church could not justifiably assert any authority over secular governments.

Lastly, the Church in the fourteenth and fifteenth centuries was steadily undermined by persistent charges of moral debasement, corruption, and mismanagement. Many late medieval and Renaissance popes were worldly men who pursued luxury, wealth, sexual conquests, and narrow, frequently nepotistic, political agendas. Symbolic of the questionable moral authority of the late medieval Church was its sale, beginning in the fourteenth century, of indulgences, described in Chapter 9. Especially in Northern Europe, where some were expressing increasing resentment of the decadent and seemingly diabolical Italian-dominated Church, faith in Catholicism was collapsing, paving the way for the Protestant Reformation. That movement, which began in 1517, would end the unity of Western Christendom once and for all.

What factors led to a decline in the powers and prestige of the papacy in the Late Middle Ages?

The Ottoman Empire

While Europe was in crisis, a new Islamic empire was coalescing in what is today Turkey. It would eventually conquer most of the Balkans, as southeastern Europe is known, and much else besides.

In the middle of the thirteenth century, invading Mongols had laid waste to large portions of the Islamic world. In the late fourteenth century, a new Mongol ruler, Tamerlane, followed in their footsteps, slaughtering whole cities. When the Mongol hordes receded after Tamerlane's death, the way was cleared for the emergence of the empire of the Ottoman Turks. Originally from Central Asia, the Ottomans were Muslims who managed to forge a remarkably diverse and resilient state. They showed a healthy respect for the empires that had come before them and thus incorporated elements of Greek and Roman, Byzantine, Arab, and Persian traditions in their administration, economy, and culture.

The greatest victory for the Ottoman Turks came in 1453, when an Ottoman army managed to break through the stout walls of Constantinople and sack the city. The Byzantine Empire, which had lasted for more than 1,000 years, was obliterated. The Ottomans then made Constantinople their opulent capital. The Ottoman Sultan even claimed the title of Roman Emperor, although his legitimacy was spurned in the West.

In the sixteenth century, the Ottoman Empire expanded still further, until it included Turkey, Greece, most of the Balkans, Syria, Israel/Palestine, Egypt and the rest of North Africa, and most of Mesopotamia and Arabia. Twice, the Ottomans made it as far as the gates of one of Europe's great cities: Vienna. They also repeatedly threatened the Persians to their east, but they could not defeat them. To some Europeans in the sixteenth and seventeenth centuries, the Ottomans seemed virtually unstoppable, especially under Sultan Suleiman the Magnificent, who reigned from 1520 to 1566. Suleiman added Hungary, parts of Serbia and Mesopotamia, and various Mediterranean ports to the Ottoman domain. Luckily for those attempting to hold back the Ottomans, their empire soon began a long-term process of decline that ended with the complete collapse of the Ottoman state after World War I. Technological backwardness, political instability and rebellions, the loss of control over trade between East and West, the overextension of Ottoman military resources, the rise of ethnic nationalism, failed experiments with constitutional monarchy, and tenuous finances all combined to produce the decline and fall of the Ottoman regime. In the Late Middle Ages, however, all of this was far in the future, and the Ottoman star was still on the rise.

The Ottoman Empire was governed by a hereditary Sultan with sweeping powers. Nevertheless, the Sultan eventually delegated much of his power to a Grand Vizier, and he was at times highly influenced by women at the Ottoman court as well as by the *ulama*, Islamic scholars who were mostly conservative in their outlook. Not surprisingly, given the religious prejudices common at the time, many Europeans reviled the Ottomans as aggressive and shameless infidels. Occasionally, though, some European monarchs, hoping to gain advantage over their Christian rivals, made common cause with the Turks. An enormous amount of trade also flowed between Ottoman lands and the West, much of it through Italian ports. This trade enriched the Ottoman elite, which in turn nurtured the development of the arts.

The Ottoman state was generally tolerant toward religious minorities such as Christians and Jews, who were permitted to run their own affairs, at least to a point, and to thrive economically. Non-Muslims were, however, segregated and subjected to varying degrees of discrimination. Some Christian children were even taken by force from their parents in order to serve in the Sultan's army and bureaucracy.

What areas were conquered by the Ottomans?

The Rise of Strong States

In the Late Middle Ages, strong royal governments that encouraged national unity and bureaucratic centralization became commonplace in much of Europe, continuing a trend that was already well established in the High Middle Ages. In the process, members of the feudal nobility, who had traditionally served as judges, collected taxes, and even raised private armies, were gradually eclipsed by agents of the king or emperor. This was partly because the nobility's military role had declined as well. By the Late Middle Ages, kings preferred to employ professional standing armies, or hire mercenaries, rather than relying on self-interested nobles and knights.

Kings increasingly entrusted the administration of their realms to civil servants. These bureaucrats often came from towns and possessed formal educations. They based their decisions on the rule of law, and those laws almost all emanated from the monarch. Although representative assemblies, such as the Parliament in England, the Estates-General in France, the *Cortés* in Spain, and the Imperial Diet in Germany, existed, they tended to be sidelined by the Late Middle Ages. The trend was instead for kings to rule more or less alone, as sovereigns—that is, as rulers with full authority over a given territory.

Kings frequently employed their sweeping new powers to make war, and this, in turn, required them to borrow money and raise taxes. Medieval taxes were laid principally on townsmen and peasants, since nobles were still influential enough to insist on exemptions.

Townspeople and peasants understood that a shift toward powerful monarchies, and away from feudalism, was taking place. The common people increasingly turned to their king or emperor rather than to the local lord for protection, guidance, and support. Kings encouraged this trend, issuing propaganda and publicly asserting their dominance.

England was one of the few countries in Europe in which the representative assembly, called Parliament, maintained or expanded its authority in the course of the Late Middle Ages. Under King Edward III, Parliament became a key component of the English government, asserting power over taxation, in particular. Moreover, one of the House of Commons' main constituencies, the gentry, that is, prominent landowners without noble titles, acquired a significant voice in policy making.

After its defeat in the Hundred Years' War, England was thrown into turmoil by a long struggle between two powerful families, both of which asserted a claim to the throne. This struggle, called the Wars of the Roses, finally ended with the enthronement of King Henry VII in 1485, who began the Tudor dynasty. Henry maximized the power of the monarchy by developing a new judicial body, called the Court of Star Chamber, to deal summarily with his opponents in the nobility and the gentry. Henry also greatly enriched the monarchy itself while avoiding expensive foreign wars, which would have required him to seek Parliament's authorization for higher taxes. Overall, despite the Wars of the Roses, England's government was strengthening. Its economy was also booming.

Although much of the French countryside was devastated by the fighting in the Hundred Years' War, France emerged from the conflict victorious. King Charles VII, who reigned from 1422 to 1461, strengthened France's government significantly. He reduced the power of the nobility, instituted large and permanent tax increases, cultivated national pride, and created Europe's most formidable standing army. He also issued the Pragmatic Sanction, which asserted the king's authority over the Catholic Church.

The progress achieved by Charles VII was built upon by his worthy successor, King Louis XI, called the Spider King because of his scheming and secretive nature. Louis built up the economy, and he defeated the Duchy of Burgundy to France's east, absorbing much of its territory.

Unfortunately, in the late fifteenth century, France's kings became obsessed with expanding their power in Italy. A long, fruitless series of wars against the Hapsburg rulers of Spain and the Holy Roman Empire, who also sought to dominate Italy, ensued.

By the late fifteenth century, Spain boasted one of Europe's strongest and most dynamic royal governments under King Ferdinand and Queen Isabella. They were steadily unifying their Aragonese and Castilian kingdoms into a single, militantly Catholic Spanish realm. In 1492, Spain defeated the last Muslim state on the Iberian Peninsula. Ferdinand and Isabella also succeeded in building an effective bureaucracy, taming the nobility and the Church, and enforcing Roman law.

The process of royal centralization unfolded in Germany and Italy just as it did in England, France, and Spain, but with one critical difference: in Germany and Italy large, unified nations did not form until the nineteenth century, and thus the strong governments that developed in these areas during the Late Middle Ages ruled over miniature kingdoms, duchies, and city-states. In Germany, the institutions of the Holy Roman Empire, such as the Imperial Diet, a convention of the German political elite, brought some degree of unity to these mini-states, but for the most part the more than 300 princely and aristocratic rulers of the component parts of the empire treated their lands as personal fiefdoms. The same problem existed in Italy. As we shall see, however, the chaotic nature of Italian politics in no way prevented the rulers of the various Italian city-states from sponsoring the artists, architects, writers, and scholars of the Renaissance. On the contrary, Italy's rulers, constantly fearful of losing their grip on power, were eager to spend freely and conspicuously on Renaissance art and literature in order to glorify and justify themselves.

Which European countries developed strong, centralized governments in the Late Middle Ages?

The Italian Renaissance

The Renaissance was an intellectual and artistic movement that occurred primarily in Italy from about 1350 to 1600. It was chronologically part of the Late Middle Ages, but in many ways the spirit of the Renaissance was antithetical to the medieval outlook.

Renaissance means rebirth. The artists and thinkers of the Renaissance thought of themselves as reinvigorating Western Civilization after a long period of ignorance and decline. They invented the term Dark Ages to describe the thousand years between the Fall of Rome and their own time. They viewed this middle period, later labeled as the Middle Ages, as an unfortunate mistake, when many of the glorious achievements of the ancient Greeks and Romans were temporarily forgotten. They saw their own principal mission as the recovery of ancient greatness, especially in the fields of philosophy, literature, and art.

First and foremost, Renaissance thinkers developed an insatiable desire to read classical texts and to learn from the wisdom therein. They did so for the specific purpose of glorifying human beings and of helping people to reach their fullest potential. Thus, they consciously allied themselves with the ancient ideal of humanism. The scholastics, by contrast, had also studied the classics, but they had employed ancient texts for the more otherworldly purpose of verifying divine revelation. Over time, Renaissance humanism also came to imply optimism, an emphasis on secular values, skepticism about traditional assumptions and superstitions, a desire to serve one's community by participating in politics, support for freedom of expression, and enthusiasm for individual talent.

Although the artists and thinkers of the Renaissance were generally believing Christians, they frequently rejected some of the presumptions of medieval Christianity. Whereas in the Middle Ages a person's fate was widely seen as predetermined by God, during the Renaissance people were more likely to think of themselves as masters of their own destinies. In addition, from a Renaissance perspective, what a person did on earth, especially to serve others, to create beautiful art or literature, and to build an honorable reputation, was considered more important than any speculation about his or her fate in the afterlife.

It is no accident that the Renaissance developed in Italy, since the traditionally minded feudal nobility there was relatively weak, and the up-and-coming merchant and banking communities, based in the cities, were comparatively strong. Italy had grown rich from trading with the East as well as from finance. Patrons of Renaissance art and scholarship tapped this wealth freely to support the recovery of ancient wisdom and the creation of new art forms, books, schools, and architectural wonders. Italy also benefited from its commercial and cultural contacts with the Byzantines and the Arabs, who were the source of a great many ancient Greek and Roman manuscripts.

Many of the first proponents of the Renaissance were philosophers, artists, writers, diplomats, civil servants, and political and military advisors who were attached in various ways to the courts of Italian rulers. In addition, urban grandees, the rising mercantile, financial, and professional classes, and craftsmen organized into guilds were captivated by the movement. As patronage became more fashionable, even seemingly conservative figures like the popes, as well as other members of the religious and political elite, began to support Renaissance artists and thinkers. Despite the popularity of the Renaissance, however, it affected primarily the privileged few. Most Italians remained poor, uneducated, and oriented more toward traditional popular religion than humanism.

As noted above, the inspiration for the Renaissance came first and foremost from the study and appreciation of great works of classical literature. Renaissance thinkers read Greek and Roman manuscripts, marveling at the elegant prose and the insights into human nature that they found there. Some went beyond the study of the Greek and Roman classics and acquired an interest in Hebrew and Arabic texts as well.

Petrarch, one of the fourteenth-century founders of Renaissance humanism, was an Italian poet, scholar, writer, and cleric. He was also an avid traveler and a hopeless romantic who pined after a beautiful married woman named Laura for more than 20 years. Petrarch encouraged his followers to learn Greek and Latin, to establish schools emphasizing classical education, and to emulate the style and philosophy of Cicero, the Roman statesman, orator, and author. Implicit in the Ciceronian ideal was the importance of making the most of one's time on earth by seeking self-improvement and helping others.

A classic statement of humanistic ideals appeared in 1486 in Giovanni Pico della Mirandola's *Oration on the Dignity of Man*. Pico, a young nobleman, asserted that human beings were capable of excellence in virtually any sphere. Pico's writings exemplified the individualism and the optimism of the Renaissance outlook.

Although Renaissance thinkers adored the classics, they were also capable of casting a critical eye over ancient texts. Whereas the scholastics had tended to take at face value all the assertions of classical philosophers like Aristotle, during the Renaissance, ancient, or allegedly ancient, manuscripts that advanced ideas that were clearly false were revealed as frauds. For example, throughout the Middle Ages, the papacy had referred to a document known as the Donation of Constantine that supposedly proved that the Roman Emperor Constantine had granted the pope full authority over Western Europe. In the fifteenth century, a Renaissance historian proved through analysis of the Latin style of the document that it was a forgery. Thus, while Renaissance thinkers certainly romanticized classical civilization, they were not starstruck fools.

One of the defining features of the Renaissance was the value it placed on education. As a result, countless schools, emphasizing classical studies, were founded in Italy and throughout Europe. In addition, some Renaissance literature, such as Baldassare Castiglione's immensely popular *Book of the Courtier*, aimed to educate and elevate its readers. Castiglione advanced a set of guidelines that a Renaissance gentleman could follow to achieve wisdom, refinement, and personal honor. In particular, he advised his readers to study the classics, polish their communication skills, and cultivate their athletic and artistic abilities.

It is often said that the humanists, following Castiglione's lead, sought to create a universal man—that is, a man who excelled in as many spheres of activity as possible and who contributed greatly to society as a result. Supporters of the Renaissance believed, furthermore, that human achievements should be recognized and celebrated. They hungered for fame and glory as much as medieval thinkers hungered for salvation.

During the Renaissance, although girls were purposefully excluded from the vast majority of humanist schools, women as well as men showed an appreciation for classical civilization, humanist thought, and new artistic forms. Wealthy and powerful Italian women provided valuable patronage to Renaissance writers, scholars, and artists. Rarely, women also became celebrated for their literary and artistic achievements. A tiny number even led Italian city-states.

One of the most important female authors of the medieval period was Christine de Pisan, who in some ways personified the transition to a Renaissance outlook. De Pisan, who grew up at the court of the French king, received an outstanding education and later supported herself as a widow by writing poetry and books. Like Castiglione, she showed a special interest in publishing advice that others, in this case women, could follow to maximize their wisdom and virtue. She also defended women from misogynistic charges that they were devoted to sin, deception, and the corruption of men. Her last work was a celebratory biography of Joan of Arc.

In the end, Renaissance thinkers played a significant role in defining modern Western Civilization's attitudes about gender. Renaissance thinkers hotly debated the qualities and abilities of women. Even when they defended women, however, they usually did so by conceding that some women could mimic virtues that were considered essentially masculine in nature.

Renaissance art was not intended simply to be beautiful. It was also a vivid demonstration of the wealth and good taste of whoever commissioned it. It should be remembered that many Renaissance patrons were, by medieval standards, *nouveaux riches* (that is, people who were newly wealthy and important). They thus had no long legacy of family honor to fall back on. For this reason, merchants, financiers, businessmen, professionals, and highly skilled craftsmen often commissioned works of art in order to bring honor to themselves. In particular, they favored portraiture, executed either in the form of paintings or sculpture, which depicted the patron himself, and sometimes herself, as a wise, virtuous, pious, generous, respected, and cultivated person.

As the demand for art increased, Renaissance artists found themselves suddenly sought after, hailed as geniuses, and, most of all, well paid. As one might expect, Renaissance architects and artists strove to imitate the ancients. Thus, in the classical tradition, Renaissance art emphasized the importance of harmony, balance, proportionality, and realism. The last quality was perhaps the most highly valued. Renaissance artists often displayed an obsessive attention to detail in their recreations of human forms and elements in nature. They experimented with revolutionary techniques that would influence Western art for more than 500 years, including new uses of light, shading, color, and especially what is known as perspective.

Giotto, a Florentine who was one of the first Renaissance painters, employed groundbreaking techniques to make his two-dimensional canvases look like three-dimensional space. Later, in the fifteenth century, other Renaissance artists, such as Filippo Brunelleschi and Masaccio, along with an art expert named Leon Battista Alberti, refined techniques of drawing and painting in perspective using the tools of mathematics.

The most famous Renaissance artists are also some of the latest, and all of them worked, for at least part of their careers, in Florence.

Leonardo da Vinci, who lived from 1452 to 1519, was a great inventor, naturalist, and engineer, in addition to possessing legendary artistic talents. His paintings of *The Last Supper* and the *Mona Lisa* are among the most exquisite and celebrated works produced using Renaissance techniques. The *Mona Lisa*, housed in the Louvre Museum in Paris, attracts over six million admirers every year.

Raphael, a masterful painter who lived from 1483 to 1520, produced captivating works including the *School of Athens*, a panoramic fresco adorning the library in the Vatican Palace. It shows ancient philosophers gathered in a classical building.

Michelangelo Buonarroti, who lived from 1475 to 1564, is perhaps the most renowned Renaissance artist of all. As an architect, he designed the famous dome of St. Peter's Basilica in Rome. As a sculptor, he created timeless works like his nude of *David*, whom he portrayed more as a Greek god than as a Hebrew shepherd boy. And, as a painter, Michelangelo is best known for his frescoes on the ceiling of the Sistine Chapel that illustrate scenes in the Old Testament.

As Michelangelo's work on St. Peter's and in the Sistine Chapel indicates, much of the finest Renaissance art was commissioned by various popes. Much of that art can be seen today in St. Peter's itself, in the Vatican Museum, or elsewhere in Rome. Nonetheless, the artistic influences spawned by the Renaissance spread to every corner of Europe, from Titian in Venice, to Albrecht Dürer in Germany, to Pieter Bruegel the Elder in the Netherlands.

What values did Renaissance artists and thinkers espouse?

Politics in the Renaissance

Great intellectual and artistic movements do not necessarily arise in conditions of political stability. Italy during the Renaissance, for instance, was a very confused and violent place. This very confusion, however, may have contributed to the achievements of humanist thought and Renaissance art, because frequent changes in government, and in the balance of power between states, created a sense of insecurity among rulers. These rulers were, therefore, more likely to become generous patrons, because they were desperate to prove their legitimacy.

The five most important Italian city-states were Milan, Florence, the Papal States, Naples, and Venice. Until the fifteenth century, most Italian city-states were republics—that is, countries without hereditary monarchs. This often meant that a city council was in charge. Voting was limited, and usually the richest and most established families in the city predominated, sharing power to a very limited extent with up-and-coming merchants and bankers, professionals and business owners, and craftsmen organized into guilds, all of whom resented their marginal political status. The poor, who represented the majority of the population, were permitted virtually no input into the political system.

During the fifteenth century, class antagonisms grew to unprecedented levels. Internal instability, including high rates of violent crime, developed in many cities. In Florence, a wild-eyed, populist friar named Savonarola briefly ruled. He ordered many allegedly unholy books and pieces of art burned before he was himself burned as a heretic.

Domestic discontent, combined with the stresses of warfare between city-states, finally led to a breakdown in the republican institutions in many Italian cities. Most city-states consequently embraced the leadership of despots, who hired mercenary armies, led by unscrupulous brokers called *condottieri*, in order to create and maintain a semblance of order.

In Florence, the headquarters of the Renaissance, the Medici family established a despotism. Lorenzo the Magnificent eliminated almost all pretense of republicanism and exercised authoritarian control over the city starting in 1480. Several Medicis later served as popes. A dynasty of despots also developed in Milan. Milan called itself a Duchy, but its Dukes were all the descendants of a strongman who had usurped control. Only in Venice did the traditional republican style of government survive. In the Papal States, of course, the pope was in charge, but the Renaissance popes participated in intrigue, repression, and violence no less than any other Italian ruler.

Starting in 1494, a series of foreign invasions by France, Spain, and the Holy Roman Empire worsened Italy's problems with political instability. The Valois family, which ruled France, and the Hapsburg family, which ruled Spain and the Holy Roman Empire, viewed the wealth of Italy as an attractive prize that might tip the scales in their long-running battle for European supremacy. In the end, France, Spain, and the Holy Roman Emperor accomplished little except mutual exhaustion in the course of their military adventures in Italy. The seemingly endless cycle of foreign invasions did achieve one thing, however: it prevented any single Italian despot from establishing his dominance over all of his peers. Thus, it also prevented Italy from being unified as a nation-state until the mid-nineteenth century, long after countries such as England, France, and Spain had developed strong national identities and centralized governments.

One Renaissance political philosopher, Niccolò Machiavelli, was inspired, by Italy's disunity and tumultuous instability, to think creatively about how a ruler ought to behave. In the process, he developed a reputation as an unscrupulous, if pragmatic, political commentator.

Machiavelli had many years of political experience under his belt. He had also watched Italy succumb to foreign invasions, and as a result he developed a heartfelt desire to see a strong Italian ruler emerge who would be able to unite the peninsula, restore order, and expel the outsiders. In 1513, Machiavelli wrote *The Prince*, which was an analysis of the attributes that a great political leader ought to possess. Unlike previous medieval political philosophers, who had sought to create an essential harmony between the behavior of rulers and the precepts of Christian morality, Machiavelli counseled Italy's leaders to be cruel, dishonest, and cunning, if necessary, to ensure the survival and prosperity of their states. Machiavelli asserted that the most successful rulers were not those who enjoyed God's favor but those who helped themselves by eliminating all opposition and pursuing military strength.

Machiavelli's secular ideas were shocking to many of his readers, but they probably seemed commonsensical to many despots. Unfortunately, from Machiavelli's perspective, however, the perfectly crafty and ruthless despot who he was hoping would arise to unite Renaissance Italy never appeared.

How did political instability and disunity in Renaissance Italy work to the advantage of Renaissance artists and thinkers?

The Renaissance in Northern Europe

Humanism, and to some degree Renaissance art, flourished in Northern Europe too, but it took a considerable amount of time before Renaissance influences made it to places such as England, France, the Netherlands, Spain, and Germany. Nonetheless, by the late fifteenth century and the sixteenth century, the Northern Renaissance was underway. It continued the humanist legacy begun in Italy, but some important differences emerged. In Italy, new architectural styles influenced by classical precedents came into vogue, whereas in Northern Europe the Gothic style remained popular. More importantly, whereas in Italy a largely secular spirit had prevailed during the Renaissance, Northern European humanists were more likely to focus on Christian piety. Although they were often free thinkers and fierce critics of the abuses of the Catholic Church, their overriding goal was to purify the Christian faith and thus to strengthen it, not to sideline it. For this reason, Northern European humanists are often known as Christian Humanists.

Exemplifying this more pious version of the Renaissance in Northern Europe was an organization called the Brethren of the Common Life, a movement of Dutch laymen, along with some clergymen. The Brethren were dedicated to classical learning, to reducing the power of theologians and priests, and to increasing the average Christian's knowledge of scripture, as well as his or her personal faith in Jesus Christ. These goals were accomplished mainly by the foundation of numerous schools in which brothers of the movement served as instructors.

One of the chief reasons for the spread of Renaissance ideas from Italy to the north was the invention of the movable type printing press around 1450 by the goldsmith Johann Gutenberg, who lived in Mainz, Germany. The production of books had previously been extremely costly, and in any case few Europeans could read them. By the fifteenth century, though, several intersecting trends altered this situation. First, the number of universities and smaller schools was surging, increasing the size of the literate population, the demand for books, and the number of authors. Second, paper-making had become more efficient and cost-effective. Lastly and most importantly, Gutenberg's innovative printing press was soon operating in many European cities and was dramatically lowering the cost of printed materials.

By 1500, although the vast majority of Europeans still could neither read nor afford to purchase a book, the number of people who had access to printed information had greatly increased. Thus, Europeans' capacity to share ideas rose to unprecedented heights, leading to a variety of exciting—and in some cases potentially dangerous—consequences. Many historians count the printing press as one of the most important inventions in all of history.

Among the greatest exemplars of the Northern European Renaissance were Desiderius Erasmus, Sir Thomas More, and William Shakespeare. All were active in the sixteenth century (and, in Shakespeare's case, also in the early seventeenth), when the Italian Renaissance was winding down.

Erasmus was Dutch, and he was educated by the Brethren of the Common Life. He therefore acquired a great respect for scholarship, especially the study of the Bible in its original ancient Hebrew and Greek versions. The message of the Bible was, he believed, so universal and valuable that even "the weakest woman" should have the opportunity to read it. When he was not teaching or writing, Erasmus traveled through Europe lecturing on the Bible and promoting his own philosophy of Christ, which emphasized kindness, toleration, simplicity, charity, strong individual faith, and criticism of corrupt and self-serving clergymen and monks. Erasmus's books were enormously popular. In 1516, Erasmus completed a Greek version of the New Testament. It became an important resource for both the proponents and the enemies of the Protestant Reformation, discussed in Chapter 9. Overall, Erasmus helped to inspire a surge in Bible scholarship that became characteristic of the Northern European Renaissance as a whole, captivating leading thinkers in France, Germany, and Spain, as well as the Netherlands.

Sir Thomas More was an Englishman and a good friend of Erasmus. He is best known for his book *Utopia*, in which he imagined an ideal island community in which private property had been abolished. More believed that greed was at the root of many of society's problems, and, therefore, if property were held in common, and a classical education was made available to everyone, a sort of morally perfect community could be built. More's idealism, and his stubborn adherence to the Catholic faith, eventually became an annoyance to England's King Henry VIII. As described in Chapter 9, More was beheaded as a traitor in 1535. Today, Saint Thomas More is widely admired, by Catholics and Protestants alike, for his integrity and courage.

Few dispute that William Shakespeare's plays are among the best ever written, but interpreting the meaning of those plays is nonetheless difficult. In one sense, though, Shakespeare's plays are thoroughly humanistic: they revolve around the strengths and weaknesses of vividly portrayed individuals, that is, characters. Moreover, Shakespeare's plays strongly suggest that man's struggle to improve himself in this life is much more important than the quest for salvation after death. Yet another sign of Shakespeare's Renaissance outlook lies in the fact that he chose to set many of his plays, including *Romeo and Juliet*, in Italy. Many of his plays also include an eclectic set of references to classical literature, history, and mythology. Shakespeare was himself something of a universal man, possessing talent not just as a playwright and a poet, but also as an actor, producer, businessman, and investor.

How did the Northern European Renaissance differ from the Italian Renaissance?

Conclusions

The end of the Middle Ages around 1500 did not necessarily imply a sudden break with tradition. On the contrary, most Europeans remained pious Catholics; most people were still peasants who toiled under the supervision, if not fully under the control, of the feudal nobility; the economy was overwhelmingly agrarian; political systems were only barely centralized; reason was still subordinated to faith; and the revolutionary outlook of the Renaissance still affected only a tiny minority of scholars, artists, writers, and members of the elite.

As we shall see, though, Europe in the sixteenth and seventeenth centuries would face a dizzying array of challenges, and, as it did so, it relied less and less on medieval assumptions and methods. Old paradigms, such as feudalism, manorialism, and scholasticism, were slowly giving way to royal absolutism, representative government, capitalism, Protestantism, and the scientific method. In a sense, however, even Europeans' ability to conduct such bold experiments in thought and practice rested on the foundation of the accomplishments of the Middle Ages. In the medieval period, despite their failures, Europeans had built a civilization that was as wealthy, productive, enterprising, militarily potent, technologically advanced, politically well organized, culturally vibrant, and fruitfully interconnected with the outside world as any that had ever existed before. As it turned out, Europeans would amass even more impressive achievements in the centuries to come.

Key Terms for Chapter 8

The Black Death—also known as the bubonic plague, it was a terrible illness that decimated Europe's population from 1347 to 1351, leading to many political, social, and economic changes.

Hundred Years' War—a long-running conflict between England and France, caused by the desire of the English monarchy to rule France. Ultimately, the French would prevail and keep their independence.

Joan of Arc—a French peasant girl who claimed to experience visions in which God commanded her to help liberate France from the English. She played a significant role in France's victory in the Hundred Years' War.

Babylonian Captivity—a phrase used to describe the period from 1309 to 1377, when every pope was a Frenchman, and the papacy was based in the French town of Avignon. The subservience of the papacy to the French monarchy was symptomatic of the weakness of the pope in the Late Middle Ages.

158   *The Late Middle Ages and the Renaissance*

Ottoman Empire—a large and resilient Muslim state, originating in Turkey, that conquered the Byzantine Empire and for centuries ruled large parts of the Middle East, North Africa, and southeastern Europe.

Parliament—England's partly elected legislature that shared power with the king. In most of late medieval Europe, kings elbowed aside similar assemblies. Parliament was the exception.

Renaissance—Rebirth. This was an intellectual and artistic movement occurring primarily in late medieval Italy. Its aim was to assist Europeans in emerging from the "Mongol Yoke," in realizing their full human potential, and in rediscovering classical philosophy, literature, and art.

Baldassare Castiglione—a Renaissance figure who wrote *The Book of the Courtier*, which described how a man could become refined, honorable, and persuasive.

Christine de Pisan—a Renaissance poet and author who sought to improve her society's attitudes toward women.

Michelangelo—one of the most widely admired Renaissance figures, and a universal man who excelled as an architect, sculptor, and painter.

Niccolò Machiavelli—Renaissance-era political philosopher who counseled Italy's leaders to be ruthless in consolidating their power.

Christian Humanists—a term used to describe the supporters of the Renaissance in Northern Europe, who were generally more devout than their Italian counterparts.

Printing press—one of the most revolutionary technological advances in history, because it made the sharing of ideas infinitely easier. It was invented around 1450 by the German Johann Gutenberg.

Review Questions for Chapter 8

1. Describe three ways in which the Black Death had a major impact on medieval society.
2. The decline of the Church, and the rise of strong monarchical governments, were two of the most important developments of the Late Middle Ages. Give two specific examples that illustrate these historical phenomena.
3. The word renaissance is often applied to a variety of reform initiatives in modern times, mainly to make these initiatives seem grand and unquestionably beneficial. First, describe the meaning of the term in a historical context. Then, give an example of an event, a process, or a policy of the last 100 years that you feel could be fairly described as embodying a "renaissance."
4. Select one of the Renaissance figures chronicled in Chapter 8 and write a biographical sketch of him or her. Then, describe which contemporary figure you feel he or she most resembles. Justify your choice.
5. Imagine that in the fifteenth century religious and cultural conservatives had succeeded in stamping out the Renaissance. Explain three ways in

which modern Western Civilization might be different if Renaissance influences were removed.

Further Reading

Allmand, Christopher. *The Hundred Years War: England and France at War c.1300–c.1450*. New York: Cambridge University Press. 2001.

Astell, Ann W. and Bonnie Wheeler, eds. *Joan of Arc and Spirituality*. New York: Palgrave Macmillan. 2004.

Biow, Douglas. *Doctors, Ambassadors, Secretaries: Humanism and Professions in Renaissance Italy*. Chicago: University of Chicago Press. 2002.

Goldthwaite, Richard A. *Wealth and the Demand for Art in Italy: 1300–1600*. Baltimore, MD: Johns Hopkins University Press. 2010.

Herlihy, David. *The Black Death and the Transformation of the West*. Cambridge, MA: Harvard University Press. 2001.

Jardine, Lisa. *Erasmus, Man of Letters*. Princeton, NJ: Princeton University Press. 2015.

King, Ross. *Michelangelo and the Pope's Ceiling*. New York: Bloomsbury. 2014.

Kirkpatrick, Robin. *The European Renaissance: 1400–1600*. New York: Routledge. 2016.

Najemy, John M. *A History of Florence: 1200–1575*. Malden, MA: Blackwell. 2011.

Servadio, Gaia. *Renaissance Woman*. London: I.B. Tauris. 2016.

Swanson, R. N. *The Routledge History of Medieval Christianity: 1050–1500*. New York: Routledge. 2015.

Witt, Ronald G. *"In the Footsteps of the Ancients": The Origins of Humanism From Lovato to Bruni*. Boston, MA: Brill. 2003.

9 The Age of Discovery, the Protestant Reformation, and the Wars of Religion, 1492–1648

Introduction

In the late 1400s, Europeans began the process of exploring and colonizing large parts of the New World, Africa, and Asia. As a result, Europe's knowledge of the rest of the world increased dramatically, as did European wealth and power.

In 1517, however, a dramatic split began to develop in Western European Christianity, as Protestants left the Catholic Church, unleashing powerful religious animosities. Much of the prosperity gained through trade with and exploitation of the New World, Africa, and Asia, therefore, was squandered in generations of religiously motivated warfare.

Today, while the conflicts of the sixteenth and seventeenth centuries have largely been set aside, the religious division of Europe into a Protestant North and a Catholic South persists. In addition, the massive changes to Western Civilization caused by increased contact with Africa and Asia, and by the settlement of the Americas, are still unfolding and reverberating. Western Civilization today is essentially a world-straddling phenomenon, and this is largely a result of the spirit of discovery and conquest that seized Europe in the century and a half after Columbus's first transatlantic journey in 1492.

Spanish and Portuguese Exploration

Before the sixteenth century, the hub of European trade was the Mediterranean region. It was Italian, Turkish, and Arab merchants who profited the most from the sale of African, Asian, and Middle Eastern luxury goods, especially textiles and spices, to rich Europeans in exchange for gold and silver. The wealth of the Mediterranean traders naturally caused jealousy among some Europeans, who longed for an alternative route to the markets of the East. This desire only increased after 1453, when the Ottoman conquest of Constantinople threatened Western access to Eastern trade goods.

Until the end of the 1400s, Portugal and Spain had been focused almost entirely on battling the Moors, Muslims who ruled the southern part of the Iberian Peninsula. When the last Moorish kingdom finally collapsed in

1492, the Portuguese and Spanish were suddenly able to concentrate on new ventures. Their ongoing desire to convert or kill infidels was a powerful motivator, as was their thirst for gold.

The Portuguese were the first to send their fast, maneuverable sailing ships, called caravels, headlong into the Ocean Sea, now known as the Atlantic Ocean. At first they established control only over several small island chains and a few trading stations on the African coast, which nevertheless allowed them to send a profitable stream of gold, spices, and slaves back to Europe.

As the Portuguese learned more about the Atlantic's winds and ocean currents, they pushed further south. In 1497, Vasco da Gama finally rounded the Cape of Good Hope at Africa's southern tip and journeyed on to India, dabbling in piracy along the way. Although 70 percent of da Gama's men never made it home, that initial voyage netted the Portuguese a cargo of pepper that made them a small fortune in Europe.

By the early sixteenth century, larger, better-armed Portuguese vessels were visiting ports and establishing bases throughout East Africa, the Middle East, India, China, and Indonesia. Portuguese ships and gunnery were so advanced that African and Asian merchants had little choice but to do business on Portuguese terms. Meanwhile, the Mediterranean traders who had once dominated Europe's dealings with the East saw their profits wither.

The success of the Portuguese drove their Iberian neighbors, the Spanish, to seek an alternate route that would allow them to gain access to the wealth of Asia. An Italian sea captain named Christopher Columbus convinced Spain's rulers, King Ferdinand and Queen Isabella, that he could reach Japan and China simply by sailing west for 3,000 miles. Columbus, like all educated Europeans at the time, assumed that the world was round, but he also believed that it was significantly smaller than it actually was.

In September 1492, Columbus departed from Spain's Canary Islands toward the west, and in October he landed on a small island that is today part of the Bahamas. Columbus made a total of four voyages to the New World before his death in 1506, but he never fully realized that the lands he had discovered were not in Asia.

The natives whom Columbus encountered were, in his eyes, strange and primitive. Many Indians, as Columbus called the Native Americans, since he assumed he had reached the East Indies, wore little clothing. None of the Caribbean Indian cultures had a written language, and none of them used iron weaponry. Some practiced human sacrifice.

Almost from the first moment that Europeans and Indians confronted one another, Europeans saw the Indians as teachable savages who would make ideal workers and passable Christians. The Indians, for their part, marveled at the Europeans' bizarre appearance and seemingly supernatural technology. Some Indians considered the Spaniards to be gods. Before long many Indians would come to doubt the Europeans' divinity as well as their good

Figure 9.1 A replica of the *Niña*—one of three ships that participated in Columbus's first voyage to the Americas.

Mike Baird/Flickr/Wikimedia Commons.

intentions, but by then the superiority of European arms, and the devastating impact of European diseases, made Indian resistance hopeless.

Although initially Europeans were apt to focus on the large-scale extraction of gold and silver from the Americas, and the introduction of Christianity to the natives in return, in reality the interaction between European and Native American cultures, environments, and economies was much more complex. America gave Europe tobacco, the potato, corn, tomatoes, cacao beans (used to make chocolate), and possibly syphilis. Europeans in turn introduced to the Americas firearms, advanced textiles, the wheel, horses, sheep, cows, chickens, wheat, cotton, and coffee, as well as many aspects of European languages, culture, and religion. Some scholars refer to this cultural back-and-forth as the Columbian Exchange.

Whatever the Europeans may have contributed in a positive sense to the Indians, the horrendous impact of European diseases, especially smallpox, often combined with harsh treatment verging on enslavement, left a more lasting impression. In many areas Indians largely or totally disappeared within a few generations. In Mexico, for instance, the number of Indians may have shrunk from around 25 million to only one to two million after less than a century. The natives on the island of Hispaniola were essentially wiped out. Some have labeled this demographic catastrophe a form of genocide, but the

Spanish did not intend to eliminate the Indians. In any case, one important consequence of this decline in the Indian population, and thus in the size of the indigenous workforce, was that the Spanish and Portuguese, and later the English, French, and Dutch, eventually chose to import vast numbers of African slaves to the New World.

Why did the Portuguese and the Spanish launch the "voyages of discovery"?

Spain Conquers the Aztecs and the Incas, and England, France, and the Netherlands Become Colonial Powers

Among the strongest and most complex of the American civilizations were the Aztecs in modern Mexico and the Incas in Peru. The Spanish quickly vanquished both empires.

Hernán Cortés landed on the Mexican coast in 1519. When he and his 500 men reached the sprawling Aztec capital of Tenochtitlán, they were amazed by its obvious wealth and sophistication. Aztec architecture, artistry, and engineering, in particular, were highly advanced. The Aztecs, however, also practiced a cruel religion that led them to sacrifice thousands of human captives each year by carving open their chests and wrenching out their beating hearts. The Indian groups that the Aztecs had conquered and exploited, many of whose people had been led to ritualized slaughter, were thus all too eager to help Cortés destroy the Aztec state. These Indian allies, along with Spanish firearms, cannons, and steel swords, made quick work of the Aztec armies, and, by 1521, Mexico had been renamed New Spain.

The Inca empire, based in the mountain city of Cuzco in what is now Peru, controlled most of the western half of South America. Its official religion was considerably less bloodthirsty than that of the Aztecs, and its agricultural economy and its system of roads were impressive. When the Spanish warrior Francisco Pizarro arrived in Peru in 1531, he brought with him less than 200 men with whom to defeat an Incan army of 100,000. Pizarro's guile and cruelty, however, combined with the Spaniards' superior weapons and the ravages of European diseases, defeated the Incas by 1534.

In both Mexico and Peru, the highest priority of the Spanish *conquistadores* (conquerors) after their rapid victories was to scoop up all the gold they could find. Only after these campaigns of plunder had run their course did the Spanish take steps to organize their new territories and exploit them more systematically. The political, economic, and social system that eventually developed in Spanish America was based on a racial hierarchy in which the *peninsulares* (Spanish-born whites) and *creoles* (whites born in the Americas) dominated the Indians, African slaves, and *mestizos* (persons of mixed race).

The three main pillars of the new society in Latin America were the Catholic Church, the colonial government, and the landowning and mercantile class. Although some Church officials, such as Bartolomé de las Casas, a Dominican monk, campaigned successfully to improve the Indians' legal standing, in practice the Church and the government looked the other way as Spanish employers worked to death millions of Native Americans. While some Indian religious and cultural practices survived in muted form, the Spanish were largely successful in molding the cities, churches, *haciendas* (ranches), and mines of the New World in the image of Spain itself. Once each year, a treasure fleet laden with American mineral wealth lumbered toward Spain. The profits of Spain's colonial empire soon spurred other European states to undertake colonial ventures of their own.

Throughout the sixteenth century, Spain dominated in the Americas, while Portugal controlled most of Europe's trade with Africa and Asia. Initially, the English, French, and Dutch were only strong enough to nibble at the edges of these great empires, often by raiding Spanish and Portuguese ships and ports. By the start of the seventeenth century, however, the English, French, and Dutch had sponsored voyages of exploration and trading expeditions throughout the globe.

During the seventeenth century, Britain and France acquired substantial empires in mainland North America, discussed in Chapter 10. Meanwhile, the Dutch muscled in on the Portuguese in the spice trade so successfully that, by 1613, they dominated the spice islands of Indonesia. The English, unable to compete with the Dutch in Indonesia, strengthened their trade ties with India instead. Portugal gradually lost most of its African and Asian empire, but it held on to its largest and most valuable colony: Brazil. Spain, England, France, and the Netherlands all controlled small islands in the Caribbean Sea by the early 1600s. There they initially grew tobacco and made modest profits, but later, with the help of African slave labor, they established sugar plantations that were a source of incredible riches.

European exploration and conquest in the Americas began, therefore, with the hunger for gold and Christian converts. It reached maturity in the craving for sweetened beverages and desserts. All along, the strong national governments, self-confident religious outlooks, well-organized commercial interests, and refined military technologies that Europeans had initially created in order to compete with each other provided vital resources in their efforts to dominate the native peoples of the Americas, Africa, and Asia. One key result was what historians refer to as the Atlantic World: a vast network of political, economic, demographic, epidemiological, religious, cultural, and environmental interconnections, with the great expanse of the Atlantic Ocean at its core. Across that ocean, an endless stream of traders, missionaries, immigrants, soldiers, slaves, and others traveled. The Atlantic World was clearly, however, a realm in which Europeans predominated.

Why were the Spanish able to conquer the Aztec and Inca empires so quickly?

Causes of the Protestant Reformation

As Europe was expanding its reach worldwide, a religious controversy was brewing that was destined to break apart the Catholic Church. The splintering of the Church, which occurred mainly during the sixteenth century, is called the Reformation. It is also sometimes known as the Protestant Reformation, because the Europeans who rejected the authority, doctrines, and practices of the Catholic Church called themselves Protestants.

Throughout the Middle Ages, the Catholic Church had been the one institution that united most of Europe. Nevertheless, even during the medieval period, the Church included people with diverse and opposing viewpoints, and ordinary Europeans often criticized official Church pronouncements—although in doing so they risked being condemned as heretics.

The Renaissance, the invention of the printing press, the discovery of the Americas, and other developments had already led many Europeans to question traditional ideas and practices. A more worldly and skeptical analysis of the Church became possible, and many Europeans became convinced that reform was vital. Scholars, for example, had begun to read the Bible in its original ancient Hebrew and Greek versions, and some were criticizing the Church's official Latin translation of the Bible as grossly distorted. Some Europeans also advocated translating the original ancient Hebrew and Greek Biblical texts into some vernacular languages (i.e., languages in everyday use), such as English and German—a practice that the Church had forbidden.

Other factors increased the frustration that many Catholics felt toward their Church. First, Church taxes, which supported the lavish lifestyles of high Church officials, were widely resented. Second, as increasingly powerful national governments squeezed their subjects for more tax revenue, Europeans became upset at the Church, which enjoyed exemptions from many forms of taxation. Third, many Church officials lived luxuriously, but they did little to earn their considerable incomes. Many had simply purchased their offices or received them due to family connections. Pope Leo X, for instance, who was pope during the early stages of the Reformation, had become a cardinal at the age of 16, largely because he was a member of the powerful and wealthy Medici family.

To make matters worse, the Church's greed even influenced its interpretation of Christian doctrine. Beginning in the fourteenth century, Church authorities had begun to offer "indulgences" for sale to Catholics, both living and dead. The definition of an indulgence has been a point of controversy ever since. Some critics of the Church alleged that an indulgence was essentially a free pass that allowed one to sin as much as one liked, and then immediately upon death receive the forgiveness of sins necessary to enter heaven. In other words, they alleged that, by selling indulgences, the Church was selling salvation. In truth, this was not what the Catholic Church intended. Forgiveness of sins, according to the Church, was granted to all Christians by the grace of God. An indulgence, therefore, was something rather different.

To be accepted into heaven, a Catholic was supposed to do penance for all of his or her sins. Normally, one would do penance by praying, going on a pilgrimage, or donating to the needy. This penance did not earn one salvation. Instead, penance paid "the wages of sin" and allowed one to enter heaven *immediately* after death. Without doing penance, one would have to spend a period of time in "purgatory," an ill-defined place or condition where sins are purged before one is deemed worthy of admittance into heaven. The purchase of an indulgence, therefore, was a substitution for performing acts of penance. An indulgence allowed any Catholic to skip some or all of the time he might have to spend in purgatory.

The problem, however, was that many Catholic officials sold indulgences aggressively, and they promised their customers more than was permitted according to Church doctrines. The sale of indulgences became a profitable industry within the Church, and many unscrupulous clergymen and salesmen made little distinction between the purchase of an indulgence and full, permanent forgiveness of any and all sins that one might commit.

Many Christians became fierce opponents of indulgences. Entrance into heaven, argued these critics, was not a commodity to be bought and sold. True, it was the Church's job to help its flock make the journey into heaven, but not to make decisions on God's behalf. Many Europeans came to believe, in fact, that there was no purgatory. Purgatory was simply a myth that the Church had created in order to manipulate its followers and milk them for profits. In the sixteenth century, most Europeans were extremely anxious to achieve salvation. Thus, the idea that the Church could be toying with the message of the Bible, and misleading Christians about the true nature of sin and redemption, made many Europeans very angry.

Why were so many sixteenth-century Europeans upset at the Catholic Church?

Martin Luther and the Protestant Reformation

Martin Luther was born and grew up in Saxony, in central Germany. His parents expected him to study law, but in 1505, at the age of 21, he became a monk instead. Luther later became a professor of theology at the University of Wittenberg. He was intensely dedicated to his Christian faith and pondered for many years how one could be righteous enough to deserve salvation.

In October 1517, Luther was ready to share his views with the world, even though he understood that this might invite severe persecution. He posted a document called the "95 Theses" on the door of a Wittenberg chapel. The document was primarily an attack on the sale of indulgences.

Word about Luther's defiance of the Church spread rapidly throughout Germany, and, over the next four years, Luther further developed his religious principles. He also began work on a German translation of the Bible. "Here I stand," proclaimed Luther, rebuffing all attempts by the Catholic authorities to silence him. Protestants—those who wished to practice their Christian faith outside of the Catholic Church—came to see Luther as a heroic opponent of Catholic tyranny and a crusader for religious freedom. Catholics, on the other hand, came to see him as a vain, self-interested heretic. In any case, Luther's followers grew rapidly in number and became known as Lutherans. Their demands were and are the minimum demands of all Protestants, so it is important to understand Lutheranism in depth.

Lutherans believed that the Catholic Church was wrong to suggest that human beings can earn, or expedite, their salvation. Luther viewed human beings as inherently sinful, and he denied that any person could ever "work off" his sins, in purgatory or elsewhere. In fact, Luther denied that purgatory existed. Salvation, according to Lutheranism, is a gift from God, based on the sacrifice of Jesus Christ on the cross. Therefore, any person who has faith in Christ as his or her savior will be saved, regardless of whether he or she does good works or is "worthy" in the eyes of the Church. Protestants called this idea "justification by faith."

Furthermore, Lutherans believed that the opinions of Church authorities are less important than the message of the Bible. Ideally, Christians should therefore learn ancient Hebrew and Greek, so that they may study the Bible in its original form, but it should also be available in vernacular languages. Church services should be conducted in the vernacular as well. Catholics, by contrast, were still insisting that all Church services and documents, including the Bible, should be in Latin, even though most Europeans could not read or understand it. Lutherans also advocated reducing the number of Church holidays and eliminating the veneration of saints so that Christians could focus on Christ himself and on the message of the Bible. In all these ways, Lutherans saw themselves as returning Christianity to its foundations.

Lutherans further believed that Church officials, including priests, were not a separate or a superior class of beings. They should not be exempted from taxation, and they should not have any special privileges. In addition, Lutherans advocated closing many monasteries and convents, which they viewed as a drain on society, and they wanted the property of these institutions turned over to the state or to charitable organizations. Protestants thus largely ignored the good work that was being done by many Catholic priests, monks, and nuns, who for centuries had been responsible for caring for orphans, the poor, the sick, and the elderly.

Because Lutherans saw priests as ordinary mortals, they believed that priests should marry—Luther himself married a former nun—and should be governed by civil authorities and by religious experts, not by the pope. Indeed, Lutherans denied that the pope should have any power whatsoever over their new church. They pointed to the corruption, assassinations, wars of conquest, deceit, sacrilege, gluttony, and sexual indiscretions practiced by many past popes as sure proof that the various "Holy Fathers" were not as holy as they claimed. A steadfast rejection of the authority of the papacy is the core belief that unites all Protestants.

Not surprisingly, the pope excommunicated Martin Luther in 1521. Luther had no choice but to go into hiding. He stayed for about a year in the magnificent Wartburg Castle, where, to conceal his identity, he impersonated a bearded knight.

The Holy Roman Emperor at the time, who had limited authority over all of Germany, was Charles V, a member of the Hapsburg family. In addition to the Holy Roman Empire, which included the Hapsburg lands in Austria, Bohemia, and Hungary, Charles ruled Spain (and its colonies), the Netherlands, and parts of Italy. Charles V, who was strongly Catholic, tried to silence Luther, but ultimately the emperor was distracted by wars against the French in Italy and against the Turks in Hungary. Throughout the 1520s and 1530s, therefore, Lutheranism managed to spread throughout northern and central Germany. Several prominent princes embraced Lutheranism, as did many self-governing towns and cities. In addition, the Scandinavian countries all accepted the Lutheran faith.

In 1555, after an abortive attempt to crush Protestantism by force, Charles V accepted that the progress of Lutheranism was irreversible. In the Peace of Augsburg, the Holy Roman Emperor recognized the right of the ruler of each of Germany's more than 300 minor states to choose the official religion of his people. Catholicism would be a crime in Lutheran areas, and Lutheranism would be a crime in Catholic areas. As a result, many Germans migrated to a new location where their faith was legally permitted. In Protestant areas, Lutheran rulers often confiscated the property of the Catholic Church, enriching themselves in the process. The leaders of Lutheran states also appreciated the fact that Protestant communities recognized the legal supremacy of secular authorities, whereas Catholics had a stubborn habit of complaining to a "higher authority," that is, the Church.

Ultimately, Lutheranism created a revolution in theology and in religious practices in large areas of northern Europe, but it did not create a social revolution affecting the class structure. Luther opposed a peasant revolt in 1524–25, and he encouraged his followers to obey their princely and aristocratic leaders. German cities remained under the control of a few privileged families, along with rich merchants. Moreover, in his old age, Luther's formerly conciliatory attitude toward Jews was transformed into bitter hatred, and he wrote a tract denouncing Jews as "poisonous . . . worms." Thus, although Lutherans struggled against what they regarded as Catholic religious tyranny, they imposed an equally rigorous tyranny on Jews—and on other Protestant groups that they believed took reform measures too far.

Lutheranism also made few substantial changes in the status of women. Protestant women gained the right to divorce their husbands, but only in the most extreme cases. Protestant women may also have had greater access to education, because they were encouraged to read the Bible. In addition, the wives of priests played an important role in many Protestant communities. Luther praised marriage in general, and he specifically condemned the extreme misogyny in some Catholic writings. Still, Protestant women, like their Catholic counterparts, were strongly urged to submit to the authority of their husbands. In addition, Protestants abolished the female dimension of Catholic religious devotion, including the proliferation of convents and the veneration of female saints, including the Virgin Mary. The Protestant

Reformation also did nothing to blunt the widespread fear of "witches" in Europe that led to as many as 50,000 deaths by 1800. In fact, the tumult of the Reformation often put religious authorities on edge, causing them to redouble their efforts to stamp out dissidents and freelance spiritualists, such as witches, who were seen as deriving their powers from the Devil. In sum, Protestantism endorsed most of the patriarchal assumptions that had governed European society for centuries. Thus, women's status and rights barely changed.

After Martin Luther's defiance of the Catholic Church, several other strains of Protestantism emerged. In the Swiss city of Zurich, Ulrich Zwingli proposed a remarkably simple form of Protestantism. Zwingli argued that all Catholic practices and beliefs that were not specifically outlined in the Bible should be immediately cast aside. This seemed rash to Lutherans. Zwinglianism never rivaled Lutheranism in popularity.

Even more radical than the Zwinglians were the Anabaptists, who believed in adult baptism. They viewed infant baptism as insufficient, because an infant cannot consent to Christian belief. Anabaptists were even more determined than Lutherans and Zwinglians to purify Christianity of all of its unbiblical components. Most Anabaptists were also pacifists, which set them at odds with the political authorities. Pockets of Anabaptists developed in Germany and Eastern Europe, but, particularly after a disastrous attempt by radical Anabaptists to rule the German city of Münster, during which one Anabaptist leader was named king and took 16 wives, Lutherans and Catholics agreed to cooperate in persecuting Anabaptists. Many were executed.

By far the most successful new strain of Protestantism during the second half of the sixteenth century was Calvinism. Its founder, John Calvin, had received an outstanding education courtesy of the Catholic Church, but by 1534, as a young man in his mid-twenties, Calvin had become an enthusiastic Protestant. Calvin eventually settled in the Swiss city of Geneva, which became the world headquarters for Calvinism.

Calvinists accepted the vast majority of Luther's religious reforms, but they went beyond Lutheranism in three key areas. First, the Calvinists believed in "predestination": they held that God had already decided who was fated to go to heaven and who would descend into hell. Nothing any person did on earth would influence God's final judgment, although the virtues that one displayed in this life might be interpreted as evidence of God's favor. Significantly, Lutherans and even Catholics had also endorsed predestination, but it was Calvinists who made it a cornerstone of the Christian faith.

Second, Calvinists believed that Christian communities should be governed by strict moral codes enforced by both the church and political authorities. In Geneva, starting in 1540, Calvin put this idea into practice. The Consistory, a church council, punished residents of the city who engaged in sinful behaviors such as missing a church service, gambling, and drunkenness. The local government, in turn, meted out banishment or death to those who committed the most serious crimes, or who opposed Calvinist beliefs. Admittedly, in the sixteenth century, it was not unusual for political and religious authorities to regulate private behavior and personal beliefs, but in Calvin's Geneva the level of intolerance was especially high.

Last, Calvinists believed in a decentralized and quasi-democratic form of church governance. Unlike Catholics, and to a lesser extent Lutherans, who were still led by a hierarchical and centrally controlled church organization, Calvinists believed that locally elected leaders known as presbyters should play a principal role in church government.

Because Calvinism promoted such a firm faith in one's predestined salvation, and because it also stressed strong moral values and the right of congregations to govern themselves, many people were drawn to Calvin's teachings. By 1560, large communities of Calvinists existed in Germany, Switzerland, France, and Eastern Europe. The most important Calvinist areas, though, were in the Netherlands and Scotland. Both the Netherlands and Britain were rising commercial and naval powers, so the association of Calvinists with these up-and-coming regions added to the appeal of John Calvin's message.

How does Lutheranism differ from Catholicism?

England Opts for Protestantism, While France Remains a Catholic Kingdom

Initially, England's Tudor King Henry VIII was disinclined to support Protestant reforms. Henry's religious views were conservative, and he had written a theological tract in 1521 that had condemned Lutheranism. Moreover, the Catholic Church in England was already largely under royal control, so Henry saw little need to pursue further changes.

Henry was ultimately persuaded to embrace Protestantism, however, because Pope Clement VII refused to grant him an annulment of his marriage to Catherine of Aragon, who had not borne Henry a son after almost 20 years of marriage. The pope would not grant the annulment partly because Catherine was a close relative of the Holy Roman Emperor Charles V, whose soldiers had recently sacked and terrorized Rome.

This impasse was resolved from 1529 to 1534, as England's Parliament passed a series of acts that separated the Church of England from Catholic control. In 1534, Parliament unambiguously declared King Henry VIII the "supreme head on earth" of the English church. By 1539, the king's key Catholic advisor Sir Thomas More had been executed, and Catholic monasteries and convents had been eliminated and their property confiscated by the government. Besides allowing the Bible to be published in English, though, Henry tolerated remarkably few changes to the practices of the Church of England.

From 1533 to 1542, Henry tried wife after wife in the quest for a son. He was married to a total of six wives, two of whom were beheaded. Henry's third wife, Jane Seymour, succeeded in bearing the king a son, an intelligent boy named Edward, but she died shortly after giving birth. Henry also had a daughter, Mary, by his original wife Catherine, and a younger daughter, named Elizabeth, by his second wife Anne Boleyn.

Upon Henry's death in 1547, Edward became King Edward VI at the age of nine. He was far too young to rule, though, so his Protestant advisors ran the government. They took the opportunity to purge many vestiges of Catholicism from the Church of England, such as priestly celibacy and rich church decorations.

Catholicism made a brief and famously "bloody" comeback in England in 1553–58, when young King Edward's death cleared the way for Henry's devoutly Catholic daughter, Mary, to become queen. Mary died in 1558 without producing an heir, however, so the crown passed to Henry's only surviving child, Elizabeth. Elizabeth had been cruelly treated by her father, and even more so by Queen Mary. She had also been raised as a Protestant. Much to the surprise of many Englishmen, she would reign from 1558 to 1603 as one of England's most successful monarchs. She safeguarded the Protestant faith in England by pursuing moderate religious policies.

Meanwhile, in France, Protestantism had begun to spread in the 1520s and 1530s, especially among nobles and townspeople, although French Protestants, called *Huguenots*, never made up more than about ten percent of the population. The Catholic monarchy periodically suppressed Protestantism, but the real struggle between Catholics and Protestants did not develop until 1559. In that year, King Henry II was succeeded by his son, Francis II. In fact, from 1559 to 1589, three of Henry II's sons ruled France. For most of this period, however, Catherine de Medici, the mother of all three sons, was in charge.

Catherine was a shrewd woman. She understood that the youth and the perceived intellectual and moral weaknesses of her sons made it likely that political factions would challenge the monarchy. One of these factions was built around the Guise family, made up of powerful and wealthy aristocrats from eastern France. The Guises were fervent Catholics and fierce opponents of the Reformation. The other principal faction was led by the Bourbon family of southwestern France. Because of the anti-Protestant views of the Guises, the *Huguenots* overwhelmingly supported the Bourbons. Although *Huguenots* were a small minority in France, perhaps a third or more of French noblemen were *Huguenots*, and their support for the Bourbons was critical.

For years, Catherine de Medici tried to play the Guise and Bourbon factions against one another, but in 1572 she appears to have made a clear choice. On August 24, 1572, France witnessed the St. Bartholomew's Day Massacre of *Huguenot* leaders. In the end, thousands of Protestants, including women and children, were slaughtered. The pope and the Guises were overjoyed. The *Huguenots* were naturally horrified, but there was little they could do.

In 1589, the last of Henry II's sons, Henry III, died, and the Valois monarchy came to an end. The rightful heir to the throne was none other than Henry of Navarre, a Bourbon and a *Huguenot*! He became King Henry IV, but, rather than take vengeance against French Catholics, he practiced religious toleration. In 1598, Henry issued the Edict of Nantes, which allowed Protestants to practice their religion freely in designated areas and even to maintain garrisons and forts. The price for securing such generous treatment for Henry's beloved *Huguenots*, however, was that King Henry IV himself had to renounce Protestantism and become a Catholic in 1593. He famously observed, "Paris is worth a mass." In changing his religion, Henry became a prime example of a *politique*—that is, a sixteenth- or seventeenth-century leader who prized stability and pragmatism over religious orthodoxy.

Despite the Edict of Nantes, Huguenots remained an embattled (and dwindling) minority in France. Nobles, in particular, rushed to abandon Protestantism. A Catholic extremist killed Henry IV in 1610. In 1685, Henry's grandson King Louis XIV revoked the Edict of Nantes, and several hundred thousand Huguenots were forced into exile. Louis's motto was "One king, one law, one faith." The faith that he chose, on behalf of all of his subjects, was Catholicism.

How did England come to be a Protestant country?

The Catholic Reformation or "Counter-Reformation," and Spain's Battle to Control the Netherlands

Even before the Protestant Reformation, some Catholics, such as Cardinal Jiménez de Cisneros in Spain, realized that the Church needed major reforms. Starting in the 1520s, in response to the rise of Protestantism, the Catholic Church began to accept that these progressive voices ought to be heeded. The resulting movement in favor of Church reforms is referred to as the Catholic Reformation, or the Counter-Reformation. Among the most noteworthy effects of this movement was the foundation of numerous new monastic orders that were dedicated to ministering to the needy and to purifying the Church of corruption and ignorance. The most important new order, begun in 1534, was the Society of Jesus, known as the Jesuits, founded by the Spanish soldier Ignatius Loyola. He saw Jesuits as "soldiers of Christ" who would help root out heresy and indoctrinate the next generation of Catholics. Protestants hated the Jesuits, mainly because they were so successful at reestablishing the vigor and self-confidence of the Catholic Church. Perhaps their most powerful weapon was education.

The most important sign that the Catholic Church acknowledged the danger that Protestantism posed was Pope Paul III's decision to call the Council of Trent, which met in northern Italy from 1545 to 1563. As it turned out, the Council of Trent refused to make any substantial changes to Catholic doctrine or rituals. Priestly celibacy, penance, indulgences, the veneration of saints, and the Latin mass were all retained. Meanwhile, an "Index of Forbidden Books" was created that forbade any Catholic to read, among other works, the Bible—in any language except Latin.

On the other hand, the Council acknowledged that the Church had been damaged by greed, arrogance, and mismanagement. After the Council of Trent, church offices would no longer be sold, nor would indulgences; church officials would be required to perform their duties themselves rather than assigning them to others; and priests had to be educated, morally upstanding, and concerned for their parishioners' well-being. In short, to combat the spread of Protestantism, the Catholic Church was prepared to follow its own beliefs more faithfully, but it refused to alter those beliefs even slightly.

This strong-willed approach was largely successful. The rapid spread of Protestantism in northern Europe was over by the second half of the sixteenth century. By 1600, northern Germany, the Netherlands, Scandinavia, and Britain were Protestant, but most of the rest of Europe remained firmly in the Catholic camp.

Throughout the sixteenth century, Europe's strongest and most emphatically Catholic state was the Kingdom of Spain. King Ferdinand and Queen Isabella had united Spain in 1479. In 1492, their armies had captured the last of the Muslim forts in southern Spain. In the same year, they had sent all Spanish Jews into exile, as both religious and racial enemies of the state. Also in 1492, Ferdinand and Isabella had sent Christopher Columbus to the New World, eventually resulting in a massive colonial empire as well as a steady flow of gold and silver that enriched Spain. It was, in short, under Ferdinand and Isabella that Spain became fabulously wealthy, immensely powerful, and utterly devoted to conservative Catholicism.

Spain's Catholic credentials were further strengthened under the rule of the Holy Roman Emperor Charles V, who was simultaneously King Charles I of Spain from 1516 to 1556. Charles was the man who struggled unsuccessfully to smother Lutheranism in Germany. But Protestants were not Spain's only enemies. The Spanish also battled the formidable Muslim Turks in the eastern Mediterranean. Spain, with the help of Venice, won a major naval victory over the Turks at the Battle of Lepanto in 1571.

The man who arguably best symbolized the ambition and the religious zeal of Spain during the sixteenth century was its Hapsburg King Philip II, who ruled from 1556 to 1598. Philip lived in a huge palace called the Escorial near Madrid. The Escorial was as much a church and a monastery as it was a royal residence. Predictably, Spain under Philip maintained a close relationship with the papacy. Philip's agents were also successful at spreading Spanish influence in Italy and the New World. Philip even acquired the crown of Portugal for himself in 1580, as well as Portugal's vast navy, merchant fleet, and colonial empire. In northern Europe, though, Spain's exuberance was finally checked.

As King of Spain, Philip II also ruled the Netherlands, where the population was increasingly restless. Calvinism and Lutheranism were spreading there, while Spanish taxation and trade regulations were becoming bothersome. During the 1560s, Dutch resistance increased, and Philip responded by sending the Duke of Alba to restore order. The Duke had a simple strategy: "Everyone must be made to live in constant fear." Thousands of Dutch rebels, mostly Protestants, were executed.

Alba's reign of terror only increased Dutch ire, which exploded after 1576, when Spanish troops killed 7,000 people, including women and children, in Antwerp. This incident, known as the Spanish Fury, led to a redoubling of rebel activity under the leadership of Prince William of Orange, a convert to Calvinism. William led the Dutch in the formation of a Union of Utrecht, which formally cast off Spanish rule in 1581. The Dutch Republic, as it became known, included most of the territories that make up the modern Netherlands. The area now known as Belgium, on the other hand, remained loyal to Spain and for many years was called the Spanish Netherlands. By 1593, Spanish forces had been forced out of the Dutch Republic, but Spain waited until 1648 to recognize Dutch independence.

Once they had evicted the Spanish, the Dutch wasted no time in building one of the strongest merchant fleets, most powerful navies, most dynamic manufacturing sectors, and most successful financial and banking systems in the whole of Europe. By the early seventeenth century, the Protestant Dutch Republic was well on its way to becoming an economic and military powerhouse, despite its small size and population.

How did the Catholic Church respond to the Protestant Reformation?

Spain versus England: Queen Elizabeth I and the Defeat of the Spanish Armada

During the 1550s, relations between Spain and England were strong. In fact, King Philip II of Spain and England's Queen Mary, a.k.a. "Bloody Mary," both of whom were Catholic, were husband and wife. In 1558, however, Mary died, and her successor was her redheaded 25-year-old half-sister Elizabeth, who shrewdly dedicated herself and the Church of England to a moderate form of Protestantism.

Anglicanism, as the English form of Protestantism is often known, is similar to Lutheranism in that, while it preserves many Catholic rituals, it incorporates many new Protestant ideas, such as justification by faith, priestly marriage, and the elimination of the veneration of saints. Anglicanism was organized by the official church, the Church of England, which observed a strict hierarchy, with the king or queen at the head of the Church, and archbishops, bishops, and priests all following a centralized chain of command. In this sense, the Church of England was and is very similar to the Catholic Church, except that in England they substitute the king or queen for the pope. These similarities made it easier for English Catholics to convert to Anglicanism, which Queen Elizabeth strongly encouraged.

Nonetheless, there were sizable religious minorities in England, mainly Catholics and members of another religious group, the Puritans. Catholics believed that the English Reformation had gone too far, while Puritans were Protestants (often Calvinists) who believed that the Church of England had not gone far enough in purging itself of Catholic ideas and practices. Some of England's wealthiest and most respected citizens were Catholics or Puritans. For rejecting some or all of the doctrines of the Church of England, they could be fined, imprisoned, or even executed.

Queen Elizabeth's most determined domestic enemies were extreme Catholics, aided by Jesuit secret agents, who plotted to kill her and replace her on the throne with Mary, Queen of Scots (not to be confused with the now deceased Queen Mary). Mary, Queen of Scots, was a Catholic, but she ruled over Scotland, which was largely Calvinist. In 1568, the Scots forced Mary into exile, and she ended up in the hands of Queen Elizabeth's government. Elizabeth did not know what to do with Mary. She was a Catholic and a potential rival, but she was also of royal blood. Elizabeth kept Mary under house arrest for 19 years, but when it became clear that Mary was plotting with the Spanish to seize the throne, Elizabeth authorized her execution. More than 100 spectators looked on as the executioner hacked at Mary's head three times with his ax until it finally rolled away. He then ran after it and grabbed Mary's red hair, holding her bloody head up to the crowd. Unfortunately, her hair was in reality a wig, and her head tumbled to the ground once more. Mary soon became a Catholic martyr.

The brutal killing of Mary, Queen of Scots, was the last straw that made King Philip II of Spain decide that Protestant England had to be defeated. Even before Mary's death, Queen Elizabeth had sponsored daring raids on Spanish ships and ports in the New World, and she had given support to Protestant rebels in France and the Netherlands. Philip II therefore decided to mount an amphibious invasion of England. Spain had a powerful navy and plentiful resources with which to amass a large invasion force. The Spanish Armada, a fleet of ships that set out to conquer England in May 1588, therefore had an excellent chance of success.

Philip's fleet sailed first to the northern coast of France, where the smaller and more nimble vessels of the English and the Dutch constantly harassed the Spanish ships. Finally, a "Protestant Wind" blew that scattered the Spanish fleet. By September 1588, about half of the Spanish Armada had been destroyed either by enemy action or by severe weather and rough seas. England had narrowly averted becoming just one more patch of earth ruled by the Catholic Hapsburg kings of mighty Spain. Not surprisingly, Elizabeth was overjoyed. Ever since, she has been regarded as one of the greatest heroines of English history.

Once the danger of a Spanish invasion had passed, Elizabethan England became increasingly prosperous and proud. It was in the last years of Elizabeth's reign, in the midst of a general flowering of English literature and art, that the career of a promising playwright named William Shakespeare took off, as discussed in Chapter 8. The bawdy humor of Shakespeare's plays underline the fact that, although Elizabethan Englishmen took their Protestantism seriously, most of them were not prudes, and they enjoyed fine living. Under Elizabeth, following the Dutch model, the English increasingly devoted themselves to making money and expanding their empire rather than to the pursuit of political and religious grudges.

Elizabeth reigned until 1603, and her policies sowed the seeds for a British empire that would, by the eighteenth century, become the world's richest and most powerful. Elizabeth herself never married, possibly in order to preserve her power as a female monarch. She was known as the Virgin Queen, after whom the Commonwealth of Virginia is named. Upon her death, James Stuart, the Protestant son of Mary, Queen of Scots, became King James I.

Why does the defeat of the Spanish Armada represent a turning point in the history of Europe?

The Thirty Years' War, 1618–48

The wars fought throughout the sixteenth and seventeenth centuries to determine the religious complexion of places such as England, France, the Netherlands, and the minor states of Germany are known collectively as the Wars of Religion. The longest and most destructive of these wars was fought from 1618 to 1648.

The Thirty Years' War, as it became known, was fought largely over a single issue. The Holy Roman Emperor Ferdinand II, who was a Catholic Hapsburg and an admirer of the Jesuits, wanted to establish firm control over the more than 300 small German states that made up his empire. Each of these states paid the emperor lip service, but they were effectively independent. A large proportion of them were also Lutheran or Calvinist, so the idea of a truly united and centrally controlled Catholic empire was frightening to many. It was because of this fear of Catholic Hapsburg domination that Protestants in Prague threw two of Ferdinand II's representatives out of a window and onto a pile of horse manure in May 1618, making war unavoidable. This was the famous Defenestration of Prague.

From 1618 to 1648, the forces of the Holy Roman Emperor, assisted by the armies of Catholic Bavaria and Spain, fought various Protestant German armies, which were in turn aided by the Czechs, the Dutch, the Danes, and the Swedes. Although religion was the primary motivator for many of the combatants, it was not an absolute predictor of each country's loyalties in the Thirty Years' War. France, for instance, which was Catholic, supported the Protestants, largely because Cardinal Richelieu, the chief minister to King Louis XIII, feared that a strong and united Holy Roman Empire would be a threat to France. Likewise, some Protestants fought on the side of the Catholic Holy Roman Emperor, mainly because the emperor was able to exploit divisions between Lutherans and Calvinists. Nevertheless, for the most part, the Thirty Years' War was a huge struggle between Catholics and Protestants to decide the political and religious future of the German states.

The fortunes of the combatant countries waxed and waned as the Thirty Years' War dragged on. The effects on the people of Germany were horrific. By the seventeenth century, battlefields were no longer dominated by knights mounted on horses. In the thirteenth century, Mongol invaders had brought gunpowder to Europe, and since then firearms and cannon technology had greatly improved. The armies that crisscrossed Germany from 1618 to 1648, therefore, were made up largely of men armed with primitive long guns, as well as pikemen, that is, soldiers with long spears. Complementing these infantrymen were increasingly powerful forces of field artillery. Armies sometimes numbered in the tens of thousands. Most of them lived off the land, and they did not hesitate to plunder, rape, and destroy. Some historians claim that by the end of the conflict more than 20 percent of the German population had died, mostly from disease or starvation.

The outcome of the Thirty Years' War was straightforward. The ambition of the Catholic Hapsburg emperor to rule Germany was thwarted. The Holy Roman Empire remained an empire in name only, and its small component states remained religiously diverse and stubbornly independent. France, on the other hand, became the single strongest power on the continent of Europe, while the English and the Dutch were becoming unstoppable on the high seas.

The Thirty Years' War ended with the Treaty of Westphalia, signed in 1648. It was arguably the first major treaty to be arranged by professional diplomats. The chief result of their labors, as we have seen, was that the independence of the small German states was confirmed. The Treaty also safeguarded Calvinist interests in Germany, rewarded Bavaria and Brandenburg (later called Prussia) with higher status, formalized the independence of the Netherlands from Spain, and added new territory to France. France's elevated status was aptly symbolized by the fact that the Treaty of Westphalia itself was written not in Latin, the dominant literary language of the Middle Ages, but in French.

What was the outcome of the Thirty Years' War?

Conclusions

Some historians argue that the diplomats who crafted the Treaty of Westphalia in 1648 consciously crafted a "balance of power" that would keep Europe at peace. If that was their aim, they did a poor job, because for the next 170 years Europe and its overseas colonies would be cursed with nearly ceaseless warfare. Indeed, the fierce competition between rival empires that began in 1492 would only intensify in the seventeenth and eighteenth centuries. In the process, European governments, economies, and societies would be transformed.

While the end of the Thirty Years' War did not usher in an age of peace, it did mark the conclusion of the Wars of Religion. From the days of the Protestant Reformation until 1648, theological disputes had arguably been the decisive force in European history. From 1648 onward, though, wars would be every bit as frequent, but they would be fought primarily for political, economic, and strategic gains—for ostensibly rational reasons, in other words—rather than to satisfy religious grudges. Whether this shifting of priorities would lead to progress, or to something altogether more sinister, remained to be seen.

Key Terms for Chapter 9

Age of Exploration—a period in the fifteenth and sixteenth centuries when Europeans, led by the Portuguese and Spanish, sailed to, traded with, and colonized parts of the Americas, Africa, and Asia.

Conquistadores—Spanish adventurers who defeated the Aztec and Inca empires.

Protestant Reformation—sixteenth-century movement of Christians desiring religious reform and wishing to cut ties with the Catholic Church.

Martin Luther—leader of the Protestant Reformation and founder of the Lutheran Church.

John Calvin—Protestant leader and founder of Calvinism.

Queen Elizabeth I—she was Queen of England from 1558 to 1603, a zealous Protestant, and vanquisher of the Spanish Armada.

Spanish Armada, 1588—a Spanish fleet that sought to conquer England and restore Catholicism there.

It met with total defeat.

Wars of Religion—a series of wars fought in the sixteenth and seventeenth centuries between Protestants and Catholics.

Thirty Years' War, 1618–48—the biggest and bloodiest European war of the seventeenth century, largely motivated by religious tensions and fought overwhelmingly in Germany.

Holy Roman Empire—a loose confederation of independent states scattered throughout the Germanies.

Review Questions for Chapter 9

1. Europe's discovery of the Americas led to many far-reaching consequences. Describe two ways in which life in the Americas was altered after 1492, and then describe two ways in which life in Europe was altered.
2. Imagine that you are a middle-class citizen of England, France, or the Netherlands around the year 1600. Many people in your country are pushing for it to undertake profitable colonial ventures such as those of

the Portuguese and the Spanish. Write a letter to a close friend in which you either support or oppose this idea.
3. The Protestant Reformation brought many significant changes to the practice of Christianity in Europe. Describe two ways in which Protestants made major alterations to Catholic ways. Then, describe two elements of Protestantism that represented a continuation of Catholicism.
4. The Wars of Religion dominated the politics of Europe for much of the sixteenth and seventeenth centuries. Choose one of these wars and describe it in detail. Then, present your own analysis as to whether the war in question was rational or irrational.
5. After 1648, few wars in Europe were caused primarily by religious disagreements. Nonetheless, some experts believe that a modern clash of civilizations, on a global scale, could produce new Wars of Religion in the future. Do you believe this is likely or unlikely? Assuming it could happen, where do you think such wars would be fought, and between whom?

Further Reading

Abernethy, David B. *The Dynamics of Global Dominance: European Overseas Empires, 1415–1980*. New Haven, CT: Yale University Press. 2013.

Baylor, Michael G. *The German Reformation and the Peasants' War: A Brief History With Documents*. Boston, MA: Bedford/St. Martin's. 2012.

Crowley, Roger. *Conquerors: How Portugal Forged the First Global Empire*. London: Faber and Faber. 2016.

Darwin, John. *After Tamerlane: The Rise and Fall of Global Empires, 1400–2000*. New York: Bloomsbury. 2010.

Frieda, Leonie. *Catherine de Medici: Renaissance Queen of France*. New York: Harper Perennial. 2006.

Hutchinson, Robert. *The Spanish Armada: A History*. London: Phoenix. 2014.

Kamen, Henry. *Empire: How Spain Became a World Power, 1492–1763*. New York: HarperCollins. 2004.

MacCulloch, Diarmaid. *The Reformation*. New York: Penguin Books. 2005.

Mullett, Michael A. *Martin Luther*. London: Routledge. 2015.

Pagden, Anthony. *Lords of All the World: Ideologies of Empire in Spain, Britain and France, c.1500–c.1800*. New Haven, CT: Yale University Press. 1998.

Parker, Geoffrey, ed. *The Thirty Years' War*. London: Routledge. 2007.

Somerset, Anne. *Elizabeth I*. New York: Anchor. 2003.

Swanson, R. N. *Indulgences in Late Medieval England: Passports to Paradise?* Cambridge: Cambridge University Press. 2011.

Thomas, Hugh. *Rivers of Gold: The Rise of the Spanish Empire, From Columbus to Magellan*. London: Penguin. 2010.

10 Politics, Colonialism, and War, 1648–1789

Introduction

During the seventeenth and eighteenth centuries, European countries divided politically into two camps. In some countries, the political power of the monarch became virtually unlimited, and the government tended toward absolute monarchy, which reached its height in France under King Louis XIV. In other countries, like Britain, the elected representatives of the people insisted that the monarch should share power with them. These countries moved slowly in the direction of representative government, although full-fledged democracy, in which all adult citizens can vote, was still considered a fanciful notion.

It was of great importance which of these two models of political organization would ultimately triumph. At stake was the political future of Western Civilization—and thus ultimately the political rights of us all.

As this momentous political debate unfolded during the seventeenth and eighteenth centuries, great powers such as Britain, France, Spain, and the Netherlands vied with one another in the race to acquire new colonies, trade routes, plantations, and, above all, gold. It was an age of cutthroat competition and increasingly savage warfare. Some nations rose to the challenge, while others were left behind.

The end of the eighteenth century held a surprise for the mighty British Empire: a rebellion by the Thirteen Colonies in North America would lead to the foundation of the United States. Europe's interminable squabbling, therefore, set the stage for at least some of its colonies to shake free from European domination. Europe's global preeminence, though, would not be threatened until the twentieth century.

Absolute Monarchy in France: The Reign of Louis XIV

Absolute monarchy, or absolutism, became not only the government of France but also the most popular form of political organization throughout Europe during the seventeenth and eighteenth centuries. It involved a government ruled by a king or emperor (and occasionally a queen or empress) who was theoretically unchecked in power. Absolute monarchs could raise new taxes, form large armies and navies, and even dictate religious policies to their subjects, all without seeking approval from anyone. Usually absolute monarchs exercised this extraordinary power in the name of the Divine Right of Kings—the idea that God himself had ordained a hereditary line of rulers for each country.

Stating a belief in absolute monarchy was one thing. Actually achieving absolute power, however, was a challenge for any king, especially since national and local elites almost always had to be consulted, and every monarch also had to pay lip service, at the very least, to the political traditions of his kingdom. In addition, laws and customs usually varied by region, so imposing a uniform system of government on an entire country was a herculean challenge.

Louis XIV succeeded in creating a system of absolute monarchy in France partly because the groundwork for absolutism had already been laid by previous French monarchs and their closest advisors. During the medieval period, important steps had been taken to improve tax collection, increase France's military strength, bring the clergy under royal control, and centralize lawmaking power in the hands of the king. It was, though, during the reign of Louis XIV's father, Louis XIII, from 1610 to 1643, that absolutism truly began to take hold. While Louis XIII was still a boy, an important milestone in France's evolution toward absolutism was reached. The Estates-General, an assembly composed of clergymen, nobles, and commoners, met for the last time in 1614—that is, until Louis XVI recalled it in 1789. Although the powers of the Estates-General had always been vaguely defined, its dormancy after 1614 represented the removal of one of the most effective checks on royal power.

Cardinal Richelieu, Louis XIII's chief minister from 1628 to 1642, was a stalwart champion of absolutism. He boldly asserted the king's authority, suppressed factionalism among the nobles, increased taxes, and curtailed the liberties of Protestants. He also reduced the autonomy of France's various regions by creating a permanent group of civil servants, accountable to the king, called Intendants.

In seeking to build a system of absolute monarchy in France, Louis XIV had to be especially cautious in his handling of the country's nobility, as well as its *bourgeoisie*—that is, its urban middle class, including merchants, business owners, and professionals. The nobility was especially formidable, as it controlled much of the country's wealth, enjoyed great prestige, and even sat on France's most powerful courts, called *parlements*. These *parlements* were not legislatures with the power to make laws, but courts with the power to review and apply laws that the king had issued.

The danger posed by the nobility was brought home to Louis XIV as a boy during a massive rebellion called the *Fronde*. In 1649, Louis had only recently become king at the age of five. Many Frenchmen, especially nobles, had resented the centralizing policies of his father's advisors. They feared that the monarchy was already too powerful, and they decided that the reign of a boy-king was an ideal opportunity to expand their political role—by force, if necessary. The resulting rebellion lasted for three years and caused Louis and his court to flee Paris. Fortunately for Louis, the *Fronde* ultimately failed, and the monarchy was fully restored in 1652. Louis learned much from the experience, but most of all he learned that nobles were dangerous when provoked, and new ways of manipulating them had to be found if absolute monarchy was to succeed.

In 1661, Louis's longtime chief advisor, or First Minister, Cardinal Mazarin, died. Louis now made the bold decision to rule alone. He did so partly to increase the loyalty of his subjects, but Louis also had grand plans for the concentration of power in the hands of the king. Until his death in 1715, he pursued four main strategies to achieve absolute monarchy in France. In the process, he dug his nation deeper into debt, but he also made France, for a while, the most powerful and glorious country on earth.

Louis's first strategy for achieving absolute rule was, as noted above, to exercise full authority on his own. This was easier said than done.

In addition to becoming his own First Minister and elbowing aside the aristocratic *parlements*, Louis was forced to rely on a series of advisors, and numerous spies, for information and advice, many of whom became skilled at misleading him for their own benefit. Louis tended to choose members of the urban middle class as ministers and bureaucrats, because he considered them less likely than self-important noblemen to defy the king's wishes. At least some of these ministers were indeed trustworthy and highly skilled. Overall, despite Louis's naivety in thinking that he could make every important decision himself, he nonetheless succeeded in creating a remarkably centralized system of government.

Louis's second strategy for achieving absolute power involved the use of what today would be called propaganda. When emissaries from the Southeast Asian Kingdom of Siam (modern-day Thailand) visited Louis's court in 1686, they were just in time to see the earliest results of a statue campaign that aimed to glorify the Sun King throughout France. These statues depicted Louis, often in bronze, either on horseback or in various triumphal poses.

Statues were just the tip of the iceberg. Louis and his advisors exploited every available art form to improve the king's image. Whereas much propaganda today aims to convince us that our leader is "one of us," Louis's image-makers instead strove to convince their audience that Louis was a semi-divine figure, excelling all other Frenchmen—indeed, all other human beings—in wisdom, piety, courage, and virtue.

Louis XIV's third strategy, which was the most effective in containing the power of the nobility, was to build a gigantic new palace on the outskirts of Paris at a place known as Versailles. The *château* at Versailles was in many ways more of a royal city than a mere residence, since it housed as many as 25,000 courtiers, servants, and soldiers. Eventually, it grew so large and elaborate that it devoured 15 to 20 percent of France's annual budget. The palace complex included numerous grand buildings, extensive gardens, the finest artwork, and over 1,400 fountains. Its style and magnificence impressed not only Louis's subjects but visitors from all over the world. Even today Versailles is one of France's most popular tourist attractions.

What really made Versailles a masterstroke for Louis, though, was its domestic political uses. The nobility, which had long been the chief source of opposition to the monarchy, was so enraptured by the splendor of Versailles that the most important nobles were easily persuaded to live there with the king. These court nobles were amused by lavish dinners, plays, musical performances, hunting expeditions, fireworks displays, and often by less savory attractions such as gambling and womanizing. Nobles were also convinced to compete with one another for the honor of performing servile duties for the king, such as helping him to put on his nightshirt, holding his candle, or watching him eat dinner. Under Louis XIV, therefore, the nobility was still treated with respect, but it increasingly became a class devoted to pleasure and status seeking rather than to political activism. Thus, for all its expense, Versailles played a vital role in Louis's plan to centralize power in his own hands.

The last major strategy that Louis employed to achieve absolutism was focused on religion. Louis XIV believed that an absolute monarch had every right to insist that all of his subjects share his faith. In fact, Louis considered the persecution of Protestants to be part of his duty as France's Catholic ruler.

In 1685, Louis moved against Protestantism by revoking the Edict of Nantes, a decades-old royal decree that had promised France's Protestants the right to practice their faith free of intimidation and harassment. Many Protestant churches were forced to close, and dire punishments were inflicted on those who refused to convert to Catholicism. As a result, more than 200,000 *Huguenots*, as French Protestants were called, fled to other European states, taking their valuable skills and their undying hatred for Louis with them.

Louis achieved Catholic domination in France, but he did so at the cost of dividing his country along religious lines. He also alienated millions of Europeans outside of France who admired Louis's accomplishments but despised his arrogance and tyranny.

By the time of Louis XIV's death in 1715, absolute monarchy was firmly established as the political system in France. As we shall see, much of Europe was trying to duplicate the Sun King's achievement.

Unfortunately, Louis's legacy was not entirely positive. Louis's expensive court at Versailles had drained the royal treasury, as had his innumerable wars. By 1715, France was deeply in debt. As a result, the impoverished peasantry was forced to shoulder higher and higher tax bills. Moreover, the nobility and the *bourgeoisie* had not been completely eliminated as potential sources of opposition. Thus, whether Louis XIV's system of absolute monarchy could be maintained in the future would depend largely on the quality of his successors.

Louis XV, the great grandson of Louis XIV, ruled from 1715 to 1774. He is remembered today more for his adventurous sex life than for his leadership. Under Louis XV, France experienced a severe financial crisis, and it suffered one of its most terrible defeats during the Seven Years' War, described later in this chapter. At the same time, the nobility began to reassert its political influence through the *parlements*, while in the towns the rising middle class grew increasingly restless. France's public debt rose inexorably. It was with good reason that Louis predicted doom for France by reportedly saying, "*Après moi, le déluge*" ("After me, the flood").

As will become clear in Chapter 12, Louis XV's grandson and successor, Louis XVI, was even more of a disappointment as king. Eventually, the French Revolution would cost him his throne and his life. Absolute monarchy may have built France into a powerful and glorious nation in the seventeenth century, therefore, but during the eighteenth century weak leadership would help to bring the country to its knees.

How did Louis XIV succeed in making France an absolute monarchy?

The Rise and Fall of Absolutism in Britain

James I, a Scotsman, was Britain's king from 1603 to 1625 (the Scottish and English crowns were united from this point on). He was a true believer in the Divine Right of Kings and had even written a book on the subject in 1598. Thus, James spent much of his reign trying to establish the dominance of the monarchy. The chief obstacle to royal absolutism in Britain was Parliament, the country's partially elected legislature.

Parliament was divided into two houses. One was the House of Lords, in which the country's hereditary nobility and its bishops, representing the (Protestant) Church of England, sat. The other house of Parliament was the House of Commons, where in theory the people were represented. In practice, only a small number of rich landowners and merchants held any real power. And, in the seventeenth and eighteenth centuries, even the House of Commons was strongly influenced by the nobility. Despite its dubious credentials as a representative body, however, the House of Commons did play an important role in British politics, especially on issues of taxation.

James I disagreed with Parliament frequently, sometimes on questions of religious policy, and sometimes regarding taxes. It was, though, when James's son became King Charles I in 1625 that the real problems began. Parliament's hostility to Charles started with his choice of a bride. Henrietta Maria, for whom the state of Maryland is named, was a French Catholic and a close relative of the King of France. Many Englishmen hated the French, and Catholics in general. Moreover, since the idea of royal absolutism was especially popular in France, many Englishmen feared that Charles's choice of a French wife indicated that he too wanted to become an absolute monarch.

During the next 20 years, the tense relationship between Charles and Parliament gradually unraveled. Three main factors contributed to their rivalry.

First, although it is not clear that Charles wished to become an absolute monarch, he nonetheless sought to expand the powers of the monarchy. For example, he tried to remove his opponents from the House of Lords and the House of Commons. Sometimes, Charles also refused to convene Parliament. In addition, Charles manipulated Britain's courts, especially the Court of Star Chamber, to punish his adversaries and obtain approval of his policies. To save money when the country was at war, Charles would order ordinary citizens to give his troops lodging in their homes. All these heavy-handed tactics made Charles appear to be a tyrant, and Parliament repeatedly stated its outrage.

Another point of disagreement was taxation. The anti-Catholicism of most members of the House of Commons often meant that they would encourage war with Catholic nations such as France and Spain. From 1618 to 1648, most of Europe was embroiled in the Thirty Years' War, and the pressure on Britain to join the fighting was intense. Ironically, however, the members of Parliament who favored war were also among Britain's principal taxpayers, and they would stubbornly refuse to fund the wars that they had supported. Charles I disagreed with Parliament again and again on issues of taxation. He attempted to go around Parliament and collect the necessary taxes without their consent, but this only made relations between the king and Parliament worse.

Finally, religious disagreements became increasingly problematic. Charles I was an advocate for the moderate policies of the Church of England, which, since it was Protestant, rejected the leadership of the pope in Rome and some Catholic religious doctrines. As discussed in Chapter 9, however, the Church of England did maintain many of the rituals of Catholicism as well as its hierarchical system of organization. What we must remember is that in the seventeenth century even seemingly minor religious differences could excite great emotions for most Europeans. Therefore, the king's support for moderate Protestantism—Protestantism that in certain ways resembled Catholicism—angered some people.

The fiercely anti-Catholic opponents of the official religion in England were called Puritans, because they wanted a Protestant church that was more fully "purified" of Catholic practices. Puritans were a diverse group, but they generally wanted a simplified, less hierarchical, and more biblically centered form of worship to prevail. Some Puritans also wanted to enforce strict moral teachings by banning entertainments such as dancing, sports, and plays, especially on Sundays. Importantly, many Puritans sat in Parliament, and they tended to be critics of Charles I. They became, in fact, one of the most important sources of opposition to the monarchy.

Finally, in 1640–42, the relationship between the king and Parliament completely fell apart. Charles therefore left London and began to raise an army for what would soon become a civil war.

What factors led to animosity between the king and Parliament in seventeenth century England?

The English Civil War, the Protectorate, and the Restoration

From 1642 to 1646, the English Civil War was fought between Cavaliers, also known as Royalists, who were supporters of the king and the Church of England, and Roundheads, who were supporters of Parliament, and often Puritans. The term Cavalier was derived from the French word for knight, whereas the term Roundheads referred to the unfashionably short haircuts sported by some backers of Parliament. The Civil War, in any case, was fought over questions of political ideology, taxation, and religious policy, but it was above all a struggle to decide who would have ultimate power in the British government: the king or the Parliament.

The war itself was brutal. Much like the U.S. Civil War, it split families apart and caused enduring bitterness. In the end, Parliament was victorious. Its New Model Army, manned largely by Puritans, proved to be better organized and more determined than its Royalist adversaries. It also benefited from the excellent leadership of one of its generals, Oliver Cromwell.

Figure 10.1 English Civil War reenactors demonstrate a musket volley.
Charlesdrakew/Wikimedia Commons.

Fired by Puritan zeal, Cromwell had risen rapidly through the ranks of the New Model Army during the Civil War, becoming its victorious commander. When, after the fighting was over, the king still refused to submit to any revised constitutional arrangements, Cromwell and his Puritan allies decided that only Charles's death and the abolition of the monarchy could end the strife of the Civil War. Thus, against the wishes of many Britons, Charles was publicly executed in London in January 1649. The House of Lords and the Church of England were also eliminated.

Immediately, Charles became known to his supporters as the Martyr King, since they believed that he had died to defend his Divine Right principles. Meanwhile, Charles's wife Henrietta Maria had wisely retreated to her native France, while the couple's eldest son, also named Charles, famously evaded capture by hiding in an oak tree. He too later went into exile.

If the people of Britain had believed that, after the execution of the king—and the elimination of the House of Lords and the Church of England—they would live in a peace-loving, tolerant democracy, they were soon disappointed. True, Cromwell instituted a degree of religious toleration, but he proved to be an inconsistent supporter of the powers of Parliament. When it appeared that Parliament might defeat his motion to execute the king, Cromwell violently purged the House of Commons of its uncooperative members. This led to the creation of a Rump Parliament that was more or less under Cromwell's control.

The government that was created in Britain after the death of Charles I, variously called the Commonwealth and the Protectorate, evolved more and more into a Cromwellian dictatorship. Since Cromwell also tripled the level of taxation, maintained a large and expensive army, enforced some Puritan religious policies, and brutally repressed Catholic Ireland, many Britons began to regret that they had overthrown their king. It seemed that they had traded one tyrant, who was partly limited by Parliament, for another, who was limited by no one.

Fortunately for the Royalists, although Charles I was dead, his eldest son Charles had managed to find refuge at the courts of a variety of European monarchs. Charles II (as he called himself, rejecting the legitimacy of Cromwell's government) sought aid from any European ruler, even Catholics, who would help him to regain the throne. When Oliver Cromwell died in 1658, Charles II saw his opportunity. After the free election of a new Parliament, Charles negotiated an arrangement that would end the Protectorate and reintroduce the monarchy to Great Britain.

What happened next is one of the most remarkable episodes in all of European history: the Restoration. On May 23, 1660, the mighty warship *The Royal Charles* brought a delighted Charles II from the Netherlands to the coast of England. He reached London on May 29, where he was greeted with banners, trumpets, ringing church bells, parading soldiers, and, above all, joyful subjects. The years of Puritan rule had deprived Londoners of many of the pleasures of life: fine clothes, sports, parties, plays, and dancing. Britons had also endured high taxes and military rule. Now, as the monarchy was reinstated, many of them experienced a great sense of relief.

Still remaining, though, was the business of revenge against Charles's nemesis, Oliver Cromwell. Inconveniently, Cromwell was already dead, but that did not prevent Charles II from having his body dug up, dragged through London, and publicly hanged. Cromwell's head was then displayed on a pike. Aside from the mutilation of Cromwell's corpse, however, the new king was surprisingly magnanimous toward those who had supported the Puritan regime.

The Restoration of Charles II, together with the House of Lords and the Church of England, had the effect of reinstating a reassuring set of political traditions. It did not, however, solve all or even most of Britain's political problems. Even after 1660, the balance of power between king and Parliament was hotly debated, as was the proper level of taxation and the degree of religious toleration that ought to be permitted to Catholics and Puritans.

Nevertheless, Charles II is widely credited with returning normality, and even a sense of optimism, to British life. The Merry Monarch, as Charles was known, made a habit of enjoying life to the fullest. He was also a celebrated patron of the arts and sciences. Britain's wealth and prestige rose, and its empire grew, while he was king.

Why did the English choose to restore the monarchy in 1660?

The Glorious Revolution

Upon Charles II's death in 1685, although he had fathered many children, none were legitimate, that is, born of a lawful marriage. This meant that the throne was due to pass to Charles's brother, James, the Duke of York, after whom New York City is named. James II was handsome and devoted to his country, but he was also Catholic, and in a Protestant nation such as England having a Catholic king was widely seen as intolerable. Many Britons feared that James would make Catholicism the official religion. There were also widespread concerns, fueled by some of James's high-handed actions once he assumed the throne, that he might try to become an absolute monarch.

James II managed these fears for several years, but when his wife bore him a son—and presumably, therefore, a Catholic heir—many Englishmen decided that they had had enough. William of Orange, leader of the Netherlands, and his English wife Mary, daughter of James II, both of whom were firm Protestants, were invited by leading politicians to invade England and restore Protestant and parliamentary control. William and Mary arrived in England in November 1688, and James's support rapidly crumbled. James ended up dropping the Great Seal, used for placing the royal signature on important documents, into the Thames River and fleeing Britain in disgrace. Parliament then pronounced the throne vacant, and William and Mary were declared the new king and queen.

The overthrow of James II in 1688, and the enthronement of William and Mary, is known today, especially to the English, as the Glorious Revolution.

(It was not so glorious in Ireland, where James II unsuccessfully tried to make a comeback in 1690 that turned into a bloodbath.) In the end, the events of 1688 accomplished a number of important goals.

First, the Glorious Revolution put an end to Catholic rule in Britain. Ever since, only Protestants have been allowed to inherit the British throne. Second, the battle for supremacy between king and Parliament was largely decided. After all, in 1688, Parliament, in the name of the people, had essentially fired one king and hired another! Third, the Glorious Revolution was also a victory for individual rights. In 1689, a Bill of Rights was passed that not only guaranteed the powers of Parliament, subjecting the judiciary and the military to unprecedented parliamentary control, but also protected some individual liberties. Simultaneously, an Act of Toleration expanded religious freedom to a limited degree. Fourth, after 1688 the size and scope of government increased, because Parliament, now that it was a full partner in politics, even a dominant one, no longer feared the growth of governmental power. An unintended side effect was an explosion in political corruption. Finally, the Glorious Revolution was the last time that the British political system was ever subjected to violent change. Since 1688, every political reform that the British have undertaken has been achieved through negotiation and has been based on the rule of law. This in itself makes the history of Britain in the modern age unique.

For all the achievements of the Glorious Revolution, Britain was still far from being a democracy in the late seventeenth century. The power of the monarchy did not simply fade away. It would be another 150 years before the political role of the British king or queen became merely symbolic. In addition, religious toleration may have been extended to most Protestants in 1688–89, but Catholics were still persecuted. They would not receive equal rights until the nineteenth century. Perhaps most importantly, representation in the British Parliament itself was still highly restricted. The average Briton still had no say in his or her government, and it would take many years to convince the political elite that real democracy and universal suffrage were worth the risk.

The real significance of the Glorious Revolution lies in the fact that it established once and for all that a government could be based on something other than the Divine Right of Kings. Specifically, the Glorious Revolution helped to promote a concept known today as popular sovereignty, which is the idea that the people are the ultimate source of power in any government. John Locke, an English political philosopher who lived in the seventeenth century, provided part of the justification for this new way of thinking. He argued that any system of government is essentially a contract between the rulers and the people. The people agree to submit to the authority of the rulers, but the rulers in return agree to respect the rights of the people. When the rulers break their word and trample on the people's rights, according to Locke, the people can and should rise up and change the government.

In truth, few of the members of the British elite who planned and executed the Glorious Revolution would have agreed with Locke's notion that the people have a right of revolution. The prevailing political philosophy in those days tended to be based instead on tradition. Nevertheless, Locke's ideas about popular sovereignty caught on, and, as explained later in this chapter, they were enthusiastically embraced by the Americans in 1776.

What were the most important consequences of the Glorious Revolution?

Mercantilism, and the Rise of Plantation Slavery

As Europeans vigorously debated the merits of absolutism versus representative government, many of their leaders, especially in Britain, France, Spain, and the Netherlands, focused on the separate but arguably related task of building large colonial empires. The question of why they did so, and why they were willing to fight nearly ceaseless wars with one another to defend and perhaps expand their colonial conquests, cannot be answered without a clear understanding of mercantilism. Mercantilism was an economic theory, but its importance went far beyond money and commerce. It also defined seventeenth- and eighteenth-century politics, diplomacy, and warfare.

Mercantilism is the idea that a country's status and wealth are based on its possession of bullion, that is, gold and silver. According to mercantilists, bullion is valuable because it can be saved and eventually spent to maximize a country's power, especially its military might. To increase a country's reserves of precious metals, mercantilists followed several strategies, one of which was the conquest and exploitation of colonies. Mercantilists also favored the protection of domestic industries from foreign competition, the manipulation of trade to produce a surplus of exports over imports, and high taxes to provide the resources for improvements in infrastructure and a strong military.

Mercantilists generally assumed that nations could best achieve greater wealth when governments actively managed and regulated domestic and international trade to the advantage of the mother country. They saw the state and its overseas colonies as forming a closed economic system that could only be expanded and enriched by shutting out foreigners and squeezing cheap raw materials out of the colonies to benefit Europe. Under mercantilism, the interests and freedoms of ordinary people, both in Europe and overseas, were frequently sacrificed in the state's unending quest for more and more gold. The purpose of acquiring all this gold in the first place was to fund a strong military, especially a strong navy. These military forces could then be used to defend a country's trade, or to expand a country's wealth by preying on the territory or commerce of its enemies.

Although initially mercantilists were obsessed mainly with gold, by 1700 mercantilism had become more sophisticated, and its focus had shifted somewhat from precious metals to the trade in commodities such as tobacco and sugar. This shift produced one of mercantilism's darkest chapters: plantation slavery, which peaked in the eighteenth century.

Perhaps surprisingly, the colonies that were most valuable to European empires in this era were mostly in the Caribbean Sea. Tiny islands such as Barbados and St. Kitts, and larger islands such as Jamaica and Hispaniola (which is today divided into Haiti and the Dominican Republic), were prized especially highly. The reason was simple: the crops raised on these tropical islands, especially sugar, produced incredible profits. Witness the fact that British trade with Jamaica in 1773 was five times more valuable than British trade with *all* of mainland North America! Taxes on this trade, moreover, could be used to fund armies and navies that could conquer even more sugar islands. Predictably, therefore, intense warfare became common in the Caribbean in the seventeenth and eighteenth centuries, but, just as tragically, Europeans tried to squeeze as much production as they possibly could out of the islands that they already possessed. They did so by the merciless exploitation of African slaves.

The use of slaves of African descent to produce sugar on plantations began in the fifteenth century on islands off the coast of Africa itself. It was the Portuguese who first discovered that these slaves survived longer—usually, for about seven years—and worked more efficiently than any other source of labor. In the sixteenth century, the Portuguese transferred many of their sugar plantations, and thousands of slaves, to their colony in Brazil. Since millions of Native Americans were dying at the time of European diseases, other European empires eventually decided to follow the lead of the Portuguese and encourage the purchase of African slaves. By the end of the seventeenth century, the plantation economy, which depended on the constant importation of unwilling Africans, was firmly established in the Caribbean and in Brazil, where the vast majority of African slaves were sent. Less than ten percent of African slaves were sent to Britain's Thirteen Colonies in North America, but here too slavery became an economic institution of vital importance.

Slave traders forced approximately ten million Africans to make the dangerous and deeply traumatic sea voyage to the New World. Once there, they would work in deplorable conditions and usually would die at a young age of overwork, malnutrition, mistreatment, or disease. African slaves in the New World were often forced to convert to Christianity, and they were also commonly separated from their families and friends. European countries, as well as African-Americans, have been struggling for several centuries to overcome the legacy of slavery.

Although racial prejudice played a significant role in the European decision to use Africans as slaves, initial attitudes about race were relatively flexible in most of Europe's colonies. For example, political, economic, and military alliances, and even romantic liaisons, between Europeans and Native Americans were common. Such relationships also existed in European colonies in Asia. Many Britons in India lived with native women and wore native dress. During the late nineteenth and early twentieth centuries, however, racial attitudes would become much stricter.

How does mercantilism differ from modern capitalism?

Great Mercantile Empires

During the sixteenth century, as Chapter 9 describes, the greatest European empires belonged to Portugal and Spain. Based on its seafaring expertise, tiny Portugal built a surprisingly large empire in parts of Africa, Brazil, and South and Southeast Asia starting in the 1400s. From 1580 to 1640, however, Portugal was occupied by Spain, and thereafter Portuguese wealth and power went into steady decline.

The Spanish experienced greater success. Their empire was based mainly in Central and South America, and it was built on the conquest of Indian peoples in the sixteenth century. The Spanish found in the Americas what they were most looking for: gold and silver. From about 1550 to 1650, Spain was Europe's richest and most powerful state. Spain squandered its bullion, though, on numerous (and mostly futile) wars in Italy, Germany, the Netherlands, and against the Ottoman Turks. Much of Spain's revenue went to service its massive debts.

These financial and military problems, combined with depopulation of the Spanish countryside, inefficient administration, fanatical religious intolerance (Jews and Muslims were expelled from Spain), an inability to develop competitive industries and modern trade, and a series of inbred and ineffective monarchs, spelled the end of Spanish dominance. Spain kept its gigantic American empire throughout the eighteenth century, but increasingly it was a second-rate power.

France under Louis XIII, XIV, and XV also possessed a great mercantile empire. French explorers were especially active in North America, where they claimed most of Canada and the Mississippi and Ohio River valleys for their king. After the initial voyages of exploration, bold adventurers and traders consolidated this American empire. One of them was Antoine Laumet de La Mothe, sieur de Cadillac, for whom the luxury brand of American automobiles is named. Cadillac claimed to have a background as a nobleman, despite his middle-class origins, and he even went so far as to steal another man's coat of arms, which is now displayed on every Cadillac vehicle.

France's most valuable possessions were its sugar colonies. Islands such as Martinique and Guadeloupe, and the French portion of the island of Hispaniola (today's Haiti), were at the center of France's colonial trade. After the Seven Years' War of 1756–1763, France willingly traded away Canada and Louisiana in order to keep its tiny sugar islands.

Meanwhile, France cultivated trade with India, where for many years Frenchmen competed successfully with their British, Dutch, and Portuguese rivals. In addition, France enjoyed excellent commercial relations with the Ottoman Turks.

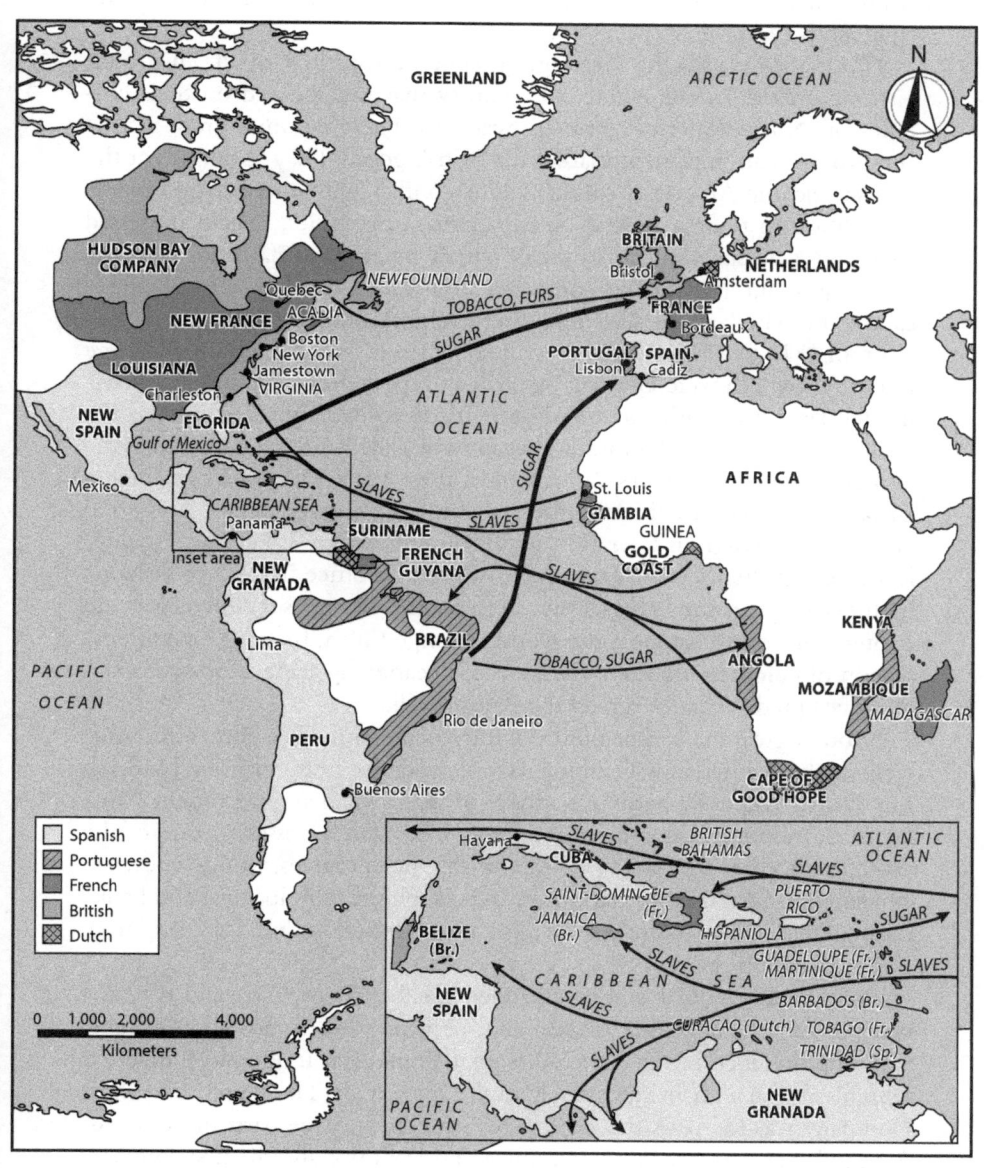

Map 10.1 The Atlantic world in the seventeenth and eighteenth centuries.

All of these trade links and colonial possessions helped to make France economically and militarily strong in the seventeenth and eighteenth centuries. France built the largest army in Europe, but its navy often fared poorly against the Dutch and the English, who ruled the seas in the seventeenth and eighteenth centuries, respectively.

The British played the mercantilist game perhaps best of all. They built a strong empire by the eighteenth century that was focused on their colonies on North America's Eastern Seaboard. These colonies grew rapidly and provided an important market for British goods. They also brought the British and the American colonists into conflict with the nearby French. In addition to their mainland North American colonies, Britain possessed numerous Caribbean sugar islands, of which Jamaica and Barbados were the most important. Britain also competed strongly for trade with India, and it captured the bulk of the slave trade in the eighteenth century.

From 1714 to 1760, Britain was ruled by King George I and then George II, both of whom were German by birth and spoke English poorly. Governing fell largely to Parliament and particularly to its Prime Minister, as the leader of the House of Commons began to be called. A faction known as the Whigs dominated Britain's Parliament in these years. The Whigs celebrated Britain's Protestant traditions, abhorred absolutism, and generally supported civil liberties, religious toleration, and economic progress. They also shamelessly helped themselves to the spoils of political office. Thanks to Britain's high taxes, when the Whigs were done raiding the treasury there was still enough left over to support the world's strongest navy. In an age when possession of colonies and the protection of oceangoing trade were so crucial, this naval predominance served the British well.

Another great mercantile power of the seventeenth and eighteenth centuries was the Netherlands. Winning its independence from Spain by 1648, the tiny Dutch Republic became a model of representative government, Protestant devotion, and commercial success. The Dutch possessed one of the most advanced economies of the day, with efficient farms, world-renowned craftsmen, a gigantic merchant fleet, and a sophisticated financial and banking system. Their extraordinary wealth allowed them to build a strong navy and a large empire.

The Dutch colonial empire included small parts of India and Africa, a number of valuable sugar islands, and, perhaps most importantly, a commanding presence in the East Indies, that is, modern Indonesia, where the Dutch enjoyed a virtual monopoly of the spice trade. The Dutch East India Company was for years the *de facto* government in large parts of Southeast Asia, and even possessed its own army and navy. It was also the first company in the world to issue stock.

Unfortunately for the Dutch, by the eighteenth century their country had peaked. The tiny Netherlands did not have the territory or the population to support a worldwide empire, and its quasi-democratic political structure failed to supply decisive leadership. The Dutch Empire did not disappear, but increasingly it took a back seat to others.

> *Which European countries possessed sizable colonial empires in the seventeenth and eighteenth centuries?*

Other Strong States, and a Few States in Decline

Despite the clear connection between mercantilism and colonialism, some countries in Europe built remarkable strength in the seventeenth and eighteenth centuries even without acquiring significant overseas possessions. First on the list would be Russia.

Russia was dominated by its Tsars (emperors), a nobility known as the *boyars*, and the Orthodox Church, which oversaw Russia's own version of Christianity, called Orthodoxy. Before the eighteenth century, most Europeans thought of Russia as backward. Under Tsar Peter the Great, this began to change.

Peter came to power in 1682, and he reigned until 1725. These were the glory days of France under Louis XIV, and Britain and the Netherlands were also strong powers. Peter decided, therefore, that if Russia was ever to overcome its backwardness it needed to Westernize.

Peter introduced various Western cultural practices to his people, especially to the nobility, and he curbed the power of the traditionally minded Orthodox Church. Economically, Peter used many mercantilist tactics to encourage industry and commerce in Russia. He also sought to acquire ports that would allow uninterrupted trade between Russia and the West. Politically, Peter moved Russia's capital from Moscow to a new site on the Baltic Sea (closer to the West) that he named St. Petersburg. He also reformed Russia's army, helped build its first navy, and expanded Russia's territory. Lastly, in pursuit of royal absolutism, Peter centralized political power in the hands of the Tsar. To emphasize the point that he was in charge, Peter sometimes participated in beheadings himself.

Many of these tactics to Westernize Russia and to increase its might were successful. Peter, however, did not plan effectively for Russia's future after his death. He even ordered his son and heir Alexis beaten to death.

After a chaotic interlude, Russia's movement toward Westernization and geographical expansion would continue under Catherine the Great, who reigned from 1762 to 1796. Catherine was famous for her political savvy. During her reign, Russia carved even more territory out of neighboring states while its economy surged. Catherine became a celebrated patron of the arts and sciences, and she communicated with many leading thinkers in the West. Although most Russians continued to live in miserable conditions of serfdom, Russia was indisputably a nation of growing importance.

Another rising power in the eighteenth century was Prussia. From the Middle Ages until late in the nineteenth century, there was no single country in Europe that united most of the German-speaking peoples. Germany was instead divided into hundreds of smaller states known collectively as the Germanies, which were very loosely organized into the Holy Roman Empire. From the fifteenth century onward, one of the most important of these small German states was Brandenburg, later known as Prussia, which was centered on Berlin.

Initially, Prussia was a small country with a primitive agricultural economy. Over the years, however, the kings of Prussia acquired new territory and new subjects, and they centralized political power. Just as importantly, Prussia's kings formed an alliance with Prussian nobles, who were known as *Junkers*, that enticed them to serve faithfully in the country's military forces. Thus was born one of the proudest military traditions in European history: the Prussian army. The rise of Prussia is enormously important historically, because in the late nineteenth century it would be Prussia and its army that were responsible for the final unification of Germany into a single (militaristic) state.

Another major power in the seventeenth and eighteenth centuries was Austria, which, along with the Germanies, was technically part of the Holy Roman Empire. Austria was dominated by the Hapsburg family, which ruled the country from the Middle Ages until 1918.

The Hapsburgs presided over an extremely diverse realm. The core of the nation was German-speaking Austria in the west. The empire also included large parts of present-day Poland, Hungary, the Czech Republic, Slovakia, Slovenia, Croatia, and Romania. Predictably, the local populations spoke many different languages and shared no common ethnic heritage. Holding such a wide array of peoples together was a major challenge.

Austria's longtime enemy to the southeast, the Ottoman Empire, was in serious decline by the late seventeenth century, which allowed Austria to expand. Austria was also able to play a major role in the Germanies, but this caused an Austro-Prussian rivalry to develop.

Like other European monarchs, the Hapsburgs tried to build an absolutist government. True absolute monarchy was elusive, though, because resistance from the nobility, the Catholic Church, and various ethnic minorities, especially the Hungarians, was too great.

Although some European countries were rising to greatness, or at least holding their own, others were in decline. Poland was a large state in Eastern Europe from the Middle Ages until the eighteenth century, but its inability to build a strong central government and army led to Poland's complete collapse and its absorption into neighboring countries by 1795.

The Kingdom of Sweden was powerful in the 1600s, but it had overextended itself by the eighteenth century and was forced to surrender much of its territory to Russia. Sweden was never conquered like Poland, but it ceased to be a major factor in European affairs.

A similar fate befell the Ottoman Empire. In the 1680s, the Ottoman Empire, ruled by Muslim Turks, included not only Turkey, but much of the Middle East, most of North Africa, parts of the Caucasus region, and all of southeastern Europe. Although the Ottoman government, based, at least in theory, on an all-powerful Sultan, was widely seen as tyrannical, it granted surprising levels of toleration to minority groups. Nonetheless, political instability, rebellions, corruption, reactionary religious influences, and technological backwardness would lead to long-term Ottoman decline. The empire was finally destroyed in World War I.

Which European countries were rising powers in the seventeenth and eighteenth centuries despite their lack of overseas colonies?

Warfare in the Age of Mercantilism, and the War of the Spanish Succession

Generals, admirals, and other officers in the seventeenth and eighteenth centuries were almost always noblemen. They were motivated by a sense of duty and a desire for glory and riches, but rarely by genuine hatred for their enemies. Usually, the object of war was not the annihilation of one's adversary but a limited victory and a favorable peace treaty. War was, in other words, an extension of mercantilist theory, which sought profit and national advantage.

On land, although the cavalry was still important, the basic unit of combat was the musketeer: an infantryman armed with a musket—a long gun that was unreliable, highly inaccurate, and awkward and time-consuming to load. To increase the effectiveness of its musketeers, most armies of the day deployed them in tightly organized lines. Once an army's lines of musketeers had advanced close enough to the enemy, the soldiers would charge forward and attack with bayonets. Casualty rates were high. Most ordinary soldiers were of the lowest social classes and fought either for monetary gain or because they were forced to do so.

By the eighteenth century, warfare often spared civilians. War was generally conducted on a relatively small scale, by modern standards, and it avoided most civilian areas entirely. In addition, army supply wagons increasingly made preying on civilians unnecessary.

Naval combat was decisively important, from a mercantilist perspective, because control of overseas colonies and maritime trade produced immense profits. The constantly shifting ownership of many small sugar islands in the Caribbean Sea attests to the importance of naval warfare in this era. It is no wonder that the British, French, Dutch, and Spanish empires came to value so highly their ships of the line, great multi-decked sailing vessels, bristling with as many as 120 cannons.

As the battle fleets of the major powers targeted one another, a window of opportunity opened for smugglers and pirates. Many pirates were actually privateers. That is, they had permission from a European government to attack and plunder the ships and bases of an enemy state.

During the Golden Age of Piracy, from 1680 to 1730, the gold and silver of the Spanish Empire and the mercantile wealth of the British, French, and Dutch tempted many adventurers to become pirates. They formed a subculture that was remarkably democratic and ethnically diverse but also uncommonly bloodthirsty. Piracy declined in the eighteenth century as European navies became stronger and colonial control over the Caribbean region solidified.

The War of the Spanish Succession was fought between 1701 and 1714 for control of the throne and extensive territory of Spain and its empire. In 1700, the Hapsburg King of Spain, Charles II, died, leaving his kingdom to Philip of Anjou, a member of the Bourbon family and a grandson of Louis XIV. This caused great concern in much of Europe, because the vast Spanish Empire, if allied to the might of France, could alter the balance of power, especially if Philip of Anjou were ever to inherit the crown of France as well as the crown of Spain. The Austrians were especially upset, since they had coveted the Spanish throne for another member of the Hapsburg family. War between Austria and France was unavoidable, but due to Louis XIV's poor diplomacy and arrogance, soon Britain and the Dutch were fighting against him too.

The war dragged on and on. Initially, France suffered terrible setbacks, leading to higher taxes and peasant uprisings. The decisive battle was fought at Malplaquet in modern Belgium in 1709. The British, Dutch, and Austrians were attempting to invade France, but they suffered such severe losses that their offensive stalled.

Peace was finally achieved in 1713 and 1714. A compromise was reached whereby Louis XIV's grandson Philip would keep the Spanish throne and control of Spain's empire in the Americas, but Spain's possessions in Italy and Belgium would be surrendered to Austria. King Philip V of Spain also agreed to renounce any future claim he might have on the crown of France.

Curiously, it was the British who profited the most from the war. They obtained Gibraltar and Minorca as naval bases in the Mediterranean Sea. Britain also gained the right to trade with Spain's American colonies, including an exclusive contract to provide African slaves to the Spanish Empire. Thus, a war that had exhausted the continental powers left the British in an even stronger position on the seas and in world trade.

How was war conducted in the seventeenth and eighteenth centuries?

The Seven Years' War, 1756–1763

By far the most important war of the eighteenth century was the Seven Years' War, known to the English colonists in North America as the French and Indian War. The Seven Years' War was so long, so costly, so bloody, and so dispersed across the globe that many historians consider it a world war.

The war had many theaters: in North America, the Caribbean, Africa, India, and on the high seas, but the most important battles were fought in Europe. The Seven Years' War pitted two great alliances against one another: on one side was Britain, with the world's strongest navy, and Prussia, with arguably its finest army. On the other side were most of the leading powers of Europe: Austria, Russia, and France, and also Spain and Sweden. On the face of it, it seemed unlikely that Britain and Prussia could survive the onslaught of so many great powers. Prussia, in particular, was exposed to attack from France to its west, from Austria to its south, and from Russia to its east. The odds of Prussian victory, or even survival, looked bleak.

Despite these obstacles, Britain and Prussia struggled to victory. How they did so is of enormous historical significance, because both countries would play critical roles in European history for the next 200 years.

The first key to Anglo-Prussian victory was the leadership of Prussia's King Frederick II, known as Frederick the Great, widely acclaimed as a military genius. Prussia's victories were based both on Frederick's strategic brilliance (he almost never allowed enemy forces to unite against him) and on his apparent disregard for the welfare of his troops and subjects, whom he forced to endure terrible sacrifices. Against the odds, Frederick held his country and his army together, often risking his own life in battle. As a result, when Russia unexpectedly withdrew from the conflict in 1762, Prussia was in a position to negotiate favorable terms with Austria and France. Frederick the Great has been beloved in Germany ever since. When Hitler was alone in his bunker at the end of World War II, he would stare for hours at a portrait of Frederick the Great, trying to find the inspiration to lead Germany to victory.

While Prussia was battling for survival in Europe, the British followed an inspired strategy devised by William Pitt the Elder, the Earl of Chatham, a popular politician. Pitt's plan was simple: he wanted to tie down Britain's mortal enemy, France, with endless, inconclusive fighting in Europe, while Britain's navy and superior colonial forces conquered France's highly lucrative overseas possessions.

Although Pitt's strategy focused on North America, the Caribbean, Africa, and India, he understood that the British needed the Prussians to put up a good fight in Europe. Pitt therefore supported Frederick the Great's army with vast amounts of money and legions of hired mercenaries. Meanwhile, Britain's Royal Navy imposed a strict blockade on French ports, defeating two French fleets when they attempted to reach open waters. Pitt then ordered British forces to attack France's colonies, especially its sugar islands. He also raised a huge army in North America, with the eager assistance of the American colonists, to invade French Canada. In 1759, a bold attack on Québec City succeeded, and all of North America east of the Mississippi fell into British hands. In addition, the British defeated the French in India. Predictably, the value of French colonial trade plummeted. Deeply in debt, humiliated on the battlefield, and chased from the seas and from most of their colonies, the French sued for peace.

Prussia gained little from the war, especially considering the immense suffering of its people. It kept the rich Austrian province of Silesia that it had taken in 1740, but otherwise Prussia's gains were mostly psychological. Prussians had proven their worth on the battlefield, and the smaller states of Germany immediately gave them greater respect.

Britain's gains were much more tangible. In the Treaty of Paris, signed in 1763, Britain gained virtually all of North America east of the Mississippi, a dominant position in trade with India, and several forts on Africa's western coast. Britain's naval, colonial, and commercial strength was perhaps never greater than directly after the signing of the Treaty of Paris.

Nevertheless, there were warning signs for the British. To achieve peace, Britain had agreed to return to France its most valuable colonies, its sugar islands. In the years after 1763, the French quickly rebuilt their economy and, more ominously, their navy. Austria and Russia were also far from decisively beaten.

Perhaps the greatest effect of the Seven Years' War was financial. Funding armies and navies that were so large and sophisticated cost all of the combatant nations more than they could reasonably afford. In Britain, taxes doubled, while the national debt skyrocketed. The war had also devastated France's economy. As Chapter 12 will explain, when the monarchy of King Louis XVI finally fell in the French Revolution of 1789–1799, it did so largely because of the crushing burden of debt that France's wars had created.

The British would attempt to pay both their debts and the ongoing costs of maintaining their military advantage over the French partly by imposing new taxes and customs duties on the American colonists. The result would be the Revolutionary War, and one of the greatest defeats in the history of the British Empire.

What countries were the victors in the Seven Years' War?

The American Revolution, and Other Setbacks for European Colonialism

From 1760 to 1820, the King of Great Britain was George III, a remarkable monarch in many respects. He was personable, hardworking, devout, and morally upright, and he avoided profanity, drinking, and even infidelity, unlike the vast majority of kings. He was also determined to reassert the influence of the monarchy, which had deteriorated under George I and George II. During the 1770s, George III successfully used royal patronage (i.e., bribery) to win control over the House of Commons. The king's influence was short-lived, however, because two misfortunes would combine to discredit him in the 1780s.

The first failure of George's reign was the loss of the Thirteen Colonies in North America. From 1763 to 1774, Parliament, at the king's urging, had tried repeatedly to raise additional revenue from the colonies. The method George III and his ministers chose was to impose new taxes, customs duties, and trade regulations in America without the colonists' consent. This was acceptable according to mercantilist theory, but it led to repeated confrontations between the British government and the disgruntled Americans. Even though the taxes at stake were minimal in scale, the colonists feared that King George III was pursuing a broad strategy to erase English liberties and ignore the people's views. "No taxation without representation" became the Americans' signature argument against British taxation schemes. At the time, though, roughly 90 percent of all adults in Britain itself could not vote, so it was unlikely that the Americans' argument would be heard. Moreover, the Americans had clearly benefited from the defeat of the French in North America. Thus, the British reasoned, why should the Americans not pay part of the bill to keep the French at bay?

Eventually, the king and Parliament grew frustrated at the colonists' defiant attitude, and stronger measures were taken to force compliance, including the dispatch of British troops. Finally, open rebellion developed, and the colonists adopted the ambitious goal of achieving complete political independence. The British were forced to undertake serious preparations for war.

In the beginning, it seemed unlikely that the improvised army of the American colonists could measure up to the British. In addition, the British controlled the seas. British tactical and strategic blunders, however, allowed the Americans to keep the initiative, and in 1777 the Americans won the important Battle of Saratoga. France, Spain, and the Netherlands now entered the war, believing that the American rebellion was an ideal opportunity to give the British a black eye. They were right.

French troops and naval forces tipped the scales in favor of General George Washington, the American commander. The result was the defeat of the British General Lord Cornwallis at Yorktown in 1781. In 1783, the British recognized the independence of the United States of America. The British Empire had suffered a terrible setback.

Fortunately for the British, as soon as the fighting was over, the Americans began trading again with Britain, and they eventually canceled their alliance with the French. Anglo-American commerce actually doubled by 1800, and in that year the British controlled an astonishing one-third of global trade.

George III, who had supported the attempt to crush the rebellion in the Thirteen Colonies, was politically damaged by the humiliating defeat of British forces. His control of Parliament was shaken. Then, in 1788–1789, George III was stricken with a sudden mental illness, accompanied by various physical symptoms. The king's physician tried to break the will of the monarch by tying him to a chair, and he also induced vomiting and encouraged blistering on the king's legs to achieve a cure. Miraculously, or so it seemed, George III's mental illness lifted after only a few months, but in the meantime Parliament, which had been asserting itself since the seventeenth century, had taken control of British politics. When George relapsed into insanity in 1801, 1804, and 1810, the monarchy's influence deteriorated even further. Britain's elected legislature has been politically dominant ever since.

Spanish imperialism, meanwhile, suffered a decisive reversal a few decades after U.S. independence. While Spain was recovering from the Napoleonic Wars, discussed in Chapter 12, all of Spain's colonies in the New

World except Cuba and Puerto Rico rebelled and managed to win their independence by 1830. (Spanish Florida was ceded to the United States.) Latin Americans had resisted Spanish rule for many of the same reasons that had led the English colonists in North America to rebel. Throughout the eighteenth century, the Spanish government had tried to impose tighter control on Latin American trade and taxation, which angered the local elites. At the same time, the Latin Americans began to feel that they no longer needed Spanish protection from the British, French, or Dutch, since the age of European colonial expansion in the Americas seemed to be over. The Latin Americans reached the logical conclusion that they would be better off without the Spanish telling them what to do. The Spanish fought back, but they were too weak to reimpose their authority. By 1830, therefore, almost all of North and South America was politically independent, although the legacy of European rule lingers to this day.

How did the American colonists manage to defeat the British in the Revolutionary War?

Conclusions

In the big picture of European and world history, the high-stakes battle between absolutism and representative government in the seventeenth and eighteenth centuries was vitally important. Whether the French or the British model of government triumphed in the end would determine nothing less than the future of Western Civilization. In 1700, it appeared to most observers that the French model was winning, since numerous other European countries were striving to adopt it. As we know today, however, ultimately representative government proved more successful and durable. The question to be addressed in future chapters is: why?

The independence of the United States of America and most of Latin America put an end to the Age of Mercantilism. The idea that a country's wealth and power could be judged solely by its possession of gold seemed to be proven false. Similarly, the idea that the ownership of colonies and the waging of constant expansionist wars was a sure route to imperial glory and riches was also discredited.

In the late eighteenth century, a Scottish professor named Adam Smith would propose a tantalizing alternative to mercantilism: *laissez-faire* (hands-off) capitalism. Smith suggested that instead of trusting in war, gold, and trade barriers to ensure economic strength, countries should let the free market work on its own. Meanwhile, peaceful commerce should be preferred over war, and governments should confine themselves to protecting basic freedoms.

Some Europeans were listening, but Smith's vision of peace and prosperity was unrealistic at the end of the eighteenth century. France, in particular, was so severely damaged by poor leadership, internal divisions, and the excesses of its costly mercantilist wars that it succumbed to violent revolution in 1789. France would eventually drag the rest of Europe with it into the abyss of total war.

Key Terms for Chapter 10

King Louis XIV—King of France from 1643 to 1715, and the best example of an absolute monarch.

Absolutism/Absolute monarchy—a system of government in which a monarch rules by divine right with unlimited powers.

Versailles—the location outside of Paris where Louis XIV constructed his main palace complex. Many French nobles were persuaded to live there.

Charles I—Britain's king from 1625 to 1649. His execution, instigated by Oliver Cromwell, symbolized the victory of the parliamentary forces in the English Civil War.

Representative government—a political system in which the elected representatives of the people rule.

Puritans—English Protestants who were dissatisfied with the doctrines and practices of the Church of England, and who strongly opposed Catholicism.

Oliver Cromwell—leader of the victorious parliamentary forces in the English Civil War, and military dictator of the British Isles from 1649 to 1658.

Restoration, 1660—the name for the reinstatement of Britain's monarchy under King Charles II.

The Glorious Revolution, 1688–89—a relatively peaceful revolution in which Parliament deposed England's Catholic king, James II, and replaced him with the Protestants, King William and Queen Mary. One key result was a permanent expansion of the powers of Parliament.

Popular sovereignty—the idea that the people should have control over the government.

Mercantilism—an economic philosophy popular in the seventeenth and eighteenth centuries that stressed government management of trade, colonialism, war, and, most of all, the accumulation of gold and silver.

Plantation slavery—an economic practice focusing on the cultivation of cash crops in the New World, and dependent on the importation and exploitation of African slaves.

Peter the Great—Russia's Tsar from 1682 to 1725. He sought to Westernize his country, to expand its territory, and to create an absolute monarchy.

Junkers—the nobility in Prussia.

Seven Years' War, 1756–1763—the largest and most important war of the eighteenth century, won by Britain and Prussia.

The American Revolution, 1776–1783—the rebellion that led to the creation of the United States of America and the temporary weakening of the British Empire.

Review Questions for Chapter 10

1. List two advantages of absolute monarchy and two advantages of representative government. Lastly, make a case for which system of government is best overall.
2. The rise of representative government in Britain during the seventeenth century set the country at odds with most of Europe, which was simultaneously moving in the direction of absolute monarchy. Explain at least three ways in which Britain's system of government after 1688 was fundamentally different from what one would have found elsewhere in Europe.
3. Although mercantilists, like capitalists, seek profit, otherwise mercantilism and capitalism are quite different. Describe one feature of mercantilism that you feel was mistaken, and describe another that you feel is superior to current capitalist practices. Justify your selections.
4. On balance, do you believe that colonialism added to a country's strength in the seventeenth and eighteenth centuries or not? If the United States were to acquire colonies today, would this make it stronger or weaker?
5. Choose one of the political or military leaders discussed in Chapter 10. Write a brief biographical sketch of him or her. Then, explain which modern figure he or she most resembles.

Further Reading

Abernethy, David B. *The Dynamics of Global Dominance: European Overseas Empires, 1415–1980*. New Haven, CT: Yale University Press. 2013.

Cruickshanks, Eveline. *The Glorious Revolution*. Basingstoke, UK: Macmillan. 2007.

Cust, Richard. *Charles I: A Political Life*. London: Routledge. 2014.

Doyle, William, ed. *Old Regime France, 1648–1788*. New York: Oxford University Press. 2009.

Fraser, David. *Frederick the Great: King of Prussia*. New York: Fromm International. 2001.

Levi, Anthony. *Louis XIV*. London: Robinson. 2005.

Massie, Robert K. *Peter the Great: His Life and World*. London: Head of Zeus. 2016.

Pagden, Anthony. *Lords of All the World: Ideologies of Empire in Spain, Britain and France, c.1500–c.1800*. New Haven, CT: Yale University Press. 1998.

Parker, Geoffrey. *The Military Revolution: Military Innovation and the Rise of the West, 1500–1800*. Cambridge: Cambridge University Press. 2011.

Rawley, James A. and Stephen D. Behrendt. *The Transatlantic Slave Trade: A History*. Revised Edition. Lincoln, NE: University of Nebraska Press. 2005.

Szabo, Franz A. J. *The Seven Years War in Europe, 1756–1763*. New York: Routledge. 2015.

Wallerstein, Immanuel. *The Modern World-System II: Mercantilism and the Consolidation of the European World-Economy, 1600–1750*. New York: University of California Press. 2011.

Woolhouse, Roger. *Locke: A Biography*. New York: Cambridge University Press. 2012.

Woolrych, Austin. *Britain in Revolution, 1625–1660*. Oxford: Oxford University Press. 2009.

11 European Society During the Scientific, Agricultural, and Industrial Revolutions, 1600–1800

Introduction

Even before the French Revolution in 1789, traditional European society faced three other revolutions: the Scientific, Agricultural, and Industrial Revolutions. Together, these earth-shattering developments would expand exponentially Europeans' knowledge of the natural world, permit a reliable food surplus to be created for the first time in human history, and, through mechanization, vastly improve the productive capacity of European manufacturing enterprises.

To label these developments revolutionary, however, is in some ways deceptive. A revolution implies a rapid and dramatic change, whereas the Scientific, Agricultural, and Industrial Revolutions all unfolded slowly over several centuries. Despite this, the accumulation of the various changes that took place before 1800 paved the way for the attitudes and beliefs, the technology and economy, and even the diet and creature comforts that Western (and non-Western) peoples take for granted today.

The Nobility

Before discussing these revolutions in detail, it is necessary to understand the society and class structure within which Europeans lived during the seventeenth and eighteenth centuries. As always, any attempt to boil down a society into separate classes is fraught with difficulties. Nevertheless, European society before 1800 can be divided into three broad classes: the nobility, the peasantry, and the urban middle class, also called the *bourgeoisie*.

The nobility had been the leading class during the Middle Ages, circa 500 CE–1500 CE, and in fact nobles would retain their dominance well into the nineteenth century. During the medieval period, the high status enjoyed by noblemen had been based partly on a sense of inborn superiority similar to racism. An even more important source of power and prestige for nobles, though, had been their military strength, which was symbolized by their coats-of-arms, designed for use on the battlefield.

By the seventeenth and eighteenth centuries, while most army and navy officers were still nobles, the nobility had lost its monopoly on the means of violence, since European militaries were increasingly controlled by kings and national governments. Increasingly, therefore, the status and power of the nobility was based not on its superior bloodlines, or on its military role, but on its property, and the most valuable and respected form of property at that time was land. In most European countries, the nobility made up only one to five percent of the total population, but it often owned 25 percent or more of the land that was suitable for farming—and in a few countries virtually all of it. In a society in which growing enough food to keep everyone alive was a constant challenge, land ownership made nobles a force to be reckoned with.

Nobles were able to translate their landed wealth into various privileges. Least important was the traditional expectation that nobles would be shown special courtesies by non-nobles, such as bowing and the use of titles. Nobles also commonly enjoyed legal advantages, such as exemption from the most humiliating forms of punishment and from some forms of taxation; they also had the ability to collect income from special dues paid by peasants, and they could even judge peasants in noble courts.

Perhaps most importantly, noble birth was a necessary qualification for many desirable jobs in the seventeenth and eighteenth centuries. Most leading government ministers and bureaucrats, most army and navy officers, and most bishops and other members of the high clergy, were either noblemen or were related by blood or marriage to noblemen. It is important to recognize, however, that the nobility itself was divided. Only those nobles with especially elevated titles, or from the oldest families, would generally be permitted to occupy the highest positions in the government, the military, and the Church. Lesser nobles often had to content themselves with holding local offices.

In addition to the nobility, a closely related group of wealthy landowners without noble titles, called the gentry, exercised considerable influence in some European countries, especially England. Members of the gentry lacked many of the legal advantages of the nobility, but their prominence in rural communities made them politically powerful.

So what was life like for most nobles? First, of all the privileges that noble status conveyed, being rich was not necessarily one of them. Many nobles were rich, of course. Some nobles owned tens of thousands of acres of land; some invested wisely in commercial enterprises such as sugar plantations, mines, or merchant shipping; others benefited from lucrative contracts or high-paying jobs in the service of the king. For every nobleman who was fabulously wealthy, however, there were many who were not. In France, for instance, most provincial nobles were poor, and they barely survived on the rents that their lands produced.

For the average nobleman, life centered on his country estate. During the eighteenth century, these estates were often built in the elegant neoclassical style, based on ancient Greek and Roman architecture. Noble estates were commonly surrounded by carefully manicured gardens or parkland.

The nobility enjoyed hunting, dances, polite conversation, reading, extravagant dining, and listening to music as forms of recreation, while gambling and extramarital liaisons were popular vices, primarily for men. Patronage of art and literature also became a major preoccupation. Although during the Middle Ages nobles had often been associated with crude and boisterous behavior, by the seventeenth and eighteenth centuries nobles usually dictated their society's ideal of good manners. Today, most people in the West eat with a knife and fork. They do so because, several centuries ago, nobles decided that it was the proper thing to do.

Noblewomen in this era found their lives tightly controlled by a male-dominated social system. The most important decision that every noblewoman faced in her lifetime was whom to marry, and typically a woman's father made this decision for her. Once married, noblewomen often managed all or part of the household, but they seldom had to exert themselves physically, since servants performed most menial tasks and children were handed over to wet nurses, governesses, and tutors. Noblewomen were expected to cultivate their beauty, manners, and artistic and musical skills in order to amuse their male relatives and their guests. Indeed, the field of manners and cultural refinement was one area in which a noblewoman could accomplish as much as any man. By bringing men together in their fashionable salons to discuss art, literature, philosophy, or politics, noblewomen could sometimes play a major, but nonetheless controversial, role in society.

What were some of the privileges that nobles enjoyed?

The Peasantry

At the very bottom of the social scale was the peasantry, which made up the vast majority of the population of all European countries. Any discussion of the peasantry in this period must differentiate between peasants in Western Europe and those in Central and Eastern Europe.

In Western European countries such as England, the Netherlands, and France, peasants were generally poor, and though they owed various amounts of labor, or payments in cash or crops, to the local lord, they were still legally free. They could marry, move from place to place, and enter into legal contracts without any nobleman's permission.

In Central and Eastern Europe, by contrast—in places such as Prussia, Austria, and Russia—most peasants were serfs. A serf was a laborer, usually a farm worker, who was legally bound to work for his local nobleman and generally was not allowed to leave the nobleman's estate without permission. His right to marry was often restricted, and his noble overlord sometimes had the power to beat or kill him for disobedience. Noblemen even traded some serfs as though they were slaves. In short, life for peasants in Western

Europe was far freer and easier than it was in Central and Eastern Europe. (For a more detailed discussion of serfdom, see Chapter 7.)

Even in Western Europe, life for the peasantry varied considerably. One of the keys to a peasant's standard of living was whether or not he owned any land. Many peasants did, but they often had to rent additional land from a nobleman or a member of the gentry to survive.

Peasants frequently grew grain, since bread was the staple of the peasant diet (cheese, potatoes, and soup were also common foods), but in the eighteenth century some farmers began to concentrate on growing cash crops and on raising cattle or sheep. Peasants might also work in their homes to spin thread, weave cloth, or perform other services that a merchant might reward. Many peasants prospered under these conditions, but others failed to adapt to new circumstances. They were forced to become day laborers or vagabonds, or to move to the cities to look for work.

All peasants faced the constant threats of famine and disease, and they bore the brunt of taxation. National and local governments, churches, and noblemen all squeezed the peasantry for money and labor in addition to agricultural produce. Mass starvation was often the result. Sometimes there

Figure 11.1 Backbreaking agricultural labor was a major feature of peasant life. Jean-François Millet, *Man with a Hoe*.

Everett-Art/Shutterstock.

were peasant revolts, which were bloody but never successful. Peasants were almost always illiterate, and this gave them very little ability to fight back when government officials, clergymen, or nobles mistreated them.

Peasants were often too distracted by the struggle for survival to maintain close family ties. Husbands were the primary breadwinners. To make ends meet they sometimes left the home to earn extra money. Wives were just as economically active as their husbands. They would help with planting and harvesting as well as bearing responsibility for cooking, cleaning, spinning, and weaving, all of which were infinitely more demanding tasks than they are today. Young children would be handed over to wet nurses, while older children commonly left the home to earn money as apprentices, laborers, or domestic servants. Children also suffered high death rates from disease, so parents would count themselves lucky if half of their children lived to see adulthood. Women faced an additional threat: due to high mortality rates in general, many women became widows. Widowhood could mean enhanced independence for a noblewoman, but it spelled lifelong poverty for most peasant women.

Peasant homes were one- or two-room shacks with dirt floors and thatched roofs. Furniture was very simple, and cleanliness was unthinkable, since animals often shared living quarters with people. Frequently, peasant villages were rife with violence and drunkenness.

Despite these challenges, life for the peasantry was not uniformly miserable. Even in Eastern Europe, where conditions for peasants were the worst, family bonds, village traditions, and religious faith were a source of comfort. Peasants would celebrate births, marriages, and other special occasions with feasting, dancing, and singing. Many modern folk traditions are the product of peasant life. Peasants were, above all, survivors. Despite their deep poverty, most peasants clung fiercely to their traditional way of life, and they opposed attempts at reform.

What was life like for peasants in the seventeenth and eighteenth centuries?

The *Bourgeoisie*, or Middle Class

The *bourgeoisie* was the class between the nobles at the top of the social structure and the peasants at the bottom. For this reason, the *bourgeoisie* is sometimes called the middle class, but this name is deceptive. When we talk about the middle class today, we mean people with moderate incomes—people who are neither rich nor poor. But the middle class of the seventeenth and eighteenth centuries, while it included many people with moderate incomes, also included some people who were fabulously wealthy. A merchant or a banker, for example, might make a fortune, but because he was neither a nobleman (at the top of society) nor a peasant (at the bottom), he was still considered middle class. Keep this in mind whenever the term *bourgeoisie* or middle class is used in reference to the seventeenth, eighteenth, or nineteenth centuries.

The *bourgeoisie* was concentrated in the cities of Europe, where in the eighteenth century a maximum of 20 percent of the population lived. Members of the *bourgeoisie* (known individually and in the plural as *bourgeois*) were often people who today would be considered professionals: doctors, lawyers, bureaucrats, editors, judges, tax collectors, teachers, professors, and clergymen. These people had special skills that they believed put them above the peasants, who they tended to view as crude and uncivilized.

Other members of the *bourgeoisie* were involved in manufacturing, trade, or finance. Perhaps they owned a business that produced clothing by loaning equipment and raw materials to peasants who worked in their own homes. Perhaps they lived in a thriving port city and owned merchant ships that brought sugar or spices to Europe from overseas. Perhaps they were bankers who loaned money to kings, noblemen, or other *bourgeois*. The *bourgeoisie*, in short, was a class engaged in a startlingly diverse array of economic activities.

Whatever their precise economic and social role happened to be, virtually all middle-class Europeans agreed on one point—they wanted their growing importance to be recognized by society. The easiest way for an individual *bourgeois* to achieve this goal, however, was not to fight for better treatment for his class as a whole, but simply to leave the *bourgeoisie* and join the nobility! This was not a fanciful aim. Rich members of the middle class could sometimes purchase noble titles from cash-strapped monarchs, or they could earn them by serving in the government, the military, or the courts. Alternatively, wealthy members of the middle class could simply buy estates in the countryside and hope that local gentry and nobles would accept them as equals. If all else failed, the middle class could at least buy the same luxury goods that noblemen consumed, imitate their manners, and try to live like gentlemen.

Ultimately, though, the nobility admitted relatively few new members, and it often treated the *bourgeois* poorly. Most middle-class Europeans therefore felt left out. Some became angry. Still, the antagonism between the nobility and the middle class during the seventeenth and eighteenth centuries should not be overstated. Both were part of society's elite, and on many issues they cooperated.

What was life like for the middle class? *Bourgeois* homes in the cities were much more spacious and comfortable than peasant dwellings, and *bourgeois* families frequently employed personal servants. The middle class also benefited from the entertainments that urban life had to offer, such as plays, concerts, social clubs, and pleasure gardens, which were similar to parks but with an admission fee to discourage the lower classes from intruding.

Middle-class children often benefited from formal education, even college education in rare cases, because the *bourgeoisie* valued learning as a path to upward mobility. Middle-class children also commonly received more love and attention from their parents than was customary for either the nobility or the peasantry. Middle-class women, however, were expected to be as subservient to their husbands as women in other social classes.

Unfortunately for the *bourgeoisie*, the world of material comfort and success that it was creating in the cities was troubled by the growing numbers of the urban poor. Some historians would even argue that the urban poor already represented a fourth class in eighteenth-century Europe. That may be an exaggeration, but certainly their importance was on the rise.

During the seventeenth and eighteenth centuries, there were few, if any, factory workers in urban areas. Most manufacturing still took place in the countryside. There was, though, a great volume of trade in the cities, involving warehousing, shipping and distribution, and wholesale and retail sales, and many poor people worked in these sectors. The urban population also included many craftsmen and household servants as well as prostitutes, beggars, the unemployed, orphans, and criminals.

Not surprisingly, as cities grew throughout the eighteenth century, and as wealth remained concentrated in relatively few hands, crime and urban discontent mushroomed. Cities also became breeding grounds for contagious diseases.

Despite these problems, at this stage the *bourgeoisie*, along with royal authorities, remained in control of Europe's cities. During the nineteenth century, however, when the pace of urbanization quickened and the factory mode of production became more popular, urban workers would begin to challenge the dominance of the *bourgeoisie*.

What were the advantages of being part of the bourgeoisie *in the seventeenth and eighteenth centuries?*

The Rise of Science

Science can best be defined as the effort to understand nature through observation and the use of reason. Science, in this sense, goes back at least to ancient Greece. During the medieval period scholasticism encouraged scientific work, although science was seen as secondary to logic and theology. The Italian Renaissance was also a period in which some aspects of scientific thinking flourished. European science has also repeatedly been nourished by the scientific discoveries made by non-Europeans.

The Scientific Revolution that began in Europe during the sixteenth century and lasted into the seventeenth and eighteenth centuries was therefore not without historical precedents. Previous efforts at expanding scientific knowledge, however, were generally less organized, less precise, less practically useful, and more reliant on religious preconceptions. They also attracted less support from powerful interests in society.

The Scientific Revolution was a critical event in European history, but in truth it developed so slowly, and initially affected so few people, that a visitor to Europe even as late as 1800 might have seen no evidence of it at all. And yet, subtly and gradually, it brought profound change.

Before 1500, most Europeans had defined what was true and right based not on science, but on tradition, on Christian doctrine, including the Bible, and on classical scholarship, especially the works of Aristotle. The idea that truth was accessible by other means, through the independent use of reason or through the experimental method of modern scientists, would not have occurred to most Europeans.

Although scientific study can follow many different paths, most modern science came to depend on what is now known as the scientific method, sometimes also called the experimental method. Scientists believe that the best way to understand nature is to use one's rational faculties, plus one's senses—especially sight—to perform experiments that yield objective results. These results are then rationally analyzed to produce broad theories that can be proven by further experimentation.

It is possible to illustrate the scientific method in a simple way. Suppose one were to ask the question: what color is the planet Mars? In 1500, an educated European would probably have consulted Catholic religious texts or the works of Aristotle to obtain an answer. A scientist, on the other hand, would look up! Not only that, but a scientist would use the best available technology, such as the telescope, to improve the accuracy of his or her perceptions. A scientist would also use the faculty of sight to look up at Mars not just once, but perhaps hundreds or even thousands of times, keeping careful notes on each observation. Mathematics might be used to organize and make sense of the resulting data. When there was enough data, a scientist would construct a theory about what color Mars is. That theory—presumably, that Mars is red—could then be tested with new experiments to ensure its validity. The final product of the scientific method is therefore not transcendent truths, but useful and revealing models of how nature normally behaves.

The scientific method may sound simple and self-evident, but the fact that more and more Europeans were thinking in these terms after 1500 was a revolutionary development. It helped to make the modern mind-set and way of life possible.

The Scientific Revolution got underway in the sixteenth century with important advances in the field of astronomy. Before 1500, the accepted model of the solar system and the universe was geocentric, meaning that everything was presumed to revolve around the earth. The geocentric theory, which was endorsed by the Catholic Church, was sometimes also known as the Ptolemaic system after one of its main proponents, the ancient Greek astronomer Ptolemy.

The Ptolemaic system was barely questioned for hundreds of years, but in 1543 a Polish astronomer named Nicolaus Copernicus advanced the provocative idea that perhaps the Earth revolved around the Sun, a concept known as heliocentrism, instead of the other way around. Because Copernicus was afraid of persecution, he waited until he was on his deathbed to publish his ideas.

As Copernicus had expected, many leading astronomers, and some Catholic and Protestant religious leaders, immediately rejected the new heliocentric theory. The Copernican system was seemingly at odds with the Bible, and, just as importantly, the evidence that Copernicus had offered in support of his theory was shaky. Some astronomers, though, were sufficiently intrigued that they began collecting data to test Copernicus's ideas.

In 1609, Copernicus's theory received important support from an astronomer working in Prague named Johannes Kepler. Kepler used advanced mathematics to prove that the Sun rather than the Earth was at the center of the solar system, and he introduced the additional refinement of elliptical orbits to make the Copernican, or heliocentric, system more accurate. According to Kepler, the planets, including Earth, revolve around the Sun in orbits that are oval-shaped instead of perfect circles. Knowledge of these elliptical orbits allows us to predict the positions of the planets in Earth's sky at any given time with great precision.

Later, further detail was added to Kepler's findings by the brilliant Englishman Sir Isaac Newton. Newton was a passionate Bible scholar and a devoted public servant, but his real claim to fame was as a mathematician and physicist. He invented calculus, studied the properties of light, and discovered many of the laws of motion, but his most important achievement was the idea of gravity. According to Newton, every object in the universe exerts a pull on other objects, proportionate to the mass of the objects and the distance between them. In other words, a heavy body, such as a planet, exerts a particularly strong pull on nearby objects, such as people, and thus we all remain firmly attached to the Earth. Newton did not fully understand what gravity was, but the idea of gravity nevertheless provided a complete explanation for why the planets revolved around the Sun: quite simply, the Sun is the most massive object in the solar system, so its gravitational force is the strongest. Based on his theories about gravity and his other scientific achievements, Newton is widely acknowledged as the greatest scientist in history.

Another important backer of the Copernican system was Galileo Galilei, an Italian scientist, mathematician, inventor, and philosopher. Galileo had been the first to use a new Dutch invention, the telescope, to observe the heavens. Galileo not only discovered unexpected features of the solar system, such as the moons of Jupiter and the rings of Saturn, but he also claimed to have found proof that the Earth revolved around the Sun. In 1632, he published his findings in a way that appeared to mock the geocentric views of the Catholic Church. The pope was outraged. The Church forced Galileo, under the threat of torture, to retract his statements and to live under house arrest for the last nine years of his life.

Galileo's fate is important, because it highlights a growing rift between religious authorities and scientists in the seventeenth and eighteenth centuries. During the sixteenth and early seventeenth centuries, relations between scientists and religious leaders had been cordial and even mutually supportive. Scientists often claimed that their scientific investigations were directly inspired by their Christian beliefs. However, in the wake of the Wars of Religion, official churches in all European countries were working hard to win over their flocks to the view that the established church was the only source of truth. Scientists were now asserting that some religious traditions could be wrong, and that experimental methods and the use of reason could establish truth on a firmer basis. This cast doubt on the authority and privileges of priests, bishops, and other church officials. Thus, relations between religion and science began to deteriorate, although the severity of the rift should not be exaggerated.

The Scientific Revolution began to move in a new and even more radical direction during the seventeenth century, when human beings themselves became the subject of scientific inquiry. The Englishman John Locke proposed that the human mind was a *tabula rasa*, or blank slate, at birth, and therefore all of a person's thoughts are supplied by his or her senses. This led to an important debate between those who believed that people's inborn traits govern who they are, and those—like Locke—who insisted that human beings are solely the product of their environment. This "nature versus nurture" debate rages even today.

Before the seventeenth and eighteenth centuries, knowledge of the human body and of how to cure its ailments was severely limited. Even the basic anatomical differences between men and women, and their roles in reproduction, were often misunderstood. Not surprisingly, therefore, medical treatments often did more harm than good. One of the most common treatments was "bleeding," that is, draining much of the patient's blood, sometimes with the aid of leeches.

Thanks to the Scientific Revolution, by the seventeenth and eighteenth centuries medical experts had access to more accurate information about the human body than ever before, particularly due to the growing acceptance of dissections. Surgical techniques improved, drugs were more sensibly prescribed, and a successful inoculation program against smallpox was undertaken. By 1800, medicine, based on a scientific understanding of the human body, was establishing its reputation as the most effective approach to fighting disease.

As the Scientific Revolution slowly took hold in Europe, new scientific societies were formed on a national or regional level to support and to lend credibility to the work of scientists. Often, monarchs personally created and funded these organizations. Rulers expected that scientific investigations would yield not only abstract knowledge but also new inventions that could make money, or, alternatively, make war.

By 1800, science as a whole was beginning to attract the attention not just of intellectuals and political leaders but of everyday people. Part of the reason lies in improvements in printing technology that facilitated the rapid spread of scientific knowledge. In addition, the spillover of science into technological innovation, and its role in producing ever higher standards of living, were instrumental in convincing more and more people that scientific know-how was invaluable.

One important consequence of the rise of science was that faith in magical or supernatural explanations for everyday phenomena diminished in modern Western Civilization, even though popular religion remained strong. This was not necessarily a predictable outcome, because initially many scientists had studied alchemy, astrology, and other forms of magic. Gradually, though, scientists developed contempt for these ideas. As a consequence, the influence of traditional healers, astrologers, sorcerers, and witches declined over time. Arguably, women, many of whom were either practitioners or consumers of magic, were especially hard hit by these changes.

What were some of the most important consequences of the Scientific Revolution?

The Population Explosion, the Agricultural Revolution, and the Beginnings of Industrialization

Two important and parallel developments occurred during the eighteenth century: a gradual but consistent increase in Europe's population, and a similar increase in Europe's production of food. Historians are still trying to sort out which was the cause and which was the effect.

The rise in Europe's population is clear. England's population grew by about 70 percent during the second half of the eighteenth century to ten million, while the already-large population of Russia underwent a similar rapid increase. France's population grew much more slowly, but it reached approximately 28 million in 1789. Europe's overall population increased by roughly 50 percent during the eighteenth century, creeping close to 200 million. Urban areas also grew. London had one million inhabitants in 1800, Paris had half a million, and other cities were breaking the 100,000 mark for the first time. One factor in this population increase was lower death rates due to better medical care and fewer epidemics. Clearly, though, the improvement and diversification of the food supply was critical.

This enhancement in Europe's ability to feed itself was due mainly to what is called the Agricultural Revolution, another gradual shift in European history, this time toward more efficient and productive farming techniques. It was the Dutch who pioneered many of these new agricultural methods in the seventeenth century, but it was the British who put them to the greatest use in the eighteenth century. New farming methods included crop rotation, the use of iron plows, and the enclosure of farmland.

Crop rotation is the practice of varying the crops that are planted in a given field from season to season in order to enhance soil fertility for each crop. With crop rotation, every piece of farmland can be in continuous use. Iron plows, meanwhile, along with a variety of agricultural implements invented during the seventeenth and eighteenth centuries, allowed for much faster and more reliable planting and harvesting of crops. Enclosure—the fencing in of land that had previously been available to peasants to farm in common, or to use as grazing land—allowed landowners to decide how to use the land for maximum profit. Many peasants resented the loss of their traditional common lands, and they were suspicious of new farming techniques.

Despite popular resistance, a more efficient and businesslike approach to farming was in place by the end of the eighteenth century.

Overall, the Agricultural Revolution produced dramatic results. In Western Europe, agricultural yields were often two or three times what they were in more backward parts of Russia. Producing a reliable food surplus was a crucial development, because it meant that less of Europeans' time, money, and labor had to be devoted to farming, and more could be devoted to achieving innovations in other areas. The Agricultural Revolution, in other words, was the prerequisite for the Industrial Revolution that followed.

Few developments in European history were as important in the long run as the Industrial Revolution. It was a transformation that ultimately would expand and enrich the middle class, swell the population of Europe's cities, and greatly diminish the grinding poverty that had always haunted the Western world. It also created new social conflicts that would define much of the history of the nineteenth and twentieth centuries.

The Industrial Revolution relied chiefly on the increased use of machinery in order to make the production of goods more efficient. Generally speaking, it is said to have begun in Britain around 1750. As a result of the Industrial Revolution, Britain would increase its power and wealth throughout the eighteenth and nineteenth centuries. Not until the last part of the nineteenth century would other countries finally catch up.

Why did industrialization begin with the British? First, Britain already had a head start, in the sense that considerable economic growth, urbanization, popularization of science and technology, and improvement in agricultural productivity had been achieved from 1550 to 1750. Second, Britain's large empire and its invincible navy meant that it had access to markets across the world. Britain was, in fact, the world leader in trade, which made it a haven for innovators and entrepreneurs. Third, Britain's financial system, built around the Bank of England, was among the most highly developed in the world. The Bank of England issued bank notes, managed the burgeoning national debt, and eased access to credit for many businesses. Fourth, Britain had abundant natural resources, including fertile land, coal, and iron ore. Fifth, navigable waterways, including 3,000 miles of canals, made the transportation of goods within Britain relatively cheap. At this stage, roads were still poorly maintained, and railroads were yet to be invented. Sixth, Britain benefited from a relatively flexible class system, in which a successful farmer or *bourgeois* could realistically aspire to advance his status through individual achievement. Lastly, Britain's government played a supportive role in industrialization by collecting taxes fairly, protecting property rights, and supporting the free exchange of ideas, including through advertising.

Thus, Britain possessed all the vital ingredients needed to make modern industrial capitalism thrive: capital (money), labor, natural resources, sound infrastructure, good governance, and a culture that valued scientific and technological progress and the accumulation of wealth. Nevertheless, before 1830 the development of an industrial economy in Britain proceeded relatively slowly. The vast majority of people in every European country, including Britain, still lived in the countryside, were involved in farming, and did not participate in industrialization in any meaningful way.

Although at this stage the factory system barely existed, eighteenth-century society still found several ways to produce manufactured goods, especially textiles (fabrics of all sorts), that were at the heart of early efforts to industrialize. This production occurred largely by two methods.

The first major approach to manufacturing in the eighteenth century, and the most outmoded, was the guild system. Guilds were located mainly in towns and cities. They were associations of master and junior craftsmen (women were usually excluded) who agreed to abide by common standards within their trade. A guild of tailors, for example, would develop rules for how much an apprentice tailor should be paid, how many hours he should work, what quality of cloth he should use, and how much a finished piece of clothing should cost. In effect, guilds were associations of small businessmen who all agreed to play by the same rules, thus eliminating competition between them and achieving security for their members. During the Middle Ages, guilds had been very popular, but by the eighteenth century most entrepreneurs found the restrictions and regulations of the guild system counterproductive. Guilds were in decline.

The second and by far the more important method of production in the eighteenth century was the "putting-out system," also called the domestic system. According to this approach, a businessman involved in, for example, the production of textiles would employ numerous peasants working in their own homes, especially when there was no planting or harvesting to be done, to complete one or more stages of the production process. Peasants in one home might spin thread, while in another home they would weave the thread into cloth. Often the entire peasant family would pitch in. Thus, by utilizing the primary existing source of labor in the eighteenth century—the peasant family—businessmen and manufacturers could produce clothing and other textiles without factories or factory workers of any kind.

The putting-out system thrived during the earliest stages of industrialization. The first inventions of the Industrial Revolution, such as the spinning jenny, a simple machine that allowed spinners to create much more thread than ever before, were clearly designed to be used within the peasant home. Inevitably, though, as British inventors produced new and more complex machines, manufacturers began to doubt the wisdom of home-based production.

One of the most significant of these early inventors was Richard Arkwright, a self-educated man who was a barber and a wig-maker before he developed a machine called the water frame that made him one of the richest men in Europe. The water frame was a brilliant innovation, but it was also expensive and difficult to maintain. It used waterpower, drawn from wheels turned by streams in the countryside, to spin thread that could be woven into pure cotton fabric, which was in high demand. Manufacturers who invested in the water frame placed it in small rural factories, often called mills, located near the homes of peasants and landless laborers. The rural lifestyle was not seriously disrupted by these changes, but moving the focus of textile production from the home to a mill was still a major step.

Some home-based workers, and some craftsmen associated with guilds, were angry enough about the trend toward mechanization that they attacked and destroyed spinning jennies, water frames, and other machines, even though they risked the death penalty by doing so. Nevertheless, the increase in production that these innovations helped to achieve was phenomenal. By 1800, cotton fabrics were Britain's main export, and the country had become the world leader in textile production. One side effect was that Britain acquired an insatiable thirst for raw cotton, most of which was produced either in British colonies or on slave plantations in the American South.

Why did the Industrial Revolution begin in Britain?

The Steam Engine and the Origins of the Factory System

Soon the remarkable advances in textile production helped to motivate innovations in other areas. The world's first cast-iron bridge, for example, was built in 1779, nestled in a beautiful valley in Telford, England. It was part of an important trend. Iron production greatly increased in Britain throughout the eighteenth century. This was critical, because iron is the most widely used mineral in modern industry. An ample supply of iron, in turn, set the stage for the greatest invention of all in the eighteenth century: the steam engine.

A number of men worked on different versions of the steam engine, but it was James Watt, a Scot, who produced the first model that was efficient enough for wide use. The purpose of the steam engine was simple: it was designed to be a source of power to run machines. Previously, machines had depended on human beings, animals, wind, or running water for power. The steam engine changed all this by harnessing the power of steam, and its tendency to rapidly condense, to move a piston up and down. Modern internal combustion engines work in a similar way.

The beauty of this new invention was that, so long as one had a portable supply of water and something to burn to generate heat, that is, wood or coal, one could use the steam engine anywhere, anytime, to produce as much power as needed. Suddenly, the limitations on the productive capacity of manufacturers were dramatically reduced. Instead of depending on a finite number of peasants to produce goods by hand, now one could call upon endless numbers of steam engines to power machines that could do the same work far more efficiently and cheaply.

James Watt and other Britons were slow to recognize the potential uses of the steam engine. After 1800, though, steam power quickly caught on.

It not only increased production but also signaled the death knell for the putting-out system. Bulky, heavy steam engines were utterly unsuitable for home-based production. They had to be placed in factories. Unlike the water frame, however, the steam engine required no nearby stream or river, so long as water and fuel could be delivered to it. Steam power therefore made it possible to locate factories in cities, where manufactured goods could then be distributed and sold with greater ease. It was the steam engine, therefore, that allowed the urban-based factory system to dominate industrial production. This would, in turn, foster a steady process of urbanization that would have dramatic repercussions not just for European economics, but for politics, society, and culture as well.

It was the *bourgeoisie* that benefited the most from these early stages of industrialization. Although some noblemen invested in industry, it was *bourgeois* merchants, manufacturers, inventors, bankers, engineers, scientists, and professionals who reaped the greatest rewards from the earliest machines and the first factories. Importantly, most members of the middle class came to believe that inventors and entrepreneurs should be given maximum economic freedom in order to encourage even more industrial progress. Increasingly, therefore, the *bourgeoisie* rejected mercantilism and embraced *laissez-faire* capitalism, the economic philosophy of Adam Smith (see Chapter 12).

Textile production was only one part of the Industrial Revolution. The production of household items, including furniture, and of many varieties of food and drink, also skyrocketed. Britain began to take shape as a consumer society, in which the consumption of new goods and services, and the expectation of a constantly rising standard of living, became commonplace, just like today.

There was a dark side to all this industrial progress and might, however. Many of the workers in Britain's new factories were women and children who toiled in deplorable conditions for very low wages. The machines they operated were often dangerous, and there was no provision for worker's compensation in case of injury. Strict discipline and organized timetables were enforced on the factory floor, and fines or beatings could be meted out as punishments for disobedience. Very long hours were also the norm. Meanwhile, pollution was severe.

Despite these drawbacks, poor Europeans often had no choice but to work in factories. Opportunities to work at home were fast disappearing. Many peasants who had depended on the putting-out system were forced to abandon their homes and fields, and to migrate to the cities to look for work in industry—or worse, they ended up toiling half-naked in the mines.

Britain may have become wealthy due to industrialization, therefore, but great social problems were created as a result. Eventually, workers would organize into unions to oppose the worst features of industrial capitalism. Some workers, notably socialists and communists, even became convinced that capitalism itself had to go.

Opposition to industrialization was also sometimes based on the connection between industry and colonialism. True, the benefits of industrial development slowly seeped out of Britain, especially to its colonies and former colonies in the Atlantic World, including the United States. But many of the raw materials that the British needed for industrial production came from overseas, and in particular from their colonies, which were not in a position to negotiate favorable terms. Thus began a relationship of economic dependency between Europe and the developing world that some experts claim has continued to the present day, even though European countries lost formal control over most of the Americas, Africa, and Asia in the eighteenth through twentieth centuries. According to one such approach, called world-systems theory, Western countries in Europe and North America today still represent the "core" of the international economy, while developing countries in Latin America, Africa, and Asia represent the exploited "periphery," or, in rare cases, the "semi-periphery." The accuracy of world-systems theory is in dispute, but impossible to deny is the fact that industrialization in the West opened up a vast gulf in living standards between the West and non-Western areas that has proved remarkably long-lasting.

What is the connection between the steam engine and the factory system of production?

Conclusions

The changes that occurred in European society due to the Scientific, Agricultural, and Industrial Revolutions were momentous, especially in hindsight, but they were slow to emerge. At the end of the eighteenth century, life for many Europeans, even in Europe's industrial heartland of Britain, remained much the same as it had been for centuries. Science was still for the most part an eccentric hobby; economic growth rates were low, by modern standards; 80–90 percent of the population still lived in the countryside; peasants and nobles predominated; and the *bourgeoisie*, despite its recent industrial and commercial successes, had trouble making its voice heard.

At the end of the eighteenth century, there was in much of Europe a sense that the existing social structure, values, and agrarian economy would endure—or at least that they would accommodate calls for reform gradually and peacefully. In 1789, however, an event occurred that would shake Europe to its foundations. The French Revolution would unleash political chaos, economic dislocation, and a generation of warfare that would make all other historical themes, including scientific discovery, agricultural efficiency, and industrialization, temporarily irrelevant.

Key Terms for Chapter 11

Serfs—peasants who are tied to the land and who live under the control of the local nobleman.

Bourgeoisie—a French term for the urban middle class.

Scientific Revolution—a period from the sixteenth through the eighteenth centuries, during which some Europeans sought to increase humanity's knowledge of the natural world through the use of observation, experimentation, and reasoning.

Scientific method—the use of one's senses and experimentation in order to amass data about the natural world that is then rationally analyzed to produce theories about how nature operates.

Nicolaus Copernicus—the sixteenth-century originator of a controversial heliocentric, or sun-centered, model of the solar system.

Sir Isaac Newton—an accomplished scientist and mathematician who lived in the mid-seventeenth and early eighteenth centuries and was the originator of the concept of gravity.

Tabula rasa—a theory of human psychology developed by John Locke, stating that the human mind is a blank slate at birth and that all of our thoughts are supplied by our senses.

Agricultural Revolution—a period from the seventeenth through the nineteenth centuries, during which more efficient farming techniques were employed, especially in Britain.

Industrial Revolution—a period from the mid-eighteenth through the twentieth centuries during which the production of goods was made more efficient through the use of machines.

Guild system—a method of producing goods popular during the Middle Ages. It involved associations of local craftsmen who all agreed to use similar business practices.

Putting-out system—a method of producing goods increasingly popular in the eighteenth century, involving manufacturers hiring peasant families to work in their own homes.

Steam engine—an invention perfected by James Watt in the eighteenth century and used to create power to run machines. It was the steam engine, more than any other innovation, that caused the rise of the factory system of production.

Factory system—a method of producing manufactured goods by bringing machines, workers, and raw materials together in one place.

Review Questions for Chapter 11

1. If you had lived in the seventeenth or eighteenth centuries, which class would you have most liked to be a part of? Which class would you have least liked to be a part of? Explain your selections.
2. Choose one of the scientists discussed in Chapter 11 and write a brief biographical sketch about him. Then, imagine how modern society might be different if his contributions were removed.
3. Briefly describe two of the accomplishments of the Agricultural Revolution. Then, describe two of the accomplishments of the Industrial Revolution.

4. One of the changes to society that the Industrial Revolution helped to bring about was the increasing level of separation between where a person lived and where a person worked. First, explain why industrialization made it difficult for many people to work at home. Then give your own opinion as to whether it is better to live and work in two separate places or whether it is better to work from home.
5. Of the various scientific, agricultural, and industrial advances discussed in Chapter 11, choose the one that you feel is the most important. Justify your choice. Then describe how modern life might be different if that advancement had never occurred.

Further Readings

Abrams, Lynn. *The Making of Modern Woman: Europe, 1789–1918*. New York: Routledge. 2016.

Adams, Christine. *A Taste for Comfort and Status: A Bourgeois Family in Eighteenth-Century France*. University Park, PA: Pennsylvania State University Press. 2000.

Allen, Robert C. *The British Industrial Revolution in Global Perspective*. New York: Cambridge University Press. 2015.

Bock, Gisela. *Women in European History*. Malden, MA: Blackwell. 2002.

Dolnick, Edward. *The Clockwork Universe: Isaac Newton, the Royal Society, and the Birth of the Modern World*. New York: HarperCollins. 2011.

Henry, John. *The Scientific Revolution and the Origins of Modern Science*. Third Edition. Basingstoke, UK: Palgrave Macmillan. 2008.

Hohenberg, Paul M. and Lynn Hollen Lees. *The Making of Urban Europe, 1000–1950*. Cambridge, MA: Harvard University Press. 2009.

King, Steven and Geoffrey Timmins. *Making Sense of the Industrial Revolution: English Economy and Society, 1700–1850*. Manchester, UK: Manchester University Press. 2004.

Lindemann, Mary. *Medicine and Society in Early Modern Europe*. Cambridge: Cambridge University Press. 2013.

Lukowski, Jerzy. *The European Nobility in the Eighteenth Century*. New York: Palgrave Macmillan. 2003.

Margolis, Howard. *It Started With Copernicus: How Turning the World Inside Out Led to the Scientific Revolution*. New York: McGraw-Hill. 2002.

Overton, Mark. *The Agricultural Revolution in England: The Transformation of the Agrarian Economy, 1500–1850*. Cambridge: Cambridge University Press. 2006.

12 The Enlightenment, the French Revolution, and the Age of Napoleon, 1700–1815

Introduction

The French Revolution was such an important event in European and world history that many historians consider it to mark the beginning of the modern era. The causes of the French Revolution were varied.

One cause mentioned already was the mountain of debt that France had built up over the eighteenth century. Another major cause was the Enlightenment, a decisive shift in attitudes and beliefs throughout Europe in the eighteenth century that was hostile to tradition and strongly advocated rational reform. It was widely assumed that the ideas of the Enlightenment would lead to progress and freedom, and that everyone would benefit. The French Revolution would prove that this was not always the case.

Indeed, the results of the French Revolution were shocking, especially to those most committed to its avowed principles of popular sovereignty, constitutionalism, individual rights, and representative government. All of these ideals were given lip service by Napoleon Bonaparte after he took power in France at the conclusion of the French Revolution in 1799, but in reality the government that he formed was a military dictatorship. For a while, Napoleon achieved French military domination of the continent of Europe, but in the end a coalition of European monarchies managed to defeat him. They made every effort to turn back the clock in Europe to a time when the ideals of the French Revolution and the naked ambition of Napoleon were unknown.

The Enlightenment

The Enlightenment was a major European intellectual movement in the eighteenth century. Although ultimately the forces of tradition prevented enlightened thinkers from accomplishing many of their goals, the movement still had a huge historical impact.

During the sixteenth, seventeenth, and eighteenth centuries, Europeans had witnessed a bewildering array of changes, including the discovery and colonization of the New World, the Protestant Reformation and the Wars of Religion, the Scientific Revolution, the beginnings of industrialization, and the rise of absolute monarchy and representative government. Educated Europeans naturally debated whether these changes were positive or negative. By the eighteenth century, a large group of literate, cultured Europeans had formed that supported many of these changes and called for even bolder reforms. This movement gradually became known as the Enlightenment. Although it was influential throughout Europe, it was chiefly based in France.

The men, and on rare occasions women, who led the Enlightenment were called *philosophes*, from the French word for philosophers. The *philosophes* were educated intellectuals from the urban middle class or the nobility. They gained notoriety either by discussing their ideas with other *philosophes*, or by publishing their views in books, newspapers, journals, and even novels, which were sold to an increasingly wide audience. Dissemination of the *philosophes'* views was facilitated by improvements in printing technology and the creation of a "print culture" during the eighteenth century. This print culture, in turn, helped to create a new force of decisive importance: public opinion. Perhaps the best example of the new print culture was the *Encyclopedia*, published in France from the 1750s to the 1780s, and distributed throughout Europe. The *Encyclopedia*, written by legions of *philosophes*, not only attempted to encapsulate all human knowledge, but it added spirited social criticism. Throughout the eighteenth century, traditional authorities used censorship to try to prevent the *philosophes'* radical ideas from spreading, but such efforts were not especially effective.

The changes that the *philosophes* supported revolved around three key concepts: reason, liberty, and reform. The *philosophes* were great believers in the use of reason mainly because they were also admirers of the Scientific Revolution. The *philosophes* were drawn to scientists because of their skeptical attitudes but also due to the spectacular advances they had made in the study of nature based on the use of their senses and their rational faculties. If the human mind and its capacity for reason could unlock the secrets of nature, the *philosophes* suggested, then why not use reason to solve other problems, such as problems of society or government? The great Prussian thinker Immanuel Kant was among the many *philosophes* who praised rational thought.

Partly because of their faith in the capacity of human reason, the *philosophes* also tended to believe that people should be given maximum freedom to live and think as they choose. *Philosophes* tended to condemn institutions that they saw as stifling liberty and enforcing conformity, such as the Catholic Church. The *philosophes'* love of freedom was due in part to their admiration for Great Britain in the eighteenth century, and the degree of freedom of speech, religious toleration, economic freedom, and representative government that was practiced there. They especially admired John Locke, who had eloquently defended many of these British liberties. The *philosophes* were not entirely consistent in their advocacy of freedom—they denied many freedoms to women, for example, they disagreed about slavery, and they sometimes showed contempt for the poor—but the connection between the Enlightenment and liberty as an ideal is clear.

Lastly, *philosophes* almost always supported reform: some touted religious reform, some political, and some social or economic reform. This prejudice in favor of change often made *philosophes* scornful of traditional institutions and of the *status quo*. The reforming zeal of the Enlightenment was somewhat blunted, however, by the fact that the *philosophes* often differed about what sort of change was best.

The image of an eighteenth-century *philosophe* can be completed by describing the man who many consider to have been the greatest *philosophe* of all: Voltaire, originally known as François-Marie Arouet. Voltaire was French, like most *philosophes*. In addition to being an accomplished lover and an occasional spy, Voltaire was a sincere believer in reason, liberty, and reform. He won international acclaim by writing about these ideals in plays, essays, and books that were filled with wit and biting sarcasm.

Predictably, Voltaire was a bitter enemy of tradition: he lampooned eighteenth-century militarism, religious orthodoxy, and political authorities. Ironically, though, Voltaire, who was fiercely anti-establishment, eventually purchased a minor title of nobility, and he was also one of the most successful *philosophes* in attracting the attention and even the patronage of kings. Voltaire's ambivalent attitude to the established order was typical of many *philosophes*: on one hand, they despised many eighteenth-century ideas and institutions, but, on the other hand, they enjoyed the money and support that monarchs and nobles could give them. Many of the lively discussions that characterized the Enlightenment also took place in the salons of noblewomen or at royal courts—in other words, in the very halls of power that *philosophes* believed were in the greatest need of reform.

What values and beliefs did the philosophes *have in common?*

Proposals of the *Philosophes*, and the Broad Impact of the Enlightenment

Although reason, liberty, and reform were the primary interests of the *philosophes*, there was another common focus of Enlightened thought that brought these three main ideas of the movement together in a concrete proposal for change. *Philosophes* usually supported enhancing religious toleration and religious freedom. Some radical *philosophes* went even further and advocated an end to traditional Christianity, with its emphasis on supernaturalism and divine revelation, and a transition to deism, a new religious perspective that revolved around reason and the scientific study of nature's laws. The majority of *philosophes*, however, could be more accurately described as secularists. Secularism is the idea that life on earth is what matters, and ideas about spirituality are of secondary importance, at best, and should be left to the individual. This was a remarkably tolerant position to take when one considers the fact that the persecution of heretics was still common in the eighteenth century.

In the realm of social policy, *philosophes* took their cue from the Englishman John Locke, who had argued that the human mind is a *tabula rasa*, or blank slate, at birth, and therefore all our thoughts are supplied by our senses. This concept implied that, by altering the environment in which people lived, better people and a better society could be created. Many *philosophes* imagined ideal communities that could develop if only the burdens of superstition and ignorance were removed. For this reason, *philosophes* tended to place special emphasis on education, and they suggested that society should reward people for their achievements, a system called meritocracy, rather than for their privileged birth. The *philosophes'* goal of improving access to education was achieved, but many schools were designed to produce model Christians and obedient subjects, not *philosophes*.

The *philosophes* had many disagreements about which form of government was best. Some seemed to endorse absolute monarchy, but they naturally encouraged absolute monarchs to pursue Enlightenment reforms. Perhaps surprisingly, some monarchs showed enthusiasm for the proposals of the *philosophes*. Prussia's King Frederick the Great, for example, sought the friendship of Voltaire. He also protected religious liberty and respected the freedom of the press. Catherine the Great, who ruled Russia from 1762 to 1796, is another example of what is called Enlightened Absolutism. She corresponded eagerly with *philosophes* in the early years of her reign. When the reform proposals of the *philosophes* became too threatening, though, she banned Enlightenment publications altogether. In short, some European rulers were prepared to experiment with Enlightenment reforms, but they were committed above all to their own power and aggrandizement.

Because Enlightened Absolutism seemed to produce such disappointing results, other *philosophes* advocated different forms of government. The Baron de Montesquieu, Charles Louis de Secondat, became famous for proposing a division of powers. Montesquieu argued that the success of limited monarchy in Britain, where the monarch, the nobility, and the common people all shared political power, was proof that his idea could work. His suggestion caught on: the Founding Fathers included the separation of powers in the U.S. Constitution.

Another *philosophe* famous for his political ideas was Jean-Jacques Rousseau. Rousseau proposed that direct democracy, in which the people themselves make the laws, was the best form of government. Rousseau suggested that all citizens (he excluded women from this category) should meet to discuss, freely and rationally, issues of mutual concern. Laws should then be crafted based on the views of the majority of citizens. Rousseau asserted that laws created in this way would be, almost by definition, just and fair. Once these laws were instituted, everyone should accept and obey them. According to Rousseau, even if the rights of individuals were sacrificed, it was society's overall interests that mattered more. This absolute faith in democracy was troubling to many people in the eighteenth century. Today, many believers in democracy assert that protections for individual rights are indispensable.

Rousseau also advocated separate spheres for men and women. Because in his view men and women are fundamentally different, Rousseau thought that men should assume all public roles in society, including voting and running the economy, while women's lives should be centered on the domestic or private sphere of home and family. Many Enlightened thinkers agreed with Rousseau that, if women were included in public life, the result would be corruption, mismanagement, and tyranny. True, a few eighteenth-century thinkers, notably Mary Wollstonecraft, advocated gender equality, but most accepted the subjugation of women as part of the natural order.

The *philosophe* whose economic views had the greatest impact was Adam Smith, who, as noted in previous chapters, advocated free-market capitalism, or *laissez-faire* (hands-off) capitalism, as it is sometimes known. Smith believed that, not only should the ownership of businesses and property be in private hands, but private individuals should be given maximum freedom to make economic decisions in their own self-interest. He assumed that, if everyone was pursuing his or her own enrichment, society as a whole would benefit, because the only way to make a profit would be by efficiently fulfilling someone else's wants or needs. Smith predicted that the forces of supply and demand, if they were fully unleashed, would produce nearly constant economic growth. Many *philosophes* agreed, although most eighteenth-century political leaders remained committed to mercantilism. Today, capitalism, although it has been greatly modified since the eighteenth century, has become dominant throughout the Western world.

Given the radical nature of many of the *philosophes*' ideas, it should come as no surprise that few of their proposals were acted upon during the eighteenth century. Reason, liberty, and reform, along with representative government, may have flourished in Britain, the Netherlands, and the Thirteen Colonies in North America, but they were generally not welcomed elsewhere. Nevertheless, the Enlightenment succeeded in planting the seeds of skepticism and doubt in the minds of many educated Europeans. For the most part, public opinion had turned decisively in the direction of reform. Now, all that some Europeans required was a good excuse, and they were ready to tear down the whole edifice of Old Europe. As it turned out, ground zero would be in France.

What form(s) of government did the philosophes *support?*

The French Revolution: The Failure of Constitutional Monarchy

Several factors combined to produce a political crisis in France in 1789. First, the credibility of the system of absolute monarchy had suffered significantly due to the bold criticism expressed by Enlightenment *philosophes*, among others. In addition, grain harvests in 1787 and 1788 had been especially bad, and the winters were unusually harsh. This worsened living conditions and inflated bread prices for the poor. At the same time, unemployment in the cities had risen to a dangerously high level.

Another factor in the political crisis was the ambition of France's urban middle class to obtain greater influence and respect. Today, Marxist historians in particular believe that the *bourgeoisie* played a decisive role in the French Revolution. Although the middle class was small in France—a mere five percent of the population—French *bourgeois* were nonetheless extremely eager to improve their position. The middle class did not in any meaningful sense plan the Revolution in advance, but its members used the opportunity that events in 1789 presented to try to redefine the nature of French society. What they wanted most was a society where one's rank was based on the possession of property (especially money) and skills, not on land ownership and noble birth.

Despite all of these contributing factors, the most immediate cause of the French Revolution was a financial crisis. As we have seen, the spending of the French government was largely out of control for much of the eighteenth century. Louis XV and Louis XVI, each of whom was prone to indecision, had faced determined opposition from the *parlements* whenever they had attempted to cure France's financial ills by raising taxes. As a result, French taxes were remarkably low, but the problem of the national debt had been left to fester and grow. By 1789, France was facing bankruptcy.

Finally, Louis XVI decided to take a major risk: he chose to call a meeting of an emergency assembly of the French people, called the Estates-General, that had not met since 1614. He hoped that the Estates-General would come to understand the dire financial peril that France was in and that it would therefore give its approval to a drastic revision of the tax laws, including an end to the immunity that clergymen and nobles enjoyed from many forms of taxation. Louis XVI anticipated that the middle class would be his greatest ally.

The Estates-General met in May 1789 in a mood of great anticipation, but there was also some confusion. Traditionally, the Estates-General had been divided into three estates, each representing one of the major groups in medieval French society. The First Estate comprised the Catholic clergy, which meant that in practice it was dominated by powerful cardinals and bishops, often of noble birth. The Second Estate consisted of the nobility itself. The Third Estate included everyone else: the commoners. The Third Estate was predominantly represented, however, not by poor peasants and urban workers, who made up the vast majority of the common people, but by wealthy *bourgeois*, especially lawyers. The Estates-General that Louis called in 1789 was still divided into these traditional three estates, but it was unclear whether each estate would have one vote, in which case the noblemen in the First and Second Estates would prevail, or whether the Third Estate, because it represented 98 percent of the French people, would be allowed greater influence. This was a critical question.

When the delegates of the Estates-General arrived at Versailles, they submitted to the king various *cahiers de doléances* (lists of grievances), mostly related to taxation, political corruption, and restrictions on personal and economic freedoms. The issue that most captivated the *bourgeoisie*, though, was power. Emboldened by the recent triumphs of the American revolutionaries, middle-class politicians were determined to use the Estates-General to gain some form of representation for themselves in France's government.

In June 1789, in the absence of strong leadership from the king, the Third Estate took bold action. It renamed itself the National Assembly, and it suddenly claimed to possess the powers of a legislature. In other words, the representatives of the Third Estate wanted to transform themselves from temporary advisors to the king into lawmakers who would permanently share political authority. Some sympathetic members of the First and Second Estates decided to join the National Assembly.

On June 20, the National Assembly hastily met on an indoor tennis court and took what is known as the Tennis Court Oath: a promise that it would not disband until the king had granted France a written constitution that clearly defined the limitations on his power. Many of Louis's noble advisors urged him to use force against the National Assembly. In July, when it appeared that the king was moving royal troops to the capital to crush his enemies, a more violent phase of the Revolution began. The working-class men and women of Paris had sympathized with the National Assembly from the start. On July 14, they stormed the royal fortress known as the *Bastille* in order to confiscate its stores of weaponry. If royal troops did enter Paris, the *sans-culottes* (i.e., poor Parisians, especially shopkeepers, craftsmen, and factory workers, as well as their family members) intended to fight to the death. The storming of the *Bastille* shocked Louis and caused him to hesitate in his plans to crush the National Assembly.

Meanwhile, urban riots and peasant uprisings developed throughout France. In a panic, clergymen and nobles in the National Assembly rushed to abandon their legal privileges, hoping that the rampaging urban workers and peasants would at least spare their property and their lives. On August 4, the National Assembly abolished the special legal status of the clergy and the nobility. Centuries of tradition had been erased overnight.

Emboldened by the king's inaction, on August 27, 1789, the National Assembly issued what was undoubtedly the most important document of the French Revolution: the Declaration of the Rights of Man and of the Citizen. It was based on the reformist spirit of the Enlightenment, on the principles of popular sovereignty and liberty as practiced by the British, and on the ideals of the American Revolution and the U.S. Constitution, ratified one year earlier. It also served as a sort of preamble for the constitution that the National Assembly hoped to write for France.

Figure 12.1 This is Jacques-Louis David's famous representation of the Tennis Court Oath in June 1789. Jacques-Louis David, *Le Serment du Jeu de paume*, 1791.
Agence Photo RNM/Wikimedia Commons.

The Declaration of the Rights of Man and of the Citizen exalted the people as the only true source of political authority, and it implied that even the king was bound to obey the people's wishes. The Declaration further stipulated that the purpose of government was to protect the rights of the people, including the rights to freedom of worship, freedom of speech, and equal protection under the law. Moreover, all Frenchmen, regardless of their birth, should be eligible for government employment, and they should be taxed based only on their ability to pay, not on their ancestry or class status. Most importantly, the Declaration required that the powers of the king and the legislature should be limited and legally defined, and the practice of absolute monarchy should end in France forever. These were ambitious goals that called for an entirely new political order. Not surprisingly, the king hesitated in accepting these conditions.

Fearing that Louis would once again resort to force, in October 1789 the militia of Paris, along with thousands of enraged and well-armed *sans-culottes* women, marched from the capital to the king's *château* at Versailles. The queen's bedchamber was ransacked and her guards butchered, and the royal family was forced to accompany the crowd back to Paris. There they would remain for three long years. Technically, the king was still the chief executive of France, but he was effectively a prisoner, and real power had passed to the National Assembly. A new phase of French history was about to begin.

Despite the confinement of the royal family, from 1789 to 1792, the French Revolution was surprisingly peaceful and orderly. The National Assembly completed its work on France's new constitution in 1791. The new government was a constitutional, or limited, monarchy. Lawmaking power was vested in a one-house Legislative Assembly that replaced the National Assembly, while the king retained power over the military and foreign policy. Most members of the new Legislative Assembly were young, educated, propertied members of the *bourgeoisie*, especially lawyers.

The first priority of these *bourgeois* legislators was achieving equality under the law and an end to all noble privileges. Measures were therefore taken to reorganize local government and the courts to eliminate noble influence. In addition, regional peculiarities that had evolved over the centuries were erased as the national government sought to standardize and centralize the country's administration. Meanwhile, unions and strikes were forbidden in order to appease *bourgeois* business owners. In short, France quickly transformed itself from a society based on tradition and hereditary privilege to one based on Enlightenment principles and the ownership of property.

Although many rights were now considered to be universal, the right to vote was not among them. Property qualifications were established for voters and for legislators. Having only recently captured control of the government, the *bourgeoisie* was unwilling to share its authority with untrustworthy peasants or the *sans-culottes*. The Legislative Assembly also ignored women. One brave woman, Olympe de Gouges, had pressed the new government to extend the rights of citizenship to both sexes. Women's political clubs pressed for similar reforms. Little was done, although divorce was legalized.

The uneasy alliance between the king and the Legislative Assembly might have lasted, and France might have evolved into a constitutional monarchy much like Britain, had France's new *bourgeois* rulers not made a key mistake. The financial crisis that had caused Louis XVI to call the Estates-General in the first place was still a serious problem. In 1789 and 1790, the Revolutionaries decided to pay off the national debt by seizing the property of the Catholic Church. In 1789, the National Assembly authorized the circulation of *assignats*, that is, bonds that were backed by the value of Church lands. They were popular investments for a time, but they ended up causing massive inflation. More importantly, the attack on the property of the Church, and the requirement that clergymen accept government supervision, were enormously unpopular. Not only were many cardinals, bishops, priests, monks, and nuns opposed to the government's new policies, but a large percentage of the peasantry, the nobility, and even the *bourgeoisie* itself perceived the new laws as an attack on their Catholic faith. The king, who was himself a devout Catholic, grew increasingly alienated from the Revolutionary regime.

By 1791, the king was so disgusted that he attempted to flee Paris in disguise with his family. He wished to join the many French nobles who had fled the country already, called *émigrés*, who were plotting against the Revolution from abroad. The famous Flight to Varennes was foiled, however, and the king was returned to Paris. It was hard to imagine how a constitutional monarchy could succeed when the monarch himself wanted to escape!

What were the causes of the French Revolution?

The French Revolution: The Republic and the Reign of Terror

By 1792, the Revolution had reached a new and more dangerous phase. A faction emerged in the Legislative Assembly called the Jacobins that pressed for far-reaching changes. They favored a republic, that is, a government without a king, but moderates balked. In April 1792, the Legislative Assembly began to fear that foreign powers were cooperating with the noble *émigrés*, and perhaps with the king, in an effort to destroy the Revolution. This convinced the French government to declare war against Prussia and Austria. The Jacobins were overjoyed, because they rightly believed that war would radicalize the Revolution.

At first, the war went badly for France. Enemy forces were advancing on Paris, and in August 1792 the *sans-culottes* decided that the royal family was to blame. They vented their rage by attacking the palace that housed (or rather, imprisoned) the king and queen. The royal family managed to escape, but the unpopularity of the monarchy, at least in the capital, was now clear.

The *sans-culottes* proceeded to institute their own extremist government in Paris that unleashed a wave of bloodletting known as the September Massacres. In this atmosphere of intimidation, the Legislative Assembly dissolved itself and allowed a more radical legislature, called the Convention, to be elected.

On September 21, 1792, the Convention, in which the Jacobins predominated, deposed King Louis XVI and declared France a republic. On the same day, a French army defeated an invasion attempt by the Austrians and Prussians at the historic Battle of Valmy. Then, in January 1793, Louis was sent to the guillotine as a traitor, and in October his wife Marie-Antoinette met the same fate. The monarchy was now finished, and the Jacobins and the *sans-culottes* found themselves suddenly in charge. Europe was aghast.

The alliance between the Jacobins, who were mostly *bourgeois* lawyers, and the *sans-culottes* was in some ways surprising. The Jacobins were strong supporters of an unregulated economy, while the *sans-culottes* were advocates of price and wage controls, and they wanted government subsidies to lower the cost of bread. Both the Jacobins and the *sans-culottes* hated the nobility, but the Jacobins wanted to create a new elite based on property, while the *sans-culottes* favored social equality. In the end, both groups could agree on little except their desire for revenge against their adversaries. Thus, the king and queen were sent to their deaths, while the war against the Revolution's foreign enemies was expanded.

By April 1793, France was at war with Austria, Prussia, Spain, the Netherlands, and Great Britain. Most Europeans believed that the French Revolution had spun wildly out of control. As early as 1790, Edmund Burke, a conservative British writer and politician, had correctly predicted that inexperienced leadership and a disregard for tradition would lead France toward instability and unnecessary bloodshed. Now, as Burke's worst predictions came true, most of Europe's leaders decided that the Revolution had to be defeated before it could spread.

Remarkably, though, the government of the Convention managed to survive and prosper. In the spring of 1793, the French Republic declared a *levée en masse*—a total mobilization of the country for war. For the first time, France sent a nationalist army into battle: an army that fought for patriotism and love of the Revolution, rather than for pay or to satisfy a nobleman's code of honor. French forces began to win great victories, and the armies of the Revolution occupied large parts of Belgium and Italy.

Meanwhile, the French government went on a determined hunt for internal enemies. In 1793, the Convention created the Committee of Public Safety. A dedicated but ruthless servant of the Revolution named Maximilien Robespierre slowly became the Committee's leader. He eagerly set himself to the task of finding and destroying anyone who opposed the government.

Robespierre and his allies abolished the right to free speech. Women who had dared to speak out were either silenced, or, as in the case of Olympe de Gouges, executed. The Committee of Public Safety also persecuted Catholics. Some priests were even forced to marry. Most importantly, Robespierre streamlined the legal process for obtaining the death penalty against suspected traitors. Crowds of gleeful *sans-culottes* would look on as sometimes hundreds of people were guillotined in a single day, many of them innocent of any crime.

The worst excesses of the Revolution were committed during the so-called Reign of Terror that lasted from autumn 1793 to summer 1794. Tens of thousands were killed, including many peasants and *sans-culottes* falsely suspected of having royalist sympathies. Eventually, the Committee of Public Safety overplayed its hand. An attempt to replace Christianity with a Cult of the Supreme Being outraged many Frenchmen, as did an effort to enforce a republican style of dress. Finally, Robespierre began to execute even loyal members of the government whom he suspected of plotting against him. The Convention had had enough. In July 1794, Robespierre himself was executed, and the leaders of France looked for a way to moderate the Revolution.

Why is the second phase of the French Revolution known as the Reign of Terror?

The Directory, and the Legacy of the French Revolution

The new government that replaced the Terror was called the Directory, which was ruled by a five-man executive council. In essence, the *bourgeois* leaders of France decided that the riotous enthusiasm of the *sans-culottes* had corrupted the Revolution. They passed a new constitution that put power firmly in the hands of the middle class. The Directory also suspended the mass executions of the Terror, and replaced them with a political purge of the Jacobins. Meanwhile, the crackdown on the Catholic Church was finally ended, while the war with Prussia and Spain, but not with Britain and Austria, was concluded peacefully.

The *tricolore*—the blue, white, and red flag of the Revolution—still flew over France, and monarchy and nobility were still outlawed, but overall the Directory took France in a more conservative direction. Women were urged to attend to their duties as wives and mothers. The poor were encouraged to work hard but to refrain from political activism. And, for their part, *bourgeois* politicians were happy to return to a system in which the pursuit of wealth and pleasure was once again tolerated. Under the Directory, fanaticism slowly gave way to greed and corruption.

Although many Frenchmen preferred it to the Reign of Terror, the new government of the Directory did not enjoy wide popular support. Many *sans-culottes* and other radicals believed that the Revolution had not gone far enough, while many royalists bided their time until another Louis could ascend the throne. The Directory was troubled by peasant uprisings and urban riots, motivated both by ideology and by the high price of bread. Increasingly, the government depended on the support of the army to stay in power.

In 1795, the Directory called upon a brilliant young artillery officer named Napoleon Bonaparte to disperse an unruly crowd that had gathered in the streets of Paris. Bonaparte did his duty, and the government was saved. Napoleon, though, was as ambitious as he was talented. In 1799, he would end the Directory, and the French Revolution, by naming himself First Consul of the Republic. He would become, in effect, a military dictator.

It is hard to escape the conclusion that, at least in the short term, the French Revolution of 1789–99 was a miserable failure. Many Frenchmen had supported the Revolution in the first place because of their enlightened faith that political reform would inevitably produce prosperity, liberty, and peace. They were wrong on all three counts. The violence and disorder of the Revolution devastated France's economy. Liberty, which had been in short supply under France's kings, was obliterated by Robespierre. And peace! France would not see peace, either within its own borders or in its relations with other European states, for a generation after 1789.

And yet today the French still commemorate the storming of the *Bastille* every July 14, and they honor the legacy of the Revolution and its enlightened values of "liberty, equality, and fraternity." Americans often like to think that they invented modern democracy in 1776, and in a sense they may be right. What they forget, though, is that in the eighteenth century the United States of America was an isolated and thinly populated country. Many Europeans scarcely noticed the triumph of democracy in America, but the end of absolute monarchy in France was an earth-shattering event.

Today, throughout the world, people who believe in democracy look just as much to the Declaration of the Rights of Man and of the Citizen for inspiration as they do to the British *Magna Carta*, the U.S. Declaration of Independence, or the U.S. Constitution. Freedom may not have flourished as soon in France as it did in America, but the French Revolution did indeed change the world. Everywhere, the privileges of monarchs, noblemen, and the Church elite were imperiled, and sometimes eliminated. The confidence of the *bourgeoisie*, in France and elsewhere, surged. Perhaps most importantly, the ideals of the Revolution—individual freedom, and representative and constitutional government—were popularized as never before. In fact, many historians believe that *ideas* were not only the primary cause of the French Revolution; they are also its most enduring legacy. Unfortunately for the French, all these achievements came at the cost of great bloodshed, which in 1799 was only just beginning.

Why is the French Revolution considered historically important?

Napoleon: Early Career and the Consulate

Napoleon Bonaparte was born on the Mediterranean island of Corsica in 1769. Corsica had only become a French possession in 1768, and in fact Napoleon's heritage was more Italian than French. Nevertheless, as a minor noble, he was able to attend a French military academy. By 1786, at the age of only 16, he had become a Second Lieutenant of artillery in the army of Louis XVI.

Napoleon, though, was not devoted to the monarchy. He supported radical factions in the early years of the Revolution. During the Terror, he received his first meaningful military assignment: he led a successful campaign to eject British forces from the French port of Toulon. After this triumph, in 1795, the Directory called upon Napoleon to crush its internal enemies. In 1796, the Directory gave Napoleon a command in Italy, one of the most important theaters in France's ongoing war with Austria and Britain. Napoleon was able to bring discipline and focus to the ragtag French Revolutionary army that was fighting there. He established French control over most of the Italian Peninsula.

Napoleon's successes in Italy, and the victories that came later in his military career, were based on several factors. Although he was capable of great initiative and inspiring leadership, many of his victories were also due to good fortune and to the ineptitude of his opponents. In addition, Napoleon

Figure 12.2 A nineteenth-century engraving of Napoleon.
Georgias Kollidas/Shutterstock.

benefited from France's *levée en masse*. France had put over one million men under arms by the end of 1794. This seemingly limitless supply of recruits allowed Revolutionary military commanders the luxury of being relatively careless with the lives of their troops. Instead of the old tactic of relying on long, tightly organized lines of musketeers, the Revolutionary army often employed columns of men, barely trained, who would charge the enemy in force. The casualties these tactics produced were horrific, but few traditional armies in Europe could withstand the human waves of fanatical patriot soldiers that France could throw at them. Since the Revolutionary armies also lived off the land, they were uncommonly mobile. France, and Napoleon, also benefited from excellent use of artillery, as well as good communications and a highly competent intelligence service.

By 1797, Napoleon's triumph in Italy was complete. He next considered an invasion of Britain. Napoleon concluded, however, that Britain's naval superiority was too great, so he decided to weaken Britain's economy and empire by conquering Egypt instead. In 1798, he convinced the Directory to support his ambitious plan.

Napoleon left for Egypt in June, and he rapidly defeated a Muslim army of 100,000 men at the picturesque Battle of the Pyramids. He then began to reorganize Egyptian society according to Enlightenment principles while a large group of French scholars and experts studied Egypt, especially its ancient past. Britain's naval strength conspired against Napoleon, though. The French fleet was badly mauled at the Battle of Abukir in August 1798. French forces could no longer be effectively resupplied by sea. By 1799, Napoleon had concluded that the Egyptian campaign was a failure.

Not for the last time, Napoleon abandoned his troops in the field and rushed back to France. There he found the Directory ready to fall. Napoleon knew that the time had come to assert himself. In November 1799, he helped to impose a three-man executive council on France, called the Consulate, but by December he had maneuvered himself into the position of First Consul. From late 1799 until 1814–15, Napoleon, for better or worse, would be the leader of France.

The Peace of Amiens halted hostilities between France and Britain in 1802. This gave France's new leader time to consider his domestic priorities. Historians have long debated whether Napoleon was a true believer in the ideals of the French Revolution, or whether he was in reality an opportunist or a conservative. The truth is that Napoleon defies easy categorization.

Napoleon clearly favored some Enlightenment reforms. For example, he was a strong believer in meritocracy, the idea that people should be judged based on their accomplishments, not on their parentage. Everywhere Napoleon went, he insisted that the privileges of the nobility should be curbed and opportunities for worthy commoners should be expanded. Napoleon also made government administration more professionalized and efficient, and he achieved a thorough reform of French law, resulting in the Napoleonic Code. In addition, Napoleon promoted religious toleration. Perhaps most tellingly, Napoleon never abandoned the pretense that he was governing on behalf of the French people. His decisions were regularly approved by plebiscite (popular referendum), although voting was frequently manipulated.

On the other hand, Napoleon's commitment to the ideals of the Enlightenment and the French Revolution was, at best, inconsistent. Napoleon may have been a believer in reason and reform, but liberty he could do without. Napoleon created a ruthless secret police force. Censorship was widespread. Napoleon also greatly increased taxes and restricted workers' rights. In addition, he had very traditional ideas about women and race. Part of the Napoleonic Code insisted that families should be headed by men, who could dispose of their property, children, and wives as they saw fit. Napoleon also sought to restore slavery in France's colonies, especially Haiti. One of Napoleon's least enlightened policies, as many former Revolutionaries saw it, was an alliance he formed with the Catholic Church. In 1801, he signed a Concordat (agreement) with the pope that established Catholicism as "the religion of the great majority of French citizens."

The question of whether or not Napoleon was an enlightened ruler may be answered by the ultimate fate of the Consulate government. In 1804, Napoleon gave up the title of First Consul and, in a grandiose ceremony at the Cathedral of Nôtre Dame, attended and blessed by the pope, he crowned himself Emperor of the French. The proclamation of the empire destroyed the republican system of government established during the Revolution and restored monarchy to France. This time, though, Napoleon Bonaparte, instead of another Louis, would rule.

How did Napoleon become the leader of France?

The French Empire: Years of Triumph, 1804–10

Even before Napoleon assumed the throne as emperor, the war between Britain and France had been renewed. This time, Napoleon convinced himself that an invasion of Britain was possible. He assembled a fleet of transports to move more than 160,000 men across the English Channel, to be protected by a French navy that had been built up to an impressive strength of roughly 75 massive ships of the line.

Napoleon's plan, though, called for a complex redeployment of French naval forces before his ships could be concentrated to support the landing in Britain. This strategy was foiled when a French fleet, with Spanish support, was set upon in October 1805 by a British fleet commanded by Lord Horatio Nelson. About half of the French and Spanish ships were lost in the resulting Battle of Trafalgar, which many consider to be the most important naval engagement in history. Napoleon's invasion plans were ruined, and Britain effectively won control of the seas for the remainder of the war.

Meanwhile, Austria and Russia had joined a renewed coalition against Napoleon, partly due to generous British subsidies, and the French troops that had been waiting to invade England were suddenly needed in the East. In Austria, Napoleon fought one of his most famous and decisive battles, the Battle of Austerlitz, in December 1805. At Austerlitz, Napoleon ingeniously deployed a French force of 60,000 men, badly outnumbered, to achieve a resounding victory. Russian forces then retreated to their homeland, while Austria signed the humiliating Treaty of Pressburg, conceding control of the lesser states in Germany to France. Napoleon thereupon abolished the largely symbolic Holy Roman Empire, and he helped reorganize the 300 or so small German states into roughly 40 larger ones, many of which he presented as gifts to his family members and closest supporters.

Austria may have been cowed into submission as a result of the Battle of Austerlitz, but Russia resolved to continue fighting, and it attracted Prussia to its side. Napoleon, though, brought overwhelming force to bear against both nations, defeating Prussia in only 19 days. In July 1807, Russia's Tsar

Alexander I signed the Treaty of Tilsit, acknowledging France's victory and consenting to the partial dismemberment of Prussia. Alexander subsequently became an ally of Napoleon. It seemed that France was now mistress of all Europe, though not of the seas that surrounded it.

As Napoleon himself said, however, "Ambition is never content, even on the summit of greatness." At the height of his power, Napoleon now proceeded to make two serious errors. First, he decided that, in the absence of an amphibious invasion of Britain, the only way to defeat his most implacable enemy was by economic means. He therefore instituted a European-wide embargo against trading with the British known as the Continental System, which even neutral states were compelled to accept. Napoleon's strategy appeared to make sense: Britain was a nation dependent on trade, and surely therefore the loss of commercial access to all the markets of mainland Europe would cause a depression, or even a revolution, in Britain.

What Napoleon had failed to consider, though, was that a cessation of trade between Britain and Europe would also hurt France. In addition, many Europeans would be strongly tempted to continue their commerce with Britain through smuggling. Perhaps most threatening to the success of the Continental System, however, was the fact that even a deep reduction in Britain's trade with Europe would not be fatal to the British economy, because markets in the Americas, Africa, and Asia would still be wide open. In short, Napoleon's Continental System was a failure, which Napoleon himself eventually admitted by selling licenses to smugglers.

In an important way, though, the Continental System did not simply fail—it backfired. It reminded all the countries in Europe subjected to Napoleon's rule that his word was law, and this indignity was just one of many. The fact that Napoleon repeatedly confiscated the wealth and resources of conquered states, and even of alleged allies, was deeply hurtful to many Europeans, as was the frequent replacement of their traditional rulers with Napoleon's friends and family members. Nationalist resistance movements against the French occupation were therefore strengthening in many parts of Europe.

Napoleon's second major error would only exacerbate his problems with local resistance to his authority. In 1808, Napoleon made the monstrous mistake of toppling the monarchy in Spain, even though Spain had been one of his most faithful allies. Napoleon then placed his brother Joseph on the Spanish throne. This high-handed action disgusted many Spaniards, whom the British encouraged to rebel. The British even sent thousands of troops and one of their best generals, Sir Arthur Wellesley, later known as the Duke of Wellington, to support the Spanish uprising, using Portugal as a base of operations. Wellington was the son of a nobleman, a rising political star as an archconservative, and, most importantly, an excellent field commander.

For the next six years, as many as 300,000 French troops were tied down in Spain, trying to enforce a hated occupation. Napoleon gained nothing from this fighting except a new and potentially powerful enemy in the Spanish people, many of whom resorted to unceasing guerrilla warfare against the French. In short, both the Continental System and the Peninsular War, as the struggle in Spain became known, were burdensome for France, but they did not in themselves spell the end of Napoleon's empire.

What country was Napoleon's nemesis?

The French Empire: Years of Decline, 1810–15

The news from Spain was bad, but there were some positive developments for Napoleon as well. In 1809, once again Napoleon convincingly defeated the Austrians, this time at the Battle of Wagram. He then imposed the punitive Peace of Schönbrunn on Austria's Emperor Francis II. Subsequently, Napoleon negotiated for the right to marry the emperor's 18-year-old daughter, the Archduchess Marie-Louise. Napoleon had decided to divorce his first wife, Josephine, because she could not bear him a son and heir. As conditions in Spain deteriorated, therefore, Napoleon and Marie-Louise concentrated on achieving conjugal bliss in Paris. Napoleon got what he most wanted out of the marriage: a son, François Charles Louis Napoleon Bonaparte. Now it appeared that the reign of the Bonapartes might last forever.

By 1810, however, major cracks were beginning to appear in the Continental System, and Napoleon's grip on his satellites and allies was loosening. Meanwhile, the Austrians and Prussians were undertaking major military and political reforms designed to make them more competitive with France in future wars. Additionally, the British economy, although it was battered by the costs of war and fluctuations in British trade, was still strong enough to underwrite huge subsidies to any country on the continent of Europe brave enough to challenge France. Finally, in 1810, Napoleon lost his trump card: Tsar Alexander canceled his alliance with France. Napoleon now decided to raise a huge army to invade Russia, hoping to establish his dominance once and for all.

The *Grand Armée* that Napoleon prepared for the invasion of Russia included roughly half a million men. Napoleon's plan was to launch this unwieldy, but seemingly unstoppable, force into Russia and fight an immediate, decisive battle. Napoleon did not prepare for a long campaign, nor did he study closely what conditions in Russia were like.

The invasion began in June 1812. Despite a French victory at the Battle of Borodino in September and the subsequent occupation of Moscow, Napoleon was unable to defeat the Russians. They craftily retreated and refused to give Napoleon the one great battle that he desired. Meanwhile, they burned crops and destroyed supplies in Napoleon's path. The Russians also exploited the fact that many of Napoleon's soldiers were conscripts from France's satellite states in Germany and Italy. Many of them deserted at the first opportunity.

In the end, Napoleon concluded that he had no choice but to retreat. From October to December 1812, the remnants of his *Grand Armée* struggled through worsening weather, harassed all the while by Russian forces, until they reached Poland. Napoleon now deserted his army and returned to Paris, leaving only 20,000 exhausted French troops to guard against a further Russian advance.

In only six months' time, the fortunes of Napoleon seemed to have reversed themselves completely. Of course, all of his enemies were delighted, and they began to orchestrate his final humiliation.

Prussia now saw its chance to take revenge on Napoleon and quickly pledged its support to the Russians. At the same time, Britain tempted Austria to join the coalition against the French. By August 1813, an impressive Quadruple Alliance of Britain, Austria, Prussia, and Russia had been assembled. Napoleon's fate seemed to be sealed.

The climactic battle of the Napoleonic Wars, called the Battle of the Nations, was fought at Leipzig in central Germany in October 1813. Numbers by this stage were on the side of the Quadruple Alliance, and Napoleon's military genius was not enough to prevent his defeat.

Napoleon fled from Leipzig to try to raise a new army that could protect France from invasion while he rebuffed efforts to negotiate a compromise peace. Napoleon was adamant that it was victory on the battlefield, not diplomacy, that determined his prestige and power. Napoleon had exhausted his military resources, however, and by April 1814 even he had to accept that he was beaten. After an unsuccessful suicide attempt, Napoleon abdicated his throne and went into exile on the small Mediterranean island of Elba. The Napoleonic Wars were over, and the traditional European monarchies had prevailed over an upstart French Revolutionary officer turned emperor, or so it seemed...

For a while, Napoleon appeared to behave himself splendidly as a prisoner on Elba: he gained weight, spent hours in the bath, and played dominoes with his mother. Eventually, though, Napoleon grew restless. In March 1815, he managed to escape from Elba and returned to France! Thus began a brief restoration of the French Empire, known as the Hundred Days of Napoleon.

Although Napoleon professed to desire peace, none of his enemies believed him. The Quadruple Alliance thus reactivated itself, and hundreds of thousands of allied troops were mobilized. Unwilling to wait for these forces to arrive in France, Napoleon decided to mount a preemptive attack on two armies—one Prussian, and one multinational, but under British command—that were based in Belgium. Napoleon hoped that a quick, stunning victory would cause the Quadruple Alliance to lose its nerve.

This time, though, Napoleon faced the Duke of Wellington, the British hero of the Peninsular War, on the battlefield for the first time. Wellington had studied Napoleon's tactics, and he had drilled superior discipline into his troops. At the Battle of Waterloo in June 1815, Napoleon's forces, including his beloved Imperial Guard, were flung carelessly at the allied lines, but this time French passion and courage were no match for British steadiness and prudence. Napoleon was beaten once and for all. He abdicated again, and was exiled this time to a more remote island in the Atlantic Ocean called

St. Helena. There he died in 1821. The cause of death was apparently stomach cancer. It was an inglorious end for an emperor to face.

Why did Napoleon's invasion of Russia in 1812 fail?

The Congress of Vienna and the Balance of Power

Once the menace of Napoleon had been definitively crushed, the members of the Quadruple Alliance found themselves in a position of total mastery in Europe. Gigantic British, Austrian, Prussian, and Russian armies covered Europe, and, if they had wished it, these four great powers could have swallowed up all the lesser states that remained. Somewhat remarkably, though, the cautionary example of Napoleon's arrogance and greed led the allied powers to rein in their ambitions. Although Britain, Austria, Prussia, and Russia all expected to be compensated for their extraordinary sacrifices in battling Napoleon, they were prepared to accept a compromise settlement, and, most of all, they desired peace and stability rather than plunder and revenge. The result was the Congress of Vienna.

From September 1814 to June 1815, representatives of all the states of Europe met in the luxurious and elegant capital of the Austrian Empire, Vienna. Three hundred ornate coaches, painted dark green and decorated with a bright yellow version of the Hapsburg coat of arms, were assembled to transport dignitaries around the city, the population of which increased by 50 percent during the Congress. Besides the pursuit of self-indulgence, these ambassadors of the European elite had the difficult task of redrawing the map of Europe to repair the damage that the Napoleonic Wars had done and to attempt to avoid a repetition of the carnage.

In the negotiations that followed, France, instead of being treated as a conquered nation, was accorded the status of a great power that was equal in rank to any other state. Thus, rather than punishing the French, and perhaps thereby provoking a war of vengeance, the British, Austrians, Prussians, and Russians chose to impose a peace that was fair to all. Their desire was to create a balance of power among the major countries in Europe that would be a disincentive to future wars. In other words, they intended to balance Austria against Prussia, and France against Britain, for example, so that no state would have anything to gain by military aggression. As it happened, their attempt to achieve stability in Europe was largely successful. From 1815 to 1914 there was no major war in Europe, although there were many small wars and considerable internal strife.

The map of Europe had changed significantly by the time the Congress of Vienna was concluded. France lost its conquests of the Revolutionary and Napoleonic eras and was reduced to the borders it possessed in 1792, roughly the same borders that France has today. Meanwhile, the government of the French Empire was eliminated, and the Quadruple Alliance agreed that the brother of King Louis XVI should take the throne as Louis

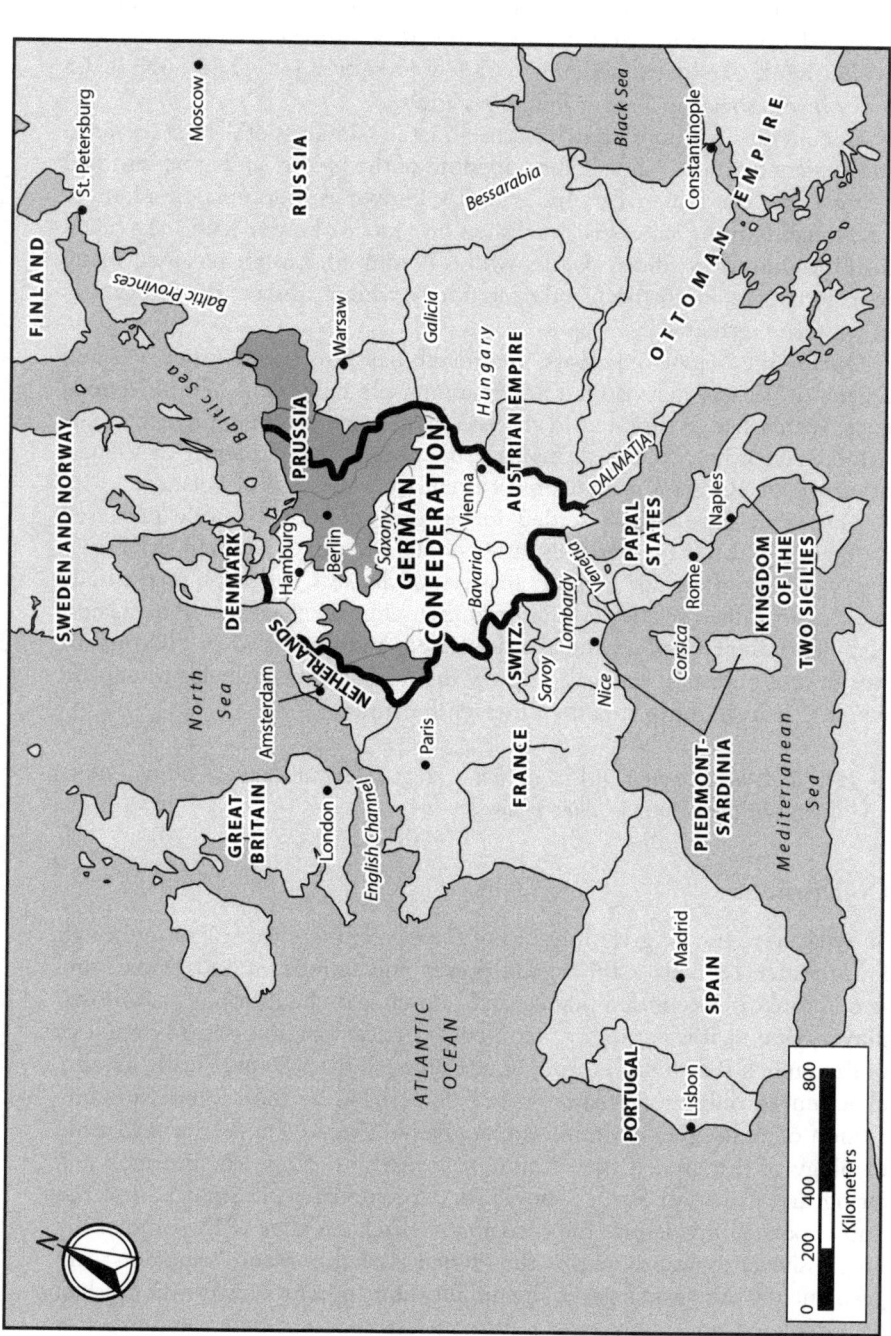

Map 12.1 Europe in 1815, after the Congress of Vienna.

XVIII (skipping over the son of Louis XVI and Marie-Antoinette, who had died uncrowned in a Revolutionary prison). Amazingly, therefore, France emerged from the ups and downs of the Revolutionary and Napoleonic periods with a restored monarchy and few territorial losses, although it did suffer severe social and economic devastation.

To contain any future French aggression, the Congress of Vienna created a strong state to France's north, the Kingdom of the Netherlands, that resumed control over the Dutch East Indies, today known as Indonesia. In addition, a reasonably strong state was established on France's border with Italy, called the Kingdom of Sardinia, also known as Piedmont. Austria regained many of its territories in northern and central Italy, while Prussia expanded greatly in western Germany.

During the Napoleonic Wars, the French had briefly established a Grand Duchy of Warsaw that had fed hopes among the Poles that their independence, which had evaporated in the late eighteenth century, might be reaffirmed. According to the terms agreed upon at the Congress of Vienna, however, the Russians gained almost exclusive possession of Poland.

Meanwhile, the British settled for several colonies formerly possessed by France and the Netherlands, most notably South Africa and Sri Lanka, that were important for Britain's mastery of the seas. Although territorially the British gained relatively little from their almost ceaseless warfare against Napoleon, their naval ascendancy increased, and their lead in commercial wealth and industrial innovation grew dramatically, which helps to explain why the British dominated the nineteenth century.

Why did the Congress of Vienna not destroy France and divide all of Europe between the victorious allied powers?

Conclusions

So what were the long-term results of the Age of Napoleon? First, although France after 1815 was still a great power, the serious wounds it had suffered more or less ensured that it would never again be Europe's preeminent power. Second, it is fair to say that Napoleon's campaign to spread the ideals of the French Revolution throughout Europe, if that was ever really his aim, experienced only modest success. In fact, perhaps the most important conclusion of all to emerge from the Congress of Vienna was the view that the ideology of the French Revolution was largely to blame for Europe's suffering, and that all of Europe should therefore return to its monarchical and noble roots. Third, despite the conservative backlash after 1815, some of the progressive changes brought by the French Revolution and Napoleon were permanent. Some privileges of the nobility and churchmen were diminished or eliminated, and many serfs and free peasants found their circumstances improved. The middle class gained in status and wealth, if not in political influence. Religious freedom was enhanced, and many administrative and legal reforms were retained. Certainly military tactics and strategy changed forever, and the expansion in the scope and cost of war was obvious. In all these ways, the French Revolution and the Age of Napoleon made an indelible mark on history.

Ironically, one of Napoleon's clearest legacies was the nurturing of nationalist sentiment. In particular, hatred of the French occupation had brought the Spanish, German, and Italian peoples together as never before. In 1871, Germany would finally complete the process of national unification, and France would face serious danger as a result. The effects of the Napoleonic Wars were profound, therefore, but they were not foreseen by Napoleon, or even by the shrewd diplomats at the Congress of Vienna.

In the short term, in the first half of the nineteenth century, Europeans returned to many of their conservative traditions and largely to monarchical and noble rule. Nevertheless, the *bourgeoisie* was waiting for an opportunity to reassert itself. The struggle for mastery in Europe was far from over.

Key Terms for Chapter 12

Philosophes—eighteenth-century thinkers who favored reason, liberty, and reform.

Adam Smith—Scottish *philosophe* who proposed the idea of *laissez-faire* capitalism, an economic system in which government plays a minimal role and property owners have maximum freedom.

Louis XVI—King of France from 1774 to 1792. He was first sidelined, and then executed, during the French Revolution.

Estates-General, 1789—an emergency assembly of the French people, including clergymen, nobles, and commoners, called by Louis XVI to address France's fiscal crisis. Instead it transformed itself into the National Assembly and ignited the French Revolution.

Sans-culottes—the poor people of Paris.

Declaration of the Rights of Man and of the Citizen—a statement of the principles of the French Revolution, including popular sovereignty, equality under the law, constitutionalism, and individual liberty.

Jacobins—a group of radical *bourgeois* politicians who wanted an end to the French monarchy. They led France during the Reign of Terror.

Edmund Burke—a conservative British politician who opposed the French Revolution and predicted it would lead to chaos and bloodshed.

The Terror—the bloodiest period of the French Revolution, from 1793 to 1794, during which Maximilien Robespierre and the Committee of Public Safety executed many suspected counterrevolutionaries.

Directory—a moderate, middle-class-dominated government that ruled France from 1795 to 1799.

Napoleon Bonaparte—a legendary French military commander and leader of France from 1799 to 1815.

Continental System—Napoleon's failed trade embargo aimed at the British.

Quadruple Alliance—a pact between Britain, Austria, Prussia, and Russia that led to Napoleon's defeat.

246 The French Revolution and Napoleon

Battle of Waterloo, 1815—Napoleon's last stand against the forces of Britain and Prussia.

Congress of Vienna—a convention of European leaders and diplomats who met after the Napoleonic Wars to craft a balance of power that would preserve the peace.

Review Questions for Chapter 12

1. Describe three Enlightenment ideas that remain influential today.
2. Imagine that you lived in France around the time of the French Revolution. Do you believe that you would have supported the Revolution or not? Would you have supported the execution of the king and queen or not? Explain your views in historical context.
3. Some of the Founding Fathers believed that revolutions were generally positive developments, because they force societies to adapt and to reconsider their priorities. Whether the French Revolution was positive or negative, however, is hotly debated. Give your own answer to this question, and then consider whether it would be desirable or undesirable for there to be a revolution in the United States today.
4. Do you consider Napoleon a hero or a villain in European history? What modern figure (of the last 100 years) do you believe most resembles Napoleon?
5. Describe two of Napoleon's actions that were successful. Then describe two of his mistakes.

Further Reading

Andress, David. *The French Revolution and the People*. London: Hambledon Continuum. 2007.
Broers, Michael. *Europe Under Napoleon, 1799–1815*. New York: I.B. Tauris. 2015.
Censer, Jack R. and Lynn Hunt. *Liberty, Equality, Fraternity: Exploring the French Revolution*. University Park, PA: Pennsylvania State University Press. 2008.
Doyle, William. *The Oxford History of the French Revolution*. Second Edition. Oxford: Oxford University Press. 2002.
Fraser, Antonia. *Marie-Antoinette*. Paris: Flammarion. 2016.
Heller, Henry. *The Bourgeois Revolution in France, 1789–1815*. New York: Berghahn Books. 2009.
Israel, Jonathan. *Democratic Enlightenment: Philosophy, Revolution, and Human Rights, 1750–1790*. Oxford: Oxford University Press. 2013.
MacMahon, Darrin M. *Enemies of the Enlightenment: The French Counter-Enlightenment and the Making of Modernity*. Oxford: Oxford University Press. 2001.
McPhee, Peter. *The French Revolution, 1789–1799*. Oxford: Oxford University Press. 2002.
McPhee, Peter. *Robespierre: A Revolutionary Life*. New Haven, CT: Yale University Press. 2013.
Mostert, Noel. *The Line Upon a Wind: The Great War at Sea, 1793–1815*. London: Vintage. 2008.
Pearson, Roger. *Voltaire Almighty: A Life in Pursuit of Freedom*. London: Bloomsbury. 2006.
Woloch, Isser. *Napoleon and His Collaborators: The Making of a Dictatorship*. New York: W.W. Norton. 2002.

13 Challenging the Conservative Order

Liberalism, Nationalism, and Socioeconomic Change, 1815–50

Introduction

After the trauma of the French Revolution and the Napoleonic Wars, conservative forces in Europe enforced tight control over all potentially revolutionary movements. Kings, nobles, clergymen, and the wealthiest members of the middle class were remarkably successful in retaining their monopoly on political power in Europe, at least until the second half of the nineteenth century. Nevertheless, they faced significant challenges in containing new movements for change, many of which the growing middle class supported.

Some Europeans still fondly remembered the ideals of the French Revolution, which they equated with the principles that guided the British and American representative systems as well. During the nineteenth century, those who wanted representative government, economic freedom, and more respect for individual rights were affiliated with a new ideology called liberalism. Also on the rise was nationalism, the idea that every group of people who share a common language, culture, and history should have the opportunity to gain political independence. Yet another strong trend in the nineteenth century was Romanticism, an intellectual and artistic movement that stressed the importance of human emotions and imagination, in addition to, or instead of, the Enlightenment's focus on reason. Finally, it should be remembered that all these new nineteenth-century "isms" arose in a period of profound economic and social change, when industrialization was beginning to spread beyond Britain for the first time.

In the years after 1850, the middle class would finally achieve its highest ambition—it would supplant the conservative elite and dominate most of Europe. In the process, liberalism, nationalism, and industrialization, rather than monarchy, aristocracy, and state-endorsed religion, would become the strongest forces in European history.

The Reassertion of Conservative Rule

After the Napoleonic Wars, the label "conservative" was applied to anyone who was supportive of European traditions, and especially of Europe's old political elite of hereditary monarchs, landed nobles, and established, that is, officially approved, churches. After 1815, conservatives were determined to reestablish their grip on power and to attack any group, idea, or movement that threatened the *status quo*.

In France, the reestablishment of conservatism meant that, after the defeat of Napoleon, the Bourbon family, which had ruled in France until 1792, was restored to power. Louis XVIII, who ruled from 1814 to 1824, is remembered more for his girth than his leadership ability. Nonetheless, as a strong conservative, Louis restricted voting to less than one percent of the population, and he handed control over France's educational system to the Catholic Church. Louis, though, was realistic enough to understand that not all pre-Revolutionary policies could be reinstated. He made no attempt, for example, to take back from the peasantry and the *bourgeoisie* land that had been confiscated from the nobility.

Louis XVIII's brother and successor, Charles X, who ruled from 1824 to 1830, was a true reactionary—that is, a conservative extremist. Charles ordered that noble landowners should be compensated for their losses during the Revolution. He also suppressed free speech and authorized a law that made sacrilege against the Catholic Church punishable by death. He carefully excluded liberals in the middle class from any political influence.

The more than 300 small states that had made up the Germanies before the Napoleonic Wars had been consolidated, by 1815, into approximately 40 states, all of which were enrolled in a German Confederation led by Austria. The most important figure in Austrian politics during the first half of the nineteenth century was Prince Klemens von Metternich, a strong advocate of cooperation and peace, but also a firm believer in royal absolutism and conservative rule. Metternich had played a central role in the defeat of Napoleon and at the Congress of Vienna, and he was determined that the order that he had helped to create would be rigorously defended.

Accordingly, Metternich did his best to prevent reform in Austria and in the Germanies. When three German states issued constitutions that compromised the power of their respective monarchs, Metternich intervened by promulgating the Carlsbad Decrees, which imposed censorship and eliminated reformist organizations of university students. Then, in 1820, the German Confederation endorsed the Final Act, which forbade serious constitutional changes or liberal reforms throughout the Germanies.

In Prussia, enthusiasm for reform peaked in 1815, but King Frederick William III quickly decided against any form of constitutional government. By 1823, he had solidified the traditional alliance between the monarchy and the conservative *Junker* nobility. He also opposed the idea of German nationalism, even though Prussia potentially had much to gain by leading the process of German unification.

Britain was by far the most liberal state in Europe. Increasingly, its elected Parliament dominated the government, which in turn respected most individual liberties. Nevertheless, an alliance of the monarchy and a handful of wealthy nobles still enjoyed tremendous influence. England's conservative elite also felt every bit as threatened by reformers as did the royal absolutists on the continent.

Under a series of Tory (that is, conservative) Prime Ministers, Britain responded to pleas for political and economic change with iron-fisted repression. In 1817 Parliament passed the Coercion Act, and in 1819 it passed the Six Acts, all of which aimed to prevent critics of the government from organizing themselves or publicizing their views. Meanwhile, Tory governments were steadily reducing support for the poor.

The will of the government to repress those advocating change was seriously tested in August 1819 by the Peterloo Massacre. A large meeting of reformers was held at St. Peter's Field in Manchester to advocate lowering the price of bread and extending voting rights to ordinary workers. Police and soldiers ordered the gathering to disperse. When the protestors refused, cavalrymen brandishing sabers attacked the crowd, resulting in 11 deaths and more than 400 injuries. The outcry that followed was embarrassing to the government, but the Tory Prime Minister Lord Liverpool supported the soldiers and police, and public agitation eventually died down.

Throughout the nineteenth century, Russia evolved into the most conservative state in Europe. Its traditional institutions of absolute monarchy, nobility, and the Orthodox Church were highly resistant to any meaningful reforms.

From 1801 to 1825, Russia was led by the handsome and amiable Tsar Alexander I, a committed autocrat. Alexander periodically claimed to sympathize with liberal ideas, but he fell under the influence of Austria's Prince Metternich and various ultra-conservative spiritual advisors, all of whom encouraged him to maintain the *status quo*.

In 1825, Alexander's brother Nicholas succeeded him as Tsar, after defeating an insurrection by reform-minded army officers. Nicholas I ruled until 1855. His sole concession to modernity was a policy known as Official Nationality that recognized nationalism as a legitimate force in Russia, but only if it served the interests of the Tsar, the nobility, and the Orthodox Church. Nicholas trampled the rights of Russia's ethnic minorities, and he strongly supported the conservative order in other parts of Europe.

An important sign of Europe's conservative mood in the years after 1815 was the formation of a so-called Concert of Europe, an agreement between Britain, Austria, Prussia, Russia, and France to work to preserve peace and stability. The Concert foundered, however, because the British refused to commit themselves to a standing alliance against all types of reform.

In the wake of the Napoleonic Wars, what actions did European governments take to protect the status quo?

First Cracks in the Conservative Order: The Emergence of Liberalism

One of the most important challenges to conservative domination came in the form of a new ideological movement known as liberalism. Importantly, nineteenth century liberalism has little to do with the liberalism of today. nineteenth-century or "classical" liberals were committed to continuing the work of the Enlightenment and the French Revolution: they wanted greater political, religious, and economic freedom for all people and more popular participation in the government. They looked to England as a place where many of their goals had already been accomplished.

More specifically, liberals believed in constitutional government—a system in which a foundational document clearly defines the powers of rulers. Liberals also wanted equality before the law, as well as guarantees of basic rights such as freedom of speech, assembly, and religion. In addition, greater separation between church and state was frequently seen as desirable from a liberal perspective. Liberals also supported popular sovereignty, or government by the people, as proposed by John Locke, in which an elected legislature has significant authority. In addition to their political goals, liberals were often proponents of *laissez-faire* capitalism: they supported minimum government interference in the economy, and maximum freedom for property owners and businessmen. Not surprisingly, most liberals were members of the middle class. It was the middle class that owned most of the businesses that would profit under a free enterprise system.

Although nineteenth-century liberals sought greater political power and economic freedom for the middle class, they were by no means convinced that workers and peasants could be trusted with the same opportunities. Liberals often believed that the right to vote should be based on property ownership or educational attainment. They also held that economic freedom should be reserved mainly for business owners, whereas workers should not have the similar freedom to organize themselves into unions. Liberals would eventually make some efforts to popularize their movement and gain working-class support, but they had limited success.

Although liberals faced a huge challenge in dislodging conservatives from power, in two instances in the early 1830s they won important victories. In July 1830, there was a revolution in France supported by the middle class that overthrew the reactionary King Charles X and installed a liberal monarchy under the Duke of Orléans, Louis-Philippe.

In many ways, King Louis-Philippe was a dream-come-true for liberals. Instead of ornate robes of state, Louis-Philippe wore an ordinary *bourgeois* business suit. He ended press censorship, expanded the right to vote (slightly), abolished the hereditary nobility, and reduced the power of the Catholic Church. Louis-Philippe also served the interests of middle-class liberals by suppressing workers' strikes and resisting calls for full democracy. Unfortunately, Louis-Philippe's government was also compromised by corruption, and it continued to favor landowners over industrialists and entrepreneurs. Nevertheless, in the context of the 1830s, the installation of France's July Monarchy was still a major victory for liberalism.

Another liberal triumph was the Great Reform Bill of 1832 in Britain. For several generations, British liberals, often called Whigs, had pressed for parliamentary reform. They rightly pointed out that, although Britain was the only major European country where an elected legislature dominated the government, just a tiny minority of the country's people could vote. Moreover, many electoral districts were so-called rotten boroughs: towns where the local landlord or nobleman manipulated voting.

Major agitation for electoral reform began in the 1820s. In 1828 and 1829, the Whigs succeeded in extending the right to hold public office to Non-Conformists (Protestants outside the Church of England) and Catholics. Then, in 1830, the Whigs proposed a major overhaul of Britain's electoral system known as the Great Reform Bill. More than 50 "rotten boroughs" were to be eliminated. Meanwhile, more representation would be given to the country's expanding cities, where many members of the middle class lived. A simple property requirement for voting would be instituted that would expand the number of voters by as much as 60 percent. True, only men would be allowed to vote, and, even after these bold reforms, only one-seventh of adult males would qualify as voters, but this was still a giant step in the direction of a government of the people. The Great Reform Bill passed narrowly in Parliament, and only after much popular pressure. Its effect was dramatic.

Although it took decades to widen the franchise to include workers and women, the Great Reform Bill put Britain on the path to democracy by enfranchising the growing middle class. It continued Britain's tradition, established during the Glorious Revolution of 1688, of gradual, peaceful reform that gave greater liberty and representation to the people. It also heralded sweeping reforms in the empire, including an end to slavery. Most of all, it preserved Britain's reputation as the most liberal state in Europe, and it proved that liberalism was by no means incompatible with wealth, stability, and national greatness.

What did nineteenth-century liberals believe in?

First Cracks in the Conservative Order: The Emergence of Nationalism

In the 1830s, as liberals were experiencing their first successes in challenging the conservative order, nationalism was also emerging as a serious threat to the *status quo*. Nationalism in many ways had begun with the French Revolution, which had stirred incredible pride and passion in the French people, who set out to conquer Europe. Nationalist sentiments then developed among the peoples of various European countries who were seeking to evict those same French invaders. By the second quarter of the nineteenth century, nationalism was becoming popular throughout the Western world.

What, then, is nationalism? Nationalism is the belief that a group of people who share a common language, culture, and history should have the opportunity to govern themselves. Nationalists assumed that the most important feature that defined a group of people was not their religious affiliation, or the hereditary monarch who ruled them, but their ethnicity. German nationalists claimed, for example, that Germany has a unique language, culture, and history, and this German identity has great value for Western Civilization. Therefore, all Germans should cultivate their Germanic roots. They should also combine into one country, and they should free themselves from foreign domination.

Because nationalists valued ethnic and cultural ties so highly, they asserted that the political arrangements that conservatives had made at the Congress of Vienna should not be allowed to dictate Europe's development forever. Not surprisingly, most nationalists were members of the middle class who were predisposed to favor change. Many nationalists were teachers, writers, artists, journalists, bureaucrats, and politicians who personally had much to gain by reinventing society along nationalist lines.

Today, nationalism is a force in international affairs that many people take for granted. It is often seen as reasonable for a group of people with a common ethnic identity to demand independence. Fairly recently, such demands led to the breakup of Yugoslavia, Czechoslovakia, and the Soviet Union into smaller, ethnically based states.

In the nineteenth century, however, most conservatives saw nationalism as a radical creed. Conservatives pointed out that nationalist movements could create enormous problems. For example, the establishment of national cultures often meant that, within a given nation, local and regional variations in language, customs, and laws had to be erased. This was a painful and difficult process.

In addition, there was the thorny question of which ethnic groups deserved nations of their own and which did not. Some ethnic groups were too small or too weak to sustain national independence. Were the Poles, the Czechs, or the Greeks, for example, capable of governing themselves? Such issues were hotly debated in the nineteenth century. Naturally, the large, multiethnic empires in Eastern Europe, notably Austria, Russia, and Turkey, resisted the idea of nationalism. They viewed traditional monarchy as a more legitimate justification for governmental authority, and they repeatedly warned that chaos and violence would result if nationalism ever became too strong.

Various hotspots for nationalism developed throughout the nineteenth century. The Austrian, Russian, and Turkish empires all included numerous ethnic groups that clamored for self-government—mostly without success. The Russians, for instance, brutally suppressed Polish uprisings in 1831 and

1863. Many Germans also dreamed of national unification, although the path was far from clear. There were no less than 40 states in the Germanies, and, until the 1860s, neither Prussia nor Austria supported their combination into a single nation. Many Italians favored the unification of the numerous small states on their peninsula into a single country, but here the influence of Austria was decisive in blocking nationalism. Many Catholic Irishmen sought an end to English rule and the establishment of an independent Ireland, despite the fact that, since 1800, the Irish had been represented in London by no less than 100 members of Parliament. The English, for their part, considered Ireland an integral part of their country, and they suppressed Irish nationalism well into the twentieth century. English leaders also worked hard to convince the Irish, the Welsh, the Scots, and the English, who had previously been very different, to embrace a unified British identity.

Throughout Europe, nationalism had to compete with other movements, such as conservatism and liberalism, for the allegiance of people who were politically aware. In Germany, for example, the complexity of the political situation forced many in the *bourgeoisie* to choose whether they valued liberal freedoms or national unification more. It would not be an exaggeration to suggest that the fate of Europe largely rested on which of these three principal ideologies—conservatism, liberalism, or nationalism—would prove dominant in the years to come.

Although the conservative elite fiercely resisted nationalist reforms, during the 1820s and 1830s some key nationalist victories were won. In the 1820s, the Greeks struggled successfully for their independence against the Ottoman Turks. Not only was Greek independence in 1832 a political triumph, but it gave nationalist movements across Europe a sense of moral superiority and even historical inevitability.

In the 1820s, the independence of most of Spain and Portugal's colonies in Latin America fanned the flames of nationalism. In addition, in 1830, Serbia (or rather, a part of Serbia) won its independence from the Ottoman Empire. Coupled with events in Greece, this established the problematic precedent that the great empires of Eastern Europe were vulnerable to nationalist revolts. Also in 1830, Belgium, which had been ruled by the Kingdom of the Netherlands, won self-government. All these nationalist achievements were impressive, but the critical question of whether nationalism would grow strong enough to build any new great powers—in Germany or Italy, for example—or to destroy old powers, like Austria, Russia, or Turkey, remained to be answered.

Which areas in Europe were nationalist hotspots?

Romanticism

Romanticism was an intellectual and artistic movement that reached its height during the first half of the nineteenth century. It has little to do with "romance," *per se*. Nineteenth-century Romanticism arose in opposition to the Enlightenment, a way of thinking that had dominated the eighteenth century. Whereas the Enlightenment had stressed the importance of reason and had exalted the model of modern science as the best route to knowledge, Romantics stressed the importance of emotion, imagination, and spirituality.

An example may help to illustrate this difference of opinion. A supporter of the Enlightenment, looking out of his or her window at a landscape of trees and grass bounded by blue sky, would see, like any good scientist, the bounties of nature waiting to be observed, categorized, and subsequently exploited for practical gain. An Enlightened thinker might also prefer that this landscape be carefully manicured and cultivated, along the lines of a formal garden. A Romantic, on the other hand, looking out of his or her window, would see the beauty and mystery of nature, which is not in any meaningful sense under human control. Wilderness, in other words, is more to the Romantic's taste. While Enlightened thinkers tended to favor science and to express confidence in humanity's ability to control its fate, Romantics tended to favor religion, and they asserted that human beings needed help from God to find their way.

Romanticism did not necessarily suggest a political program. There were, in fact, elements of Romanticism that could be harnessed to support all of the major political ideologies of the nineteenth century. Nevertheless, Romanticism developed its strongest political connection to nationalism. "Romantic nationalism" is a phrase often used to describe nationalist movements in the nineteenth and twentieth centuries that were inspired by a strong emotional connection between a certain group of people and the national identity that they cherished.

Romantic nationalists tended to follow several strategies. They often sought to purify a national language, ridding it of foreign influences and regional inconsistencies. Modern Norwegian and Greek were among the first languages to be reinvented for nationalist purposes. Romantics also sought to recover an original national culture in the form of folklore, music, or classic literature. The Grimm Brothers in Germany collected fairy tales that were meant to convey the wisdom of traditional Germanic folk culture. Often Romantics also sought to establish a clear link between a nation's people and the territory of its beloved fatherland or motherland, and sometimes they tried to define the nation in racial or biological terms. Romantic nationalists generally accorded women a central role in the future of the nation, since they were seen as the guardians of its racial purity, as well as the creators and nurturers of the next generation of patriots. As the nineteenth century wore on, nationalism became much more than a mere political movement—it became a quasi-religion that stirred incredible passions throughout Europe.

Romantic art in its various forms struggled to give expression to human emotions, and in the process it generally disregarded artistic conventions. Romantic art is perhaps most recognizable in the form of painting. In England, painters such as J.M.W. Turner and John Constable reveled in idealized depictions of nature. Constable was famous for his hauntingly beautiful landscape paintings of the English countryside. Other Romantic painters pursued exotic or historical themes, such as dark, supernatural Gothic imagery from the Middle Ages.

Romantic music is equally celebrated. Ludwig von Beethoven was one of the first and greatest of Romantic composers. Other Romantics would develop new forms of musical expression laden with sentimentality, such as nocturnes and rhapsodies, and they would attempt to tell stories with music. Opera was one of the favorite vehicles for the expression of Romantic ideals in musical form.

Romantic literature included some outstanding poetry. In Britain, two Romantic poets, who were also friends, William Wordsworth and Samuel Taylor Coleridge, highlighted the spiritual power of nature and the emotional complexity of the human experience. Romantic poetry often expressed a melancholy mood that was also in evidence in Romantic novels. Mary Shelley, wife of the English poet Percy Bysshe Shelley, was the author of *Frankenstein*, a typically Romantic Gothic tale.

Religion, which is often associated with an emotional experience of faith in the supernatural, flourished during the Romantic era. During the eighteenth and nineteenth centuries, Methodism, a new sect that stressed a deep faith in Christ, prospered in Britain and America. In the mid-nineteenth century on any given Sunday approximately 60 percent of all able-bodied Britons were in church. In Catholic countries, the story was no different. There was a strong religious revival in nineteenth-century France.

Another outlet for Romantic yearnings was the growing industry of tourism. Just as Christians flocked to their churches, so middle-class travelers streamed toward picturesque seaside resorts, quaint peasant villages, historic sites like the Waterloo battlefield, and sometimes even exotic foreign destinations to which many Europeans had an imperial connection. Tourism today is still based on these Romantic longings.

How did Romantic thought differ from Enlightened thought?

The Revolutions of 1848

In 1848, a remarkable series of revolutions throughout Europe seemed to imperil the conservative order. Middle-class liberals and nationalists, backed by angry workers, revolted in numerous countries. The two main causes of these revolts were middle-class resentment of continuing monarchical and noble dominance, and misery and starvation among workers and peasants caused by crop failures, unemployment, and government indifference. The latter problem was seen most notably in the inadequate assistance granted by the British government to starving Irishmen in the Potato Famine of 1846–48. As many as one million people in Ireland died, and an equivalent number emigrated, many to America. Britain and Ireland, however, would not be among the epicenters of revolution in 1848.

Although the middle class and many workers and peasants were allies in the revolutions of 1848, in the long term their goals were incompatible. Whereas workers and peasants often sought more aggressive and expensive government programs to address the problems of poverty, unemployment, and high food prices, the middle class tended to seek instead more political representation for itself, national unification, and *less* government spending on the poor. This divergence of opinion between the two chief constituencies of the revolutions of 1848 helps to explain their ultimate failure everywhere in Europe, with the sole exception of France.

In February 1848, French middle-class liberals held a series of banquets designed to increase support for an expansion of the right to vote. King Louis-Philippe tried to prohibit the banquets, but the resulting protests ultimately forced the king to abdicate. The liberals appeared to have won, and a Second Republic was established (the First Republic existed during the French Revolution) that called for elections based on a broad franchise to a new National Assembly. The *bourgeoisie*, however, dominated the National Assembly that was elected in April, and so some discontented Parisian workers rebelled in June, leading to hundreds of deaths, but the middle class remained in control.

As it turned out, liberal government in France was short-lived, as was the Second Republic. In late 1848, Napoleon Bonaparte's nephew, Louis Napoleon Bonaparte, was elected President. Louis Napoleon was sometimes known, because of his short stature and his inability to live up to his uncle's example, as The Little Napoleon, but, although he was no legendary conqueror, Louis Napoleon was an able politician and a gifted opportunist. In 1851, he staged a bloody coup to prolong his term in office. Then, in 1852, he abandoned republicanism and declared himself Emperor Napoleon III (Napoleon I's unfortunate son, who had died in 1832, was considered Napoleon II.) Napoleon III was hardly the liberal savior hoped for by the middle class. He courted workers with progressive social policies and expensive public works projects. He also suppressed dissent and refused to allow the elected legislature to challenge his will. In a peculiar irony, therefore, the Revolution of 1848 in France followed the same trajectory as the Revolution of 1789. In both cases, France went from constitutional monarchy, to republic, to chaos, to dictatorship, and then finally to repressive empire.

The revolution in France in February 1848 soon sparked similar revolts elsewhere. In Italy, Austrian forces barely managed to keep control of Milan. Meanwhile, in 1849 French troops defeated a brief attempt to found a liberal republic in Rome—perhaps a precursor to Italian unification.

Revolts also developed throughout the Austrian Empire. In 1848 the Hungarians rebelled, demanding greater autonomy. They overplayed their hand, however, and by 1849 the Austrians had suppressed the Hungarian uprising with help from Russia. Similar revolts in Prague and Vienna were also defeated.

In March 1848, violence in Berlin motivated Prussian King Frederick William IV to promise that he would call an assembly to write a constitution. In 1849, though, the king issued a constitution of his own design. It gave the right to vote to all Prussian men, but the legislature would have only limited powers, and wealthy citizens would be overrepresented.

Potentially much more significant historically were events in Germany as a whole. Specifically, revolutionary violence throughout Germany led to an ambitious attempt in 1848–49 to reorganize the German Confederation into a fully unified liberal state. Had this effort succeeded, nationalism and liberalism could both have flourished in Germany, and the history of Europe in the nineteenth and twentieth centuries might have been very different.

The assembly that was convened to discuss constitutional changes in Germany, known as the Frankfurt Parliament, finished writing a constitution in March 1849. It then offered the crown of the German nation to the King of Prussia. He refused it, though, because he viewed the rights of a monarch as a gift from God, not from an assembly of reformers.

In the end, the Frankfurt Parliament was probably Germany's best chance, at least for the next 100 years, to achieve national unification and true liberal reform simultaneously. Increasingly, after the Parliament's failure, the nationalist and liberal movements in Germany separated, and nationalists made accommodations with conservatives that excluded liberals altogether. Some historians go as far as to say that Germany's rejection of liberalism from 1848 to 1945 means that the country pursued a *Sonderweg*, or alternative path, that separated it from Western Civilization as a whole. Be that as it may, in 1871, Germany finally achieved national unification under Prussian leadership, but as a conservative monarchy dedicated to militarism rather than as a liberal democracy.

It is easy to dismiss the revolutionary violence of 1848 as inconsequential, because in most of Europe the conservative elite remained in power. In fact, though, conservatives learned in 1848 that it was dangerous to ignore the demands for reform coming from the middle class, and they also learned that the urban poor were an increasingly dynamic force in European history. Conservatives accepted, therefore, that ultimately the interests and views of these groups would have to be respected. In the second half of the nineteenth century, the conservative grip on power would steadily loosen, and the political influence of the middle class, peasants, and urban workers would increase exponentially.

Why were the revolutions of 1848 so historically important, despite the fact that most of them failed?

Industrialization Continues: The Machine Age Arrives in Europe

As Europe redefined itself politically and culturally during the first half of the nineteenth century, momentous economic changes portended even more political, cultural, and social development in the years ahead. Britain's Industrial Revolution spread in the early 1800s to other parts of northwestern Europe, especially France, Belgium, the Netherlands, and western Germany. Slowly, the Machine Age crept into Southern and Eastern Europe as well. In the process, Europe's power over nature and its material wealth surged, but at the same time new conflicts arose between the middle class and urban workers.

The most potent symbol of industrialization in Europe in the second quarter of the nineteenth century was the railway, a bold new application of the steam engine. The first railways were called tramroads and used wooden rails and horse-drawn carts. Gradually, iron rails became more popular, and steam-driven locomotives were designed to replace the carts. The world's first modern commercial railway line, the Stockton and Darlington Railway, opened in England in 1825, but the first successful line designed exclusively for steam-driven locomotives was the Liverpool and Manchester Railway, established in England in 1830.

Railway companies quickly discovered that the demand for rail transportation, for the movement of both goods and people, was exceedingly high. This led to a Railway Mania in Britain in the 1830s and 1840s. As railways spread and as shipping costs diminished, prices for food and fuel actually fell in some cities. Passengers, needless to say, gained unprecedented mobility.

The success of the railways in Britain caused Europeans in other countries to want to develop railway systems of their own. By the 1840s, significant railway networks were developing in France, Belgium, the Netherlands, Germany, and Austria.

Figure 13.1 A replica of *The Rocket*, a steam locomotive designed by Robert Stephenson for the Liverpool and Manchester Railway.

Tony Hisgett/Wikimedia Commons.

Perhaps more important than railways in the long run was the increasing shift in the early nineteenth century from the production of goods in peasant homes and rural mills to factory-based production in cities. Factories in the early nineteenth century were most common in Britain, but the factory system was spreading rapidly elsewhere.

As economic opportunities contracted in the countryside, and as jobs became relatively plentiful in the cities, millions of Europeans became urban dwellers for the first time. This sped up industrial development, but it also subjected many urban workers to miserable working conditions and to life in crowded, violent, polluted, and disease-ridden slums.

In the early part of the nineteenth century, large numbers of women and children were hired to work in factories, partly because they were easier for foremen to intimidate, and partly because they earned only 25–50 percent of a man's wage. By the second half of the nineteenth century, however, male workers were preferred in most factories. Increasingly, even women of the working class remained in the home once they were married, although they might still earn some money through part-time employment or home-based labor.

In defense of the factory system, the wages that factories paid were generally far better than those that could be earned in agriculture or in home-based production. These relatively high wages created not only a more comfortable lifestyle but also the chance to give one's children an education and the opportunity for social advancement. The factory system also greatly increased the efficiency of production, thus lowering the cost of a wide variety of goods.

By 1850, thanks to the ongoing process of industrialization and urbanization, half the population in Britain lived in cities (it would be 80 percent by 1901). In France and Germany, roughly one-fourth of the population was urbanized, but this figure was quickly increasing. The populations of Paris, Berlin, and St. Petersburg all doubled in the first half of the nineteenth century.

Predictably enough, rapid urbanization led to ballooning crime rates. In response, professional police forces were introduced in London and Paris by 1829, and prisons were reformed and expanded. In addition, gaslights were installed so that criminal gangs could not lurk in the darkness. Capital punishment became rarer, but many who broke the law were punished with transportation to a far-flung colony, such as Australia for the British. By the end of the nineteenth century, crime rates had diminished somewhat.

Although one might expect that the middle class, which often lived in cities, would have felt sympathy for the urban poor, *laissez-faire* capitalism taught that it was counterproductive to try to improve the lot of the less fortunate. Two influential economists, Thomas Malthus and David Ricardo, argued that higher wages for the poor would only cause them to have more children. More children would mean more workers, which would cause wages to fall and misery to increase. The best remedy for poverty, therefore, would be to teach the poor to help themselves.

In 1834, Britain reformed its Poor Law, requiring those who received government assistance to live in prison-like workhouses. Meanwhile, strikes were prohibited, because liberals valued the right of employers to bargain with individual workers as they pleased. Thus, the working poor had little leverage with which to seek improvements to their wages and working conditions.

The liberal commitment to a *laissez-faire* approach in dealing with the poor was matched by a commitment to free trade. In 1846, Britain began the era of free trade by repealing its Corn Law, which had imposed tariffs on imported grain. The result was that foreign grain became cheaper, and food was less expensive for urban workers. Free trade was also achieved in the Germanies by a customs union in 1834. The drive for free trade, therefore, which is such a major, albeit controversial, theme of capitalism and international relations today, began more than 150 years ago in Europe.

What were the pros and cons of life as an early nineteenth-century factory worker?

Conclusions

To many observers, Europe in 1850 might have seemed largely unchanged since the end of the Napoleonic Wars. There were still more peasants in Europe than factory workers. Industrialization was still largely confined to Britain. Conservative monarchs and nobles still predominated in most governments, and liberals and nationalists struggled to achieve their goals. Additionally, Romanticism was still a movement that primarily affected a small number of intellectuals, artists, and writers. Nevertheless, irresistible forces for change had been unleashed.

In the second half of the nineteenth century, industrialization would cease to be a mere trend and would become a way of life for most Europeans. Conservative governments would be toppled in some countries, and everywhere else conservatives would have to make compromises with middle-class liberals and nationalists, and often with newly politicized workers. Thanks to the spread of public education, Romantic ideas, especially Romantic nationalism, would be popularized as never before. In fact, nationalism would go on to become one of the most potent forces in world history.

The second half of the nineteenth century would see the final conquest of political, social, and economic power by the middle class. Middle-Class Europe was about to be born, therefore, but the *bourgeoisie* would very soon face opposition from below.

Key Terms for Chapter 13

Conservatism—a political ideology favoring tradition and entrusting power to monarchs, nobles, and clergymen.

Prince Metternich—an Austrian statesman who strove to maintain the conservative *status quo* in Austria and the Germanies.

Concert of Europe—a loose alliance of the major powers that sought to keep the peace and defend conservative governments throughout Europe.

Liberalism—a political ideology that favors representative government, constitutionalism, individual rights, equality under the law, and limited government interference in the economy.

Great Reform Bill, 1832—a major overhaul of Britain's electoral system, granting the right to vote to many in the middle class.

Nationalism—an ideology supporting the right of a group of people with a common language, culture, and history to govern themselves.

Romanticism—a nineteenth-century intellectual and artistic movement stressing the importance of emotion.

1848—a year in which many failed revolutions occurred in Europe.

Napoleon III—Napoleon I's nephew, and Emperor of France from 1852 to 1870.

Frankfurt Parliament—a political convention that met in 1848–49, but failed to achieve its goal of a unified, liberal state in Germany.

Railways—a major innovation in European industry and transportation that initially blossomed in Britain during the 1830s and 1840s.

Urbanization—the movement of people from the countryside to the cities, a process sped up by Europe's steady industrialization.

Review Questions for Chapter 13

1. The United States is often considered a liberal state, in that it tends to adhere to ideals similar to those of classical liberals. Describe one way in which the modern United States is definitely liberal, and one way in which it has strayed from liberalism.
2. Which nineteenth-century "ism"—conservatism, liberalism, or nationalism—do you find most appealing? Which do you find least appealing? Explain your selections.
3. Do you believe that the average person is more enlightened or Romantic in his or her thinking? Do you consider yourself more enlightened or Romantic? Explain your views.
4. Imagine that you are a member of the Frankfurt Parliament. Write a speech in which you either favor or oppose Germany's unification as a liberal state. Include in your speech a prediction about what Germany's future will be like if your position on unification and liberalism is adopted.
5. Urbanization was one of the most important consequences of the Industrial Revolution. List two positive features and two negative features of nineteenth-century urbanization.

Further Reading

Atterbury, Paul and Susanne Fagance Cooper. *Victorians at Home and Abroad*. London: V&A. 2001.

Bilenky, Serhiy. *Romantic Nationalism in Eastern Europe: Russian, Polish, and Ukrainian Political Imaginations*. Stanford, CA: Stanford University Press. 2012.

Blanning, Tim. *The Romantic Revolution: A History*. New York: Random House. 2011.

Broers, Michael. *Europe After Napoleon: Revolution, Reaction and Romanticism, 1814–1848*. New York: Manchester University Press. 1996.

Hahn, Hans Joachim. *The 1848 Revolutions in German-Speaking Europe*. New York: Routledge. 2016.

Kahan, Alan S. *Liberalism in Nineteenth-Century Europe: The Political Culture of Limited Suffrage*. New York: Palgrave Macmillan. 2014.

Kitchen, Martin. *A History of Modern Germany, 1800–2000*. Malden, MA: Blackwell. 2010.

Schulze, Hagen. *The Course of German Nationalism: From Frederick the Great to Bismarck, 1763–1867*. Cambridge: Cambridge University Press. 2003.

Seward, Desmond. *Metternich: The First European*. London: Thistle. 2015.

Simmons, Jack and Gordon Biddle. *The Oxford Companion to British Railway History: From 1603 to the 1990s*. Oxford: Oxford University Press. 2003.

Sykes, Alan. *The Rise and Fall of British Liberalism, 1776–1988*. Harlow, UK: Longman. 1997.

Vick, Brian E. *Defining Germany: The 1848 Frankfurt Parliamentarians and National Identity*. Cambridge, MA: Harvard University Press. 2002.

14 Middle-Class Europe

The Triumph of Liberalism and Nationalism and the Rise of Socialism, 1850–1914

Introduction

The Great Exhibition, held in London in 1851, was essentially a world's fair that showcased the latest manufactured goods and machines that were contributing to Europe's industrial progress. Ceremonially opened by Queen Victoria, the Exhibition marked the dawning of the age of Middle-Class Europe, when finally the political, social, cultural, and economic priorities of the *bourgeoisie* became predominant. In the second half of the nineteenth century, middle-class ideals such as liberalism and nationalism would experience their greatest triumphs.

The inexorably expanding working class would not, however, be ignored. As the nineteenth century drew to a close, movements seeking to empower the lower classes, including trade unionism, socialism, and communism, would rise in popularity and influence. Middle-Class Europe was thus in peril almost as soon as it came into existence.

Figure 14.1 The Crystal Palace, built to house the Great Exhibition in 1851. It symbolized the extraordinary industrial and technological progress of nineteenth-century Europe.

Hein Nouwens/Shutterstock.

The Middle Class, 1850–1914

Polls have repeatedly shown that if you ask an American today what class he or she belongs to, the response as much as 90 percent of the time will be the middle class. For whatever reason, few Americans will admit to being either rich or poor. Of course, if everyone is middle class, then the term has little meaning.

In the nineteenth century, it was not necessarily any easier to define the middle class, because a transition was occurring in the concept of the class structure. During the eighteenth century, the term *bourgeoisie* or middle class had referred, broadly speaking, to anyone in society who was not a nobleman (at the top of the social scale) or a peasant or an urban worker (at the bottom). Thus, the middle class included many professionals, merchants, and business owners, at least some of whom became fabulously wealthy. Today, these rich members of the *bourgeoisie* would probably be called upper class, but in the seventeenth and eighteenth centuries they were still thought of as middle class.

In the nineteenth century, some people still defined the middle class in eighteenth-century terms. Others, however, were beginning to think of the term middle class in its modern sense, denoting people with moderate incomes. Luckily for us, in most cases the two definitions overlapped.

It is important to keep one vital difference between today's middle class and the middle class of the nineteenth century in mind. Today, most people in all Western countries are middle class. In the nineteenth century, on the other hand, the *bourgeoisie* was not a majority of the population in any European country. The middle class was large and growing, but peasants, factory workers, and other groups were still much more numerous. England had the largest middle class, but it still made up only 25 percent of the population in 1900. Thus, the middle class became the most powerful class in Europe in the second half of the nineteenth century even though it was still in the minority.

What was life like for the nineteenth-century middle class? First, in terms of gender relations, separate spheres for men and women, as Jean-Jacques Rousseau had advocated in the eighteenth century, were considered normal and natural. Ideally, the public sphere, including politics and business, was considered to be the preserve of men, while the private sphere of home and family was considered to be the proper focus for women. Thus, women lacked the right to vote, they were often discouraged from working outside the home, and they lacked many of the educational opportunities and legal rights that women take for granted today. Obtaining a divorce, for instance, was difficult or impossible for women in most European countries. Nevertheless, Victorian society valued women very highly. (The Victorian Age coincided with the reign of Britain's Queen Victoria from 1837 to 1901.) Something called the Cult of Domesticity arose during the nineteenth century. The Cult of Domesticity was a viewpoint that celebrated the domestic, that is, home-based, role of women as wives and mothers. Women were seen as natural nurturers, whose virtues of compassion, loyalty, and self-control were widely praised. In other words, Victorians respected women—as long as they upheld society's strict gender norms.

It is sometimes said that the Victorians invented childhood in the modern sense. Before the nineteenth century, relatively little effort was made to understand child psychology or to prolong the joys and innocence of childhood. All this changed as middle-class fathers and mothers became increasingly devoted to their children. By 1900, birth rates were declining across Europe. Families had fewer children overall, so that more time and money could be spent on each child. Corporal punishment became increasingly rare and was banned in French schools. Toys and books for children were sold in vast quantities.

The second half of the nineteenth century saw all the major Western countries institute compulsory elementary education, which the government often provided free of charge. This dramatically expanded literacy, which in turn contributed to Victorian society's voracious appetite for reading material. Books, newspapers, and journals proliferated. Prominent writers were popular and influential, and sometimes very rich.

Partly because of their enchantment with Romanticism, middle-class Europeans often became passionately religious, and they tended to insist on rigid adherence to conventional standards of morality. Prominent Victorians therefore practiced, or at least praised, virtues such as sobriety, frugality, honesty, hard work, cleanliness, self-reliance, self-control, and politeness. They also evangelized on behalf of moral improvement among the poor and in foreign lands. Christian missionary zeal was never stronger than in the nineteenth century. Meanwhile, *bourgeois* humanitarians addressed problems as diverse as slavery, public health, animal cruelty, housing reform, the plight of orphans, and education. Many of the most successful reformers, and the most tireless volunteers, were women.

In social relations, respect and formality were very important—first names were almost never used. Young women from good backgrounds would never interact with men outside their families unless a chaperone accompanied them. Dating in the modern sense was unthinkable, and out-of-wedlock births were extremely rare.

Although it is commonplace to imagine that nineteenth-century marriages were characterized by sexual repression, this appears not to have been the case. Sex within marriage was widely heralded as natural and healthy. Partly for this reason, the use of contraceptives became common in middle-class households. Condoms were in wide use by the 1860s.

The middle class in the nineteenth century was obsessed with the new and ingenious products that were available for it to buy (thanks in part to the Second Industrial Revolution, described in Chapter 15). Throughout the nineteenth century, middle-class homes became steadily larger, and furnishings became more elaborate and luxurious. Sanitary improvements like flushable toilets served to improve hygiene, while laborsaving devices such as sewing machines, telephones, typewriters, washing machines, and electric lights were available by 1900. The spread of advertisements, first in print and later in the form of colorful billboards, encouraged a growth in consumerism. Shopping, meanwhile, was revolutionized by department stores, the first of which, called *Le Bon Marché*, opened in Paris in 1852.

Men's and women's fashions underwent huge changes during the nineteenth century. In 1800, elite men wore elaborate costumes including wigs, colorful and often intricately embroidered shirts and jackets, and knee-breeches (short trousers that ended at the knee), along with stockings to cover their calves. Men's fashions were accessorized with jewels, feathers, ribbons, and gaudy hats. By 1900, even noblemen had forsaken such extravagant fashions for the austere *bourgeois* business suit, usually in black or gray.

By contrast, Victorian women's clothing, especially evening wear, was often highly ornamental. The decorative function that women served (from the perspective of men) was highlighted by the wide use of the corset, an extraordinary contraption worn under a woman's clothing that molded her figure to achieve the sought-after look of wide hips, a small waist, and a generous *décolletage*, or cleavage. At the same time, respectable women avoided makeup altogether.

Sports became a major feature of middle-class life during the nineteenth century. Depending on where they lived, middle-class Europeans might watch or participate in sports such as tennis, ice skating, skiing, rugby, swimming, golf, boating, gymnastics, cricket, croquet, field hockey, and cycling. The Wimbledon tennis championships and the modern Olympic games both began in the nineteenth century.

Leisure travel became increasingly popular. By the 1850s, hordes of middle-class vacationers were already visiting seaside resorts, which became progressively more elaborate. The White Star Line, famous for losing the *Titanic* in 1912, launched the first luxury steamship in 1871.

When members of the middle class sought recreational opportunities closer to home, they might visit parks, cafés, restaurants, social clubs, concert halls, museums, the theater, opera, or ballet. They avoided popular music halls and pubs, due to their reputation for rowdiness and a lower-class clientele. In the home itself, crafts and games were very popular, as was singing, listening to music, and reading aloud. It was in the nineteenth century that it became common for animals, especially dogs, to be kept as pets.

What must never be forgotten about nineteenth-century society was that it was much more rigidly divided along class lines than Western societies are today. Above all, familiarity or friendliness across class lines was almost unthinkable. Even within the middle class, variations in rank and status were considered highly significant.

Since the typical middle-class family enjoyed an income roughly ten times that of an unskilled or semiskilled worker, most middle-class families were able to afford domestic servants. In 1881, 16 percent of all employed persons in England were domestic servants, mostly women and girls. This brought the different social classes into regular contact with one another, and it necessitated the creation of strict rules to govern their interactions. Servants were to speak to their masters only when necessary, and only using formal titles; they were to walk behind their masters; and they were not to smile, laugh, or otherwise show an attitude of familiarity.

Under these circumstances, it is not surprising that some members of the working class, whether they were domestic servants or simply employees of a self-important middle-class boss, developed a strong dislike for their *bourgeois* overlords. In many parts of Europe, this resentment would eventually have important historical consequences, as this chapter's discussions of trade unionism, socialism, and communism will make plain.

What was life like for members of the middle class in the nineteenth century?

The Triumph of Nationalism in Italy

The middle class achieved some remarkable victories for the *bourgeois* political movements of liberalism and nationalism during the second half of the nineteenth century. One of the first major successes for nationalism was the unification of Italy, accomplished in 1861–70.

Ever since the collapse of the Roman Empire, Italy had been divided into numerous small political units that outside powers such as Spain, France, and Austria often dominated. In the first half of the nineteenth century, it was Austria that had the most influence over the Italians.

In the 1850s, two strong movements in Italy sought to evict the Austrians and establish a unified nation-state. One was the Romantic Republicans, who advocated Romantic nationalism and a united government for Italy without a monarch. Giuseppe Mazzini and Giuseppe Garibaldi were the leaders of the Romantic Republicans, and they used guerrilla warfare, political intrigue, and foreign financing to pursue their goal of a Republic of Italy. They had little success.

The second movement for Italian unification achieved better results. The strongest and most independent of all the Italian states was the Kingdom of Sardinia, often known as "Piedmont," which was the area in northwestern Italy that it ruled. In 1852, Piedmont's king appointed Count Camillo Cavour as his Prime Minister. Cavour, a believer in Italian unification, decided to cooperate with a group called the Nationalist Society. Cavour, however, was not a republican: he wanted a united Italy to be a monarchy, and he wanted his monarch to become the new King of Italy. To a large extent, Cavour achieved his goals by 1861. He did so by deftly exploiting several diplomatic and military opportunities.

In 1858, Cavour formed an alliance with Emperor Napoleon III of France, who wanted to help liberate Italy from Austrian control. In 1859, French and Piedmontese forces defeated the Austrians in two major battles, and Cavour moved quickly to encourage a union between Piedmont and many of the states in northern Italy, including Tuscany. In addition, an attempt by the Romantic Republicans to found a republic in southern Italy was exploited by Cavour as an opportunity to send Piedmontese troops to occupy Naples and Sicily. By late 1860, most of northern, central, and southern Italy had accepted Piedmontese rule, and, in 1861, King Victor Emmanuel II of Sardinia/Piedmont was proclaimed King of Italy.

Cavour died a few months later, but the process of Italian unification continued. The only major parts of Italy that remained to be absorbed into the Kingdom of Italy were, first, the area around Rome governed by the pope; second, Venice, which the Austrians still controlled; and, third, the Trentino region of northeastern Italy, also under Austrian occupation.

Two of these three regions were brought under Italian rule in short order. Italy conquered Venice in 1866 (with help from Prussia). Rome was seized in 1870 and was promptly declared Italy's new capital. The pope was left with virtually no territory of his own, ensuring bad blood between the Kingdom of Italy and the papacy for decades. The Trentino region, however, remained under Austrian control well into the twentieth century. Italy's desire to conquer the Trentino was one of its chief motivations for joining the Allies in World War I.

The creation of a united Italian nation was a spectacular achievement, but the Kingdom of Italy was also a disappointment to some groups. Republicans and liberals were dismayed that Italy was united as a monarchy. Business owners were upset that Italy's new government granted workers, some of them socialists or communists, political rights. Supporters of the Catholic Church were angry that the new Italian state had shown such disrespect to the pope. Italians as a whole were disappointed that their new government was so corrupt. Major differences between Italy's industrialized north and its agrarian south weakened the new state as well. Italy managed to join the ranks of the great powers after 1870, but it never quite matched the British, the French, or the Germans in terms of political stability, economic development, and military strength.

How did the Kingdom of Sardinia/Piedmont achieve the unification of Italy?

The Triumph of Nationalism: German Unification

Ironically, it was a conservative, aristocratic politician, Otto von Bismarck, serving a traditional monarch, King Wilhelm I of Prussia, who would achieve the most important victory for nationalism, an overwhelmingly middle-class movement.

German unification in 1871 was a critical turning point in European history. For hundreds of years, the German peoples had been divided into many small states, few of which were strong enough even to defend themselves. In 1871, though, the Germanies fused into the German Empire, a conservative, monarchical state, albeit with liberal and parliamentary elements, that possessed one of the strongest armies in world history. The balance of power that the Congress of Vienna had created in 1815 was shattered forever.

More than anyone else, Otto von Bismarck (after whom the capital of North Dakota is named) was responsible for German unification. Bismarck was a *Junker*, that is, a member of the traditional nobility in Prussia that owned most of the farmland in the country and staffed the army officer corps and the bureaucracy. Historically, the Prussian monarchy and the

Junkers had been close allies. Bismarck, as a conservative, wanted to keep the king and nobles in power for as long as possible.

In 1861, King Wilhelm I, who had just succeeded to the throne of Prussia, began to have serious trouble with the country's elected legislature, which middle-class liberals dominated. Aiming to put the legislature in its place, Wilhelm asked Otto von Bismarck to become Prussia's new Chancellor (the German equivalent of the British Prime Minister.)

Many liberals in Prussia initially attacked Chancellor Bismarck as a reactionary. Bismarck, however, was a gifted politician, diplomat, and military strategist. While he was conservative, he was also realistic enough to understand that Prussia needed to change. Bismarck sensed that the liberal and nationalist movements in Prussia, and throughout Germany, were strong, and he was determined to co-opt and manipulate them to maintain the power of the Prussian monarchy and *Junker* elite. The strategy he chose was simple: he planned to use conservative institutions and methods in order to achieve German unification. Bismarck believed that this would appeal to middle-class nationalists who would, out of gratitude, accept a united Germany that the monarchy, the army, and the nobility still ruled. In other words, Bismarck bargained that the middle class would be willing to trade away liberalism in return for national unification.

In 1866, Bismarck put his master plan for German unification into effect by provoking a war with Austria. Historically, Austria had been Prussia's main rival in exercising influence over the smaller states that made up the Germanies, so to achieve Prussian domination over Germany Austria needed to be out of the picture.

Cleverly allying with Italy while securing the neutrality of France and Russia, Bismarck engineered the defeat of Austria after just seven weeks of fighting. Bismarck thereupon took control of all of the German states north of the Main River, forcing them to join a new entity called the North German Confederation, led by Prussia. Most of Germany was now united under Prussian rule. Liberal politicians in Prussia now began to praise Chancellor Bismarck!

The last phase of German unification was Bismarck's plan to bring the independent states of southern Germany, notably Bavaria, under Prussia's control. In 1870, Bismarck engineered a diplomatic crisis between Prussia and France. Bismarck reasoned that, although the southern Germans might be suspicious of Prussia, they were far more hostile to France. If Prussia could provoke France into behaving aggressively toward the North German Confederation, then the south German states would rally to the side of their fellow Germans. Nationalist passions would then make German unification unstoppable.

In July 1870, France's Emperor Napoleon III foolishly declared war on Prussia. By September 1, however, the Prussian army had once more proven its superiority. French forces were in full retreat, the French emperor was a German prisoner, and the south German states were fighting alongside Prussia. All that remained was to complete the negotiations to establish a united Germany under Prussian domination.

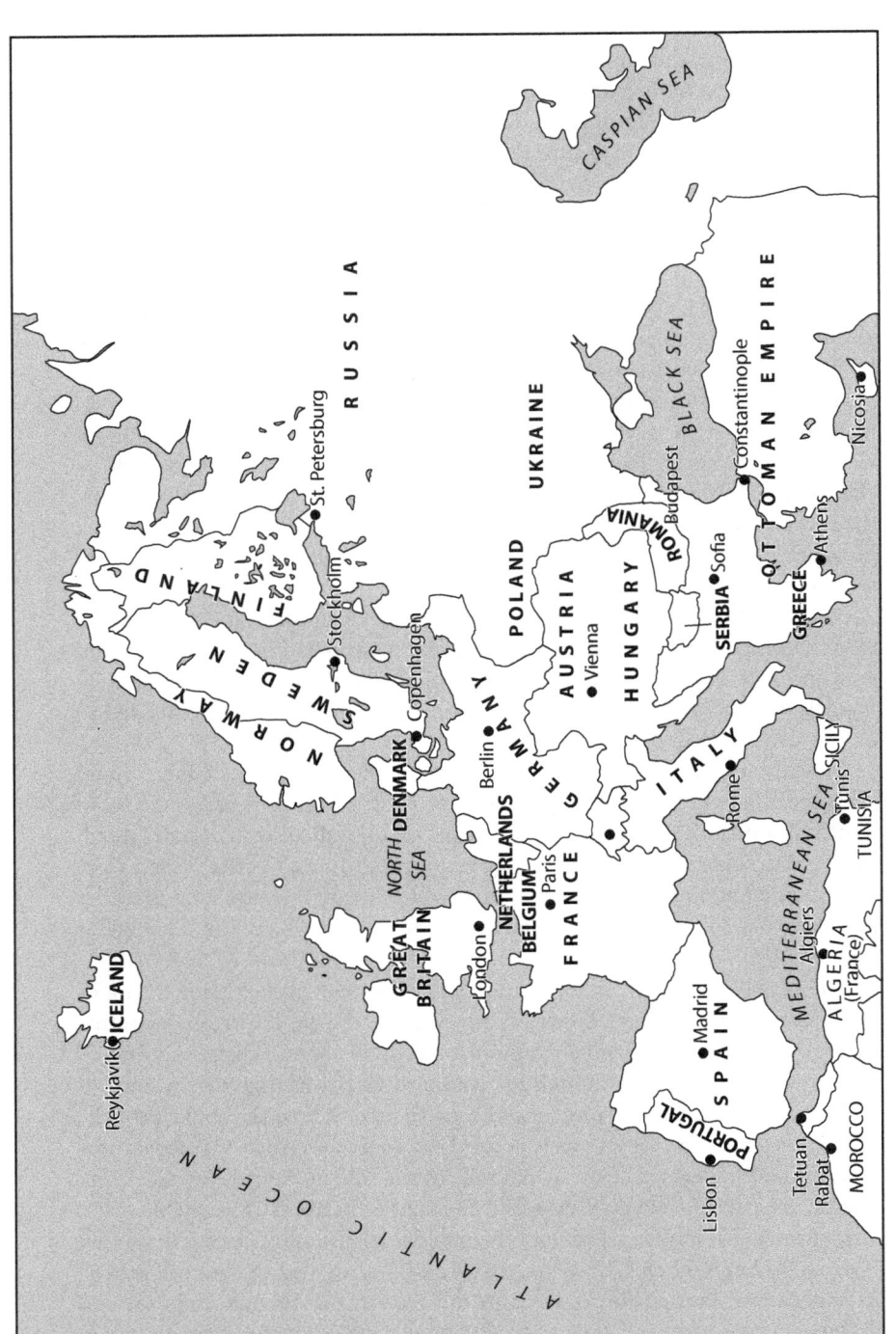

Map 14.1 Europe in 1871.

On January 18, 1871, Bismarck achieved his ultimate goal. On that day, in the Hall of Mirrors at the Palace of Versailles, which was in a part of France then under German occupation, the birth of the German Empire was declared. King Wilhelm I of Prussia became German Emperor (or *Kaiser*) Wilhelm I. An ingenious combination of subtle diplomacy and naked force had worked to achieve German unification.

Germany was united as a constitutional monarchy in which all men had the right to vote for a popular legislature called the *Reichstag*. Germany's various states also retained some powers of self-government. Most real power, however, was still in the hands of the emperor, his *Junker* advisors, and the (highly conservative) army leadership. National unification appeased the German middle class, therefore, but it did not empower it.

Almost overnight, a new country had been born in the middle of Europe. Germany was now indisputably one of the great powers, and it had the potential to outstrip all of its neighbors in military and industrial strength. In many respects, the nineteenth century had belonged to the British. Would the twentieth century belong to Germany? That remained to be seen.

What was the historical significance of German unification?

The Triumph of Liberalism: Democracy Comes to Europe

One of the most important developments in Europe in the late nineteenth century was the extension of the right to vote, at least in most countries, to all men, regardless of income or social class. Universal male suffrage was a huge step toward democracy, although at this stage women were still excluded from the franchise. *Bourgeois* politicians took this leap of faith, extending the right to vote to peasants and workers, largely because liberalism taught that it was the right thing to do—and common sense suggested that the poor would be far less menacing as voters than as potential revolutionaries!

Britain led the way throughout the nineteenth century in extending the right to vote to increasing numbers of people. By 1884, Britain had enfranchised the majority of its male citizens for the first time, including millions of workers, and in the early twentieth century universal male suffrage was secured.

Politics in Britain during the second half of the nineteenth century was dominated by a contest for power between the Conservative and Liberal parties. For most of the 1860s, 1870s, and 1880s, the two parties' respective leaders, Benjamin Disraeli and William Gladstone, alternated in the office of Prime Minister. The Conservatives generally supported the powers and privileges of the traditional elite as well as a strong role for government in guiding the economy and protecting workers' rights. The Liberals supported liberal goals such as free trade, the expansion of voting rights, low taxes, and limited government. It is important to note, however, that there were few serious ideological disagreements in British politics, much less instability or violence. Although they argued frequently, both the Liberals and Conservatives were committed to maintaining Britain's (now largely symbolic) monarchy, its empire, its commitment to individual liberty, and its brand of industrial capitalism.

Napoleon III's Second Empire, which lasted from 1852 to 1870 in France, achieved many social reforms as well as impressive economic and industrial growth, but it failed to attract strong popular support. When Prussian armies defeated French forces in the Franco-Prussian War of 1870–71, France's legislature renounced the empire and created a Third Republic, which extended voting rights to all male citizens.

The Third Republic faced many political challenges. First, it had to endure the Paris Commune of 1871, during which Parisian radicals took over the city and refused to submit to the new republican government in France. In the end, the Paris Commune was defeated at the cost of over 20,000 lives, and France was once again whole. It lost territory to the new German Empire in the peace settlement at the end of the Franco-Prussian War, though, and was forced to pay handsomely to end the German occupation of parts of France. This humiliation established a passionate French desire for revenge against Germany.

France faced yet another serious political crisis at the turn of the century. A Jewish officer in the French army, Captain Alfred Dreyfus, was convicted of espionage. Liberals and socialists in France came to believe that Dreyfus had been framed because of anti-Semitism, that is, hatred of the Jews, while conservatives defended his conviction. A political firestorm developed over the Dreyfus Affair that eventually led to a presidential pardon and Dreyfus's vindication in a civilian court. Many conservatives were embittered by this outcome.

France had struggled to define itself politically ever since 1789. Under the Third Republic, internal political disagreements would continue to be France's Achilles' heel.

As Western European and some Southern European countries were granting the right to vote to all male citizens during the late nineteenth century, countries in Central and Eastern Europe either avoided mass participation in politics altogether, as in Russia, or they introduced democracy without giving substantial power to the people's elected representatives.

In Germany, as we have seen, all men had the right to vote as soon as the empire was formed in 1871, but the will of the people, and liberal freedoms, were not always respected. At various times, Bismarck sponsored political persecution of socialists, Catholics, and ethnic minorities such as the Poles and the Danes. The elected legislature was also subordinated to the emperor, the Chancellor, and the *Junker* elite.

Although Bismarck was not a true believer in democracy or individual rights, he did come to realize that Germany's workers could not simply be ignored. In the 1880s, Germany led the way in Europe in enacting health insurance, accident insurance, and old age pensions for workers.

In 1890, Bismarck was fired as Chancellor by Germany's impetuous young Emperor Wilhelm II, who had succeeded to the throne in 1888. As Chapter 16 will show, Wilhelm's aggressive policies helped to provoke the First World War.

In Austria, advocates of democracy were frustrated by the continuing influence of the monarchy and by the country's ethnic diversity. Many Austrians feared democracy, because they predicted that it would encourage ethnic minority groups to make nationalist demands for independence. Indeed, in 1866–67, the Hungarian minority revolted, seeking internal self-government and equality with the German-speaking Austrians. In 1867, Austria's Emperor Franz Josef agreed to an *Ausgleich* ("Compromise") that literally renamed the country Austria-Hungary. The *Ausgleich* reconciled Austrians and Hungarians, but it left open the question of the ultimate fate of Austria-Hungary's many millions of Czech, Polish, Ruthenian, Romanian, Croat, Slovak, Serb, Slovene, and Italian subjects.

> *Why did so many European countries embrace universal male suffrage in the nineteenth and early twentieth centuries?*

The Rise of the Working Class, and the Formation of Trade Unions

At the end of the nineteenth century, the urban working class, especially factory workers, emerged as a powerful force in European politics. Previously, urban workers had intervened intermittently and largely ineffectively in European history. During the 1830s and 1840s, for example, in the midst of economic hard times in England, a movement called Chartism had emerged that pressed for democratic reforms. Ultimately, Chartism failed, largely because its working-class membership lost interest once economic conditions had improved.

By 1900, all this had changed, and workers had become numerous enough—and also knowledgeable and disciplined enough—to organize themselves into powerful trade unions, political parties, and ideological movements. Middle-Class Europe faced a serious test.

For the most part, the middle class defended its privileged position in society successfully, but it had to make compromises. In Russia, compromise proved impossible, and both the middle class and the conservative elite were swept aside by the Bolshevik Revolution of 1917.

Ever since the inception of the Industrial Revolution, a huge gap had existed between the wealth of the *bourgeoisie* and the poverty and desperation of the workers. Not only were workers' wages low (they barely covered rent and food, in most cases) but their working conditions in terms of hours, workplace safety, job security, and fringe benefits were often deplorable. The neighborhoods in which workers lived with their families were also overcrowded, violent, and unhealthy.

To make matters worse, conditions for some workers were deteriorating, thanks to a process known as proletarianization. Before the Industrial Revolution, many urban workers in Europe had been artisans, that is, skilled laborers or craftsmen who owned some of the tools of their trade, helped set their own working conditions, and hoped one day to become business owners themselves. By the end of the nineteenth century, though, many of these skilled laborers had been effectively replaced by machines that could do the same work far more efficiently and cheaply. These former artisans, as a consequence, were transformed into unskilled wage laborers, often factory workers, who relied on a capitalist businessman to provide the tools needed for production and to set all the conditions of work. They were also paid low wages and had few avenues for advancement.

The large pool of unskilled workers that toiled, especially in factories, at the end of the nineteenth century was known as the proletariat. Socialists viewed late nineteenth-century urban society as divided into two basic classes: the *bourgeoisie*, which owned capitalist enterprises and therefore benefited from industrial capitalism, and the proletariat, which worked for the *bourgeoisie* and received meager wages and exploitative treatment in return. Advocates for the working class began to suggest a number of remedies that could alleviate or eliminate this exploitation. One potential answer was unionization.

By the end of the nineteenth century, wage hikes, free public education, and improvements in urban living conditions had addressed some of the complaints of the working class, but the gulf between life for the middle class and life for the workers remained enormous. One of the most successful approaches to improving wages and working conditions for the new proletariat was the formation of trade unions, which are organizations of workers who negotiate collectively with their employers for better treatment.

Given the effectiveness of trade unions, it should come as no surprise that many *bourgeois* businessmen initially opposed the union movement. Prominent capitalists argued that unions artificially interfered with the mechanisms of the free market. For much of the nineteenth century, *bourgeois* politicians ensured that trade unions were illegal in most European countries. Toward the end of the century, though, Britain, France, Germany, and many other European states legalized union activity. The grievances of the workers were so widely accepted, and the danger of revolution if those grievances were ignored was so great, that even many businessmen accepted unions as a necessary evil.

By the twentieth century, powerful coalitions of trade unions had emerged in several European countries, such as the Trades Union Congress in Britain and the *Confédération Général du Travail* in France. By 1900, more than two million workers in Britain were unionized. Skilled workers were the first to join, but eventually many unskilled workers did too. Male workers were always more likely than their female counterparts to join unions. Historically, in fact, many unions were openly hostile to women, who they saw as a source of economic competition for men.

Trade unions differed in their tactics, but the ultimate weapon of most unions was the strike. The general strike, in which workers from a number of major industries refused to work simultaneously, was a particularly potent weapon in the hands of the union movement.

What was the relationship between trade unions and the proletariat?

Socialism and Communism

Some Europeans did not see trade unions as a sufficient response to the exploitation associated with the capitalist system. More radical workers, and their allies within the middle class, favored socialism.

Socialism is the idea that economic life should be characterized by cooperation rather than competition, and that many economic enterprises should be publicly owned and controlled. Socialism is also characterized by dedication to the interests of ordinary people, skepticism toward the profit motive, and a desire to achieve greater equality in the distribution of wealth. In the late nineteenth century, socialists concentrated their ire on the *bourgeoisie*. Socialists referred to the accumulated wealth of the *bourgeoisie* (made up of machines, buildings, raw materials, land, etc.) as "capital" or the "means of production." The redistribution of capital, or the placement of the means of production in public hands, was, and remains, the core objective of socialism.

Before the second half of the nineteenth century, there were a variety of socialist movements, including forms of agrarian and utopian socialism, but these were largely ineffective. However, once workers acquired the right to vote, and once socialism adapted itself to modern conditions, including industrialization and urbanization, socialists were able to form political parties that sometimes acquired mass support.

The Labor Party in Great Britain, formed in 1906, sought recognition of the right of workers to strike; improved wages, social services, and benefits for workers; and, in theory, government ownership of the economy. It accomplished the first two goals, but gradually lost sight of the third. Even though the Labor Party won few seats in Parliament before the 1920s, it still had a major impact on British politics.

In Germany, the most important socialist organization to emerge was the Social Democratic Party, known by its German initials SPD (for *Sozialdemokratische Partei Deutschlands*.) The SPD was formed in 1875 and was somewhat more extreme than the Labor Party in Britain. During the 1870s and 1880s, Bismarck persecuted the SPD, which he, along with many conservatives and liberals in Germany, viewed as revolutionary. When the SPD continued to increase its share of the popular vote, however, Bismarck largely abandoned his anti-socialist crusade.

In 1891, the SPD committed itself to a new plan of action known as the Erfurt Program. The SPD declared in the Erfurt Program that it opposed capitalism, but it would not seek to overthrow the *bourgeois*, capitalist system by violent means. This opened up a major rift between moderate socialists in Germany, who supported the SPD and the Erfurt Program, and radicals, who still wanted revolution. Most radicals became communists.

Communism, the most extreme form of socialism, was a small movement at the end of the nineteenth century. In simple terms, communism is the belief in an economic system in which private property is eliminated and all businesses are owned and controlled by the state. Because the goals of communism were so ambitious, most communists rejected any possibility of cooperating with the *bourgeois* establishment. Instead, they advocated revolution.

Modern communism relies heavily on the ideas of Karl Marx, the most influential socialist thinker of all time, and the founder of communism. Marx was a German middle-class intellectual (not a worker, as one might suppose) from a family with Jewish origins. His Jewish roots would later become important to many anti-Semites, who viewed communism as a Jewish plot. Marx proposed a completely systematic version of radical socialism that he dubbed "communism." He did so in the *Communist Manifesto*, which he and co-author Friedrich Engels published in 1848. Marx's followers are usually known either as communists or as Marxists.

According to Marx, nineteenth-century history was dominated by conflict between the *bourgeoisie* and the proletariat. Only the *bourgeoisie*, because of its ownership of capital, was in a position to benefit from economic growth. The *bourgeoisie*, however, was growing ever smaller, said Marx, because a tiny number of rich industrialists, merchants, and financiers were hoarding more and more wealth to themselves. Meanwhile, the proletariat was growing ever larger, and the gap between the rich and poor kept increasing.

Marx predicted that eventually the proletariat would grow so large and so angry that revolution would result. The *bourgeoisie* would then be overthrown and eradicated, private property would be abolished, and a perfect egalitarian society would arise. In this new communist golden age, even the desire to exploit one's fellow man would be unthinkable. Traditional religion, which Marx viewed as a *bourgeois* illusion, would also disappear. Marx backed his analysis with carefully chosen references to the ideas of previous thinkers, while also giving his pronouncements a scientific gloss. To many Europeans, his arguments appeared very convincing.

In retrospect, historians know today that many of Marx's claims about the nineteenth-century economy were false. Wages and working conditions for the proletariat were not getting worse—they were getting better. The middle class was not shrinking—it was rapidly expanding. Ownership of capital was not restricted to a few lucky millionaires. On the contrary, increasingly, many members of the middle class and some workers possessed stock, insurance policies, and other investments that made them part owners of the capitalist system. In addition, government actions to improve the educational opportunities, and housing of the working class made communist revolution unlikely. Perhaps most importantly, the proletariat was not united as a revolutionary class—it was instead riven by divisions based on skills, income, ethnicity, age, gender, regional background, education, ideology, union affiliation, and religion.

In most European countries, the *bourgeois* establishment could afford to laugh at the radical slogans of the communists. In Russia, though, communism would emerge as a deadly serious threat to the *status quo*.

Why is communism considered to be an extreme form of socialism?

The Last Days of Tsarist Russia, and the Rise of the Bolsheviks

By the time Tsar Nicholas II took the throne in 1894, Russia was socially and economically one of the most dynamic countries in Europe. In 1861, Russia's serfs had been freed, at long last. Millions of them were now streaming into the cities to toil in factories and businesses, and their hard work helped to enrich a growing middle class. Russia's population and economy were both booming. Between 1880 and 1917, Russia's population grew from 100 million to 182 million. Meanwhile, economic growth was over three percent per year and foreign investment surged—facts symbolized by the completion of the mighty Trans-Siberian railway in 1916.

Russia's social and economic progress, though, was not matched by political reforms. The government remained an absolute monarchy, and the democratic institutions that had blossomed in the rest of Europe were almost completely absent.

Because of the activity of the Tsar's secret police, the opposition had no choice but to organize in secret. One group, called the Populists, believed that Russia needed to recapture the traditional, communal way of life of its peasants. Another group, the Social Democratic Party, brought communism to Russia. A third group, called the Constitutional Democrats, or Kadets, favored liberalism.

Ultimately, the Social Democrats would be the most successful of these movements for change. One of their leaders, Vladimir Illich Ulyanov, known as Lenin, founded the Bolshevik faction of the Social Democratic Party in 1903. It was the Bolsheviks who would assume control over Russia after the October Revolution of 1917, which created the world's first communist state.

Lenin came from a middle-class family. As a young man, he was strongly influenced by the execution of his older brother Alexander for participating in a plot to assassinate the Tsar. Lenin became a convinced Marxist, who believed strongly in the violent overthrow of the Tsarist government, the complete destruction of the *bourgeoisie*, and the elimination of private property. Nonetheless, to people who met him, Lenin often came across as an amiable intellectual rather than as a revolutionary firebrand.

Importantly, Lenin added two new elements to Marxist thought—and thus the resulting ideology was sometimes called Marxism-Leninism. Lenin believed that the working class itself could not lead a revolution. It required a dedicated group of highly intelligent and organized professionals, called a revolutionary vanguard, to direct it. Lenin's other revision to traditional Marxist theory was his suggestion that, because both groups were oppressed in Russia, workers and peasants should unite to seek a communist revolution. Marx, on the other hand, had ignored and even insulted peasants.

In the early years of the twentieth century, it seemed unlikely that Lenin would ever get a chance to lead Russia, because he was in exile. Moreover, the government of the Tsar clung stubbornly to power, despite an abortive democratic revolution in 1905. As we shall see in Chapter 16, however, World War I would produce major changes in the political landscape that would give Lenin and his Bolsheviks a golden opportunity to seize power and create a communist regime. Europe would never be the same again.

What important modifications did Lenin make to Marxism?

Conclusions

The rise of communism was a warning sign to Middle-Class Europe as a whole, but it did not signal the death knell of *bourgeois* rule everywhere. Middle-class governments, once they recognized the great danger that working-class discontent and socialist and communist propaganda entailed, worked hard to win over the workers to, as they saw it, more responsible forms of political, social, and economic organization. Liberalism, capitalism, nationalism, conservatism, and a host of other "isms" all competed for the loyalty of the working class. Luckily for the *bourgeoisie*, Europe's workers never united behind the ideology of Karl Marx.

As the twentieth century dawned, Europe was experiencing a dizzying pace of change, and the rise of nationalism, democracy, trade unionism, socialism, and communism could only partly explain this sense of dislocation. The next chapter will consider other important changes in European society and intellectual life.

Little did most Europeans know that, as confusing and frightening as the early years of the new century sometimes were, the future they were facing—two catastrophic world wars in a 30-year span—was considerably worse.

Key Terms for Chapter 14

Cult of Domesticity—a mainly nineteenth-century point of view asserting that home and family are the natural and proper domains of women.

Kingdom of Italy, 1861—Italy, the first new major power created by nineteenth-century nationalism, was brought into being by the Piedmontese politician Count Camillo Cavour.

Otto von Bismarck—the Prussian, and later German, Chancellor who led the process of German unification.

Franco-Prussian War, 1870–71—a war provoked by Bismarck in order to bring all the German states under Prussian control.

German Unification, 1871—after their victory over France, the German people united under the banner of the German Empire, led by a *Kaiser*, that is, emperor.

Third Republic, 1870–1940—after the Franco-Prussian War, the Second Empire was replaced with a republican government that endured until Hitler's invasion of France in World War II.

Dreyfus Affair—one of many political crises to affect the Third Republic. It centered on accusations of spying made against a Jewish army officer.

Trade unions—organizations of workers who negotiate collectively with their employers.

Socialism—an economic system or ideology that stresses the importance of cooperation, as well as the need for public ownership of large parts of the economy.

Social Democratic Party (SPD)—a major political party in Germany starting in the 1870s, and one of the most successful moderate socialist parties in all of Europe.

Communism—the most extreme form of socialism, advocating an end to private property. Communism is also known as Marxism, after its founder, Karl Marx.

Nicholas II—Tsar of Russia from 1894 to 1917. Opposed to serious reforms, he was overthrown and eventually executed.

Lenin—leader of the Bolsheviks, a group of Russian communists, and from 1917 to 1924 the head of Russia's new communist government.

Review Questions for Chapter 14

1. Describe two ways in which middle-class life in the nineteenth century was similar to middle-class life today. Describe two ways in which it was different.
2. In general, do you believe that German unification was a positive or a negative development? Discuss two ways in which twentieth-century history would have been different if Germany had never been unified.
3. Democracy, in the form of universal male suffrage, came to Europe in the second half of the nineteenth century. What do you believe is the best argument in favor of democracy? What is the best argument against it?
4. Imagine that you are an impoverished factory worker living in the second half of the nineteenth century. Which of the following "isms"—conservatism, liberalism, nationalism, trade unionism, socialism, or communism—would you have found most attractive? Which one would you have found least attractive? Explain your selections.

5. Describe two reasons why some Europeans were adamantly opposed to socialism and communism in the late nineteenth century. Then describe two reasons why some Europeans strongly favored these new "isms."

Further Reading

Auerbach, Jeffrey A. *The Great Exhibition of 1851: A Nation on Display*. New Haven, CT: Yale University Press. 1999.

Cahm, Eric. *The Dreyfus Affair in French Society and Politics*. New York: Longman. 1996.

Gay, Peter. *Schnitzler's Century: The Making of Middle-Class Culture, 1815–1914*. New York: Norton. 2002.

Hearder, Harry. *Italy: A Short History*. Cambridge: Cambridge University Press. 2001.

Hewitson, Mark. *Nationalism in Germany, 1848–1866: Revolutionary Nation*. Basingstoke, UK: Palgrave Macmillan. 2010.

Kitchen, Martin. *A History of Modern Germany, 1800–2000*. Malden, MA: Blackwell. 2010.

McLellan, David. *Karl Marx: A Biography*. New York: Palgrave Macmillan. 2014.

Mitchell, Sally. *Daily Life in Victorian England*. Westport, CT: Greenwood Press. 2009.

Nord, Philip. *The Republican Moment: Struggles for Democracy in Nineteenth-Century France*. Cambridge, MA: Harvard University Press. 1998.

Pelling, Henry and Alastair J. Reid. *A Short History of the Labour Party*. Twelfth Edition. Basingstoke, UK: Palgrave Macmillan. 2005.

Read, Christopher. *Lenin: A Revolutionary Life*. New York: Routledge. 2005.

Saunders, Robert. *Democracy and the Vote in British Politics, 1848–1867: The Making of the Second Reform Act*. New York: Routledge. 2016.

Schulze, Hagen. *The Course of German Nationalism: From Frederick the Great to Bismarck, 1763–1867*. Cambridge: Cambridge University Press. 2003.

Wetzel, David. *A Duel of Giants: Bismarck, Napoleon III, and the Origins of the Franco-Prussian War*. Madison, WI: University of Wisconsin Press. 2002.

15 Industrialization, Imperialism, and Intellectual and Social Change, 1850–1914

Introduction

In the late nineteenth and early twentieth centuries, Europe's industrial and technological lead over the rest of the world was greater than ever before or since. Moreover, Europeans were ruthless in utilizing that industrial and technological edge to dominate "lesser" peoples in Africa and Asia. The result was a renewed wave of European conquest known as the "New Imperialism." At the same time, important intellectual, cultural, and social changes were percolating in Europe that would contribute to the creation of a more recognizably modern mind-set. Europe in the years before 1914 was as confident and powerful as ever, but its priorities and self-image were rapidly changing.

The Second Industrial Revolution and the Growing Pace of Urbanization

From 1850 to 1914, an intensification of the process of industrialization occurred in Europe that is often termed the Second Industrial Revolution. It is distinguished from the first phase of the Industrial Revolution, lasting from 1750 to 1850, in two ways.

First, the initial Industrial Revolution was centered on Britain, whereas the Second Industrial Revolution created new industrial powerhouses such as Germany, the United States, and Russia. By 1913, Germany slightly outpaced Britain in industrial production. Meanwhile, the largest industrial power in the world was the United States. Even countries in Southern and Eastern Europe were starting to industrialize. The extensive geographic scope of the Second Industrial Revolution led, in turn, to a huge expansion in international trade.

The second major distinction between the two phases of industrialization in Europe is that, from 1750 to 1850, industry had focused on the production of textiles, iron, steam engines, and railways. The Second Industrial Revolution, by contrast, expanded into new areas such as steel, the internal combustion engine (leading eventually to the automobile), chemicals, and electricity.

Steel, a metal alloy that is stronger than iron, was first produced on an industrial scale after innovations in metallurgy pioneered by the Englishman Sir Henry Bessemer in the 1850s. Steel had numerous applications, but its use in building construction was especially important. Before the 1880s, it was virtually impossible to build any structure over six stories tall. Once buildings could be constructed with steel frames, however, the modern skyscraper was born. As elevators and central heating were added, skyscrapers became increasingly popular.

Steel could also be turned to more destructive uses. Long before the outbreak of the First World War in 1914, the German Krupp family was famous for its steel foundries and its massive factories that produced high-tech weapons, especially artillery.

Equally significant was the invention of the internal combustion engine, which by 1886 was powering primitive motor cars designed to run on gasoline, refined from petroleum. By 1914, automobiles were rapidly replacing horse-drawn transportation in Europe and North America, thanks in part to the highly efficient factory-line system of production that the trailblazing American automaker Henry Ford had developed. Ford was a generous but demanding employer. He doubled his workers' salaries, but he also scrutinized their private lives—even pressuring them to spend their Saturday nights square dancing!

In 1903, a gasoline-powered internal combustion engine lifted the first airplane into the skies. As the internal combustion engine caught on, the oil industry surged. In those days, the world's leading oil producers were the United States, Russia, and Romania.

It was in Germany that the modern chemical industry first boomed, leading to the development of new dyes, fertilizers, and plastics. One of the most intriguing new applications for plastics in the early twentieth century was in creating film for motion pictures. The invention of modern chemical explosives would also prove historic. The discoverer of dynamite, Alfred Nobel, a Swede, felt so guilty for unleashing such awesome destructive potential on the world that he created and funded the Nobel Prize Committee.

Arguably the most important innovation of the Second Industrial Revolution was the use of electricity as a source of power. Scientists and engineers had known about electricity at least since the eighteenth century. It was only during the 1880s, though, that it became practical for electrical power to be used in homes and businesses. Before long, thanks to Thomas Edison's invention of the light bulb, candles and gas-lit lamps had become obsolete. In addition, electrically powered laborsaving devices such as refrigerators, vacuum cleaners, and washing machines transformed daily life for Europeans and Americans alike (although housework remained overwhelmingly a female responsibility). Electricity also made it possible to communicate over long distances. By 1866, a message could be sent between London and New York via an undersea telegraph line. Telephones gradually became commonplace in the homes of the well-to-do, while an Italian, Guglielmo Marconi, pioneered wireless telegraphy, which would evolve into radio.

During the early phases of industrialization, before 1850, life for workers in Europe's cities had been, by any standard, miserable. Overcrowding, crime, disease, harsh working conditions, and the lack of educational and social services combined to create despair and, occasionally, revolutionary violence.

After 1850, during the Second Industrial Revolution, many cities undertook major efforts to improve conditions for the poor. Gas and electric lighting networks, subsidized housing developments, expanded public education systems, better law enforcement, public water and sewage systems, and the enforcement of building standards and health codes all made life easier for many working-class families. What is remarkable about these reforms is that they came about in a period when the populations of major European cities were surging, thanks to an influx of not just factory workers but also office workers, retail clerks, domestic servants, middle-class professionals, and others. By 1914, London was still by far the most populous city in Europe, with over seven million inhabitants, but Berlin, Moscow, Paris, St. Petersburg, and Vienna had all passed the one million mark.

Thanks to the construction of trams and underground railways, residential areas increasingly shifted toward the suburbs. City centers were given over to major retailers, offices, government buildings, parks, libraries, museums, and theaters. Despite the persistence of slum conditions in some areas, most of Europe's cities became showcases for industrial growth, architectural splendor, and cultural vitality. By 1914, the majority of Britons, Frenchmen, and Germans lived in cities, and those cities were more dynamic and prosperous than ever before.

How did the second phase of the Industrial Revolution, 1850–1914, differ from the first, 1750–1850?

The New Imperialism

In addition to fostering urbanization, Europe's industrial progress allowed it to expand its control over large areas of Africa and Asia between 1880 and 1914. This so-called New Imperialism followed a lull in Europe's acquisition of additional overseas colonies that had lasted for most of the nineteenth century. Scholars talk of European colonialism in the fifteenth through the early nineteenth centuries as producing an interconnected Atlantic World. Starting with the New Imperialism, though, scholars usually talk instead about globalization. From a world-systems perspective (see Chapter 11), one might say that at this stage the core (i.e., rich) countries of the West succeeded in expanding the list of poor and exploited countries in the periphery to include virtually the entire globe.

By the end of the nineteenth century, Europe's industrial and technological might made a renewed campaign of conquest seem easily achievable. Improvements in steamship technology allowed Europeans to traverse African river systems for the first time. Rapid communication via telegraph lines allowed European governments and armies to coordinate their subjugation

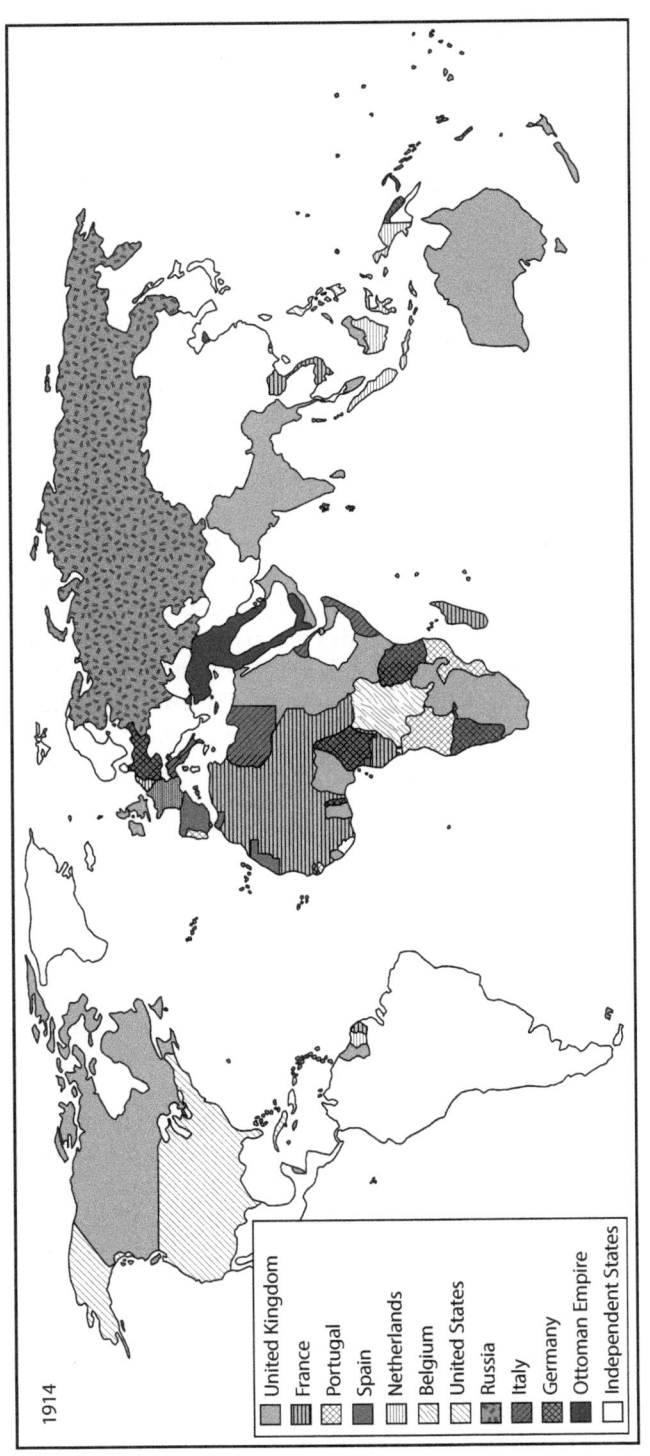

Map 15.1 Global empires in the Age of the New Imperialism, circa 1914.

of weaker native states. The development of quinine to combat malaria made it possible for Europeans to live in tropical areas that previously had been off-limits. Perhaps most importantly, improvements in firearms technology allowed Europeans to obliterate native resistance. The Maxim gun, a rudimentary form of machine gun, was already mowing down Africans by 1893.

All these technological advances made European domination of Africa and Asia *possible*, but they do not explain why Europeans went out of their way to expand their overseas possessions. After all, many Europeans argued that conquering and governing "inferior" peoples was expensive and unnecessary, so why bother?

One reason was population expansion in Europe itself. Between 1850 and 1900, most European countries experienced population growth of 40–60 percent. Europe's cities could absorb only so many surplus workers, and, even for the middle class, life was becoming increasingly hectic and competitive. Many politicians, therefore, suggested that encouraging some people to settle overseas was the answer. In reality, however, most Europeans who emigrated left for the Americas, not for colonies in Africa or Asia. Between 1850 and 1930, more than 50 million Europeans emigrated, the majority of them to a single country: the United States.

Another reason for the New Imperialism was the pressure that Christian missionaries placed on European governments to provide security for their work overseas. Missionaries were often among the first European explorers and settlers in Africa and Asia. The European drive to Christianize these areas, although always controversial, was partially successful. Today, countries that were once colonies of Europe are home to hundreds of millions of Christians.

An additional motivator for the New Imperialism was fierce economic competition. European states often wanted colonies in order to secure access to raw materials as well as markets for the finished goods that European industry produced. This would, in turn, create economic growth and provide jobs for angry workers. In reality, while the economic argument for imperialism often seemed persuasive, there is strong evidence that most colonies were too underdeveloped to serve as strong markets for European goods. In fact, many newly acquired colonies required huge infusions of European investment in order to become minimally viable.

There was also a cultural argument for imperialism. Many Europeans felt a strong sense of superiority relative to Africans and Asians, who they commonly viewed as backward, cowardly, effeminate, unwashed, lazy, superstitious, lustful, ignorant, dishonest, and cruel. The French, for instance, tended to assume that their empire was built around a "civilizing mission," and that their colonial subjects would benefit from French education, technical expertise, and government. Meanwhile, Rudyard Kipling, a British apologist for imperialism, talked of the "White Man's Burden." Kipling suggested that, although natives would never appreciate European rule, they could still benefit from Western influences.

In many cases, European efforts to promote economic development, modern education, and medical advances among their colonial subjects did produce positive results. Numerous new roads, hospitals, and schools were built. Be that as it may, Europeans' sense of cultural superiority tended to produce a sense of racial superiority as well. Many Europeans sincerely believed that the weaknesses of African and Asian societies were due to racial factors. They explained European conquest as a natural and inherently just process that would teach natives their proper place.

Despite these various technological, demographic, religious, economic, and cultural explanations for the New Imperialism, the strongest explanation of all is essentially political and psychological. During the late nineteenth century, European states were forced to navigate through an increasingly competitive and unstable environment. The power balance in Europe had been shattered by the emergence of Italy and Germany as new nation-states. British dominance was fading, and countries such as the United States and Russia seemed destined to play major roles in twentieth-century history. Europe's dedication to peace, enshrined in the agreements made at the Congress of Vienna in 1814–15, seemed to be in rapid decline. Many Europeans believed that a major war, even a world war, was right around the corner.

As a consequence, the acquisition of new overseas colonies served a critical purpose. Even if it could be argued that most colonies were money-losers, any European state that acquired a large empire created the political and psychological impression that it was powerful, virile, and dynamic. In other words, it was the *image* of imperial greatness that mattered most. Few Europeans stopped during the age of the New Imperialism to weigh rationally all the costs and benefits of colonial expansion—they simply wanted "in" on the colonial game before all the best "prizes" were taken. They assumed, based on the British example, that imperial expansion equaled national prestige, power, and wealth. In retrospect, they were often mistaken.

What factors led to the New Imperialism, circa 1880 to 1914?

The Scramble for Africa and the Partition of Asia

So which European states carved out the largest empires? Before 1880, thanks to their naval and commercial preeminence, the British had already captured control over many of the most strategic points in Africa and Asia. In Africa, they occupied Egypt and thus controlled the Suez Canal, which linked the Mediterranean Sea to the Indian Ocean. They also controlled most of South Africa, its mineral wealth, and the critical sea-lanes surrounding it. In addition, Britain occupied Singapore, a vital Southeast Asian port, and India, which allowed Britain to dominate South Asia and much of the Middle East. Britain also controlled Australia and New Zealand. Imperialist expansion after 1880, therefore, by countries such as France, Germany, Italy, Spain, Portugal, and Belgium—and, eventually, Japan and the United

States—aimed largely at scooping up the territories that England had not already claimed.

The most famous example of the New Imperialism was the so-called Scramble for Africa, from about 1880 to 1900, during which virtually all of the continent was parceled out among the European powers. As recently as 1850, the European presence in Africa had been limited to a few small coastal trading stations, left over from the days of the transatlantic slave trade, which was largely abolished in the early nineteenth century. During the 1860s and 70s, however, European explorers began to chart the African interior. Many

Figure 15.1 Henry Morton Stanley, one of the most famous explorers of Africa in the nineteenth century.

Everett Historical/Shutterstock.

of them argued that the "savage" peoples that they encountered there could only benefit from European influences. Henry Morton Stanley was one of these intrepid explorers, who alternately studied and shot at the Africans in his path.

In 1884–85, at the Berlin Conference, European governments agreed on a process that would lead to the partition of Africa and, they claimed, would secure the "moral and material well-being" of the natives. Although antislavery and free-trade rhetoric prevailed at the Berlin Conference, its main purpose was the cynical division of African territory.

The race to establish African colonies was astoundingly swift. By the end of the nineteenth century, only two African countries, Liberia and Ethiopia, had preserved their independence. The rest of Africa was firmly under British, French, German, Italian, Belgian, Portuguese, and Spanish rule.

The exploitation that European colonialism unleashed was at times extreme. Some historians believe that the greedy and tyrannical rule of Belgium's King Leopold II in the vast Congo Free State, which was his personal property, caused a holocaust that killed ten million people. Despite a slick public relations campaign to justify his rule, Leopold's terrible treatment of the Africans, along with his scandalous affair with a French prostitute, caught up with him. The Belgian parliament took control of the colony in 1908. It was renamed the Belgian Congo.

Discrimination and segregation became common in colonial Africa. Some colonies, such as British-controlled Kenya, Rhodesia, and South Africa, and French-occupied Algeria, became popular destinations for European settlers. Not surprisingly, relations between the settlers and the natives tended to be poor. Many whites insisted on denying economic opportunities and basic rights to Africans. In the Kenyan Highlands, for example, the best farmland was reserved for whites, and Africans were compelled to become laborers by a strict tax code and a Masters and Servants Ordinance. Algeria, meanwhile, because of its large white population, was legally defined as part of France. Its indigenous population, however, was denied political influence. In other parts of Africa, racial discrimination was less of an issue, because the white settler community was small or nonexistent. In these areas, often Western rule could only be maintained by compromising with the native elite.

As Africa came under European control, so did large parts of Asia. When Ottoman power began to recede in the Persian Gulf, the British eagerly stepped in. Britain and Russia also shared informal domination of Persia, today known as Iran, while most of the major European powers demanded special privileges in China, which was still technically independent. Much of Asia, though, was fully subordinated to Europeans. The Dutch ruled Indonesia, and the French conquered Vietnam.

Most famously, India became the "Jewel in the Crown" of the British Empire. There, British settlers and administrators, who were less than one percent of the population, successfully dominated a proud civilization, thanks largely to their technological superiority and their ability to exploit ethnic and religious divisions. True, a mutiny briefly imperiled British rule in 1857, but, after a few months, British forces, supported by loyal native *sepoys* (soldiers), reestablished colonial control. They were not subtle in their methods. The rebels in Cawnpore, for instance, who had herded the European women and children of the town into a brothel where they were butchered *en masse*, were forced, before they were hanged, to lick the blood of their victims from the floor.

In the western Pacific, a major rivalry was brewing between Japan and the United States. Japan had made the momentous decision in 1868 to modernize and Westernize in order to avoid falling victim to European imperialism. As a result, Japan built strong industries and an equally formidable army and navy. Japan defeated China in 1895 and Russia in 1905, and as a consequence built its own large empire that included Korea, Taiwan, small parts of China, and many Pacific islands.

The late nineteenth-century mania for imperialism also seduced the United States. In 1898, the United States won a war with Spain and purchased, at gunpoint, Spain's colony in the Philippines. This put Japan and the United States on a collision course in Southeast Asia and the western Pacific. One might say, therefore, that the New Imperialism helped to sow the seeds not just for World War I, but for World War II as well.

Which parts of the world fell under European control during the age of the New Imperialism?

Scientific Progress, and Darwin's Theory of Evolution by Natural Selection

During the Second Industrial Revolution, public interest in science greatly increased, as did government support for scientists. Ironically, science itself also became far more analytically and mathematically complex, so that, to the average person, many scientific theories were incomprehensible.

In chemistry, the famous Periodic Table of the Elements was formulated, and many new industrial applications for chemical knowledge were developed, while in physics radiation was discovered and explained by scientists such as Henri Becquerel, Ernest Rutherford, and Marie Curie. The atom, which had previously been seen as indivisible, was found to have several components, and Albert Einstein and other physicists speculated that splitting atoms could potentially unleash huge amounts of energy. Thus, the seeds for nuclear power and nuclear weaponry were sown in the Victorian Age.

In geology, Charles Lyell used fossil evidence to help prove that the Earth was much older than previously thought. He demonstrated that natural processes such as erosion and volcanic eruption could explain the surface features of the Earth, and therefore God had not instantaneously created these features in 4004 BCE, as many Christians believed.

In medicine, Louis Pasteur developed the bacteriological theory of disease. He also invented numerous vaccines. Meanwhile, anesthesia and the sterilization of medical instruments greatly improved the safety and effectiveness of surgical procedures.

The most important and controversial scientific discovery of the nineteenth century was Charles Darwin's theory of evolution by natural selection. Darwin was, to say the least, a very systematic thinker. In 1838, he carefully considered the pros and cons of matrimony: a wife would be a "constant companion . . . better than a dog anyhow," but she would also mean "less money for books." In the end, he married.

In 1839, Darwin published a book based on an earlier sea voyage to the Galapagos Islands, off the coast of Ecuador. In it, he marveled at the diversity of species he had encountered there, and he began to speculate on how those species had evolved, or changed, over time. In 1859, after a period of reflection (some would say procrastination), and after a long detour into the study of barnacles, Darwin published another book called *The Origin of Species*. It laid out a simple theory that explained how evolution might work.

Darwin claimed that every species produces too many offspring to survive in the environment. There is thus a fierce competition for food and other resources that only the strongest organisms can win. These organisms survive and reproduce, and their superior characteristics endure in future generations and thus influence the evolution of the species. The inferior characteristics of weaker organisms, however, are not preserved, because the organisms themselves die off. Thus, evolution is dictated by an automatic process by which nature "selects" which characteristics and organisms are best adapted to the environment. Decades later, biologists and chemists suggested that genes and DNA might be the cause of the different characteristics that organisms exhibit.

Darwin's theory of evolution by natural selection had revolutionary implications, which he, who had once trained to become an Anglican priest, readily understood. Publishing his ideas was "like confessing a murder," he wrote. Darwin did not shrink from controversy, however, and in 1871 he followed up his *Origin of Species* with a new book, *The Descent of Man*, that outlined how human beings, and even their religious sensibilities, had been created by natural selection.

Many Victorians were outraged. Darwin's account of the creation of human life denied God any significant role, and it contradicted the teachings of the Bible. Moreover, if man was the product of natural selection, then he was not made in the image of God, but, more accurately, in the image of apes. Many Victorians caricatured Darwin as a fool for believing that apes could ever evolve into human beings. They also questioned what the purpose of human life could be if a cold, mechanistic process of nature had created it. These issues remain controversial to this day. Darwin himself, one of the greatest scientists of all time, was refused a knighthood by Queen Victoria because the Church of England opposed it.

Although Darwin was widely hated, many Victorians praised him. Some even sought to apply a garbled version of his idea of natural selection to society as a whole. Social Darwinism was a movement that advocated unrestrained competition in economics and society to permit the "strong" to dominate, and the "weak" to perish. These ideas seemed to justify the subjugation of the poor, of women, and of natives in Africa and Asia by "fitter" individuals, who were coincidentally the same white, upper- and middle-class men who had created the Social Darwinist movement in the first place. Importantly, Darwin himself opposed many Social Darwinist ideas.

What were the most significant innovations in science during the nineteenth century?

The Questioning of Religion, and the Emergence of Psychoanalysis

Darwinism, and the rise of science more generally, was a powerful challenge to the influence of traditional religion during the nineteenth century, but there were other forces at work leading to a decline in Europe's Christian faith. First, millions of urban workers and their family members lived in an environment where the Christian message was not usually heard, because the infrastructure of Christianity was still located primarily in the countryside. Increasingly, therefore, many residents of urban areas became thoroughly secularized. One symptom of this transformation was a spectacular rise in the percentage of illegitimate births, especially in the working class.

Second, strong voices among intellectuals and politicians were attacking Christianity directly. Writers like the philosopher Friedrich Nietzsche argued that Christianity's emphasis on self-denial contradicted the human need to be proud and assertive. Nietzsche called Christianity a "slave religion," and he proclaimed the "death of God." Meanwhile, historians like Ernst Renan questioned the accuracy of the Bible and suggested that early authorities of the Catholic Church had written and revised it for selfish purposes. In addition, many politicians and social critics viewed Christianity as a traditionalist creed that distracted the masses from more important priorities. Marx famously compared religion to an addictive and debilitating drug. This drumbeat of criticism directed toward Christianity had a cumulative effect: some Europeans abandoned the Church, while others remained nominally Christian while downgrading the importance of faith in their lives.

The most serious challenge that Christianity faced came not from intellectuals, but from governments. Throughout the nineteenth and early twentieth centuries, *bourgeois* governments struggled to build public unity and to achieve the goals of middle-class movements such as liberalism and nationalism, which were largely secular. In France, for instance, liberals often viewed the Catholic Church as an intransigent force opposed to positive reforms. They noted that the Church had sided with the monarchy during the French Revolution, and subsequently with tyrants such as Napoleon and his nephew, Napoleon III. In 1905, anti-clerical forces won a great victory when church and state were legally separated in France for the first time since the Revolution.

The Catholic Church faced similar challenges in Germany. During the 1870s, Bismarck persecuted Catholics, not because of any liberal inclinations on his part, but because of his desire to solidify German nationalism. He believed that the loyalty of some Germans to the pope might weaken their allegiance to the German emperor. Bismarck's anti-Catholic campaign, called the *Kulturkampf* (Cultural Struggle) was a failure, and he ultimately abandoned the effort, but all across Europe the Church felt that it was under siege.

In 1870, the pope responded to the widespread hostility to traditional religion by proclaiming the idea of Papal Infallibility, which asserted that, whenever the pope formulates Catholic doctrine under the inspiration of the Holy Spirit, he is not subject to error. In the increasingly secular environment of the nineteenth century, this was a claim that even many Catholics shrugged off. Although the vast majority of Europeans remained practicing Christians before the First World War, organized religion was clearly facing a crisis.

In 1886, a Jewish doctor in Vienna named Sigmund Freud began a medical practice that specialized in treating hysteria, that is, mental illness. Freud at first experimented with some of the most daring treatments of his day, including hypnosis and the prescription of cocaine, but gradually he came to the conclusion that no existing approach to the treatment of mental illness was sufficient. Instead, he invented his own approach to the study of the mind that he called psychoanalysis. It rested on three central assumptions.

First, Freud argued that sexual desires are at the core of human psychology, and the mental state of all human beings, even infants and children, is dictated by their struggle either to fulfill or to repress their sexual needs. Second, Freud suggested that the human mind is far less rational than many Enlightenment thinkers had supposed. Instead, vast regions of human thought and emotion are buried beneath the surface, within what Freud called the unconscious. This unconscious can only be unlocked through the analysis of dreams, or by careful, prolonged investigation into a person's past experiences. Lastly, Freud argued that the mind itself can be divided into three parts: the id, the ego, and the superego. The id Freud associated with man's instinctual, animal urges, such as the drive for sexual gratification. The superego, according to Freud, was the part of the mind that internalizes the values that one is taught by one's parents, peers, and society in general. The ego, then, is the part of the mind that mediates the battle between the id and the superego. It is a person's rational, conscious self that decides whether, in a given situation, he or she will give in to selfish drives, or what is considered socially responsible.

All of Freud's views were deeply controversial in the late nineteenth and early twentieth centuries, and they remain so today. Probably the most accepted of Freud's theories is his idea that the unconscious mind plays a major role in defining who we are. Freud's idea that all human beings—even infants and children—are sexual beings still scandalizes many psychologists and ordinary people alike, while his division of the human mind into the id, ego, and superego is often criticized as simplistic.

> *Why did many Christians in the nineteenth century feel that their religion was under siege?*

The Rising Tide of Racism and Anti-Semitism

Whereas the Enlightenment had tended to emphasize human similarities, nineteenth-century Romanticism taught people to value the differences between individuals and between groups. Not surprisingly, there was strong support in the Victorian era for nationalism, which taught that a person's ethnic background was the most important part of who he or she was.

As the nineteenth century drew to a close, the emphasis on nationalism and ethnic pride led many Europeans to become increasingly intolerant of anyone who did not share their particular ethnic heritage. At the same time, many scientists, especially biologists, were suggesting that racial factors might be the "key to world history," as British Prime Minister Benjamin Disraeli once put it. According to this view, the differences between groups were not merely cultural—they were biological and thus rooted in a person's blood. Racial conflicts were therefore increasingly seen as irresolvable, except by the domination or extermination of one race by another.

As these views were becoming common, economic hard times encouraged some intellectuals, journalists, and politicians to find scapegoats to blame. The Jews were a frequent target, as the Dreyfus Affair in France, discussed in Chapter 14, demonstrated. Simultaneously, many Europeans began to argue that the technological edge that white Europeans enjoyed over Africans and Asians, which was undeniable during the nineteenth century, was proof of Europeans' racial superiority. They suggested that white supremacy and white racial purity should be carefully maintained. Thus, by 1914, a strong movement in favor of anti-Semitism and racism existed in Europe, long before fascism or Nazism were ever conceived.

Although many forms of racism existed in the nineteenth and early twentieth centuries, ultimately the most influential was a movement called Aryanism. According to men such as Count Arthur de Gobineau and Houston Stewart Chamberlain, who invented the movement, the original Aryans were a group of racially pure, light-skinned whites who lived thousands of years ago and settled much of Europe and Asia. To support this claim, proponents of Aryanism cited historical evidence of a mother tongue that Aryans had introduced to regions as diverse as northern Europe, Iran, and India.

Believers in Aryanism, moreover, suggested that the Aryans were not merely a historical phenomenon; rather, their superior blood was the origin of all of the great achievements that humanity had ever made, and ever would make, in art, literature, science, technology, government, and many other fields. The defects in modern civilization, on the other hand, were caused solely by the fact that the Aryans had unwisely contaminated themselves by intermarrying with lesser races.

Houston Stewart Chamberlain was more specific than many other Aryanists about the problem of racial mixing and its potential solution. He suggested that the Jews were the chief source of racial contamination that had hurt the Aryan race in Europe. According to Chamberlain, controlling the threat that the Jews posed, and using eugenics to rebuild the purity of the Aryan race, offered the best hope of restoring the greatness of Aryan civilization. Importantly, Adolf Hitler and many other twentieth-century racists were deeply impressed by Chamberlain's arguments.

Aryanism condemned both non-Europeans and Jews to permanent inferiority, at best, and slavery and death, at worst. It should come as no surprise, therefore, that the conclusions of Aryanism, and other racist movements, were sharply resisted by many non-Europeans and Jews.

In Europe's colonies, such as British-ruled India, nationalist resistance movements disputed the claim that whites were superior, or were destined to rule the world (they also opposed claims that the natives themselves could be sorted into higher and lower racial groups). Starting in 1885, the Indian National Congress demanded that the British treat Indians and whites equally, and that they prepare India for eventual self-government. Some Europeans, notably socialists and communists, were sympathetic to this egalitarian and anti-colonialist agenda.

At the same time, Jews began to perceive the dangers that they faced from the rising tide of anti-Semitism. Hatred of the Jews had long roots in Europe. It had led, during the Middle Ages, to the expulsion of Jews from countries such as England, France, Spain, and Portugal—often because of religious, cultural, or economic resentments. During most of the nineteenth century, however, outside of Russia, European Jews had benefited from a movement known as Jewish Emancipation. It had produced a decrease in traditional prejudice against the Jews, and a growing acceptance of Jews as full citizens entitled to political and economic rights. By the 1880s, though, public attitudes toward Jews once again became hostile. In response, many Jews decided to join movements such as liberalism, socialism, and communism, which preached equality and tolerance. Other Jews chose to support a form of Jewish nationalism, called Zionism, that advocated the establishment of a Jewish homeland, perhaps in Israel. Few Jews, though, could imagine the horrors that lay in store for them during the 1930s and 1940s.

Why were racism and anti-Semitism on the rise toward the end of the nineteenth century?

The Emergence of Feminism, and the Dawn of Women's Suffrage

Feminism is the belief that women should enjoy equality, independence, and respect in society and in their relationships with men. Before the late nineteenth century, there were few Europeans of either sex who could realistically be called feminists. By the late 1800s, though, traditional patterns of male domination were on the decline. Public education reached girls as well as boys, and educated women, some of whom attended universities, increasingly demanded rights and opportunities that previous generations of women had lacked. At the same time, industry was creating new jobs for women—as telephone operators, retail clerks, and typists, for example. Some women were even able to support themselves as teachers, writers, nurses, or government workers.

In another sign of change, during the second half of the nineteenth-century women began to organize themselves politically to promote certain causes. Women's suffrage was high on the agenda, but improving access to health care and social services, achieving better treatment for the working class, enhancing education for women and girls, restricting the sale of alcohol, and abolishing prostitution were other common goals. Most female activists were of the urban middle class. All of them took on substantial risks by becoming politically active, since, by transgressing nineteenth-century gender norms, they were inviting ostracism, harassment, and sometimes imprisonment. Nevertheless, many reform movements led by women produced impressive results.

In Britain, Josephine Butler led a successful campaign to repeal the Contagious Diseases Acts, which had tacitly legalized prostitution and had subjected prostitutes to mandatory physical exams and medical treatment for venereal diseases. In 1885, a massive crowd of 250,000 people attended one of Butler's demonstrations. Progress for women also extended into family relationships, as women demanded and often received a stronger role in the management of their households and greater power over the rearing of their children. Many European women were also granted easier access to divorce and the right to own private property.

Despite all these victories for feminism before 1914, the Cult of Domesticity, which had argued that women should concentrate on private sphere of home and family, remained dominant throughout Europe. In fact, the organized resistance to feminism was often stronger than feminism itself.

Traditional gender roles were defended in a variety of ways. Many Victorian intellectuals and scientists, such as Charles Darwin and Sigmund Freud, emphatically opposed the idea that women and men were biologically equal. In addition, one of the most popular arguments against feminism was that it would destroy womanliness and femininity. Many Europeans also opposed feminism because of its connections to radical movements like socialism and communism. Finally, Almroth E. Wright, a crusader against feminism in Britain, spoke for many when he claimed that liberating women would lead to a decline of the military spirit. This would be especially dangerous, because a world war seemed to be looming.

Despite the vigorous campaign against feminism, female activists won further victories in the twentieth century, the most important of which was the right to vote. As early as 1869, a prominent British philosopher and politician, John Stuart Mill, had advocated complete equality between the sexes in a book called *The Subjection of Women*. Mill was a liberal who believed in the principle of equality of rights, but he also suggested that the only reason women had been sidelined for so long in Western societies was because men had the sheer muscle power to dominate women, and so they did—all their rationalizations were merely excuses.

Not surprisingly, it was in Britain, the most liberal country in Europe, that Mill's ideas found the most acceptance. Local voting rights were extended to women in 1869. Strong organizations to promote women's suffrage on the national level developed after 1900, including Emmeline Pankhurst's Women's Social and Political Union, which used vandalism, arson, and civil disobedience to pressure the government. These violent tactics failed to impress Parliament, but World War I proved to be a turning point for feminists. Almroth Wright's fear that women would stand in the way of Britain's military strength proved to be unfounded. On the contrary, women contributed so mightily to the war effort that, partly in gratitude, Parliament gave some women the vote in 1918.

The women's suffrage movement made similar progress in other parts of Europe. Even before the First World War, Norway and Finland had granted women the right to vote. Women were enfranchised in Germany in 1919, due in large part to the country's catastrophic defeat in World War I, which brought liberals and socialists to power. In France, Hubertine Auclert argued that women's suffrage would create a motherly state that would keep the peace internationally and provide more social services to the people. French women were finally granted the right to vote in 1944. Fascist Italy granted women the right to vote in local elections in 1925—and then banned local elections! Italian women would not receive full voting rights until 1945.

The Cult of Domesticity was shaken as a consequence of these historic developments, but it was not yet destroyed. In fact, as future chapters will make clear, in the interwar years and again in the post–World War II era, strong backlashes against feminism would emerge in many parts of Europe.

Why did so many Europeans resist the extension of new rights to women?

Conclusions

Europe had witnessed many jarring changes in the years leading up to the outbreak of the First World War, and yet the middle class retained a sunny optimism about Europe's future. After all, who could deny the rising standard of living? Who could ignore the manifold benefits of modern technology and scientific knowledge? Who did not feel a sense of pride as Europe flexed its muscles on the world stage, and non-Europeans were compelled to kneel and obey? And, in the final analysis, were not many of the cherished goals of the middle class, including individual liberty and national unity, steadily being achieved in most corners of Europe? It was, in short, a time perhaps to worry about the frightening pace of change, but it was also a time to exult in the continuing strength, vitality, and progress of Western Civilization.

Sadly, in August 1914, as British Foreign Secretary Sir Edward Grey put it, the lights went out all over Europe. Europe's prosperity and its self-confidence would be the first casualties of World War I.

Key Terms for Chapter 15

Second Industrial Revolution, 1850–1914—a continuation and expansion of the process of industrialization begun in the eighteenth century, involving new technologies and many new countries as industrial powers.

Electricity—a flexible source of power, and the most important innovation of the Second Industrial Revolution.

The New Imperialism, 1880–1914—a term describing Europeans' renewed interest in acquiring colonies in Africa and Asia, much of which fell under European rule.

Scramble for Africa—during a 20-year period at the end of the nineteenth century, virtually all of Africa was divided between various European powers.

Charles Darwin—a nineteenth-century British biologist who developed the controversial theory of evolution by natural selection.

Sigmund Freud—the father of psychoanalysis, a new approach to understanding human psychology and to treating mental illness.

Unconscious—Freud's new field of psychoanalysis assumed the existence of vast regions of the human mind that were irrational and hard to access.

Anti-Semitism—hatred of the Jews, which had existed in Europe for centuries, but which was increasing by the late nineteenth century.

Aryanism—a white supremacist ideology that was popular in Europe during the nineteenth and twentieth centuries.

Feminism—the belief that women should enjoy equality, independence, and respect in society and in their relationships with men.

Women's suffrage—voting rights for women, obtained in most European countries in the first half of the twentieth century.

Review Questions for Chapter 15

1. Describe three ways in which the Second Industrial Revolution was different from the forms of industrialization that occurred before 1850.

2. Imagine that it is the late nineteenth century, and you live in an area in Africa or Asia that is in danger of falling under European control. Write a letter to the leader of whichever European country has its eye on your homeland. Provide at least three good reasons why he would be wise to resist the temptation to add your land and its people to his country's empire.
3. Ever since Charles Darwin offered up his theory of evolution by natural selection, it has excited great controversy. First, summarize Darwin's theory. Then give your opinion as to whether it is compatible with Christianity or not.
4. Which element of Freudian psychology do you find most persuasive? Which element do you find least persuasive? Explain your views.
5. Describe two reasons why many Europeans became feminists in the late nineteenth century. Then, describe two reasons why many Europeans opposed feminism.

Further Reading

Abernethy, David B. *The Dynamics of Global Dominance: European Overseas Empires, 1415–1980*. New Haven, CT: Yale University Press. 2013.

Abrams, Lynn. *The Making of Modern Woman: Europe, 1789–1918*. London: Longman. 2002.

Appleby, Joyce Oldham. *The Relentless Revolution: A History of Capitalism*. New York: W.W. Norton. 2011.

Bock, Gisela. *Women in European History*. Malden, MA: Blackwell. 2002.

Burrow, J. W. *The Crisis of Reason: European Thought, 1848–1914*. New Haven, CT: Yale University Press. 2002.

Darwin, John. *After Tamerlane: The Rise and Fall of Global Empires, 1400–2000*. New York: Bloomsbury. 2010.

Gay, Peter. *Schnitzler's Century: The Making of Middle-Class Culture, 1815–1914*. New York: Norton. 2002.

Hochschild, Adam. *King Leopold's Ghost: A Story of Greed, Terror, and Heroism in Colonial Africa*. London: Pan Books. 2012.

Jonnes, Jill. *Empires of Light: Edison, Tesla, Westinghouse, and the Race to Electrify the World*. New York: Random House. 2003.

Larsen, Timothy. *A People of One Book: The Bible and the Victorians*. Oxford: Oxford University Press. 2012.

Paletschek, Sylvia and Bianka Pietrow-Ennker. *Women's Emancipation Movements in the 19th Century: A European Perspective*. Stanford, CA: Stanford University Press. 2006.

Quammen, David. *The Reluctant Mr. Darwin: An Intimate Portrait of Charles Darwin and the Making of His Theory of Evolution*. New York: W.W. Norton. 2007.

Stansell, Christine. *The Feminist Promise: 1792 to the Present*. New York: Random House. 2011.

Weller, Shane. *Modernism and Nihilism*. New York: Palgrave Macmillan. 2011.

Wilson, A. N. *God's Funeral*. New York: Ballantine. 2000.

16 World War I, 1914–18

Introduction

Between the unification of Germany in 1871 and the outbreak of the First World War in 1914, the balance of power in Europe steadily unraveled. A system of alliances took shape that arguably made war more likely. Fierce competition in economics and in empire-building further increased the probability of war, as did a rising tide of nationalist sentiment.

Unfortunately, that war, when it came, proved far more protracted and bloody than any of the combatants had imagined possible. Europe's technological and industrial supremacy, which had been a source of great strength, now became a curse. From 1914 to 1918, Europeans slaughtered one another with unprecedented efficiency.

The nineteenth century had been, for the most part, a century of peace, prosperity, and progress. The twentieth century would be marked instead by bloodshed and uncertainty.

Bismarck Tries to Preserve the Peace

After Prussia's victory over France in 1871, and Germany's unification in the same year, Bismarck pronounced himself satisfied with Germany's borders. Peace, however, was far from assured, because France was likely to desire revenge against Germany. If France were able to attract powerful allies to its side, Germany's territory, or even its existence, could be jeopardized. To protect Germany from this threat, Bismarck sought alliances with other great powers in Europe.

The strongest alliance that Germany was able to forge was the so-called Dual Alliance, formed in 1879. The Dual Alliance united Germany and Austria-Hungary, which made good sense, considering the geographical, commercial, and cultural ties that bound the two countries together.

Bismarck went further, though, and sought additional security for Germany in a Three Emperors' League that would unite the three Central and Eastern European empires of Germany, Austria-Hungary, and Russia. The League was inaugurated in 1873, and it lasted throughout most of the 1870s

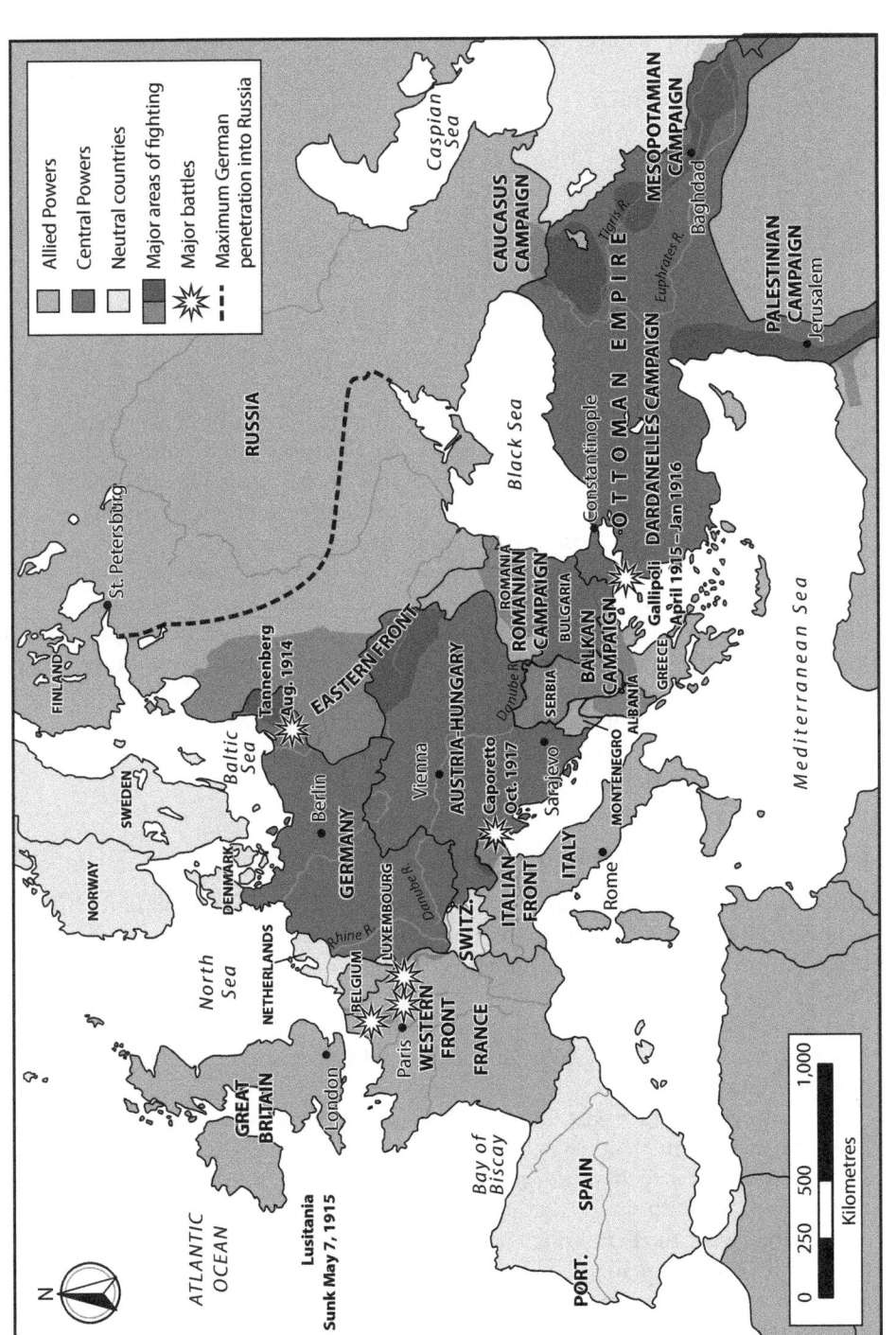

Map 16.1 World War I in Europe.

and 1880s. In 1882, in fact, Bismarck strengthened the League by creating a secret Triple Alliance between Germany, Austria-Hungary, and Italy. Now, in theory, no less than four great powers were united against France. Thus, a French war of revenge against Germany would have been suicidal.

Luckily for France, in 1888 a new emperor took the throne in Germany. Wilhelm II was young, arrogant, and far more aggressive in his international outlook than Bismarck. He soon established a reputation throughout Europe as a bombastic buffoon. (Tellingly, his closet contained over 400 military uniforms, plus a solid-gold helmet.)

Wilhelm II fired Bismarck as German Chancellor in 1890, and Bismarck's alliances rapidly fell apart. By 1894, Tsarist Russia had formed an alliance with France. Italy, meanwhile, maintained its membership in the Triple Alliance, but it secretly planned to hedge its bets in the event of war. In effect, therefore, within just a few years of Bismarck's dismissal, Germany was left with only one reliable ally: the Austrians. Moreover, in the event of war, Germany would have to fight on two fronts: against France in the west, and against Russia in the east. It was a strategic nightmare.

By 1894, the contours of World War I were already set, at least in part. On one side would be Germany and Austria-Hungary, while on the other side would be France and Russia. In retrospect, this division made sense, because the two hottest rivalries after 1871 were between France and Germany, caused by Germany's defeat of France in the Franco-Prussian War, and between Austria-Hungary and Russia, caused by the desire of each country to dominate southeastern Europe.

Still, three major powers remained free agents. If war were to break out, which side would Italy, the Ottoman Empire, and Britain choose? Italy presumably would wait to see which side would offer it a better deal, and the Turks might well do the same. The Ottoman Empire had sputtered throughout the nineteenth century, failing to compete technologically, economically, and militarily with the other great powers. Some successful political and economic reforms had been undertaken after 1839, but seething discontent among the empire's ethnic minorities, combined with the Europeans' brazen conquest of much Ottoman territory, combined to make Turkey "the sick man of Europe" long before 1914. A world war therefore offered the Turks a chance at a comeback.

But what about Britain? Britain had the largest empire, the strongest navy, and the most financial resources of any country. If it joined with either the Germans or the French, it could be a powerful ally, even a decisive one. Wisely, the Germans courted the British, who were tempted by Germany's advances, until the pride of Emperor Wilhelm II got in the way.

Germany's *Kaiser* was determined to make his country a naval power. Accordingly, in 1898 Germany began a major buildup of what would later be known as its High Seas Fleet. The British were petrified. Ever since the eighteenth century, Britain had been mistress of the seas. Now the Germans, with their massive industrial resources, were challenging Britain to a naval arms race.

By 1904, the *Kaiser* was calling himself the Admiral of the Atlantic. Understandably, the British began to see Germany as a threat. The irony is that the Germans, despite all their efforts, remained distinctly inferior to the British in naval strength, and so the *Kaiser*'s shiny new fleet ultimately did him no good.

Finally, between 1904 and 1907, aggressive German policies pushed the British to make a choice. In 1904, Britain agreed to an *Entente Cordiale* (that is, a Friendly Understanding) with France. It was technically not a formal alliance, but it amounted to the same thing. In 1907, Britain also resolved its differences with Russia. Now Britain, France, and Russia were united in a Triple Entente.

The two sides in any future war seemed to be determined. It would be the Triple Entente of Britain, France, and Russia versus the Dual Alliance of Germany and Austria-Hungary. The status of the Italians and the Ottoman Turks would be decided later. Critically, the Germans doubted the resolve of the British (as did the French), but otherwise the strategic situation was fairly clear. The only question was, who would be foolhardy enough to start a war that promised to be so destructive?

What major alliances were in place prior to the outbreak of World War I?

Dress Rehearsals for World War I, the Balkan Powderkeg, and the Strategic Balance

In retrospect it is fairly obvious that the First World War was bound to be long, bloody, and arguably not in the interests of any of the participating countries, but before 1914 many Europeans actually looked forward to the fighting. Since 1815, Europe had largely been at peace. The few wars that had been fought on the continent had been relatively quick and decisive. Simply put, no European alive in 1914 could remember a time when war was a terrifying specter of bloodshed and carnage.

But if Europeans had assessed their recent military history more carefully, they might have reached a far more sobering conclusion. For instance, in 1854–56, Britain, France, and Turkey had fought against the Russians in the Crimean War. None of the combatant countries were well prepared, and war correspondents had made headlines describing the ineptitude of the commanders and the suffering of ordinary soldiers. That misery was only partly relieved by the noble efforts of Florence Nightingale, who nursed many British servicemen back to health.

From 1899 to 1902, the British had fought the Boer War in southern Africa against white settlers of mainly Dutch descent. The British had won, but the war had exposed the lack of readiness in Britain's army. To make matters worse, to defeat a raging insurgency the British had crisscrossed South Africa with barbed wire, and they had herded Boer women and children into concentration camps, where more than 27,000 of them died. War in the twentieth century, it seemed, would be exceptionally cruel.

Finally, in 1904–05, the tactics employed during the Russo-Japanese War foreshadowed many of those used in World War I. Russian and Japanese soldiers huddled in long trenches, endured horrible weather conditions and endless artillery barrages, and, when ordered to attack, suffered appalling casualty rates.

These wars provided a chilling forecast of future military conflicts. Another set of wars, though, helps to explain the timing of World War I itself.

From 1878 to 1913, a series of conflicts were waged in the Balkans, a.k.a. southeastern Europe. For centuries, the Ottoman Empire had ruled most of southeastern Europe, but by the late nineteenth century the Ottomans were in retreat. They were forced to concede independence to minor Balkan states such as Greece, Serbia, Bulgaria, and Romania, all of which were poor, rural, and backward, by Western European standards.

Because of the presence of many Orthodox Slavs in the Balkans, Russia felt it had a right to hegemony in the region. From 1830 on, Russia was the primary backer and ally of Serbia, which, with Russian support, dreamed of uniting all of the south Slavic peoples.

The Russians' chief competition in the race to dominate the Balkans came from Austria-Hungary, which in 1878 had occupied the Ottoman province of Bosnia, a region peopled partly by ethnic Serbs. Since this was territory coveted by Serbia, Austria-Hungary and Serbia became enemies. Austria-Hungary did not attack Serbia, however, because of the danger of a Russian response.

Minor wars engulfed the Balkans in 1912 and 1913. By 1914, tensions were running very high. The Austrians were determined to destroy Serbia once and for all, while Russia was itching to come to the rescue of the Serbs. Because of the network of alliances that existed throughout Europe, any war between Austria-Hungary and Russia would likely produce a world war. All that was required was a spark to ignite the conflict.

If a world war did arise, who would have the strategic edge? In terms of naval strength, the advantage would clearly rest with whichever side attracted the support of Britain—and thus with the Triple Entente. By 1914, the German High Seas Fleet boasted 29 capital ships (that is, battleships and battlecruisers), but the British had 47. The war at sea, therefore, would presumably be brief.

On land, the situation was somewhat more promising for the Dual Alliance. German and Austro-Hungarian forces were centrally located in Europe, and Germany could also count on its outstanding tradition of inspired military leadership, efficient logistics, and technological sophistication. Perhaps most importantly, the Germans believed that they could mobilize their reserves for battle much more quickly than their enemies could. The Germans therefore planned to go on the offensive and defeat their adversaries before they were even ready to fight. If the war became protracted, though, Germany was in trouble. In terms of overall manpower, Germany and Austria-Hungary were completely outclassed by the

Triple Entente. With respect to economic and industrial resources, here too the advantage clearly rested with the Allies, as the countries of the Triple Entente became known. In 1913–14, in terms of defense expenditures, Britain, France, and Russia outspent Germany and Austria-Hungary by about two to one.

After 1914, it also became apparent that the countries of the Triple Entente had superior political resources. The Western democracies, especially Britain and France, had good relationships with neutral powers, such as the United States, and they proved to be more skilled at using propaganda. When the Germans invaded Belgium in 1914, lurid, and often exaggerated, stories about civilian massacres there helped to win worldwide sympathy for the Allied cause. Starting in 1915, the Allies could also point to alarming reports of widespread atrocities targeting Christian Armenians in the Ottoman Empire—the first genocide of the twentieth century. Ultimately, this continuous stream of Allied propaganda was very influential. It helped to convince the United States to join the war in 1917. That development would shift the strategic balance even more sharply against Germany and Austria-Hungary.

What strategic advantages did the Allies and the Central Powers possess?

An Assassination Leads to War, and Stalemate in the West

On June 28, 1914, Archduke Francis Ferdinand, the heir to the Austro-Hungarian throne, and his wife made an official visit to Sarajevo, the quaint capital city of the Austro-Hungarian province of Bosnia. Many Serbs lived there, and some of them longed to be ruled by Serbia rather than by Austria-Hungary. On June 28, one of those angry Serbs, who was affiliated with a terrorist organization called the Black Hand, shot and killed the Archduke and his wife. The Austrians, however, were not terrorized. They were enraged.

With some justification, the Austro-Hungarian leadership placed the blame for the assassination on the government of Serbia. Serbia had been a thorn in the side of the Austrians for years. Now seemed like a perfect time to wipe Serbia off the map. With any luck, the rest of the world would be so sympathetic to the Austrians because of the death of the Archduke that not even the Russians would intervene. Accordingly, on July 28, 1914, Austria-Hungary declared war on Serbia, and it mobilized its forces for an invasion.

There were a number of questions still to be answered. Would the Germans support an Austrian attack on Serbia? The answer in July 1914 was an emphatic yes, although the Germans hoped that the conflict would not escalate. What then of Russia? Would it follow through on its pledges of support to Serbia and invade Austria-Hungary? If it did, would France intervene to support Russia? In those days, France was enjoying its *belle epoque*, an era of cultural vivacity and general prosperity. Would France risk everything for the sake of its eastern ally? If the answer to all these questions was yes, then a general war in Europe was inevitable. Ultimately, the Austrians and the Germans decided that they were prepared to take that risk.

At the end of July, Russia made the fateful decision to mobilize its forces for a possible attack on Austria. Now Germany's hand was forced. Mobilization in Russia meant that the Russians would be prepared to attack within weeks. Germany's master strategy for winning a two-front war, however, called for a massive German attack against France, and then a secondary attack against Russia more than a month later. If the Russians had a head start, Germany was doomed.

Thus, on August 1, 1914, Germany ordered full mobilization. The Germans simultaneously ordered the activation of the Schlieffen Plan, which called for a massive invasion of Belgium, Luxembourg, and France. The idea was that, while France launched a futile frontal assault on the Franco-German border, an immensely strong column of German armies would pour through Belgium into northern France, through Paris, and then wheel to the east in order to attack the main French army from the rear. In theory, the French would be outflanked and defeated within six weeks. From there, Germany would rapidly redeploy its forces to the east and defeat the Russians in turn.

By August 4, 1914, Germany had invaded Belgium and France. Almost immediately, things began to go wrong.

First, the Belgians, who had been neutral before the German invasion, fought far more valiantly and effectively than the Germans expected. Second, although the Germans had hoped that Britain would stay out of the conflict, Britain declared war on Germany as soon as Germany invaded Belgium. Britain's belligerence changed the whole nature of the war. Now, all the resources of the British Empire would be turned against the Central Powers, as the Dual Alliance became known. True, the relatively small British Expeditionary Force would take some time to arrive in France, but now the Royal Navy would chase the German fleet and merchant marine from the seas. Germany had better win the war quickly, therefore, or its economy would be shattered.

In September 1914, a huge battle was fought near the banks of the Marne River in northern France, only 35 miles from Paris. The Germans were desperately trying to complete their encirclement of the French army. After much hard fighting, though, the Germans were pushed back 40 miles. The Schlieffen Plan had narrowly failed.

What came next disappointed the politicians and generals on both sides, and it tormented ordinary soldiers. A stalemate developed on the Western Front, which stretched 466 miles from the English Channel coast to the southern reaches of the Franco-German border. All along this front, both sides built networks of trenches to defend the ground that they held. These trench systems were elaborate, and they were protected from advancing enemy forces by barbed wire and murderously efficient machine gun emplacements. When soldiers were periodically ordered "over the top" to charge across "no man's land" at the enemy, their only hope of victory was a massive artillery bombardment that preceded their attack. With any luck, these shells would kill and injure enough of the enemy troops that the attack would meet with minimal resistance. It seldom happened that way.

In 1916, at Verdun and at the River Somme, the Germans and the British, respectively, launched massive attacks to try to break the deadlock. At Verdun, shells rained down on the French at the rate of 100,000 per hour. The successful defense of Verdun gave the French their greatest hero of the war, Marshal Henri Philippe Pétain, who would later become the leader of the collaborationist French Vichy government during World War II. In Pétain's own words, those who survived Verdun "sagged beneath the weight of horrifying memories." At both Verdun and the Somme, approximately one million men were either killed or wounded. But it was not only men who suffered from this carnage: women served near the front lines too, usually as nurses and ambulance drivers.

A quick death during a hopeless charge at the enemy's trenches was in many cases not even the worst fate that could befall a soldier on the Western Front. Day in and day out, men lived underground, harassed by rats and surrounded by mud. In these damp conditions, food rotted and wounds became infected. It was extremely hard to bury the dead, and enemy artillery fire frequently scattered corpses and body parts around the battlefield. During the war, it is estimated that the British fired no less than 170 million artillery rounds. These frequent bombardments terrorized many soldiers, leading

Figure 16.1 Canadian soldiers training to go "over the top."
Everett Historical/Shutterstock.

often to nervous collapse, while periods of inactivity sapped morale. A single mistake, such as peering for a brief moment over the top of the trench, could lead to instant death at the hands of an enemy sniper.

Many officers in the rear seemed insensitive to the plight of the men on the front lines. They ordered attacks that seemed suicidal, and they lived comfortably while their men suffered. It is no wonder that, in 1917, after three years of hard fighting, a large fraction of the French army mutinied. Discipline was restored only through the administration of draconian punishments.

It would be a mistake, however, to see life for ordinary soldiers in the First World War as uniformly miserable. For many, there was the joy of comradeship and a strong sense of pride and honor, which the distribution of medals and awards helped to foster. For others, diversions such as gambling, drinking, and prostitution offered a form of comfort. There was also the promise of periodic rotations to the rear of the battlefield, which could mean sojourns in quiet villages, or perhaps training in new military procedures or equipment. The average soldier, in fact, spent relatively little time on the front lines, and he rarely engaged in battle. Still, all the armies of World War I were based on a draft, and thus soldiers had to be compelled to fight. In America in 1917, they euphemistically called it "selective service," but it amounted to the same thing.

In reality, Allied and German commanders were fully aware of the suffering of their troops, but, after so much sacrifice, it seemed unimaginable to accept anything less than total victory. The inclination of the generals was to seek that victory by escalating the scale of their attacks. When this failed to produce the expected results (at least, until 1918), the generals put their faith in technology instead.

What was life like for soldiers on the Western Front?

New Weapons Fail to Break the Deadlock, and the Emergence of Secondary Theaters

Many important innovations in military technology were employed during the First World War. The Germans, for example, fielded numerous artillery pieces of unprecedented size, range, and destructive power. The Paris Gun, for instance, hit Paris from a distance of 75 miles. The armies of World War I had even better luck with smaller artillery pieces that relentlessly pounded enemy troops, and with machine guns, which cut down horrific numbers of young soldiers.

In 1915, the Germans were the first to use chemical warfare. They hoped that gas would be the decisive weapon of the war. It injured or killed over a million soldiers, but it offered no solution to the stalemate.

Both sides used aircraft extensively in the war, primarily to observe the enemy. Dogfights were also common. The leading ace of the war was the

German, Manfred von Richthofen, known as the Red Baron, who shot down 80 Allied planes. Bombing occurred only on a very minimal scale.

The British tried in 1916 to break the deadlock with a stunning invention: the tank, so called because it resembled a water carrier, and military authorities did not want to give away its real purpose. The earliest tanks had a top speed of only a few miles per hour, and thus they were highly vulnerable to artillery fire. Nevertheless, had tanks been available in sufficient numbers, and had the Allies understood how to use them, the results could have been disastrous for the Germans. As it was, only by the end of the war were the Allies using tanks and infantry together to hit the Germans with a one-two punch.

Thanks to these technological innovations, the fighting on the Western Front developed into mechanized slaughter on a gargantuan scale. Day by day, the Allied and German commands invented artful new ways to send men to their deaths, but, before 1918, they could devise no way to end the war.

Both sides understood that the conflict would likely be decided on the Western Front. Still, in the East battles were waged involving similarly vast numbers of men, and inflicting comparable misery. On a front that stretched from the Baltic coast down to the Black Sea, millions of German and Austro-Hungarian troops confronted the Russian "steamroller" that could draw on virtually limitless reserves of manpower.

Initially, the execution of the Schlieffen Plan in France distracted the Germans, and Russia was able to advance clumsily into East Prussia. The Germans then made the fateful decision to strengthen their eastern armies, at the expense of their forces in the West. The elderly Field Marshal Paul von Hindenburg was named the German commander in the East. His triumphs there made him a national hero and led to his election in 1925 as German President.

In 1915, Germany and Austria-Hungary attacked and advanced deep into Russian territory. The headlong Russian retreat exposed the incompetence of the Russian commanders and the inadequacy of their efforts to supply the troops. By 1916, military discipline was beginning to collapse, while the Russian economy sputtered. Tsar Nicholas II rushed to the front to take personal command, but he proved no more effective as a general than he was as head of state.

Sensing the weakness of the Russians, in 1915 the head of Britain's Royal Navy, Winston Churchill, developed a plan that was designed to make it easier to send men and supplies to help the Tsar and his troops. The Ottoman Empire had entered the war on the side of the Central Powers in November 1914. This allowed the Central Powers to take firm control of the Balkans, except for Greece. More importantly, Turkey, through its control of the Turkish Straits, which connect the Mediterranean and Black Seas, was able to prevent any serious Allied effort to send supplies to Russia. Churchill's plan to reverse this situation involved sending British battleships to pound the forts that guarded the Straits, and subsequently to launch an amphibious invasion that would seize the waterway and possibly force Turkey out of the war. The plan's execution in 1915–16, however, left much to be desired. In fact, the Gallipoli campaign, as it became known, was a fiasco.

The Allies had more success in attacking the Ottoman Empire's Arab provinces. From 1914 to 1918, the British brought thousands of troops from India, Africa, Australia, and New Zealand to help evict the Turks from modern-day Saudi Arabia, Jordan, Israel, Syria, and Iraq. The British (notably T. E. Lawrence, known as Lawrence of Arabia) were even able to convince the Arabs to help liberate their lands from Turkish oppression. By December 1917, Jerusalem and Baghdad were in British hands.

Meanwhile, Germany's African colonies fell easily into the hands of the British, French, and Belgians, except for Tanganyika (modern-day Tanzania). Here, German Colonel Paul von Lettow-Vorbeck mounted a spirited guerrilla resistance that continued until November 1918. Throughout the conflict, white supremacy was rigidly enforced by both sides, even though Africans did most of the fighting.

In 1915, Italy, after a series of secret negotiations, betrayed its alliance with Germany and Austria-Hungary and joined the war on the side of the Allies. British and French promises of territorial concessions were the main inducement. Italy was a great power, so its entrance into the war should have been significant. In reality, though, the Italians fought poorly. They required help from Britain and France to prevent a complete collapse of the Italian army after its defeat at the Battle of Caporetto in 1917.

Where besides the Western Front was World War I fought?

The War at Sea, and America Enters the War While Russia Quits It

Naval combat was not as important in World War I as in World War II, because the Central Powers never seriously contested British naval dominance. Nevertheless, naval strategy would prove influential in determining the political and economic fortunes of the combatants.

As early as 1915, contrary to international law, the British were enforcing a strict blockade against any merchant ships traveling to Germany, even those carrying food for civilians. The Germans replied in two distinct ways.

First, in May 1916, for the only time in the war, the Germans sent their whole High Seas Fleet to engage the British in the North Sea. At the Battle of Jutland, the British Grand Fleet suffered heavier losses, but the German fleet still retreated and was never heard from again.

Second, the Germans decided that, if they could not control the surface of the sea, then perhaps they could use submarines, which they called U-boats, to attack British warships and, more importantly, the British merchant fleet. If enough merchant ships could be sunk, the British, who depended on international trade and foreign supplies of food, might be forced to leave the war. The German U-boat strategy, however, ended up backfiring on Germany, and in a spectacular fashion.

Although in spring 1917 German submarines sank a quarter of the merchant vessels entering and leaving British ports, by the summer Allied convoys had greatly reduced the U-boat menace. Much more important in the long run, though, was the fact that the German U-boat strategy radically increased American anger at Germany, since American passengers on British and French liners were often casualties of U-boat attacks. The most famous example of German aggression on the high seas was the sinking of the British ship *Lusitania* by a U-boat in 1915. Twelve hundred passengers died, including 128 Americans. In reality, the *Lusitania* was also carrying munitions to be used against Germany, but since this fact was not disclosed its sinking made many Americans furious. To soothe American public opinion, therefore, later in 1915 the Germans had agreed to suspend their practice of "unrestricted submarine warfare," which had categorized any Allied vessel in the waters off Britain or France as fair game. The Germans, however, then resumed unrestricted submarine warfare in January 1917. This decision, more than any other factor, caused the United States to enter the war on the side of the Allies, despite strong isolationist sentiment.

Several other factors were at work, however. Beginning early in the war, the United States sold huge amounts of ammunition and other war supplies to the Allied powers, and it loaned vast sums of money to Britain, France, and Italy. Thus, the United States had a vested interest in an Allied victory. In addition, U.S. President Woodrow Wilson secretly wished to bring America into the fighting on the Allied side. In January 1917, the German Foreign Secretary, Arthur Zimmermann, sent a telegram to Germany's ambassador in Mexico that helped Wilson to achieve his goal. Zimmermann proposed a German-Mexican alliance against the United States! The Zimmermann Telegram, deliberately revealed by British intelligence, made headlines, and it goaded many Americans into supporting war. At the same time, President Wilson cannily described the First World War as a war "to make the world safe for democracy." All these arguments, combined with the impact of unrestricted submarine warfare, had a cumulative effect. Congress accordingly passed a declaration of war against Germany on April 6, 1917.

It would take time, though, for American troops and industrial prowess to make a difference. Indeed, the U.S. Army was in such a sorry state that it was more than a year before it was usefully employed on the Western Front.

There were other signs in 1917 that it might be too late for America to influence the outcome of the conflict. The mutiny of the French army in spring 1917 threatened to cause a collapse of the Allied forces on the Western Front. Even more significant was the October Revolution in Russia, which brought Lenin and the Bolsheviks to power, and led to Russia's speedy exit from the war.

In 1914, Tsar Nicholas II had brought Russia into the First World War on the side of the Allies. As we have seen, the results were disastrous. Russian troops were often poorly led, malnourished, and ill-equipped. By 1917, their German and Austro-Hungarian opponents had pushed deep into Russian territory. Simultaneously, economic and social conditions had become unbearable for most civilians. Finally, the influence within the royal family of a drunken, lecherous, and ill-mannered mystic, named Rasputin, caused public opinion to shift decisively against the well-meaning Tsar. In late 1916, Rasputin was poisoned, bludgeoned, shot, and drowned in an icy river. His death, however, could not reverse the damage he had done to the Tsar's public image.

In spring 1917, a revolution erupted in Russia that shocked Tsar Nicholas II into abdicating. The Romanov dynasty, which had ruled Russia for more than 300 years, was now finished. One year later, communists brutally killed Nicholas, along with his wife and children.

After the Tsar's abdication, a Provisional Government, dominated not by the Bolsheviks but by the Constitutional Democrats, or Kadets, briefly took over in Russia. The Kadets were determined to create a liberal state built around individual rights, capitalism, and representative government. They also, however, wished to maintain Russia's involvement in the First World War. Unfortunately, the war continued to go badly for Russia, and conditions for soldiers and civilians alike deteriorated even further.

Sensing an opportunity to cause even greater chaos, the Germans now smuggled Lenin, who had been in exile, back to his homeland. The Germans hoped that Lenin would unleash another wave of revolutionary violence that would force Russia to quit the war. They got their wish in the fall of 1917, when, in a stunning turn of events, the Bolsheviks ignited the October Revolution that ousted the Provisional Government and brought Lenin to power. Lenin's Russia now became the world's first communist state.

In March 1918, Russia fully capitulated to the Germans by signing the Treaty of Brest-Litovsk. The war on the Eastern Front was over. Germany was suddenly the proud owner of Poland, Ukraine, Estonia, Latvia, and Lithuania. More importantly, the Germans were now able to move 44 divisions to the West. It seemed therefore that the war had taken a dramatic turn in favor of the Central Powers.

What role did German U-boats play in the outcome of World War I?

Germany's Last Offensive, and the Paris Peace Conference

In the spring and summer of 1918, before the American colossus had made a major impact on the fighting, the Germans planned to capitalize on their success in the East by launching a massive, decisive attack in the West. Despite the perilous condition of the German economy and increasing divisions at home, the German army made impressive territorial gains, once again advancing close to Paris. Finally, though, British, French, and American troops were able to push them back.

By the fall of 1918, much to everyone's surprise, the German retreat was turning into a rout. German resolve was shattered. On November 9, the *Kaiser* suddenly abdicated, and a republic replaced the German Empire. Germany now faced a terrible choice. Should it fight on and almost certainly lose? Or should it surrender immediately, hoping for a favorable peace treaty? In the end, the new German government chose the latter option.

Germany signed an Armistice, that is, a cease-fire, that took effect on November 11, 1918. It did so for three principal reasons.

First, Germany's economy and military were close to collapse. Food was so scarce that by 1919 as many as 750,000 Germans had died of hunger.

Second, Germany reached the conclusion that it could not continue to fight after all the other Central Powers had surrendered. By early November, Austria-Hungary, Turkey, and Bulgaria had all capitulated after the collapse of the Balkan and Middle Eastern fronts.

Lastly, the Germans surrendered because they had the realistic hope that the Allies would treat them fairly. President Wilson, earlier in 1918, had proposed his 14 Points, which promised a new and better world characterized by democracy, free trade, open diplomacy, disarmament, national self-determination, and peace. To the Germans, this did not sound so bad.

On November 11, 1918, therefore, the guns fell silent on the Western Front. World War I was over. Approximately 70 million men had fought, and as many as ten million had died. No nation had suffered more in proportional terms than Serbia, whose government had helped to instigate the war. Perhaps a quarter of the Serbian population had been wiped out. European governments had also mobilized every financial resource available, going deeply into debt. In addition, rationing, food shortages, strikes, and unrest had plagued many countries, ensuring that civilians, as well as soldiers, suffered throughout the war. Sadly, when the war was over, there was no respite, because a vicious strain of influenza rapidly spread worldwide. It killed 30 million people.

The worst feature of the Armistice was that it left the most vital questions still unanswered. Would a stable peace be negotiated? Were nationalist hatreds resolvable? Could another world war be prevented? It fell on the politicians and the diplomats to address these momentous issues.

Beginning in January 1919, the representatives of the victorious nations in the First World War, including the United States, Britain, France, and Italy, gathered in Paris to draft the terms of a final peace treaty. Ominously for the Germans, they were excluded from the negotiations, as were the Russians, who had left the war early and had embraced communism, a widely despised ideology. Thus, as much as Woodrow Wilson had declared the Allies to be seeking a "peace without victors," it seemed that something less noble was taking place. The winners were preparing to divide the spoils.

The negotiations that followed were intense. At one point, French Prime Minister Georges Clemenceau offered to fight a duel with British Prime Minister David Lloyd George. Luckily, though, U.S. President Wilson, always the peacemaker, separated the two men before they embarrassed themselves any further.

The Paris Settlement, when it was finally signed, was divided into five separate treaties, one for each of the countries in the defeated Central Powers. The most famous of these accords was the Treaty of Versailles, which was imposed on Germany. Four other treaties were imposed on Bulgaria, Turkey, Austria, and Hungary (the last two had already been divided into separate countries).

The cumulative effects of the latter four treaties were massive. The Austro-Hungarian Empire was dissolved. The far western provinces of the empire, populated by ethnic Germans, became the Republic of Austria. Meanwhile, the Kingdom of Hungary was granted its independence, but it lost huge amounts of territory, and many ethnic Hungarians were forced to live under foreign rule. A Republic of Czechoslovakia was created that housed Czechs and Slovaks, but also many discontented Germans, Hungarians, Poles, and Ukrainians.

The minor states in Eastern Europe that had chosen to side with the Allies—Romania, Greece, and Serbia—all received generous slices of Austria-Hungary, Turkey, or Russia in compensation. Serbia, in fact, was allowed to realize its dream of becoming the nucleus of a larger state, Yugoslavia, which united Serbs, Croats, Slovenes, Bosnian Muslims, and others. In addition, based in part on an effective lobbying effort by Poles during the war, the Allies decided to reestablish an independent Poland. Polish nationalists were overjoyed, but their new country, by necessity, included territory that used to belong to Germany and Russia. Thus, the new state of Poland was instantly unpopular in Berlin and Moscow.

The Russians suffered even more humiliations. Finland, Estonia, Latvia, and Lithuania were all granted independence, and Russia was only able to hold on to Ukraine, Belarus, and the Caucasus after some bitter fighting.

All these territorial adjustments in Eastern Europe were made, superficially at least, in order to satisfy Wilson's goal of ethnic self-determination, a.k.a. nationalism. Arguably, though, the Paris Settlement had only succeeded in creating a patchwork of small, weak, unstable, and impoverished Eastern European states. Once the Germans and the Russians had recovered their strength, presumably these Eastern European nations would be easy prey.

Like Austria-Hungary, the Ottoman Empire was also destroyed. A Republic of Turkey succeeded it, but Turkey lost all of its territory in the Middle East to Britain and France, which claimed these areas as "mandates" (colonies in all but name). During the war, Britain had promised the Arabs that they would become independent, but these promises were not immediately kept.

The most famous element in the Paris Settlement was the Versailles Treaty, which officially ended the war between Germany and the Allies. The terms imposed on Germany were harsh, although not as harsh as the Germans would have imposed on the Allies, had they won the war.

In Article 231, the war was officially blamed on German aggression. As a consequence, the Germans would face a number of punishments. First, Germany would forfeit all of its colonies to the Allies. In theory, these colonies would be put on the road to independence, but in fact they were treated as conquered territories. More importantly, in Europe, the Germans would lose the provinces of Alsace and Lorraine to France, and significant territory in the east to Poland. Germany would also be partially occupied, west of the Rhine River, by British, French, and American troops, and its army would be permanently limited to only 100,000 men. No German air force or submarine force would be permitted. Lastly, the Germans were expected to repay the Allies for all of their expenses and losses associated with the war. The full extent of Germany's reparations bill, though, was not immediately disclosed.

To the Germans, especially to veterans of the recent war, these seemed like monstrously unjust terms. What about the 14 Points, the Germans asked? What about Wilson's "peace without victors"? But no one on the Allied side was listening.

The only concessions that the Allies made to Wilsonian idealism in the Treaty of Versailles were, first, they allowed the Germans to retain their national unity, and, second, they created a League of Nations, similar to the modern-day United Nations, dedicated to keeping the peace. It was symbolic of the Allies' attitude to peace, however, that the Germans and the Russians were excluded from the League of Nations from the start. In the United States, President Wilson praised the new League, claiming that the "hand of God" had formed it. (In reality, it was Wilson's idea.) The U.S. Senate, though, was not convinced, and America never joined. The League of Nations, therefore, got off to a very poor start.

The new regime in Germany that was forced to accept the Versailles Treaty was called the Weimar Republic, because its constitution was written in the city of Weimar. It was a generally liberal government that was dominated initially by moderate socialists from the SPD—a party loathed by many Germans, especially conservatives. As a result, the myth grew up in Germany that the country's army had been "stabbed in the back" in the First World War by socialists and Jews, who had conspired to engineer a German defeat so that they could take power. While this was an absurd explanation for Germany's downfall, in fact, on several occasions in 1919, Marxists, some of whom were Jewish, did try to take over in Germany. They were narrowly defeated.

As soon as it was created, therefore, the Weimar Republic was tainted in the eyes of many Germans by its connections to military defeat, socialism, liberalism, and (much less plausibly) Judaism. Extremist movements developed throughout Germany that promised a stronger, more prosperous nation, and revenge against those who had caused Germany's humiliation. The Nazis, formed in 1919, were just one of these movements.

Marshal Ferdinand Foch of France called the Versailles Treaty a "20-year truce," rather than a final settlement. He foresaw that Germany would rise again, and France would be imperiled as a result.

Despite the fact that Foch's prediction eventually came true, this was not necessarily because the Versailles Treaty was too harsh. Germany was not destroyed by the Treaty, but it *was* disgraced and enraged. In retrospect, a settlement that angered Germany, but did not lastingly deprive it of the tools to seek vengeance, was the worst possible result that the Paris negotiations could have produced.

In a sense, though, it was not the Treaty itself that made renewed conflict likely, but rather it was the lack of effective enforcement of its provisions during the 1920s and 1930s. The framers of the Treaty did the best that they could, but they did not foresee how conditions would change in the next 20 years. The Great Depression, in particular, would obliterate the established order on which the Treaty was based.

Once the United States made the fateful decision in 1919 to return to isolationism, another potential check on future German aggression was removed. As Foch suggested, it was arguably just a matter of time before war again ravaged Europe.

Why did the Germans find the Treaty of Versailles so objectionable?

Conclusions

Even before the First World War, it had become fashionable for progressive intellectuals, writers, artists, and musicians to criticize middle-class ideals such as liberalism and nationalism, and to point out the contradictions and cruelty in middle-class life. This critique of modern, *bourgeois* society gathered momentum after the trauma of World War I. Ezra Pound, an American poet, acidly referred to the West as a "botched civilization," unworthy of the millions of lives that had been lost to defend it. In short, an overpowering sense of uncertainty, combined with a cynical rejection of tradition, infiltrated not just the arts but also science, politics, and religion.

In the midst of this cultural ferment, many Europeans insisted on the need for reform. Some of the strongest voices calling for change were those of women, many of whom had worked in factories during the war and were now demanding equality and respect. Laborers, who had toiled to supply frontline troops, were calling for political and economic rewards, and sometimes for socialist reforms. Governments, which had exercised unprecedented power during the war, especially economically, remained insistent on their authority, and they expanded social welfare programs. Veterans, who had sacrificed their youth, and often their health, demanded compensation, and sometimes they called for revenge against enemies at home and abroad.

What Europe needed most in 1918 was rest and a return to "normalcy," as U.S. President Warren G. Harding put it. It would receive neither. During the 1920s and 1930s, Western Civilization unraveled even further, leading in 1939 to the most horrific war in human history.

Key Terms for Chapter 16

Dual Alliance, 1879—a close alliance between Germany and Austria-Hungary that lasted until the end of World War I.

Triple Entente, 1907—an understanding between Britain, France, and Russia that they would fight together against the Dual Alliance.

Archduke Francis Ferdinand—heir to the throne of Austria-Hungary. He was assassinated by a Serb terrorist in June 1914, leading Austria to declare war on Serbia. This touched off the First World War.

Mobilization—the process of preparing an army to fight.

Schlieffen Plan—Germany's strategy for victory in the First World War, involving a massive attack on France, followed by an attack on Russia.

Western Front—the most important front in World War I, located in Belgium and Northern France. Both sides became bogged down in trench warfare.

Eastern Front—the second most important front, along which the Germans and Austro-Hungarians made slow but steady progress against the Russians. The Russian military collapsed in 1917, and Lenin took Russia out of the war.

U-boat (*Unterseeboot*)—German submarine. Germany's subs had some success in targeting Allied shipping, but their predatory attacks also motivated the United States to join the war.

Woodrow Wilson—President of the United States from 1913 to 1921. He led the United States into World War I and played a major role at the Paris Peace Conference.

Bolshevik Revolution, 1917—a.k.a. the October Revolution, this was Russia's second revolution in 1917, which brought Lenin to power and created the world's first communist state.

Treaty of Brest-Litovsk, March 1918—an agreement between the new Russian government under Lenin and the Central Powers, according to which Russia left the war and surrendered large amounts of territory.

Paris Peace Settlement—this refers to the peace treaties formulated by Allied leaders and imposed on the defeated Central Powers. The Versailles Treaty, affecting Germany, was widely viewed as overly harsh.

Review Questions for Chapter 16

1. Describe three of the causes of World War I.
2. Imagine that you are a soldier fighting on the Western Front in World War I. Write a letter to your parents in which you describe the challenges

that you face. Then make a case for why the war is either justified or unjustified.
3. What do you believe was Germany's biggest mistake in World War I? Could Germany have won the war if this mistake had been avoided? Explain your views.
4. Describe why the United States entered World War I. Do you feel that the United States was wise or unwise to do so?
5. Many Germans bitterly resented the terms of the Versailles Treaty. List at least five reasons why Germans found the Treaty unfair.

Further Reading

Boemeke, Manfred F., Gerald D. Feldman, and Elisabeth Glaser, eds. *The Treaty of Versailles: A Reassessment After 75 Years*. New York: Cambridge University Press. 2006.

Burrow, J. W. *The Crisis of Reason: European Thought, 1848–1914*. New Haven, CT: Yale University Press. 2002.

Chickering, Roger. *Imperial Germany and the Great War, 1914–1918*. Third Edition. New York: Cambridge University Press. 2014.

Englund, Peter. *The Beauty and the Sorrow: An Intimate History of the First World War*. London: Profile. 2012.

Fleischer, Wolfgang. *Military Technology of the First World War: Development, Use and Consequences*. Barnsley, UK: Pen and Sword Military. 2017.

Grayzel, Susan R. *Women's Identities at War: Gender, Motherhood, and Politics in Britain and France During the First World War*. Chapel Hill, NC: University of North Carolina Press. 1999.

Keegan, John. *The First World War*. London: The Bodley Head. 2014.

Morrow, John H. *The Great War: An Imperial History*. London: Routledge. 2016.

Philpott, William. *Three Armies on the Somme: The First Battle of the Twentieth Century*. New York: Vintage. 2011.

Read, Christopher. *From Tsar to Soviets: The Russian People and Their Revolution, 1917–21*. New York: Routledge. 2013.

Robb, George. *British Culture and the First World War*. London: Palgrave. 2015.

Sondhaus, Lawrence. *The Great War at Sea: A Naval History of the First World War*. Cambridge: Cambridge University Press. 2014.

17 Interwar Europe, 1919–39

Introduction

Between the end of World War I and the beginning of World War II, Europeans made futile efforts to recapture the prosperity and optimism of the pre-1914 era. Americans, meanwhile, concluded that their participation in the First World War had been a mistake, and they attempted to avoid involvement in any future European conflicts.

Both the victors and the vanquished in World War I were generally unhappy with the terms of the Paris Peace Settlement. Europe was simmering with resentments, and a very strong hand would have been required to keep them in check. Unfortunately, no such force able to guarantee peace and stability arose. Europe therefore drifted toward renewed conflict. The shape of that conflict, though, remained unclear. It was, more than anything, the Great Depression, and the political changes that it helped to cause, that determined the nature and the ambitions of the regimes that unleashed the Second World War. In particular, the Depression led directly to the creation of the Nazi regime in Germany, with fateful consequences for Europe and for the world as a whole.

Sources of Political and Economic Instability, and the Great Depression

As much as the peoples of Europe had hoped that the conclusion of World War I would bring an end to suffering and uncertainty, it soon became apparent that "normalcy," stability, and prosperity would be hard to recapture. Germany was smarting from the wounds inflicted both by its catastrophic military defeat and its subjection to the harsh terms outlined in the Versailles Treaty. In Eastern Europe, newly established nations struggled to build sound governments while seething with ethnic tensions. Meanwhile, much of Europe quaked at the menace that the Soviet Union, as communist Russia now called itself, seemed to pose.

These political challenges were exacerbated by a European economy that performed dismally. Germany, in particular, faced a seemingly limitless reparations bill that did severe damage to German finances. In 1923, the German government defaulted on its reparations obligations. In response, the French swooped into the Ruhr Valley, Germany's industrial heartland, and confiscated the value of the reparations in the form of coal. As a consequence, Germany's currency imploded. By late 1923, the German Mark had fallen to one-trillionth of its pre-war value.

To fight the specter of inflation, governments throughout Europe followed conservative fiscal policies that limited growth and investment. As a result, stagnation and unemployment spread. In the early 1920s, the United States was virtually alone in escaping this economic malaise. The U.S. economy, fueled by Allied arms purchases, had boomed during the war, and it continued its ascent after the fighting was over.

During the mid-1920s, as the American stock market soared, increasing amounts of U.S. capital were invested in Europe, leading to a short-lived economic boom. The German economy would grow significantly from 1925 to 1928. As European economies recovered, sincere efforts were made to overcome the divisions that the Paris Peace Settlement had caused. Burning national hatreds had been reduced to a manageable level, at least for the moment.

In 1924, and again in 1929, American initiatives made reparations easier for Germany to pay. In 1925, Britain and France consented to Germany's admission to the League of Nations. Also in 1925, the British, French, Germans, and Italians met at Locarno, Switzerland, where they agreed that the new Franco-German border would stand. In return, France would accelerate the withdrawal of its occupation forces from Germany's Rhineland region.

An air of optimism gripped Europe after these negotiations. The peaceful mood of the late 1920s was epitomized in 1928 by the signing of the Kellogg-Briand Pact, a worldwide agreement to forsake "war as an instrument of national policy." If the signatories to the Pact were to keep their word, then apparently World War I really would be "the war to end all wars."

From 1929 to 1939, however, an economic depression of unprecedented severity would plague every capitalist country in the world. Some nations suffered more than others, but everywhere the mood of optimism of the late 1920s was forgotten. A radicalization of European politics occurred that would lead, in time, to the Second World War.

The Great Depression began in the United States with Black Tuesday on the New York Stock Exchange. On October 29, 1929, stock values plummeted. By 1933, U.S. stocks had lost 80 percent of their value, industrial production had fallen 50 percent, and almost a third of U.S. workers were unemployed.

Even before the stock market crash, U.S. capital had begun to dry up, and a number of European banks had collapsed as a result. Governments could have tried to spend their way out of the crisis, but the fear of inflation made this seem too risky. Instead, many national governments responded to the

Great Depression by instituting tariffs—that is, special taxes on imported goods. Tariffs were supposed to reduce imports and stimulate demand for domestically produced goods and foodstuffs. Instead, when virtually all nations used tariffs simultaneously, their cumulative effect was to choke off international trade, which fell by as much as two-thirds. This only produced more hardship, and unemployment spread even further.

Although the Depression impacted every capitalist country, some were hurt more than others. Germany and the United States endured the highest rates of unemployment: 30 percent or more. In France, by contrast, unemployment hovered around 15 percent.

Also very significant is the fact that the Soviet Union, as the only communist country in the world, was completely isolated from the effects of the economic downturn. In fact, the Soviets were able to achieve massive economic growth throughout the 1930s. This naturally increased the appeal of communism in the eyes of some Europeans.

By 1933, the worst of the economic crisis was over, although it would take years for the world economy to recover fully. In 1932, many debts, including German reparations payments, had been effectively canceled. Many governments also cautiously applied Keynesian policies in order to stimulate economic growth. John Maynard Keynes, a British economist, had suggested that governments should not cut their spending during a recession or a depression in order to maintain a balanced budget and avoid inflation. Instead, governments should *increase* spending, and even go deeply into debt, in order to stimulate demand and employment. By the mid-1930s, expensive government programs, such as Franklin Roosevelt's New Deal in the United States, were showing some positive results. Unfortunately for Europe, however, it was Adolf Hitler in Germany who had the greatest success in applying the lessons of Keynesian economics. He used huge amounts of government spending, including public works programs, to produce dramatic economic and industrial growth, much of it designed to prepare Germany for war.

What countries were most strongly and least strongly affected by the Great Depression?

Interwar Britain and France

After World War I, Britain faced serious economic problems. Throughout the 1920s, unemployment remained above nine percent. In addition, Britain's currency, the pound, had ceased to be the most important world currency during the war. It was surpassed by the U.S. dollar. Throughout the interwar period, the British struggled vainly to recapture their financial preeminence.

Partly as a consequence of this economic tumult, starting in 1923 the Labour Party replaced the Liberal Party as the chief opposition to the Conservatives. Liberal politicians, it seems, were too condescending to workers to win their support, and middle-class voters increasingly drifted into the

Conservative camp. The withering of the Liberal Party, and the rise of Labour, made many Britons nervous. Their fears were assuaged in 1923, when Ramsay MacDonald became Britain's first Labour Party Prime Minister. MacDonald, a charming and surprisingly restrained socialist, was so successful at improving the public image of the Labour Party that in 1931 King George V asked him to lead a "National Government." This involved MacDonald's Labour Party supporters forming a coalition with the Liberals and Conservatives, all of whom would cooperate to deal decisively with the effects of the Great Depression. The National Government was largely successful. Britain prevented its banks from collapsing, aided struggling workers, began a modest military buildup, and encouraged trade within the British Empire. Between 1931 and 1937, the number of unemployed Britons fell by almost half. As a result, fascism and communism never seriously threatened Britain's capitalist democracy.

During the interwar years, while the Royal Navy still commanded the seas, the British Empire began to decline. True, it was still larger than any empire in world history, but its size was deceptive. The bonds of loyalty and submission that held the empire together were rapidly dissolving.

In 1919, a civil war broke out in Ireland over the issue of independence from Britain. In 1921, the conflict was resolved by the creation of the Irish Free State, a nominally independent Dominion of the British Empire. Northern Ireland, which was mostly Protestant, was detached from the Irish Free State and continued to be under British control. Many Catholic Irishmen rejected this arrangement. In 1949, the Irish Free State withdrew completely from the British Empire and became The Republic of Eire. Civil strife between Catholics and Protestants then emerged in Northern Ireland, also known as Ulster. The British tried to resolve the Irish Question in 1921, therefore, but it was a resolution that left many dissatisfied.

Ireland was arguably England's first colony, and its loss was a signal that the British Empire was past its prime. During the 1920s and 1930s, the Indian National Congress and its spiritual leader, the nonviolent activist Mohandas Gandhi, sharply criticized British rule in India. Gradually, the British relented and pledged more powers of self-government to the Indians. In addition, in 1931, Britain issued the Statute of Westminster, which granted full powers of self-government to the "white Dominions" of Canada, Australia, New Zealand, the Irish Free State, and South Africa. Although technically still within the empire, if Britain ever went to war, these countries would choose for themselves whether or not to support her.

The Third Republic had been founded in France in 1870. Although it was repeatedly challenged from the left and from the right, it endured until 1940.

After the First World War, although rebuilding the economy was a serious challenge, France's highest priority was securing itself from the danger of future German aggression. Accordingly, French governments insisted on rigorous enforcement of the Versailles Treaty. Nevertheless, the French still felt threatened by Germany, so France concluded a series of alliances with small Eastern European states such as Czechoslovakia, Romania, Yugoslavia, and Poland. To boost France's ability to defend itself still further, it also constructed a defensive line, called the Maginot Line, on its border with Germany.

Politically, although France remained a democracy, it suffered from chronic instability. Parties on the left and on the right feuded constantly. Government coalitions came and went with astonishing speed. Not surprisingly, under these conditions, extremist political movements had more success in France than they did in Britain. France had a large communist party. There were also two large quasi-fascist organizations on the right: *Action Française* and *Croix de Feu* (meaning Cross of Fire).

In 1936, a so-called Popular Front government was elected in France, and Léon Blum, a Jewish socialist, became Prime Minister. Blum's government was a coalition of democratic socialists and communists who had temporarily put aside their differences at the urging of Stalin, along with some liberal elements. Although Blum pursued moderate policies, many conservatives were outraged that a Jew with socialist beliefs had risen to a position of leadership. A mob of right-wing Frenchmen once physically attacked Blum, and he only narrowly escaped.

During the interwar years, France was a nation politically divided. When its government faced the ultimate test of a German invasion in 1940, the Third Republic fought valiantly, but it finally imploded.

In what ways was the British Empire weakening in the interwar years?

The Soviet Union: Civil War and Communist Reforms Under Lenin

By late 1917, the Bolsheviks had realized their dream of making Russia the world's first communist state. Lenin, who led the country from 1917 to 1924, promptly took Russia out of World War I. A civil war then developed between the supporters of Bolshevism and those who wanted monarchy, military rule, or liberal democracy instead.

To win the civil war, Lenin devised a policy known as War Communism, under which the bureaucracy and the Communist Party took full control of the economy. Factories were regulated by the state, workers were compelled to accept low pay and long hours, and peasants faced forcible requisition of their grain. Every economic enterprise was exploited to provide resources for the communist Red Army, led by Lenin's ally, Leon Trotsky.

In the end, the communists won the civil war, but at a terrible cost. Ten million Russians died in the fighting, or as a result of famine or disease. Two million were forced into exile. No less than half a million died in the custody of the Bolsheviks' feared new secret police force, the *Cheka*. Meanwhile, by 1921, industrial production had fallen roughly 80 percent, and millions of Russians had fled the cities because conditions there had become unbearable.

Lenin realized that Russia was in a desperate situation, and many citizens had come to resent their new communist overlords. To reverse this situation, Lenin made a crucial strategic decision. In 1921, he retreated from his old policy of War Communism and instead imposed a New Economic Policy, also known as the N.E.P.

The N.E.P. called for a mixture of free enterprise capitalism in some sectors, and state-management, or communism, in others. Major banks, heavy industries, and transport companies remained under state control, while retail shops and farms were often placed in private hands. Lenin was especially hopeful that the profit motive would inspire peasant farmers to increase the food supply and thus reduce the danger of food riots in the cities.

The N.E.P. was largely a success. Russia's economy rebounded, and pre–World War I production levels were restored by 1927. The downside, as many fervent communists saw it, was that Lenin had betrayed Marxist principles, which called for the *total* abolition of private property. Indeed, in the countryside, farmers who prospered under the N.E.P., called *kulaks*, were resented by poorer peasants, who saw the *kulaks* as a new capitalist elite.

Under Lenin, the Soviet Union's foreign policy also underwent major changes. Lenin was a believer in world revolution. To maintain the momentum of global communism, therefore, Lenin decided to organize a Third International, a worldwide federation of socialists, also known as the Comintern. The Comintern laid out the Twenty-One Conditions that governed which socialist parties of any country could join the Comintern. In effect, Lenin was informing democratic socialists in the West that they should stop cooperating with *bourgeois* governments, they should work for revolution, they should call themselves communists, and, most importantly, they should take orders from Moscow. Some socialists in Western countries accepted Lenin's commands. Understandably, they became known as communists during the 1920s and 1930s. Others, however, refused to accept Soviet leadership. They continued to work for socialist goals peacefully and democratically. They were generally known in the 1920s and 1930s as socialists or democratic socialists. The net result of Lenin's Comintern and the Twenty-One Conditions was that the socialist movement worldwide became increasingly divided. In fact, so-called socialists and communists often despised one another. It should come as no surprise, therefore, that Lenin's goal of spreading communism globally was not achieved.

In the field of social reform, Lenin was exceptionally bold. Among the successes of Soviet communism was the complete subordination of the media, the arts, and intellectuals to party goals. Lenin sponsored the use of propaganda to convince the masses that a utopian socialist future lay in store. He also lived simply to drive home the message that, in the Soviet Union, no one was privileged. Meanwhile, religious organizations were suppressed. In addition, the Bolshevik secret police, called the *Cheka*, terrorized anyone who stepped out of line. Russia's system of *gulags*, or labor camps for enemies of the state, was founded under Lenin. These *gulags* were places where men and women did hard labor, often in extreme cold, and received little food, clothing, or medicine in return. For all practical purposes, many *gulags* were extermination camps.

Lenin also sponsored changes in family life and in the status of women. From the beginning of the Bolshevik movement, women had participated as party members and activists. During the civil war, however, the Communist Party had become militarized, and Bolshevik women had lost much of their influence. Nevertheless, their dedication to communism was rewarded, to a point. In 1918, divorce and abortion were legalized. Furthermore, some Soviet leaders, especially Alexandra Kollantai, the head of the Women's Department, advocated equality in marriage for husbands and wives, as well as full economic opportunities for both sexes. A few Bolsheviks even criticized the institution of marriage, which they saw as perpetuating the exploitation of women. They hoped that, in the future, the state, rather than wives and mothers, would have primary responsibility for raising the young.

In reality, under communism, family life changed little for many women, and most radical experiments with family policy were abandoned, or simply were never implemented in the first place. Moreover, feminism was anathema to Stalin, who succeeded Lenin as Soviet dictator. Stalin abolished the Women's Department, and he made divorce much more difficult to obtain. Abortion was also outlawed in order to promote higher birth rates. Stalinist propaganda encouraged women to devote their time to housework and childcare as well as to laboring in factories or on farms.

The Bolshevik Revolution made bold promises of freedom in 1917. In the end, it delivered on remarkably few of them.

What policies did Lenin implement?

The Soviet Union: Industrialization and Terror Under Stalin

Lenin died in 1924. His body was embalmed and elaborately displayed in Lenin's Tomb in Red Square, Moscow, while his brain was removed and closely studied because of Lenin's extraordinary "genius." A struggle for power soon developed between two of Lenin's followers: Leon Trotsky, former head of the Red Army, and Joseph Stalin, General Secretary of the Communist Party. Lenin had expressed profound distrust of both men before he died.

Stalin was from the Soviet republic (i.e., province), of Georgia. He came from humble origins and apparently had been brought up in conditions of terrible physical and emotional abuse. As a young man, Stalin studied for a while to become an Orthodox priest, writing poetry on the side, but later he became a fearless Bolshevik revolutionary instead. Although Stalin showed some rare signs of humanity and tenderness, for the most part his defining characteristic was an utter indifference to the suffering of others. When in the early 1920s his son shot himself, but survived, Stalin observed coldly,

"He can't even shoot straight." Stalin's track record in Lenin's government, moreover, suggested that he would rule the Soviet Union with brute force and without moral scruples.

Nevertheless, Stalin prevailed in the leadership struggle with Trotsky, largely because of his organizational abilities, his intelligence, and his iron will. By 1927, Stalin had maneuvered Trotsky out of the government and into exile in Siberia. In 1940, Stalinist agents killed Trotsky in Mexico with an ice-ax of the sort preferred by mountain climbers.

What Stalin chose to do with his newfound power was astonishing. In some areas, admittedly, Stalin simply continued or modified Lenin's policies. For example, like Lenin, Stalin used his secret police force, which he renamed the NKVD, to terrorize his opponents. In other areas, however, Stalin departed completely from Lenin's example.

Unlike Lenin, Stalin believed in "socialism in one country." In other words, he thought that communism could succeed in Russia whether or not there were similar communist revolutions elsewhere. After 1934, in fact, fascist successes in Italy and Germany so worried Stalin that he authorized communist parties around the world to cooperate with democratic socialists. He was willing, therefore, to defer the goal of world revolution if Russia's national interests were served by doing so.

Another difference between Lenin and Stalin was that Lenin was relatively selfless in his pursuit of communist ideals. Stalin, by contrast, shamelessly promoted a personality cult that made Stalin himself the centerpiece of Soviet life.

Stalin's more fundamental break with Lenin came in the realm of economic policy. Stalin had campaigned for the leadership of the Soviet state as a supporter of the New Economic Policy. Stalin had argued that, because the N.E.P. had created steady economic growth and social stability, it should be continued. Trotsky, on the other hand, had opposed the N.E.P. He advocated an even more ambitious policy than War Communism. Trotsky wanted the complete collectivization of agriculture, meaning that private farms would be confiscated and subjected to state management, and all farmers, even successful *kulaks*, would become state employees. The agricultural sector would then be squeezed for profits, and the resulting revenue would be pumped into (centrally controlled) industry. Trotsky wanted to achieve rapid industrialization, no matter what the cost.

During the mid-1920s, Stalin rejected these arguments. As soon as Trotsky was out of the picture, though, Stalin reversed himself, turning his back on Lenin's N.E.P. and embracing Trotsky's radical proposals for reform. In 1928, Stalin instituted the first Five Year Plan for the economy, which was designed to bring every single enterprise under state control. In 1929, he began the collectivization of agriculture.

The results of Stalin's decision to support collectivization and rapid industrialization were far-reaching. On paper, it would appear that Stalin chose rightly. The Soviet economy boomed during the late 1920s and throughout the 1930s. These were the years of the Great Depression in the capitalist world, so the fact that, in the same period, the Soviet Union was able to achieve a huge increase in industrial production was impressive, to say the least.

Although the production of consumer goods was neglected, the improvements to Soviet infrastructure were massive. Whole cities were built in the Soviet wilderness, new industries were created from scratch, and vast numbers of Soviet engineers and technicians were trained in the latest technologies. There is no doubt that, under Stalin, the Soviet Union became an industrial colossus. Importantly, the Soviet Union now had the resources to fight a major war, as Hitler would discover in 1941–45.

In addition, by the mid-1930s, the agricultural system had been brought under full state control. Even though the collective farms never produced as much food as Stalin had predicted, now the government no longer had to rely on the goodwill of the *kulaks* in order to ensure a steady food supply to Russia's cities.

Many left-leaning Westerners visited Russia during the 1930s and praised Stalin's accomplishments, but the social costs were horrendous. To achieve the collectivization of agriculture, Stalin had made the decision to eliminate the *kulaks*. Despite the fact that they were the Soviet Union's best farmers, the *kulaks* were shot, starved, or shipped off to labor camps. In the process of enforcing collectivization, Stalin caused chaos in the countryside that led to the migration of 12 million Soviet citizens to urban areas. Collectivization also produced as many as 10 million deaths, many of them in Ukraine, where the famine of 1932–33 is now known as the *Holodomor* and is often condemned as a form of genocide. Coming on top of the ten million deaths that had already taken place during the civil war, all this carnage produced a serious drop in the Soviet population. This fact, however, detracted from Stalin's image of the Soviet Union as a happy, vibrant, and expanding nation, so it was simply covered up.

Meanwhile, in Soviet factories and in the cities, workers and their families endured conditions more wretched than any that Europeans had faced since the advent of the Industrial Revolution. Food and clothing were scarce, families were packed into single room apartments and military-style barracks, and workplace safety was ignored. The Soviet people only accepted such sacrifices because Stalinist propaganda promised them a better future—and the NKVD promised them death if they complained.

Stalin's economic policies were brutal, but successful. His political policies were even more brutal, and arguably a complete disaster. Stalin's primary political goal was to acquire total control over the Soviet Union for himself—and in the process to eliminate anyone who might pose a threat to his dictatorship. Propaganda was a part of Stalin's strategy, but terror was his trump card. Beginning in 1934, Stalin initiated a series of political trials, imprisonments, and executions known collectively as the Purges. The Purges began with the assassination of a prominent Communist Party official, Sergei Kirov. Stalin claimed to be outraged about Kirov's murder, but many historians believe that Stalin himself ordered it. Whatever the case may be, Stalin used Kirov's death as an excuse to begin hunting for enemies of the state. Although Stalin did face opposition, the primary cause of the Purges appears to have been Stalin's own deep-seated paranoia, perhaps aggravated by his grief at the death by suicide of his wife, Nadya.

From 1934 to 1938, millions of Soviet citizens were subjected to arrest, torture, and sometimes confinement to a labor camp or summary execution. Of the hundreds of thousands of Soviet citizens who were killed outright, many were prominent members of the Communist Party whom Stalin distrusted. Sometimes "show trials" were held to "prove" the guilt of the accused, but, more often, Stalin's version of justice was meted out secretly. By 1939, the majority of the members of the Communist Party's Central Committee and its Party Congress had been killed.

Worse still, Stalin next turned his attention to the military. In 1937 and 1938, the vast majority of the high command of the army and navy was liquidated. Many of these men were experienced, battle-hardened officers. When Germany attacked the Soviet Union in 1941, therefore, incompetent leadership paralyzed the Soviet military.

All in all, the death toll from Stalin's tyranny—before, during, and after the Second World War—exceeded the numbers killed in the Nazi Holocaust. Stalin may have modernized Russia, therefore, making it a superpower by his death in 1953, but he accomplished this feat at an astounding cost. Russians still debate whether Stalin's rule was a blessing or a curse.

How did the Soviet economy change under Stalin?

Italy: The Birthplace of Fascism

Many Americans confuse fascism and communism. Although there are significant similarities between them, including their opposition to liberal democracy and their practice of military aggression, they are highly distinct.

Fascism is generally seen as a radical right-wing movement, while communists are described as leftists. At the core of fascism is extreme nationalism, while communism preaches the solidarity of workers across the world. Fascists permit private property, while communists insist that all economic enterprises should be owned and controlled by the state. Most importantly, during the 1920s, 1930s, and 1940s, fascists and communists hated each other. It is unlikely that Mussolini or Hitler ever would have come to power as fascist dictators if the people of Italy and Germany, respectively, had not desperately wanted protection from the dangers of Bolshevism.

The first country to adopt a fascist government was Italy. It is reasonable to ask how a great power like Italy could succumb to such a novel, extreme, and at times farcical right-wing movement.

Italy had been on the winning side in World War I, but many Italians were unhappy with the Paris Peace Settlement. Italy had gained new territory, but many Italians believed that they deserved much more. There was also economic turmoil in Italy after the war. Strikes were common, and many urban workers and angry peasants agitated for socialist or communist reforms. This terrified the middle and upper classes. At the time, Italy's government was a constitutional monarchy that an elected parliament dominated. Italy's leaders were notoriously corrupt and ineffective, however, and by 1922 many Italians were ready to give up on democracy.

Benito Mussolini offered Italians a simple solution to their problems: fascism. Initially a socialist, Mussolini underwent a transformation during World War I and became fiercely nationalistic and militaristic instead. After the war, he advocated a dictatorial form of government that would abolish corruption, end the confusion of multiparty politics, and eliminate socialists and communists. Mussolini promised that under his leadership Italy would recover its past greatness, and, in particular, the ancient glory of the Roman Empire.

By 1921, with the aid of a brilliant propaganda campaign, Mussolini had won a large following. Mussolini's black-shirted fascist squads, meanwhile, terrorized the opponents of fascism.

In October 1922, Italy's King Victor Emmanuel III was forced to make a difficult choice. Fascist paramilitary forces were beginning a March on Rome, and they were demanding that Mussolini be made Prime Minister. The king would either have to agree, or he would have to send the army to fight the Fascists, which could lead to civil war. He chose, in the end, to make Mussolini Prime Minister.

Many Italians expected Mussolini's government to fall apart quickly, but he surprised them. Mussolini changed the election laws to favor Fascist candidates, he acquiesced in the murder of Giacomo Matteotti, a critic of fascism, and in 1926 he outlawed all parties except the Fascists. Mussolini had become *Il Duce*, The Leader, whose will was beyond questioning. All along, Mussolini's greatest asset was the extreme fear that many Italians had of communism.

Fascist economic policy is usually known as corporatism. Essentially, Mussolini divided the Italian economy into 22 corporations that organized production and labor relations according to government priorities. In theory, capitalists still owned their businesses, and workers were still organized into unions, but their freedom of action was sharply limited. This system produced many show projects that made Italians proud—and it allegedly made the trains run on time—but it did not save Italy from the Great Depression. Corruption also remained a serious problem.

Fascist social policy was largely traditional, but it also aimed to promote unity under the banner of fascism. Mussolini wanted an Italy that was masculine and militaristic, and so every schoolchild was taught about the importance of courage and self-sacrifice. An elaborate personality cult, meanwhile, revolved around *Il Duce* himself. Mussolini advocated a modified version of the Cult of Domesticity. He believed that the number of women in the workforce should be minimized, and women should be encouraged to have many children and to stay at home to raise them. One fascist slogan told women: "You are . . . serving the Fatherland when you sweep your own house." Mussolini also forbade abortion and birth control.

In 1929, in a move that pleased conservatives, Mussolini reached an accommodation with the Catholic Church, called the Lateran Accord. Although Church-state relations remained troubled, the Accord gave the Church substantial control over education and marriage law, and it compensated the Church for lands that Italy had taken from the pope in 1870.

Italy's Fascist government pursued an aggressive foreign policy. In 1896, the Italians had been ignominiously defeated in an attempt to conquer Ethiopia. In 1935, Mussolini decided to even the score. He invaded Ethiopia and used aircraft, artillery, and poison gas to pound the backward country into submission. World opinion was outraged, but Mussolini pressed on to victory. In 1939, he also added Albania to Italy's empire.

Italy's aggression soured the country's relationship with its former allies, Britain and France. Italy therefore drifted steadily into the arms of Hitler's Germany. A Rome-Berlin Axis was in place by 1936.

Why did fascism succeed in Italy?

Figure 17.1 Benito Mussolini and Adolf Hitler.
Everett Historical/Shutterstock.

Germany: The Weimar Republic and the Nazi Conquest of Power, 1919–33

The Weimar Republic was battling for its survival from the very start. It had been born in November 1918 in the context of military defeat and national humiliation; it was initially dominated by ineffective liberals, Catholic centrists, and socialists in the widely hated SPD, or Social Democratic Party; and it presided over a weak economy that, during the massive inflation of 1923, teetered on the brink of total collapse.

To make matters worse, in 1919 and 1920, there was a series of strikes, assassinations, and uprisings throughout Germany. Communists even briefly took over in Bavaria. Many of the leaders of the communist uprising had been Jewish, which led an increasing number of Germans to blame the Jews for Germany's plight. The turmoil climaxed in November 1923, when a small political party known as the Nazis staged a coup in Munich, called the Beer Hall Putsch. It was easily defeated, but to many Germans it appeared that their country was falling apart.

Adolf Hitler was an unlikely savior for Germany. Although he was ethnically German, he was born and grew up in Austria, not Germany. Once an aspiring artist and architect in Vienna, during World War I he had served as a lowly corporal in the German army on the Western Front, where he was decorated for bravery. Unlike most Germans, he was a teetotaler who never drank, smoked, or ate meat. His Austrian accent immediately marked him as an outsider. There were also false rumors that Hitler had Jewish blood.

More important than Hitler's background was his political philosophy. Hitler was convinced that he understood why Germany had lost the war, and why the country had been plunged into chaos ever since. Hitler claimed that the German army had been "stabbed in the back" by politicians, especially socialists and Jews, who had caused Germany's defeat so that they could take power. Now, those same politicians, and their friends in business and the media, were profiting from the suffering of the German people.

In 1918, Hitler was just one of millions of irate Germans who had their own pet theories about the nation's predicament. Starting in 1919, though, Hitler was able to play a role, albeit a modest one, in German politics. In that year, the German army hired him as a political officer. In effect, his job was to spy on right-wing political organizations. One of his initial assignments was to keep tabs on a group that would become known as the National Socialist German Workers' Party (its German initials were NSDAP). Hitler soon impressed the Nazis with his skillful oratory and his passionate German nationalism. He was acclaimed as the Nazi leader by 1921. In their early days, the Nazis modeled their party on Mussolini's Fascists. The famous Nazi raised-arm salute, for example, was taken from the Fascists, who in turn had taken it from the ancient Romans.

Hitler was not the only strong personality in the Nazi movement. Hermann Göring, a World War I flying ace, joined the party early on. He was handsome and popular at first. During World War II, though, Göring's morphine addiction, his self-indulgent lifestyle, and the failures of the *Luftwaffe* (the German air force), which he commanded, all combined to discredit him. Another early Nazi was Heinrich Himmler, a former agriculture student who would later lead the much-feared Nazi *Schutzstaffel*, or SS. Himmler was a complex man. He was by nature a colorless bureaucrat who enjoyed playing chess, drank mineral water, and nearly fainted at the sight of an execution. He also emerged as the chief organizer and justifier of the Jewish Holocaust.

The goals of the Nazis were often unclear, but Hitler definitely wanted to abolish the Versailles Treaty. He also desired an end to reparations, the withdrawal of all occupation troops from German soil, plus a rapid reconstruction of German military might in order to conquer new lands in the East. In addition, Hitler sought to overturn the liberal institutions of the Weimar Republic, to crush communism, and to institute an authoritarian regime. On most other points, however, the Nazis seemed to change their views over time, or emphasize different points with different audiences.

One of Hitler's personal obsessions was with the connection between communism and world Jewry. Hitler believed that the Jews, even if they sometimes posed as capitalists, were engaged in a diabolical conspiracy along with the communists. The goal of this conspiracy was global domination and the destruction of the Aryan race. Hitler devoted much of his political career to battling the forces of communism and Judaism, both of which he passionately hated.

Why, though, did Hitler choose to target the Jews so relentlessly? For centuries, many Christian Europeans had attacked Jews as "Christ-killers," they had resented Jewish economic success, and, since the nineteenth century, they had noted the Jews' apparent affinity for reformist, even radical, ideologies such as liberalism, socialism, and communism. Anti-Semitism was therefore widespread in Europe long before the rise of Nazism. Moreover, there was also, by the 1920s, a century-long tradition of casting the Jews' alleged wickedness in biological terms. Jews were compared to a plague or an infection that could potentially be removed by some form of "racial hygiene." Hitler even went as far as to suggest, echoing nineteenth-century Aryanism and Social Darwinism, that there was an epic struggle for survival underway between Aryans and Jews, and only one side could prevail. Hitler's anti-Semitism was largely, therefore, an amalgam of old stereotypes and ideas, but it nonetheless had the effect of greatly raising the stakes in the battle against "Jewry."

To many Germans in the 1920s and early 1930s, Hitler's anti-Semitic logic was puzzling, and his intentions if he became Germany's leader were ambiguous. Sometimes the Nazis talked about "extermination," and sometimes they suggested less extreme remedies to the "Jewish-Bolshevik" conspiracy, such as excluding Jews from full German citizenship. Many Germans, in the final analysis, chose to close their eyes to Nazi anti-Semitism. The Nazis promised them national unity, strength, and prosperity, as well as the destruction of communism. The German people were largely content to let Hitler work out the details on his own.

Yet another source of ambiguity in Nazi proposals lay in Hitler's economic policies. Initially the Nazis were quite socialistic. They attacked war profiteers and appealed for support to industrial workers. Later, though, the Nazis instead courted middle-class and rural voters, along with business interests. In the end, the Nazis never advocated an end to private property, although they did believe that businesses and labor unions should subordinate their interests to the overriding goal of a strong Germany.

The mid and late 1920s were challenging times for Hitler and his Nazis. The failure of the Beer Hall Putsch in 1923 had embarrassed the movement. For many Germans, Hitler became a joke. He served less than a year in prison, though, and soon the Nazis were again vigorously campaigning for support.

After the Putsch, Hitler decided that persuasion, rather than violence, would be the primary means that the Nazis would use to win power. This was easier said than done, however, because, from 1925 to about 1928, the German economy surged. Meanwhile, Germany negotiated various compromises with Britain and France, including the Locarno Agreements. These compromises seemed to suggest that Germany could overcome the legacy of World War I without waging a war of vengeance against the Allies.

In this atmosphere of prosperity and peacemaking, support for the bellicose Nazis withered. In 1925, Field Marshal Paul von Hindenburg, a strong conservative and a war hero, was elected as Germany's President. Most Germans preferred to entrust the defense of the Fatherland against communism to von Hindenburg rather than to hotheads like the Nazis. In 1928, the Nazis received less than three percent of the vote.

More than any other factor, it was the Great Depression that lifted Hitler and the Nazis into power. Before the Depression, the Nazis were politically irrelevant. Once the German people had confronted the specter of 30 percent unemployment and an explosion in communist agitation, however, Nazism began to seem much more appealing.

The Depression in Germany was indeed more severe than in any other country in the world. By the early 1930s, six million workers were unemployed, and many Germans were destitute. In fact, many German men joined the paramilitary forces of the communists or the Nazis not out of idealism, but simply because they needed food and something to do. The Nazis' militia, called the *Sturmabteilung*, or SA, known in the English-speaking world as the Stormtroopers or Brownshirts, was especially successful, eventually attracting several million members. Street battles raged constantly between the SA and the communists.

By 1932, the Nazis had become the single largest party in the *Reichstag*, the German parliament. They received more than 37 percent of the vote. War veterans, the young, Protestants, farmers, and members of the lower middle class were most likely to support the Nazis. Party rallies, like the annual gathering in Nuremberg, fired many Germans with frantic enthusiasm for Hitler. The Nazis also devised a brilliant campaign for support known as "Hitler Over Germany." Hitler traveled the nation in an airplane, attending multiple rallies each day and sending the message that the Nazis were technologically advanced and even futuristic in their thinking.

The Depression put President von Hindenburg in a difficult position. He detested communism, but he was unwilling to make common cause with the Nazis because he considered them too radical, populist, and unruly. His initial response to the political and economic crisis was to use the emergency powers that the Weimar constitution granted him to govern without the consent of the *Reichstag*, which had become ineffectual. Von Hindenburg appointed a series of conservative Chancellors—Heinrich Brüning, Franz von Papen, and Kurt von Schleicher—who ruled as virtual dictators. None of them, though, proved able to end the Depression or attract mass support.

Finally, in January 1933, von Hindenburg's advisors convinced him that Hitler had to be made Chancellor. The alternative appeared to be a communist revolution. Regretfully, von Hindenburg offered Hitler the chancellorship, and Hitler accepted it on January 30, 1933. Nazi Stromtroopers paraded triumphantly in Berlin, but conservatives in von Hindenburg's inner circle were confident that Hitler could be manipulated. They were sadly mistaken.

How did Adolf Hitler and the Nazis come to power in Germany?

Hitler's Germany, 1933–39

Once Hitler became Germany's leader, his first task was to eliminate all of his rivals for power. In February 1933, an arsonist burned down the *Reichstag* building. The timing was exceedingly convenient for the Nazis, because Hitler could use the incident to inflame the German people's fear of communism. According to Hitler, a communist had committed the crime, and the fire was a signal that was intended to start a Soviet-style revolution. In March 1933, Hitler convinced the *Reichstag* to pass the Enabling Act, which granted him dictatorial powers. In a period of national emergency, Hitler argued, strong leadership was necessary, and civil liberties were a luxury that Germany could not afford. By July 1933, the trade unions had been brought under Nazi control, and all other political parties were outlawed. It had taken Mussolini four years to achieve a one-party state in Italy. It took Hitler only six months.

Hitler's next task was to remove potential rivals within the Nazi Party itself. Although many people assume today that the Nazis all moved in lockstep with Hitler, in reality there was considerable corruption, confusion, bureaucratic infighting, and personal jealousy within the party, some of which Hitler encouraged. There were also ideological disagreements among the Nazis. Some were essentially socialists, while others favored aristocracy and monarchy. Some were forward-thinking, favoring industry and urbanization, while others looked to the past, hoping for a return to the soil. Some Nazis despised the Jews, while others scarcely noticed them. Some lusted for war, while others feared its consequences. These important differences were never fully resolved.

In the end, the biggest threat to Hitler within the party came from Ernst Röhm, the leader of the SA, the Nazi's main paramilitary force. Röhm was widely popular, but his extreme views and his ambition made Hitler conclude that he was a liability. The German army also wanted Röhm out of the picture, because his SA threatened to become the nucleus of a new and more populist army.

On June 30, 1934, the SS, a Nazi paramilitary force that was smaller, more elite, and more loyal than the SA, moved against Röhm and his allies, who were plotting a coup, according to Hitler. In the Night of the Long Knives, Röhm and at least 80 other Germans, mostly high-ranking Nazis, were killed.

Hitler's grip on power was solidified even further in August 1934, when the death of the elderly von Hindenburg allowed Hitler to combine the offices of President and Chancellor. Now, with both titles in his pocket, Hitler truly was *der Führer* (The Leader), and his power was absolute—although in practice he delegated it extensively to subordinates. In August 1934, Hitler also cannily required all military officers to swear an oath of personal loyalty to him.

Two other institutions in Germany contributed to the popularity and power of the Nazi Party. One was the Ministry of Public Enlightenment and Propaganda, which was ably led by the gaunt womanizer, Dr. Josef Goebbels. Goebbels coordinated the media and the arts in Germany, including the press, music, literature, radio, and film. In doing so, he made use of many talented artists and writers to mobilize support for Nazism. In addition, pageantry, often in the form of huge rallies, gigantic swastika banners, and parading Nazis (always in uniform), communicated the pride and enthusiasm of the movement. Perhaps the most remarkable demonstration of Goebbels' Nazi idealism was the exhibition of "degenerate art" in 1937 that showcased modern and abstract art that the Nazis condemned as "un-German." Overall, Goebbels' Ministry was highly effective in encouraging loyalty to Hitler, even in the darkest days of World War II. Indeed, active opposition was virtually nonexistent.

The other asset upon which Hitler could rely was the *Gestapo*, the secret police, which was, beginning in 1934, administered as a branch of Heinrich Himmler's SS. Germany's legal system essentially gave free rein to the *Gestapo* to hunt down ruthlessly all enemies, real and imagined, of the regime. As Hitler himself wrote, "Terror ... will always be successful unless opposed by equal terror." Needless to say, no one could equal the *Gestapo*.

The SS, composed only of those who could prove they had pure Aryan ancestry, included the secret police, but it also played a much wider role in the Third Reich. Himmler's SS branched into areas as diverse as education, industry, technical research, publishing, culture, history, archaeology, racial science, and even warfare—SS divisions served alongside the regular army, and they sometimes engaged in terrible atrocities. Although the SS is usually portrayed as a hyper-efficient and elite organization, recent research has demonstrated that many of its operations were poorly managed. Nonetheless, by the end of the Nazi era, the SS was an empire unto itself, with its own bureaucracy, economy, army, and culture, and a heroic self-image to match.

In the realm of economic policy, Hitler achieved a stunning success: he rescued Germany from the Great Depression. Arguably, many of Hitler's public works programs, such as the famous highways, or *Autobahn*, were inherited from previous governments, but Hitler still got the credit. By 1939, thanks to massive public spending, full employment had been restored, and the breadlines of the Depression were a distant memory.

To end the disorder caused by strikes, Hitler dissolved the unions and created a Nazi Labor Front. This effectively deprived workers of collective bargaining power, but businesses too were expected to make sacrifices. Germany remained a nominally capitalist country under Hitler, but ultimately its business leaders and its workers all took their orders from the state. Meanwhile, a program offering subsidized entertainment and holiday trips, called "Strength through Joy," helped to increase public support for Nazi economy policy.

One of Hitler's most important economic goals was "autarky," that is, economic self-sufficiency. Hitler knew that, in any future war, Britain was likely to cut off Germany's maritime trade through a naval blockade, as it had during World War I. If Germany could produce its own raw materials, foodstuffs, and industrial products, therefore, the British threat would be neutralized.

Overall, Nazi economic policy was hugely successful. By 1939, the German economy, especially its military-industrial complex, was immensely stronger than when Hitler had taken power.

Nazi social policy was guided by a desire to protect the unity and the purity of the "Aryan race," under the broad rubric of German nationalism. Accordingly, the Nazi Party sponsored clubs and organizations that put the stamp of Nazism on virtually every activity. The goal was for every citizen to be "merged completely in the Germanic herd," as one American journalist put it. Churches, women's organizations, charities, cultural groups, and sports and outdoor activities were all subordinated to the party and state, at least in theory (practicing Christians were especially resistant). The most famous of these attempts to enforce conformity to Nazism was the Hitler Youth, which by law enrolled every school-age boy. In addition to ideological and racial purity, it stressed physical and psychological training that would prepare boys and young men for military service. A League of German Girls also existed.

In the 1920s, a New Woman had emerged throughout Europe—independent, educated, fun-loving, and self-confident. The Nazis were generally distressed by this trend toward female emancipation. They viewed women first and foremost as mothers, and thus as the creators and nurturers of the next generation of Aryan Germans—and the Nazis were adamant that they wanted as many Aryan children as possible. Under the Nazi regime, therefore, special allowances and tax breaks were granted to families with numerous children. The Nazis achieved a 40 percent increase in the birthrate, and they occasionally expressed theoretical enthusiasm for polygyny. Women were by no means excluded from the workforce, but they were generally encouraged to view the three Ks—*Kinder, Kirche, Küche*, or Children, Church, and Kitchen—as their main functions in life, in addition to living as model Nazis. Ironically, although the Nazis praised marriage and parenthood, Hitler never had any children, and he did not marry until the last hours of his life. From 1936 to 1945, Hitler's mistress, Eva Braun, lived with him at his picturesque mountain retreat, known as the *Berghof*, in the Bavarian Alps.

Some groups in Germany did not live up to the Nazis' Aryan standards, and they were harshly persecuted. For instance, while most Germans were encouraged to have many children, those who were judged to be insufficiently Aryan, or who were seen as physically or psychologically defective, were sometimes medically sterilized. Some mental patients were even killed by poison gas, setting a precedent for wartime atrocities against the Jews and other groups.

The Nazis targeted the Jews as soon as Hitler came to power in 1933. Many lost their jobs as teachers or bureaucrats. In 1935, the Nazis went further and passed the Nuremberg Laws, which denied full German citizenship to Jews and legally defined them as a separate race that was not allowed to intermarry or have sexual relations with Aryans. In 1938, during *Kristallnacht*, the Night of Broken Glass, Nazi mobs vandalized or burned to the ground many synagogues, as well as Jewish homes and businesses. Much of the property and wealth of Jews was also confiscated by the government.

All these measures were designed to make life unbearable for the Jews. At this stage, the goal was not extermination. It was to convince the Jews, who were less than one percent of the population, to leave Germany, which more than half of them did. Some refused to flee their homeland, however. Others could find nowhere else to go.

As early as 1933, the Nazis had built the first concentration camp at Dachau, but not to house or murder the Jews. Initially, such camps were essentially prisons, and their inmates, while often guilty only of political opposition, were given adequate food and shelter, and many of them were eventually released. As time went on, more concentration camps were built, and the number of victims of Nazi terror multiplied. Jews, communists, and Gypsies were among the most likely to be persecuted. By 1939, the precedent for a more thorough and deadly campaign against the perceived enemies of the Aryan race had been set.

What policies did the Nazis pursue in Germany from 1933 to 1939?

Weakness and Instability in Eastern Europe

Northwestern Europe remained overwhelmingly democratic during the 1930s, despite the turmoil of the Depression. Norway, Sweden, Finland, Denmark, the Netherlands, Belgium, Luxembourg, and Switzerland were all liberal democracies when World War II broke out in 1939.

In Eastern Europe, though, every democratic government that had been formed at the end of World War I, except that of Czechoslovakia, was eventually toppled from within. Poverty (worsened by the effects of the Great Depression), corruption, political instability, and ethnic and religious discrimination plagued many of the Eastern European states. Most had been ruled before 1914 by Germany, Austria-Hungary, or Russia, and thus they had no strong historical tradition of self-government to fall back on. Most of these Eastern European nations eventually became quasi-fascist dictatorships.

In Poland, a substantial Jewish minority, representing roughly ten percent of the population, faced persecution at the hands of the Catholic majority. The government sponsored numerous discriminatory laws targeting Jews. In addition, the Poles mistreated the large Belorussian and Ukrainian minorities living in the eastern part of the country. To make matters even more complicated, one million disgruntled Germans lived in the western part of Poland, on land that had belonged to Germany as recently as 1919. It was inevitable that Germany would seek to recover these areas. Meanwhile, Poland's democratic constitution was subverted in 1926, and Marshal Josef Pilsudski emerged as military dictator.

At the end of World War I, Hungary had been separated from Austria. In 1919, a communist regime under Béla Kun arose in Hungary, but it was soon replaced with a regency government under the conservative Admiral Miklós Horthy. Admiral Horthy collaborated closely with the Nazi regime in Germany, largely in an effort to recover lands in Transylvania that were populated partly with ethnic Hungarians, but which the Paris Settlement had assigned to Romania. To curry favor with the Nazis, and also due to rampant anti-Semitism in Hungary itself, Horthy's government introduced anti-Jewish laws in 1938.

Austria and Czechoslovakia showed the greatest promise as potential democracies, but only the Czechs and Slovaks managed to keep their liberal governments in place until 1939. Czechoslovakia was unique in Eastern Europe in that it possessed a large middle class and modern industries. Czechoslovak democracy was troubled, however, by Czech-Slovak rivalry, and by the presence of several million ethnic Germans in the German-Czech border region, known as the Sudetenland. Many of these Germans would have preferred to live under Nazi rule. They got their wish in 1938–39, when Hitler conquered Czechoslovakia.

In Austria, political confusion led to a "Christian Socialist" dictatorship in 1934. One of Hitler's most cherished goals was the union of his native

Austria, which was populated with ethnic Germans, with Germany itself. He accomplished this union, or *Anschluss*, in 1938.

Estonia, Latvia, and Lithuania—commonly known as the Baltic states—also succumbed to authoritarian rule. Like Czechoslovakia and Austria, they too were absorbed by a stronger power: in this case, the Soviet Union.

In southeastern Europe, also known as the Balkans, ethnic divisions among Serbs, Croats, Bosnian Muslims, and others plagued the new Kingdom of Yugoslavia. Here, and also in Romania and Bulgaria, kings ruled as dictators. In all these countries, primitive forms of fascism and anti-Semitism flourished.

Greece was among the victors in World War I, and in the Paris Settlement it had been promised a slice of Turkish territory. A Turkish general by the name of Mustafa Kemal—later known as Atatürk, or "Father of the Turks"—expelled the Greeks from Asia Minor, however, and Turkey emerged as a partially Westernized one-party state. Greece experienced considerable instability in the interwar years, despite its close ties to Britain. A military regime took power there in 1936.

What factors produced chronic instability in Eastern Europe in the interwar years?

Conclusions

It is fitting to end a chapter on interwar Europe with a survey of the weak authoritarian regimes in Eastern Europe. By the 1930s, both Germany and the Soviet Union were recovering their strength and confidence. Both countries increasingly eyed the territory and resources of Eastern Europe, and they concluded that these were nations that could easily be conquered. The only questions were: who would begin the process of subjugating the region, and when would they strike? And how would Britain and France react? World War II, just like World War I, would begin in the East, but it would spread much further.

Key Terms for Chapter 17

Locarno Agreements, 1925—peace accords reached between Britain, France, Italy, and Germany that seemed to suggest that another war was unnecessary.

Great Depression—a very serious economic downturn from 1929 to 1939 leading to reduced output and high unemployment in capitalist countries, as well as much political turmoil.

National Government—a coalition government in Britain starting in 1931 including members of the Labour, Liberal, and Conservative Parties, all of which cooperated to deal with the Great Depression.

War Communism—Soviet economic policy under Lenin from 1918 to 1921 that put all economic activity under state control, with the goal of providing the Red Army with the necessary resources to win the Russian Civil War.

New Economic Policy (N.E.P.), 1921—revised Soviet economic policy that mixed some elements of capitalism with elements of socialism, the goal of which was to produce economic growth and a steady food supply.

Joseph Stalin—an associate of Lenin, and Soviet dictator from 1927 to 1953. He was best known for achieving collectivization, initiating the Purges, and leading the Soviet Union to victory in World War II.

Collectivization—the process of bringing all agricultural activity under state control. In the Soviet Union, this involved destroying the *kulaks* (wealthy independent farmers) as a class.

Purges—a wide-reaching series of political arrests, trials, imprisonments, and executions in the Soviet Union, directed by Stalin, lasting from 1934 to 1938.

Fascism—an ideology defined by extreme nationalism, authoritarianism, anti-communism, and militarism.

Adolf Hitler—from 1921 to 1945, leader of the Nazi Party, and, from 1933 to 1945, dictator of Germany. He is best known for leading Germany to catastrophic defeat in the Second World War.

Heinrich Himmler—prominent Nazi and head of the *Schutzstaffel* (SS), which took charge of Germany's police forces and of the Nazi Holocaust.

Paul von Hindenburg—conservative war hero who, as President of Germany from 1925 to 1934, acquiesced to the Nazi takeover.

SA (*Sturmabteilung*)—large Nazi paramilitary force, known in the West as Stormtroopers or Brownshirts.

Josef Goebbels—prominent Nazi and head of Hitler's propaganda machine.

Nuremberg Laws, 1935—the first systematic attempt by the Nazis to persecute the Jews. This new approach defined who was Jewish, excluded Jews from German citizenship, and prohibited marriage or sex between Jews and Aryans.

Review Questions for Chapter 17

1. Describe two reasons why the Great Depression is considered one of the most severe economic downturns in world history. Then, describe two of the political consequences of the Great Depression.
2. Imagine that you are a Soviet citizen living during the late 1930s. Write a diary entry in which you discuss in detail one of Stalin's accomplishments and one of his mistakes.
3. Explain three of the distinguishing features of fascism.
4. If you had lived in Germany in 1932–33, do you believe that you would have voted for the Nazis or not? Give at least three arguments to support your position.

5. Write a short biography of either Stalin, Mussolini, or Hitler. Then consider whether a similar leader could come to power in a Western country today. Explain your views.

Further Reading

Bosworth, R.J.B. *Mussolini's Italy: Life Under the Fascist Dictatorship, 1915–1945*. New York: Penguin. 2007.

Clavin, Patricia. *The Great Depression in Europe, 1929–1939*. Basingstoke, UK: Macmillan. 2000.

Fest, Joachim C. *The Face of the Third Reich: Portraits of the Nazi Leadership*. London: Tauris Parke Paperbacks. 2011.

Friedlander, Saul. *Nazi Germany and the Jews. Volume I: The Years of Persecution, 1933–1939*. London: Phoenix. 2014.

Kershaw, Ian. *Hitler, 1889–1936: Hubris*. Toronto: Penguin. 2001.

Kershaw, Ian. *Hitler, 1936–1945: Nemesis*. London: Penguin. 2001.

Kershaw, Ian. *The Nazi Dictatorship: Problems and Perspectives of Interpretation*. London: Bloomsbury. 2012.

Kitchen, Martin. *A History of Modern Germany, 1800–2000*. Malden, MA: Blackwell. 2010.

Koonz, Claudia. *The Nazi Conscience*. Cambridge, MA: Belknap Press. 2005.

Kuromiya, Hiroaki. *The Voices of the Dead: Stalin's Great Terror in the 1930s*. New Haven, CT: Yale University Press. 2007.

Maier, Charles F. *Recasting Bourgeois Europe: Stabilization in France, Germany, and Italy in the Decade After World War I*. Princeton, NJ: Princeton University Press. 2016.

Overy, Richard. *The Twilight Years: The Paradox of Britain Between the Wars*. New York: Penguin. 2010.

Service, Robert. *Stalin: A Biography*. London: Pan Books. 2010.

Steiner, Zara. *The Triumph of the Dark: European International History, 1933–1939*. Oxford: Oxford University Press. 2015.

18 World War II, 1939–45

Introduction

The German invasion of Poland in September 1939 marked the beginning of what would become the bloodiest and most destructive war in human history. More so than any other conflict, the Second World War unfolded on a truly global scale, involving major campaigns in Europe, Africa, and Asia. Although there were many reasons for the conflict, the ambitions of Germany, Italy, and Japan—states that felt that the Paris Peace Settlement had not treated them fairly—were critical. Equally important was the unwillingness of the Soviet Union and the Western democracies, principally the United States, Britain, and France, to exert themselves to restrain the military aggression of the fascist powers.

Although the Allies possessed overwhelming human and material resources, the outcome of the conflict was by no means assured, because initially the Axis powers enjoyed the strategic initiative. For a variety of reasons, though, the tide of battle would turn in 1942–43, and the Axis powers would go down to total defeat.

Hitler's Quest for *Lebensraum*, and Europe's Path to War, 1933–39

During the interwar years, there was one point on which Hitler and most other German leaders were absolutely consistent: Germany's eastern borders, as they had been drawn in the Versailles Treaty, were utterly unacceptable. Many ethnic Germans had been forced to live outside the borders of Germany, in countries such as Poland, Czechoslovakia, and Austria. At a minimum, most Germans wanted to lay claim to these ethnically German communities as well as the land on which they stood.

Hitler, however, wanted to go much further than this. He desired *Lebensraum*, or living space, for Germany, by which he meant that Germans should pursue a program of massive territorial expansion in the East. Vast areas of Poland and the Soviet Union ought to belong to Germany, according to Hitler. The fact that tens of millions of Slavs—mainly Poles, Russians, and

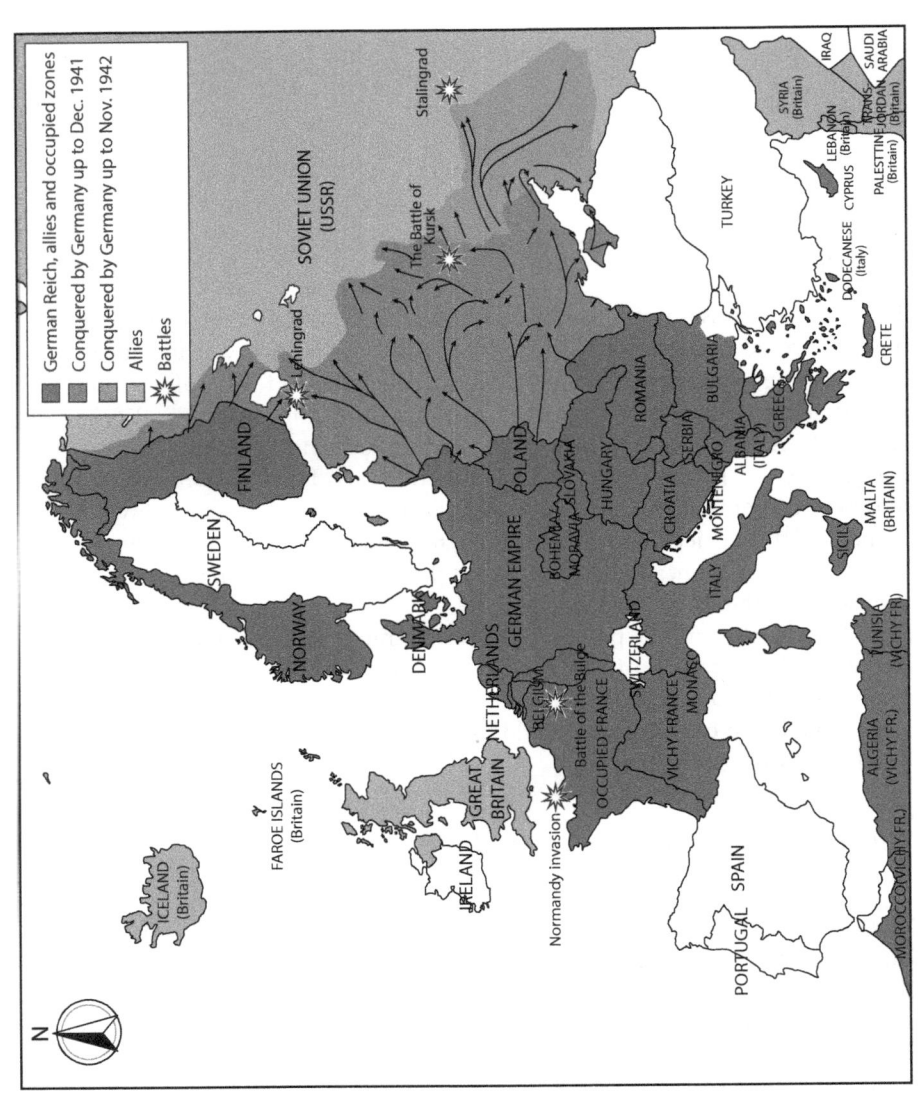

Map 18.1 World War II in Europe.

Ukrainians—already inhabited these regions was, for him, not a concern. These "subhumans" could be relocated, enslaved, or killed.

Although Stalin also had designs on Eastern Europe, it was Hitler who took the initiative from 1933 to 1939. One potential obstacle was the League of Nations, which aimed to enforce "collective security" by applying sanctions against any nation practicing "aggression." Luckily for Hitler, Japan had humiliated the League in 1931. Japan had invaded Manchuria, a province of China, and the League had done little or nothing in response. The League also failed to stop Mussolini from conquering Ethiopia in 1935–36. As a result, Hitler was confident that the League of Nations could be brushed aside.

A more serious obstacle to the conquest of *Lebensraum* was the Allies that had opposed Germany in the First World War, especially Britain, France, and Italy. The United States was now firmly isolationist. France, in particular, was determined to resist German aggression, but it required help, and Britain and Italy were indecisive. No one was eager to fight another World War. Many Britons also felt sympathy for the Germans, who arguably had been unjustly treated in the Paris Peace Settlement. In addition, since Hitler sometimes claimed in public to have designs only on territory that was populated by ethnic Germans, to many Europeans it seemed that he was simply a German nationalist whose goals were limited.

From 1933 to 1939, Hitler successfully exploited these doubts and divisions in the Allied camp. In 1936, 1937, and 1939, he signed treaties with Italy, pulling Mussolini closer to Germany. He also signed a naval agreement with the British in 1935 that soured relations between Britain and France.

Hitler then decided to renounce the disarmament clauses in the Versailles Treaty, which Germany had been secretly violating since the 1920s. Simultaneously, Hitler began a massive military buildup, increasing the size of the German army to 500,000 men and creating a modern and well-equipped *Luftwaffe* (air force) and *Kriegsmarine* (navy). Germany was also building thousands of panzers, that is, modern tanks. The British and French, by comparison, lagged far behind in military preparedness, although the Royal Navy still commanded the high seas.

Hitler's next major step was to send German troops into the Rhineland region in western Germany in March 1936. According to the Versailles Treaty, the Rhineland was supposed to be demilitarized, so Hitler's actions were a clear provocation. Britain and France would have been justified in declaring war. At that stage, Germany probably would have been easily defeated. Instead, Britain and France did nothing.

Many German generals had been wary of Hitler's occupation of the Rhineland, because they feared Allied retaliation. Hitler's success therefore caused many previously skeptical Germans to see their new leader as a miracle-worker. The next time Hitler wanted to act aggressively, few Germans thought to question him.

From 1936 to 1939, a civil war was fought in Spain between leftist republicans, including many communists, and homegrown fascists, bolstered by conservative Catholics. This was a critical opportunity for Britain and France to stop the spread of fascism. Once again, they proved unwilling to act. Germany and Italy, by contrast, sent men and military supplies to help General Francisco Franco, who led the fascist armies. The Germans also sent the Condor Legion, a modern bomber force, which pulverized the Spanish city of Guernica, killing many civilians. Finally, in 1939, Franco's forces defeated the republicans, and Spain succumbed to fascism.

In 1938, Germany became much bolder in its foreign policy. Hitler had always wanted to annex his homeland of Austria, which was populated with ethnic Germans. He had failed in an attempt to do so in 1934, but in 1938 he struck again. Germany mounted a bloodless invasion of Austria in March of that year, and Hitler journeyed to Vienna to proclaim the *Anschluss*, or union, of Germany and Austria to cheering crowds. Amazingly, the Allies made no move to stop Germany.

Later in 1938, Hitler announced his determination to annex the Sudetenland, a region in western Czechoslovakia that was populated by ethnic Germans. Czechoslovakia objected, and a diplomatic crisis ensued. At the last minute, Neville Chamberlain, the British Prime Minister, traveled to Munich and negotiated a compromise. Germany could have the Sudetenland, as long as Hitler promised that his territorial expansion would stop there. Hitler cunningly agreed, and Czechoslovakia was forced to hand over the Sudetenland. This effort by the British and the French to reach an understanding with Hitler was known as "appeasement." Chamberlain boasted that he had secured "peace for our time."

In March 1939, though, Hitler broke his promise and conquered the rest of Czechoslovakia. Now the weakness of the British and the French, who had done nothing to help their Czech allies, was becoming embarrassing. Hitler began to feel as though he could do anything he pleased. The Allies, however, were finally developing some resolve. On March 31, 1939, the British and the French solemnly declared that if Hitler attacked Poland they would declare war on Germany. They did not, however, make any effective plans to assist the Poles.

There was little doubt that Hitler wanted to invade Poland. He despised the Poles as "subhuman" Slavs, and Polish territory was absolutely essential to his goal of *Lebensraum*. Hitler knew, though, that Britain and France might follow through on their pledge to help Poland. If they did so, and if Poland did not fall quickly, Germany might be compelled to fight simultaneously in the west and in the east. A two-front war had not gone well for Germany before. How could this be prevented? The answer was strategically obvious, but ideologically repugnant: Germany should strike a deal with the Soviet Union. With Stalin's help, Poland could easily be subjugated, and Germany could turn its full attention to the west.

The position of the Soviet Union in the European power balance was ambiguous. Hitler's regime was fiercely anti-communist, and Stalin had made no secret of his contempt for fascists and Nazis, so it appeared to the Allies as though a Nazi-Soviet agreement was impossible. Britain and France mounted a diplomatic effort in 1939 to win over the Soviets to an alliance with them. They hoped that, in the event of a German attack on Poland, Russia would do most of the fighting against Germany. In reality, though, an alliance of this sort was unappealing to Stalin. Britain and France were offering the Soviet Union nothing except bitter fighting without the prospect of territorial gains. The Nazis and the Soviets, on the other hand, shared a common goal: territorial expansion in Eastern Europe. If they could agree on how to divide the spoils, then why not do so?

Hitler dispatched his Foreign Minister, Joachim von Ribbentrop, a dapper former champagne salesman, to Moscow to negotiate a deal. On August 23, 1939, the Nazi-Soviet Non-Aggression Pact was announced to the world. Jaws dropped in Berlin and Moscow no less than in every other world capital. The fascists and the communists, bitter enemies up to now, were suddenly friends. Communists around the world dutifully followed Stalin's orders and supported the Pact.

Importantly, the Pact had secret clauses. Hitler agreed that Stalin could conquer the Baltic states and parts of Poland and Romania, if in return the Soviets gave Germany certain strategic materials and a free pass to fight Britain, France, and Poland without Russian interference. It was not an alliance—in fact, it was more like an uneasy truce—but the Nazi-Soviet Non-Aggression Pact gave Hitler the strategic edge he wanted. Now he could attack Poland and, with any luck, Britain and France would once again prove too cowardly to act. If they did declare war, however, Hitler was confident that, once the backward Poles were defeated, Britain and France could be beaten too.

Why did Britain and France fail to confront Germany until 1939?

Blitzkrieg: The Fall of Poland and France

On September 1, 1939, Germany attacked Poland. German forces used a new military strategy, with roots in the First World War, called *Blitzkrieg*, or "lightning war." *Blitzkrieg* involves rapid advances behind enemy lines using mobile columns of tanks, other armored vehicles, and trucks, supported by air cover in the form of fighters and bombers. Above all, *Blitzkrieg* calls for a war of movement, unlike the trench fighting in World War I, in which the front had barely moved for years. Hitler had fought on the Western Front and had experienced the frustration of trench warfare firsthand. He was determined that World War II would be fought differently. Although it was risky, *Blitzkrieg* offered the possibility of the quick encirclement and defeat of enemy armies.

Blitzkrieg, and modern warfare in general, depends on accurate intelligence. Although it was far from apparent in 1939, as the war progressed the Allies would develop a decisive advantage in intelligence gathering. In 1943–44, for instance, the British would build the world's first electronic programmable digital computer—for the sole purpose of breaking German codes.

Germany's invasion of Poland was followed just two days later by British and French declarations of war against Germany. Hitler was unfazed, however, because his armies were making superb progress in the East, and the Western Allies took a passive approach to the war. Despite promises that they would rush to the rescue of Poland, Britain and France did nothing as Poland was quickly overrun.

In mid-September, the Soviets, following the conditions spelled out in the Nazi-Soviet Non-Aggression Pact, invaded eastern Poland, sealing that country's fate. The fall of Warsaw on September 28, 1939, marked the effective end of the Polish campaign, and the beginning of a grueling occupation.

From September 1939 to April 1940, there was a "Phony War" in the West. Although Britain and France were at war with Germany, there was no fighting, except at sea. Britain and France, thinking back to the pointless, bloody charges on the Western Front in World War I, refused to attack. The Germans, for their part, were not quite ready to strike. Finally, in April 1940 Hitler unleashed *Blitzkrieg* on Denmark and Norway. Although these countries were neutral, Hitler wanted them for strategic reasons. They fell with relative ease.

Then, on May 10, 1940, Hitler invaded the Netherlands, Luxembourg, Belgium, and France. The Allies were convinced that the Germans would bypass the Maginot Line, a fortified defensive barrier located on the Franco-German border, and advance straight through Belgium, as they had in 1914. The French were well prepared for such an attack. Their plan, once the Germans made their move, was to invade Belgium from the south and meet the Germans in central Belgium. This would mean that World War II would be fought primarily on Belgian soil.

The Germans, though, outsmarted the French generals. The Germans pretended to attack through Belgium, as the French expected, but they sent most of their tank forces through the Ardennes Forest around Luxembourg, an area that the French thought was impassable. The highly mobile German land forces, superbly reinforced by air power, advanced relatively unopposed toward the west, and eventually they drove a wedge between the Allied armies in Belgium and those in France. Stunned, the Allied forces disintegrated. The British, French, and Belgians were routed in just six weeks. Clearly, in the early stages of World War II, the Germans were prepared for a war of movement, while the Allies were not.

On June 14, 1940, Paris fell to Hitler's armies. France, which had successfully resisted German attacks from 1914 to 1918, was now defeated, and Hitler was acclaimed a military genius. He toured Paris in late June 1940, visiting the Eiffel Tower and Napoleon's tomb. Britain was thus left alone to face Germany. Much of the British Army's equipment had been lost, but 200,000 of its soldiers were rescued at the last minute from the beaches of the French town of Dunkirk.

France was understandably in shock as its armies collapsed. In July 1940, the French parliament voted to hand over dictatorial power to a conservative hero of the First World War, Marshal Henri Philippe Pétain. The new government was based in the resort town of Vichy, and thus France under

Pétain became known as Vichy France. Pétain's first task was to negotiate France's surrender to Germany. Hitler spitefully insisted that the French sign the capitulation agreement in the same railroad car in which the Germans had surrendered in 1918.

The terms of the surrender were harsh. Most of France would be occupied, and French citizens would pay the occupation bill. Eventually, Vichy officials were also asked to cooperate with German efforts to round up the Jews (some Frenchmen were quite happy to oblige). Today, the French still debate whether or not the leaders of Vichy France were traitors.

Most Frenchmen, whatever they thought of the Vichy regime, longed for an end to the German occupation. In 1940, General Charles De Gaulle of the French Army had fled the German advance and retreated to London. There, he launched the Free French movement. Free French forces served alongside British units for the remainder of the war. De Gaulle also encouraged "the Resistance" in France, which continually harassed the Germans. When France was finally liberated after the D-Day invasion in June 1944, De Gaulle became France's new leader, and many Vichy officials were imprisoned or executed.

How did Germany defeat Poland and France so rapidly?

The Battle of Britain

Once France was defeated, Hitler offered peace to Britain. He promised to respect the integrity of Britain's empire, all of which stood at Britain's side throughout the war, if the British in turn would acknowledge Nazi domination of continental Europe. After the fall of France, Britain was desperate, so it might have agreed to Hitler's terms. There seemed to be little chance that either the United States or the Soviet Union would come to Britain's aid. In May 1940, though, Neville Chamberlain, the architect of appeasement, had resigned as Prime Minister. His replacement was Winston Churchill, a fierce enemy of Nazism.

Churchill came from one of England's leading aristocratic families, and as a young man he had served bravely as a cavalry officer and a war correspondent. He was a great writer, and in 1953 would win the Nobel Prize for Literature. Like Hitler, Churchill enjoyed painting, but unlike Hitler he was a hard drinker and loved cigars. As First Lord of the Admiralty during World War I, Churchill had led the planning of the disastrous Allied attack on the Turkish Straits, which led to the Battle of Gallipoli. He was subsequently fired, but rather than shrink into obscurity he had requested the opportunity to fight on the Western Front. During the 1930s, as a member of Parliament, he was one of the strongest critics of the appeasement policy. Churchill was adamant that the Nazis were a terrible threat. In May 1940, he finally got his chance to lead Britain.

As France fell to Hitler's armies, Churchill could only promise the British people "blood, toil, sweat and tears" in the ongoing fight with Germany, but he vowed that Britain would never surrender. Hitler, therefore, authorized hasty planning for Operation Sea Lion: an amphibious invasion of Britain itself.

Germany faced a crucial challenge in conquering Britain. As an island, Britain was protected by the sea, which its vast navy controlled. Only by obtaining local air superiority over the waters of the English Channel and over the coastline of southeastern England could the Germans hope to mount a successful invasion. Accordingly, in July 1940, the Germans launched a massive bombing campaign that was designed to destroy British airfields, ports, and other vital military targets—mostly in the area where the Germans planned to land their invasion force. Despite heavy German losses, the plan seemed to be working, but, just at the pivotal moment, the Germans shifted their strategy.

On August 24, 1940, German planes had accidentally bombed a residential area in London. The British retaliated by bombing Berlin. Enraged, Hitler responded by launching "the Blitz." Instead of attacking only military targets, the Germans would now engage in the terror bombing of British cities. By killing thousands of civilians and destroying whole neighborhoods, Hitler hoped to bully the British into submission.

The Blitz was a horrific experience for ordinary Britons. Bombing raids often occurred on a nightly basis, and casualties and damage were high. At the sound of shrieking air raid sirens, civilians would huddle in basements, bomb shelters, and subway stations. A total blackout was enforced at night. The Germans bombed many landmarks, including Parliament and Buckingham Palace, and entire streets went up in flames. Meanwhile, many British children were sent to live in the countryside.

Hitler expected British morale to crumble as a result of the Blitz, but he was wrong. Churchill, with the help of King George VI and a continuous stream of patriotic BBC broadcasts, roused the courage of his people. Meanwhile, a coalition government carefully organized the wartime economy. Between 1939 and 1943, British production of armaments increased eightfold, while the production of many consumer goods declined.

Perhaps most importantly, German attacks on British cities distracted the *Luftwaffe* (the German air force) from its original strategy of striking only vital military and industrial targets. Thus, Britain's RAF (Royal Air Force) was given the opportunity to recover its strength. Thanks to Britain's superior intelligence networks, to a brilliantly organized air defense system, and to the invention of radar, the RAF inflicted terrible losses on the *Luftwaffe*. As a result, Operation Sea Lion was effectively canceled. By spring 1941, German air raids had become less frequent and less intense. Britain had prevailed in the Battle of Britain, the most important battle ever fought purely in the skies.

Britain was still a thorn in Germany's side, but Hitler felt confident that the British posed no direct threat to the Third Reich. Now was the ideal time, he believed, for German land forces to strike elsewhere.

Why did Germany decide against launching an amphibious invasion of Britain?

War Comes to the Balkans and Africa, and Germany Begins Operation Barbarossa in the East

At first, Mussolini kept Italy neutral. By June 1940, though, it had become obvious that France was on its knees. Mussolini decided to launch his own symbolic attack against southern France. Italy also attacked British positions in the Mediterranean region. In September 1940, Italian forces in Libya struck into British-occupied Egypt. Mussolini also invaded Greece, a British ally. All these campaigns were abysmal failures.

Hitler came to the rescue of the Italians in early 1941. He sent German troops to attack Greece and Yugoslavia, and he sent General Erwin Rommel, the "Desert Fox," to lead Germany's new *Afrika Korps*. Rommel quickly established a reputation for strategic brilliance and scrupulous honor.

By May 1941, German and Italian forces had occupied Greece. Yugoslavia was defeated in just ten days of fighting. It was subsequently partitioned among Germany's Croat, Hungarian, Bulgarian, and Italian allies, who helped the Germans to enforce a savage occupation. Also in 1941, the British army in Egypt was sent reeling by Rommel's *Blitzkrieg* attacks.

If there was one fatal flaw in Hitler's strategy in World War II, it was hubris, or overconfidence. Hitler repeatedly attacked in new areas, and he picked fights with new enemies before he had decisively beaten his old ones. In December 1940, while Britain still fought, Hitler made plans to widen the war. Despite the Nazi-Soviet Non-Aggression Pact, he ordered his generals to prepare for an invasion of the Soviet Union.

Why did Hitler want to attack the Soviets? First, the timing seemed right, since the Red Army was still weak because of Stalin's Purges. The Germans also knew that Stalin had aggressive intentions, so if Germany did not strike now it might be attacked itself in the future. In addition, anticommunism was a powerful motivator. Many German soldiers, as well as troops from throughout Europe, fought proudly in the East in order to stamp out Bolshevism.

The most important reason of all for the German attack on Russia in June 1941, though, was Hitler's personal obsession with the racial inferiority of the Slavs, and the need for Germany to conquer *Lebensraum* in the East. Hitler prepared to unleash SS death squads on communists, Jews, and other perceived enemies of Germany as soon as his invasion of Russia had begun. He wanted to pacify the region quickly and settle it with Germans.

Operation Barbarossa was set to commence in mid-May 1941. The attack was delayed until June 22, however, because of fighting in the Balkans, and due to adverse weather. In the end, this delay would prove critical. Starting the operation six weeks late meant that the Germans would need to reach their objectives quickly, or else the war might drag on into the harsh Russian winter, and Germany's chances of victory would be sharply reduced.

The scale of Germany's invasion of the Soviet Union was massive. Over three million German troops, plus 3,000 to 4,000 tanks and 2,000 aircraft, were mobilized for the attack. Facing the Axis onslaught were 2.5 million Soviet troops and at least 15,000 Russian tanks. The battle on the Eastern Front would soon become the greatest and deadliest land campaign waged in the history of warfare.

At first, the invasion went astonishingly well for Germany. Over 1,000 Soviet aircraft were destroyed in the first 24 hours of the campaign. In the first six months of fighting, moreover, half of the soldiers in the Red Army were wounded, killed, or captured. By December 1941, much of the most densely populated portion of the Soviet Union had been occupied. The Ukraine was in German hands, and Leningrad had been besieged. The Germans were nearing Moscow. It seemed that Russia would meet the same fate that had befallen Poland and France. In October 1941, Hitler had even boasted that the war was effectively over, and Germany had won!

In late 1941, however, several factors combined to halt the German advance. First, extremely severe winter conditions descended on the German troops trying to take Moscow. Second, the Soviets had destroyed or removed crops, raw materials, factories, and critical infrastructure in the areas that the Germans had occupied, making their advance wholly dependent on their own over-stretched supply lines. Third, Stalin managed to move reinforcements from Siberia to central Russia at a critical time. Fourth, the Germans were staggered by the sheer vastness of Russia's territory, its limitless reserves of manpower, and its plentiful and modern armaments. Fifth, British, and later on American, aid to the Red Army became an important factor in bolstering Russia's fighting strength. Sixth, the Nazis made little effort to win over Soviet citizens in conquered areas, despite the fact that many of these "subhumans" might have been easily persuaded to join a war against Stalin. Soviet POWs were also treated with utter contempt. The Germans took three million Soviet prisoners in 1941 alone. Due to starvation and ill treatment, two-thirds of them were dead by spring 1942. Lastly, the Soviet Union did not collapse in 1941 because Stalin proved to be a capable and determined wartime leader. In October 1941, he made the important decision not to abandon Moscow. Instead, Stalin called on all Soviet citizens to rally around him and fight a Great Patriotic War to defend Holy Russia from fascist aggression. He even welcomed the support of the Orthodox Church. The Soviet people responded to Stalin's call by struggling against Hitler with unshakeable resolve.

By December 1941, the German advance had stalled. Both sides hoped that 1942 would bring them final victory.

Why did Operation Barbarossa narrowly fail?

America Enters the Fight

In December 1941, as the German advance on Moscow ground to a halt, another development made a German victory in the Second World War increasingly unlikely. In 1937, Japan had launched a bloody invasion of China. Ever since, relations between Japan and the United States had gone from bad to worse. The United States, with its large Pacific base at Pearl Harbor in Hawaii and its colony in the Philippine Islands, appeared to the Japanese to be the single greatest obstacle to their goal of establishing a "Greater East Asian Co-Prosperity Sphere," a euphemism for Japanese domination of East Asia and the Western Pacific. Japan's leaders were keen to remove the American threat, but how?

U.S. President Franklin Delano Roosevelt had already led America through the worst years of the Great Depression. At the start of World War II, he made no secret of his contempt for fascism and his determination to lend assistance to Great Britain. Even before the formal U.S. entry into the war, Roosevelt had initiated a draft, begun a military buildup, and described America as the Arsenal of Democracy. Although the United States was officially committed to a policy of neutrality, FDR authorized the shipment of weapons to Allied countries, and he ordered the U.S. Navy to provide armed escorts for convoys sailing to Britain. Roosevelt also bolstered American military forces in the Philippines, and he put an embargo on oil sales to Japan. By 1941, Roosevelt was actively planning America's entry into the war. Both Hitler and Japanese Prime Minister Tojo were furious at the United States.

Accordingly, the Japanese decided to launch a surprise attack on the U.S. fleet at Pearl Harbor. Their aim was not to invade the United States, but to weaken its long-term ability to block Japanese expansion. Ultimately, the Japanese hoped that the Americans would be so stunned by Japanese victories that they would accept Japanese domination in the Pacific. This was a terrible mistake. The American people, once roused by the Japanese "sneak attack," would demand nothing less than the unconditional surrender of Japan.

Incredibly, Hitler, who was allied to Japan under the terms of the Anti-Comintern Pact, had tacitly encouraged the Japanese to go on the offensive. He even pledged that Germany too would declare war on the United States. Once again, Hitler added needlessly to the list of Germany's enemies at a time when defeating Britain and the Soviet Union should have been his foremost goals. Even more incredibly, the Germans did not insist that the Japanese mount their own assault on Russia. This would have placed the Soviet Union in a truly desperate position.

Initially, the Japanese offensive in late 1941 and early 1942 was a spectacular success. Many U.S. battleships were damaged or destroyed at Pearl Harbor, although the American carriers were at sea and escaped unscathed. The U.S. colony in the Philippines was overrun, as were many Pacific islands. All of Southeast Asia fell into Japanese hands, including the oil resources of the Dutch East Indies, now known as Indonesia, and the British stronghold at Singapore. Western imperialism had been dealt a crushing blow. By the middle of 1942, the Japanese were close to launching invasions of India and Australia.

This Japanese momentum was not to last. The contributions of the United States to the war in Europe, Africa, and Asia would eventually help the

Allies—Britain, the Soviet Union, the United States, and dozens of friendly nations around the world—to defeat the fascist powers once and for all.

Why did Japan attack the United States in late 1941?

The Tide of Battle Turns: 1942–43

1942 marked the height of the "Battle of the Atlantic," the most important naval battle of the 20th century, during which Germany launched many powerful new surface ships in an attempt to defeat the Royal Navy and choke off British trade. The most famous of these German warships was the gigantic battleship *Bismarck*, which was sunk in 1941, thanks to continuous hounding by British torpedo bombers. Indeed, the principal theme in naval warfare during the Second World War was the surprising domination of air power over surface ships. The British and the Americans, who possessed numerous aircraft carriers, were able to rain destruction from above on the German, Italian, and Japanese navies.

The Battle of the Atlantic climaxed with another German U-boat offensive. The Germans hoped that submarines would succeed in cutting off American aid and reinforcements that were being sent to Britain in convoys. The U-boats were highly effective at first, but by 1943 Allied technological improvements and long-range air cover had neutralized the undersea threat. A steady stream of U.S. supplies and soldiers poured into Britain, and so Hitler ordered the hasty construction of an "Atlantic Wall," mainly on the French coastline, to keep the British and the Americans at bay.

The Japanese were no more successful at sea than the Germans. As early as May and June 1942, the Allies won important naval victories at the Battle of the Coral Sea and the Battle of Midway. The Japanese lost a large fraction of their carriers in these battles.

Beginning in 1943, the Allies in the Pacific—with the United States, Britain, and Australia in the lead—went on the offensive with a strategy of "island hopping." Instead of attempting to retake every Pacific island that the Japanese had conquered, the Allies would hop from one island to another, steering their advance toward Japan. The goal was to secure air bases that would allow for the bombing of Japanese cities. If necessary, island hopping would continue until Japan itself was invaded.

As these amphibious operations proceeded in the Pacific, British forces also attacked from India into Japanese-controlled Southeast Asia, while the Chinese continued to resist the Japanese invasion of their homeland. Throughout the Asian and Pacific theater of war, the fighting was incredibly cruel. The Japanese, who considered surrender to be dishonorable, usually insisted on fighting to the death—and most Allied soldiers were only too happy to kill them.

One of the clearest signs that the Allies were gaining ground was the conclusion of the fighting in the North African theater in 1943. In 1941 and 1942, Rommel's *Afrika Korps* had repeatedly threatened the small British army defending Egypt. In November 1942, however, British General Bernard Montgomery, known as "Monty," defeated Rommel at El Alamein, Egypt. Almost simultaneously, American troops landed in Morocco and Algeria to attack the *Afrika Korps* from the west. By May 1943, Axis forces had been cornered in Tunisia, and there they surrendered.

Next, the British and Americans launched an amphibious invasion of Sicily. This devastated Italian morale, and in July 1943 Mussolini's own Fascist Grand Council deposed him. Marshal Pietro Badoglio became the new Italian leader. He pretended to continue Italy's alliance with Germany, but amazingly, when the Allies began an invasion of the Italian Peninsula in September 1943, Badoglio's government switched sides in the war! Instantly, Germany lost the support of the Italian military on all fronts. The Germans, though, recovered quickly. German reinforcements ensured that the Allied armies advancing from southern Italy toward Rome moved much more slowly than expected.

By far the most important signal of a shift of momentum in the war was the Battle of Stalingrad, which was fought between Germany and Russia on the Eastern Front between August 1942 and February 1943. During the winter of 1941–42, German troops had just barely managed to hold their ground. In June 1942, they were finally ready to resume the offensive. They planned to drive deeply into southern Russia and capture the oil fields of the Caucasus region.

The German territorial gains in their 1942 offensive were impressive. By August 1942, German units had advanced into the northern Caucasus, and they had reached the industrial city of Stalingrad on the Volga River. Partly because of its strategic importance, and partly because the city was named

Figure 18.1 Stalingrad was just one of many cities reduced to rubble during World War II, either by artillery or by bombing.

Everett Historical/Shutterstock.

after Stalin, both the Soviets and the Germans were absolutely determined to control Stalingrad.

The fighting there was intense. Almost a half million Soviet soldiers died, often in house-to-house fighting, but in November 1942 a sudden Russian counterattack succeeded in isolating the German forces that remained in Stalingrad. The remnants of those forces finally surrendered in February 1943. It was the first major Soviet victory in the war. It had also been the single largest and bloodiest battle in human history.

From now on, despite staggering Soviet losses, the Red Army steadily drove the Germans back to the west. The Germans tried to make a comeback at the Battle of Kursk in July 1943, but by then the Soviet superiority in manpower, tank strength, and artillery was overwhelming. The sheer quantity of Soviet military power, in addition to its rapidly improving quality, awed the retreating Germans.

As much as Americans like to brag that they saved Europe during World War II, the truth is that the German army was defeated on the Eastern Front. Eighty percent of German battle casualties occurred in the East. The epic scale and the extraordinary viciousness of the fighting there almost defy description.

Why was the Battle of Stalingrad so important in determining the outcome of World War II?

The Defeat of Germany: 1943–45

By 1943, Germany's prospects in the war looked bleak. The war in Africa had already been lost, the Russians were advancing relentlessly from the east, parts of Italy had fallen, and German U-boats were being hunted to the point of extinction.

To make matters worse, the British and the Americans began to engage in large-scale strategic bombing against targets in Germany. While tactical bombing aims to destroy a specific military asset, strategic bombing aims to disrupt or destroy the enemy's ability or willingness to fight.

First and foremost, strategic bombing called for Allied attacks against German factories, railways, ports, bridges, mines, military bases, oil and gas infrastructure, and research and development facilities. If the German economy and transportation network could be severely damaged, the Allies hoped that the war could be shortened. The Allies went even further, however, and began to use terror bombing against German civilians, sometimes in so-called thousand-bomber raids. The dropping of incendiary bombs in order to cause fire storms in major cities was especially controversial. By the end of the war, hundreds of thousands of German civilians had been killed, and seven million Germans were made homeless.

Nevertheless, German morale remained strong. In fact, Propaganda Minister Dr. Josef Goebbels managed to convince the German people to fight even harder. The merciless nature of the British and American air attacks, combined with the danger posed by "the barbarian hordes advancing from the east," persuaded many Germans to oppose the Allied onslaught with all their might. Significantly, the Allies were united in demanding unconditional surrender, which seemed to spell ruin for Germany. The Allies had even discussed the Morgenthau Plan, which called for the transformation of Germany into a nation of backward peasants.

Toward the end of the war, Goebbels began to promise that "miracle weapons" would soon be available that would reverse the tide of battle. Germany did succeed in deploying the world's first jet-powered fighter-bomber, the sleek and futuristic Me 262. German scientists and engineers also made major advances in rocketry. The German V-2 rocket was so ahead of its time that its design served as the basis for the U.S. and Soviet space programs during the 1950s and 1960s. These advances in German military technology were impressive, but they were too few and too late to change the outcome of the war.

On June 6, 1944, the British, Americans, and Canadians landed thousands of men on the beaches of Normandy, France. Many were killed in the first few hours of bitter fighting, but the Allied assault succeeded. The D-Day invasion, which U.S. General Dwight D. Eisenhower commanded, breached Hitler's Atlantic Wall. The Germans had planned to destroy the Allied beachhead quickly, but Allied control of the skies made this impossible. By late July, the Allies had built up a force of 1.5 million men in Normandy. Now, the Western Front reemerged.

After D-Day, a group of German officers decided that the war had become hopeless. They plotted to kill Hitler and negotiate peace. On July 20, 1944, a bomb exploded at the *Führer*'s headquarters. Hitler, though, was only slightly injured. The coup plotters were almost all killed or compelled to commit suicide. Understandably, by this stage, Hitler was becoming irritable and depressed, but he showed no desire to step down as Germany's leader.

In August 1944, the Allies used a variant of *Blitzkrieg* strategy to advance beyond Normandy and into the rest of France. In September, Paris was liberated, and Allied servicemen began to talk optimistically about defeating Germany before Christmas.

In December 1944, Hitler authorized one last surprise offensive on the Western Front, known as the Battle of the Bulge. Its failure, due largely to German fuel shortages, led inexorably to Germany's defeat. In March 1945, the British and the Americans finally crossed the Rhine River in western Germany, the last major obstacle in their path.

As the Western Allies advanced, the Soviets closed in on Berlin. Earlier, in 1944, in a series of spectacularly bold and swift offensives, the Red Army had finally pushed the Germans out of Soviet territory, and out of most of the countries of Eastern Europe as well. Partisans, that is, guerrillas operating behind German lines, aided the Soviet advance in many areas. They were especially active in Poland and Yugoslavia, and also in France and Italy in the west. In Yugoslavia, the partisans managed to tie down numerous Axis divisions—and to kill each other in astoundingly high numbers. Some partisans were communists, but most were simply stubborn locals who wanted to evict the Germans from their homelands.

Figure 18.2 An old woman is horrified by the devastation in a defeated Germany. World War II injured, killed, and displaced more civilians than any other conflict in history.

Everett Historical/Shutterstock.

By April 1945, the Soviets were ready to mount the last major offensive in the European theater: the attack on Berlin. Much as Stalin had done in 1941, Hitler decided that he would not abandon Germany's capital city.

On April 30, 1945, Hitler decided that the battle was lost. He shot himself in the head just hours before the Soviets completed their occupation of Berlin. Many of his henchmen met a similar fate. Goebbels, for instance, shot his wife and then himself outside Hitler's bunker—after the couple had killed their six children. Just as Goebbels had predicted, the Soviets now took vengeance on the German people. Many Soviet soldiers were encouraged to rape German women and girls, and millions of Germans fled in terror toward the West.

The surviving leaders of the Nazi state and the German military recognized that the war was effectively over. They surrendered unconditionally. May 8, 1945 became known as V-E Day, for "Victory in Europe."

Why did Germans continue to fight in 1944–45, despite facing such long odds?

The Fall of Japan

In April 1945, the war in the Pacific was altered by two significant developments: first, Franklin D. Roosevelt died, and Harry S. Truman succeeded him as President and Commander-in-chief. Second, the United States began an amphibious assault on Okinawa, the most isolated of the Japanese home islands. The fighting there was fierce, punctuated by Japanese *kamikaze* attacks on U.S. ships, but Okinawa had fallen by July.

By August 1945, Japan faced annihilation. The Americans had recaptured the Philippines, the British had taken Burma, and a massive Soviet army had invaded Manchuria. Japan had also lost arguably the largest naval battle in history, the Battle of Leyte Gulf, and its navy and air force had been decimated. Japan's Greater East Asian Co-Prosperity Sphere was crumbling rapidly.

To avoid launching a series of bloody amphibious invasions of the main islands of Japan itself, President Truman decided to employ the ultimate weapon: the atomic bomb. In 1941, American scientists had begun work on the Manhattan Project, which aimed to create an immensely powerful bomb based on the fission, or splitting, of uranium atoms. There was no guarantee that the project would work. The Germans, Soviets, and Japanese were working along similar lines, but they had made little progress.

On August 6, 1945, the American bomb was ready. A B-29 long-range bomber, nicknamed the *Enola Gay*, dropped it on the Japanese city of Hiroshima, killing 70,000 people and subjecting thousands more to disfiguring injuries and radiation sickness. Three days later, Nagasaki was struck. The Japanese government wavered. Surrender was still unacceptable to many Japanese leaders. After all, they argued, American bombing raids using conventional explosives had already killed hundreds of thousands of civilians. Plus, how many atom bombs could the Americans have? The Japanese also doubted whether the United States had the stomach for a full-scale invasion.

These arguments did not convince Emperor Hirohito. He knew that the time had come for Japan to give in. Although he refused to call it surrender, for the first time ever he addressed the Japanese people on the radio and informed them that the war was over. President Truman accepted Japan's capitulation.

Now World War II truly was finished. Approximately 60 million people had died, most of them civilians. No war, before or since, can compare with the Second World War in terms of sheer carnage and loss of life. The suffering was distributed unevenly, however. In terms of debt, the British were in the worst position. They had essentially mortgaged their empire, accepting U.S. financial and commercial preeminence in the bargain. Meanwhile, Germany and Japan had experienced total military defeat and national humiliation along with the obliteration of most of their cities. But it was arguably the Soviet Union that had lost the most. Around 27 million Soviet soldiers and civilians had died in the Great Patriotic War against Nazi Germany.

After so much sacrifice, the Soviets demanded compensation, in the form of territorial adjustments, reparations, and greater influence in Eastern Europe. These demands, which seemed excessive to the Americans and to the British, sowed the seeds for a Cold War between East and West. In 1945, no one bragged even for an instant that World War II would be the "war to end all wars."

What factors led to Japan's surrender at the end of World War II?

The Holocaust

If the Second World War had been only a military confrontation, it would still be remembered as the blackest chapter in twentieth-century history, but it was much more than that. World War II is also infamous for the extraordinary inhumanity that the Axis powers inflicted on innocent civilians. Although the Japanese were guilty of using slave labor, slaughtering women and children, and mistreating prisoners, the worst crimes were committed by the Nazis. Approximately 10 to 12 million people died as a result of the Nazi Holocaust from 1941 to 1945. Half of them were Jews, the people Hitler had always blamed for Germany's misfortunes. The Nazis practiced genocide against the Jews. That is, the Nazis tried to wipe them out as a people.

The Holocaust was a complex event. It began with the German conquest of Poland in 1939. The Germans considered the Slavic, Catholic majority in Poland to be subhuman. Catholic Poles were therefore exploited as cheap labor and given inadequate food rations and medical care. Polish intellectuals, political and cultural leaders, and professionals were often killed. Poles were also discouraged from reproducing. The intent was to reduce the Poles to the status of an uneducated servant class, and to kill off as many as possible so that German settlers could take their place.

As badly as the Germans treated the Slavic, Catholic majority in Poland, they treated the Polish Jews much worse. Initially, Heinrich Himmler's SS, which took charge of the "Jewish problem," chose to segregate the Jews into "ghettos": sealed urban neighborhoods where hunger and disease ran rampant. The death rates in the ghettos were high, but not high enough, by SS standards.

In the summer of 1941, as the Germans advanced into the Soviet Union, *Einsatzgruppen* (Task Forces) carried out mass killings. They targeted communist officials and Jews, in particular, who were assumed to be natural enemies of the German occupation and potential partisans. The *Einsatzgruppen* killed hundreds of thousands of Soviet Jews. The success of the *Einsatzgruppen* encouraged the Nazis to consider using similar brutal methods in other parts of Europe.

In January 1942, Nazi leaders met at a stylish villa in Wannsee, a suburb of Berlin. Although Hitler took no part in the discussions, the meeting assumed that a decision had been made at the highest level to pursue the "final solution" of the "Jewish question."

At Wannsee, Nazi officials discussed measures that would accelerate the murder of Jews—not just Eastern European Jews, but Jews from every corner of Europe. A vast network of extermination camps would be built, mostly in Poland, that would kill Jews and other supposed undesirables with maximum efficiency.

The most important of the death camps would be at Auschwitz-Birkenau, where several large German corporations produced war materials. Inmates at Auschwitz who were deemed unfit to work, as well as many women and children, who might have carried on the Jewish race in future generations, were promptly killed. Most died in gas chambers, and their bodies were subsequently ransacked for valuables and then cremated. Over time, this grim process was "perfected" so that Jews, and other victims, could be killed on an industrial scale—tens of thousands of people could be murdered in a single day. Most inmates who were not immediately killed were worked to death. In all, over one million people died at Auschwitz.

Even though Jews were the primary victims of the Nazi death camps, Russian POWs, Poles, communists, and Gypsies were also killed in large numbers. In most cases, the Nazis conceived of these groups much as they conceived of the Jews: as irreconcilable racial enemies of the German people.

Sometimes Jews resisted the implementation of genocidal Nazi policies. In 1943, for example, the 60,000 Jews who remained in the Warsaw Ghetto rebelled. Virtually none survived the Nazi counterattack. Occasionally Jews became partisans. Some Jews also received protection from Christians, who risked their lives by hiding Jews or helping them to escape. Nevertheless, the overall impact of the Holocaust was devastating. Of the nine million Jews in Europe in 1939, only three to four million survived the war, and many of them, facing ongoing persecution, migrated to Israel or the United States. In some countries, such as Poland and the Netherlands, the Jewish community was almost completely destroyed. Today, European Jewry is a pale shadow of what it was when World War II began. The Nazi effort to wipe out Europe's Jews was thus very nearly successful.

In the last few months of the war, the SS leader, Heinrich Himmler, tried and failed to strike a deal with the Western Allies using death camp inmates as pawns. In April 1945, he even greeted a member of the World Jewish Congress by saying, "Welcome to Germany . . . It is time you Jews and we [Nazis] buried the hatchet." Needless to say, the time for reconciliation had passed. At the end of the war, the liberation of the camps, and the exposure of the brutal conditions in which inmates were held, was cited by many Allied leaders as the ultimate vindication of their efforts to stamp out fascism.

Historians continue to debate the lessons of the Holocaust. Should Germany and ordinary Germans, for instance, be held responsible for the mass murder conducted primarily by the SS? Some historians, citing the history of violent anti-Semitism in Germany, the participation of Germans outside the SS in atrocities, and the generally high level of support for Nazism, say yes. On the other hand, it is important to recognize that most ordinary Germans' knowledge of the Holocaust was limited. In addition, in a wartime environment, many Germans, and indeed many Allied leaders and soldiers, viewed the suffering of the Jews as less important than winning the war. In the end, although virtually every historian acknowledges that Hitler and the SS played a commanding role in the Holocaust, there is no clear consensus on whether anyone else should be held responsible, or on what, if anything, should be done to atone for the Nazi campaign of genocide against the Jews.

The Nazi Holocaust was not the largest episode of mass murder in history. Stalin in the Soviet Union and Mao Zedong, the communist leader of China, were each responsible for more deaths. Neither was the Nazi attempt to obliterate an entire ethnic group unique. The Holocaust was remarkable, however, in that it was carried out by the representatives of a country that claimed to be among the world's most civilized, and it employed advanced, industrial technology and organization to destroy its victims with maximum efficiency. For many people, these factors make the Holocaust an unparalleled example of the human capacity for evil.

At the end of the war, it would be the German people's turn to suffer. As Soviet rule took hold in the East, approximately 12 million Germans became refugees or expellees, and two million of them died—and this came on top of the 7.5 million German soldiers and civilians who had already died during the war. Moreover, it is not an exaggeration to say that Germany in 1945 was a wasteland. Its cities were in ruins, its economy and industries were shattered, and its people were hungry and destitute. The startling rebirth and recovery of Germany, and Japan, after 1945—as nations dedicated to peace, rather than war—is, therefore, one of the most incredible chapters in human history.

In what ways was the Holocaust unique?

Conclusions

At Yalta, a seaside resort on the Black Sea coast of the Soviet Union, the Big Three—Churchill, Roosevelt, and Stalin—met in February 1945. They hoped to plan the future of Europe and Asia. Churchill and Stalin wanted to divide the world into spheres of influence, but Roosevelt wished instead to create a United Nations (UN) organization to keep the peace. Churchill and Stalin agreed to support the UN, but Stalin extracted major concessions in return.

The leaders of Britain, the United States, and the Soviet Union met again in July 1945 in the Berlin suburb of Potsdam, which was now in Soviet hands. Here they agreed to divide Germany into four occupation zones, one each for Britain, France, the United States, and the Soviet Union. Furthermore, the worst Nazi war criminals would be tried at Nuremberg. Many were executed. All of Germany would be subjected to a rigorous program of disarmament and denazification. Still, the long-term future of Germany was unclear.

The subject that divided the Allies most sharply in 1945 was the future of Eastern Europe. Russia, which had long dreamed of dominating Eastern Europe, and which had twice been invaded from the west during the twentieth century, wanted a guarantee that Eastern European governments would be friendly to Soviet interests. The British, French, and Americans, on the other hand, sought to protect the independence of the Eastern European states. They wanted democracy and capitalism to thrive there.

Stalin made some conciliatory gestures, but ultimately the Soviets assumed control over most of Eastern Europe. Stalin shamelessly replaced Eastern European governments that would not accept Soviet-style communism.

During the war, Stalin had been known affectionately in the West as "Uncle Joe." By 1946, though, Winston Churchill was already speaking of an "Iron Curtain," a phrase coined by Goebbels, that had come to divide Western Europe, which was free, from Eastern Europe, which was under Stalin's tyranny.

This fundamental disagreement over the future of Eastern Europe, more than any other factor, explains the beginning of the Cold War. The Cold War would be fought primarily in Europe, but most European countries had little control over the struggle. Increasingly, in the second half of the twentieth century, it would be the United States and the Soviet Union that dominated.

Key Terms for Chapter 18

Lebensraum—living space, that is, territorial expansion for Germany. This was one of Hitler's overriding goals.

Appeasement—the Allied policy of avoiding war by negotiating with Hitler and meeting some of his demands.

Nazi-Soviet Non-Aggression Pact, August 1939—an accord between Nazi Germany and the Soviet Union that divided Eastern Europe between them, and committed the Russians to remaining neutral in any war between Germany and the Western Allies.

Blitzkrieg—lightning war. In World War II, Germany used tanks and aircraft to strike deep behind enemy lines, often leading to the rapid collapse of enemy forces.

Winston Churchill—British Prime Minister from 1940 to 1945 (and again from 1951 to 1955). An implacable enemy of Nazism, Churchill led Britain's stubborn resistance to German expansion.

Battle of Britain—an aerial battle fought to control the skies over Britain. In September 1940, the German *Luftwaffe* (air force) switched from attacking military targets to the terror bombing of civilians, allowing the Royal Air Force to recover its strength and ultimately prevail.

Operation Barbarossa, June 1941—Germany's ill-fated invasion of Russia, which was designed to achieve victory before the onset of winter.

Franklin Delano Roosevelt—President of the United States from 1933 to 1945. A strong enemy of fascism, Roosevelt supported Britain before the United States entered the war, and after the Pearl Harbor attacks he led the American war effort until his death in April 1945.

Battle of the Atlantic—a struggle between Germany and the Allies to control the Atlantic Ocean. It climaxed with the efforts of German U-boats to sink Allied ships in the sea-lanes around Britain. The U-boats were effectively defeated by 1943.

Battle of Stalingrad, August 1942–February 1943—a major confrontation on the Eastern Front, and Russia's first major victory in the war.

Strategic Bombing—large-scale aerial assaults on targets such as factories, infrastructure, and residential areas, designed to destroy the enemy's economy as well as enemy morale.

D-Day, June 6, 1944—the date of the Allied landings on the Normandy coast of France, leading to further Allied offensives, including the invasion of Germany itself.

Partisans—guerrilla soldiers who fight to liberate their homeland from foreign occupation.

Auschwitz—the largest Nazi death camp, at which over one million people were killed, the great majority of them Jews. It was also a huge industrial complex.

United Nations—a new international organization conceived by President Franklin D. Roosevelt in order to encourage cooperation and peace after World War II.

Review Questions for Chapter 18

1. Describe three events that helped to cause World War II.
2. What do you believe was Germany's biggest mistake in World War II? Could Germany have won the war if this mistake had been avoided? Explain your views.
3. Do you believe that strategic bombing is an effective approach to fighting a modern war or not? Do you believe that the strategic bombing of civilian areas is morally acceptable or not?
4. Imagine that you live in a German-occupied area in Europe in 1943. You have the choice of becoming a collaborator, becoming a partisan, or sitting on the fence. Which role would you select? Make your case in historical context.
5. The Western Allies were confronted with a major moral dilemma in World War II. Although they found many Nazi practices, including the extermination of the Jews, repugnant, they also fiercely disagreed with the mass murder perpetrated by Stalin's regime in the Soviet Union, to which they were allied. Is it true that "the enemy of my enemy is my

friend," or did the Western Allies make a mistake by helping Stalin? If a similar choice confronted the United States today, should we be prepared to work with a brutal dictator?

Further Reading

Allen, Michael Thad. *The Business of Genocide: The SS, Slave Labor, and the Concentration Camps*. Chapel Hill, NC: University of North Carolina Press. 2005.

Bartov, Omer, ed. *The Holocaust: Origins, Implementation, Aftermath*. New York: Routledge. 2000.

Collingham, Lizzie. *Taste of War: World War II and the Battle for Food*. New York: Penguin. 2013.

Hastings, Max. *Armageddon: The Battle for Germany, 1944–1945*. London: Pan Books. 2015.

Jackson, Julian. *France: The Dark Years, 1940–1945*. Oxford: Oxford University Press. 2003.

Kershaw, Ian. *Hitler, 1936–1945: Nemesis*. London: Penguin. 2001.

Lyons, Michael J. *World War II: A Short History*. Fifth Edition. New York: Routledge. 2016.

Mackay, Robert. *The Test of War: Inside Britain 1939–45*. London: Routledge. 2003.

Mazower, Mark. *Hitler's Empire: How the Nazis Ruled Europe*. New York: Penguin. 2008.

McKale, Donald M. *Hitler's Shadow War: The Holocaust and World War II*. New York: Cooper Square. 2002.

Meacham, John. *Franklin and Winston: An Intimate Portrait of an Epic Friendship*. London: Granta. 2005.

Megargee, Geoffrey P. *War of Annihilation: Combat and Genocide on the Eastern Front, 1941*. Lanham, MD: Rowman and Littlefield. 2007.

Murphy, David E. *What Stalin Knew: The Enigma of Barbarossa*. New Haven, CT: Yale University Press. 2008.

Slepyan, Kenneth. *Stalin's Guerrillas: Soviet Partisans in World War II*. Lawrence, KS: University Press of Kansas. 2006.

Wintle, Michael and Menno Spiering, eds. *European Identity and the Second World War*. New York: Palgrave Macmillan. 2011.

19 The Cold War and the End of European Dominance, 1945–present

Introduction

One of the great tragedies of the Second World War is that, for all the suffering it entailed, once it was over, oppression and the constant threat of renewed conflict persisted for many Europeans. Eastern Europeans were faced with Soviet occupation and with the replacement of their governments by communist puppet regimes. The entire world was threatened by the Cold War that emerged between the Western democracies and the Communist Bloc, led by the Soviet Union. The related threat of nuclear annihilation made the prospects for peace and stability look particularly dim.

And yet Western nations and communist states avoided direct conflict, including nuclear war. The second half of the twentieth century was marked by dramatic improvements in the standard of living enjoyed by Europeans—and by most of the world's people. The conclusion of the Cold War in 1989–91, and the collapse of communism in Eastern Europe and in its Russian heartland, paved the way for an end to the arms race and for the extension of democracy and capitalism to most of Europe's people for the first time in history.

Today, Europe is as free, peaceful, and prosperous as ever, but its role in the world is much reduced from the heady days of the nineteenth and early twentieth centuries. As this chapter and the Epilogue will make plain, Europe's place in global affairs, and its relationship with the United States, will undoubtedly undergo further significant changes in the years ahead. Luckily, the study of European history can help illuminate the directions in which those changes are likely to lead.

The Emergence of the Cold War, 1945–49

When Germany surrendered to the Allies, the future of Europe and the world as a whole was a subject of sharp disagreement. The Soviets intended to maintain control over Eastern Europe, and they believed that communist parties in Western European countries and in the Middle East would create opportunities for the further expansion of Soviet influence. The United States, Britain, and France, on the other hand, foresaw a world in which

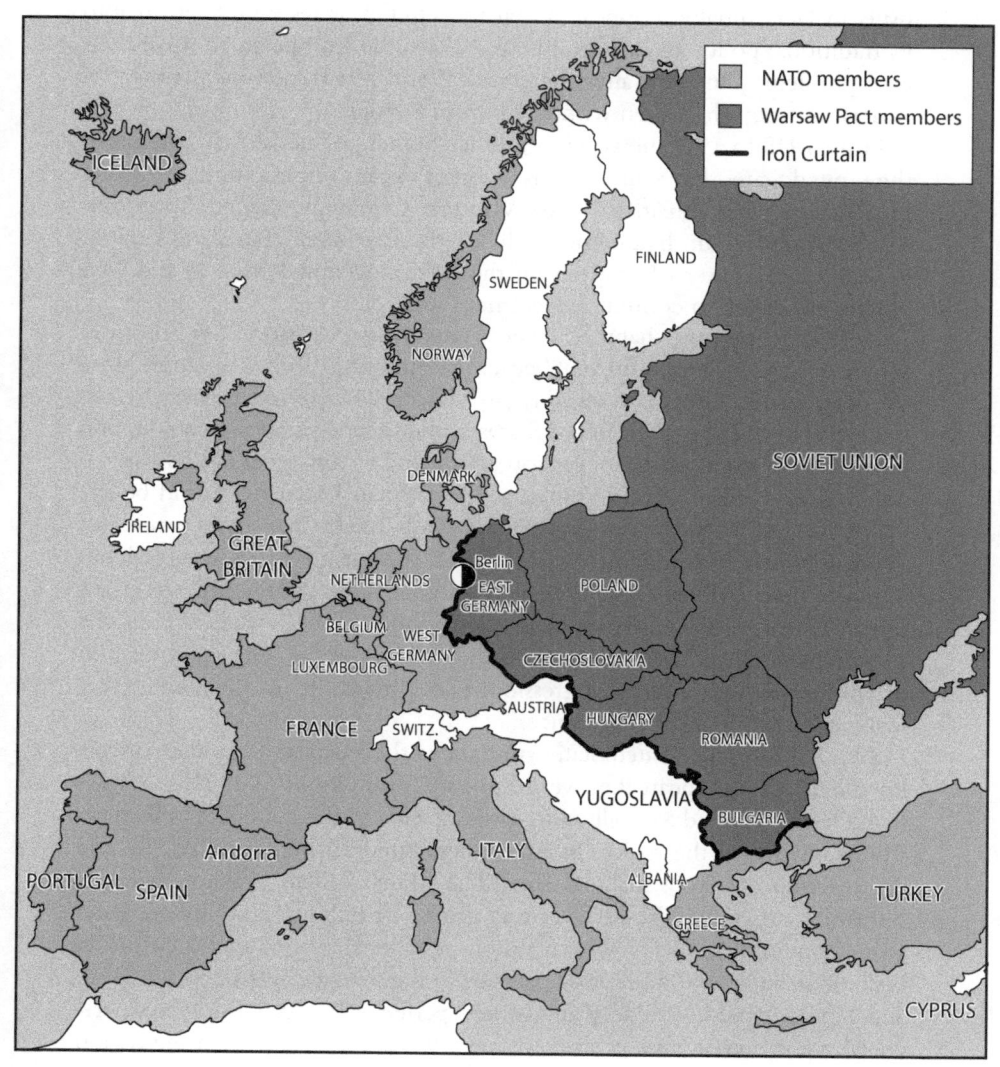

Map 19.1 The Cold War in Europe.

capitalist democracies would predominate. The Western Allies were divided in their opinions of European imperialism—the United States was decisively opposed—but they were united in urging the Soviets to respect the independence of all the countries of Eastern Europe. Nevertheless, none of the Western powers was prepared to fight yet another bloody war over the issue. In fact, initially it appeared that the United States might retreat into its traditional policy of isolationism and allow the Europeans to solve their own problems. One year after the end of World War II, the vast majority of American troops had been withdrawn from Europe.

From 1945 to 1949, however, aggressive Soviet policies slowly convinced the United States that Stalin and his brand of expansionist communism were indeed a terrible threat. In 1946, Winston Churchill warned Americans that an Iron Curtain had come to divide the free, democratic, and capitalist nations of Western Europe from the Soviet-occupied zone in the East, where authoritarian communist regimes took hold.

In 1947, it appeared that the Soviets were trying to expand their European sphere of influence even further, because communist rebels were attempting to take power in Greece. In response, in March 1947 President Harry S. Truman announced that the United States would give assistance to any nation threatened by communist subversion or attack. The new goal of U.S. foreign policy, under what became known as the Truman Doctrine, would be the "containment" of Soviet power. In other words, the United States would not attack the Soviet Union, or any of the territories it presently occupied, but it would fiercely resist—by political, economic, diplomatic, and if necessary military means—any effort to expand Soviet power into new areas. Thus, the United States abandoned isolationism and embraced the long-term mission of confronting communist aggression. The United States has been deeply involved in world affairs ever since.

Also in 1947, the United States announced the Marshall Plan, alternatively known as the European Recovery Program. From 1948 to 1951, the Marshall Plan distributed $13 billion in economic aid to the countries of Western Europe. Much of the region had been devastated during World War II, and some Europeans were malnourished. The Marshall Plan was not merely a humanitarian gesture, however. It was also smart politics. The United States gave economic aid to its Western European allies largely so that they would become stronger and more loyal partners in the struggle against communism and Soviet expansion. The plan worked perfectly. Western Europe experienced massive economic growth, and by 1949 most countries in the region had eagerly joined a military alliance with the United States and Canada called the North Atlantic Treaty Organization (NATO).

NATO committed the United States to the defense of its European allies from potential Soviet attack, but it also committed the Europeans to fight together, alongside the United States, against Soviet expansionism. The Soviets recognized the strength of NATO, and they responded in 1955 by forming the Warsaw Pact, a military alliance between the Soviet Union and its satellite states in Eastern Europe. These Eastern European states and the

Soviet Union became known collectively as the Eastern Bloc, the Soviet Bloc, or the Communist Bloc. Now Europe was effectively divided into two armed camps.

As NATO came into being in 1949, the future of Germany was also clarified. In 1945, the war-ravaged country had been divided into four occupation zones—one each for the United States, Britain, France, and Russia. The capital of Berlin had also been divided into four zones, even though the city itself was located deep within the Soviet sector of Germany.

In 1948–49, Stalin had attempted to blockade West Berlin and its small garrison of American, British, and French defenders. The people of West Berlin looked as though they might be starved into submission, but the U.S. policy of containment worked. Instead of buckling under, the United States, Britain, and France airlifted ample supplies to the Berliners—eventually including candy bars that arrived by tiny parachutes. In 1949, Stalin gave up on his blockade. In that same year, the American, British, and French zones of occupation throughout Germany were combined into the democratic and capitalist country of the Federal Republic of Germany, popularly known as West Germany, which joined NATO in 1955. The Soviets responded by sponsoring the creation of the German Democratic Republic, or East Germany, in their zone, which became a hard-line communist state and a member of the Warsaw Pact. Now the Iron Curtain ran straight through Germany, and the citizens of West and East Germany would not be reunited until 1990.

From 1945 to 1949, what steps did the United States take to achieve the containment of Soviet communism?

The Strategic Balance in the Cold War

Throughout most of the Cold War, the balance of conventional armed forces in Europe (men, tanks, artillery, etc.) was stacked decisively in favor of the Soviet Union. Why, then, did the Soviet Union not launch an immediate invasion of Western Europe and defeat NATO once and for all?

Part of the answer lies in the severe trauma that the Second World War had produced for all the participating countries. No one was eager to start yet another devastating war. The main reason the Soviets hesitated to attack in Western Europe, though, was that in the modern world conventional weapons pale in significance to nuclear weapons. Because of their massive destructive power, nuclear weapons exert a broad, or strategic, influence on global politics. Simply put, a Soviet tank rolling into Munich might achieve a small tactical victory, but an American atomic bomb dropped on Moscow would be an effective strategic response. Thus, as long as the United States was the only country in the world with nuclear weapons, as it was in 1945–49, the Soviet Union was not prepared to risk a major confrontation with the Americans.

After 1949, the strategic balance became more complicated. The Soviets exploded their first atomic bomb in that year, and the British and the French followed suit in 1952 and 1960, respectively. Communist China detonated its first atom bomb in 1964.

The Soviet nuclear program, in particular, was enormously significant to the evolving dynamics of the Cold War. From 1949 onward, there was a race between the United States and the Soviet Union to build more and more nuclear weapons with greater destructive power and more reliable and flexible delivery systems.

At first, both the United States and the Soviet Union depended on bombers to deliver their atom bombs. Eventually, though, both countries switched to much more powerful hydrogen bombs, based on the fusion, or combination, of atoms of hydrogen. They also increasingly employed ballistic missiles, launched either from silos in the ground or from submarines lurking off the American and Soviet coasts, as their primary delivery systems. The *Typhoon* class submarines that the Soviets launched in the 1980s were the largest submarines ever built. They were remarkably quiet, and their 20 missiles, with up to ten nuclear warheads each, were capable of destroying most of the cities on either coast of the United States in less than ten minutes.

All this nuclear hardware was immensely expensive. The United States spent over $3 trillion on its nuclear weapons during the Cold War. Nuclear technology was an even greater economic burden for the Soviet Union, which was significantly poorer. Nevertheless, the Soviets achieved nuclear parity with the United States by the 1970s. Each country's arsenal was also sufficiently powerful to destroy human civilization several times over.

Needless to say, the nuclear dimension to the Cold War made the conflict incredibly frightening. Some leading thinkers predicted that nuclear weapons would cause the extinction of humankind. Government advisories to schoolchildren to hide under their desks to avoid the effects of a nuclear blast were hardly comforting. Some citizens planned to huddle in their basements in case of a nuclear war, but the long-term effects of radiation made instant death arguably more attractive than temporary survival.

Despite these widespread fears, no nuclear or conventional war was ever fought between NATO and the Warsaw Pact, or between the United States and the Soviet Union. This was primarily because of an idea known as Mutually Assured Destruction (MAD). According to the doctrine of MAD, the only conceivable result of one superpower launching a nuclear attack on its superpower enemy would be that both countries, and most of the world, would be destroyed by nuclear retaliation. In other words, according to MAD, nuclear war is unwinnable.

Ultimately, the leaders of the United States, the Soviet Union, and the other nuclear powers agreed with the idea of MAD. Although they competed for power and influence by other means—including participating in bloody conflicts in the Third World—they were not prepared to escalate any confrontation to a level that would produce nuclear devastation.

How did nuclear weapons help to keep the peace between the United States and the Soviet Union?

The Dynamics of the Cold War Take Shape

Because direct military confrontation between the superpowers seemed so ill-advised during the nuclear age, for the most part the Cold War was waged by peaceful means. For example, both superpowers battled to achieve economic growth and a higher standard of living for their citizens. The United States had a major lead in this struggle, which it kept until the Soviet Union's demise.

Throughout the Cold War, although the Soviet economy often grew quickly, the Soviet Gross Domestic Product (GDP) was never more than 40 percent of America's. The United States could also count on the support of wealthy, high-tech allies such as Canada, Britain, France, West Germany, and Japan. The Soviet Union, by contrast, could count only on its small Eastern European satellite states, and those countries were loyal mainly because they were coerced.

In addition to economic rivalry, there was also cultural competition between the United States and the Soviet Union. Although the Soviets never excelled in the production of consumer goods, they produced ballet dancers and classical musicians at an astounding rate. When colorless Soviet bureaucrats made their periodic attacks on the alleged decadence of American pop culture, though, they had to compete for the world's attention with pop icons such as John Wayne, Madonna, and Muhammad Ali. It was an uphill battle.

In the technological arena, the Soviets made some major breakthroughs. In 1957, the Soviets launched the first Earth-orbiting satellite: *Sputnik*. In 1961, they launched the first man into space: Yuri Gagarin. By 1969, however, the Americans had beaten the Russians in the race to the moon. Thereafter, Soviet technology would fall further and further behind. In fact, some historians believe that the American edge in computer and telecommunications technology in the 1970s and 1980s helps to explain the Soviet Union's defeat in the Cold War.

One of the few arenas in which Americans and Russians battled each other directly during the Cold War was in international sports competitions. The Soviets exulted in the fact that they often won the medal count at the Olympics, and Soviet athletes were indeed champions in many sports. The Americans celebrated when they won the gold medal in ice hockey at the 1980 Winter Olympic Games at Lake Placid, mainly because the Russians were heavily favored.

There was a dark side to the communist successes in sports, though. Many athletes from the Eastern Bloc chose to defect to the West to escape oppression. Communist sports authorities also sometimes forced athletes to use powerful steroids. For years, East German women, who appeared suspiciously masculine, triumphed at the Olympics. Only later was it discovered that many of those women had been drugged without their consent.

Although the economic, cultural, technological, and athletic competition between the superpowers was important, the military campaigns that they

370 *The End of European Dominance*

Figure 19.1 The Apollo 16 mission lifts off. The moon landings marked the culmination of the Space Race.

NASA/Wikimedia Commons.

waged during the Cold War were arguably more decisive. The Americans and the Soviets never fought against each other directly, but they each fought in a number of smaller wars, most of them in Africa, Asia, or Latin America.

The United States fought a war in Korea in 1950–53. Communist North Korea had invaded the non-communist south. Eventually, troops from communist China also fought on the side of North Korea, while the Soviet Union furnished North Korea with military aid. Unlike the Soviets, the United States intervened directly. About 35,000 American soldiers were killed, but the goal of containment was achieved. Although North Korea remained communist, South Korea remained capitalist and friendly to the West, as it is today.

The most bloody and destructive Cold War conflict was fought in Vietnam, to which France had granted independence in 1954. From 1965 to 1973, U.S. troops struggled to prevent the spread of communism from North Vietnam to South Vietnam. The Soviets sent arms and military advisors to help the North Vietnamese, but no combat troops. Ultimately, U.S. forces withdrew, and the communists conquered all of Vietnam in 1975. The Vietnam War was America's biggest defeat during the Cold War, and it aroused great opposition in America itself and in Western Europe.

Luckily for the United States, the Soviets repeated some of America's mistakes by invading Afghanistan in 1979. The Soviets became bogged down in vicious fighting against U.S.-backed guerrillas, many of them Islamic fundamentalists. In 1989, the Soviets withdrew from Afghanistan in disgrace.

For the most part, the various Cold War military conflicts helped to confirm the most basic fact of the Cold War: the world had become essentially bipolar. In other words, there were now only two superpowers that dominated, whereas before 1945 there had been many great powers that shared global hegemony. This bipolarity was driven home by events in 1956.

In October 1956, the Hungarian communist leader, Imre Nagy, attempted to take his country out of the Warsaw Pact. He also requested the removal of Soviet troops. In response, the Soviets used force to overthrow Nagy's government. Nagy himself was executed. The lesson was clear: the Soviets made the rules in Eastern Europe.

At roughly the same time, the British and the French invaded Egypt, with Israeli support. They were trying to retake control of the Suez Canal, which had been nationalized by Egyptian President Gamal Abdel Nasser. The invasion was a success, but the United States was so embarrassed by this act of imperialist aggression that it applied financial pressure that forced Britain and France to back down. Again, the lesson was clear: just as the Soviets dominated in the East, the Americans dominated in the West. Moreover, the Americans, as we shall see, chose to exert strong pressure on their European allies to dissolve their colonial empires, thus further weakening European influence worldwide.

Name several American and Soviet victories in the Cold War.

Life Behind "The Wall," 1961–89

Since 1989, Eastern Europeans have happily embraced Western European practices such as free-market capitalism, free speech, and democracy. Before the fall of communism and the Berlin Wall in 1989, however, Eastern Europeans, as well as ordinary citizens in the Soviet Union, lived under an oppressive system in which the state and the Communist Party controlled not just politics but also economics, education, leisure activities, and even religion.

In 1961, during a particularly tense period of the Cold War, the East German government built a wall that separated East Berlin, which was the capital of East Germany, from West Berlin, which was part of West Germany and in which capitalism and democracy thrived. Before 1961, East Germans had been free to travel to West Berlin. Roughly 2.5 million of them had visited the West and chosen to stay there.

In August 1961, the East German government decided that, if it did not stop the flow of refugees to the West, the East German economy would collapse. With Soviet permission and assistance, therefore, the Berlin Wall—often simply called "The Wall"—was built. Eventually, there were actually two high concrete walls surrounding West Berlin, with a "death strip" in-between. The Wall quickly became the most powerful symbol of Soviet and communist oppression in Eastern Europe.

To deal with widespread discontent, communist governments in Eastern Europe prevented the formation of independent groups—political parties, labor unions, clubs, and sometimes even churches—that might serve as a focal point for an opposition movement. The Communist Party attempted to coordinate all aspects of everyday life. Censorship was rigorous. All the countries in the Soviet Bloc also maintained large secret police organizations. The best known of these was the Soviet KGB, but the East German *Stasi* was a close second. The *Stasi* controlled a network of informers that included hundreds of thousands of East Germans. It also maintained files on approximately one-third of all East German citizens. Amazingly, *Stasi* officers were five times as numerous as their *Gestapo* predecessors.

Another challenge with which all Eastern Europeans had to contend was shortages of food and consumer goods. By the 1960s, Western Europeans had come to expect that most consumer goods would be plentiful and affordable. In the East, on the other hand, obtaining necessary items was often very difficult. Many Eastern Europeans and Soviets had to enter their names on a list and wait years for a car or an apartment. Frequently, a person could only obtain what he or she wanted by standing in line, paying a bribe, or exploiting personal connections. Furthermore, the gap between living standards in the West and in the East, which was initially small, gradually widened to become an unbridgeable chasm.

What was worse, even when Eastern Europeans got access to consumer goods, they were often of inferior quality. A famous example was the *Trabant*, a small car manufactured in East Germany. Its two-cylinder motor belched smoke, while its body was made of cheap, thin plastic. The *Trabant*'s design remained essentially unchanged for 30 years. This points out an area of special weakness in the communist command economies: their inability to respond to changes in "fashion" and consumer expectations.

Given the lack of political freedom and material rewards in Eastern Europe and the Soviet Union, it should come as no surprise that levels of public dissatisfaction were high. Because of the efficiency and brutality of the secret police, however, it was virtually impossible to organize any effective opposition to the communist system. There were only a few exceptions.

Initially, intellectuals often provided the nucleus of an opposition movement. Another focal point for the critics of communism was the Catholic Church, which was popular in areas such as Poland, Czechoslovakia, and Hungary. Because of the Church's international influence and prestige, the communist authorities never dared to suppress it altogether, even though all of the Soviet Bloc regimes were officially atheistic.

The election of a Pole, Karol Wojtyla, as pope in 1978 was especially problematic for the communists. Pope John Paul II was a fierce critic of communism. He visited his homeland as pope in 1979 and received an enthusiastic welcome. Eventually, the Soviets decided that he had to be eliminated. An assassin who narrowly failed to kill the pope in 1981 was almost certainly employed by the Bulgarian secret police, acting under Soviet orders.

Ordinary laborers could also be a source of opposition to communism, even though communist ideology expressed so much sympathy for the working class. Eastern European workers were often well aware that their pay, benefits, and conditions of employment were substandard. They sometimes used protests and illegal strikes to extract concessions from the communist authorities. The most successful of all the worker movements in Eastern Europe was the independent Solidarity labor union in Poland. During the 1980s, Solidarity grew so popular that the communist government agreed to negotiate and meet some of the union's demands.

Solidarity was unusual, however. For most of the Cold War, and in most of the Soviet Bloc, there was no official or organized opposition, and ordinary citizens were at the mercy of the communist system. The few benefits of communism—improved education systems; economic and social equality; reliable, if substandard, social services and health care; and enhanced economic opportunities for women—were never enough to win over the peoples of Eastern Europe. They overwhelmingly viewed communism as a defective system that had been imposed on them by force.

What were the downsides to living in Soviet-dominated Eastern Europe?

The Rise and Fall of the Soviet Union

Joseph Stalin ruled Russia from 1927 until his death in 1953. After Stalin's demise, the world watched with great interest to see what sort of successor would emerge. In the context of the Cold War, the very fate of the world was at stake. By 1956, Nikita Khrushchev had become the new leader of the Soviet Union. Khrushchev was an impulsive but intelligent man who had risen from peasant origins to become one of Stalin's cronies. He had managed to survive Stalin's Purges during the 1930s, but he never forgot the unspeakable terror that Stalin had used against his friends and enemies alike.

One of Khrushchev's first acts as Soviet leader was to give a speech in 1956 to Communist Party officials that condemned "the crimes of Stalin." Khrushchev argued that Stalin had been too quick to use violence and intimidation, and he had shown too little regard for the suffering of his own people. Khrushchev therefore insisted on the elimination of Russia's *gulags*, and he redirected the economy so that it would produce more consumer goods. Khrushchev even boasted that living standards in the Soviet Union would soon surpass those in America. "We will bury you," he said, rather optimistically.

Although Khrushchev sought a better quality of life for his people, and although he was willing to concede them slightly more personal freedom than under Stalin, he was not a believer in capitalism or democracy in any sense. Under Khrushchev, the Communist Party continued to monopolize political and economic power, and critics of the government, called dissidents, were routinely harassed or imprisoned.

In addition, Khrushchev was determined to compete successfully with the United States in the Cold War. He visited the United States in 1959 and made peaceful gestures toward the West, but he also pursued the Soviet Union's foreign policy goals aggressively. Khrushchev gave permission to the East German government in 1961 to build the Berlin Wall. He also attempted to place nuclear missiles in Cuba, an ally of the Soviet Union, in 1962. This decision precipitated the Cuban Missile Crisis. To pressure the Soviets to withdraw their missiles, U.S. President John F. Kennedy imposed a naval blockade on Cuba. The United States also prepared to invade the communist nation. Khrushchev backed down, and the nuclear missiles were dismantled and shipped back to Russia. World opinion assumed that the Americans had bested the Soviets. That was debatable, but clearly the Soviet Union and the United States had come perilously close to all-out nuclear war.

Ultimately, the communist elite in the Soviet Union was not impressed with Khrushchev's leadership. Many Soviet officials believed that their country had been humiliated during the Cuban Missile Crisis. Khrushchev had also shown signs of irrationality. Once, during a speech at UN headquarters, Khrushchev had removed his shoe and banged it on a table in a gesture of contempt. In 1964, Khrushchev was forced to resign.

From 1964 to 1982, the leader of the Soviet Union was Leonid Brezhnev. The few personal freedoms that Khrushchev had permitted were largely retracted under Brezhnev. The Soviet economy had boomed under Khrushchev, but in the last decade of Brezhnev's term in office the economy began to sag under the weight of mismanagement, corruption, and inefficiency. Simultaneously, social problems, such as alcoholism, drug use, and crime, exploded, while serious environmental problems, leading in turn to higher rates of cancer and infant mortality, strained Soviet society all the more.

Brezhnev himself was too busy enjoying the perks of office to notice many of Russia's problems. He enjoyed wearing expensive Western clothes and driving fast foreign cars. Brezhnev also had many mistresses, and he was known for granting himself undeserved medals and awards.

Despite the Soviet Union's limited resources, Brezhnev pursued an active foreign policy. He acquired new client states for Russia in Africa, Asia, and Latin America. In addition, Brezhnev crushed a pro-democracy movement in communist Czechoslovakia in 1968 and announced the Brezhnev Doctrine, which stated that the Soviet Union had the right to interfere in the domestic affairs of other communist states. Brezhnev greatly increased the size and strength of the Soviet military, including its nuclear forces.

Despite all of these aggressive moves on the international stage, Brezhnev recognized that stable relations with the United States were desirable from a Soviet perspective. Brezhnev and U.S. President Richard Nixon pursued *détente*, that is, the relaxation of tensions, during the early 1970s. Trade between the two superpowers increased, and some arms control treaties were signed, but ultimately no lasting improvement in U.S.-Soviet relations was achieved.

The Cold War took an unexpected turn in 1972 when President Nixon visited communist China. The thawing in U.S.-Chinese relations greatly worried the Soviets. China and the Soviet Union, the world's two largest communist states, had been allies from about 1949 to 1960. Then they became competitors. After 1972, the Soviets worried that the United States and China might be working together against them. The Soviets were forced to station a large percentage of their conventional armed forces on the Soviet-Chinese border, thus straining Russia's military and economic resources all the more.

Brezhnev died in 1982, and his two initial successors both followed him to the grave after very short terms in office. By 1985, the Soviet Union was desperately looking for new leadership to solve the serious problems that Brezhnev had ignored.

First and foremost, the Soviet Union was clearly overextended in a strategic and economic sense. It sent military and economic aid and sometimes troops to help friendly communist governments all around the world. Its armed forces were a match for those of the United States, but the Soviet economy, which was one-third the size of America's, lacked the necessary resources to fund both military and civilian needs. The Soviet economy had also become overreliant on petroleum exports, which had boomed during the 1970s. Any reduction in the value of oil was bound to cause an economic crisis.

To make matters worse for the Soviets, in 1980 Ronald Reagan had been elected President of the United States. Reagan made no secret of his view that the Soviet Union was an "evil empire." Not only did Reagan give aid to anti-communist rebels in Nicaragua and Afghanistan, but he also pursued a gigantic U.S. military buildup. In addition, Reagan sponsored research into a space-based missile shield that could protect the United States from a Soviet nuclear attack. The proposed missile shield was known as the Strategic Defense Initiative (SDI). Many Americans made fun of Reagan's idea, which involved satellites that could shoot down Soviet missiles with laser beams. They referred to SDI as "Star Wars." The Soviets, though, took the program seriously, and they increased their defense budget accordingly.

By the mid-1980s, thanks to excessive Soviet military spending and poor economic management, the economic malaise that had begun under Brezhnev had turned into a serious crisis. Shortages of food and consumer goods became acute, and the patience of ordinary citizens in the Soviet Bloc was running out.

In order to breathe new life into the communist system, the Soviets chose as their new leader a young and vigorous party official named Mikhail Gorbachev. Gorbachev had worked as a tractor operator before becoming a law student and then a Communist Party administrator. In 1985, at the age of 54, he took the reins of power and immediately started shaking up the whole Soviet system. One of his first acts was to attack (vainly) the problem of alcoholism.

Mikhail Gorbachev was a sincere believer in communism, but he also thought that the Soviet regime had become rigid and corrupt. Although ultimately the Soviet Union collapsed with Gorbachev in charge, that was never his goal. On the contrary, Gorbachev tried to make Russia stronger.

Gorbachev's first instinct was to tackle the country's economic problems through a set of reforms he labeled *perestroika* (restructuring). *Perestroika* was meant to improve the quality of life for ordinary citizens by increasing the production of food and consumer goods. It was supposed to achieve this goal by loosening central control over economic decision making and reducing military spending. In order to make military cutbacks feasible, Gorbachev reached out to the West and signed several major arms control agreements with President Reagan, who proved to be a surprisingly flexible and farsighted Cold Warrior. Gorbachev also withdrew some Soviet troops from Eastern Europe, and he ended the Soviet occupation of Afghanistan.

As a consequence of these peaceful gestures, Gorbachev became wildly popular in Western countries, where he was affectionately known as "Gorby," but he was less and less popular at home. His economic reforms, far from leading to renewed growth, destabilized the economy and made a bad situation worse. Gorbachev compounded the problem by switching back and forth between market-based and socialist policies, while party bureaucrats obstructed serious reforms.

Eventually, partly because public anger was rising over the economic crisis, Gorbachev decided to pursue political reforms as well. He bargained that, by granting more freedom to the Soviet people, he could increase public support for the Communist Party. Gorbachev instituted a policy known as *glasnost* (openness) that permitted extraordinary levels of free speech, freedom of worship, and honest media coverage in the Soviet Union. He also took steps to allow critics of the Communist Party to be elected to public office.

As Gorbachev predicted, the Soviet people enthusiastically embraced *glasnost*. However, they used their newfound freedoms not to praise communism, but to condemn it. In the past, the failings of the government had always been covered up, but now every mistake that the Soviet bureaucracy made was widely reported. What was worse, the various ethnic minorities in the Soviet Union—Ukrainians, residents of the Baltic states, and Central Asian Muslims, for example—began to demand autonomy from Moscow. Russia was only one of 15 republics, that is, provinces, in the Soviet Union, and it appeared as though most of the other republics wanted to break away from Soviet rule. It was an open question whether the Soviet Union could survive such grave challenges.

How did the failures of Mikhail Gorbachev's predecessors contribute to his decision to pursue perestroika *and* glasnost?

Freedom for Eastern Europe, and the Soviet Union Becomes Modern Russia

As the Soviet economy unraveled, and as public dissatisfaction and ethnic unrest mounted, Gorbachev reached the radical conclusion that, in these adverse circumstances, the Soviet Union could no longer afford to occupy and repress Eastern Europe. To improve relations with the West, and to make further cuts in military spending possible, therefore, Gorbachev renounced the Brezhnev Doctrine in October 1989. In other words, he declared that the Soviet Union would no longer try to dominate Eastern Europe, which would be free to chart its own course.

The reaction was almost instantaneous. By the end of 1989, every country in Eastern Europe had renounced communism, and most communist leaders had left office peacefully. New governments that embraced democratic and capitalist reforms, and usually some version of nationalism, now took over.

Nowhere was the fall of communism more dramatic than in East Germany. In October 1989, large demonstrations of East Germans had developed. The secret police, the *Stasi*, did not know how to respond. The East German government hesitated, and then, on November 9, 1989, the East German authorities allowed crowds to pass freely through the checkpoints in the Berlin Wall. German families, many of which had been divided for decades, were suddenly reunited. World television audiences looked on as ecstatic Germans began to demolish the Wall with sledgehammers. By late 1989, all border restrictions had been abolished.

In October 1990, East Germany and West Germany combined into a single democratic and capitalist state. Many in the West celebrated the fall of the Berlin Wall and German reunification as the effective end of the Cold War.

Sadly, the initially festive atmosphere in Eastern Europe dissipated during the early 1990s. Most shockingly, a civil war developed in the former Yugoslavia. As that country broke apart, Serbs, Croats, and Bosnian Muslims battled for control of Bosnia-Herzegovina. More than 100,000 people died in the worst episode of violence in Europe since the end of World War II. NATO intervention in 1995 finally ended the fighting, but in the meantime most of Bosnia had undergone a frightful process of "ethnic cleansing."

Happily, such horrors were avoided in the other newly liberated countries of the former Communist Bloc. After 1989, these Eastern European nations suffered from severe economic recession, environmental devastation, and social dislocation, but not civil war. Ultimately, Eastern Europeans overcame these transitional problems. They successfully cast aside communism, embraced democracy and capitalism, albeit with a socialist twist, and most of them joined NATO and the European Union.

In the Soviet Union, despite Gorbachev's receipt of the Nobel Prize for Peace in 1990, events in Eastern Europe were not viewed as positively as they were in the West. The Soviet empire in Eastern Europe had evaporated, but the Soviet people still were not seeing any benefits from Gorbachev's reforms. The economy continued to decline. In a sign of hard times, Gorbachev effectively canceled the Soviet space shuttle program.

By 1991, it appeared to many diehard communists that Gorbachev's reforms were a disaster. The Communist Party was steadily giving away its power, and the country was growing more impoverished and unstable every day. Ethnic unrest was reaching vast proportions, and the scaled-down Soviet military could not cope with the violence.

In August 1991, hard-line communists tried to overthrow Gorbachev. They failed, but Gorbachev was temporarily arrested and the charismatic leader of the Soviet Union's Russian republic, Boris Yeltsin, led the popular movement to defeat the coup. Yeltsin claimed that the communist hard-liners wanted to plunge the Soviet Union back into Stalinist tyranny. When the coup finally unraveled, it was Yeltsin, rather than Gorbachev, who reaped the political benefits.

By December 1991, Gorbachev had accepted that his Soviet government was doomed. The Union of Soviet Socialist Republics, born under Lenin, officially ceased to exist on December 25, 1991. Separatist movements succeeded in establishing each of the Soviet Union's 15 republics as an independent country. The largest of these new countries was the Russian Federation, and Boris Yeltsin became its first President. Almost in the blink of an eye, the Cold War had ended, and the Soviet Union had ceased to exist!

Russia experienced hard times throughout the 1990s. Many Russians had assumed that, after giving up their empire and much of their military strength, Western aid, plus democratic and capitalist reforms, would lead to rapid improvements in their quality of life. They were sadly mistaken. Russia's economy imploded during the 1990s, crime rates skyrocketed, alcoholism spread, health standards declined, and Russian pride reached new lows. Many Russians regretted their newfound freedom.

In December 1999, Yeltsin left office and was replaced as President of Russia by a savvy former KGB officer, Vladimir Putin. Putin has engineered an impressive recovery in the Russian economy. Russia has emerged as one of the world's top oil producers, and the country's industries and public services have rebounded. Meanwhile, Moscow has become one of the world's most prosperous, and expensive, cities. Even after so much turmoil, Russia still maintains an active space program, and its nuclear arsenal is the world's second largest. Crime, disease, ethnic strife, income inequality, and corruption plague modern Russia, but nonetheless it has successfully reestablished itself as a major power.

Since Putin took office, Russia's relationship with the United States and NATO has been severely tested. When President George W. Bush ordered an invasion of Iraq in 2003, Russia was among the countries that harshly criticized his decision. Russian aggression in neighboring countries such as Georgia and Ukraine has also led to Western condemnation. In addition, Russian intervention in Syria's civil war generated controversy. It remains to be seen whether a new Cold War will emerge between Russia and the

West, and whether democracy will truly take hold in Russia. Putin is sometimes labeled a dictator in the West, although for now he is overwhelmingly popular at home.

> *What events led to the fall of communism in Eastern Europe and the Soviet Union from 1989 to 1991?*

Europe Turns Inward: Decolonization, the European Union, and Domestic Politics

During the Cold War, European colonial empires began to shrivel up. This was because the major Western European colonial powers—Britain, France, the Netherlands, Belgium, Spain, and Portugal—concluded that maintaining their empires, especially in the face of escalating "native" resistance, was too costly. In addition, after 1945, the ideology of white supremacy was widely viewed as morally bankrupt. Lastly, the United States put pressure on its Western European allies to pursue decolonization. The Americans feared that if the Europeans waited too long rebellions would proliferate throughout Africa and Asia, and communists would benefit from the chaos.

The wave of decolonization began in 1947 when the British gave up the Jewel in the Crown of their empire: India. In 1949, Indonesia gained independence from the Dutch. France withdrew from Vietnam in 1954. After the Suez Crisis in 1956, the pace of decolonization quickened. Britain granted independence to Ghana in 1957. In 1960, a massive wave of decolonization began, mainly in Africa, that lasted throughout the decade. In 1962, the French finally parted with their most valued possession in Africa: Algeria. Hundreds of thousands of French settlers who lived there fled to France. The last European colonies in Africa—Portuguese Angola, Guinea-Bissau, and Mozambique—became independent in 1975.

Often, decolonization produced just the sort of chaos that the Americans had hoped to avoid, and communists benefited from the instability. By the 1980s, the Soviet Union had acquired client states scattered across the globe.

Decolonization played a major role in causing the Vietnam War, but the most long-lasting conflict that decolonization helped to create has been between the Arabs and the Israelis. In the first half of the twentieth century, hundreds of thousands of Jews had migrated from Europe to the British mandate, that is, colony, in Palestine, angering the Arab majority there. In the wake of Jewish losses in the Holocaust, support for Zionism, or the creation of an independent Jewish homeland in Israel, surged among Jews worldwide. In 1948, the British withdrew from Palestine and turned over the management of relations between Arabs and Jewish settlers to the United Nations. No broadly acceptable solution emerged, however, and in May 1948 the new Jewish state of Israel declared its independence. Various Arab countries immediately attacked Israel but failed to defeat it. During the Cold War, the United States generally supported Israel, while the Soviets generally supported the

Arabs. Wars were fought between Israel and its Arab neighbors in 1948, 1956, 1967, 1973, and 1982. Today, militarily, Israel is stronger than ever. Palestinian Arabs, though, are still seeking an independent state of their own.

The end of European empires in Africa and Asia was a watershed development in European and world history. From the sixteenth century until the middle of the twentieth century, European nations and their empires had dominated the world. Today, more than 80 percent of the world's people live in countries that during the last 500 years were entirely or partially ruled by Europeans. In many of these countries, the legacy of European rule is still a cause of resentment.

Arguably, colonial mismanagement, followed by hasty decolonization, helped to produce long-term instability in Africa and the Middle East, which in turn has contributed to many current global problems. Some residents of the developing world also claim that a version of colonialism, or rather neo-colonialism, is still in place In the developing world, but that it now takes an economic rather than a political and military form. As we have seen, believers in world-systems theory would tend to agree. It is important to note, however, that today economic growth rates in the developing world are generally much higher than those in the West, so Western economic predominance may be coming to an end.

During the Cold War, as Western Europe relinquished its hold on Africa and Asia, it increasingly conceded global hegemony to the superpowers and began to pursue the goal of European unity instead. Six major Western European countries, with France and West Germany in the lead, founded the European Economic Community in 1957. The EEC coordinated Western European economic policies and created a free-trade zone. The United States applauded and actively supported these developments, because greater unity and prosperity in Western Europe made it less likely that communism would spread there. The EEC was so successful in building economic growth in Western and Southern Europe that its membership consistently grew, and, after a period of consolidation in the 1970s and 1980s, in 1992 it broadened its mission and renamed itself the European Union (EU).

The EU has attempted, so far with modest success, to coordinate European politics, foreign affairs, defense policy, and legal systems, in addition to encouraging economic union. There is even a European Space Agency, affiliated with the EU, that competes with NASA. The EU's greatest accomplishment so far has been in creating in 1999 a single currency for most of Europe: the *Euro*. While the new currency has been controversial, and some EU countries have declined to use it, overall the transition to the *Euro* has been a success. Another important accomplishment of the EU has been that, since the fall of communism there in 1989, the European Union has expanded its membership in Eastern Europe. The EU today is a vital link between Western and Eastern Europe, and it has helped to strengthen democratic and capitalist institutions in what used to be the Communist Bloc.

The future of the EU is uncertain. Some believe it has already unified Europe as much as possible, while others forecast that the EU will become a United States of Europe. The latter prediction is plausible, but not in the short term, due to several key obstacles to further integration. First, an attempt to create an EU constitution in 2005 was defeated by referenda in France and the Netherlands, indicating considerable popular resistance to the EU. Even more damaging was the decision of the British electorate in June 2016 to vote in favor of "Brexit": Britain's exit from the EU. In addition, a major rift has developed in Europe over whether Turkey, a predominantly Muslim country located partly in Europe and partly in Asia, should be permitted to obtain EU membership. There has also been little agreement about how to formulate a unified EU foreign and defense policy. European relations with the United States and Russia have proved particularly difficult to coordinate. Lastly, the bureaucratic structure of the EU displeases many Europeans. There is an elected EU parliament, but its powers are limited, and much of the time diplomats and EU officials effectively run the organization behind closed doors.

As Western Europeans pursued greater unity from the 1950s onward, almost all of their national governments were democratic and capitalist in nature. (The exceptions were Spain and Portugal, which remained quasi-fascist until the 1970s.) For the most part, Western European democratic politics during the Cold War settled into a contest between Christian Democrats and socialists. Christian Democratic parties favored free-market economics, conservative social policies, and strong relations with the United States. Socialist parties favored a mixture of free-market capitalism and socialism, progressive social policies, and strong relations with the United States, but also peaceful coexistence with the Soviet Union.

The political system in West Germany is a good example of the historical phenomenon of competition between Christian Democrats and socialists. From 1949 to 1966, the Christian Democratic Union (CDU) governed West Germany and pursued conservative policies not unlike those which the U.S. Republican Party favors. After 1966, periodically the Social Democratic Party (SPD) governed West Germany. The SPD has played a major role in German history since the 1870s. It pursues policies that put it somewhat to the left of the U.S. Democratic Party. Meanwhile, from 1945 to the present, no political party that advocated dictatorship or extremism garnered significant support from the West German electorate. Today, with the Cold War a distant memory, the CDU and the SPD still dominate German politics.

For the most part, therefore, multiparty democracy and capitalism flourished in Western Europe after 1945. This does not mean, however, that the established order was never threatened. A wave of violence washed over much of Europe in 1968, for example, as university students, among others, protested the Vietnam War, antiquated educational systems, alleged government repression, and other social ills. Some of the protestors active in 1968 subsequently turned to terrorism (The Troubles in Northern Ireland between Catholics and Protestants began around the same time). Although this revolutionary dynamism petered out in the early 1970s, many American and European leaders today are former 1960s radicals who still retain traces of their former idealism. The key point, though, is that, even in 1968, the Christian Democratic-Socialist political consensus in Western Europe remained intact. By and large, it continues to predominate in European politics today.

The appeal of moderate socialism and of generous social welfare programs to many Western Europeans, not just during the Cold War but also today, has helped to produce one of the most important long-term differences between U.S. and European politics. In Europe, many citizens support a much stronger role for the government in the economy than most Americans will accept. For instance, some European industries are government-owned. Subsidies are also common. European subsidies for agriculture, in particular, are enormously costly, and they have led to the production of considerably more food than anyone can eat. Socialist parties in Europe have also helped to create a complex and expensive system of welfare and social programs. For example, most Europeans enjoy guaranteed lifetime access to health insurance, which is often funded by taxpayers. Education, including higher education, is generally much cheaper in Europe than in the United States, primarily due to high levels of state support. By law, most Europeans work fewer hours than most Americans, and they often enjoy four weeks or more of paid vacation time each year. Moreover, European workers are protected from layoffs, and, in the rare event that they do lose their jobs, they receive generous unemployment benefits.

Most Europeans believe that their progressive laws and expansive social programs give them a higher quality of life than can be found in America. The costs of these policies are very high, though, and they are rising at an alarming rate. In most European countries, government expenditures account for 40–50 percent of the total economy, leaving a bare majority of spending in private hands. Europeans already pay higher taxes on average than Americans, and, as Europe's population ages and shrinks, some analysts believe that the welfare state will become impossible to maintain.

Since the 1980s, therefore, many Europeans have turned away from socialism and have embraced neoliberalism—that is, they favor a return to the more radically capitalist, *laissez-faire* policies of nineteenth-century liberalism, often called classical liberalism. Many right-wing Americans applauded neoliberal European politicians, such as "The Iron Lady," Margaret Thatcher, a member of the Conservative Party and British Prime Minister from 1979 to 1990. Thatcher strove to lower taxes, curb the power of labor unions, privatize government-owned industries, and reduce government regulation of the economy. It remains to be seen whether free-market capitalism, or a mixture of capitalism and socialism, will ultimately triumph in Europe.

What successes have been achieved to date by the European Union (EU)?

Social Change in Western Europe, 1945–present

Many of the social changes in post–World War II Western Europe mirrored those that occurred in the United States. Religious belief and church attendance have waned in both areas, but more so in Europe. In some Scandinavian countries, less than five percent of the population attends church services on any given Sunday. Nevertheless, the vast majority of Europeans remain Christians.

One trend that traditional European Christianity was unable to counteract was the Sexual Revolution of the 1960s and 1970s, during which the younger generation engaged in sexual activity that older generations considered promiscuous and dangerous. Premarital sex became commonplace, while marriage itself became less popular. Traditionalists especially lamented the sexual liberation of young women, who previously had been held to an ideal of chastity. In Europe, as in America, the precondition for the success of the Sexual Revolution was the widespread availability of birth control and abortion. Today, the growing acceptance of homosexuality in Europe, including the legal recognition of homosexual marriages in a rapidly growing list of countries, is a sign that, in some ways, the Sexual Revolution is ongoing.

Enhanced sexual freedom was not the only change demanded by Western European feminists after World War II. Feminism is the belief that women should enjoy equality, independence, and respect in society and in their relationships with men. In 1949, European feminism received a boost from the publication of Simone De Beauvoir's *The Second Sex*. De Beauvoir argued that women deserve not just formal legal equality but also equal opportunity to work in all sectors of the economy and equal status within family life. Modern feminists have called for nothing less than the total abolition of the Cult of Domesticity.

Feminist organizations were few and far between in Europe during the 1940s and 1950s. In those years, in reaction to the extraordinary mobilization of women as workers during the Second World War, there was a temporary revival of the ideal of domesticity, exemplified in the United States by television programs that praised traditional family values. Then, in the 1960s, women's organizations started to form at the grassroots level. By the 1970s, the feminist movement had acquired an irresistible momentum. Women's activists successfully pressed Western European governments to repeal aspects of family law that gave husbands authority over their wives or that failed to deal decisively with spousal abuse. European governments also instituted numerous new subsidies and tax breaks for families raising children. During the 1970s, the signature issue of European feminism was abortion, which was legalized in the vast majority of European countries by 1980.

Since 1945, the proportion of married women who work outside the home, either full or part time, has dramatically increased in Europe, as it has in the United States. Many professions that were previously closed to women are now open to both sexes, and in some countries, notably in Scandinavia, women have even become high-ranking politicians in large numbers.

Most Europeans are proud of their societies' progressive attitudes toward women, and they point especially to the generous benefits and maternity leaves that many European mothers receive. Surprisingly, though, women make up a smaller percentage of the workforce in most European countries than they do in America. Many predominantly Catholic countries in Europe also remain heavily male-dominated.

Another way in which life in Europe and America has changed since 1945 is in the extraordinarily high levels of geographical mobility that many people experience. The mass migration of Americans and Europeans from the countryside to the cities began in the nineteenth century, and it continues today. As a result, most modern Western European countries are highly urbanized. In France, more than 75 percent of the population lives in urban and suburban areas. It is also common for modern Europeans to move from city to city, or even from country to country. Never before in European history have ordinary people been so mobile—and so uprooted from traditional communal life.

Another form of mobility that Western Europeans have experienced recently is immigration from Africa, Asia, Latin America, and the Middle East. Before 1945, European populations were overwhelmingly white. Since the 1960s, however, large numbers of Africans, Asians, Latin Americans, and Middle Easterners have migrated to Europe, many of them seeking a higher standard of living. Some of these immigrants have arrived illegally, while others have become legal residents and sometimes citizens. Today, racial minority groups make up as much as 10–15 percent of the total population in countries such as Britain, France, Germany, the Netherlands, and Sweden.

Whereas Americans have a tradition of assimilating immigrants from all parts of the world, the presence of racial minorities, who often speak foreign languages and practice a diverse array of religions and cultures, is distinctly alarming to some white Europeans. Many of these immigrants are Muslims from Africa and the Middle East. So far, they have been only partially integrated into mainstream white European society. Meanwhile, a disproportionate number of immigrants receive public assistance, representing a major expense for cash-strapped European governments. Some immigrants also form criminal gangs or participate in civil disobedience. Perhaps inevitably, therefore, some white Europeans have joined anti-immigrant movements, while the most radical members of Europe's Muslim minority have affiliated themselves with terrorist organizations such as *Al Qaeda* and ISIS. Nevertheless, despite all of these concerns, many Europeans strive to welcome immigrants, who are frequently seen as valued members of the communities in which they live.

Another change that has occurred in European society since 1945 has focused on environmentalism, which has been a concern for Americans and

Europeans alike since the first Earth Day in 1970. Europeans, though, tend to be much more passionate about environmental issues than Americans. In Germany, there even is a popular environmentalist political party, the Green Party, which has participated in government coalitions.

The environmentalist movement in Europe received a boost in 1986 when there was a serious accident at the Soviet nuclear facility in Chernobyl, Ukraine. Over 100,000 people had to be evacuated from the area. The explosion at Chernobyl released a radioactive cloud that eventually threatened large parts of Europe and even reached the United States. Partly because of their memories of this accident, many Europeans are skeptical of nuclear power. Nonetheless, nuclear power stations are common in Europe, especially in France, where their safety record is excellent.

Another sign of Europeans' environmentalism is their opposition to the wasteful use of natural resources such as oil, which EU countries import in large quantities from the Middle East. Most European governments tax gasoline heavily in order to discourage its use. As a result, the average European pays roughly two to three times as much as an American for a gallon of gas. European governments have also invested heavily in public transportation. Finally, in recent years Europeans have struggled to reduce their emissions of carbon dioxide, which are related to climate change. Per capita emissions in Europe are in almost all cases far below those in the United States.

Another social change that Western Europeans have experienced since 1945 is a growing emphasis on consumerism. Americans and Europeans both like to have access to the latest creature comforts and technological advances. By the 1960s, Americans and Western Europeans could take for granted a degree of material abundance, in the form of plentiful food supplies, and the widespread availability of modern conveniences such as automobiles, clothing, and household appliances. To cite only a few revealing statistics, in 1956, only eight percent of British homes had refrigerators; in 1971, it was 69 percent. In 1958, only 12 percent of Italian families owned a television set; in 1965, it was 49 percent. In France, meanwhile, during the 1960s, average wages doubled, and spending on consumer goods and vacations surged. In the Communist Bloc, by contrast, the good life was much more elusive. In fact, Eastern European jealousy of American and Western European living standards, more so than any abstract commitment to capitalism and democracy, was arguably the main factor leading Eastern Europeans to abandon their faith in communism in the late 1980s.

Yet another major social transformation that has washed over Europe during the last 60 years is Americanization. American pop culture, in the form of movies, television, music, fast food, and fashion, has profoundly influenced Europe. Today, as much as some Europeans may lament the fact, Mickey Mouse is more popular than Monet.

What social changes affected both Europe and the United States from 1945 to the present?

Conclusions

Europe today is arguably as prosperous and peaceful as it has ever been. Levels of crime and violence are low, by American standards, and the Cold War, along with the threat of nuclear annihilation, is a distant memory. The standard of living is exceptionally high. Life for most Europeans is what might be considered ordinary and comfortable in America. And yet, as quiet and contented as most corners of contemporary Europe may seem, there are several fundamental questions hanging over Europeans that have yet to be answered. These we will consider in the Epilogue that follows.

Key Terms for Chapter 19

Truman Doctrine—a policy announced in 1947 that the United States would help any country threatened by communists. The overriding goal would be the containment of Soviet influence where it already existed.

Marshall Plan—a major financial effort by the United States designed to support capitalist democracies in Western Europe.

NATO/Warsaw Pact—the main alliances during the Cold War. NATO was led by the United States, and the Warsaw Pact was led by the Soviet Union.

MAD—Mutually Assured Destruction was the idea that no one should start a nuclear war, because the only conceivable result would be the obliteration of civilization.

Suez Crisis, October 1956—an episode in the Cold War involving a successful British/French/Israeli invasion of Egypt that was aborted because of U.S. pressure.

The Berlin Wall, 1961–89—a heavily guarded barrier surrounding democratic and capitalist West Berlin, which was located deep inside communist East Germany. It was built to prevent the citizens of East Germany from fleeing to the West.

Solidarity—an opposition labor union in communist Poland that, because of its popularity, succeeded in forcing the government to meet some of its demands.

Nikita Khrushchev, 1956–64—Stalin's successor as dictator of the Soviet Union, which experienced many successes under his rule, but was also humiliated during the Cuban Missile Crisis, leading eventually to Khrushchev's forced retirement.

Leonid Brezhnev, 1964–82—Khrushchev's successor as dictator of the Soviet Union. Soviet power peaked under Brezhnev, but the Soviet economy began to stagnate, setting up the country's disintegration under Gorbachev.

Mikhail Gorbachev, 1985–91—the last leader of the Soviet Union, known for his policies of *perestroika* (restructuring) and *glasnost* (openness). Gorbachev's bold reforms led to instability and economic decline, and eventually to the breakup of the Soviet Union.

Vladimir Putin—current President of Russia. Putin has to a considerable degree rebuilt Russia's economic and military strength, but he has also reinstituted some authoritarian practices and soured relations with the West.

Decolonization—the process by which Europe's colonies in Africa and Asia received their independence. The vast majority of decolonization occurred between 1945 and 1975.

EEC/EU—the European Economic Community, later known as the European Union. It is one of the most ambitious attempts in history to bring unity—especially economic union—to the peoples of Europe.

Immigration—since the 1960s, large numbers of non-whites have settled in Europe, creating cultural and racial tensions to which many white Europeans are not accustomed.

Chernobyl, 1986—the site of a major nuclear accident in the Soviet Union, which motivated many Europeans to work to preserve the natural environment.

Americanization—the process by which Europeans, and others, adopt elements of American culture.

Review Questions for Chapter 19

1. Name and describe in detail three measures undertaken by the United States during the Cold War to help achieve the containment of the Soviet Union.
2. Describe two important factors that influenced the creation of the European Economic Community in 1957. Next, describe two major achievements of the EEC/EU.
3. Two of the most interesting differences between Europeans and Americans that have evolved since 1945 are Europeans' greater level of concern about environmental issues, and Europeans' greater acceptance of socialist practices. Illustrate these different European and American attitudes with at least four brief examples.
4. During the Cold War, how did life in the Communist Bloc differ from life in Western Europe? If you had lived under communism, would you have tried to flee to the West? Why or why not?
5. One of the most critical dynamics in the Cold War was the nuclear arms race, coupled with MAD—the idea that nuclear war should be avoided because it is unwinnable. Write an alternative history of the Cold War that assumes that nuclear weapons had never been invented. How would the struggle, and its outcome, have been different?

Further Reading

Bock, Gisela. *Women in European History*. Malden, MA: Blackwell. 2002.

Castells, Manuel. *The Information Age: Economy, Society, and Culture*. Malden, MA: Wiley-Blackwell. 2010.

Darwin, John. *After Tamerlane: The Rise and Fall of Global Empires, 1400–2000*. New York: Bloomsbury. 2010.

Fursenko, Aleksandr and Timothy Naftali. *Khrushchev's Cold War: The Inside Story of an American Adversary*. New York: W.W. Norton. 2007.

Gaddis, John Lewis. *The Cold War: A New History*. London: Penguin. 2007.

Geddes, Andrew and Peter Scholten. *The Politics of Migration and Immigration in Europe*. Second Edition. Thousand Oaks, CA: Sage. 2016.

Harrison, Brian. *Seeking a Role: The United Kingdom, 1951–1970*. Oxford: Clarendon Press. 2011.

Hitchcock, William I. *The Struggle for Europe: The Turbulent History of a Divided Continent, 1945 to the Present*. New York: Anchor. 2013.

Holton, Robert J. *Globalization and the Nation State*. Second Edition. Basingstoke, UK: Palgrave Macmillan. 2011.

Jenkins, Philip. *God's Continent: Christianity, Islam, and Europe's Religious Crisis*. New York: Oxford University Press. 2010.

Judt, Tony. *Postwar: A History of Europe Since 1945*. Ashland, OR: Blackstone. 2011.

Kenney, Padraic. *The Burdens of Freedom: Eastern Europe Since 1989*. New York: Zed Books. 2006.

Marquand, David. *The End of the West: The Once and Future Europe*. Princeton, NJ: Princeton University Press. 2011.

Stitziel, Judd. *Fashioning Socialism: Clothing, Politics, and Consumer Culture in East Germany*. New York: Berg. 2007.

Zubok, Vladislav M. *A Failed Empire: The Soviet Union in the Cold War From Stalin to Gorbachev*. Chapel Hill: UNC Press. 2009.

Epilogue

Europe, the United States, and the World in the Twenty-First Century

The European Achievement, and Europe's Three Challenges

Europe today represents a triumph for the ideology known as classical liberalism, which is a blend of ideas from the British parliamentary tradition, the Enlightenment, the American and French Revolutions, and free-market economics, a.k.a. capitalism. Liberals have battled for centuries in Europe to create political systems and societies based on representative government, free speech, freedom of religion, and private enterprise. Although today some European countries practice a mixture of socialism and capitalism, by and large, most of the goals of liberalism have been achieved throughout modern Europe. Europe today is arguably more united, prosperous, and peaceful than it has ever been in its history, and there is widespread agreement in all European countries that every citizen is entitled to enjoy political, economic, and religious freedom. Since the end of the Cold War in 1989, these ideas have become as much a part of life in Eastern Europe as they are in the West. Given the utter devastation that covered Europe in 1945, and the oppression that shrouded Eastern Europe for 40 additional years, these achievements are more than remarkable—they are nearly miraculous. The triumph of liberalism, moreover, has forged an enduring bond between Europe and the United States, both of which are strongly committed to democratic and capitalist values. Increasingly, these values are being popularized worldwide.

The victory of democratic and capitalist ideas in Europe may convey the impression that European history has reached a happy ending, but this is not necessarily the case. Europeans still face three major challenges.

Politically, Europeans must decide how interconnected and interdependent they wish to be. Will the EU, for instance, ever become a fully integrated United States of Europe? If so, what will its relationship be with the United States of America, Russia, and other major powers?

Economically, Europeans must decide to what degree they wish to modify their form of capitalism by adding substantial elements of socialism and government management. As some are now asking, is the European welfare state even affordable any longer?

And finally, culturally, Europeans must decide how and to what degree to include non-white immigrants in their traditionally homogeneous

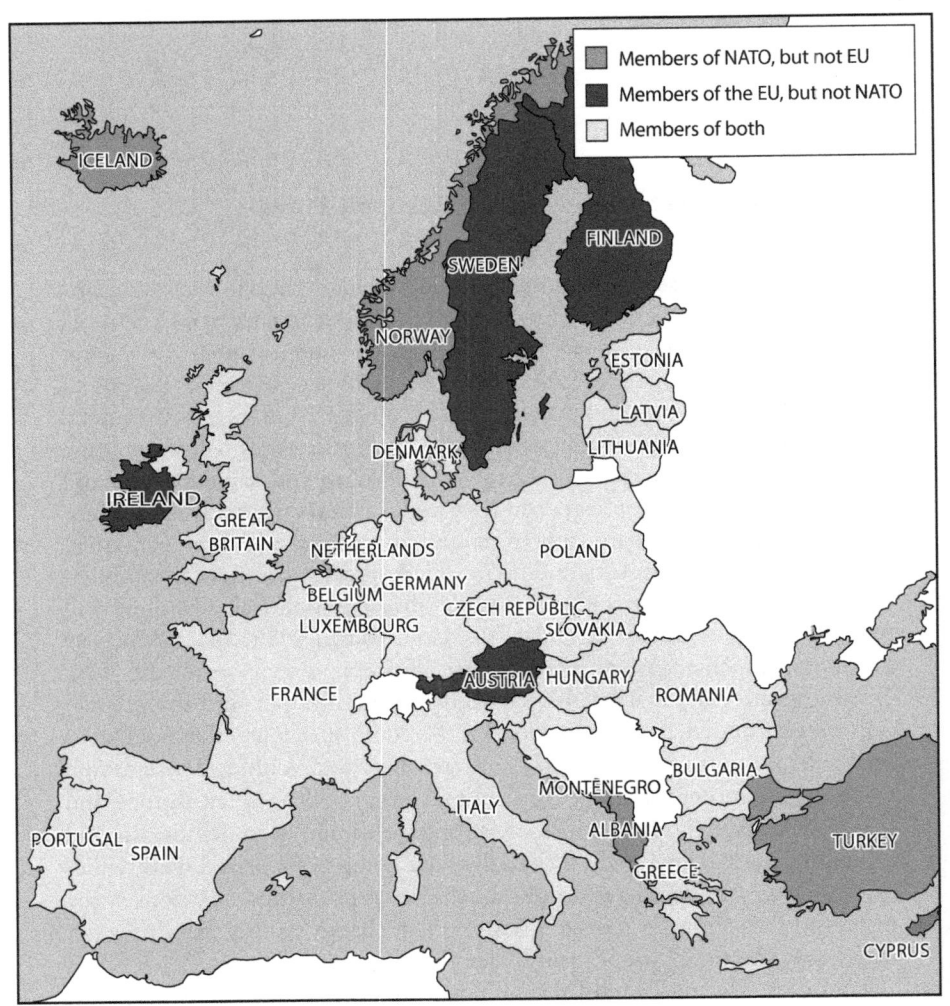

Map 20.1 Modern Europe.

and nationalistic cultures. Will Muslim immigrants, in particular, ever be acknowledged as full Europeans? Do they even want to be?

Finding the solutions to these three major challenges will not be easy. Despite all the historical evidence that this book has considered, it is extremely hard to predict how Europeans will respond to these complex problems. We can only hope that Europeans will choose wisely, because, beyond any doubt, their choices will affect us, as Americans, profoundly. After all, our cultures—not to mention our governments and our economies—remain indelibly linked.

The U.S.-European Relationship, and the Future of the West

Today, despite its closeness, the relationship between the United States and Europe is increasingly difficult to characterize. Prior to the twentieth century, it was mainly Europe that provided a model for Americans to emulate. In other words, Europe would lead, and Americans would follow, especially in a cultural sense. During the Cold War, however, it was the United States that led the Western alliance, turning the traditional Euro-American relationship on its head. In addition, today, even though European culture continues to influence America, the trend of Americanization in Europe, and beyond, is arguably more powerful. Furthermore, the traditionally positive and cooperative relations between the United States and most of Western Europe are under threat. True, the United States and Europe sometimes work closely together, as in some NATO operations, but at other times they seem bitterly antagonistic. How, then, can one make sense of all these mixed signals? To make matters even more complicated, given the growing cultural, religious, and racial diversity in the United States and Europe, even the term "Western Civilization" seems, at times, anachronistic.

We are, it would seem, entering a phase in which many traditional assumptions about the West no longer apply, and in which the future contours of Western and world history are hard to predict. Even the certainties of Western thought, the bedrock principles of modern Western Civilization—democracy, capitalism, individual rights—may be challenged by forces and events that no one can foresee.

Perhaps one of the few observations that one can make about the world we live in, without any great danger of oversimplification, is that it is a more interconnected world than has ever existed before. The incredibly rapid and voluminous flow of information from place to place, and from person to person; the remarkable fluidity of cultural barriers and the prevalence of cultural exchange; the massive rise in international trade and investment; even the insidious spread of globe-straddling terrorist movements, such as *Al Qaeda* and ISIS, taken together, all indicate a world in which "globalization" has progressed beyond mere theorizing and sloganeering to become an established and historic trend.

In a sense, therefore, even to talk in this day and age about Europe and the United States as though they were discrete realities may be a mistake. After all, today, a banker in London may have more in common with a stockbroker in San Francisco, or a journalist in Shanghai, than he does with a factory worker or a retail clerk who lives just a mile or two away from his home. This does not mean, however, that the differences between ethnic groups and nations have become irrelevant, and that we now live, or will live soon, in a harmonious "global village." On the contrary, in an interconnected world, the conflicts between groups may have more far-reaching consequences than ever before, simply because their cancerous effects can spread so widely and so quickly.

What the rising crescendo of globalization does mean, though, is that, increasingly, to understand America, Europe, and the world as a whole, one will need to think more broadly—to move beyond the simple categories that have constrained human understanding in the past. As a professor who teaches both history and international relations, I often find myself explaining the world's myriad problems to my students, but I continually return to a single, overpowering, and in many ways desperately unsatisfying theme: "It is complicated, and it depends on how you look at it." Europe today, and the United States, Latin America, Africa, and Asia, are indeed complicated, and they are only becoming more so every day. There are, however, two certainties that I can offer you at the close of this book.

One, whatever shape the world may take in the years ahead, the rich heritage of Western Civilization will always play a powerful and important role in global affairs. Even the modern phenomenon of globalization is, more often than not, a continuation of some form of Westernization, even if few are willing to admit it.

And two, you, having learned the history of Europe up to the present day, which is intimately related to the history of your own country, its people, and the world as a whole, are in as good a position as anyone to interpret and navigate the numerous changes that will take place in the twenty-first century. It is time, therefore, armed with these insights, to go beyond the mere study of history, and to make history yourselves.

Index

Page numbers in italic indicate a figure.

14 points 312
"95 Theses" 166

Abbasid dynasty 107
Abraham 14
absolutism 203; in Britain 184–186; in France 180–184
Acropolis 21, *41*
Act of Toleration 189
Action Française 322
Actium 62
Aeneid, The 82–83
Aeschylus 40
Afghanistan, Soviet invasion of 371
Africa: Berlin Conference 288; Boer War 302; Scramble for Africa 287–288, *287*, 297
Afrika Korps 349, 352–353
Age of Pericles *see* Classical Greece
agora 21, 38
Agricultural Revolution 215–216, 221; review questions 221–222
agriculture: collectivization 326; crop rotation 128; irrigation 6; in Middle Ages 128; in Neolithic Age 2; Neolithic Revolution 2; in Roman Republic 74–75
Ahura Mazda 25
Akkad 4–5
Al Qaeda 384, 391
Albigensianism 99
Alcuin 104
Alexander I, Tsar of Russia 249
Alexander the Great 18, 30–31; Battle of Chaeronea 30; Battle of Granicus River 31; Battle of the Hydaspes River 32; death of 32; invasion of Persian Empire 31–33

Allah 105
alphabet: Cyrillic alphabet 98; Phoenician 13
Amazons 44
American Revolution 200–203
Americanization 385, 387
Anabaptists 169
Ancient Egypt *4*; battle at Qadesh 8; *Book of the Dead* 11; Great Sphinx *10*; hieroglyphics 7; Kingdoms 5; Pharaohs 10, 11; pyramids 9–10, *10*; religion 11; territorial aggrandizement 8; women's status in 12
Ancient Greece: Acropolis *41*; architecture 41; Bronze Age 18–20; daily life in Athens 42–44; Dark Ages 20–22; divination 39; drama 40; festivals 39; Greek mythology 39; humanism 40; oracles 39
Ancient Rome *see* Roman Republic or Roman Empire
Anglicanism 174–176
animals, domestication of 2
Anschluss 344
Anti-Comintern Pact 351
Antigone 40
Antigonid rule of Macedonia 32
anti-Semitism 297; Dreyfus Affair 272; of Hitler 331; the Holocaust 358–360; in Middle Ages 100; Nuremberg Laws 339; twentieth century 293–294
Apollo 39
Apollo 16 mission *370*
appeasement 361
Arabic numbering system 129
Archaic Greece: the Assembly 24; craftsmen 38; Greek colonization 22,

37; hoplites 22; map of *23*; phalanx 22; Sparta 24
Archimedes 49
architecture: Gothic churches 138; Greek 41; in High Middle Ages 134–135; Roman 83–84
archons 24
Ares 39
arete 20, *21*, 33–34, 38
Arianism 89
Aristagoras 26
Aristarchus 49
aristocracy 21, 47
Aristophanes 40
Aristotle 29, 47, 50
Ark of the Covenant 12–13
Arkwright, Richard 217–218
art: "degenerate art" 334; drama 40; Giotto 152; Michelangelo 153; the Renaissance 149–153; Romanticism 253–255; sculpture in Ancient Greece 41
Aryanism 293–294, 297, 331
Asia: European colonization of 288–289; Korean War 370; Vietnam War 370–371
Aspasia 45
assassination: of Archduke Ferdinand 304; of Julius Caesar 61
Assembly, the 24, 28
assignats 231
Assyrian Empire 5, 8
astronomy: Copernicus, Nicolaus 49, 212–213; Galileo 213; geocentric theory 212–213; in Hellenistic world 49; Kepler, Johannes 213; in Middle Ages 136; Newton, Sir Isaac 213, 221; Scientific Revolution 136, 211–212, 214–215
Athena 39
Athenian democracy 27–28
Athens 34; Acropolis *41*; *archons* 24; the Assembly 28; Battle of Salamis 26; daily life in 42–44; Delian League 26; Epicurus 49; Peloponnesian War 28–29; Thucydides 42; *see also* Classical Greece
athletics, *arete* 20, *21*
atomoi 46
Auclert, Hubertine 296
augurs 76
Augustan Principate 63–65, *64*
Auschwitz-Birkenau 359, 362
Ausgleich 273

Austria 196; *Anschluss* 344; *Ausgleich* 273; Prince von Metternich 248; War of Spanish Succession 198
Austria-Hungary: assassination of Archduke Ferdinand 304; Dual Alliance 299; Three Emperor's League 299–301, *300*; Triple Alliance 301
Autobahn 335
Averroes 129
Avicenna 129
Avignon 144
Aztecs, Spanish conquest of 163

Babylonia 4–5; law code of Hammurabi 7–8, 11–12
Babylonian Captivity 13–14; of Late Middle Ages 144, 157
Badoglio, Pietro 353
Balkans: Central Powers' control of 308; ethnic division in 338; instability of 303–304; World War II in 349
barbarians 68, 72; *comitatus* 94; Goths 69–70; in Middle Ages 94–95
Barbarossa, Frederick 110
Barca, Hamilcar 57
Barracks Emperors 72
Bastille, storming of 229
Battle of Agincourt 143
Battle of Austerlitz 238
Battle of Bouvines 110
Battle of Britain 347–348, 361
Battle of Chaeronea 30
Battle of Granicus River 31
Battle of Hastings 111
Battle of Kursk 354
Battle of Legnano 110
Battle of Leyte Gulf 357
Battle of Pharsalus 60
Battle of Plataea 26
Battle of Poitiers 107
Battle of Salamis 26, 37
Battle of Stalingrad 353–354, *353*, 362
Battle of the Atlantic 352, 362
Battle of the Hydaspes River 32
Battle of the Nations 241
Battle of the Pyramids 237
Battle of Trafalgar 238
Battle of Wagram 240
Battle of Waterloo 241–242, 246
Battle of Zama 57
BCE (Before the Common Era) 17
beauty, Classical ideal of 41
Beer Hall Putsch 330

Beethoven, Ludwig von 255
Belgium, German invasion of 304
Benedictine Rule 90
Beowulf 135
Berghof, the 336
Berlin Conference 288
Berlin Wall 371–373, 386; fall of 377
Bessemer, Sir Henry 282
Bible, The 91; Hebrews 12–14; Old Testament 13; standardization of 88–89
Bismarck, Otto von 268–269, *270*; *Kulturkampf* 292; Three Emperor's League 299–301, *300*; Triple Alliance 301
Bismarck, sinking of 352
Black Death 140–143, *142*, 157; buboes 141; economic effect of 142–143; nobility, impact on 141–142; serfdom, impact on 142–143
Black Hand 304
Blitzkrieg 345, 361; in Africa 349
Blitz, the 348
Blum, Léon 322
Boer War 302
Bolshevik Revolution of 1917 273, 310–311, 316; Lenin, Vladimir 277
Bonaparte, Louis Napoleon 256
Bonaparte, Napoleon 223, 245; alliance with Catholic Church 237–238; Battle of Austerlitz 238; Battle of the Nations 241; Battle of the Pyramids 237; Battle of Trafalgar 238; Battle of Wagram 240; Battle of Waterloo 241–242; as commander in Revolutionary army 235–236; Continental System 239; early career 235–238; as First Consul 237; *Grand Armée* 240–241; review questions 246; role in French Revolution 234–235
Book of the Dead 11
Bosnia, "ethnic cleansing" 377
Boudicca 67
bourgeoisie 125, 138, 220; Bolshevik Revolution of 1917 273; communism 276–277; in nineteenth and twentieth centuries 264–267; role in French Revolution 228–229; in seventeenth and eighteenth century Europe 209–211; working class, rise of in nineteenth and twentieth century Europe 273–275
boyars 195
Brethren of the Common Life 155

Brezhnev, Leonid 374, 386
Britain: absolutism in 184–186; Coercion Act 249; conservatism in nineteenth century 249; Corn Law 260; Glorious Revolution 188–190; Industrial Revolution 216–217; mercantilism 194–195; National Government 338; Poor Law 260; popular sovereignty 189; the Restoration 187–188; rotten boroughs 251; Seven Years' War 198–200; Six Acts 249; urbanization 259; *see also* British Empire
British Empire 286; Boer War 302; Central Powers 305; *Entente Cordiale* 302; India 288–289; Indian National Congress 294
Bronze Age: agriculture in 3; King Minos 18; Mycenaean culture 19–20
Brown, Peter 67
buboes 141
bubonic plague *see* Black Death
bullion, mercantilism 190–192
burghers 125
Burke, Edmund 233, 245
Butler, Josephine 295
Byzantine Empire 93; Caesaropapism 97; *Corpus Juris Civilis* 99; Cyrillic alphabet 98; Empire of the Greeks 98; Justinian 99; military successes 98–99
Byzantium, occupation by Ottoman Turks 99

Caesar Augustus, Augustan Principate 63–65, *64*
Caesarion 62
Caesaropapism 97
cahiers de doléances 229
Caligula 65
caliphate 106
Calvin, John 169–170, 178
Canaanites 12–13
Canon of Medicine, The 129
Canterbury Tales (Chaucer) 135
Capet, Hugh 110
capitalism 216–217, 389; *laissez-faire* 219, 227, 250
Cardinal Mazarin 182
Cardinal Richelieu 181
Carolingian dynasty 103–104, 116; Holy Roman Empire 108–110
Carthage 56–57; Battle of Zama 57; First Punic War 57; Second Punic War 57
Castiglione, Baldassare 158

casualties from World War I 312
Catharism 99
Catherine the Great 195, 226
Catholic Church 95; Babylonian Captivity 144; clergy 122–124; Conciliar Movement 145; Council of Constance 144; crusade against Cathars 99; Duke of Alba 174; excommunication of Henry IV 96–97; Glorious Revolution 188–190; Gothic churches 134–135; Guise family 171; "indulgences" 165; *Kulturkampf* 292; Lateran Accord 329; lay investiture 96–97; masses 126–127; Napoleon's alliance with 237–238; Peace of God movement 103; penance 165–166; persecution of the Jews 100; Pope Gregory VII 96; Pope John Paul II 372–373; Pragmatic Sanction 148; purgatory 166; reform movements 145; split with Orthodox Church 97–98; Thirty Years' War 176–177; Truce of God movement 103; Waldensians 99; weakening of in Late Middle Ages 144–146; *see also* Protestant Reformation; Protestantism
Catholic Reformation 172–174
Cato the Elder 81–82
causes of Protestant Reformation 164–166
Cavour, Count Camillo 267
CE (Common Era) 17
Central Powers 305; control of Balkans 308
centurions 54
Chamberlain, Houston Stewart 293–294
Chamberlain, Neville 344
chansons de geste 135
Charlemagne 104–105, 116
Charles I, King of Britain 203
Charles II, Restoration of 187–188
Charles V 168
Charles VII, King of France 148
Charles X, King of France 248
Chartism 273
Chaucer, Geoffrey 135
Cheka 322
Chernobyl 385, 387
China, Nixon's visit to 375
chivalry 101–103, *102*, 138
Christian Democratic parties 381
Christian Humanists 155, 158

Christianity 72; Anabaptists 169; Constantine's adoption of 69, 88–89; conversion of Germanic tribes 94–95; conversion of Saul of Tarsus 86; the Crusades 107–109; emergence of 85–88; the Gospels 85–86; heresies 89; "justification by faith" 167; Messiah 16; missionaries, influence on New Imperialism 285; monasticism 89–90; Nero's persecution of Christians 66; Orthodox Church 97–100; persecution of Christians 88; religion, questioning of 291–292; St. Augustine 89; the Trinity 89; *see also* Catholic Church; Protestant Reformation
Churchill, Winston 308–309, 361; Battle of Britain 347–348
Cicero 82, 91
Circus Maximus 78
cities: capture of 9, 20–21; urbanization 259
Classical Greece 27–29; the Assembly 28; Athenian democracy 27–28; craftsmen 38; Delian League 28; "Golden Age of Classical Greece" 46; Peloponnesian War 28–29; *poleis* 29
Claudius 65–66
Cleopatra, Queen of Egypt 32, 62
clergy 122–124; friars 124, 138; monastic life 123
clothing: of Roman citizens 78; of Victorian Age 266
Clovis 103
Cluniacs 116
Coercion Act 249
Cold War, the 364; Berlin Wall 371–373; collapse of the Soviet Union 373–376; decolonization during 379–382; *détente* 374–375; economics of 369; emergence of 364–367, *365*; Korean war 370; MAD 368; NATO 366–367; Nixon's visit to China 375; nuclear weapons, development of 368; *perestroika* 376; strategic balance in 367–368; Vietnam war 370–371; Warsaw Pact 366–367
Coleridge, Samuel Taylor 255
collapse of the Soviet Union 373–376
collectivization 326, 339
colonialism 191–192; American Revolution 200–202; review questions 204
colonization: of Africa 288; Greek 37
Colosseum, the 66

Columbian Exchange 162
Columbus, Christopher 161–163, *162*, 173
Comintern 323
comitatus 94
Committee of Public Safety 233
Commodus 66
communism 275–277, 279; Bolshevik Revolution of 1917 277–278; collapse of the Soviet Union 373–376; collectivization 326; Eastern European renouncement of 377; *glasnost* 376; Lenin, Vladimir 277; *perestroika* 376; revolutionary vanguard 278; Social Democratic Parry 277
Communist Bloc 364
Communist Manifesto (Marx & Engels, 1848) 276
concentration camps 336; *see also* the Holocaust
Concert of Europe 249, 261
Conciliar Movement 145
Concordat of Worms 97
Condor Legion 344
condottieri 154
Confédération Général du Travail 274–275
Confessions, The 89
confinement of the French royal family 230–231
Congress of Vienna 242–244, *243*, 246
conquistadores 163, 178
conservatism 248–249
Consistory 169–170
Constantine the Great 69; Christianity, adoption of 88–89
Constantinople as Ottoman capital 146
Constitutional Democrats 277
constitutional monarchy, failure of as cause of French Revolution 227–232
consumerism in European society 385
Contagious Diseases Acts 295
Continental System 239, 245
conversion of Saul of Tarsus 86
Copernicus, Nicolaus 49, 212–213, 221
Corcyra 28
Corinth 28
Corn Law 260
Corpus Juris Civilis 99
Corsica 235
Cortés 115
Cortés, Hernán 163
Council of Constance 144
Council of Clermont 108

Council of Trent 172–173
craftsmen, in Archaic and Classical Greece 38
Crassus 60
criticism of Christianity 291–292
Croix de Feu 322
Cromwell, Oliver 186–188, *186*, 203
crop rotation 128, 215–216
Crusades, the 93–94, 107–109, 116; Council of Clermont 108; First Crusade 108; *Reconquista* 108
Crystal Palace *263*
Cuban Missile Crisis 374
Cult of Domesticity 264, 278, 296
culture 2; Americanization 385; Arab contributions 129; *arete* 38; Columbian Exchange 162; Greek cultural influences on Rome 81–82; in Hellenistic world 48; High Middle Ages 119; Mycenaean 19; nationalism 251–253; and New Imperialism 285; *Romanitas* 70, 74; *symposium* 38; trade between Eastern and Western Europe 128–130
cuneiform 7, 16
Cynics 48
Cyrillic alphabet 98

da Gama, Vasco 161
da Vinci, Leonardo 152–153
daily life: in Ancient Greece 42–44; in Roman Republic 77–79
Dante Alighieri 135
Darius I, King of Persia 26; Battle of Granicus River 31
Dark Ages 93; *see also* Greek Dark Ages
Darwin, Charles 289–291, 297
David 13
D-Day 362
De Beauvoir, Simone 383
de Gaulle, Charles 347
de Gobineau, Count Arthur 293–294
de las Casas, Bartolomé 163–164
de Medici, Catharine 171–172
de Pisan, Christine 158
de Troye, Chrétien 135
death camps, the Holocaust 358–360
Declaration of the Rights of Man and of the Citizen 229–230, 245
decolonization, post-war pursuit of 379–382, 387
defeat of Spanish Armada 174–176
"degenerate art" 334

Delian League 26, 28
Delphi 39
democracy 21–22; Athenian democracy 27–28; voting rights, European expansion of 271–273
Democritus 46
Descent of Man, The (Darwin, 1871) 290
destruction of the Jewish Temple 13
détente 374–375
development of writing 7
Diocletian 68–69
Diogenes 48
Dionysus 40
Directory, the 234–235, 245
discovery *see* exploration
disease: Contagious Diseases Acts 295; impact on Native Americans 162–163
Disreali, Benjamin 271–273, 293
dissolution of the Soviet Union 378
divination 10–11, 39
Divine Comedy, The (Dante) 135
Divine Right of Kings 181, 187
domestic system 217–218
domestication of animals 2
Dominican Order of friars 124
Domitian 66
Donation of Constantine 151
Doomsday Book 111–112
drama 40, 50
Dreyfus Affair 272, 279, 293
Dual Alliance 299, 316
Duchy of Normandy 111
Duke of Alba 174
Duke of Wellington 239; Battle of Waterloo 241–242
Dutch Republic 174

East Germany: Berlin Wall 371–373; fall of the Berlin Wall 377
Eastern Front 316
Eastern Roman Empire, adoption of Christianity 88–89
ecclesiastical reform in Catholic Church 96
economics: capitalism 389; of the Cold War 369; Continental System 239; Keynes, John Maynard 320; *laissez-faire* capitalism 227, 250; mercantilism 190–195, *193*; *perestroika* 376; socialism 275–277; "Strength through Joy" 335; world-systems theory 220
Edict of Milan 88

Edict of Nantes 172
Edison, Thomas 282
education: in High Middle Ages 132–133; Renaissance emphasis on 151; in Roman Republic 79; scholasticism 133–134, *133*, 138; universities 138
Edward III 143
Edward VI, King of England 171
EEC (European Economic Community) 380
ego 292–293
Egypt: Battle of the Pyramids 237; Ptolemaic dynasty 32; Queen Cleopatra 32; Suez Canal 371; *see also* Ancient Egypt
Einsatzgruppen 358
Einstein, Albert 289
Eisenhower, Dwight D. 355
Elizabeth I, Queen of England 178
empire: post-WWII decolonization 379–382
Empire of the Greeks 98
Encyclopedia 224
Engels, Friedrich 276
engineering, in Roman Republic 84–85
England: adoption of Protestantism 170–171; Battle of Hastings 111; defeat of Spanish Armada 174–176; establishment of English monarchy 111–113; exploration 164; *Magna Carta* 112; Parliament 148; Plantagenet dynasty 112; shires 112; Wars of the Roses 148; *see also* Britain
English Civil War 186–188, *186*
Enlightened Absolutism 226
Enlightenment, the 223–225; Kant, Immanuel 224; Napoleon's support for 237; proposals of the *philosophes* 225–227; Rousseau, Jean-Jacques 226–227; Voltaire 225; *see also* Romanticism
Enola Gay 357
Entente Cordiale 302
environmentalism in European society 384–385
ephors 24
Epic of Gilgamesh 11
Epictetus 83
Epicureanism 83
Epicurus 49
Erasmus 156
Erfurt Program 275

Estates-General 111, 181, 245; *cahiers de doléances* 229; meeting of 1789 228–229
Ethiopia, Italy's invasion of 329
Etruscans 53, 71
EU (European Union) 380–381
Euclid 49
Euripides 40
European feminism 383–384
European Space Agency 380
excommunication of Henry IV 96–97
experimental method 212
exploration: Columbus, Christopher 161–163, *162*; Cortés, Hernán 163; da Gama, Vasco 161; Pizarro, Francisco 163; review questions 178–179

factory system 218–221, 259
Fall of Rome 67–71; barbarians 68; Odoacer 70; Severan dynasty 67
fall of Soviet Union 373–376
fall of the Berlin Wall 377
family law, law code of Hammurabi 11–12
farming: in Bronze Age 3; crop rotation 128, 215–216; Gracchi 59; irrigation 6; *kulaks* 326; *latifundia* 58–59, 67–68; in Mycenaean culture 37; in Neolithic Age 2; peasants 120–121; in Roman Republic 74–75
fascism 327–329, *329*, 339; *see also* communism
feminism 295–297; European feminism 383–384; in Soviet Union 324
Ferdinand, Francis 316; assassination of 304
Ferdinand, King of Spain 173
Ferdinand II, Thirty Years' War 176–177
festivals 39; *Saturnalia* 76
feudalism 100–103, *102*, 116; knights 101–103, *102*; oath of fealty 100; vassals 100
Final Act 248
First Consul of the Republic 234–235; Napoleon as 237
First Crusade 108
First Estate 122, 228–229
First Punic War 57
Five Good Emperors 66, 75
Flavian dynasty 66
flexibility: of Catholic Church 96; of Roman policy toward religion 77
Foch, Marshal Ferdinand 315

food of Roman citizens 77
Ford, Henry 282
forum 90
founding of modern state of Israel 14, 379
France: absolutism in 180–184; *Action Française* 322; Avignon 144; *Croix de Feu* 322; establishment of French monarchy 109–111; Estates-General 181; exploration 164; *Île-de-France* 110; interwar period 320–322; July Monarchy 251; liberalism in nineteenth century 250; Maginot Line 346; mercantilism 192–195, *193*; Paris Commune of 1871 272; *parlements* 181; Revolution of 1848 256; royal centralization in Late Middle Ages 148; Second Republic 256; Third Republic 272; Triple Entente 302; urbanization 259; Versailles 182–183; Vichy France 347; War of Spanish Succession 198; *see also* Bonaparte, Napoleon
Franciscan Order of friars 124
Franco-Prussian War 279
Frankfurt Parliament 257, 261
Frankish Kingdom 103–105; Alcuin 104; Battle of Bouvines 110; Capet, Hugh 110; Carolingian dynasty 103–104; Charlemagne 104–105; Clovis 103; establishment of French monarchy 109–111; Merovingian dynasty 103; Philip Augustus 110
Frederick I 115–116
French and Indian War 198–200
French Revolution 223; Committee of Public Safety 233; confinement of the royal family 230–231; Declaration of the Rights of Man and of the Citizen 229–230; the Directory 234–235; failure of constitutional monarchy as cause of 227–232; Jacobins 232–233; *levée en masse* 233; Napoleon's role in 234–235; Reign of Terror 232–233; review questions 246; September Massacres 232; storming of the *Bastille* 229; Tennis Court Oath 229
Freud, Sigmund 292–293
friars 124, 138; Savonarola 154
Fronde, the 181–182

Gagarin, Yuri 369
Galileo 213
Gallic War, The 60
Gallipoli campaign 308–309

400   Index

Garibaldi, Guiseppe 267
Gaugamela 31
Gaul: Roman conquest of 60;
    Vercingetorix *61*
gender rights: European feminism
    383–384; feminism 295–296
Gentiles, conversion to Christianity 86
gentry 148
geocentric theory 212
George III, King of Great Britain
    200–202
Germanic tribes: barbarians 94–95; sack
    of Rome 70
Germany: admission to League of
    Nations 319; *Afrika Korps* 349; Allies'
    defeat of 354–356, *356*; *Anschluss* 344;
    Condor Legion 344; Dual Alliance
    299; *Entente Cordiale* 302; Final
    Act 248; Franco-Prussian War 279;
    Frankfurt Parliament 257; High Seas
    Fleet 301–302; Hindenburg, Paul
    von 308; the Holocaust 358–360;
    invasion of Belgium 304; invasion of
    Poland 341, 344–345; *Lebensraum* 341;
    Locarno Agreements 332; nationalism
    251–253, 268–271, *270*; Nazi-Soviet
    Non-Aggression Pact 345; occupation
    of Rhineland 343; *Reichstag* 271;
    Richthofen, Manfred von 308; royal
    centralization in Late Middle Ages 149;
    Schlieffen Plan 305; Second Industrial
    Revolution 281–283; signing of
    cease fire 312; sinking of the *Lusitania*
    310; *Sonderweg* 257; SPD 275; Three
    Emperor's League 299–301, *300*; Treaty
    of Versailles 313–314; Triple Alliance
    301; U-boats 309–310; unification of
    268; urbanization 259; V-2 rocket 355;
    Weimar Republic 314–315, 330–331;
    see also Hitler, Adolf; Nazi party
Gestapo 334
Genghis Khan 113
Giotto 152
gladiators 78–79
Gladstone, William 271–273
glasnost 376
globalization 283; *see also* New
    Imperialism
Glorious Revolution 188–190, 203
Goebbels, Josef 334, 339, 354
gold, mercantilism 190–195, *193*
Golden Age of Piracy 198
"Golden Age of Classical Greece" 46

Golden Horde 113
Gorbachev, Mikhail 375–376, 386
Göring, Hermann 330–331
Gospels, the 85–86
Gothic style of architecture
    134–135, 138
Goths 69–70
government: aristocracy 21; the Assembly
    24, 53; Carthaginian 57; democracy
    21–22; hereditary monarchies 8;
    oligarchy 21–22; representative
    government 203; separation of
    powers 226
Gracchi brothers 59, 72
Great Depression 319–320, 338
Great Exhibition 263
Great Pyramid at Giza 9–10
Great Reform Bill of 1832 261
Great Sphinx *10*
Greece: Archaic Greece 22–25, *23*;
    Bronze Age Greece 18–20; Classical
    Greece 27–29; colonization 37; Greek
    Dark Ages 20–22; Hellenistic world 34,
    47–49
Greek colonization 22, 37
Greek Dark Ages 20–22; *acropolis* 21; *agora*
    21; *arete* 20; government 21–22
Greek philosophy 45–47; Aristotle
    47; *atomoi* 46; Democritus 46; Plato
    46–47; *Republic, The* 47; Socrates 46;
    Sophists 46
Green Party 385
guilds 125–126, 138, 221;
    manufacturing 217
Guise family 171
gulags 323–324
gunpowder, use of in Middle Ages 136
Gutenberg, Johann 155–156
gymnasium 21, 43

haciendas 164
hadith 105
Hammurabi 5; law code 7–8
Hannibal 57
Hapsburgs 196; War of Spanish
    Succession 198
Hebrews 12–14, 16; Ark of the Covenant
    12–13; Babylonian Captivity 13–14;
    battle with Canaanites 13; David 13;
    destruction of the Jewish Temple 13;
    emphasis of religion on character
    14–15; founding of modern state of
    Israel 14; as God's "Chosen People"

14–15; marriage 15; Solomon 13; Ten Commandments 12, 14
Helen, of Troy 44–45
heliocentric theory 212–213; astronomy 47, 129, 136, 212; Copernicus 49, 212–213, 221; Scientific Revolution 211–215, 221
Hellenistic world 34, 47–49; Epicureanism 49; philosophy 48–49; science 49; Stoicism 49; virtue 49
helots 24, 29
Henry V (Shakespeare) 143
Henry VIII, King of England 170–171
Hercules 38
hereditary monarchies 8; Divine Right of Kings 181; Hapsburgs 196
heresies 89; Albigensianism 99; Conciliar Movement 145; Inquisition 116
Herodotus 42
hieroglyphics 7
High Middle Ages 119; architecture 134–135; clergy 122–124; crop rotation 128; education in 132–133; literature 135; monastic life 123; nobility 119–120; politics 127; review questions 138–139; scholasticism 133–134, *133*; scientific achievements 136; serfs 120–122; townspeople 124–126; troubadour poetry 135
High Seas Fleet 301–302
Hildegard of Bingen 123, 138
Himmler, Heinrich 334–335, 339, 359
Hindenburg, Paul von 308, 339
Hippocratic Oath 42
Hitler, Adolf 199, 294, 320, 326–327, 329–337, 339, 341, 343–352, 355–356, 358, 360; anti-Semitism of 331; and Aryanism 294; the *Berghof* 336; Night of the Long Knives 334; renunciation of Versailles Treaty 343; suicide 356
"Hitler over Germany" campaign 333
Hittite Empire 5; Qadesh 8
Hohenstaufens 109–110
Holocaust, the 358–360
Holodomor 326
Holy of Holies 13
Holy Roman Empire 108–110, 178, 196; Hohenstaufens 109–110; Protestant Reformation 166–170; Thirty Years' War 176–177
Homer 19
Homeric epics 40; *arete* 20; *The Odyssey* 36

Homo sapiens sapiens 1
homosexuality in Ancient Greece 43
honestiores 75–76
hoplites 22, 34
Horthy, Miklós 337
Huguenots 171–172
humanism 40, 50, 89; the Renaissance 149–153, 155–157
Hundred Years' War 143–144, 157
hunter-gatherers 1–2, 16; disappearance of in Middle East 3
Hus, Jan 145
Hussites 145
hypocaust 84

id 292–293
ideologies: communism 275–277, 279; conservatism 248–249; fascism 327–329, *329*, 339; liberalism 250–251, 389; nationalism 247, 251–253, 261; neoliberalism 382; socialism 275–279
Il Duce 328
Île-de-France 110
Iliad, The 19–20
immigration 387; in post-WWII Europe 384
imperator 62
Imperial Diet 149
imperialism, review questions 297–298
Inanna 8
Incas, Spanish conquest of 163
"Index of Forbidden Books" 173
India 288–289
Indian National Congress 294
Indo-European languages 7
"indulgences" 165
Industrial Revolution 216–218, 221; domestic system 217–218; factory system 218–220; manufacturing 217; review questions 221–222; steam engine, invention of 218–220; textile production 219; water frame 217–218; world-systems theory 220; *see also* Second Industrial Revolution
industrialization in the Soviet Union 324–327
inheritance of noble status 120
Inquisition 116
Intermediate Periods 5
internal combustion engine, invention of 282–283
interwar Europe: France 320–322; Germany 330–333; Germany's

admission to League of Nations 319; Great Britain 320–322; Great Depression impact on 319–320; Italy 327–329, *329*; Kellogg-Briand Pact 319; review questions 339–340; Soviet Union 318

inventions: chemical explosives 282; Dutch 213; first writing systems 7; internal combustion engine 282–283; light bulb 282; printing press 155–156; radar 348; steam engine 218–220; tank 308

Ionia 25

Irish Free State, formation of 321

irrigation 6

Isabella, Queen of Spain 173

ISIS 384, 391

Islam 93; Abbasid dynasty 107; Allah 105; Battle of Poitiers 107; caliphate 106; the Crusades 107–109; *jihad* 106; Muhammad 105; Ottoman Empire 146–147; Quran 105–106; rise of in Middle Ages 105–107, *106*; Sharia law 106; trade with Western Europe 128–130; *Ulama* 147

Israel 4; founding of modern state 14, 379; Hebrews 12–14; Jericho 9; Jewish Temple, destruction of 13; Zionism 294

Italian Renaissance *see* the Renaissance

Italic languages 53

Italy: ancient Rome 53, 55–61, 70, 90; city-states 153; fascism 327–329, *329*; invasion of Ethiopia 329; Kingdom of Italy 267–268, 278; Mussolini, Benito 328–329; nationalism of nineteenth century 267–268; post-WWII era 296, 383; royal centralization in Late Middle Ages 149; the Renaissance 211; Triple Alliance 301; in World War II 353

Ivan the Great 114

Ivan the Terrible 114

Jacobins 232–233, 245

Jacquerie 142

James I, King of Britain 184–186

James II 188

Japan: Allies' defeat of 357–358; imperialism 289; invasion of Manchuria 343; Pearl Harbor, surprise attack on 350–352; Russo-Japanese War 303

Jericho 9

Jerusalem, destruction of Jewish Temple 13

Jesuits: Catholic Reformation 172–174; Thirty Years' War 176–177

Jesus of Nazareth 15, 91; rise of Christianity 85–88, *87*

Jewish Temple 16; destruction of 13

Jews: anti-Semitism 293–294; anti-Semitism in Middle Ages 100; Babylonian Captivity 13–14; Dreyfus Affair 272; as God's "Chosen People" 14–15; Hitler's obsession with 331; the Holocaust 358–360; mistreatment of in Eastern Europe 337; Nazi party targeting of 336; Nuremberg Laws 339; reaction to spread of Christianity 86; Ten Commandments 14; Zionism 294; *see also* Hebrews; Judaism

jihad 106

Joan of Arc 143, 157

Judaism: emphasis on character 14–15; Ten Commandments 12; *Yahweh* 14; *see also* Hebrews

Julio-Claudian dynasty 65

Julius Caesar 60, 72; assassination of 61; as dictator 61

July Monarchy 251

Junkers 196, 203, 248

jus civile 54

jus gentium 54

"justification by faith" 167

Justinian 99

Kadets 277, 311

kamikaze attacks 357

Kant, Immanuel 224

Kellog-Briand Pact 319

Kennedy, John F., Cuban Missile Crisis 374

Kepler, Johannes 213

Keynes, John Maynard 320

Kievan Rus 113

King Alfred 111

King John 112

King Minos 18

King of Kish 5

King Solomon's mines 13

Kingdom of Italy 267–268, 278

Kingdom of the Franks *see* Frankish Kingdom

Kingdoms of Ancient Egypt 5

Kirov, Sergei 327

knights 101, 120

Knossus 19

Koine 48, 50

Kollantai, Alexandra 324
Korean War 370
Kriegsmarine 343
Krupp family 282
Khrushchev, Nikita 373–374, 386
kulaks 323, 326
Kulturkampf 292

La Convivencia 138
Labour Party of Britain 321
laissez-faire capitalism 219, 227, 250, 382
land ownership: gentry 148; Gracchi 59; *latifundia* 58, 67–68; medieval manors 121; in Mesopotamia 6; nobility of High Middle Ages 119–120; patricians 53–54; serfs 120–122; *see also* feudalism
language: of barbarians 68; earliest development of in humans 2; Indo-European languages 7; Italic languages 53; *Koine* 48; nationalism 251–253; Semitic languages, predominance of in Middle East 7; *see also* writing
Late Antiquity 67; barbarians 68; Constantine the Great 69; *latifundia* 67–68; sack of Rome 70; Severan dynasty 67
Late Middle Ages: Babylonian Captivity 144; Black Death 140–143, *142*; Catholic Church, weakening of 144–146; Conciliar Movement 145; the Renaissance 149–153; review questions 158; royal centralization 147–149; scholasticism, weakening of 145–146
Late Republic 59; Triumvirate 60
Lateran Accord 329
latifundia 58–59, 90; in Late Antiquity 67–68
Latium 53
law: code of Hammurabi 7–8; *Corpus Juris Civilis* 99; *jus civile* 54; *jus gentium* 54; *Magna Carta* 112; Napoleonic Code 237; Sharia law 106; Ten Commandments 14; Twelve Tables 54
Lawrence of Arabia 309
lay investiture 96–97
Le Bon Marché 265
League of Corinth 31
League of German Girls 335
League of Nations 343; Germany's admission to 319
Lebensraum 341, 361
legacy of the French Revolution 234–235
legions 54, 72

Legislative Assembly 231; Jacobins 232
Lenin, Vladimir 277, 322–323
Lepidus 62
Lettow-Vorbeck, Paul von 309
levée en masse 233
liberalism 247, 250–251, 261, 389; voting rights, European expansion of 271–273; *see also* socialism
Lighthouse of Alexandria 48
literature: in High Middle Ages 135; Romanticism 253–255; troubadour poetry 135
Livy 82
Locarno Agreements 332, 338
Locke, John 189, 214, 224; *tabula rasa* 226
logos 49
Lollards 145
Louis XIII, King of France 181
Louis XIV, King of France 172, 180–184, 195, 198, 203; French absolutism 180–184; Versailles 182–183
Louis XVI, King of France 181, 184, 200, 228, 231–232, 235, 242, 244–245, 248
Louis-Philippe, King of France 250
Lucretius 83
Luftwaffe 343; the Blitz 348
Lusitania, sinking of 310
Luther, Martin 166, 178; "95 Theses" 166; *see also* Protestant Reformation
Lutheranism: "justification by faith" 167; Thirty Years' War 176–177
Luxor 9
Lyell, Charles 289
lyric poets 40

MacDonald, Ramsay 321
Macedonia: Alexander the Great 30–31; Antigonid rule of 32; Battle of Chaeronea 30; Battle of Granicus River 31; invasion of Persia 31–33; Roman invasion of 58
Machiavelli, Niccolò 154–155, 158
Machine Age 257–260, *258*
MAD (Mutually Assured Destruction) 368, 386
Maginot Line 346
Magna Carta 112, 116
Magyars 115
Malthus, Thomas 259
manors 138
manufacturing 217; factory system 218–220; Great Exhibition 263
Mao Zedong 360

map of Ancient Greece 23
Marconi, Guglielmo 282
Marcus Aurelius 66, 83
Maria, Henrietta 184–185
Marius 59–60
Mark Antony 62
marriage, in Hebrew tradition 15
Marshall Plan 366, 386
Marsiglio of Padua 145
Martyr King 187
Marx, Karl 276
Mary, Queen of Scots 171, 175
masses 126–127
mathematics: Arab contributions 129; Euclid 49; Pythagorean Theorem 42
Maxim gun 285
Mazzini, Giuseppe 267
Medici family 154; de Medici, Catherine 171–172; Pope Leo X 165
medicine: *The Canon of Medicine* 129; Hippocratic Oath 42; Middle Ages achievements 136–137
medieval manors 121
medieval romances 135
Memphis 9
mercantilism 190–195, *193*, 203; Golden Age of Piracy 198; review questions 204; War of Spanish Succession 198; and warfare 197–198
merchants 127
meritocracy 226
Merovingian dynasty 103
Mesopotamia 4, 16; Alexander the Great's occupation of 31–32; divination 10–11; land ownership 6; *naditu* 10; Queen Puabi 8
Messiah 16
Michelangelo 153, 158
Middle Ages: agriculture 128; anti-Semitism 100; astronomy 136; barbarians 94–95; Byzantine Empire 93; Catholic Church 126–128; chivalry 101–103, *102*; Concordat of Worms 97; the Crusades 93–94, 107–109; establishment of English monarchy 111–113; feudalism 100–103, *102*; guilds 125–126; Holy Roman Empire 108–110; Kingdom of the Franks 103–105; knights 101–103, *102*; lay investiture 96–97; medicine 136–137; peasants 120–121; rise of Islam 105–107, *106*; scientific achievements 135–136; serfs 120–122; townspeople 124–126; trade between Eastern and Western Europe 128–130; warfare in 101–103, *102*; women's role in society 130–132; *see also* Byzantine Empire; Frankish Kingdom; High Middle Ages; Late Middle Ages
middle class: in nineteenth and twentieth century Europe 264–267; review questions 279–280; in seventeenth and eighteenth century Europe 209–211
Middle East 4; ancient weapons 8; Assyrian Empire 5; Babylonia 4–5; cities, capture of 9; early farming in 2; Hittite Empire 5; hunter-gatherers, disappearance of 3; irrigation 6; Persian Empire 5; Semitic languages, predominance of 7; ziggurat temples 9–10; *see also* Mesopotamia
Middle Kingdom 5
military reforms during Augustan Principate 63–65, *64*
Mill, John Stuart 296
Ministry of Public Enlightenment and Propaganda 334
Minoans 18–19, 33; Knossus 19
Mirandola, Giovanni Pico della 151
missionaries, influence on New Imperialism 285
mobilization 316
Mona Lisa 152–153
monarchy: Britain, absolutism in 184–186; establishment of English monarchy 111–113; failure of constitutional monarchy as cause of French Revolution 227–232; France, absolutism in 180–184; French monarchy, establishment of 109–111; July Monarchy 251; Valois monarchy 143
monasticism 89–90; *Benedictine Rule* 90; ecclesiastical reform in Catholic Church 96; in High Middle Ages 123
Mongol Empire: Golden Horde 113; Russian domination by 113–114
monks 91
monotheistic religions 11; Judaism 14
Montesquieu 226
Montgomery, General Bernard 353
More, Sir Thomas 156
Moses 12
Mount Olympus 39
Mt. Vesuvius, eruption of 77
Muhammad 105, 116

Mussolini, Benito 328–329, *329*
Mycenaean culture 19, 34; farming 37
mystery cults 39, 85
mythology, Greek 38–39

naditu 10
Nagy, Imre 371
Napoleon I *see* Bonaparte, Napoleon
Napoleon III 261
Napoleonic Code 237
Napoleonic Wars 201, 240–242, 244–248, 260
National Assembly: circulation of *assignats* 231; Declaration of the Rights of Man and of the Citizen 229–230; replacement with Legislative Assembly 231; Tennis Court Oath 229
National Socialist German Workers' Party *see* Nazi party
nationalism 247, 251–253, 261; in nineteenth century Germany 268–271, *270*; in nineteenth century Italy 267–268; and Romanticism 253
Native Americans: impact of disease on 162–163; Seven Years' War 198–200
NATO (North Atlantic Treaty Organization) 366–367, 386, 391
natural selection 289–291
naval combat: *Kriegsmarine* 343; in World War I 309–311
Nazi party: Aryanism 335–336; Beer Hall Putsch 330; death camps 358–360; *Gestapo* 334; Hitler, Adolf 333–336; "Hitler over Germany" campaign 333; Jews, targeting of 336; Ministry of Public Enlightenment and Propaganda 334; Night of the Long Knives 334; Röhm, Ernst 334; *Schutzstaffel* 331; social policy 335–336; "Strength through Joy" 335; *Sturmabteilungen* 332; three Ks 336
Nazi-Soviet Non-Aggression Pact 345
neoliberalism 382
Neolithic Age, farming in 2
Neolithic Revolution 2, 16
N.E.P. (New Economic Policy) 323, 325, 339
Nero 66
New Imperialism 281, 283–286, *284*, 297; British Empire 286; Scramble for Africa 287–288, *287*
New Kingdom 5
Newton, Sir Isaac 213, 221

Nicholas II, Tsar of Russia 277, 308, 311; abdication of 311
Nietzche, Friedrich 291
Night of the Long Knives 334
Nightingale, Florence 302
Nineveh 5
Nixon, Richard 370, 374–375
Nobel, Alfred 282
nobility: Black Death impact on 141–142; *boyars* 195; in High Middle Ages 119–120; *Junkers* 196, 248; in seventeenth and eighteenth century Europe 205–207
noblewomen 130–132, 207, 225
Normandy, establishment of English monarchy 111–113
Normandy invasion 355
Normans 111
Northern European Renaissance 155–157; Erasmus 156; More, Sir Thomas 156; printing press, invention of 155–156; Shakespeare, William 156–157
nuclear weapons: Cuban Missile Crisis 374; MAD 368; SDI 375
number systems, Sumerian 7
Nuremberg Laws 339

oath of fealty 100
Odoacer 70
Odyssey, The 20, 36
Oedipus 40
Old Kingdom 5; Memphis 9; pyramids of Egypt 9–10; Thebes 9
Old Stone Age 1–2
Old Testament 13
oligarchy 21–22
Olympic Games 18–20, 27, 39, 266, 369; during Cold War 369
Operation Barbarossa 349–350, 362
Operation Sea Lion 348
Ophir 13
Oracle at Delphi 39
oracles 50
Oration on the Dignity of Man (Mirandola) 151
Order of Preachers (Dominicans) 124
Order of Saint Benedict 90
Origin of Species, The (Darwin, 1859) 290
Orthodox Church 97–100, 116; Catholic Church 226; split with Catholic Church 97–98
Ottoman Empire 146–147, 158, 197; decline of 147; *Ulama* 147

paganism 95
painting, Romanticism 255
palaistra 43
Paleolithic Age 1–2
Pankhurst, Emmeline 296
Paris, German occupation of 346
Paris Commune of 1871 272
Paris Gun 307
Paris Settlement 313
parlements 181, 184, 228
Parliament 148, 158; absolutism in Britain 184–186; Roundheads 186
partisans 362
Pasteur, Louis 290
pater familias 81, 91
Patriarch of Constantinople 97
patriarchs 12
patricians 53–54, 71; Sulla 60
Peace of Amiens 237
Peace of God movement 103
Peace of Schönbrunn 240
peasants 24, 53–54, 69, 71, 75, 81, 100, 102, 108, 110, 114, 119–123, 126, 128, 131, 137–140, 142–144, 148, 157, 168, 183, 198, 205–210, 215, 220–221, 228–229, 231, 233–234, 244, 248, 250, 255–257, 259–260, 264, 271, 277–278, 322–323, 328, 355, 373; in seventeenth and eighteenth century Europe 207–209, *208*
Peasants' Revolt 142
pederasty 43
Peloponnesian War 28–29, 34; Thucydides 42
penance 165–166
peninsulares 163
Pepin III 103–104
perestroika 376
Pericles 27, 45
Periodic Table of the Elements 289
persecution of Christians 88
Persian Empire 5, 34; invasion of Greece 25–26; King Darius I 26; Macedonian invasion of 31–33; *satraps* 25; *Shahanshah* 25; Xerxes 26; Zoroastrianism 25
Pétain, Marshal Henri Philippe 346
Peter the Great 195, 203
Peterloo Massacre 249
Petrarch 150–151
phalanx 22
Pharaohs 10–11, 16
Philip Augustus 110

Philip II, King of Macedon 30–31, 34
Philip II, King of Spain 173–174; defeat of Spanish Armada 174–176
Philip VI 143
philosophes 224–225, 245; Kant, Immanuel 224; Locke, John 224, 226; Montesquieu 226; proposals of 225–227; Rousseau, Jean-Jacques 226–227; Smith, Adam 227; Voltaire 225
philosophy: Cicero 82; the Enlightenment 223–225; Epicureanism 83; Greek philosophy 45–47; Hellenistic 48–49; *logos* 49; questioning of religion 291–292; the Renaissance 149–153; virtue 49
Phoenicians 13
"Phony War" 346
piracy 198
Pitt, William 199
Pizarro, Francisco 163
Plantagenet dynasty 112
plantation slavery 191, 203
Plato 29, 46–47, 50
playwrights in Ancient Greece 40
plebeians 53–54, 71
poetry: in Ancient Greece 40; *chansons de geste* 135; medieval romances 135; of Roman Republic 82–83; troubadour poetry 135
Poland: Auschwitz-Birkenau 359; German invasion of 341, 344–345; Jewish mistreatment by 337; solidarity 386; Warsaw Ghetto 359; Wojtyla, Karol 372–373
poleis 20–21, 34; *acropolis* 21; *agora* 38; Aristotle's conception of 47; Athenian democracy 27–28; *gymnasium* 21; Peloponnesian War 28–29
politics 18–35, 53–73, 93–118, 180–204; Cicero 82; in High Middle Ages 127; of Renaissance period 153–155
polytheistic religions 10; in Ancient Egypt 11, 38; in ancient Greece/Rome 76, 94
Pompeii 77
Pompey 60
Poor Law 260
Pope Boniface VIII 144
Pope Calixtus II 97
Pope Clement VII 170
Pope Gregory VII 96, 116
Pope Innocent III, crusade against Cathars 99

Pope John Paul II 372–373
Pope Leo X 165
Pope Urban II, Council of Clermont 108
popular sovereignty 189, 203
population explosion of the eighteenth century 215
Portugal: da Gama, Vasco 161; mercantilism 192–195, *193*; plantation slavery 191–192
Poseidon 39
Potato Famine of 1846–1848 255–256
Pragmatic Sanction 148
precious metals, mercantilism 190–192
"predestination" 169–170
Prince von Metternich 248
princeps civitatis 62
Prince, The (Machiavelli, 1513) 154–155
print culture of the eighteenth century 224
printing press, invention of 155–156, 158
professionalization of the Roman army *64*
proletariat 276–277
propaganda: Louis XIV's attempt at absolute power 182; Ministry of Public Enlightenment and Propaganda 334
proposals of the *philosophes* 225–227
Protectorate 187
Protestantism: "95 Theses" 166; Anabaptists 169; Anglicanism 174–176; Calvin, John 169–170; causes of 164–166; England's adoption of 170–171; *Huguenots* 171–172; Puritans 203; rejection of the papacy 167; review questions 178–179; Thirty Years' War 176–177; Zwingli, Ulrich 169
Provisional Government 311
Prussia 177, 196, 198–199, 203, 207, 224, 226, 232–234, 238–242, 244–246, 248–249, 253, 257, 268, 269, 271–272, 279, 299, 301, 308; Seven Years' War 198–200
psychoanalysis 292–293
Ptolemaic theory 49
Ptolemy 32
Punic Wars 57, 72
Punici 57
purgatory 166
Purges, the 326–327
Puritans 203
Putin, Vladimir 378–379, 387
putting out system 217–218, 221

pyramids of Egypt 9–10, *10*, 16
Pythagorean Theorem 42

Qadesh 8
Quadruple Alliance 241, 245; Congress of Vienna 242–244, *243*
Queen Puabi 8
questioning of religion 291–292
Quran 105–106, 116

racism: Aryanism 293–294; Indian National Congress 294
RAF (Royal Air Force), defense against the Blitz 348
railways 261; and the Machine Age 257–260, *258*
Raphael 153
Rasputin 311
rationalism 50
Reagan, Ronald 375
Reconquista 108, 115
reform: of Catholic Church 96; Catholic Reformation 172–174; the Enlightenment 223–225; Hus, Jan 145; Peterloo Massacre 249; social reform in Soviet Union 323–324; Wycliffe, John 145; *see also* Protestant Reformation
Reichstag 271, 332
Reign of Terror 232–233
rejection of the papacy by Protestants 167
religion: in Ancient Greece 38–40; Catholic Church 95–97; clergy 122–124; divination 39; festivals 39; flexibility of Roman policy toward 77; Islam 93; monotheistic religions 11; polytheistic 10; questioning of 291–292; in Roman Republic 76–77; and secularism 225–226; theology as scholastic pursuit 134; Wars of Religion 176; ziggurat temples 9–10; Zoroastrianism 25; *see also* Catholic Church; Christianity; Islam; Protestantism; theology
Renaissance, the 149–153, 158; Brethren of the Common Life 155; da Vinci, Leonardo 152–153; education, emphasis on 151; Giotto 152; Machiavelli, Niccolò 154–155; Medici family 154; Michelangelo 153; in Northern Europe 155–157; Petrarch 150–151; politics 153–155; Raphael 153; review questions 158; Savonarola 154; women's contributions to 152

Renan, Ernst 291
representative government 203
Republic of Eire 321
Republic, The 47
Restoration, the 187–188
review questions: Agricultural Revolution 221–222; Ancient Greece 34–35, 51; challenging the conservative order 261; early humans and the dawn of civilization 16–17; end of European dominance 387; French Revolution 246; imperialism 297–298; Industrial Revolution 221–222; interwar Europe 339–340; Late Middle Ages 158; Middle Ages 117–118; middle class Europe 279–280; Napoleon 246; politics, colonialism, and war 204; Protestant Reformation 178–179; the Renaissance 158; Roman Empire 72–73; Roman Republic 72–73, 91; Scientific Revolution 221–222; social change 297–298; society and culture in Middle Ages 138–139; World War I 316–317; World War II 362–363
Revolutions of 1848 256
revolutionary vanguard 278
Rhineland, German occupation of 343
Ribbentrop, Joachim von 345
Ricardo, David 259
Richthofen, Manfred von 308
right to vote, expansion of in Europe 271–273
rise of Christianity 87; Constantine's conversion 88; conversion of Saul of Tarsus 86; monasticism 89–90; standardization of *The Bible* 88–89
Robespierre, Maximilien 233
Roger II 115
Röhm, Ernst 334
Roma 77
Roman Catholic Church *see* Catholic Church
Roman Empire: Augustan Principate 63–65, *64*; barbarians 68; Caligula 65; Christianity, adoption of 88–89; Claudius 65–66; Constantine the Great 69; decline and fall of 67–71; Diocletian 68–69; Five Good Emperors 66; Flavian dynasty 66; Greek cultural influences 81–82; *honestiores* 75–76; Nero 66; *Pax Romana* 53, 65–67, 72; reign of Tiberius 65; review questions 72–73, 91; rise of Christianity 85–88, 87; sack of Rome 70; Severan dynasty 67; Theodosius 69
Roman Republic: agriculture 74–75; architecture 83–84; army recruitment 54–55; assassination of Julius Caesar 61; the Assembly 53; *centurions* 54; Cicero 82; class system 75; conquest of Gaul 60; daily life in 77–79; destruction of 62; education 79; engineering 84–85; Etruscans 53; expansion of 56; Gracchi 59; Julius Caesar 60; land ownership 53; Late Republic 59; legions 54; Marius 59–60; Octavian 62; poetry 82–83; *princeps civitatis* 62; religion 76–77; review questions 72–73, 91; Scipio Africanus 57; sculpture 83; slavery 58; soldiers 54–55; status of women in 79–81; Struggle of the Orders 54; Tiber River 53; trade 75; Triumvirate 60, 62; Twelve Tables 54; urban life 78; *see also* Augustan Principate; Roman Empire
Romanitas 70, 74
Romantic Republicans 267
Romanticism 247, 253–255, 261
Rommel, Erwin 349
Romulus Augustulus 70
Roosevelt, Franklin Delano 351–352, 362
Rosetta Stone 7
rotten boroughs 251
Roundheads, English Civil War 186–188, *186*
Rousseau, Jean-Jacques 226–227, 264
Royal Charles, The 187
royal governments 8, 101, 107, 113, 115, 121, 147, 149; centralization in Late Middle Ages 147–149; *see also* government
Royalists, English Civil War 186–188, *186*
Rump Parliament 187
Russia: Alexander I, Tsar of Russia 249; Bolshevik Revolution of 1917 277–278, 310–311; *boyars* 195; conservatism of nineteenth century 249; Ivan the Great 114; Ivan the Terrible 114; Kievan Rus 113; Lenin, Vladimir 277–279, 310–311, 316, 322–325, 338–339, 378; Mongol domination of 113–114; Napoleon's invasion of 240–241; Nicholas II, Tsar of Russia 277, 308; Operation Barbarossa 349–350; Provisional Government 311; Putin, Vladimir 378–379; Rasputin 311; Russo-

Japanese War 303; Second Industrial Revolution 281–283; Social Democratic Party 277; Three Emperor's League 299–301, *300*; Triple Entente 302; *see also* Soviet Union
Russian Federation 378
Russo-Japanese War 303

sack of Rome 70
sacramentum 56
sans-culottes 229, 245; alliance with Jacobins 232
Sargon 5
satrapies 25–26
satraps 25
Saturnalia 76
Saul 13
Saul of Tarsus 86
Savonarola 154
Schlieffen Plan 305, 316
scholasticism 133–134, *133*, 138; weakening of in Late Middle Ages 145–146
School of Athens (Raphael) 153
Schutzstaffel or SS 331
science 50; achievements of in Middle Ages 135–136; Arab contributions 129; Archimedes 49; *atomoi* 46; heliocentric theory 212–213; in Hellenistic world 49; Periodic Table of the Elements 289; Pythagorean Theorem 42; Scientific Revolution 211–215, 221; Theory of Evolution 289–291
scientific method 212, 221
Scientific Revolution 211–215, 221; Copernicus, Nicolaus 49, 212–213, 221; Galileo 213; heliocentrism 212; Locke, John 214; Newton, Sir Isaac 213; review questions 221–222
Scipio Aemilianus 57
Scipio Africanus 57
Scramble for Africa 287–288, *287*, 297
sculpture: in Ancient Greece 41; in ancient Rome 83
SDI (Strategic Defense Initiative) 375
Second Estate 122, 228–229
Second Industrial Revolution 281–283, 297
Second Punic War 57
Second Republic of France 256
Second Sex, The 383
secularism 225–226
Seleucid dynasty 32

Seljuk Turks, Council of Clermont 108
Semitic languages, predominance of in Middle East 7
senate 72
Seneca 83
separation of powers 226
sepoys 289
September Massacres 232
serfs 120–123, 125–128, 138, 141–143, 207, 220, 244, 277; Black Death impact on 142–143
Seven Wonders of the Ancient World: Lighthouse of Alexandria 48; pyramids of Egypt 9–10
Seven Years' War 184, 198–200, 203
Severan dynasty 67
Sexual Revolution of the 1960s and 1970s 383
Shahanshah 25
Shakespeare, William 175–176
Sharia law 106
Shelley, Mary 255
Shelley, Percy Bysshe 255
shires 112
Sicily, as monarchy 115–116
sinking of the *Bismarck* 352
sinking of the *Lusitania* 310
Six Acts 249
Skeptics 48
slavery: in Ancient Greece 43–44; impact on Roman technology 84; plantation slavery 191, 203; in Roman Republic 58; Spartacus 58
Slavic groups 114–116
Smith, Adam 219, 227, 245
social change, review questions 297–298
Social Darwinism 291, 331
Social Democratic Party 277; in Russia 277
socialism 275–279; and Christian Democratic party 381; collectivization 326; Labour Party of Britain 275; SPD 275
society 36–51, 74–91, 119–139, 205–222; clergy of Middle Ages 122–124; *honestiores* 75–76; of Latin America 163; nobility of High Middle Ages 119–120; townspeople of Middle Ages 124–126; women's role in Middle Age society 130–132
Socrates 46, 50
soldiers in Roman Republic 54–55
Solidarity 386

Solomon 13; destruction of the Jewish Temple 13
Solon 24, 43
Somme, Battle of 306
Sonderweg 257
Sophists 46
Sophocles 40
South Africa, Boer War 302
Soviet Union 318; Battle of Stalingrad 353–354, *353*; Brezhnev, Leonid 374; *Cheka* 322; the Cold War 364, 366–379, 381, 386–387; collectivization 326; Comintern 323; Cuban Missile Crisis 374; dissolution of 378; fall of 373–376; feminism in 324; *glasnost* 376; Gorbachev, Mikhail 375–376; industrialization 324–327; invasion of Afghanistan 371; Khrushchev, Nikita 373–374; launching of *Sputnik* 369; Nazi-Soviet Non-Aggression Pact 345; N.E.P. 323; Operation Barbarossa 349–350; *perestroika* 376; the Purges 326–327; social reform 323–324; Stalin, Joseph 324–326; *Typhoon* class submarines 368; War Communism 322; Warsaw Pact 366–367; *see also* the Cold War
space exploration: Apollo missions 370; European Space Agency 380; *Sputnik* 369
Spain: Catholic Reformation 173–174; Columbus, Christopher 161–163, *162*; Conquest of the Aztecs 163; Conquest of the Incas 163; *conquistadores* 163; Cortés, Hernán 163; defeat of Spanish Armada 174–176; *haciendas* 164; mercantilism 192–195, *193*; *peninsulares* 163; *Reconquista* 115; royal centralization in Late Middle Ages 149; War of Spanish Succession 198
Sparta 24, 34; *helots* 29; Peloponnesian War 28–29; women's status in 45
Spartacus 58
SPD (*Sozialdemokratische Partei Deutschlands*) 275, 279, 330, 381
sports, *arete* 20, *21*
Sputnik 369
SS *see Schutzstaffel*
St. Augustine 89
St. Francis of Assisi 124
St. Helena 88
St. Paul 86
St. Thomas Aquinas 124, 134, 138

Stalin, Joseph 324–327, 339, 349–350; the Purges 326–327
Stanley, Henry Morton 288
Stasi 372
Statute of Westminster 321
steam engine, invention of 218–221
steel 282
Stoicism 49, 51, 83
strategic balance in the Cold War 367–368
strategic bombing 362
"Strength through Joy" 335
Struggle of the Orders 54
Sturmabteilungen odr (SA) 332
Subjection of Women, The (Mill, 1869) 296
Sudetenland 337
Suez Canal 371
suffrage movement 296–297
Suleiman, the Magnificent 146–147
Sulla 60
Sultan, ruler of Ottoman Empire 147
Sumeria 4–5; cuneiform 7; number system, development of 7; Uruk 8
Summa Theologica 134
superego 292–293
surprise attack on Pearl Harbor 350–352
symposium 38, 50

tabula rasa 214, 221, 226
Tacitus 82
Tamerlane 146
tanks, use of in World War I 308
tanks/panzers in WWII 343
technology: Middle Ages achievements 136; printing press, invention of 155–156; slavery's impact on 84
temples 10; in Ancient Greece 39; ziggurat 9–10
Ten Commandments 12, 14, 16
Tennis Court Oath 229
terrorist organizations: Black Hand 304; ISIS 384, 391; Al Qaeda 384, 391
textile production 219
Thatcher, Margaret 382
Theban plays 40
Thebes 9
Theodosius 69
theology: Lutheranism 168–169; "predestination" 169–170; as scholastic pursuit 134
Theory of Evolution 289–291
Third Estate 122, 228–229
Third Punic War 57

Third Republic 272, 279
Thirty Years' War 176–178
Three Emperor's League 299–301, *300*
three Ks 336
Thucydides 42
Tiber River 53
Tiberius 65
tolerance, flexibility of Roman policy toward religion 77
townspeople of Middle Ages 124–126; burghers 125; guilds 125–126
trade: Black Death, economic effect of 142–143; colonialism 191–192; Columbian Exchange 162; Continental System 239; Corn Law 260; between Greek colonies 38; guilds 125–126, 138; merchants 127; in Middle Ages 128; in Roman Republic 75
trade unions, emergence of in Europe 274–275, 279
tragedies 40
tramroads 258
Treaty of Brest-Litovsk 316
Treaty of Versailles 313–314; Hitler's renunciation of 343
Treaty of Westphalia 177
tribune 54
Tribune, Rome 54
tribunicia potestas 63
Trinity, the 89
Triple Alliance 301
Triple Entente 302, 316
Triumvirate 60, 62
Trotsky, Leon 324–327
troubadour poetry 135
Troy 19; Helen 44–45
Truce of God movement 103
Truman, Harry S. 357, 366
Truman Doctrine 366, 386
Tudor dynasty 148
Turkey 5, 7, 19–20, 25, 31–32, 58, 69, 78, 93, 98, 107, 146, 158, 197, 252–253, 301–302, 308–309, 312–313, 338, 381; Gallipoli campaign 308–309
Twelve Tables 54
Twenty-One Conditions 323
Typhoon class submarines 368

U-boats 309–310, 316; Battle of the Atlantic 352
Ulama 147
Ulster 321
UN (United Nations) 360, 362
the unconscious 292–293, 297
unification of Germany 268–271, *270*
Union of Utrecht 174
United States: American Revolution 200–202; Cuban Missile Crisis 374; current relations with Europe 391–392; entrance into World War II 350–352; Great Depression 319–320; Marshall Plan 366; post-WWI 319; Second Industrial Revolution 281–283; surprise attack on Pearl Harbor 350–352; Truman Doctrine 366; Vietnam War 370–371; in World War I 307
universities 138; in High Middle Ages 132–133
urban life in ancient Rome 78
urbanization 259, 261; Second Industrial Revolution 281–283
Uruk 8
Utopia (More) 156

V-2 rocket 355
Valens 69–70
Valois monarchy 143
vassals 100
V-E Day 356
Vercingetorix *61*
Verdun 306
Versailles 182–183, 203
Versailles Treaty, Hitler's renunciation of 343
Vespasian 66
Vesta 76
Vichy France 347
Victor Emmanuel III, King of Italy 328
Victorian Age 264–265; clothing 266; Cult of Domesticity 296; feminism 295–296
Vietnam War 370–371
Vikings 111, 116; Kievan Rus 113
Virgil 82–83, 91
virtue 49; Stoicism 83
Voltaire 225
voting rights, European expansion of 271–273

Waldensians 99
warfare: in age of mercantilism 197–198; American Revolution 200–203; *arete* 20; *Blitzkrieg* 345; Boer War 302; gunpowder, use of in Middle Ages 136; hoplites 22; Hundred Years' War

143–144; Korean War 370; in Middle Ages 101–103, *102*; Napoleonic Wars 240–241; Peloponnesian War 28–29; phalanx 22; Russo-Japanese War 303; Seven Years' War 198–200, 203; *see also* Punic Wars; World War I; World War II
Wars of Religion 178
Wars of the Roses 148
Warsaw Ghetto 359
Warsaw Pact 366–367, 386
Washington, George 201–202
water, irrigation 6
water frame 217–218
Watt, James 218
wealth: mercantilism 190–195, *193*; redistribution of, socialism 275–277
weapons in ancient Middle East 8
Weimar Republic 314–315, 330–331
Wellesley, Sir Arthur (Duke of Wellington) 239
Western Front 316
Whigs 251
White Star Line 266
Wilhelm II 301
William of Ockham 145
William of Orange, the Glorious Revolution 188–190
William the Conqueror 116; establishment of English monarchy 111–113
Wilson, Woodrow 310, 316; 14 points 312
wireless telegraphy 282
Wojtyla, Karol 372–373
Wollstonecraft, Mary 227
women: Amazons 44; in Ancient Greece 44–45; ancient societies, role in 11–12; Aspasia 45; Cult of Domesticity 264–265; European feminism 383–384; feminism 295–296; medieval society, role in 130–132; noblewomen 130–132; Renaissance contributions 152; in Roman Republic 79–81; in Spartan society 45; status of in Ancient Egypt 12; suffrage movement 296–297; three Ks 336
Women's Social and Political Union 296
Woolley, Sir Leonard 8
Wordsworth, William 255
working class, rise of in nineteenth and twentieth century Europe 273–275
World War I: 14 points 312; assassination of Archduke Ferdinand 304; beginning of 300–301; casualties from 312; Central Powers 305; daily life of soldiers 307; Gallipoli campaign 308–309; German surrender 312; High Seas Fleet 301–302; naval combat 309–311; Paris Gun 307; Paris Settlement 313; post-war negotiations 313; review questions 316–317; Richthofen, Manfred von 308; Schlieffen Plan 305; signing of cease fire 312; sinking of the *Lusitania* 310; tanks 308; Treaty of Versailles 313–314; Triple Entente 302; Battle of Verdun 306
World War II *342*; *Anschluss* 344; in the Balkans 349; Battle of Britain 347–348; Battle of Kursk 354; Battle of Leyte Gulf 357; Battle of Salamis 353–354, *353*; Battle of the Atlantic 352; the Blitz 348; *Blitzkrieg* 345; defeat of Germany 354–356, *356*; fall of Japan 357–358; fall of Paris 346; German invasion of Poland 344–345; German occupation of Rhineland 343; Germany's military buildup 343; the Holocaust 358–360; Maginot Line 346; Marshall Plan 366; Normandy invasion 355; North African theater 352–353; Operation Barbarossa 349–350; Operation Sea Lion 348; "peace for our time" pronouncement 344; review questions 362–363; surprise attack on Pearl Harbor 350–352; United States' entrance into 350–352; V-2 rocket 355; V-E Day 356; Vichy France 347
world-systems theory 220
writing 7, 16
Wycliffe, John 145

Xerxes 26, 37

Yahweh 12, 14
Yalta 360
Yeltsin, Boris 378
Yugoslavia, formation of 252, 303, 313, 322, 338, 349, 355, 377

Zeus 39
ziggurat temples 9–10
Zimmermann, Arthur 310
Zionism 294, 379
Zoroastrianism 25
Zwingli, Ulrich 169